GW01458403

354
>PIES

Keiretsu Economy – New Economy?

Keiretsu Economy – New Economy?

Japan's Multinational Enterprises from a Postmodern Perspective

Rainer Kensy

Foreword by Seiichi Mitani

palgrave

First published 2001 by
PALGRAVE
Houndmills, Basingstoke, Hampshire RG21 6XS and
175 Fifth Avenue, New York, N.Y. 10010
Companies and representatives throughout the world

PALGRAVE is the new global academic imprint of
St. Martin's Press LLC Scholarly and Reference Division and
Palgrave Publishers Ltd (formerly Macmillan Press Ltd).

ISBN 0–333–92175–5

This book is printed on paper suitable for recycling and
made from fully managed and sustained forest sources.

A catalogue record for this book is available
from the British Library

Library of Congress Cataloging-in-Publication Data
Kensy, Rainer
     Keiretsu economy – new economy? : Japan's multinational enterprises
from a postmodern perspective / by Rainer Kensy.
       p. cm.
     Includes bibliographical references and index.
     ISBN 0–333–92175–5
     1. International business enterprises – Japan. 2. Japan – Foreign
economic relations. I. Title.

HD2907 .K44 2000
338.8′8952–dc 21
                                                                    00–048295

10   9   8   7   6   5   4   3   2   1
10   09 08 07 06 05 04 03 02 01

Typeset in Great Britain by
Aarontype Limited, Easton, Bristol

Printed and bound in Great Britain by
Antony Rowe Ltd, Chippenham, Wiltshire

Contents

Contents vii

List of Tables

List of Figures

Foreword

Reading this comprehensive work on the strategies and special characteristics of Japanese firms was an extremely interesting and revealing experience. The perspective used by a young European to explain well-known Japanese facts is entirely new to me and has given me much to think about. Unusual combinations used in this book bring to light some fascinating perspectives, which for myself and my colleagues, not only in Japan but also in other places around the world, are extremely useful and valuable.

I consider it important that, for once, this book demonstrates undogmatically that Japan is not a strong, impregnable fortress but a country which has, by centuries of extremely hard work and perpetual improvement of the status quo, successfully transcended an evolutionary phase (and is just entering a new one), for which we should all be heartily grateful. The fragile nature of good fortune has been demonstrated to us and the world by the recent earthquakes, some volcano catastrophes and the current problems in our financial and corporate world.

Rainer Kensy uses many examples to demonstrate the importance of fully comprehending difficult situations, that American-style 'quick fixes' can never lead to a long-term result and that it is only a commitment to education and communication which can guarantee success. I hope that, for numerous other researchers of current affairs, as well as for many others who, in their positions of responsibility, have cause to contemplate the future of their companies, their markets and their workforce, this type of study will represent an exciting concept which will serve to stimulate new impetus. Hopefully, it will also help readers, who are not directly involved with Japan, to take on board the problems and solutions of Japanese companies and adapt them to achieve new and constantly higher levels of productivity, efficacy and values in all multinational companies, for the benefit of all the company's 'stakeholders': employees and their families, customers and consumers as well as shareholders and creditors.

New visions are necessary in an ever-more rapidly changing world, in which mutual understanding is often the resource in shortest supply. I am convinced that the questions which Dr Kensy attempts to answer in his study are among the most important of this decade, at the turn of the millennium. I hope the following pages will present a fascinating stimulus for debate and communication. I wish this book great success.

November 1999   SEIICHI MITANI
                        (former) Executive Director, Mitsubishi Bank, Tokyo

xi

Preface

This whole book is but a drought – nay a draught of a draught.
Oh, Time, Strength, Cash, and Patience!
H. Melville, Letter to Duyckinck, p. x

'Japan embracing the postmodern will be the role model for the New Economy':
a phrase combining three of the nowadays most-used catchwords. The importance
of these terms, all of which conceal hegemonic claims and are surrounded by
myths, is continually being extended in the economic and/or intellectual debate.

The myths surrounding Japan On the one hand, Zen, cherry blossoms, geishas and
the Samurai; and, on the other, mass application of high-technology, just-in-time
systems (or any other management gadget) and the provocation and intrusion
presented by Japan's economic might. We frequently fail to notice that these myths
often adopt a Disney-like character and are frequently used to play down or dis-
tort, whilst being far removed from the core issues.

The myth surrounding the postmodern Debate about this term is often sophisticated and specialized and the current vogue is to categorize all kinds of phenomena
as 'postmodern'. Consequently, to the outsider, the term remains unclear in content
and its existence and effect on everyday life uncertain.

The myth surrounding the New Economy It is hailed as the ultimate solution to all
our worldly problems. For everything, from poverty to spiritual growth, Internet/
New Economy/IT is the seemingly obvious answer. Yet, naïve proponents are walk-
ing on very thin ice as there are no theoretical foundations to be seen on which an
architecture of concepts can be constructed; the revolution just happens to happen.

In this study, we attempt to counter the effects of this tendency to (unintentionally)
create a mythology in these areas. Our aim is to demonstrate (a) that the description 'postmodern' can be usefully employed to investigate, from a totally different
angle, the most important research topic around today, that is, the multinational
companies; (b) to show that the New Economy is an emanation of the postmodern
philosophy; and (c) that Japan is a most interesting contemporary puzzle as it
combines (a) and (b).

This theme is both topical and explosive, due to the way in which it combines the two elements. Consequently, there is a perceived need to preoccupy
ourselves urgently with this problem, which is documented by a flood of literature in 'each specialist area'. Unfortunately, this literature consists mainly of
monofactorial models – *à la* 'Kaizen – the Secret of Japan', 'the Kata Faktor',

xii

'the MITI –Miracle' or 'Samurai Management'. But can we generate a new, broader way of looking at Japan's economy? Is there really any hope of combining two diffuse, apparently separate, phenomena to form a coherent 'explanation'? Is the only possible outcome an empty vacuum?

In order to prevent this approach degenerating into a multicoloured pot pourri, we have consistently set a number of focal points. In all thematic areas we have endeavoured to use *information processing*, *decision-making structures*, the *structure of the networks* and *historical genesis* as the guiding categories to get some discipline into the analysis. Even if we do not always manage completely to achieve our objectives in all areas, we have certainly been able to clarify two points:

Firstly, both definitions – Japan and the postmodern – must be seen as a challenge; and a failure to rise to this challenge would lead to long-term disadvantages. On the one hand, Japan's supremacy (whether it is intentional or unintentional, welcomed or resisted is open to question), not just in market and production sectors but also in cultural, social and normative spheres, is spreading unnoticed (some quarters of economic stagnation notwithstanding). On the other hand, the omnipresent disintegration of social structures, the compartmentalized nature of lifestyle elements and sub-elements, cultures and sub-cultures can no longer be understood other than by adopting a postmodern perspective, since hardly any alternative perspective is able to assimilate and interpret all of these contemporary phenomena. In fact, the widespread term 'New Economy' serves only as a denominator for the postmodern influence into the economic and business world.

Secondly, we should again point out that Japanese phenomena, whether they relate to the economy, the political or social arena or to culture and everyday life, must never be over-hastily interpreted one-dimensionally or ahistorically. Only a perspective which focuses on the whole and is capable of considering all aspects integratively (even those which seem far-fetched to the Western eye) can do justice to Japan and the Japanese.

During the research and preparation stages of this book, the author was dependent in many instances on a great deal of assistance from countless people. I should like, certainly not purely for formal reasons, to thank all those, including unnamed participants, for their support and for the forbearance occasionally demanded of them. In particular, I would like to thank Mrs Motoko Ezaki, Mr Edward Dodson (Credit Suisse, Tokyo) and Mr Ross A. Pollack (Cambridge Hewitt, Tokyo) for their participation in hours of debate over the enigmata of the Japanese economy, language and culture. I am especially grateful to Mr Seiichi Mitani (Executive Director, Mitsubishi Bank, Tokyo) for the friendly way in which he explained some of the background behind complex Japanese peculiarities. My thanks also go to Dr J. Timothy Cloyd (Vanderbilt University), Mr Timothy H. Dwight Sr (US Department of Agriculture) and, above all, to Prof. Tom Schneeweis (University of Massachusetts) for their 'American input'. In spite of all this assistance, I bear sole responsibility for any errors, omissions or lack of clarity.

Now having started to mention some, I must add to the list my wife for her unorthodox, candid and creative comments which were always welcomed, and Leo

Buchmann for the long debates on the radical changes in today's world, the incredible impact it will have on philosophy and the existential need for lateral thinking and cross-breeding ideas.

As my texts resemble more a thorny thicket than a crisp cricket field,[1] Anne Richner's help with the English version has been very valuable. Some of the literature were not used in their original editions but in the print available to me. In the dilemma between philological exactness and productivity, I have opted for the latter.[2] Also, quotations from German, French or Japanese were translated by me, and so all inaccuracies are mine. If an English-language edition is currently available, it is mentioned. To publish with Macmillan is a fascinating and extremely effective venture; needless to say that my thanks to Stephen Rutt and his team are not lip service as they provided the competent and, most importantly, patient help I so much needed.

Not to clutter the taxonomy, strategic alliances, partnerships and all forms of new internet business models are treated as subforms of networks, as some of these business models have not been proven to make sense nor to last. Similarly, emphasis has been placed on the postmodern side of the New Economy in order to better display the intellectual roots of this phenomenon, which is not at all only IT-related. The cursory reader can skip it, but should bear in mind that, generally speaking, the New Economy is a real-life projection of the abstract term postmodern.

Recent developments in Japan – the creation of the largest bank in the world by Mitsubishi; the reorganization of the financial world; the active revitalization of economic growth promoted by the state; the smooth handling of the – already forgotten – Kobe earthquake crisis; the struggle with recession and the current big 'sellout' of the Japanese car-makers – which have taken place during the writing of this book, can be perceived almost as associated case studies. Although they may often fail to make the headlines, Japan's momentous dynamics are still at work and unfettered, with the will and aim to create a strong Japanese platform in this wondrous New Economy. Following this (r)evolution will remain an exciting exercise. I hope the benign reader will analyse the current developments in Japan within the context of the arguments proposed in this book and feel that we are moving ahead in understanding our times and Japan.

Tokyo and Zurich, Spring 1996–Spring 2000   RAINER KENSY

Notes

1   Someone once said, that 'to read the footnotes is the most productive of all study'. As I subscribe to that academic version of 'no pains–no gains' I strongly encourage the reader to jog that extra mile for it may give him a clearer view on which foundations I have based my arguments while giving the interested reader some more avenues to explore should he want to dare further into the jungle.
2   But I have refrained myself from spraying URL's and links into the text as it is a book to read and to reflect upon rather than an excuse to rush to the computer.

List of Abbreviations

CAD   computer aided design
CAM   computer aided manufacturing
CIM   computer integrated manufacturing
CNN   Cable News Network
DKB   Daiichi Kangyo Bank
EPA   Economic Planning Agency (Japan)
ESOP   employee stock ownership plan
FAZ   *Frankfurter Allgemeine Zeitung*, Frankfurt
GATT   General Agreement on Tariffs and Trade
IBJ   Industrial Bank of Japan
IT   information technology
JIT   just in time
JTB   Japan Travel Bureau
LDP   Liberal Democratic Party (Japan)
ME   Mitsubishi Electric
MHI   Mitsubishi Heavy Industries
MIT   Massachusetts Institute of Technology
MITI   Ministry of International Trade and Industry (Japan)
MNE   multinational enterprise
MNC   multinational corporation
MoF   Ministry of Finance (Japan)
MTV   music television
NIE   newly-industrialized economies
NZZ   *Neue Züricher Zeitung*, Zurich
OAG   German East-Asiatic Society, Tokyo
OECD   Organization of Economic Cooperation and Development
R&D   research and development
RoI   return on investment
SCAP   Supreme Command of the Allied Powers (Japan)
TQC   total quality control

Part I

The Framework

1 Introduction

There is no point in using exact
methods where there is no clarity
in the concepts and issues to
which they are to be applied.

J. v. Neumann and O. Morgenstern,
Theory of Games and Economic Behavior, 1953, p. 4

I TERMINOLOGY

Postmodern modes of thought, Japanese economic structures, multinational
Japanese conglomerates, New Economy models: these are the corner stones
which define the course this work will follow. In this introduction we take an initial
look at these terms, without defining them too precisely, in order to produce an
preliminary framework. We will highlight the individual areas more specifically
and expound upon them in greater detail, one by one, in the course of the
argumentation.

Postmodern Thought Categories

Today, the term 'postmodern' is as familiar as an everyday household object but is
all too frequently used merely in a predicative and discursive sense. A more precise
analysis of the apparently boundless 'postmodern' phenomenon is seldom
conducted.[1] Discussions focus on origin, subject, object and method, in short, all
that is intense and contradictory: 'Postmodern? Obviously there is not much
consensus here about whether the term ought to be used at all, let alone where or
when.'[2] Is there any point in discussing it in the first place? Is it, positivistically-
speaking, a fictitious problem? Doesn't the entire concept become bogged down in
vagueness and capriciousness as a result of the absence of any real conviction?[3]
However, one can map the course of this trend which is clearly bidirectional:

3

- One of these directions represents *openness* and *vagueness* Here, diversity and multi-dimensionalism are the dominant issues: 'postmodernism is present wherever fundamental pluralism of language, model and procedure are practiced, although not juxtaposed in various works but rather in one and the same work, i.e. interferentially'.[4] Postmodernism[5] means a 'propagation of juxtaposed linguistic games which adopt an indiminishable diversity, thus preventing, right from the outset, any global totalitarianism of interpretation or thought'.[6]
- The focus of the second direction is more on the *relational*. There is no place here for definite, formal, generally-accepted truths. Everything depends on context, perspective and subject. Equal treatment is bestowed on historical, social and psychological meaning, as well as rational dimensions. 'There are no "hard facts of the matter" and all these concepts are relative to a specific conceptual scheme, theoretical framework, paradigm form of life, society, or culture.'[7]

A synthetic viewpoint is needed to take account of all these trends if we are not to degenerate into trivial tautologies, *à la* 'anything which calls itself "postmodern" is de facto "postmodern"' or into Feyerabend's 'anything goes'[8] style. This would, however, place the preoccupation with defining 'postmodern' too firmly centre-stage. In an initial approach, postmodern thinking can be channelled into the above profile. The following theses do not depend on universal truths and none of the analysis results can be either totally valid or totally invalid. In the interpretation of falsification proposed by Popper, the hypotheses will be subjected only to a 'validity test',[9] with the aim of enhancing comprehension of the two terms 'postmodernism' and 'Japan'. In so doing, the project will be seen, according to Bateson's interpretation, as a *quest for patterns which combine to produce mutual meaning*.[10]

Japanese Economic Structures

In general terms, the phrase 'economic structure' describes the cursory division of the national economy into state, enterprise and private households and the subdivision of enterprise into industrial sectors.[11] However, in this work we adhere to a clear perspective in which Japanese economic structures are seen as highly operationalized and based on the interaction between industrial groups. Thus the focus of our attention is on *these industrial groups and their most important elements – Japan's multinational enterprises –* the aim being to counteract the temptation of describing as many phenomena as possible, without ultimately being in a position to determine abstractable structures. Nonetheless, we shall also consider industrial conglomerates in terms of the network of economic, social, political, legal and cultural associations with other economic constituents, since this is an important element in the search for internal mechanisms. This analysis will, however, focus unequivocally on internal relationships within this sector; that is on multidimensional links between individual industrial conglomerates and their collective response to changing conditions in (world) markets as well as internal relationships within industrial groups. Statements made in the pages which follow also apply *cum grano salis* to other vantage points but must subsequently be carefully modified in the course a further analysis.[12]

Japanese Multinational Enterprises

Multinationals, international companies, transnational corporations, multi-domestic firms:[13] the variety of terms used to describe 'multinational enterprises' (MNEs) indicates that this is a phenomenon deserving of our consideration from a number of different viewpoints. It is currently seen as the most complex development stage in the theory of the firm.[14] These different viewpoints can be divided into three sections:

(a) the *geographical perspective*: cross-border company control, direct foreign-investment, relationships between homeland and host country;[15]
(b) the *'entrepreneurial' perspective*: production and marketing in several countries and the problem structures resulting from it;[16]
(c) the *'group-oriented' perspective*: a MNE comprises independent companies which together form international commercial units which maintain strong trade links with each other and operate, in principle, on an international level.[17]

According to Buckley,[18] we can also differentiate between four sub-definitions:

(a) *operational approach*: formal control over production facilities in several countries;
(b) *structural definition*: organization beyond national borders;
(c) *performance criterion*: quantification of international success;
(d) *behavioural assumptions*: structure, philosophy and scope of global management.

These perspectives also include nuances which facilitate the definition of even clearer subdivisions.[19] By pursuing these definition methods, we pinpoint, in this work, group-orientated perspectives together with focal points relating to structural and behaviour-oriented definition. This general definition must now be specified in a Japanese context. As a rule, major Japanese companies do not readily fit into this type of framework since they frequently:

• do not operate indiscriminately in all world markets; but
• maintain a strong presence only in certain, strategically selected product/market matrix areas;
• consciously neglect other areas;[20] or
• remain typically Japanese in terms of management and production structure, irrespective of location.[21]

In amplification, Kobayashi sets out a *behaviour-oriented definition of a multinational company*:

> In order for an enterprise to be multinational, its activities must have a certain impact upon the economy ... The management must have a global perspective and a strategy that surpasses nationalities and boundaries. It must work to advance the enterprise by utilizing the differences among various managerial resources and by setting regulations that limit corporate activities. The multinational enterprise must be supported by the overall system of control and organization in order to act as an entity. It must have enough flexibility to adapt to the demands for localization and customs of the society and government of the host country. Only when these five conditions are fulfilled can an enterprise be called multinational.[22]

In the case of commonly used Japanese definitions, we need to differentiate between two main terms:

Kaisha   This is the role model for modern Japanese conglomerates and is synonymous with all internationally-known companies, such as Honda, Toyota, Matsushita, Mitsubishi, Sumitomo.[23] This comprehensive description also includes companies which would not necessarily be called 'multinational', since the term 'Kaisha' also includes some major but purely national companies which, although active on the international market, are, in every other respect (e.g. production, personnel, finances) Japanese through and through.[24]

Zaibatsu   A second group of expressions relates to the term Zaibatsu, often used in the past, and usually translated as 'industrial grouping'. In Western languages this has the same meaning as the word *Keiretsu*, a more formal term used in the postwar era to describe these business structures.[25] To simplify matters, it is sometimes translated simply as 'big business';[26] although the best interpretation of the word Zaibatsu is 'a group of gigant [sic] diversified companies under the control of a family-owned holding company'.[27] Keiretsu is seen as the *network-type successor* to these hierarchically-structured companies (see Chapter 5, sections III and IV and the later part of section II). The list of companies with which this is most commonly associated include some of the most famous names: Mitsui, Mitsubishi, Fuyo and Sumitomo. In this context, 'younger companies' – although some are even more famous globally, such as Sony, Toyota, Honda, Matsushita, NEC and Nomura – should also be included under the heading 'other Kaisha'.[28]

Thus, in the chapters which follow, the term *Japanese multinational enterprise* primarily refers to *Keiretsu* (and also to Zaibatsu and Sogo Shosha if appropriate from a contextual point of view), although, in principle, the statements made could equally apply to other (multinational) Kaisha.

The Business Revolution called New Economy

As with the advent of the PC, the impact of the net' was and still is underestimated and misunderstood. No one talks about products anymore, exploring the assumed vast potential of e-business, i-business, m-business and so forth, while forgetting the roots of this New Economy. However, behind this search for meaning in the current revolution now taking place in the business world, after it has mutilated our social and private world (where this process was called postmodernization), a grand picture emerges. It is one of a technologically-enabled, ultra-flexible, open, non-spatial network of relations that transgresses the old borders between supplier–producer, client–firm, individual–nations, products–services, and so on. Things just break up at lightning speed without really making sense.

But, after the IT craze concerning technological possibilities, the real questions will be in the limelight: How will we be modelling this new world? What kind of relationships, communication forms, consensual decision-making systems and contractual agreements will emerge as standard operating procedures? Japan and the postmodern philosophy might well serve as tools in answering these questions.

So, in this sense, the New Economy is seen as the economic reality of postmodern theories. As the New Economy and the Internet are true revolutionaries, there is not a structured set of theories behind them but a colourful debate. Hence the link between the postmodern and the New Economy is maybe not yet fully understood and has to be axiomatically assumed here. Therefore, instead of speculating about the possible forms the New Economy might take, or praising the powers of IT, we will leave that level in order to examine the theoretical foundations found in the postmodern forum that might well serve for the architecture of the New Economy to be better grounded.[29]

Objectives

After having introduced the individual elements, we must now forge the links which bind these apparently unrelated images. To start with we consider three concepts:

1 Japan has demonstrated more long-term dynamism than any other country in the world and can therefore be considered as a challenge, a *reference model* and study case. To some extent Japan (and particularly Japanese multinational companies) might also be seen as a further stage in the development of a new paradigm for the economy and society.[30]
2 In general, there is only *partial understanding* of Japan as a country (socially, economically and in terms of cultural history), with the result that other areas are subsequently neglected, despite their ubiquitous presence. Consequently, there is a hidden risk that misconceptions about other dimensions can subconsciously creep in at other levels and thus drastically impair the picture when individual dimensions are analysed. And this applies particularly in the case of Japan.

3 The more frequent use of the expression *postmodern* in any given context has unfortunately resulted in *increased confusion* surrounding the term, so that it is rarely used in a plausible, pragmatic way. Likewise, the hailing of the New Economy is rarely based on sound analysis and a nexus between the postmodern and the New Economy is not yet described.

These three concepts show where the general theme of this work originated. We shall attempt to evaluate the concept of 'postmodernism' and 'Japan' for potential compatibility. Though this is not plausible at first sight, and despite the divergence of their origins, it is conceivable that a fruitful, informative collaboration might emerge from this association. We will specifically explore the following issues:

• Can the concept of postmodernism be used instrumentally in order to describe and understand Japan more effectively?
• Is it possible to produce a new, potentially hermeneutic, view of Japanese economic structures which would, in addition to political economy, social or quantitative analyses, contribute to the formation of a more complete picture of Japan?
• Looking at it from another perspective, could Japanese MNEs also act as a 'fruitful' research subject, allowing us to elucidate postmodernism in a more plausible, promising and forward-looking manner?

II RELEVANCE OF THE RESEARCH

The Postmodern Discussion or: a Discussion of 'the Postmodern'

The sheer volume of published material dealing with the most diverse of phenomena in a postmodern context would lead the unbiased observer to conclude that this is a research field with clear, predetermined subject areas, representing a canon of basic ideas for which boundaries to neighbouring disciplines have been well-defined as a result of continuous discourse. Conversely, readers who are more familiar with the material will conclude that these orthodox scientific criteria represent precisely the war zone in which advocates of postmodern thinking are battling. In proportional terms, an almost inverse relationship exists between the exponentially rising volume of publications and the level of consensus of any type on the nature of the term 'postmodernism' and its use in reports on the human environment. But this diversity is more than just a short-lived fashion which can be arbitrarily replaced by another, without consequence, in a couple of years' time. And it is certainly more than just a purely scholastic dispute among academics who constantly go round in circles in the same way, becoming embroiled in increasingly conceited forms of bizarre peculiarities, producing art for art's sake, with a level of efficacy confined to stunned, uncomprehending amazement from those around them, as in the Middle Ages.[31]

The postmodern current is a reaction both to a concrete *philosophical emergency* and to the contemporary intellectual understanding of our times. In the analysis of the American philosopher, R. Rorty, he determines that traditional philosophy has been forced into stubborn, self-inflicted isolation from which it is unable to deliver any relevant commentary whatsoever on the diversities and complexities of contemporary life.[32] Consequently, philosophy bears some of the responsibility for the way in which we shape our world. To deny this responsibility and persist with an illusionary project is tantamount to abdicating all rights and exposing oneself to ridicule.[33] Philosophical theory must now climb back down into the real world from its remote and somewhat elevated throne and make a pragmatic contribution to knowledge. In this context, postmodernism is a reflection of the spirit of the times. 'The spirit of the times or the spirit of the epoch, one of the new words inspired by Hegel, characterizes the present as a transitional period which is absorbed in an awareness of acceleration and the expectation of a different future.'[34] The diversity and contradiction, fragmentation and fuzziness in apparently each and every intellectual routine concept is a sign of our times. This is interpreted as an expression of the end of an epoch and as fertile ground for a new era. This end-of-an-era atmosphere by necessity brings with it a host of designs for the future. Prophets of doom as well as prophets of new golden eras are legion but only a few (like Sakaiya)[35] incorporate contemporary postmodern trends in their argumentation. This is also being expressed in many different forms in the precursory studies of the 'new-age movement' which is proliferating in every field, even in the economic disciplines.[36] As yet, no autonomous explicit vision of a postmodern future exists except the constant reiteration that a New Economy exists, though such reassurances are usually without any conceptual theoretical backbone. Implications for a perspective on the future can be abstracted only indirectly from theoretical discourse, but nevertheless, postmodernism sees itself as a go-between between today's set of norms and the set of values needed in the future, thus enabling us to comprehend current (global) trends and collaborate in their creation.

This embodies two divergent orientations which need to be balanced, which is what postmodernism is attempting to do. On the one hand, postmodernism takes account of this *multidimensionalism*, and to some extent takes it on board, in order to comment more fully on reality. Architecture, art, literary criticism, the fine arts, the dramatic arts, sociology and music are all eager to proclaim their postmodernity. A broad spectrum of topics is available, and nothing escapes this eclectic attempt to interpret reality.[37] On the other hand, this is the very reason why postmodernism is deeply embroiled in the discussion surrounding *modernity*. Modernism, which is also synonymous with the concept of the industrial age as something which should be overcome, is seen as a given handicap, as an instable and unsatisfactory starting point. It is the inevitable starting point of pragmatic postmodernism. The relationship between modernism and postmodernism is a frequently discussed topic: postmodernism as a later form of modernism; postmodernism as a separate innovation, as a foundation for modernity;[38] postmodernism as an inaccurately formulated catalogue of unresolved problems created by the modern. Neither view provides a clear standpoint and this naturally calls into question *the very existence of postmodernism and its legitimization*. This reappraisal of its own origins is necessary, however, in order to assert independently and, once and for all, a postmodern standpoint of any given type, which makes its own claims to relevance and wishes to be taken seriously.[39]

The economy, as the sector which has had the greatest global influence on people's lives, has largely been ignored in postmodern approaches, leaving aside for once short-lived faltering journalistic attempts and general investigative action.[40] Since economic activity always reflects the intellectual mood of society, any postmodern attempt to help in the quest for perspectives, designed to offer an understanding of current processes and the development of economic and social systems, should not be ruled out. Conversely, emerging theories on the New Economy still (involuntarily) leave out the postmodern material. The following questions make the postmodern discussion both interesting and topical:

- Does postmodernism exist at all as a separate, distinctive entity? Is the relation to the New Economy just spurious or is it a true parallel? What is it based on, what is its global relevance and can it make a pragmatic contribution?
- Is it the eagerly sought new paradigm which will embrace the dynamism of today's world and can it provide an operating framework and facilitate designs for the future?

Japan as the Focus of Attention

Japan has always commanded great respect in its dual role as cultural 'fascinosum' and economic power. It has a unique culture, combining two completely different personas. The first is that of a technological nation: efficient, forward-thinking, socially and economically homogeneous, sacrificing itself for the sake of the good of the nation with all the forces of Japan marching in rank and file, in a manner of speaking, at the same tempo along the straight road to growth, ahead of all other nations. However, it is also a country which values tradition very highly, a country which lovingly nurtures a sensitively refined culture and which has developed a markedly subtle, intense communication and social system. This duality alone ensures that Japan is compelling. But why is it now necessary to conduct a more thorough study, extending beyond the 'normal' accepted criteria applied to super-powers such as Japan, America, Russia or, now once more, Europe? The reasons why Japan presents itself so forcefully as a special subject for investigation can be explained through four arguments:

1 *Japan has attained and elevated herself to the status of a superpower in economic terms.* Japan is home to the largest banks and the most highly capitalized stock

exchange. It is the largest trading partner of the EU and NAFTA and has the highest life expectancy in statistical terms. These facts appear to speak for themselves.[41] Vogel's vision which warns of: 'Japan As Number One',[42] has now become reality and some American opinion-makers are finding the loss of their supremacy or 'pole position' painful. Leading economists, like Galbraith, see Japan as a global trendsetter, a precursor, though not in an ethical sense but rather as a system worthy of imitation, after it has undergone a cultural adaptation, rendering this system more digestible and more practicable for us Westerners.[43]

2 *In principle, Japan has never abandoned its hegemonic objectives.* There are many arguments in Japan's history to support this theory of hegemony. For example, it was voiced very clearly before the Second World War, in 1930, by General Arakiin in his work: To the entire Japanese race, which was distributed widely in Japan: '[T]the true mission ... is to spread and glorify the Imperial Way [i.e. Japan's Power] to the end of the four seas. Inadequacy of strength is not our worry. Why should we worry about that which is material?'[44] The Second World War brought about changes in the Japanese psyche which, historically-speaking, are without precedence (cf. Chapter 4). For the first time in the entire history of Japan, a foreign, alien power had set foot on Japanese soil. The desire to make amends for this disgrace *vis-à-vis* (a) their ancestors, (b) Japan and (c) themselves, has become a (subconscious) objective during the postwar period. At the end of the Second World War, when all hope had been lost, this urge for dominance moved to the economic sector: Americans and, to an increasing extent, Europeans as well, are again talking in economic terms of a frontal assault equivalent to Pearl Harbor. Here, belligerent vocabulary is used as the appropriate style: battles are waged using camouflage tactics, the element of surprise and unexpectedly aggressive moves.[45] And one often places a mythical interpretation, relating to Japan's sense of mission for world dominance, on questions as to the aim and purpose of putatively aggressive, strategic action on the part of the Japanese.[46]

The publication, *'No' to ieru Nihon*,[47] written by the politician S. Ishihara, is of interest in this context as it strikes a chord in the Japanese psyche by arguing in favour of a strong, dominant, one might almost say superior, role *vis-à-vis* America and Europe, *driven by Japan's sense of mission.* The *Neue Züricher Zeitung* commented as follows: 'Washington sees this pamphlet as proof of the theory that *Japan's commercial policy has non-commercial objectives* ... [48,49]. Articles like '1992: Europe's Counterattack: Japanese Industry will be shut out'[50] are conspicuously common in the Japanese press. Extracts, which highlight meta-economic symbolism and (national) moral values such as 'Europe is preventing us from pursuing our national objectives ['nihon do' proliferation of the Japanese way;] ... we must put up our shields, otherwise we will become the poor relation of the world instead of its master' appear not infrequently in articles of this type.[51] This point of view is not confined merely to economic and political matters; Japan is also exerting ever-greater influence over our daily lives. A cause for reflection is that we are being confronted by Japan in increasingly diversified ways, whether it is in the commodities sector, in articles about Japan, or even if only in terms of the greater spread of Japanese cuisine: this cultural invasion of our living environment is not declaring itself directly and openly as such (contrary to the way in which the American way of life was glorified throughout the whole of Europe in the postwar years), but is taking place very subtly. It is important for Europe and the USA to recognize these subliminal influences and adopt an appropriate stance towards Japan. Since Europe is making heavy weather of purely economic affairs, for example in respect of trade agreements, one can but estimate how disproportionately more complicated it is in cultural areas.

3   *In a temporal perspective different modes of action come to a head: or, expressed differently, the timing is right.* If Japan is to maintain the steep growth curve it has enjoyed over the past 30 years, disregarding 'flaws' in some quarters, it will need to extend its influence far beyond the domestic market and establish dependable markets outside its own island. The launch of a new 'Heisei' era in 1989, following the death of Emperor Hirohito, had a definite objective: in the official interpretation; it was translated as the final struggle for eternal peace. A different version of the Kanji allows a more striking interpretation 'the final major struggle before ultimate victory is achieved' (or, in more graphic terms: 'knock-out round').[52] Involuntarily, Caesar's *pacem facere* springs to mind, which was usually translated as 'bringing peace to the people', or 'pacifying, in the sense of conquering and showering with Roman culture'. Ohmae's[53] triad is now in the process of being established and the first steps to isolate individual triad forces are already in process, together with ensuing raids on each of the other 'territories'.

For Japan, the year 2000[54] is the target date for securely establishing dominance. The current (1998/99) economic low-growth/recession/reform phase is just slowing Japan down; it now merely defers the target into 2001 or 2002 and, more importantly, it even 'sharpens the blade' – the unfettered mind remains unerringly set on the 'great goals' established long ago. Japan has been pursuing an *extremely expansionist economic development strategy* for years, and this trend will undoubtedly continue. Japan is reinforcing its strategic position in the world and Europe and America are on the defensive.[55] Publicists take a clearer view of this trend: 'Japan's Trojan horse, i.e. investments in assembly plants, with low value added and a lack of control on the part of the host country, is a time bomb ticking away, at a frightening rate, right at the heart of western, industrial competitiveness ... and time is irrecoupably running out.'[56]

4   *Points 1–3 are probably also the reason why Japan is increasingly under the media spotlight.* Unfortunately, the basic concept of integral understanding is being lost in the flood of essays and short reports on rather arbitrary Japanese facets. This accounts for the superficial, one-dimensional or mythified, incomplete views held in Europe and the USA Hardly any attempt is ever made to piece together this multidimensional puzzle.

An integrated approach is still considered unconventional but is already becoming clearer in some works. For example, Kendrick[57] proposes the theory that the tension between social, communal and harmony-oriented forces and interests aimed at competition and victory within an individuum, but also within and between groups, forms the core of the Japanese motivation structure. This theory is elucidated in many examples from the world of work, law and economic policy and leads Kendrick to conclude that: 'The Japanese have become so expert in the art of practical compromise to achieve consensus and harmony yet being very ambitious and goal oriented, that when they see the advantages to their clan of working constructively with other groups or nations, they could play a leading role in world management.'[58] A further example of an integrated attempt at elucidation is put forward by Frischkorn,[59] who makes an empirical attempt to detect the effects of Buddhist thinking and practice on the Japanese work ethic, personnel management and top management. Up to now, the West has failed to make associations of this type due to a lack of formulated hypotheses, and it has neither been commented upon nor encouraged by the Japanese, as, for them, it is a natural almost unconscious and consequently unremarkable practice.

This discovery of the underlying forces influencing the Japanese economy is also hindered by the image which Japan promotes of itself abroad. Japan is selective in revealing its image to the outside world and this image differs substantially from the domestic view of Japan: to the outside world Japan portrays itself as a harmless, nature-loving and harmony-oriented country which still has much to learn and catch up on.[60]

The Japanese *self-portrait*, however, is very different: one intellectual constant in Japan is the debate about what it means to be Japanese (*Nihonjin-ron*). For a Japanese, the distinct dichotomy between 'we' and 'the others' (*uchi-tanin*) is ever-present multidimensionally, in the form of a linguistic, intellectual and ethical concept.[61] In Western sources, this discrete self-portrait of Japan is presented as an ethnological phenomenon: 'The Japanese formed a sort of *gigantic modern tribe* ... It is almost as if they regarded themselves as a different species from the rest of the world.'[62] A non-Japanese will have great difficulty in setting out clearly-structured, circumspect analyses, given this diversity of Japanese character, a difficulty which is further compounded by the Machiavellian manner in which the Japanese exploit this situation: 'They [the Japanese] confound and confuse those in the West who have become unwitting partners in Japan's economic aggression.'[63] Western analyses seldom probe beneath the surface of the (Western) image of Japan.[64] Social, psychological and personal dimensions could supplement this image – the habits and attitudes of the Japanese people are possibly even more foreign to Westerners than Japan's economic strategy. Up to now, much concerning the Japanese debate has been distorted or dealt with only inadequately or superficially. If proper account is taken particularly of the first three points – Japan's economic might; its political and cultural objectives and its hardening attitude towards trade (or global business cooperation in general) – there is an urgent need for those in the Western world to understand the fundamental driving forces behind Japan and not allow themselves to be diverted by confusing detail.

The Multinational Enterprise as a Research Subject

Multinational enterprises have long been a subject for research in the context of a 'theory of the firm', but they are now being subjected to even greater scrutiny due to the burgeoning internationalization of individual national economies.[65] Specific studies into the international features of industrial giants were not undertaken in the English-speaking world until relatively recently,[66] and those which have been conducted have so far failed to come up with a 'unified conceptual notion'[67] of multinational companies. This field of research continues to produce high levels of heterogeneity among research paradigms.[68] These research problems can probably be attributed in part to the research subject itself: no other company category comprises such a uniqueness of the various phenotypes. One could come up with a postmodern company classification simply by reading a brief, general description of the characteristics of the ideal, modern multinational enterprise: (1) simultaneous decentralized, virtual omnipresence; (2) assimilation and implementation of a diversified strategy (for example, production cost variations or different target group-dependent preferences); (3) incorporation of varying 'regional' cultures into overall management style; (4) maintenance of an open structure, not excluding anything *a priori*; and (5) amoeba-like adaptation to the 'global environment'.

A new paradigm for multinational enterprises is required to explain these trends, since companies are undergoing radical transformations necessitated by far-reaching changes in the global economic environment. '[There is a] need to restructure according to the organizational principles of a new production paradigm in the face of social inertia resulting from the legacy of a past industrial order.'[69] This statement – widened by the multidimensionality of the paradigm (which means that not only the production perspective but also organizational, cultural and consumer-oriented perspectives take their rightful place in the new paradigm) – is the current challenge which globally-oriented companies (and academic research) are setting themselves. Some companies are already well-advanced in the formulation and implementation of the new concept of a future-oriented (postmodern) company. In many cases, Japanese companies are cited – Matsushita or Toyota, Hewlett-Packard, IBM Japan, Nissan and Fuji-Film, Ogilvy or BSN, to name but a few.[70]

Multinational enterprises are actively confronting the challenge of a changing future. The proactive, strategic, structural and organizational projects undertaken in preparation for the Common European Market, even before bureaucrats and politicians had even mentioned it in meaningless rhetorical declarations of intent, is one example of this. Multinational enterprises set and anticipate trends, acting to a degree as role models for the (other) 'national' industries (cf. Chapter 5, section II). These 'paradigmatic' companies are reasonably certain of their role and also of their potential for success. An extensive quotation from a speech given by the founder of Matsushita, K. Matsushita, on the differences between American and Japanese production companies, goes some way to proving this:

> We will win and you will lose. You cannot do anything about it because your failure is an internal disease. Your companies are based on Taylor's principles. Worse, your heads are tailorized too ... We have passed the Taylor-stage. We are aware that business has become terribly complex. Survival is very uncertain in an environment filled with risk, the unexpected, and competition. We know that the intelligence of a few technocrats – even bright ones – has become totally inadequate to face these challenges. Only the intellects of all employees can permit a company to live with the ups and downs and the requirements of the new environment. Yes, we will win and you will lose. For you are not able to rid your minds of the obsolete Taylorisms that we never had.[71]

This post-Taylorist knowledge coupled with the specific Japanese know-how embodied in these enterprises needs to be analysed, fully documented, selectively adapted, adopted and implemented in other (read: Western) companies, although careful account of transcultural aspects should necessarily be taken, to ensure future survival in the face of changing frameworks especially in terms of the competitive environment and ever-changing consumer needs.

Previous Research

In answer to Morgenstern's rhetorical question as to whether economic data were ever accurate enough, Grilliches said: 'There are basically four responses to his criticism and each has some merit. (1) The data are not that bad. (2) The data are lousy but it does not matter. (3) The data are bad but we have learned how to live with them and adjust for their foibles. (4) That is all there is – it is the only game in town and we have to make the best of it.'[72] These four statements apply quite specifically to the topics dealt with here. A major imbalance exists in the general *data situation* in respect of specific research topics relevant to this work. Material is available on the individual topics (postmodernism, Japan, multinational enterprises), and is for the most part comprehensive, but the links between these topics have largely been ignored.

Multinational enterprises have been examined from many standpoints (as in section I of this chapter), but a genuinely postmodern approach has yet to be considered. Although cultural aspects have been included as parameters, these falter at the half-way stage, for two reasons. Either the cultural aspects are considered *exogenous* and are considered, non-specifically, as an effect resulting from national differences or variations in administrative forms (dictatorship, bureaucracy, management, chaos),[73] or the word 'culture' is used *endogenously* in the sense of *corporate culture*.[74] An interdisciplinary, eclectic viewpoint is evident in only a few pilot projects.[75]

Our preoccupation with Japan as an entity has led to a vast amount of research covering every conceivable aspect. Literature on the Japanese economy can be roughly divided into four categories: cultural-history-based works,[76] eye-witness reports,[77] studies on specific economic aspects[78] or a sectoral view of the interaction between individual industries taking account of major exogenous influences such as politics and foreign countries.[79] *The first link in the chain between cultural phenomena and the economy has yet to be forged completely*, since the vast majority of works attempt to pinpoint cultural influences on Japanese companies with the intention of elucidating their productivity (Western viewpoint)[80] or supremacy (Japanese viewpoint).[81] This analysis of cultural and social influences often gets bogged down in generalizations[82] or is incomplete and inadequate in conception, shuddering to a halt when enumerating a few seemingly transparent cultural parameters.[83]

In Japan, postmodernism is analysed only very sporadically and only in professional circles within the framework of theoretical specialist debate.[84] A reflection which ventures beyond the obligatory treatment of a predefined topic, producing independent comment as a result of its own concrete situation, has so far failed to materialize. Equally, a postmodern view of Japan[85] can be found only in very few non-Japanese sources. The economy is not a major topic for postmodern authors, any more than postmodern approaches are to economists.[86] If these handicaps are viewed in combination, the paucity of the research situation becomes clearly apparent which can, in itself, be characterized as a postmodern phenomenon. Well-developed structures do exist in relation to the individual topics of these two groups (comparable to Lyotard's narratives), but the central seam linking them together remains open and raw.

The exploding volume of New Economy literature has still not yet taken on the copious body of postmodern work of the last ten years which awaits application to the business sphere.[87,88] To my best knowledge, there is basically no New Economy literature developed on the basis of postmodern material.[89] As a result, the combination of the New Economy and Japan usually leaves this out as well.[90] As a research topic, the postmodern aspects of Japan's multinational enterprises (or, equivalently, postmodern aspects of Japan's economic structure) must be classified as *terra incognita*, since individually established fields of research have omitted this area up to now.

III DEMARCATION LINES

The following demarcation lines have been drawn in order to pinpoint the perspectives included, the sub-areas which deserve special attention, and the areas which will be largely relegated to the wings. This is intended primarily to enhance the sharpness of the overall picture and (in optical terms) to optimize focus. We must step back somewhat in order to facilitate full documentation of each of the three types of phenomenon and avoid a 'can't see the wood for the trees' scenario. Conversely, certain specific details require closer inspection as they may *add plausibility to the overall argument. This adjustment of focus is not undertaken ad libidum,* but in support of the objective which is to consider individual phenomena integrally whilst allowing their relationship to one another to remain fluid.

The Terms 'Postmodernism'/'Postmodern'/'Postmodernity'

The postmodern should not be seen as a single, isolated discussion topic, as the intention is not to intervene directly in the debate surrounding postmodernism.[91] It is more a case of presenting a pragmatic view derived from the debate associated with Rorty: 'Rorty praises pragmatism as "post-philosophical philosophy" ... [H]e sees pragmatism at the center of a postmodern philosophical revolution in the very nature of truth and knowledge.'[92,93] This is the reason why our realities, which are always provisional, contradictory and at best asymptotic, must be subjected to sustained examination and interrogation.[94] Thus, postmodernism assumes a two-dimensional character: it serves as a *paradigm for contemporary society* and may consequently be seen as a practical method, an *instrument*, to help us understand, categorize and actively form economic phenomena. A laborious argument that the New Economy is postmodern philosophy in interaction with economics and business is not prepared, as that axiom should implicitly develop itself during the course of the investigation.[95,96]

It should also be made clear at the outset that it is not the purpose of this study to filter out postmodern influences in the overall intellectual debate in Japan; the question as to whether and to what extent Japan has a postmodern school of thought is rather irrelevant here. A few studies on this issue already exist in other areas.[97] The basic premise that Japan is postmodern or has postmodern characteristics should be seen more as the *starting point* on which this study is based.

The View Taken of Japan

Especially where a large number of dimensions interact simultaneously, particularly around the research subject 'Japan', it is impossible to assign the same priority to all these levels and to deal with them all at once. At the top end of the abstraction – Japan as an economic structure – the framework is clear: economic relationships, information- and decision-oriented behaviour and the structural characteristics of the economy are central topics. Here, economy is understood to include all companies and company-type organizations such as trade associations, unions, para-governmental commissions, regulatory bodies and so forth. Individual entities, the consumer and the employee are intentionally included only on the fringes. Enterprises merged together in company groups are a focal point, representing in the context of a macroeconomic analysis, trades, industries and sectors, and forming from a microeconomic perspective a bundle of company strategies, conglomerates and business entities.

The *historical dimension*, as an explicit category, must be left to historians of economics, whilst the argument of historicism – that is the historically-dependent economic structure and economic behavioural structure created from antecedents – is strongly reinforced. Primarily due to a lack of space, it is impossible to present a detailed picture of the forces that, as a result of historical developments, shaped the status quo, although that would form an interesting topic in itself.[98]

Within our framework, we will focus on the situation within Japan itself. References to Japanese *foreign* commitments (e.g. Japanese direct investment projects; Japanese managers abroad or the external trade links maintained by Japanese companies) would serve only to dilute the picture, since, in these aspects, Japan's '*modus operandi*' is no longer clearly visible due to the extensive exchange and adoption of Western patterns of behaviour, organization and thought. Only in Japan, where the Japanese persona is left to flourish largely undisturbed and undistorted, does the area of conflict between old and new, Japanese and non-Japanese, traditional, modern and postmodern become most apparent.

The *political dimension* also lies beyond our field of vision. Since political forces exert a strong influence on economic life, and are themselves affected enormously by the economic environment, the Japanese economy and political situation should then be seen as an inseparable unit, in need of global analysis. Nevertheless, this divide is necessary to make the complexity of the subject more manageable and to allow clearer representation of the main arguments.[99] To date, no other analyses, such as a postmodern interpretation of political events in Japan, have been published, either in Japan or abroad. Equally, purely political analyses[100] based on the strong interdependence between politics and economy fail to reach the heart of the argumentation present here.

The *social situation*, everyday life and private life are also considered only where social processes are fundamental to the discussion. This would include, for example, the special significance of group processes in decision-making, the Confucian principle of seniority hierarchies or the extremely important concepts of 'guilt' and 'duty' (*giri* and *on*; Chapter 3, section IV), which, for the Japanese, play a central role in every aspect of life. A psychologically-oriented view of the individual and groups is equally unsustainable and is convincingly represented in many studies.[101] It has been left to future research to trace an overall view of the psychological and social origins of the modern and postmodern aspects of the Japanese economy.

In consequence, this investigation remains open at the core: Japan as an abstract concept is only of secondary significance, the main focus of our attention being on the multinational enterprises, which are embedded in their Japanese tradition and in their contemporary Japanese environment.

Methodological Limitations

Crosscultural research has considerable advantages over mono-dimensional approaches: one forsakes self-centredness; becomes more sure-footed in the analysis of international business; discovers optimization possibilities; and knowledge of one's self is enhanced by observing other systems.[102] The current status of research on multinational enterprises sets clear, interculturally verifiable, global test statistics as its methodological ideal and takes the view, that 'traditional methods cannot and will not be used for interdisciplinary research topics'. Irrespective of the extent of diversity and non-convergence applicable to the individual cultural elements, it is possible to generate coherent images from the juxtaposition of appropriate individual pieces.[103]

Parallel to this, postmodernism views things in 'decontextualized' terms, providing no indication as to context or, in the form of quotations, with no trace as to the historicity of the quotation, or as polyvalent symbols with more than one possible meaning.[104] Contradictory meanings are condoned, for they permit comparison between an infinite variety of meanings and, consequently, contexts and cultures. A single culture can provide only an incomplete interpretation; only multiple polycultural interpretations (decentre cultures) can provide meaning.[105,106] Consequently, the postmodern concept transcends traditionally defined cultures. The aim of postmodern research is not therefore to be crosscultural but *transcultural*. Thus, a contest of paradigms is taking place, the temporal outcome of which, if definable at all, remains open. Meanwhile, in reality, practical problems remain to be solved. Armchair economics[107] or a desktop economy[108] are as much a luxury as a professorial philosophy for professors of philosophy[109] and we can afford neither at the present time. Rorty's preferred strategy is to abandon all claims to uniqueness and try out anything that is available.[110] Thus, in order to solve a problem one should start with an eclectic movement[111] and thus create a discussion which is diverse, hermeneutic and contradictory. An hermeneutic economic science is extremely pragmatic in its principles and aims to explain, assist and advise but not to assess or direct; thus it is positive rather than normative. Friedman, one of the doyens of this approach, defines a positive economic science quite pragmatically: '[Positive economics asks] what is and not what ought to be ... Economics as a positive science is a body of tentatively accepted generalizations about economic phenomena that can be used to predict the consequences of changes in circumstances.'[112] Johnson sums up the descriptive aspect in clearer terms: 'By positive or non-normative knowledge, we mean knowledge about conditions, situations and things which does not have to do with their goodness and badness.'[113] Nor is the choice of method made *a priori*, but in the context of a 'constructive hermeneutics'.[114] Phenomena *per se* do not exist independently of the relevant paradigm of the observer, but are construed only by paradigms manifest in the observer, that is, are brought to life and defined.[115] Concretely, within the framework of this work, terms like 'Japanese economic structures' and 'postmodern thought categories' are formed during the course of the argumentation, for these terms are referring to each other when these terms need to be defined. This standpoint is based on Maturana and Varela, among others, who comprehensively describe a system of *epistemological constructivism*. According to them: 'we will, in fact, present a view which looks at understanding, not as a representation of the outside world but rather as a

continuing evolution of a world via the process of life itself'.[116] Each act of perception is synonymous with the creation of a world with mutual structural dependency: The 'object' of perception is created in the exchange with the perceiving
'subject', and vice versa.[117]

For this reason, postmodernism can be considered a method in its own right.
If the postmodern debate also chooses to see itself as a discourse between methods,
there is an indication that it might be used instrumentally.[118] 'Since many theoretical, deductive systems are possible ... [and] a presumably infinite number of logical
worlds likely',[119] the go-between must make provision for them. Postmodernism
wishes actively to attempt this. It is unclear *a priori* whether it is valid as a *metatheory* in the terms of scientific theory.[120] In any case, the intention in this work is
to attempt to demonstrate that postmodernism is not simply a lifestyle, an attitude
to life or a philosophy for life,[121] but rather a concept whose aim is to act as a go-
between between lifestyles and methods, is able to function to some extent as a
method in its own right, with the objective of preventing a breakdown in communications between the divergent lifestyles and methods.[122]

Although the method used for testing these hypotheses should be called empirical,
that is employing reality as arguments, it tends to be deductive and hermeneutic,
considering phenomena in their entirety rather than in a mono-dimensional,
rational-analytical context. The result may very well be merely hints and facets,
indicating possible compatibility between 'postmodernism' and 'Japanese multinational enterprises'; completeness or total exhaustion of the empirical facts of the
matter is not achievable: 'An empirically saturated theory of postmodernism is not
available and it is unlikely that one would strive to achieve this goal, given the
premises on which postmodernism itself is based.'[123]

IV STRUCTURE OF HYPOTHESES

Basic Approach

Even if one is not a Japanese specialist, it is impossible to shut out the news and
information disseminated regularly on a wide variety of subjects: Japan, a challenge
for Europe and America; Japan, the major banking force; Japan, the most active
direct investor, and so on. We think we are being kept well-informed but it is only
when we delve deeper into the detail that we become aware of the amount of
contradictory and 'extremely controversial images portrayed of Japan'.[124] But the
belief still remains (when viewed at a distance) that it is feasible to blend these
diverging facets into one single picture. This belief is totally destroyed when one
becomes privy to 'the special intensity of daily life in Japan':[125]

> ... [W]hat hits you with one, almighty blow, on arriving in Japan is the transition
> from quantity to quality, the transformation of the small worker into opulent

diversity ... they are different in innumerable ways and there is no intolerance to the feeling of being [just] one of the many, no subversion whatsoever against the system.[126]

Newly-discovered and assimilated categories disintegrate and the spotlight diffuses, with increasingly regularity, on conundrums of every conceivable dimension: 'Our reality dissolves' under the influence of other classifications, or a 'different syntax', into a disjointed, loose juxtaposition without a centre. The growing image in Western minds of an enigmatic Japan provides an incentive to search for patterns in order to regain our bearings. Barthes talks of the liberal, arbitrary and consequence-free exchange of significants; significants – signs in Brownian motion. Tokyo is a symbol of this: a city with a symbolically empty city centre which cannot *de facto* be reached. This refers to the giant imperial presence enthroned intrusively, impassably and quasi vacantly in the city centre. In its total openness, this city with no street names, subdivisions or cartography has no points of reference to assist the uninitiated. 'Tokyo reminds us that rationale is simply one of many systems.'[127]

After 70 years of intensive dealings with Japan, the former Harvard professor and ex-US Ambassador to Japan, E. Reischauer, concluded with resignation: '[T]he Japanese society is too complex and too rapidly changing to fit into any tight, neat model'.[128] Nevertheless, the problems of personal daily life force one to confront the issue of the Japanese condition, irrespective of whether it relates to a businessman based in Japan or a Central European consumer. The only thing remaining in our 'intellectual superstructure' is an awareness of the contradictory, diverse and arbitrary perspectives, and the vagueness and diffuse uncertainty of each structure. This is exactly where we must search for the connection between Japan and post-modernism, this is the point where the two topics merge. A new postmodern era will proclaim randomness of background; any 'histoire', any 'narration' becomes quotable in tandem. Fundamentally everything is applicable anywhere, in any desired combination, whether of Western or Eastern origin, in order to give meaning.[129]

Hypothesis of the Postmodern Economic Model

If the postmodern trend is considered a dominant model for explaining social change, this explanatory approach can also be applied in the economic domain and thus one could speak in terms of a postmodern *economic model* (thus widely overlapping with the New Economy idea). The expression 'economic model' should not be understood in the sense of an economic order or economic system, but rather as a set of all interpretations of practical phenomena with the same provenance, to explain phenomena on the macro-, meso- and micro-economic levels. The definitions 'economic system' and 'economic order' demonstrate precisely that these terms are too hermetic and too orthodox and are therefore specifically inappropriate when used together with postmodernism, due to the openness, vagueness and parataxis of postmodernism. Sombart, for example, understands the term *economic system* to mean:

a type of economy which can be seen as a coherent unit, in which each of the fundamental components of the economy take on a certain shape ... it is this type of economy which is seen as an intellectual unit which is a) dominated by a specific economic ethos, b) possesses specific order and organization and c) employs a specific technique.[130]

It is primarily point (a) of this definition, the economic ethos, which corresponds to a postmodern economic model.[131] The term *economic order* is also too hermetic and hierarchical in structure to coincide with a postmodern economic way: 'By economic order we mean a complex of real and idealistic determining factors which are moulded into a single entity of economic reality by a power-driven creative desire, which is historically embedded.'[132] The term 'economic way' can be seen as synonymous with the American usage of the term 'economic system' or 'economic model' (analogue to business model). This terminology is usually defined as follows: 'An economic system is a complex of organizational patterns among individuals and groups engaged in activities of fulfilling human material needs.'[133]

But all these terms – most of them based on the post-Second World War pioneering German school of economics – remain problematic. In English, which is a more pragmatic language, the description 'postmodern economic model' is, for our purposes, expressed more simply and easily as 'a postmodern reading of business'.[134] On this basis, the term 'postmodern economic model' means the presence of strategies, business practices, theories and classification groups in business life to which the description 'postmodern' applies. The concepts of postmodernism can be used to explain the latest, long- and medium-term trends and the New Economy is therefore postmodern philosophy in action.

In short, the hypothesis of a postmodern economic model way could be proposed as follows:

> Based on the axiom of the social, paradigmatic relevance of postmodernism, it is possible by using different developments in economic research to demonstrate that the postmodern body of thought plays a forward-looking role both in the theory and practice of the economy and business. These newest developments point to a postmodern approach (in the future) and, specifically, to a postmodern *modus operandi* in terms of the economy. It is the very heart of the New Economy.

Hypothesis of Japan's Postmodernity

In a second stage, this hypothesis of a postmodern economic model is defined in concrete terms. It is assumed that Japan, a *trend-setter* for social development in the postwar era, must *per se* represent postmodernism in a clearer and more diverse manner than other countries, based on the premise of postmodernism as a social explanation or an expression of the times (Hegel's 'Zeitgeist'-concept seems to be too broad in this connection, and encumbered with disproportionately large claims). Particularly in Japan, where cultural traditions are of major structural significance and affect behaviour, the rules and nature of human coexistence have been perfected and 'tested' over an extended period of time. The Western world is only now encountering some parameters which have always been valid for Japan: the restricted nature of the living environment, a total (and correspondingly menacing) shortage of resources, population density, and 'harmonious' coexistence (whilst acknowledging the diverse nature of attitudes) as a social objective.[135] It is only now that these limitations, which have always been significant from a theoretical viewpoint, are flooding into the Western comprehension of economic activity in the form of critical conditions of thought.

The Western world views postmodern concepts as a new instrument (new to them) with which to circumvent these limitations. Historically-speaking, Japan has always been good at developing circumvention methods and structures: Japan's structure is what we, in the Western world, now refer to as 'postmodern'. We aim to demonstrate this by using Japanese multinational enterprises as an example, since they, like practically no other institutions, link the past with the future. Their structures, strategies and the behavioural demands on those actively involved in them, represent an evolution spanning centuries. At the same time, their present role is a dominant one and they represent a major force in the realization of the future.

In short, the hypothesis of Japan's postmodernity reads as follows:

> Special features which are referred to as 'postmodern' exist in relation to economic structures which have developed historically, as well as to the economic practice adopted by Japan's multinational enterprises. By juxtaposing them with postmodern thoughts and concepts, they can be identified and thus represent a novel attitude to and understanding of Japan.

Structuring the Task

In the context of a short overview, we shall proceed to comment on the logical structure of this work. This should not be seen as a detailed research programme,[136] but simply as a disclosure of the background assumptions made in relation to the two hypotheses set out above. In addition, we split these hypotheses into research questions which will then, in operationalized form, determine the course of the argumentation.

The following axioms form the starting point for the study:

1 *The existence of postmodernism*: 'postmodernism' does exist as an independent school of thought. It sees itself as a 'serious' attempt to explain reality and not

as unrealistic, irrelevant speculation on rival platforms. Equally it is not a reformulation of established schools of thought.

2 *The objective of postmodernism to be a comprehensive explanatory tool*: as a plausible paradigm with contemporary significance, it is not confined to just a few social phenomena of a culture, but internationally encompasses, in correspondingly adapted form, the human cultural environment of the most highly developed or post-industrial countries.

3 *Japan as a challenge*: Japan, as a nation, is considered by the Western cultural hemisphere to be a challenge in many areas, due to its economic standing. A cursory view from both an economic and social standpoint serves as a reference model which challenges 'conventional' Western social paradigms.

4 *Multinational companies are an ideal research model*: Japanese multinational enterprises, grew out of trading companies, unique to Japan, which, still today remain at the heart of their crystallization. They represent plausible examples from which to elucidate fundamental Japanese characteristics, which are, in a Darwinian sense, Japan's 'fittest' entities, having been successful over the centuries in the face of dynamic changes in every basic condition.

We have described these axioms, together with the origins of the basic research question, in this chapter. The hypotheses set out above are generated from these basic assumptions. In specific terms, the axioms relating to the existence of postmodernism and its overall validity can be seen as the origins of the hypothesis for a postmodern economic model. The hypothesis for Japan's postmodernity can then be generated from the second group of axioms, that of the reference role of Japan and the use of Japanese multinational enterprises as a model.

Chapter 2 provides an overview on the understanding of postmodernism. Special attention will be devoted to social visions derived from postmodern concepts and to the economic understanding of postmodernism. In view of the complexity and ambiguousness of the term, it seems vital to operationalize this concept, which will then act as a reference in the chapters which follow.

The third part of the work (Chapters 3–5) adopts the descriptive methods employed by Best to explain competitive structures.[137] Chapters 3 (culture as a basis for competitiveness; relevant social principles for Japan's postmodernity), 4 (industrial policies and economic macro- and meso-coordination as a competitiveness strategy; individual building blocks of coordination mechanisms in the Japanese world) and 5 (structure and organization of the MNE as a competitiveness facilitator; Japanese MNEs as postmodern business models) deal with the basic dimensions of culture, strategy and organization of production. Figure 1.1 summarizes the above.

V INITIAL SUMMARY: *MODUS OPERANDI*

The aim of this first chapter has been to present the explanatory and causal relationships contained in this work.[138] We have tried to demonstrate the relevance

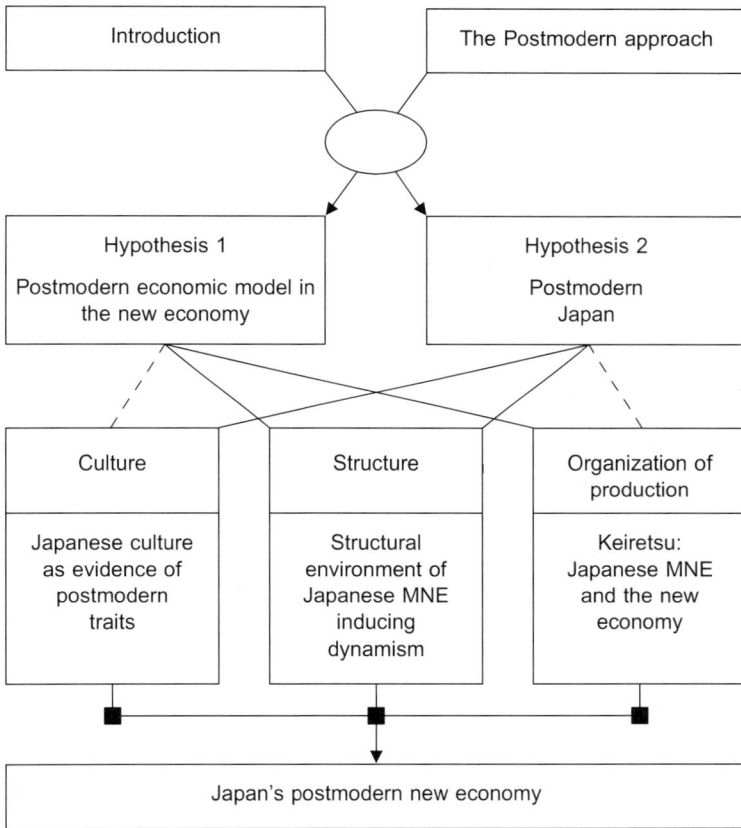

Figure 1.1 *Flow chart of the book*

of the task as well as its definition. Taking the definitions of the individual components and their explicit limitations as a starting point, we have generated hypotheses which were subsequently operationalized within a problem structure. A number of methodical considerations proved to be necessary as an interim stage, which, listed separately, are:

1 The *relevance of Japan as a research subject* is explained by:

- its position as an economic leader;
- the potentially latent presence of Japan's hegemonic objectives;
- the diversity of misunderstandings or conundrums with which Japan continually confronts the West; and finally by

- the current explosive nature of the global political situation (the further disintegration of the Soviet Union, European unification, uncertainties in America's domestic policy, etc.)

all of which are grounds for a strategically far-sighted but nevertheless expeditious course of action.

A framework for the term 'Japanese economic structure' needs to be selected in relation to:

- analysis levels (we shall confine our argumentation to sectors/industrial groups, referring to individual companies as examples only for clarification purposes);
- classification in terms of area and time (concentration on the domestic economy, without setting out a detailed outline); and
- focus definition (emphasis has clearly been placed on economic criteria, without excluding social and political aspects or diverse relationships to other internal structural mechanisms, such as the socio-cultural environment).

2   The *topicality of postmodernism* and its media presence, which makes the conceptual uncertainty surrounding it even more astounding, and the aim of postmodernism, seen as a reflection of the spirit of the time, to be a concept with which to manage our present world, were the main points intended to clarify the relevance of postmodernism. In so doing, we did not view postmodernism as the attribute of a single discipline, within the framework of a single science, but rather in its entirety, that is as a postmodern thought structure initially defined primarily by means of relational, contextual dependencies, its multidimensionality and its openness. Nor do we intervene in the theoretical professional debate but represent a rather more pragmatic view of postmodernism as a method. Additionally, the New Economy is not seen as a separate phenomenon *sui generis* but is the economic reality created by the postmodern currents.

3   The justification for using *Japanese multinational enterprises* as the basis for our work can be found in the increasing globalization of all economic phenomena and in the paradigmatic role of multinational companies *vis-à-vis* all other firms, whereby only Japanese multinational enterprises which have evolved over many years out of family-owned trading companies and which are preeminent in shaping the future, have been considered.

The aim of this work is to combine the three elements of this problem and to enhance our understanding of the Japanese multinational enterprise by looking at them from a postmodern viewpoint and, secondly, to obtain greater clarity on the characteristics of postmodernism by applying it to a defined and practical research subject.

Building on this, it was possible to establish the following two research hypotheses:

1 The postmodern economic model is a new kind of economic thinking, which has already been imbued with increasingly significant, postmodern concepts.
2 Postmodern constellations do exist within the economic structure of Japan and particularly within the structures and plural processes of Japan's multinational enterprises.

Methodologically, we focus on a deductive, pragmatic and constructivistic approach. This *modus operandi* appears appropriate, taking account of the given conceptual complexity and its dynamism and vagueness. The data situation can be seen as difficult, since substantial research is only available on peripheral topics – that is, on the specialist areas of Japanese, postmodern and multinational company research – with no published material available at the intersection of these two sets. This empty set needs to be filled.

Part II

Economics and the Postmodern

2   Postmodern Principles

What distinguishes those futurologists
who foresee merely an 'advanced technological society'
in the offing from those who herald a 'new society'
is that the former perceive only an upgrading,
while the latter believe that the main framework
and social paradigm of industrial society will be replaced
by forms as radically different from what we have known
as medieval society was different from modern.

T. Sakaiya, *The Knowledge-Value Revolution*, 1991, p. 5

I   OVERVIEW

As already mentioned in the previous chapter, it is not feasible to present an amoeba-like, formless but, nevertheless, descriptive concept such as postmodernity like a butterfly pinned out in a display case.[1] It is equally impossible to provide a detailed history of the term or a fundamental history of the concept, since it is not possible to identify any linearity in the course of the argument, nor is this the aim of postmodernism.[2] The dominate discussions within postmodernism concern the issue of the independent existence of postmodernity within or after modernity and the issue of the content of the postmodern debate. Whitehouse aptly comments: 'Like Postmodernism itself, then, the debate [about it] is a markedly eclectic event.'[3]

The structure of this chapter endeavours to do justice to these difficulties by adopting several different perspectives. *Independence as a conceptual approach* can be demonstrated by its emancipated relationship to modernity (to industrial society and its guiding concepts). Building on this, we clarify the extent to which post-modernism is capable of depicting a comprehensive picture of (contemporary, post-industrial, Internet based) society. From this, we develop the concept of *postmodern economic understanding*, which is then provided, in a generalized form, as the working model for future work. The intention here is to create a bridge between the theoretical view of the feasibility of a postmodern economy and its discovery, as a reflection, in contemporary economic literature.[4]

II APPROACHES TO THE POSTMODERN

The aim of this chapter is to mark out the area which the term 'postmodern' wishes to address. It is, however, impossible to illuminate all areas thoroughly – this would be beyond the scope of the present work. If we were to attempt to capture the hundreds of separate opinions on postmodernity and postmodernism, we would completely destroy the possibility of obtaining any overview, since there would then be no coordinated starting point or generally accepted position from which to work through the individual disciplines, but only a discordant cacophony of babble. After conducting a study of the genealogy of postmodernism[5] (or rather the impossibility thereof) and its origins, we shall use two examples to demonstrate how postmodernism has made the transition from ethereal, 'pure' theory to a real, 'practical' application. Architecture was one of the first areas in which postmodern sensations took on a physical form of expression and put down visible markers for postmodernity. Secondly, theory of science has, particularly in recent times, been in the unusual position of achieving discoveries – though on a purely modern basis – which no longer fit into any familiar overall concept, but which can be interpreted in a postmodern manner.

We will use the history of the term, its initial and its (for the time being) ultimate application to demonstrate the extent to which postmodern thinking has proliferated and why it is therefore more than just a few concepts within different disciplines. On the other hand, we also intend to demonstrate that postmodernism has an inherent claim to a *comprehensive global interpretation*, comparable in intensity to all other (earlier) concepts of global interpretation.

The Genealogy of Postmodernism

Even 15 years ago, during the 'postmodern wave', no consensus on the origins of postmodernism was apparent; too many intellectual trends from the past were seen as its origins. In his study of genealogy, Köhler was forced to conclude that 'there is still a lack of consensus on the part of authors as to what can be classified as "postmodern"'.[6] Five years later, Hassan dismissed the issue of genealogical classification in an equally terse manner: 'The question of postmodernism remains complex and moot.' Since then, no other serious studies based on a historically detailed analysis of postmodernism have been conducted; it is accepted that it is impossible to interpret its origins or course of development linearly, since they remain inextricably intertwined.[7] Summation attempts generally detect its earliest signs in the America of the 1950s, when modern industrial society first experienced a glut. One was obliged to distance oneself from an oversatiated society, in a manner which was radically removed from the fixed, ossified categories of a bigoted affluent society.[8] It was a period of liberation, of negative influences, followed by a positive, constructive mood in which the pop and hippie movements of the 1960s then proliferated: 'The present was no longer viewed as the anticlimax to the end of an era but as a new start, bursting with promise.'[9] Total rejection was abandoned in favour of a counterculture, which was not merely a postmodern culture; its scope was too wide for this. However, postmodernism was able to gain some momentum from its creativity and radical methods of analysis.[10] This led to the propagation of a new type of sensuality which frivolously and unpretentiously employed superficiality as a value *per se.*

Meaning remained always concealed in modernism and had to be surgically removed by means of interpretation and comprehension. Sonntag and Fiedler opted for the direct approach to superficiality, as all that exists apart from the thought structures of the observer, actor or author involved. Instead of transmitting messages, there is a free flow of energy which anyone can formulate as they wish.[11] When, in the 1970s, postmodernism once again started to deal with the issue of modernism, although this time in the emancipated form of a discovery of its own roots, it encountered frustrated disillusioned contemporary forces bitterly opposed to postmodernism, whose aim was to initiate a 'cultural backlash'. This conflict spread and became polarized in Habermas[12] on the one hand, and Lyotard[13] on the other. The lengthy rearguard action fought by modernism was conducted with vehemence and rhetoric, obliging Nägele to speak of a religious war between 'Frankfurters and French Fries'.[14]

Although this modern vs postmodern discussion flares up now and again, the issue of 'modernity or postmodernity?' neutralized itself in the 1980s, since postmodern authors to some extent lost their enthusiasm for it; areas of conflict have diminished and the modern is classified as a facet of the postmodern:

> What appears on one level as the latest fad, advertising pitch and hollow spectacle is part of a slowly emerging cultural transformation in Western societies, a change in sensibility for which the term 'postmodern' is actually, at least for now, wholly adequate. The nature and depth of that transformation are debatable, but transformation it is ... However, in a major sector of our culture, there is a noticeable shift in sensibility, practices and discourse formations which distinguishes a postmodern set of assumptions, experiences and propositions from that of a preceding period.[15]

Instead of a historical or logical succession, the foundations on which modernity was built have been removed, which is what happened to technology in the 1960s. *The cornerstones supporting modernity have been pawned to postmodernity*. The only conflicts which now remain unresolved concern method and metatheory:

> Thus the term 'postmodernism' indicates a situation, in which opposites exist, unresolved, in close proximity. In this context, the term is less significant from

a historic and chronological viewpoint but does, to a greater extent, indicate a specific relationship between practical and theoretical opposition.[16]

The links between modernity and postmodernity dissolve during the transition to a fateful stage of ever-increasing complexity in all dimensions – from scientific analysis to everyday life.[17]

Taking into account the number of lifestyles and fearing the inability of postmodernism to live with these superficial, subtle changes with their own inherent and fulminate consequences, some authors even speak rather over-hastily of the end of postmodernism or even of a post-postmodern era,[18] while another group generally refers to a melancholia resulting from a 'fin de siècle' mood which is an active feature of postmodernism.[19] If, therefore, a main perspective concerning the future of postmodernism does indeed exist, it would appear to be this: a new phoenix, heralding the dawn of a new era, is rising from the ashes of modernism and industrial society.[20]

An important phenomenon which should be mentioned in this connection is the ability of postmodernism to approach from apparently irreconcilable positions and successively integrate them, with the result that postmodernity has now become a general phenomenon, a *general cultural dominant*.[21] Whereas the main shoots of postmodern thinking were more often identifiable in literary and artistic critiques, now not even the most remote or trivial of areas is excluded from the post-modern debate.[22]

Architecture and Postmodernism

Architecture was one of the first 'concrete', 'practical' disciplines to provide fertile soil for postmodern thinking,[23] and the postmodernist movement has brought about fundamental rejuvenation and lasting changes in that field.[24] Portoghesi defines this transition as a rejection of rigidity, clarity and intransigence, and the boredom associated with it,[25] even if contemporary architecture does, in fact, in historical terms, employ the practically endless memory of architectural language. It is not, however, used as a means of creating modern uniqueness or unity. Today's objectives are the suitability of a building for its environment and to use the building, as a form of communication, as a rich tissue which embodies many historical textures.[26,27] The outcome is a postmodern building in the form of a playful eclectic text, rich in ambiguity (a double coding, according to Jencks[28]), complexity and contradiction.[29] In the words of Deleuze, postmodernity is repetition with a difference, a small variation.[30,31] The grammar of modernity demands unity, clarity and harmony. The grammar of the postmodern demands diversification, ambiguity, fragmentation, networking and openness to prevent the exclusion, *a priori*, of potential realities which reflect contemporary society, and to promote living environments with their clashes, conflicts and pollination.[32] 'So the post-modern world is here, whether we like it or not. It was not invented by the revisionist critics. It was spawned by the modern masters themselves, and by many of their failures. And now, what are the alternatives?'[33]

The failure of modernism, as a result of its simple perpetuation of the status quo, is clearly voiced in the pathetic slogans used at the beginning of the 1980s. 'Return to the City', 'Urban Revitalization Movement' and so on are the swansongs of modern urban culture, and add to the debit balance of its problem-ridden forerunners like New York and Los Angeles.[34] This final plea for help from the old structure falls on deaf ears and has no effect. And even the last dinosaurs are become extinct: Corporate America has always built giant structures as monuments to its ego.[35] One could relive America's economic history through the Woolworth Building, the Pan Am Building and the Trump Tower; AT&T, with its postmodern headquarters, may well have laid the final demarcation stone.[36] Hard on its heels comes 'No-style', the last word on New York's architectural scene: confidence in a style incorporating self-strength has given way to a cost-conscious, downsizing of symbols, offering only sparse frivolities or symbolic symphonies in which opulence plays practically no part. Instead of personifying rigid egos, the main objective is flexibility of use and interesting but discrete diversity coupled with in-built ambiguity: No-one knows what type of company culture the next occupier will embrace, when the present one goes bust.[37]

Thus, postmodernism's infiltration of architecture is complete. Building blocks have gradually been conquered and other connotations placed upon them, without any direct, belligerent confrontation ever taking place between two fronts, thus circumventing, to an increasing extent, the intransigent positions of the old ones.[38]

Postmodern Infiltration of Science

This transition is currently in full bloom in the natural sciences. For some time now the Cartesian/Newtonian vision of the world has been too confined, but it is only recently that a number of separate issues have merged to form a constructive new beginning. Instrumental reasoning is on the retreat and the principles of uniformity and transcendence have been rejected in favour of plurality and immanence.[39] The uniform framework which Foucault described as classical epistles, the 'mathesis universalis', providing consistent and universal representation, is being destroyed. In the twentieth century, science is no longer a matter of classifying, collating, describing and botanizing; it now focuses more on a structural association model, fuzzy logic and knowledge as research topics in their own right. The reasoning with which it is associated is also undergoing a parallel transition.[40]

As a result, postmodernism may be interpreted as the logical development of contemporary innovation, based firstly to some degree on Einstein's theory of relativity and Heisenberg's Unschärferelation, on Gödel's theory of incomplete sets and, finally, on Mandelbrodt's fractals and Eigen's concept of biological self-organization.[41] Thus, '[p]ostmodernism, which advances this view of reality, is not the invention of dreamers but a definite progression towards plurality. This pluralism, as evidenced by science itself, is flanked on either side by the arts, and by the developments of social structures.'[42] This *pluralism of models*, meaning various models are used simultaneously, and, in its most strict form, the agnostic model (we will never know whether the right model exists or which combination of models is correct) are the unintended products of rigid modern research.[43]

The reverse, the blatant use of science in postmodernism, is also true. In 1996, an article entitled 'Transgressing the Boundaries: Toward a Transformative Hermeneutics of Quantum Gravity' was published in the cultural studies journal *Social Text*.[44] Packed with recherché quotations from 'postmodern' literary theorists and sociologists of science, and bristling with imposing theorems of mathematical physics, the article addressed the cultural and political implications of the theory of quantum gravity. Later, to the embarrassment of the editors, the author revealed that the essay was a hoax, interweaving absurd pronouncements from eminent intellectuals about mathematics and physics with laudatory – but fatuous – prose. The authors of the hoax contend that abuse of science is rampant in postmodernist circles, both in the form of inaccurate and pretentious invocation of scientific and mathematical terminology, and in the more insidious form of epistemic relativism. At best, 'elegant nonsense' is the result. This is the unfortunate reverse side of the coin and it shows that postmodern thinking is coping in vain with expansion of our knowledge base. Without the luxury of an elaborated base, excursions into other fields prove dangerous.[45]

The consequences of the knowledge explosion are evident – it is no longer possible to identify or define 'research status' or the 'frontiers of research' in even the most minor of scientific fields and, in consequence, individual sciences are merely degenerating to expert-cultures within their sanctioned, legitimized, internally-discursive habitat.[46] The correlate for this in our everyday world is the fragmentation of our life and of our living environment, which common sense can no longer fully register and in which traditional interpretations are hopeless in the vain and outdated search for unity of meaning.[47,48] If viewed more positively, scientific findings and objectivity are no longer seen as absolute but rather as an attempt at clarification, in which science becomes a mesh or interdependent network. Terms like 'local ontology' or 'the polyparadigmatic nature of scientific findings' are symptomatic of attempts to bridge the gap between the two camps.[49]

This is ultimately where the affinity to postmodern thought patterns becomes clear.[50,51] In consequence, and as also postulated by Lyotard who echoed the argumentation put forward by Kuhn and Feyerabend, science in the postmodern era must focus on the following issues: indeterminables, controllability boundaries, quanta, conflicts produced by incomplete information, 'fracta', catastrophes and pragmatic paradoxes. In addition, it has to blur 'the boundaries between common sense and paralogism'. Interaction instead of objectivity, interactive paradigms instead of the mono-directional causal principles, poly-ocularity instead of fixed approaches are all key-words, illustrating the distance which science has travelled from its modern base towards postmodernity.[52] Taking the natural sciences as an example, a second process, also fundamental to the successful proliferation of the postmodern, becomes apparent: the *endogenous disintegration* of the tight, rigid straightjacket of contemporary scientific rationality and all its paraphernalia is forcing individual disciplines to search for new frameworks and parameters, making them more receptive to new ways of looking at themselves and the world around them.

In summary, it is true to say that three elements are the root causes of the extensive encroachment of postmodernism: firstly, as a tool it is *universally applicable* through its reflections of multiple reality (multivalence, multicultural, multidimensional, multi-etc.). Secondly, postmodernism has avoided creating a defined front thanks to its *subtle incorporation of the status quo*. Thirdly, it is being warmly embraced by individual disciplines in their *quest for a new meaning*. With this to reinforce its general relevance, postmodernism as 'leading edge', or 'cutting edge', is making an appearance on a wide front. It has certainly become the spirit of the times and the best catchword of the Zeitgeist. Whether it is really the keenly sought after and eagerly awaited new paradigm or simply a promising intermezzo, only the immediate future will tell.

III SPECIAL FEATURES OF THE POSTMODERN DEBATE

If we are to comprehend and operationalize the principal, contextual message conveyed by postmodernism, we must now define the individual points in concrete terms. For this we have selected to represent three eminent philosophers whose opinions in the debate on postmodernity are widely recognized: the German, J. Habermas, the American, R. Rorty and the French, J.-F. Lyotard. These three philosophers form, what might be called, centres of gravity, from which we can crystallize the chain of thought leading from the existence of the postmodern, via its structure in society, to economics.[53]

Habermas, or the Existence of Postmodernity

Habermas' interpretation of the present

As a supporter of modernism, Habermas has assumed, *nolens volens*, the role of the sparring partner of self-creating postmodernism in shaping the basic understanding of postmodernism. Assuming, and this is not just some frail hypothesis, that the model of modernism which he presents is workable, it is easy to identify in his attitude the struggle between postmodernism and modernism for clarity of comprehension. For him, the real task of postmodernism is to relegitimize and prove the project of modernism, taking account of the change in circumstances.

In his philosophical work, Habermas' main aim is to demonstrate the feasibility and delineate the structure of a rational society.[54] The convergence point of this objective is a theory of rationality which harbours a universal claim to validity.[55] Consequently, the first question to be answered in this connection is what rational actually means: '[Rational] arguments are the means of creating inter-subjective recognition of what exactly is a proponent's hypothesis, thus making it possible to transform opinions into knowledge.'[56] Which means that only rationality-based standpoints are accepted in the debate with the aim of eliminating anything which is unclear.[57] Ergo, if multiple and non-congruent cultures are mutually excluded as a permanent situation, how, therefore, does the simple process of agreeing to a statement function, according to Habermas?

Here too, the analytical apparatus of rationality acts as a yardstick, the purpose of which is to assess and check divergence between non-congruent cultures or positions. In this context, Habermas is operating in the Enlightenment's tradition, since he believes in reason as the ultimate arbitrator and rejects everything which reason does not understand and is unable to legitimize.[58] Thus, processes to achieve agreement unfold in the form of a contentious argument, with reason in the not entirely ambiguous dual role of plaintiff and judge. We are therefore forced to concede that different forms of argumentation have different claims to power, although practical rationality is assigned a higher claim to power[59] since its primary objective is, after all, to control the environment and people's lives.[60] However, the normative power of this theory is exhausted after it reaches the formulation of baseline conditions and final outcomes, failing to explain the process itself meaning the creation of a consensus in practical life.

The practical side, the actual process to reach agreement, is the main theme of his next work *Faktizität und Geltung*,[61] which presents an analysis of a frail theory based on the thin ice of contemporary law and politics. Here, his argument is based on three key elements: (a) a performance-oriented view of debates (all parties involved want to achieve results); (b) a radical democracy approach (the conflict stemming from the definitions of needs); and (c) a belief in commitments resulting from the interaction ('keeping one's promises'). These are the elementary forces which, in the practical coping with daily life, implement the theoretical conception of communicative rationality.[62] This is how the theory of rational action becomes embedded in a social environment which then broadens it to a theory of communicative action in the reality.

In this theory of communicative action, Habermas, based on the legacy of occidental rationalism,[63] searches for the shape of social consensus on which rules and which actions can be called rational and which not. Rational argumentation between rational discussion partners is the *modus* to achieve this consensus, with the pure reasoning of the Enlightenment being replaced by an 'ideal' communication community devoid of all power-games, in which discussion participants of equal standing arrive at a rationally motivated consensus by adopting a communication-oriented view and by sincerely trying to understand each other. Although this debate is accompanied implicitly by a discourse on power, Habermas alludes only in passing to the risks of a potential 'terrorism' of reason *vis-à-vis* other types of discourse.[64]

The exclusive focus placed on rational, Western culture could be considered a further example of risks embodied. Other views of the world, which could also produce powerful outlooks on life, are discredited by Habermas. In comparing the rational and occidental, on the one hand, with the mythical and primitive on the other, he attempts to demonstrate by means of evolutionary arguments that the rational image of the world is best, as it is unencumbered by traditions and influences and consequently occupies the highest rung of rationality. Thus, he forces Asiatic worlds of thought towards metaphysics, without allowing them to make relevant statements concerning the structure of society.[65]

In its ideal form, the outcome of the argumentation is a non-authoritarian consensus of Western calibre, which is, at the same time, the *modus operandi* of a rational society; not, however, a fatalistic status quo but the product of free and open communication:

> The discursively formed may be called rational because formal properties of discourse and of the deliberative situation sufficiently guarantee that a consensus can arise only through appropriately interpreted generalizable interests, by which I mean needs that can be communicatively shared.[66]

Here, Habermas' basic principles are the free exchange of information, the ability to comprehend, truth, sincerity, 'the force of the better argument' and normal problem-solving.[67] He banishes strategic action, lies and manipulations from this ideal world and, therefore, contrary to Lyotard and Foucault,[68] does not distinguish between the two levels of discourse: power and truth.[69]

Thus, Lyotard's critique of Habermas does not entirely hit home as far as 'Technoscience' (gr.: lógos kai techné) is concerned, for, in addition to using technical instrumental reasoning as a method, the primary essential aim of Habermas' mechanisms remains the emancipation of the people by means of critical self-reflection.[70] In the tradition of the Enlightenment, Habermas is of the opinion that this major intellectual aim – critical self-reflection – has not yet reached its final stage. Habermas' objectives include the alteration of contemporary industrial society further but rather from the inside out, whereas postmodern writers claim that reason is dependent on external assistance. Habermas has himself also mentioned this, insofar as he bemoans, on the final pages of his theory of communicative action, the broadening of the range of action of modern societies in terms of the ever-increasing number of subsystems that pervade our 'normal' living environment, thus increasing breadth and complexity of life without generating more 'meaning'.[71]

Rationality, in the form of a differentiation process, has accompanied modernism but has now been divided by modernism into many special rationalities, resulting in a dispersion of values and fragmentation without hope of unification.[72] The inherent dynamism of modernism is flagging and has degenerated into a 'yes-man' culture, in which things are simply left to run their own course. As a result, internal self-contradictions have finally surfaced.[73] Rationalization of our living environment has caused the system to become more complex and it is now so hypertrophied that the powers of comprehension of the normal human being, as well as the complexity of day-to-day life have reached their breaking point and the logic of dispersion is causing an irreversible, ever-increasing long-term conflict of life-styles.[74] Habermas is unable to explain why the subsystems have acquired this irreversible centrifugal dynamism of their own; he still desires 'the establishment of a new form of social integration' which has not yet been operationalized.[75]

Thus the reasons behind the disintegration have now been determined endogenously. The main protagonist can be identified as the process of secularization (with all its associated manifestations): rationalization and the demystification of the world, in the favouring of purpose-oriented rationality and the disfavouring of value-based rationality, and the substitution of religion by science are the results of this secularization movement.[76] Following on from Adorno and Horkheimer, Habermas is indirectly of the same opinion, in principle: 'The process of Enlightenment can be understood ... as a decentralization of the view of the world [Weltbild].'[77]

Fragmentation of consumer markets, decentralization, a 'new lack of transparency', the legitimization crisis in politics and, finally, the ungovernability of states are headlines boding the collapse of the social system.[78] Baudrillard, as Bataille before him, specifically referred to these *excesses of modernism*. For him, the prototypes of these anomalies are: hypertrophy (cancerous growth), obesity (a shapeless, physical excess), unrestricted growth and control (a surfeit of dynamism or its repression), torture (excessive suffering and total hopeless submission), pornography (excessive emotionless sexuality) and terrorism (excessive, irresponsible and unregulated violence).[79] These routine, modern-day abnormalities have been brought about by dispersion and not by the conscious exclusion of subjects and the damnation of their actions, for normal core values no longer exist and society is fragmenting into a spectral society, in which all actions and values are of equal worth.[80] The fundamental evil of this fragmented society is the *disassociation of the individual from reality*. Distances and times are being eradicated by transcontinental flight, videoconferencing and chatrooms; direct personal contact is being replaced by indirect methods of communication; the body as an experience in itself becomes useless (a trend which a despairing body culture and fabricated hedonization are trying in vain to reverse).[81] Content, depth and meaning are giving way to an obliging but non-pervasive, superficial external view. (A simple proof might be the stark contrast between the incredible number of websites and their often non-existent content or meaning.) Baudrillard's unified hyperreality and simulated subjectivity are apparently the end products of modernism.

This leads Habermas to the issue of the two possible future courses of action: either attempting to create total uniformity based solely on logic or yielding to the progressive effects of diffusion.[82] In this dilemma, Habermas argues against diffusion and in favour of rational logic, which is a precondition for every form of burgeoning social organization, and he opts therefore for modernism rather than postmodernism.

The creation of a rational society is modernism's uncompleted project. Habermas himself defines the project of modernity as an effort aimed at 'objectivity of science, universality of moral and society and the autonomy of art in accordance with their inherent logics'.[83] (Almost) total communication, as a fundamental principle, is essential in a rational society in order to do justice to these objectives. 'Rationality presumes communication, because something is rational only if it meets the conditions necessary to forge an understanding with at least one other person.'[84] This conceals implicitly a relative approach which is similar to that of Lyotard insofar as true and false are no longer appropriate as absolute criteria, since they are assessed pragmatically for functional suitability as products of consensus. The difference between this and Lyotard is that Habermas does not accept a meta-discourse on consensus.[85] However, it should at least be feasible to reach consensus on dissent, without allowing the consensus mechanism to imperialistically dictate contents and outcome via the choice of methods and rules for decision-making. Equally questionable is the decision as to when to consider consensus-finding complete and how durable this type of consensus can possibly be. Gadamer already emphasized that, in principle, a discursive dialogue can never be considered as definitely closed.[86]

If modernity has finally reached its goal to complete the Enlightenment's tasks of differentiating all possible subtleties of reasoning, then no further metadiscourse can be allowed, since all debates on the levels of the individual discourses are secondary to the primacy of rationality of reason.[87] Thus, communicative consensus excludes any dissent.[88] Seen in these terms, the project of modernity is transformed from epoch to ideology.[89] Rorty criticizes these Habermasian manoeuvres as a 'language game known as the question of legitimacy'.[90] Lash sums up Lyotard's detailed critique of Habermas in four main points:

1 Habermas' theory is based on the '*"major narratives", the credibility of which is now badly dented'*.[91]
2 Habermas attempts to use his 'strong notion of universality' to regulate language games; to this extent language games are not an obstacle for him insofar as they ultimately converge at a single point, that is universal rationality. Internal conflicts are soluble, but external disputes, the conflict between different types of discourse, are not. Precisely this *autonomy of various types of discourse* is subsequently described by Lyotard as 'le différend' [the conflict, the need to differ].[92]
3 Habermas still owes us an answer as to how he intends to achieve, in practice, the Kantian split between aesthetic, practical and theoretical categories, which are acknowledged by him as the characteristics of modernism.[93] Thus, Habermas perpetuates an error which was not eradicated right at the start of the age of Enlightenment: the far too *rigid commitment to a purpose-oriented rationality* as the driving force behind human development. 'The growth of purposive-instrumental rationality does not lead to the concrete realization of universal human freedom, but to the creation of an 'iron cage' of bureaucratic rationality from which there is no escape.'[94]
4 A necessary change does not see itself as a 'new barbarity', but particularly as a shift of importance from norms to *signs*, from objective reality to *hyperreality*,

from a single culture of reason to a *decentralized culture*, (now) held together by media and technology. '[Habermas] ... misses in its entirety the key tendency of postmodern existence: the death of the social ("modernism with its repre-sentational logic") and the triumph of an empty ("signifying culture").'[95] Symbolization, not socialization; Baudrillard's simulacrum, rather than Gehlen's institutional discourse; simulation, not rationalization are the key words uttered by the souffleur. The world is increasingly degenerating into

> an empire of voyeurs held together by up-scale titillation effects (from the valorization of corpses to the crisis jolts of bad news and more bad news) and blasted by the laser beam into the pulverized state of Sartre's 'serial being' and **not** [emphasis in original] the old boring 'structure of roles' held together by the 'internalization of need-dispositions'.[96]

This perception of the clear restrictions placed on the potential success of the realization project for theoretical modernism extends the criticism levelled at Habermas to a general criticism of modernity and to a portrayal of its crisis.[97] How can one control this crisis? In the best of modern traditions, industrial society is trying to use internal solutions to overcome the crisis. This is brilliantly portrayed in Wolfe's symbolic novel *The Bonfire of the Vanities*: in a soliloquy, the Wall Street hero, McCoy, who is totally unsuited to everyday life, worries himself into his worst crisis: ' "Get yourself together! Regroup! Think this thing out! There's no way you can let it collapse after all this! Call him back and be yourself, the best producer of Pierce & Pierce! – Master of the Universe!" ... He lost hope.'[98] Unfortunately modernity is no longer in a state to launch a powerful rescue attempt of this type; the patient is suffering from 'nervous exhaustion',[99] in which reason, which was once celebrated as a new mythology, is no longer able to develop any creative and constructive power whatsoever.[100] Here, decadence is seen as an escape from decrepit structures, dragging a wave of creativity along behind it. New eras have always been heralded as high-speed, ephemeral and muddled. Gryphius, Goethe, Marx,[101] Baudelaire, Dostojevski, Proust and Musil already provided evidence of this.[102] And, in this context, Eco also concludes that each epoch has its own postmodernity and thus even modernism deserves 'its own' postmodernism.[103]

The crucial relationship between postmodernity and modernity

Postmodernity sees itself as the termination point of modernity which is also the starting point for something new. Postmodernism's view is that modernism has now been declared bankrupt, a fact indicated by the unnecessary complica-tion and alienation, the isolation of contemporary life and the schizophrenic technical destruction of our natural environment. But modernism should not simply be abandoned, but destroyed or 'liquidated' during the creation of a post-modern era.[104]

Rather than being negative, however, this should be seen as creative destruction *à la* Schumpeter, involving the remoulding of serviceable components. Only modernism's mode of thought is destroyed. Just as modernism is a critique of the previous epoch of 'Victorian' naïve realism, postmodernism is now a ' "*critique de la critique*", an *enlightenment of the Enlightenment'*.[105] In a world which, due to its irrational selection of a value system (in this case that of science), is in danger of degenerating into a mass of technicians and social engineers, the only theory which can help, according to Habermas, is one which not only improves management of material and immaterial objects, thus changing everything into a world of goods, but rather persistently drives forward the interest of reason towards maturity and autonomy of decision. Precisely this attempt is seen by postmodernism as a futile attempt to sustain life. Idolization of reason and despair about the future are the ambivalent results of this; the mechanism which was once meaningful now becomes the opposite.[106,107]

This postmodern critique of modernity necessarily leads one to examine a list of all familiar or known objects. This comprehensive examination of grammar and society, and the outlook on the world and the individual, results ultimately in the deconstruction of the subject, coupled with a radical review of the Enlightenment's concept of reason and its epistemological implications. This ends in the rejection of pure empiricism and pure natural science as a strategy to obtain knowledge and leading from a paradigm of consciousness to a paradigm of language. In principle, even Habermas could agree with all these points, although contemporary conflicts in 'professional philosophy' are distorting the picture.[108] Whether modernism will be ultimately overcome or not still remains, in itself, a modern issue which does not confront postmodernism in the same way, since its impetus is forward-facing, aimed more at the present than the past.[109] Thus postmodernism represents *a pragmatic approach*:

Therefore the flashy question of "Zeitgeist" diagnostics, whether we are actually living in a modern or postmodern era, must be subjugated. The objective is to dissect layers in which to observe behavioral phenomena, 'observe' used, of course, in its broadest sense, involving several methods. An attempt must be made to describe real world; when this is done, it then becomes clear that the label 'modern' is no longer entirely appropriate.[110]

The relationship between modernism and postmodernism is not easy to chart and it is therefore unsurprising that inconclusive and ambivalent statements are predominant:

Modernism in its heroic phrase is a retrospective revolt against a retrograde, mechanical industrialism, postmodernism is an ahistorical rebellion without heroes against a blindly innovative information society.[111]

Postmodernism is a 'condition' following the death of metaphysics.[112]

The relationship between the two is primarily that no solution, no end can be found; these types of situations are known colloquially in Spanish as 'faena', i.e. the sensation experienced by bullfighters who look death in the eyes with every 'corrida', or the sensation experienced when painting with the wrong (left) hand.[113]

No one exactly agrees as to what is meant by the term, except, perhaps, that 'postmodernism' represents some kind of reaction to, or departure from, 'modernism'.[114]

Postmodernism has become an essentially contested concept.[115]

Even a definite, determined representative of postmodernism such as Hassan decreed circumspectly that the postmodern was created as a result of the trans- formation of the modern, although it still remains unclear whether it represents a redevelopment of modernity or a transformation from modernity to a new separate ideology. Derrida also refers to this point when he uses the motto 'repartons' (let's set out again). At any rate, the view that postmodernity is rooted in 'modern origins' denotes a complex relationship resulting from consistent succession, difference and dependency.[116] But there are also those who prefer to see post- modernity simply as the final throes of modernity:

Things look totally different, if one dutifully accepts that the postmodern displays itself not only as a novelty when compared to the modern, but, more radically, it sees itself as the end of all novelties, as the "end of history", and not just as another, more or less progressive, chapter of the same history.[117]

The 'end of a history' not, however, as a farewell to modernism but rather as a radical questioning of it.[118] Postmodern critique puts its finger on a gaping wound when it exposes the unacknowledged monism of modernity as contradictory. Postmodern philosophy validates plurality as a form of reason. Thus, postmoder- nity is not just a simple sequel to modernity but has attempted to assert itself, posing, in a manner of speaking, as the (potential) fulfillment of early modern commitments, and thereby solving the long-term hidden self-contradictions of the whole process of the Enlightenment.[119]

Thus, viewed from this angle, postmodernity becomes the fulfillment of moder- nity and its logical culmination as a 'sophisticated' later form.[120,121] 'The affix "post-" clearly indicates a break, separating the postmodern from the develop- ments within the modern and applying expressively the idea of surpassing the level of mere critique towards creating new foundations, taking up the loose ends left by Nietzsche and Heidegger in their attempt of a critical review of Western thought.'[122] Welsch and Lyotard view postmodernity as a radicalized modernity: 'Postmodernism does not take up a position after modernism or oppose it. It was already included in it, merely concealed.'[123] Postmodernism puts the spotlight on issues implicitly, latently or intentionally omitted by modernism. Its role is not simply that of a counter-explanation or revolt within or against modernism, in the manner attempted, for example, by Marxism: '... [P]ostmodernism at its deepest level represents not just another crisis within the perpetual cycle of boom and bust, exhaustion and renewal, which has characterized the trajectory of modernist culture. It rather represents a new type of crisis of that modernist culture itself.'[124] A view which describes postmodernism as being immanent to modernism cannot bear fruit. 'The very term signifies a simultaneous continuity and renunciation, a generation strong enough to dissolve the old order, but too weak to marshall the centrifugal forces it has released.'[125] Integration not apposition is the more successful relationship between two completely incommensurable positions.[126] Welsch graphically described this duopoly as the convergence of postmodernity, irrationality, Francophonia and a plural historical understanding of overlapping stories, on the one hand, and modern rationality, Germanophonia and a direct historical succession of linear events, on the other.[127] The postmodern sees itself as a *mature follow-on movement* but in systemic rather than epochal terms. So postmodernism is not a 'polite plea for communication',[128] not a slack extension of modernism nor its total rejection, but a radical inspection whose intention is to identify components which are still serviceable and to classify problem areas, tidying up loose ends in preparation for the new beginning. This process can, to some extent, be compared with the audit of an insolvent company or a full autopsy (ironically, referred to in English medical terminology as a post-mortem).[129] Something new is *in statu nascendi*: postmodernism is assuming the symbol-laden role of midwife. But it also plays the role of a testamentary executor or undertaker or even that of a butcher who processes animals for profit.

Thus the postmodern does not act as a utopia, as an alternative design, but as a heterotopia in the sense Foucault uses the term, as an opposing position which takes over the real positions and objects present, for example, in a culture and subjects them to an alternative system of coordinates, another perspective.[130] This is where the difficulty lies: both perspectives are trained on the same object – today's world – which no longer entirely conforms to modern categories but which, equally, cannot be clearly described in postmodern terms.

But the postmodern is slowly appearing as 'a cultural dominant'. However, this should not be interpreted in hegemonic terms but rather as a liberation from modernism, whilst still remembering its forerunner.[131] Considered in these terms, postmodernism cannot function as a *programmatic reconstruction* but represents more of an *interludium*, a *gain in time*, necessitated by ubiquitous disruptions caused by instrumental global reason.[132] Interludium, gain in time, but not, in fact, an epoch – the definition of this term is too broad (in any event, it is a term from the linguistic arsenal of modernism). But we should interpret this complex relationship in a postmodern way: 'How I learned to stop worrying and started loving postmodernism.'[133] Seen in more simple terms, it is irrelevant whether it represents a break with or the advancement of modernity. An appropriate outcome, which both camps consider valid, confirms the existence of postmodernism as a new method of interpreting and understanding the world. This independent entity offers but the initial possibility of a workable design for the future, which modernism is not in a position to create (on its own). Postmodernism has already made a start on the theoretical dimensions of this design for the future, and today's world gives us a practical indication of the opportunities offered in the immediate future.[134] The profession of critics also confirm the independence of postmodernism to the extent that they continually call upon it, in their work, as a reference point when they are in need of assistance.[135] There is one final indication of its *emancipated independence* and that is the fact that some voices repeatedly proclaim that postmodernism has decreed its own demise or has committed suicide so that work can finally commence on the creation of something new.[136]

The rapid advances of IT which brought us a global community of a billion 'facettes' helped to start the sacking of modernity and its fellow the industrial society. Without it, postmodernity would still not be emancipated and the progress from the final (or post-) industrial society to the postmodern society and its New Economy could not have been that brisk. New ideas, new forms of human interaction are currently tested, questioning the time-honoured (Western) principles of human understanding. And it seems the enlightenment and its *homo economicus* have taken a serious beating.[137]

From the debate on the complex relationship between modernism and postmodernism, we have been able to dissect the uncertainty which has arisen about Western rationalism of industrial society that is fundamental to the existence of postmodernism. This led to increasing differentiation and greater divergence of the debates which originated in modernism, in consequence resulting in a heightening of system complexity (fragmentation, decentralization, delegitimization) in (almost) all areas of life, especially in the economic sphere. This trend has been detrimental to the subject, which has been robbed of orientation and grasp, and is therefore no longer able to function as one of the cornerstones of a human being. It is here that the postmodern is used as an independent novelty, which can self-assuredly criticize the old from its own standpoint and attempt to create a new understanding.

In the major emancipation process of modernism from its crises and their resolution to the initial stages of a design for the future, we can perceive the postmodern as a truly new basic constellation, which differs fundamentally from simple trends, revisions and reformulations of the old.

Rorty, or Postmodern Society

Rorty's image of society

As we have seen in the previous chapter, a mature postmodernity does indeed exist and it is more than just a 'post-something or the other'. In its main features, the global view adopted by postmodernity is not clearly defined but presents more of a vague, open, flexible, situation-dependent image. Thus, postmodernism cannot be simply interpreted in short as merely a critique on modernism, but must be seen as the vanguard of a new self-interpretation of the world and society '... [P]ostmodernity is a complex of competing, often contradictory discourses each of which seeks to configure the afterlife of the modern in its own particular way.'[138] Therefore the main impetus is not primarily that of critique but that of tackling the question of how to interpret the present and how to prepare for future trends and dynamics of our society and our cultural environment. Consequently, postmodern discussion continually revolves around the enigma of a theoretical concept of a new society, the foreplay of which has long been evident.[139] The debate associated with this is the extent to which postmodernism is socially viable, in the sense of its ability to shape society, and whether or not everything is dissolving into disjointedness and negative chaos. The American philosopher Rorty, who, together with Habermas, Walzer and Taylor is frequently listed under the main heading 'contemporary communitarianism', has focused a substantial part of his oeuvre on this question.[140]

Rorty's first main work *Philosophy and the Mirror of Nature*,[141] criticized progressive modernism as a method of human perception, particularly in the social sciences.[142] His work centres on the quest for fundamental truths within modernism: 'Modern philosophers, both empiricists and rationalists believe in ultimate foundations of knowledge which are independent of the particular framework of the observer.'[143] The purpose of the modernism project, according to Habermas, is to develop scientific, moral and artistic areas in accordance with their own internal logic.[144] This is precisely the position which postmodern philosophers, especially Rorty, attack. This quest for certainty and the concept of ahistoric, generally-accepted, finite principles creates 'the illusion of foundationalism'[145] Rorty describes these fundamental truths as 'the longest lie ... The lie that there is something beyond mankind to which it is man's duty to be faithful.'[146] An escape route is provided by what is viewed as pragmatic postmodern philosophy which attempts 'to liberate our new civilization by giving up the notion of "grounding" our culture, our moral lives, our politics, our religious beliefs, upon philosophical bases'.[147]

If we therefore accept that languages (global views of the world) are manufactured and do not, *a priori*, exist just waiting to be discovered, then we must also accept by the same token that truths can only ever be manufactured:

Truth cannot be out there – cannot exist independently of the human mind – because sentences cannot so exist, or be out there. The world is out there, but the descriptions of the world are not. Only descriptions of the world can be true or false. The world on its own – unaided by the describing activities of human beings – cannot.[148]

Here, one can detect an extremely clear affinity to the biologically based, epistemological designs of Maturana and Varela, which have explored the basic issue of how perception and coordination are biologically possible.[149] Maturana and Varela's fundamental theory is that each act of perception conjures up a veritable world in its own right which, as an organizational principle, can only result in *autopoietic organization*[150,151] (self-generating organization).

The nervous system does not 'receive information', as is often stated, but rather produces a world by deciding which configurations of the environment represent perturbations and which changes in the organism are triggered by them.[152]

But on this basis how is it possible to circumnavigate the cliffs of the 'Whorf–Sapier hypothesis' which, assuming irreconcilable diversity of languages, conjectures totally different consciousnesses and incommensurable worlds. Under such a hypothesis people of one language community have nothing in common with other communities, nor can there be a meaningful exchange between these groups.[153]

The escape route sought here by postmodernism lies in a mistrust of the claims to uniqueness made by 'meta-narratives', that is of the (seemingly) ubiquitously-valid, general or background knowledge of the language group in question. This goes hand in hand with the *delegitimization of metaécrits*, the aim of which is to destroy any claim to hegemony made by a language game.[154,155]

Harvey describes the first steps which convert this diversity to a unifying force as a useful but fragile web consisting of many different threads.[156] Rigid channels of communication no longer dominate but dissolve into a flexible network of language games, which uses the individual meta-narratives as modules in an open system of constant interchange. In this context, the issue of the transition point between language games is one of the main topics dealt with by postmodern theory which perceives growing differentiation as the genuine tendencies of emancipation. From this, postmodernism hopes to achieve a creativity advantage, to the extent that the individual language games point ahead and beyond themselves by means of 'a murmur which redoubles itself, through setting up en endless "play of mirrors"'.[157] Thus, Rorty issues an invitation to actively seek and multiply language games in order to increase the number of possible discourses. Rorty's preferred strategy is to abandon all claims to uniqueness and attempt anything which may be available in terms of methods, language games, etc. Thus, what was formerly virgin truth becomes serene agreement: 'These truths are themselves only relative; they are interesting "stories", even possible temporary strategies for living. But, in the final analysis, they are ephemeral, provisional, cognitive frames.'[158] Therefore, it is pointless to enquire whether propositions – that is, descriptions of the world – are true or false; we can only determine their efficacy or inefficacy in a problem-solving context. Successful results prove the accuracy of a description of the world. Nietzsche already saw the world as a world of relationships rather than as a world of objects;[159] dispute within these relationships is fruitless, not least because the conflicting paradigms are incommensurable, lacking common methodological features which would aid mediation. The aim should much rather be 'to keep the conversation going'[160] and to strive against any attempt 'to close off conversation by proposals for universal commensuration through the hypostatization of some privileged set of descriptions'.[161]

This produces an open concept of understanding and truth which comes into existence only in a community. 'Truth is what presently counts as such in the ongoing plural discourse of civilized exchange.'[162] Thus truth can never be final but only asymptotic. It is a dynamic understanding of knowledge which moves away from the laboratory bench of rational analysis of the objective disinterested observer, to become an active component in the constant debate (conducted with changing constellations) surrounding group and individual interests.[163]

The basic building blocks of postmodern societies

Currently, we are witnessing the disintegration of society into two sections: one perceives itself as exposed to the *challenge of complexity*, and the other to the older, more terrible *challenge of survival in integrity*. This divide is possibly the main cause for the failure of the project of modernity.[164] Our aim is to show, briefly, taking the example of four manifestations of modernity, the extent to which it would be possible to mould the old components into a new social theory.[165] The key words are: *information overflow, loss of identity,*[166] *excess* and *capriciousness.*

The general torrent of information, which incessantly pours down upon us, does not have to result in general stupefaction. If we accept the quantity and train our perception, we will be able to move to a situation where diversity of information is perceived as productive rather than confusing. Therefore, we are not moving towards computer imperialism of the information society,[167] but are using global, informal, open networks to build ourselves a diffuse information network, which may have adopted the basic optimism of technology but whose aim is, in fact, to cross quite different dividing lines. The objective is not to send a man to the moon but to create simulated computer worlds (virtual reality, cyberspace), in which man can credibly play an active role using a dataglove and a helmet monitor to interact with (or even to act in the Internet as) avatars (virtual characters).[168] In these virtual worlds, it is possible to 'realize' every conceivable type of world in the same way as the human spirit can 'realize' anything imaginable.[169] Instead of degeneration into total capriciousness and a society like the one portrayed in post-human, apocalyptic films like *Mad Max, Blade Runner* or *Terminator*, it is possible to identify, amongst the ashes, the young shoots of a new species, which do not appear disorientated by the too-much-of-everything but consider their existence as being enriched by it. Equally, one can lament the disintegration of groups and the individual brought about in the last stage of modernity; subjects drift aimlessly around[170] and their 'personal identity has been rendered soft, fluid endless'.[171] Already decades ago, Anders had drawn attention to the crisis of the bourgeois subject, no longer able to cope with its actions and the worlds it has created.[172]

Individual and collective identity are losing themselves and become decentralized. '[T]he ego is anything but fixed ... the group is flexible and permeable.'[173] No longer are different events lined up in nice rows but, in the search for identity, events and situations are investigated from all angles to find an exhaustive set of all possible perspectives.[174] Even theories of class are being eroded: postmodern society has no use for any type of class identity. For both Habermas and Lyotard, class is now a spent force in society.[175] This is why Bourdieu uses the broader term 'fields' (champs): for example, juridical, aesthetic, political, cultural fields, and so on. These fields replaced the rigid layers and also created themselves (differentiated themselves) in modern times and are now dedifferentiating themselves in postmodern times.[176]

Excess or surfeit is the third stigma marking the end of modernity.[177] The hypertrophy described by Bataille, including obesity (shapeless, physical excess), being held hostage (excessive suffering and total hopeless submission), pornography (excessive emotionless sexuality) and terrorism (excessive, irresponsible and unregulated violence) as archetypes of anomalies, indicates the excrescence of modernism, its final traces. The main feature of them all, caused by the industrial system,[178] is unrestricted growth, bereftness of content (lethal hyperdisposability and hypersaturation, including the hope for unlimited control). Therefore, according to Malraux, the world may be perceived only as a provisorium, as the types of relentless economic, religious and civilization conflicts being waged today can lead only to disaster.[179]

These crisis scenarios may lead to the realization that the chains which bind discourses, ideologies and power strategies are unbreakable.[180] The 'reciprocal interpermeability of the discourses' is increasing to such an extent that it is impossible to clearly define the individual positions.[181] Given these inextricable interrelationships, one can only achieve consensus in the area of dissent, which is still our best chance despite all its difficulties.[182] As a result, our capacity to record greater quantities of different data is gradually increasing, signalling a rise in general competence which, in turn, enables the creation of increasingly differentiated systems. Competition between individual subsystems is the norm and this, subsequently, enhances output and efficiency, extending the curve of social production opportunities outwards, in a manner of speaking.[183]

This demonstrates that we can still use many of the building blocks without denigrating them as revolutionary and iconoclastic.[184] Thus, our objective is not destruction but more of a deconstructive, differentiated and novel interpretation of the old components. In practice this means that we no longer have a common solid centre to use as a guideline.[185]

The outlines of a postmodern society

We are now off-limits, in the precise sense of the word. Society is becoming a multidimensional area in which a state of hyperpluralism[186] is being created by an almost interminable number of gravitational centres (or, to use trendy language: 'strange attractors'). Whether this space is perceived as a system comprising 'an ordered cluster of possibilities'[187] or as fundamentally opaque, fluid, inevaluable and unidentifiable can be considered irrelevant,[188] the *main aspect of this cultural, political and social polyphony is the concept of the fundamental difference of components without oppositional relationships.*[189]

Consequently, the dichotomies 'postmodern versus modern', 'old economy versus New Economy', or 'utopia versus alternative futures' are untenable. The postmodern dynamism, fuelled by modern intentions, is just the logical next step for society.[190] If we accept radical plurality as the core of postmodernity, we create, by pluralizing living environments and styles, a constellation in which hetero-geneous life-forms overlap each another and, in their difference to one another, learn from one another without being dependent on a common core.[191,192] 'In this way, growing complexity in most fields, including everyday "lifestyles" will dominate the horizon in [the next] ... century.'[193] Our everyday life is made up of incommensurable components and we have developed the ability to link them together so that heterogeneity stimulates rather than taxes us.[194]

These worlds or, in everyday pragmatics, lifestyles, no longer created by a single dimension (class divisions by birth), are now, comparatively speaking, no longer rigid. These lifestyles are self-generated along a plethora of coordinates (preferences, resources, history, etc.) and are indistinctly defined in puncto exclusivity, duration and overlap. Only by adding together every possible lifestyle aspect,[195] is it possible to establish the 'world as whole'. Goodman summarized the consequences of this world creation as a general commitment to plurality, an acknowledgement of the impossibility of completeness; the view that reality cannot exist in itself and the recognition of ontological relativity.[196]

How can we create worthwhile living environments in view of this multiplicity, incompleteness and relativity?

> According to one variety of solipsism, only I exist but this holds for each of the many people in the world. Somewhat analogously, one might say that there is only one world but this is true for each of the many worlds. In both cases the equivocation is stark – yet perhaps negotiable.[197]

Thus, Habermas is able to state, using the concept of living environment as a basis, that the problem of postmodernism is principally political[198] since the largest success of a postmodern society is precisely its *effectiveness in coordination*, in terms of the *creation of cooperation between divergent views of the world*. This coordi-nation potential conforms to postmodern theory, not by means of well-structured general staff plans, but by interweaving (or networking) all perspectives which have viscous, fluid, and amoeba-like locomotive properties.[199] Here, communica-tion is characterized by words like heterarchy, meta-orientation (as opposed to object-orientation), flexible, rotating roles, *ad hoc* social networking or multiple models.[200] Deleuze and Guattari aptly use the botanical example of a *rhizome*: not a traditional branch hierarchy but a jungle of roots each with equal standing; the roots and shoots are indistinguishable. The rhizome invades everywhere and forges transversal links between diverging components. It is not monadically but nomadically unsystematic.[201]

How can a theory of postmodern society exculpate itself from these accusations of sceptical agnosticism, subjectivism, irrationality, nihilism and relativism? A defense is the argument that the denial that objective rational criteria for establishing the truth do exist, is in itself not necessarily negative, but can be seen positively and constructively instead. Hence agnostic, subjective, nihilistic, etc., are attributes which have simply been incorrectly combined with relativism and the rejection of *a priori* principles.[202]

Thus, all that is left of the accusations is the lack of absolute criteria to define truth. In this context, the brutal stance 'either-solid-truth-or-total-chaos' is unnecessary;[203] a 'neither–nor' scenario is more applicable to the relativistic core of the postmodern. This denial of absolute criteria does not imply that criteria do not exist or that they are purely subjective or irrational, but is relativistic insofar as it applies the whole truth only relatively with respect to those involved in the discussion. 'To accept the contingency of all starting points is to accept our inheritance from, and our conversation with, our fellow humans as our only source of guidance.'[204] Thus, values are functionally dependent on changing constellations in the environment.[205] Truth is created within society in the first place[206] and, as a result it is context-dependent and only ever provisional.[207]

Human interpretation, evaluation, choice and desires become accordingly more significant in the creation of the truth. Moreover, tradition, the debate around an evaluation of statements, ethical-political assessments of our interaction with others, are useful once again.[208] In the absence of any absolute rational criteria, no computer (as the apex of modern rational logic) can produce decisions. Now, there is a 'moral obligation of seeking to validate claims to truth through argumentation and opening ourselves to the criticism of others'.[209] The community context is considered more significant in the postmodern era than in the modern era, where the communal ideal has always been opposed to the fulfilling freedom of the individual:

> Our identification with our community – our society, our political tradition, our intellectual heritage – is heightened when we see this community as ours rather than nature's, shaped rather than found, one among many which men have made. In the end ... what matters is our loyalty to other human beings clinging together against the dark, not our hope of getting things right.[210]

No wonder then that the Internet communities soar and provide meaning and comfort.

Rorty refers to this developing social form of the future as a 'post-philosophical culture',[211] in which precisely this denial of *a priori* values reinforces communal cohesion: 'If we give up this hope [to find absolute criteria], *we shall lose* what Nietzsche called *"metaphysical comfort"*, *but we may gain a renewed sense of community*.'[212] Being dependent on tradition and culture is providing an incentive for the individual to improve his understanding of his own cultural heritage, to be aware of these roots and adopt an attitude towards them and then to influence culture by articulating his view.[213] Despite all attacks, postmodernism is precisely what is needed to create a stronger association with a community.[214]

How can we briefly outline a postmodern society? The most important point for Rorty is the *self-supporting approach*[215] of a society which 'asserts itself without [being] bothered to ground itself'.[216] Here, delegitimization of metadiscourses means a distrust *vis-à-vis* claims of uniqueness, knowing that all attempts to gain insights into fundamental truths are futile. Plausible histories which prove to be pragmatic in practice are given priority over inorganic, rigidly classified systems and hierarchies. This creates worlds of relationships (as opposed to object worlds) which increasingly subdivide and emancipate themselves into a flexible fluid network, in which open, fast and intense continuous exchanges of information prove to be vital. In this network, all the individual components of this society have equal standing towards each other, paratactically, paralogically and non-hierarchically, and are mutually pervasive without being aggressive. There is mutual interest in the individual cultures which together form a loose bond, characterized not by rigid features but by consensus on some points, regardless of standpoint. Learning and acceptance rather than conversion are the main links which bind the groups. The constellations constantly change their focus, preventing the development of clearly defined boundaries between the groups. Furthermore, the trend is away from mega-groups ('Catholics', 'labourers', 'Communists') and towards extremely small and transparent groups in which similar attitudes to values and cognate behavioural/consumption patterns prevail.[217]

A society in which this type of dynamism is seen as a provisional arrangement is not comparable to the Tower of Babel built by modernism, but has much in common with the Nomads, who rest at always changing different (spiritual) camp fires. Primacy of action over structure, action rather than retention, is the dominant style.[218]

Loyalty and cohesion in the community are produced within a network resembling a jungle of roots or an inextricable web comprising all standpoints, worlds, discussion types and language games and are based on the view that no single, individual solution is feasible. Individual and group identities are weakened in favour of a situative, relational temporary definition, which heightens the sensitivity of the players still further to the diversity of potential frameworks and the puzzle of partial responsibilities.

Despite total openness to anarchy, schizophrenia and inflation of meaning, postmodern society is not nihilistic or quietist but can build a type of transit camp from the remains of modern society, in which values like openness, detachment, the will to live, the willingness to comprehend and community spirit are fundamental values.

Lyotard, or the Postmodern Economy

Lyotard's theoretical framework

The aim of this chapter is not to venture further into the differences between individual positions of professional professorial philosophy, and we shall not deal

with any of the following problem areas:[219,220] opposing conceptions; differences in
the interpretation of modernity and postmodernity; differing strategic proposals of
choice for action; postmodernism seen as a phase within modernism or as an
autonomous new beginning; or the issue of common features. As Kunneman aptly
stated: 'The positional warfare which the exponents of these two trends [Habermas
and Lyotard] have waged for years is just as useless as it is unproductive and only
serves to miss the opportunities which do exist.'[221]

Lyotard can be credited with having written the most telling essay on postmodernism, *La condition postmoderne* (The Postmodern Knowledge).[222] After
having written somewhat reflective works on daily politics (Second World War
responsibility, the Algerian question, etc.) in the 1950s and 1960s, Lyotard's
interest, since the early 1970s, increasingly focused on psychoanalytical topics.[223]
In this, he attempted to create a link between French Marxist theory and
psychoanalysis, designed to form the basis for a total rejection of social structures
and geared, in a quasi idealistic tradition, to the use of abstract ideas and content
as social ideals and guidelines.[224,225] In addition, he determines that truth as an
absolute yardstick is pointless; 'truth' can never be. Everything proclaimed as truth
is derived from a desire for the truth. This desire alone, rather than the truth it
manifests, can be understood by everybody as genuine, as 'true' and, as such,
as human.[226]

And thus Lyotard takes up one of Nietzsche's concepts – that the foggy world of
desires is the only true world, as opposed to a world of false truths. This latter
world based on 'lies, generally referred to as reality',[227] is perceived now only as
one possible narration, an interpretation, a heightening of desire for the truth
(a desire for reality). Therefore, religion, science and art are merely variants.
Consequently, for Lyotard, there is only one single escape route out of these blind
alleys. Mankind must abandon the (modern) path, together with its aim of a
unified, rational explanation of the world, and stand back in order to gain clarity
on the relationship between desire and desired reality and other potentially
desirable realities. We must abandon theories and even reject the concept that there
could be just one clarification. In this context, the final sentence of the 'économie
libidinale' states: 'You have to let the disrupting forces play to get intensity. This
strategy proves invulnerable as it is without hierarchy or headquarters, without
master-plan or project and it throws thousands of little hooks into the vast body
of symbols.'[228]

In 1979, *La condition postmoderne* incorporated these thoughts in the form of an
analysis of information processing within the knowledge society. This work, which
appeared somewhat by accident (originally it was an essay commissioned by the
Supervisory Board for Canadian universities), was welcomed as a postmodern
agenda and elevated to the status of a general reference work on the postmodern
theme. The essay is a situation documentary on modern society and its inherent
inability to develop. Lyotard's theory is that knowledge, structures, groups and
educational institutions are also changing in the course of the far-reaching
transformation from an industrial to a post-industrial society, and together are

ringing in the postmodern era, a period which is seriously different from any in the past. The ancillary theme which runs through this work is the role of language as an agent for social change and social stabilization.

The last remaining role of science is that of one language game among many, although even this function is being undermined by science itself in the course of an internal erosion process in which, due to the specialization and classification of science and its applications and, consequently, those of society too, it corroborates the suspicion that a single unifying narrative no longer exists, only several juxtaposed narratives (which are still perceived as competing views of the world expounded by different scientific disciplines).[229] Science is itself exposing its own myth of 'objective rationality' as a myth which, in the absence of a challenge from any other system, represents the self-destruction of modernism.[230] For Lyotard, this endogenous process has two distinctive characteristics: on the one hand science is changing to an even greater extent due to the priority placed on application in an output-producing technology. Society expects scientific activity to lead to effectiveness rather than comprehension. On the other hand, individual disciplines are now, by themselves, narrowing down the scope of their statements and, as a result of this increasing specialization and atomization of knowledge, venturing less and less frequently onto the thin ice towards other disciplines or onto the poorly regarded interdisciplinary platform. Scientific specialists are nowadays retreating into statements that have little general relevance and possess only paradigm dependent validity (i.e. they are useless for the most part).

Lyotard transfers this figure of thought to (modern, Western, i.e. the most highly developed) society, in the form of a comprehensive loss of legitimacy. This basically throws up again the global issue of legitimacy of narratives, since *postmodernism directs all previous modern methods of legitimization back to their relative position.*[231] In the postmodern era, no conceptual approach can claim to have discovered total truth. We can only decree provisional, ultimate pragmatic truths, the boundaries of which are defined by the type of discourse from which they originate. A discourse which is capable of objectivity, can speak for everyone or lay claim to general legitimacy (as Marxism did, for example) is not available. According to Lyotard, legitimacy is not achieved by consensus but, on a more restricted level, is reached within each individual discussion[232] (a view not shared by Habermas and Rorty). Thus, each discourse is perceived as a language game which draws up and monitors its own rules (agreements). Parties to the relevant discourse are required to learn its language (and social conventions) and to apply the rules in order to be understood. However, this applies only within a language game. For this reason individual discussions are basically incommensurate, incapable of reference to an (inexisting) meta-narrative in which they could all be united. But these individual discussions do not lie peacefully dormant next to each other like monads but are interrelated in competitive exchange.

A far-reaching crisis in terms of legitimization ('distrust regarding unifying theories'),[233] can be attributed to this fundamental conflict between individual discussions, and this crisis is manifested in society as dissemination and deconstruction (the dispersal or division of reason) to use Derrida's terms.[234] The dissolution of familiar social structures, the collapse of goal hierarchies, the blurring of meanings all follow the same pattern, which is also displayed in the deconstruction of the subject:

> In this dispersion of all language games, the subject, the individual itself will be disintegrated. The social cohesion is language-based, though is clearly not just one thread, but rather like a tissue where at least two (though many more in reality) language games interweave, each with its own separate set of rules.[235]

Lyotard does not, however, take a pessimistic or resigned view of this contemporary, ubiquitous departure from old structures but perceives it more as forward-thinking and dynamic in character.[236] Not a remote analysis but an active debate, and making moves in the game of language, is the way to develop new meanings and improve the situation in the context of creative destruction described by Schumpeter.[237]

Fundamental prerequisites for this are the complete autonomy of individual discussions and the 'purity' of their relevant rules. From Lyotard's viewpoint, this allows undisturbed, internal development in every discussion and permits each discussion to be measured fairly and justly against the others.[238] Awareness of one's ignorance and the perception of one's own weaknesses reveal new areas of knowledge and provide access to a new type of interaction with other discussions (language games): that of *paralogism*.[239] The fundamental transaction in this competition, the basic move in this game, is the exchange of information. This creates a link which is reinforced by a series of moves. In this way, a historical network of moves binds the discussions together, guaranteeing intercommunication.

Discussion participants can occupy only fluid positions between the 'islets of determination'.[240] The associated legitimization model can no longer be biased towards technical solutions, efficiency or performance, but must be designed as a positive difference, or paralogism.[241] Dissent is welcomed and presented to the scientific consensus system as a productive, creative and innovative counter-model.[242] Because unwanted moves can be neutralized, Lyotard perceives the consensus of a scientific society as extremely hostile to innovation, as well as static and anti-dynamic: 'The stronger a strategic move in the game is the more likely it abandons the areas of a minimal consensus, just because the rules of the game on how to achieve consensus are altered by this very move.'[243] This argumentation applies equally on the level of the dialogue interspersing the discussions. The structure of actions in this paralogic state is still unclear. An initial approach would be to admit the heteromorphology of the language games and strive for an evolutionary dynamism of social interaction (social interactions in the form of local and temporary agreements).[244] A preliminary result of this would be in the form of lower costs (material as well as idealistic) and a general increase in efficiency and effectiveness, which ultimately 'benefits the operational output of society'.[245] This study of postmodern knowledge breaks off without further elaborating this new procedural model of paralogism.[246]

We have now worked our way through Lyotard's central theme, namely the *interaction between discussion types*. This theme is subjected to further analysis, on a theoretical level, in Lyotard's subsequent major work, *Le différend* (The Conflict). Once again it is based on the philosophy of language, although in this case not that characterized by Wittgenstein, but rather in terms of the linguistic logic of the grammatical rules system appertaining to the various discussion types. No category of metadiscussion is available which is capable of uniformly and fairly presiding over the conflicts within the different discussion types.[247] The only outcome which we can finally achieve is a plethora of mutually conflicting discussions.[248] It is to these principal structures that Lyotard attributes the statement, that no systematic or compelling statements of a universal nature whatsoever can exist and also that sentences from dissimilar, heterogeneous control systems are not translatable. It follows, therefore, that conflict is not only unavoidable but there is no possibility of resolving the conflict.[249] The reason for this is that the antiquated concept of singular equations '{a symbol (name, proposition) = an object in the world}' is being broken down into a system comprising of several equations,[250] in which nothing can be omitted or implied silently. 'A sentence can embody more than one meaning, refer to more than one object, can be addressed to more than one type of reader, can be emitted by more than one originator.'[251] Here, Lyotard supports Derrida's deconstruction theory which does not merely acknowledge atomization passively, but actively, yet responsibly, attempts to produce it.[252] Lash presents an opposing view which perceives postmodernism as a de-differentiation, as a levelling following the modernist phase of differentiation.[253]

To Lyotard, these facts point, in linguistic terms, to the *absence of a uniform language with which to settle the conflict between discussion types*. This fundamental heterogeneity not only essentially incites conflict, it also fundamentally frustrates its settlement. A 'just' hegemony of one type of discussion over the other is thus inconceivable.[254] This is the distinction between a legal dispute (in which the parties refer back to common legal methodology and trust in an abstract community), and a conflict (in which no constructive communication exists between the two worlds).[255]

Of preeminent importance, at this stage of analysis, is not only the recognition of this basic lack of heterogeneity but, specifically, an awareness of the individual types and the inner logic of the individual forms of discussion involved in the conflict. This awareness, this understanding allows a productive exchange of information to take place. Analogies, symbols or juxtaposed synoptic comparisons can enhance the exchange,[256] which is why Lyotard also promotes small narratives which attempt, at least partially or temporarily,[257] to interpret different discussions in a more modest way than their predecessors, the larger narratives. Thus Lyotard reverts once again to his objective, declared programmatically in *La condition postmoderne*, to find a *modus operandi* in which the desire for fairness between different types of discussion and the desire for something new and unknown are both fulfilled in equal measure.

But how should we resist one-sidedness, the oppressive dominance of one paradigm (as, for example, in scientific modernism)?[258] In principle, Lyotard mistrusts social consensus which, despite its theoretical attempt to ingratiate itself, has frequently failed in practice. Consensus is much too easy to manipulate and has little to do with fairness, given the pressures generated by regulation and the imperative goal to reach consensus.[259] Only a 'natural' mistrust of any theory or set of criteria can ensure constant vigilance. Lyotard often employs the ideal of the heathen,[260] who does not believe in just one God but, pragmatically, has a portfolio of Gods. Thus, decisions take on a radical new form and are conducted using criteria adapted to suit the relevant circumstances. Without preconditions the world does indeed emerge as unreservedly superficial, just as for the primate in prehistoric times a simple and one-dimensional goal of survival was the only criterion. Vigilance, a certain artfulness, a *qui-vive*, as well as unlimited sensitivity to all opportunities ensures the survival of individuals and the enhanced performance of all the individuals within the group.

Knowledge as the powerhouse of postmodern change

Thus, one can detect two fundamental influences in Lyotard's work: firstly, human knowledge which is perceived as a major factor in current and future human dynamics;[261] and, secondly, economic thought is always apparent in Lyotard's patterns of thought.[262]

This fundamental, economic influence in postmodern thinking is evident in many other approaches to postmodernism (as well as aesthetic, psychological and other influences).[263] As a result, we shall methodically develop this concept. Postmodernism is even seen as a *new economic order*,[264] in which *multinational enterprises are the major feature of this new trend*.[265] The capitalism of this century was merely a preliminary step designed to help the global market capitalism of multinational companies to serve postmodern consumer preferences. Postmodernity and economic structure are inextricably linked. For Jameson, every opinion on postmodernity is an implicit and explicit statement on multinational capitalism.[266]

The link between both areas is knowledge. Know-how as its accumulative dimension and information as its dynamic process, is the only thing with any durability at all given the radical and rapidly changing parameters.[267] Although valuable, science in this context is ultimately perceived as merely an extra raw material (like money), an additional productive input. The motto of these 'ancillary sciences' is now efficiency rather than truth.[268] Knowledge, comprising firstly technical and organizational know-how, and secondly and more importantly symbolic competence, will become the major factor as far as production is concerned and the focus of an intense struggle in an extremely volatile global market, lacking exclusive hegemonies.[269] In this market, an alliance will be forged between wealth, efficiency and truth: 'No truth without money.'[270] Truth, money and power are becoming increasingly dependent on just one thing, which is, however, extremely complex and fleeting in character – information. Therefore the New Economy really is an IT-based economy with knowledge (or the network, the rhizome of information) as the most scarce resource and knowledge management as the most precious skill.[271]

Lyotard clearly addresses the underlying issue of *information control*.[272] Information, or rather access to information, is the central criterion for power and profit. Information is perceived as a commodity, but also as one of the highest privileges. This status is not granted by the traditional institutions (the state, society, the church, etc.), for it is precisely these institutions which are the weakest, leaving aside the currently fading spectre of 'big brother'.[273] Databases, Internet backbones, microcomputers, international corporations and independent 'think tanks' will all be interfaces on the information highway. Whoever controls information logistics and learning has a positional advantage.[274] In the context of Lyotard's perceptions, a torrential flood of changing economic parameters (globalization, flexibility of capital, monetarization, fragmentation of consumer markets, etc.), combined with changes in the technological sphere (digitalization, increased mobility, low-cost technology, the faster pace of innovation, etc.) are totally redefining the economy.

International currency markets are a prime example of this disintegration of exclusive legitimacy: the rules of the game are determined chiefly by active market players – international banks, international traders and other financially powerful, major institutions. Governments, or rather their central banks who were originally 'the guardians of currencies', now exert the least influence in terms of rule-making. After relinquishing the gold standard and, later, fixed exchange rates, the players have slowly broken free of a regime to determine exchange rates increasingly quasi-autarchically. Although the central banks can now cap rates thanks to their disproportionately large resources, a diminishing number of them are now in a position to do so. Smaller countries (even within Europe) are obliged to indulge in risky speculation. (From a market viewpoint, these transactions are nothing more than bets which the central banks place on a rate which are designed to prop up currencies to a politically desirable level.) In 'a worst case scenario', the result of assuming enormous financial commitments on the swap market, for example, could be the short-term insolvency of the sovereign state concerned. Equally, some countries are unable to hold their currency at an 'agreed' level and introduce (provisional) types of currency (or interest rate) management. Currency controls can be circumvented in seconds with a dexterity not found on any other market. In an information and knowledge-based society like ours, international companies are next in line, after the financial markets, to change to a new *modus operandi*.[275]

In a perspective of the national economy, the use of language games and discussion modes becomes clearer if we look at one or two firms and concepts. Which principles should the world adopt: monolithic company control, *à la* IBM; the diffuse conglomerate, such as Mitsui; or is a more general neo-mercantilism, a communism or Keynesian economic theory the regulatory framework within which we should operate?

Ultimately, the question of authority and legitimization cannot be resolved completely. Authority cannot be extracted from somewhere, 'it just happens'. Any attempt to legitimize authority logically leads to a *petitio pricipii* – who authorizes the authorization? Thus authority can never be determined on the basis of a single regulatory framework, it can only be situative, frail, contextual and provisional, without ontological foundations.[276] This network of perspectives no longer needs a supreme interventionist power to control it but is, in a manner of speaking, self-organizing and self-sufficient in its own right.[277]

The symbolism of postmodern change

In addition to knowledge, symbolism is another highly significant metaphor in a postmodern reading of the economy. Here, one basic hypothesis might be: *the significance of symbolism (in the form of signs, status, privileges) and conceptual content is growing rapidly in general economic behaviour and, more specifically, in products themselves.* Postmodern ideas have been introduced into the economy through a kind of postmodern 'symbology', that is via the world of symbols.

The production of symbols, or the creation of the symbolic features of a product or service, is becoming increasingly important in its process of material production.[278] This is also one of the reasons for the current obsession with packaging, held in high esteem in Japan and perceived as an indication of the sophisticatedness of the purchaser.[279] The completely new way in which symbolic concepts are reproduced in a product is set apart from any influence exerted by logic, money and power. The success of a product is no longer based on functionality, durability and so forth, but to an increasing extent on its marketing concept, ultimately its image. The significance of the functionality of a product is dwarfed by the plethora of meanings bought/sold with the product. Status, identification, image, value-enhancement, lifestyles, the feel-good factor and enjoyment are the pillars underpinning this symbolism. This advance into symbolism is actively taken by the economy, which is obliged to accede to a self-inflicted compulsion to achieve higher sales targets in an increasingly saturated consumer environment. Since new goods must always be produced, aesthetic idealistic innovation is becoming increasingly an important 'structural' role and function.[280]

The number of arbitrary sign systems is rising tremendously, although the overall sum of significance has not risen in parallel, indicating a fall in the significance of individual items as a consequence of this surfeit of potential symbolic meanings. Although the motto of the defined symbols is 'all that can (must) be said and thought',[281] the plethora of potential universes of meaning causes the object to appear strangely blank and ill-defined. The underlying principle in this is aptly described by Lash as an *oversupply of significants/symbols/meaning* (the popular examples of MTV and CNN come to mind) and, given a constant demand, quantified in terms of significates/goods, a 'price crash' or loss of contextual meaning is the result along with field of ruins of insignificant significants/useless symbols without much meaning.[282] As a consequence of this process, the significant (the symbol, the meaning, the object, the good) starts to look weathered. It no longer represents the reference object against which copies are measured; its importance diminishes, the copies become independent, acting as references for each other. The reference value is abolished, leaving only a structural value association behind. This should not, however, be perceived as a conflict between symbols and production but as the integration of the human world of symbolism into the economic system.[283] This *dissociation of significantes from signifikat* is apparent in the split between wages and work, in the separation of production from social reference and in the dissociation of money from production.[284] For this reason, the concept of a branded product or brand-name again becomes extremely important. Today, a label sums up hundreds of different diffuse meanings, sometimes without even presenting or naming the product or referring to it in any other way. Colours, shapes and unambiguously identifiable attributes make any direct reference to the brand name almost obscene.[285,286]

This contradicts the traditional economic model of direct, physical competition and the subliminally profound monotony of the products, but it is successful in restimulating demand. For the freedom achieved by the product manager to let the products mean whatever is required, gives the consumer, for the first time in his history, the complete freedom to realize his 'bundle of needs' not only in a material but also in an idealist context. This is why today's addiction to consumerism (particularly in Japan) resembles more a general hysteria than the actions of the ideal *homo economicus*. Consumers live in a self-service society in which everyone is responsible for creating his own meaning, and preprocessed modules of 'meaning' are used to create one's own individual living environment. Thus consumption is transformed into a system of meanings which performs an essential function similar to that of language or family relationships or systems of belonging (e.g. religion, myths). Adopting Say's and Galbraith's models, demand is substantially stimulated only by production (of meaning). In this way, needs are generated which would not otherwise exist were it not for production.[287]

So this is how we explain, in a postmodern context, the fragmentation of society into a myriad of different consumer groups. Flexibility, an elasticity of the significance of an object is the prerequisite for this. This is Baudrillard's phenomenon of *simulation*. The original loses its value; it can be reproduced, copied, changed and improved at will and its value is therefore no greater than that of a copy, which is practically zero. Systems are now merely simulations of systems; simulations have now taken the place of politics and the economy.[288,289] Therefore, instead of living in reality we now live in a kind of *hyperreality*. Meaning is no longer classified rationally but, simply, it just happens, without valid reference, provisionally, in the knowledge that it is an arbitrary referral.[290,291]

A simpler way of looking at this hyperreality is to see it as an endless stream in which, unlike in the traditional economy, nothing accumulates, stops or ceases. *To some degree, production and consumption flow interminably in all directions.*[292] Money is the best example of this. Whereas, once upon a time, it was saved or hoarded for future purchases and investments, it now has to be in perpetual motion, 'working'. Twenty-four-hour trading of financial devices on the financial markets is now the norm. Money can be transferred electronically around the globe 'at the speed of light', as a result of which antiquated concepts like the right of coinage or fiscal sovereignty have become objects of ridicule. Money, when seen in this context, is the *pure simulacrum*. It is obscene and is no longer tendered shamefully, as in the past. Money is traded for profit, which is circulation, pure and simple, without any regard for its origin, aim, purpose or meaning.[293] Capital is undergoing a metamorphosis from object to process; the increased turnover rate is now an asset in itself.[294] This is precisely the reason why Lyotard also perceives monetary realism as capricious realism.[295]

Financial trading, which is at the very heart of economic perception, clearly demonstrates the transition from a modern, rational view to a postmodern, symbolic view.[296] Perceived in simple terms, goods are exchanged for money, equalizing the value of the goods with that of the money. This process of equalization can, however, be subdivided into functional logic of value in use (utility); economic logic of exchange value (pricing); differential logic of brand value (symbolic value); and idealistic logic of symbolic exchange (abstract valuation of symbols through comparing by economic agents). Tangible economic activities can be explained by combining individual components. By combining 'value in use' with 'pricing', we get 'normal consumption' (goods for money). The combination of 'value in use' and 'symbolic valuation' refers to the equation of a product with its symbolic content (conspicuous consumption, consumption of art, and buying an original rather than a colour copy, for example). Thus, combining 'symbolic exchange value' with 'pricing' can now explain Andy Warhol's ability to generate a huge business by selling symbols (symbol commercialization).

This places a new interpretation on the traditional concept of equating utility to exchange value, that is equivalence of symbolic meaning (symbolic value) and symbolic exchange value (the subjective value comparison). This results in (a) the *redefining of utility through symbolic value* (the value of the ideas and lifestyles which the product represents), and (b) the *replacement of exchange value by symbolic valuation* (symbolic, instead of monetary prices).[297] These equations also explain why, generally speaking, the symbolic content of the products continues to rise (the symbolic content is now the actual utility of the product)[298] and why some of today's price relationships can be considered, in a traditional context, as surreal and out of proportion to everyday life. The old pricing formula is now being replaced by a comparison of the different symbols which are being exchanged (just as gold has been obliged to relinquish its reference status, symbols are now taking over the right claimed by money to be seen as a reference value).[299]

The emphasis placed by modernism on monetary exchange is now diminishing and, in essence, products are now losing their character as physical goods. Both these developments are caused by (a) marginally decreasing utility functions (as in the neoclassical model), and (b) the sheer infinite demand for symbols (a monotonically increasing linear function).[300]

It is becoming evident that material production is necessarily linked to the symbolic realm. This link with the realm of desires and concepts is so intense that symbols and signs/significants could even achieve primacy: 'Production is nothing but letting fantasies become realities, or differently put, production of expressions.'[301] Thus the *theory of material exchange* is broadened to a *theory of symbolic exchange*. From this, we can place a new interpretation on economic events, one which is based purely on symbols and symbolic value. *Postmodernity leads to a proliferation of symbols and their potential meanings.* This language of symbols has now entered the very core of business activities, together with all its consequences of non-rational evaluation, the acceptance of multiple meanings and the irrelevance, in a hyperreal world, of differentiation between original and copy.

Postmodern man as an economic agent

What kind of people can live in this hyperreal world? Does the image of the profit-maximizing *homo economicus* not become too limited when it is based on the premise that postmodern theory represents genuine postmodern reality? Can we not interpret the transition to postmodern economic behaviour patterns as a function, as a result of the special mood of our postmodern times?

Once again, the players in the financial world can illuminate the scenery. The 'enigmatic' events, some of which were illegal or at any rate excesses, around people like Boesky, Milken, Gutfreund, or Leeson are representative of tens of thousands of epigones. The apex for a rational profit-maximizer involves money and power, the evangelism of Wall Street.[302] Devoid of all other goals 'the golden boys' pursue with unfettered focus the ideal of unlimited acquisition of money and power, skimming along the surface of things, losing touch with (other) realities. This successful type is the epitome of a moribund society from which there is no escape.[303] This is no longer Nietzsche's light-hearted profound superficiality,[304] nor is it Habermas' decentralized subjectivity, free of all the imperatives of work and usefulness.[305] Sheer surface becomes valuable in itself. A new superficiality is creating an intense emotional mood in which genuinely superficial views are gratefully accepted, whether they result from overload or a desire to avoid adopting too profound a view.[306]

The result, in terms of the individual as well as groups, is *fundamental decentredness inevitably accompanied by schizophrenia.*[307] Consequently, we can no longer build social groups which can be identified as supporters of the emancipation of social progress. The elite are being resocialized, the bourgeoisie and the proletariat are being debilitated into a consumer society. Aesthetics is being downgraded to a lifestyle. The welfare society, which somehow does still exist, ultimately normalizes everything. Each aspect of avant-gardism is subdivided into a myriad of mini-avant-gardes and would-be groups, which allow no new major social development to take place fostering only singular, private interests.[308,309] Each individual group is incidental and self-legislating, even though their living environments are mutually pervasive. Many new global groups are being created with codes like Yuppies, Dinks, Eurokids, Yeppie, Techie, and so on,[310] but these are just the major groups in a myriad of consumer groups.[311] Here again we can successful apply Bourdieu's concept of social fields.[312] The 'fields' cover this new kinetic since they explode the concept of static classes in favour of more open fields without boundaries. Their energies are not so much spent on external struggle (a struggle with 'those of other opinions' as a result of clashes in symbolism, such as clothing or eating habits), but are introverted, aimed at group cohesion and the creation of a group identity.[313]

In this world, society is *atomized into a flexible network* of language games and forces, evenly distributed across its space and occupied by a modest subject, which is also its elementary unit.[314] The individual, the ego of bourgeois society, is replaced by *nomadic subjectivity* which appears unstable in every dimension.[315] Lacking any cocky self-assuredness, it has not isolationist differentiation as its aim, but rather the creation of a community based on non-hierarchical principles of diversity and difference. Symbolic modules can be combined, allowing individuals to live not just in one form of existence but in several.[316] This rules out any subjection of the individual to hubris, egomania or megalomania and also, conversely, to autistic isolation.[317] The individual is becoming less and less important. The information network interface, the crystallization kernel of social and relational forces, or just the consumption pattern are better identifiers.[318] Perceived in this context, the post-industrial economy has seized complete control of all human life and is forcing it towards what is rapidly becoming a disposable society, without taking account of psychological changes.[319,320]

Just as modernity represented a new way of dealing with time and space, so postmodernity has brought about the accelerating changes in spatial and temporal categories, although, this time, we can no longer keep pace with developments.[321] The *disintegration of spatial and temporal notions* is now unstoppable. Today, we can order Japanese sushi as an appetizer, Argentinean steak as a main course with French cheese to follow, accompanied by (American) Coors lager, rounded off with Israeli plums in Barbadian rum and Egyptian cigarettes, without being aware of the cultural and spatial connotations. This would have been impossible in 1970 and unthinkable in 1950.[322] The trendsetter, once again, was the financial world. The globalization of financial markets does not only alter technical details: 'Banking is rapidly becoming indifferent to the constraints of time, place and currency.'[323] One can no longer speak of 'business as usual' in any context whatsoever. The debt crisis in Latin America has (again) been shelved until the next decade, the magic world of 'financial engineering' is capable of producing highly flexible financial tools, which can evade any attempt to pin them down in terms of familiar categories such as space, time, nation and so on. The resulting delocalization and deterritorialization and the loss of all temporal references and rhythms completely disorient people in their daily lives, leading them to seek refuge in a *world of signs and symbols*, where they can assemble easily their own world of symbols.[324]

But these consequences should not only be considered negative; they are also accompanied by a departure into a new type of social performance. This post-modern mode of economic action has itself resulted in efficacy and performance, and by encouraging active participation it reduces to some extent entropy, since each new move necessarily affects other players forcing them to reevaluate the situation which results in new moves. A new style of business competence is prerequisite for this new system to be productive. Hence the call for a new (i.e. knowledge-based) economy.[325] This refers more to new capabilities needed, new strategies required by the postmodern world (such as circumspection, common sense and cleverness),[326] than to the implementation of a fundamentally new image of the human being.[327] Welsch specifies this new strength as *aisthetic competence*, seen here as the 'special ability to understand differences, an awareness of hetero-geneity, a sensitivity to divergence and dissent'. These are the first traces of a new economic style. The qualities with which this competence is imbued are softness, sensitivity and imagination, perceptiveness for differentiation, suppleness, alert-ness to heterogeneity, mergeability and, in particular, a heightened sensitivity to information and communication.[328]

Authority and power are no longer institutionally linked to physical forces, they are merely the names of constellations, of strategic situations, in which a multi-dimensional force-field shapes a society without centre or hierarchy.[329] Just as the conundrum of the guerrilla has replaced the chessboard of war,[330] a different kind of trust today forms the basis for economic activities. In terms of human history, mankind has progressed from a naïve direct trust in trading partners, through hostage-taking[331] and spiritual sanctions (taboos, religion) to a conditional trust in business partners. The innovation of the contract has meant that greater trust is now placed in the abstract virtue of the law.[332] Apparently, a further step towards abstraction is now needed. All trust has been lost, both in one's fellow man and social abstracts. A *general indifference and openness* towards one's fellow man has led to a new fairness, since everyone is unreservedly careful when dealing with others. This is where the picture again coincides with Rorty's argumentation, which foresees the creation of a new, revolutionary type of community.[333,334]

When examining a synopsis of the chapter, we can determine, in close conver-gence with Lyotard's chain of thought, just how postmodern basic constellations in the area of knowledge, the world of symbols and the field of the human aspects of economic interaction can point the way to new economic paths. Paralogy and dissent together form the basis for a productive exchange and for innovative impetus, culminating in a plethora of small strategies without any need for commit-ment to a major project. Science is degraded to a profitable and necessary language game of only limited temporary legitimacy. New economic priority is given to meaning, signs and symbols at the expense of the ability to differentiate between what is real and what is simulated, a distinction no longer applicable in today's hyperrealism. By taking the fundamental transaction of trading the reinterpretation of business activities as an exchange of symbols is exemplified: money as an abstract, currency markets and the international financial market in general, are used to demonstrate how the heart of the global economy has changed into a postmodern market in which nothing can be fixed and everything is in a state of flux.

> In this way, the modern economy developed into a multiple perspective on business which perceives the world as countless decentralized but omnipresent markets, whose reactions are highly sensitive to information. It is equally impossible to define, statically, the relevant decision-makers; they gain more contours when perceived as a flexible rhizome of information interfaces. The features of these frail subjects, whose pragmatic aim is to benefit at least to some extent from these complex dynamics, are constant alertness and innovative performance, plus a sensitive nose for diversity. Naïve trust in one's fellow man (directly or via the legal system) has given way to an indifferent openness which sets no preconditions but, equally, excludes nothing and is sufficiently flexible, responsive and vigilant to promise the communication of meaning and exchange opportunities which everyone desires.

IV DIGRESSION: JAPAN'S RECEPTION OF THE POSTMODERN

Our aim in this chapter is not to provide a postmodern interpretation of contemporary Japan, as is more the role of Chapters 3, 4 and 5 in the context of a general introduction to the Japanese sphere. Our objective is rather to conduct a special study in order to determine whether and to what extent Japan's contemporary thinkers perceive and assimilate the postmodern. Here we must proceed with great caution in order to avoid committing the insidious Western sin of jumping to conclusions or overinterpreting, one example of which was the flawed attempt to describe the contemporary Zen movement as postmodern. The (misconceived) hypothesis would be that Zen definitely does promote vagueness and openness and must ergo (erroneously) be 'postmodern'.[335] If we take a cautious look, however, it is possible to identify the reception of postmodern thinking in Japan on three levels:

1 *The contemporary reception of traditional scripts and cultural elements*
In the Western world, classical texts are being constantly reinterpreted and reassessed, adapting them to the new surroundings.[336] Theoretically, this might also be the case in Japan, but if we survey contemporary interpretations of traditional cultural elements such as Buddhist scripts, the tea ceremony, martial arts or horticulture, this theory must be disputed. It is impossible to identify any radical new interpretation whatsoever, or any application of postmodern points of

view. Mostly, the Japanese reception of classical thoughts and cultural elements is limited to conservative exegesis and cautious development of these bodies of thought within predefined limits.[337,338]

In this context, techniques, codes of behaviour, values and concepts are transmitted without any demand for reinterpretation or development. Where changes are really necessary, they must correspond to the inherent meaning of the relevant tradition, and external secular influences are for the most part rejected.[339] This basically weakly developed self-reflectiveness may be a disadvantage which retardively affects cultural development. But, conversely, the rigid accentuation of cultural forms (*kata*) acts as a positive reference framework insofar as the cautious adaptation of reforms is concerned. Just as modernization was jump-started, at the very beginning, by the Japanization of imported 'modernity', we now initially anticipate the Japanization of postmodern influences, designed to allow the application of postmodern interpretations to its own roots, thus creating its own Japanese 'postmodernity'.[340]

2 *The postmodern reading in 'professional' Japanese philosophy*

In this context one is faced with the fundamental difficulty of summarizing Japanese thinking into a concept of Japanese philosophy, as this would result in the omission of a number of areas not covered by the conventional body of Western philosophy. For in doing so one would omit, to take an example, Zen and religious thought in general as well as the philosophical interpretation of crafts or the theatre (particularly the No-theatre).[341] By assuming a broader definition of philosophy, we can at least identify references to a postmodern body of thought, although, even here, no explicit postmodern assessment of positions is conducted.

Already in 1971 the Japanese philosopher, Hisamatzu, attempted to break up the traditional, personalized fixed dialogue (master/class) of Zen teaching and broaden it into a general diffuse human dialogue. During this procedure 'the boundaries and problem areas themselves are breached from ground level upwards', effecting a radical awakening and thus ending modernity.[342] Equally, Ohashi,[343] for example, draws interesting conclusions in his observation of the current relationship between Zen and philosophy. Today, philosophy is in crisis: its philosophical principles are juxtaposed but irreconcilable and therefore incapable of recreating philosophical unity *per se*. A far-reaching modernist crisis is also detectable in our society. Since Zen is very far removed in nature from both, it is ineffectual in terms of assistance or communication. But Zen methods can alleviate man's plight, in situations of discontinuity (irreconcilability) as well as continuity (a positive, progressive outcome to the confrontation), by means of an equal but non-committal cooperation with Western philosophy.[344] Nevertheless, this Zen concept is not overcoming its traditional ambivalence towards other viewpoints; active difference or an open juxtaposition is not searched. For this reason, we can say that although this new understanding of Zen is reconcilable with postmodern views, it has not yet taken the step towards an active postmodern dispute which actively embraces opposing positions.

Postmodern thought appears to be more poorly represented in the field of academic publications when compared to the English-speaking,[345] French-speaking or German-speaking areas. The cause of this disinterest could be the superficial similarity of postmodernism and some traditional structures of thought. By traditional structures of thought we mean values which the Japanese have considered ideal for a very long time. Irrespective of their specific origins, these might also be included in a compilation of postmodern items and the following list contains what could be considered examples of this type of values:

(a)   in aesthetic terms, a preference for asymmetry, intended coincidence and the combination of simple shapes capable of producing symbolic stimulation;[346]

(b)   in philosophical terms, the obligation to view divergent, contradictory individual values integratively, as a unit. This refers to the paradoxes of the Zen *koan* or the general structure of classical Japanese philosophy, which Nakamura characterizes as the tendency to neglect the rules of logic in favour of symbolism, a lack of coherence and an emphasis on all that is intuitive and emotional;[347]

(c)   in ethical terms; the obligations arising from even the smallest of favours (*on, giri,* etc.; cf. Chapter 3, section IV), leading to the creation of a network of obligations which inevitably becomes extremely complex and can incorporate major contrasts and total contradictions. Thus, in spite of all the antinomies for each individual, strict yet uncoded customs and traditions and all commitments, irrespective of nature, must be respected in external relationships.[348]

Because of these or similar notions, there is a kind of blind spot which inhibits acknowledgement of the innovation and global relevance of postmodern thought. Consequently, Western discussion is relegated to a disjointed, coarse attempt to mimic the traditional principles of Japanese thinking. Since this aping by the West appears too awkward for the Japanese taste, it is considered unworthy of mention and consequently remains unreported. However, we cannot follow the course of this argument in detail here. Otherwise, postmodernism is deemed to be just one of many 'schools', with postmodern writing used to differentiate and identify an academic in an otherwise indistinguishable mass of philosophy teachers within a conservative, rigid educational system.[349,350] The hypothesis, that the postmodern plays a more important role in Japan than the West assumes, is confirmed by Miyoshi, a Japanese philosopher primarily concerned with postmodern thinking, who denigrates postmodernism as a purely Western affair.[351] Asada *et al.* place another interpretation on postmodernism,[352] comparing postmodern methodology to a well-equipped tool box which is able to apply know-how in order to achieve the fulfillment of claims to power in a general context.

All the above authors, however, ignore the convergence of new Western thinking with traditional Japanese life patterns and thought structures. Surprisingly enough, no reference has yet been made by any Japanese thinker to this convergence, perhaps because the difference to modernity or pre-modernity is not evident. For the Japanese, there is a difference, not least for purely historical reasons, between the Japanese and the Western body of thought which, as dogma would have it, cannot correspond. In the context of this maxim, the discussion between modernism and postmodernism is perceived purely on the basis of the Western world of thought.

3 *Assimilation of a global phenomenon in individual cultural areas such as architecture or literature*

These are the areas in Japan which appear to have been mostly affected by the postmodern atmosphere. Recent, internationally recognized architectural feats like the Tsukuba Science City Project or Tokyo's postmodern luxurious suburb Tama have clear postmodern characteristics. Arata, a prominent architect, explains his design in the following terms:

> ... I crushed the clear system – of the kind usually preferred for institutional architecture – with the result that fragments overlap, setting up friction, betraying, and then being stitched together with a vague hope that a new statement will emerge from among the sutures ... In order to deal with this ambivalence, I made the center simply a space – a void ... Everything is situated around a void.[353]

The language of postmodern architecture flows smoothly into the repertoire of Japan's urban planners and architects, leaving traces which turn out to be 'serenely spectacular',[354] always leading one to the possible conclusion that this is merely an infantile enactment of a fashion statement, randomly determined *ad acta* when a new trend appears, rather than an expression of the spirit of the time. This assumption is reinforced even more strongly by the fact that, in Japanese architecture, Western influences are never really combined with traditional form language. A conglomeration of Western templates is regularly used, presenting, to a degree, postmodernism in its purest form. In the postmodern context two things are interesting even with a project as international as, for example, the famous hotel erected in Fukuoka, a small provincial town, which is an avant-garde design by a number of European and Japanese architects. Firstly, the absence of cohesion between individual architectural concepts and between the hotel and its small-town environment. Diversity and the avant-garde function here as a compulsory exercise lacking in concept. Secondly, it should be noted that the hotel rooms themselves are, again, designed and decorated in traditional Japanese style. Postmodernity is used only for the contemporary exterior design, but the internal environment, which is the functional aspect, remains classically Japanese, unruffled and unaffected by the facade.[355]

This superficial desire to be 'in' by employing the latest concepts is not emphasized so forcefully in Japan's modern literature, although the status of the postmodern is similar. In recent years, the interest of Japanese literature in postmodern themes has increased[356,357] but has not taken root as securely as in the USA or in Europe.

Currently, the most famous postmodern Japanese novel is probably *nanotaku kurisutaru* (Somehow it's a crystal).[358] This novel is not based on a structured story but merely communicates a sense of loss of identity, a chance existence in a consumer culture. Despite being denigrated by critics – Miyoshi called it a 'crude apologia for affluence'[359] – it has held onto its position as an example of a postmodern Japanese novel thanks to immense public interest. It reflects the abandonment felt by the younger generation[360] and its quest for identity in the irrational over-consumption of branded goods. These young Japanese lack a primary identity, beyond the phony identity offered by the image portrayed by brands. For them, 'Japan' is ultimately nothing more than a branded article. Field[361] portrays the problems of this atmosphere as the area of conflict between identity, 'Japaneseness' and consumer freedom (monetary affluence). This novel is provocative but is equally very indirect in its suggestiveness, since it fails to extrapolate an abstract postmodern position but merely presents a snapshot of Japanese youth. An inherent feature of more recent literature appears to be that it reflects reality without commenting upon it, provides no framework and lacks definition as far as values and terminology are concerned. Here, postmodern literary techniques are employed to produce collage-like variations, incorporating extreme eccentric characters, experimenting with textual settings and inducing diverse perspectives of interpretation.[362] Since this represents a literary visualization of the spirit of the times, we can detect a new distinctive form of realism in its original sense,[363] which runs through the more recent Japanese literature, collating and portraying postmodern atmospheres but not actively creating them or advancing them by way of comment. But even in this limited role, it does represent postmodernity since it 'searches for new representations, not to enjoy them but to leave behind a more profound impression of what is unrepresentable'.[364,365]

In conclusion, we can say that although the Japanese are aware of the postmodern and do use it, it is not a self-sufficient basic influence in the wider intellectual life of Japan. Postmodernity is rather understood as an exogenous variable, without a life of its own (like for example 'existentialism' in Paris in the 1960s had). In the attempt to identify and explain the profound phenomena which have existed for years in Japanese life, which are otherwise expressed primarily in forms which one could not call postmodern,[366] an independent, 'emancipated' form of postmodernity is not clearly distinguishable in Japan.

V THE POSTMODERN IN THE NEW ECONOMY

Nearly every aspect touched upon when characterizing postmodern theory and the atmosphere in general can serve as a description of the emerging processes, rules and codes of the Internet world and the New Economy. Rereading this chapter having replaced the term 'postmodern' with 'New Economy' would feel easy and would make intuitive sense.

After the emancipation from modernity on the theoretical level, now the implementation in everyday life takes another step. From atmospheres, niches in academia or art, the postmodern amoeba grows into the business and political worlds.

Economic literature is usually terse in embracing ideas stemming from areas other that the hard-core natural sciences. Therefore, only few but a growing number of traces can be found.[367] Nevertheless, there are some signs that the economic sphere is opening up and uses the postmodern reading of the world and the concepts developed. Some authors cite the compression of space and time, fueled by IT, as the driver for social change; some develop notions of postmodern capital; others respond to the contemporary economy of signs with postmodern marketing. Bell sees the New Economy as essentially a knowledge economy without hierarchical structures, organized organically as a gigantic ultra-flexible network ('capitalism without capitalists' as he phrases it).[368]

This rapprochement is particularly visible in the general-reader business literature where, by virtue of the dynamics of the Internet, nearly every aspect of standard business behaviour is being questioned and replaced by new concepts that are analogous to postmodern ideas, whereby the New Economy is often unaware of the close relation between the two views of the same coin.[369] A special case in point is the work of Siegel, the reputed web-strategist. His view of the market as a communicative forum in the virtual world where people live online in communities held together by situational common interests is strikingly parallel to some ideas of Habermas and Rorty.[370] The eight C's of the web – community (virtual tribes), continuity (spatial and temporal disruption do not matter anymore), convenience (speed), customization (my identity in the net), commerce (real transactions), content (meaning), commitment (relative to the setting I commit myself temporarily) and (self-)control – seem like a reiteration of the characterization given earlier in this chapter of *homo postmodernus*.[371] Powered by the global interconnectivity, the individual as a free agent roams the virtual net and shares limited (temporary or issue-specific) experiences with others, thus forming communities and tribes and consequently creating a performance economy as a natural outgrowth of the truth economy and relativity.[372]

Thus, the postmodern changes from a theoretical description, an attribute, from an atmosphere to a project and to an active verb. The New Economy is then the operationalization, the praxis of the postmodern theoretical and emotional fabric.[373] But how can such postmodern qualities be succinctly described from the postmodern side to then serve as a yardstick for the creation of New Economy concepts?

VI SUMMARY TWO: THE POSTMODERN CHARACTER

We have demonstrated the successful dissemination of postmodernism, using architecture and the natural sciences as an example. A fundamental feature is, on the one hand, the endogenous breaching of the armour-plating of modernism and industrial society, which has generally become too confined and inflexible, combined with the active quest for separate discussions on new goals and meaning. An additional factor for success is, on the other hand, the universal applicability of postmodern terminology. Subtle external infiltration and inducing evolution via examples from other unrelated debates widen dissemination of the postmodern body of thought.

In principle, we support the theory that the postmodern trend is a reflection of the tendencies present in reality, thus portraying a spirit of the times. On its own admission, postmodernism is not a new paradigm but rather an interlude, a pre- and post-treatment. By studying Habermas' position, we have demonstrated its independent existence whose role is that of a new response to a changed world (a new reading). The indicators for this are chiefly the failure of modernism, resulting from self-induced crisis, the constructive criticism of it voiced by post-modernism and the emancipated, consciously reflective and forward-looking pragmatic viewpoint adopted by postmodernism in terms of its behaviour towards modernism.

This method of positive expansion of the status quo into new constellations is becoming increasingly important from a social point of view, for it provides a means with which to resist the forces of disintegration. This is Rorty's starting point. Elements of a synthesis into a postmodern picture of society are charac- terized by their dynamism, their dependency on their situative context and their self-definition in the form of a non-committal provisorium. Due to the super- abundance of potential argumentation forms and the inextricably intertwining of all the discussions as a given, the acceptance of the temporary character of any solution is the only passable route. The major challenge presented by this complexity, which stems from its vagueness and general openness and the desire to survive, produces the necessary minimal communal solidarity, loyalty and cohesion.[374] The changes which human societies are undergoing are more extensive and also further advanced in the economic sphere than anywhere else. Hence it is no wonder that technology-induced new blueprints for our world are now originated in the form of the New Economy.

According to Lyotard, the main agent in the transition to a postmodern *modus vivendi* is human knowledge, the structures of which have fundamentally changed so that it now effects fundamental changes in the economy. The metaphors of this change are the symbols, the signs. The basic content of economic activity (production and commerce) are being transferred from the physical sphere ('goods' in a traditional sense) to an immaterial sphere (symbols, status, concepts, etc.). Meaning, signs and symbols are being given a new economic priority at the expense of the ability to distinguish between real and simulated, a distinction which no longer applies in today's hyperrealism. Thus a world with an endless plethora of globally linked, non-localized markets is being created, which reacts highly sensitively and rapidly to the flood of information. The *homo postmodernus* associated with this, re-enacts the specific moods of the postmodern era: indifferent openness, alertness, flexibility[375] and innovative performance as well as an instinct for differences and change. These are the characteristics of postmodern decision-makers, whose aim is not the dutiful implementation of plans and projects but simply being successful: surviving by pragmatically taking account of an increasingly complex, uncertain and dynamic economy.

In principle, this positional representation of postmodernism is constantly used as a backdrop when we reflect on the working hypothesis of the postmodern economic model and the hypothesis of Japan's postmodernity (cf. Chapter 1, section V). Postmodernism must be operationalized so that it can be used productively to resolve the issue of the effect of postmodernism on the global economy and management, as well as the question of the postmodern dimensions of Japanese culture and economic structure, particularly in respect of Keiretsu. This is why the following *working definition of postmodernism* will be used further on:

1 Postmodernism presumes absolute *equivalence* of all discussions which, although competing, do not seek to create fixed hierarchies but prefer to function *multidimensionally* as a type of *network* (rhizome), the purpose of which is to create meaning.

2 Starting with the legacy of modernism, postmodernism attempts to construct provisional, situative, temporary interpretations of the world by *deconstructing* and *reassessing* all values.

3 Postmodernism introduces a variety of *symbols with multiple meanings*, which have superseded 'logic' and create a world of signs in which endless superficial layers are simulating reality and therefore appear 'more real' than the naïve view of 'reality'. Rigid boundaries are broken down into open *indeterminables*, which, in a blended and disorientated fashion, produce a perspective-dependent, hypothetical truth.

4 *Transmorality, immanence* and *indifference* are the intellectual signs of postmodernity and their targets are *paralogy, performance, pragmatism* and *liquid dynamism*.

5 Postmodern thought avoids identifying the subject and any 'traditional' groupings. *Identities are simulated*; society is disseminated thanks to the partial absorption of multicultural fragments. Temporary communities (as symbolized by the myriad found on the Internet) is the only possible from of association.

6 The atomization of society is creating a *diffuse distribution of power* within a network of singular responsibilities; loose, flexible coordination between the many lifestyles is the only organizational structure available.

7   Maximum activity in terms of *information* and *communication*, coupled
    with the embrace of technology is strengthening capitalism in global
    delocalized markets in which there are no dominant players, with roles
    constantly changing. The impracticability of control and organization is
    allowing efficiency drivers such as *imagination, charisma, total awareness*
    and *sensitive, rapid response* to appear on the scene and to function as the
    chief components of success.

Part III

Japan: New or Old – Postmodern all the Same

3 Postmodern Indicators in Japanese Culture

Both roads
– that of the classical Far East and that of the modern West –
ultimately lead to the same perception:
the totally reflective goal, 'finality amidst emptiness'
is the goal of all experience – an emptiness
not of hopeless nihilism but of the plentitude of nothing,
from which man, highly-developed in his sense of awareness
can easily create whatever he cares to imagine,
including pleasure and pain, paradise and hell.

C. Kellerer, *Der Sprung ins Leere*, 1982, p. 189

I OVERVIEW

After presenting a general overview of research on Japan we now examine the country's cultural aspects, taking into account its postmodern dimension, since this affects economic and social behaviour and economic structures to a far greater extent than in any other country. Because of its special features, it also contributes to the international success of 'Japan Inc'. As already indicated in Chapter 1, section V, we now examine more closely the thesis that Japan's culture and tradition have general characteristics which can, from a contemporary perspective, be labelled 'postmodern'. In this argument, the theory that Japan has always been postmodern only serves to confuse. A more accurate formulation would be that some of Japan's basic characteristics, developed during its history, are (again) now just as prevalent as prior to Japan's modernization (during and after the Meiji period, i.e. from 1868), and today hold a special supportive position since they promote precisely the features considered essential for survival in the postmodern era.[1] For this reason, it is dangerous to compare premodern, modern and postmodern in a Japanese context, since this would hypothesize a discrete temporal process, which would be inaccurate.[2]

77

Traditional fundamental values coexist simultaneously with modern influences in Japan's contemporary social structure, and this combination of diverse stimuli continues to act as the formative driving force. On closer inspection we can divide this dialectic into several backdrops which set the scene for Japan in the world of today. From early historical times the Shinto model has managed to retain its formative influence, supplemented by the Buddhist and imperialistic ideals of the Nara and Heian periods around AD 750, and subsequently by the chivalrous ideals of the Samurai from the twelfth century onwards. The more sophisticated art forms of the fourteenth and fifteenthth centuries brought the aesthetic model to bear and this was supplemented by bourgeois and democratic (western, technical) prototypes during the subsequent Tokugawa (1600–1868) and Meiji (1868–1912) periods.[3]

All these models now exert equivalent influence on contemporary Japan. The fundamental objective of this chapter is to demonstrate, by means of some examples, how greatly the relevance of a few traditional influences, the characteristics of which are indistinguishable from those now required to deal with the 'postmodern world' and which function as *historic building blocks* in a postmodern context, has been enhanced. These traditional concepts should be perceived as somewhat analogous to postmodern qualities. Their nature precludes any attempt at an exhaustive, postmodern analysis of the cultural assets concerned. It is more important, and suffices here, to demonstrate that Japan is well-equipped for the postmodern era.

II THE STRUCTURE AND FUNCTION OF THE
JAPANESE LANGUAGE

To the Japanese, the concept that language is at the very heart of their culture and nation is very deep-rooted. In the Japanese comprehension, speaking Japanese is equivalent to being Japanese, so that language becomes a means of national self-esteem, a mythology and a symbol, binding a group together in spiritual terms.[4]

Writing, Speaking and Interpreting

Japanese can be written and read in three directions – horizontally, from left to right or right to left, and vertically from top left to bottom. There are four types of script – 'hiragana' or feminine script, 'katakana' or foreign script, 'romaji' or Japanese in Latin script, and 'kanji' which is symbolic script which can be read in two ways: Chinese or Japanese. In addition, an attempt has been made to adopt terms from the European world of thought. For example, there was no word in Japanese for philosophy; it was referred to as the Japanese spirit (*yamato damashi* or the Japanese soul), skillfulness (methods, *jutsu*) or ways (attitudes of mind, *do*), but no thought structure of an abstract nature, *per se*, has been registered.[5] 'The pure original Japanese has never been able to serve as a medium for expressing philosophical concepts.'[6]

Similarly, Western legal or medical concepts, which stood in stark contrast to earlier Chinese jurisprudence and medicine, had to be introduced into the Japanese world. Terms were adopted straight from the German, so that neurosis (in German: 'neurose'), for example, is now *noiroze* in Japanese and hysteria ('Hysterie') is 'hisuteri'. The third wave was a whole range of modern inventions for which no correlate whatsoever existed in Japan. Here, too, terms were translated mechanically and phonetically into Japanese. From English, taxi or *takushi* and car or *kaa*; from German, Gelegenheitsarbeit (temporary work) as *arubaito*; and even a French ideomatic expression for girlfriend (*avec*; literally, 'with', interpreted somewhat strangely as 'being with someone') became the Japanese word *aweku*. Cheese or *cheesu* did not exist in Japan prior to the Second World War and was accepted, phonetically at least, by consumers[7]. It could therefore be said, somewhat heretically, that the modern Japanese language consists only partly of 'real' Japanese, with the predominate part consisting of 'japanned' foreign terms.[8]

This realization may serve to explain why the Japanese have retaliated by redefining their language to act as a clear, distinguishing feature between Japanese and non-Japanese. The cumbersome untranslatability of specific Japanese concepts (*mu* = the non-existent; *amae* = the passive; or the desire to bond with other people = *haragei*, the pre-relational (or trans-relational) creation of compatibility between two discussion partners),[9] and the postulated unlearnability of the Japanese language are the central themes arguing in favour of the uniqueness of the Japanese language. These factors turn the national language into a national bulwark, a weapon or natural resource, with the objective to help in the process of self-referential identification and to boost Japan's competitiveness.[10] If a foreigner speaks a little Japanese, the Japanese praise him like child or a trained dog. If, on the other hand, he speaks Japanese extremely well, they continually criticize him and draw attention to his 'mistakes' or, worse still, they constantly pretend not to understand and speak to him in English since they cannot accept that a foreigner can speak their language. (The Japanese call their language 'the national language', *kokugaku*, rather than identifying it as the same Japanese which is spoken by foreigners, *nihongo*, or the language of the country which foreigners call 'nihon'/ 'nippon', that is Japan.)[11]

In this interpretation, the diversity of script described above reinforces group identity, since this diversity involves an enormous task in interpretation terms and is dependent not on meaning, like Chinese, but rather on the context of use. Thus, Japanese is a contextual language and its function as a 'high context system' is comparable with insider jargon.[12]

The visual aids provided by the script characters, by symbols and context are required to differentiate these meanings. For example, the word 'driver' ['doraiba'] can mean either a screwdriver, a golf club or a motorist; boring (as in dull), bowling and boring (as in drilling) are all called 'boringu' in Japanese; food and a hood are both translated as 'fudo'; a 'ron' is a loan or a lawn; 'barubu' can mean a light bulb or a valve, and so on. The list is endless but the problematic nature of this polylexy and homonymy soon becomes apparent. T. Suzuki conducted experiments in which groups of ten Japanese had to read and interpret short, complex texts. Inevitably this produced 10 different versions.[13] From this, one can conclude that uncertainty is an inherent feature of the Japanese language, which can only be overcome by interpretation and a mutual understanding of context (word context but also, in its widest sense, the situation in which it is used). But also in a broader picture, the Japanese language remains incomprehensible and vague even to the Japanese. R. Mouer and Y. Sugimoto conducted a study of the comprehensibility of Japanese sayings and idioms ('kotozawa'), in which 850 students took part, and they reached the conclusion that usage, understanding and interpretation could hardly be described as homogeneous.[14] I. v. Neustupny also supports the hypothesis that the Japanese language is an extremely vague language, using the word 'vague' to indicate great complexity, combined with intrinsic indeterminability and a wealth of nuances.[15]

The Ambiguity of Meaning

Therefore the ambiguity of Japanese is in no way attributable to incompetent translators but is rather an inherent and intentional feature of the language.[16] 'The features of this language are not logical clarity, organic structure or solid certainty but effortless, limitless wavering, a talent rich in nuances and overt uncertainty.'[17] We quote here some examples of this linguistic ambivalence: Nakamura speaks of the 'non-logical character of the Japanese' using, in a grammatical context, the lack of distinction between substantive and adjective, and the indeclinability of the substantive as examples. In connection with linguistic structure, Schinzinger refers to the argument of indifference, as opposed to logical exactness and a predilection for ambiguity, irrationality and intuition, combined with a dislike for symmetry and formal logic.[18] The Japanese language fails to express precisely and exactly the individual conditions which relate to states of being. No distinction is made between the singular and plural of nouns and articles, and genders do not exist. The assumption is that this information will become apparent to the communicant from the unspoken context.[19] It is only with considerable difficulty that one can indirectly construe relative pronouns, which therefore promotes a lack of clarity. It is very difficult to express relationships of action–reaction or of cause and effect; the relationship between the pairs is, in itself, more important than the direction. Extraordinary significance is attached to honorary or hierarchic forms of address, particularly when addressing someone face to face (the well-known suffixes -*san* and -*sama* are used in a personal context).[20] It is extremely difficult to select the correct one which is not simply a question of social status. Doi perceived that, in addition to other features, the use of correct suffixes can pacify those of a higher status and create harmony. They are also often used simply to enhance the grace and beauty of the language used. The speaker is considered vulgar and common if he fails to use honorary forms of address.[21]

In the same way, the desire for aesthetic language is expressed by the existence of a *delicate distinction in nuance, both in emotional and sensual terms.* Definitions and characterizations are condensed into words with an overabundance of connotations, multiple overtones and ambiguities, which presupposes general familiarity with the basic richness of words chosen. This is why reference is sometimes made to a (language) culture of silence, since much is considered self-evident and to discuss it would be foolish.[22]

Blurring of the Subject

In common Japanese speech, the subject of a sentence is often omitted and an intuitive comprehension of what is being described is necessary, based on a familiarity with the scenario (cognizance of the people, references to narratives, fables, stories and the general situation) created prior to the discussion by means of the social and psychological links between the communicants, in order to comprehend the meaning of the sentence.

Personal pronouns are disproportionately more difficult in Japanese than in other languages, and choosing the correct one in a given situation is a constantly recurring problem. Special pronouns depending on rank (superior, inferior, equal), degree of acquaintance (family, friend, colleague, stranger) and sex are opportune.[23] When the Japanese converse among themselves, it fundamentally makes no difference who is speaking; what's more important is to promote a harmonious atmosphere in interpersonal relationships. Thus, the notorious word '*hai*' simply implies 'yes, I am answering you' and not, as is cursorily assumed in the West, 'yes, that's right'. The reply relates not so much to the facts under discussion but has a positive effect on the interrogator. In general, the use of rituals and special terminology in conversation is dependent more on hierarchical considerations and perceptions than on logical associations. Japanese focus to a much greater extent on a world of social relationships than on a world of impersonal, logical facts.

Therefore, the linguistic ego of a Japanese is not a monolith but is always identified in relation to one's fellow beings. From a Western perspective, this constitutes the development of a weak ego.[24] The first person is basically defined only in the context of interpersonal correlations,[25] which is why specific words are used to express familial relationships: *nesan* is the older sister, *ototo* the younger brother, *imoto* the younger sister, *nisan* the older brother, and so on. According to the Japanese way of thinking, the question 'Who am I?' is only conceivable if formulated as: 'What relationship does my opposite number have to me?'[26] Equally, a title or a function is used whenever possible (e.g. *sensei*, a teacher or father) rather than *anata* (you). For example, a man will refer to himself as uncle (*ojisan*) *vis-à-vis* a neighbour's child; but *vis-à-vis* his students at school he would be *sensei*; *boku* would be the correct first person to use when addressing colleagues;

watakushi in the case of the principal; or *washi vis-à-vis* his own reproachful father. Each of these different ways of expressing the first person[27] is based on a deluge of connotations, so that in using a particular expression the speaker demonstrates a specific attitude in terms of personality.[28] Initially, the *fragile, fluid ego* is temporarily stabilized by this *relative self-definition* towards one's opposite number and the situation. Specifically, indifference surrounds impersonal relationships, which makes it difficult for the Japanese to deliver objective statements. The main purpose of the Japanese language is mutual comprehension or communication of inner aspects.[29]

The Japanese language avoids *objective representations* and the narrator is the constant reference point of the narration. Thus knowledge is always subjective and, even if theoretically each subject reaches the same conclusion, it remains subjective rather than objective as far as the Japanese understanding of linguistics is concerned. 'The way of thinking used to acquire knowledge, is not by objective methodology but through human relationships.'[30] Intuitive perception, human context and utilitarianism are the guiding principles applicable here.[31] Universal statements are extremely difficult to formulate in Japanese and the assumption of a common background renders them too obvious and crude, and therefore inappropriate and uncultivated. The method adopted is to reel off individual features. Actual circumstances and dissimilarities with the familiar are the main features. Realia are, in a broader context, far more important in the Japanese language than concepts and theories. Nakamura calls this specific thinking, which is the opposite of conceptual Western thinking.[32]

Pragmatism in Communicating

Isolated functional elements, if perceived as practical, are used and, if necessary, pragmatically adapted and transformed. Examples of this fundamental pragmatism are also to be found in the etymology of everyday terms. The Japanese word for cat, *nekko*, is supposedly derived from the phrase 'nezumi no koo matsu' (waiting for baby mice).

Nature and the human disposition are accepted *per se*, without question, thereby ensuring the worldliness of Japanese thinking. Thus Japanese mythology never comments on future worlds, distant skies or even on life after death. The absence in Japanese grammar of a future tense linguistically reflects this, with the result that it is extremely difficult to express the future in anything but indirect terms.[33] Contrary to the Indians, who perceive death as the main concept from which their thinking evolves, the Japanese see life as both the beginning and end of their thinking. Birth and death are not the cardinal factors governing human existence but are, in fact, rather irrelevant. It is more important to live life in the intervening period, that is during one's actual existence, without concern for anything else. Life-orientation, rather than life itself which as a value *per se* is held in low esteem, is one of the main themes running through Japanese fables (and TV soap operas).[34] Thus, both worldliness and pragmatism constitute an important part of the Japanese language.

This cursory look at the Japanese language serves to demonstrate that such a fundamental and ancient cultural form of expression contains some major basic characteristics which could serve to indicate that postmodern thinking might well prosper and bear fruit if planted on such fertile ground. Conversely, some skills that are essential in a new world are natural to the Japanese, which stresses the distinct advantages the Japanese possess in only having to adapt and move on compared to the Westerner who needs to fully reorientate and completely regroup his bearings.

Nevertheless, despite the fact that the Japanese language is, for the most part, based on foreign elements, it is perceived and defended as a major con-tributor to self-definition, a definition which becomes *ambiguous* and *context-dependent* as a result of the many different ways in which Japanese sentences are read, heard and interpreted. This ambiguity and context-dependency is perpetuated in the loosely defined and strongly relational structure of the language, as well as in its abundant nuances and elaborate *symbolism*. The general absence of fixed points or anchors in terms of subject and object, leads to *multiple objectivity* (reality, surface, worlds) as a result of the seemingly boundless flexibility in defining the self, the ego, the narrator. However, the welcome afforded to ambiguity does not founder in feeble, static aesthetics but is based rather on a powerful *pragmatism* of this world.

III ZEN PRINCIPLES

Japan – a Multireligious Nation

It is not our intention to explore here the finer details of Zen principles or to expound the theory of Zen's postmodernity.[35] Instead, we will attempt to elucidate briefly a few of the points which form the basis of this system and which still play a major role in Japanese society, whilst also suggesting how traditional Zen thinking can make a coherent contribution to a postmodern image or postmodern reading of Japan.[36]

According to Doi, no system of coordinates whatever exists which would compulsorily and unicausally integrate Japanese thinking into everyday life. Never-theless Zen thinking, particularly when combined with the Japanese language, gives rise to themes which flow right through the dense rootball which is the Japanese vision of the world.[37] However, contrary to the language, Zen does not appear to suffer from any ethnocentric handicap, for although it has a powerful effect on Japanese life, Japanese influences have not affected Zen doctrine to any great extent, which has retained its self-sufficient autonomy.[38]

All religious practices in Japan have polydirectional features. Religious illumination is achieved without centre, focus or rigid organization; individuals reach enlightenment via their own set of familiar religious practices and preoccupations.[39] The simultaneous presence of several juxtaposed religious convictions is considered acceptable.[40]

Zen and Rationality

However, the *focus* of all religious movements is primarily on the *transrational*, the *intuitive*, the *emotional* and the *aesthetic*. Particularly in Zen, this focus is strongly and clearly pronounced. Japanese Zen propagates the theory that things are of greater significance in themselves and have more dimensions of significance than reason alone is capable of recognizing. Intellectual thought is transcended and an alogical, irrational vision of the world promoted. 'True' vision can only be achieved when instinctive and intuitive cognitive forces come into their own as well, rather than being subordinated to intellectual control which leaves them stranded in a cul-de-sac.[41]

This does not mean that critical, rational thought does not exist in Japan. Paul attacks this mystifying view of Japan and China as an irrational tradition of thinking. 'One of the most stubborn and also most absurd prejudices which exists in relation to "Japanese" or even "Eastern" thinking, is that a specific Japanese or Eastern logic exists.'[42] The point of departure for Paul is the universal principles of human logic, which have become pronounced in a variety of different forms. In early Japan, logic (combined with rhetoric) was a lowly-regarded, sub-discipline of Buddhism. Japanese logicians were more interested in human interaction and the psychology of logical debate than in abstract, logical, content. Logic, in common with sword-forging and (at its onset) Zen, was a secret study which both impeded its proliferation and damaged its reputation.[43] Today it is an alternative method of thought, 'existing in tandem with conventional thought'.[44] The principle Zen practice, apart from *zazen* (meditation in a sitting position) and *mondo* (the lesson), is *koan* (meditating a paradox). *Koan* involves the formulation of questions which cannot be solved using intellectual powers alone but which must be confronted spontaneously without guided thoughts. In the West, probably the most famous *koan* concerns the sound produced by single-handed clapping. Each *koan* is consciously conceived in such a way as to ensure that all possible rational methods of problem-solving are misleading.[45]

Trying to understand Zen by intellectual means alone leads into blind alleys. *Koan* aims to correct this mistake and the purpose of its paradoxes is to demonstrate the breakdown of intellect, thus helping to promote enlightenment. Answers are not fully definable; too many possible meanings lie hidden in this short paradox which, by definition, rules out a solution. In the course of discussions with the student, the teacher establishes that the problem has been understood and resolved, which implies that the student has now broken the bonds of primacy of reason.[46] In principle, this method of 'learning what is not rational' is employed in many other Japanese art forms. Stone gardens, like the famous Rioanji in Kyoto, can be interpreted as visual *koans*, and short poems (*haiku*) can be seen as aesthetic *koans*.[47]

The Pragmatism of Zen

The aim of these exercises is not other-worldly meditation, but rather the enhancement of existence within the real environment of everyday life:[48] 'Human nature is transcended not in the sense of a hereafter but in its innermost here and now.'[49] If considered from this viewpoint, Zen teaching is less of a doctrine, a solution-providing religion or theory and more of a concrete understanding of reality and permanent ongoing practice.[50]

Dogma-free concrete experience, rather than pre-prepared rational concepts of the world, helps human beings confront pragmatic challenges.[51] '[T]he epistemology of Zen is, therefore, not to resort to the mediumship of concepts.'[52] If perceived as *homo faber*, man is no longer the master of his (worldly, technical) objects. According to Zen teachings, he reacts in the same way also towards philosophical concepts, and needs to relativize these concepts and accept alternative, irrational concepts.[53] Parallels between Zen and the basic positions of postmodern thought can be drawn: (a) the multiple realities perceived by different observers of a single situation or, in the case of a single observer, a hopping backwards and forwards, in situative terms, between realities; (b) indifferent, detached but alert attentiveness; (c) fluid integrative comprehension; and (d) the continual, impermanent interchange of elements.[54] This ambiguity in an interpretation of the world and its changeability is specifically intended.[55] Dogen, a Zen master, described this objective as: 'the fluid aspect of impermanence is in itself the absolute state'.[56]

Frequently, Zen writings refer to existence as continual change, lauding the intermediate states, the tentative existence in the here and now.[57] The spirit is perceived as nomadic and fluid and not to be overshadowed by the one perspective of rational intellect. Active repositioning is encouraged to promote all-embracing global awareness. Subject and object are irrelevant words, submerged in a dynamic relational interpretation in which differences are clearly evident but nonetheless permeate reciprocally.[58] In this context, one could perceive enlightenment as acceptance (and mastery) of a plethora of standpoints.[59] Students of the doctrine are left even more uncertain of their own identity and position as a result of extreme pragmatism combined with almost arbitrary, context-dependency. But then this is the aim of Zen practices.

Permanent practice and dogma-free action are also pillars of the arguments favouring a strong business ethic based on Confucian and Zen principles. As it was more a moral argumentation before the advent of the New Economy, now exactly the character traits that are necessary to master the demands of the upcoming business and economic models (e.g. fluidity, standpointlessness) are the ones that are stressed by Japanese religious practices.[60]

The Dissolution of Self

A constant topic in Zen's catalogue of objectives is the dissolution of self. The ego is perceived as the product of fleeting images or objects, a product which has lost its gravitational attraction. One can overcome the 'artificial' divide between subject and object, reality and unreality by relinquishing this frail self.[61] Parallels to observations of a dissolved self in contemporary Western literature are near at hand, albeit that this state is usually bemoaned in Western culture as the death of the individual, whereas it is seen in the East as a prerequisite of a liberation of the person enabling the evolution of one's self towards a more 'performing' state of mind.[62]

This is also the fundamental concept behind an *empty spirit*, which films a mirror image of the environment *mutatis mutandis* and in consequence reacts better, that is more correctly, rapidly and effectively.[63] Thus the theory of the 'no-track-mind' (thoughtless or *mu nen*) applies here. This is a spiritual state (mental structure) in which one is free to take action without pausing for reflection, whilst deliberately and intentionally perceiving all of one's own environment and activities.[64] In this context, 'action' is not used in a purely active sense but rather to signify (passive or active) acceptance of 'things happening'.[65]

Digression: the *No*-Theatre

A brief digression into the classical *No* (or *Noh*) dramatic genre may serve to clarify this type of action. *No* is considered to be the institutionalized form of pure Zen. 'The study of the "No" play is really the study of Japanese culture generally.'[66,67]

Coarse in nature, this dramatic form can convey the most subtle of mood nuances. Its stylized symbolism is able to elucidate complex Zen concepts through a kind of ring-fencing with assortments of hints. It explores the sensation of time and space like the Greek drama, but in a manner completely unfamiliar to Western audiences.[68] Plots of strange complex plainness, moods and images, the dramaturgical use of silent actions or inaction, empty rooms and unnatural breathless falsetto voices produce an atmosphere of unreality. Total alienation (similar to, but much more extreme than Brecht's *Verfremdungseffekt*) is the dominant impression generated by those artistic devices. '[T]he No space is obviously a poetic space not at all coextensive with any physical dimensions.'[69]

It produces a virtual space in which everything is highly concentrated: surroundings, action, symbolism, all attempting to express meaning in a condensed form without drawing attention to the individual, his character or personality. Here, one can muse about the conspicuous similarities to the interactors on the Internet. *No* portrays sensory communications in the most effective way, using pure symbolism without having to resort to the niveau of language, personality or action.[70]

The Zen Value System

A list of adjectives including 'selflessness', 'wordlessness', 'spontaneity of is-ness', 'nowness', 'oneness', 'goallessness', 'boundlessness' are often used in connection with the general spiritual state expected. The extent to which these short descriptions apply is open to question.[71] Nevertheless, in the course of this characterization of a general state of mind we can identify three trajectories which form the main framework Zen practice strives to achieve: *alertness*, a *deliberate lack of fixed positions* amidst all the possibilities and *solidarity*.

The first term, alertness, signifies an integral and integrated perception of the world in which 'transcendental aloofness amidst of multiplicities' dominates.[72] The term for this is *wabi*, a rough translation of which is humble, non-acquisitive, not dependent on fashion or trends. It denotes an unencumbered positive view which is able to spontaneously understand the nature of things without prejudice or hindrance. Suzuki described this attitude of mind as *dynamic intuition*.[73]

The 'deliberate lack of fixed positions' intends to convey a certain disinterest in and dissociation with concepts, perceptions and advance information, favouring observation from afar, identifying and promoting details and differences.[74] Aesthetically, this attitude is characterized by a preference for asymmetry, incompleteness, improvization and imbalance.[75] Emptiness is no longer negative but incorporated as the sum total of all the different options available. According to Suzuki, this understanding of difference, inconsistency and irrationality is Zen's greatest strength.[76] The postmodern concept of multiple, conflicting standpoints can thus be perceived as a preliminary step towards the acceptance of the paradox of equality and difference.[77]

The third strand, solidarity, concerns a specific, positive basic attitude to all things. This includes loyalty, forbearance, virtue and disinterest and is based on sincerity (*makoto*). In the Kamakura period, at the time when Zen was brought over from China and chivalry was flourishing, self-sacrifice was day-to day business, and loyalty equated to royalism. Together they acted as the link between Zen and the Samurai, from which both profited significantly. Zen was a perfect complement to the military, Spartan, cultivated lifestyle of the warrior class.[78]

One can establish an affinity with postmodern positions even from this short summary of Zen. The promotion of irrational discourse, contradictions and paradoxes; the recognition of multiple realities and situative, momentary definitions; the acceptance of inherent dynamics; the attempt to reject limitations set by the false necessity to be an individual, an ego, and the unwillingness to categorize fixed points, relating to subject, object, time and space, together with unprejudiced acceptance of diversity in order to reach an 'amicable arrangement', are all traits evident both in Zen and the postmodern.

IV SOCIAL MODELS AND THE SOCIAL MECHANISM OF JAPAN

The Web of Individual Relationships

Sketches from everyday life

One can identify a surfeit of postmodernism in Japanese everyday life, from the postmodern world of media and advertising to the seamless mingling of Western and Japanese patterns of behaviour and thought and the unconscious dissolution of the individual into the amorphous stream of society.[79]

At first sight, the basic pattern which runs right through everyday Japanese life is an attitude of mind which can be called the 'Disneyland-approach to the contemporary world'. Take marriage for example: brides are 'married' on three different levels – firstly, in a Japanese environment at a Shinto ceremony dressed in a traditional kimono; immediately thereafter in a social setting, dressed in an American wedding gown; and in the evening in a social sphere, among friends, dressed in a French evening dress. All these events are equally important and constitute an essential part of the 'social spectacle of marriage', although the first setting might be called 'deeply ritualistic', the second 'formal but superficial' and the third 'status-ridden but informal'. Three irreconcilable levels which are nevertheless an inseparable part of Japanese marriage. Clothing, in general, is also an interesting aspect of postmodern Japan. Depending on which type of clothing is appropriate for the occasion, kimonos are seamlessly exchanged for conventional Western dress or 'ultramodern in-wear', accompanied by the image with which they are associated. Thus in any given location, for example a posh hotel lobby, a group of traditionally dressed party-goers celebrate side by side with businessmen in pinstripe suits and a group of rich children dressed in Hip-Hop 'uniforms', without these worlds conflicting with one another. They do, however, assert themselves co-extensively and are created entirely naturally and consciously, lived and then set aside, as appropriate.

This would lend credence to stories claiming that, in Japan, cosmetic surgeons earn astronomical sums due to the surprisingly high percentage of women who make use of their services not once but several times. Prior to marriage, the European look (nose, eyes, cheeks) is favoured but, afterwards, they revert to classical Japanese features.

It is evident in many things that continuity of the individual or values takes a back seat. Momentary performance is all important. Anything *kawaii* (cute), *omoshiroii* (charming) or interesting is a desirable goal. So society and the rest of the world represent a unique way of playing this game, the best example of which is the Japanese approach to travel. In travel agencies all over Tokyo can be found offers like: 'seven countries in five days' (London–Amsterdam–Brussels–Luxembourg – a boat trip down the Rhine–Neuschwanstein and Mozart's Salzburg, with the Lake of Zurich as an add-on)), 'ride the highways of Germany' (five days racing around German motorways in a BMW, preceded by a 'course in speed driving' in Japan).[80] Everything is surface, placatingly 'attractive'; but the underlying sensation of being a stranger in a foreign land as well as within one's own society and the world in general cannot be disguised. Insecurity in an unfamiliar country, insecurity within Japan's complex social network; personal insecurity; racial and national insecurity – all compel the Japanese to search for coziness close to their fellow humans. The group is the place where it all makes sense, the place where the Japanese persona is formed. Although this 'social and mental space, ruled by an unaccustomed geometry' institutionalizes intangible, fluid contradictions,[81] which an unrefined Western viewpoint dismisses as 'a herd-like existence',[82] it does demonstrate, in a pure form, the major traits of the Japanese persona – that is, the *primacy of the relational*, of the '*human nexus*'.[83]

The function of the social nexus as a central theme

Living in contradictions is not that complicated when being constantly reminded that Japanese society and its thinking is intuitively and emotionally based on the principle of overall understanding of the group, the family, the clan and the nation.[84]

This understanding is called *ningen kankei* (a narrow and cooperative collaboration between human beings in a mutually enhancing relationship[85]). Behind this lies fundamental functionality, which at its core is targeted entirely unemotionally at efficacy and performance rather than naïve, romanticized spiritual unity. However, this is not measured on an individual level, but on a group level. Success is always group success, and scant attention is paid to individual success.[86] Thus, Mouer speaks of the 'dry relationships' which make up Japan's social network.[87] This author goes even further: 'Japanese do not spontaneously form groups or associations. Indeed, one might say that the flag, the symbol of the Japanese travel group, and the leader are there precisely because there is no real group.'[88] Thus, this close group formation is based on a pragmatic *do ut des* (give that you shall receive),[89] through which the individual achieves total security via his horizontal links with others and vertical links with 'higher situated leadership units' (it will become clear later in the book why it would be inaccurate to talk about leaders, bosses or chiefs in this context). In return, the individual is completely loyal and self-sacrificing.[90] In this way the group or community creates its own existence and world.[91]

This creates a postmodern concept of reality in which relative group behaviour is more important than anything else, protecting the position of the Japanese both emotionally and materially within the group and shielding them from epistemological, existential, religious and political issues.[92]

The role of the primary group as the smallest social unit

The smallest social unit is not an individual but the family, in which the individual is an indistinguishable part. The basic constellation in Japanese comprehension is that of the large family ('*ie*'). The primary source of group identification is the *ie* spirit.[93] But this large family, this domestic commune, is not simply an extended family but rather a 'managing body', a social structure similar in nature, for example, to the big farmhouses of former times, with all their farm workers and tenant farms, which today could equally be labelled a 'company family'.[94] In this respect, the Japanese *ie* is on a par with the individual in the West.[95] This household structure should be perceived as an existential unit. The individual is completely absorbed within the internal structure (*marugake* or enclosed, wrapped up) whose existence is defined by the relevant circumstances.[96,97] This is why the class concept did not prevail in Japan; officially it was rendered obsolete by the Meiji restoration. In any event, Japan fundamentally never developed a class system; two worlds existed, one for the rulers and one for the simple man, although both these worlds were subdivided into further spheres. Both have always been kept strictly apart in terms of language, clothing, behaviour, contact and traditions, in short, all forms of interpersonal communications.[98]

The best way of tracing the course of this extensive *stratification* of Japanese society is, once again, to look at the development of the language. This social stratification produced total bilingualism (the Japanese of the elite vs the Japanese of the simple man). Although this peculiarity was for its most part overcome after the Second World War, the segmentation of contemporary society has yet again created *separate networks*, with their own behavioural and linguistic rules.[99] However, in sociological terms these represent clans, cliques, 'clusters', communities, tribes, or simply consumer groups rather than classes.[100]

The basic social concept

In the absence of an Orwellian totalitarian central authority, Japanese society strives to be *diversified yet homogeneous, capable of multiple permeability, accepting contradictory values* and allowing, to a certain extent, infinite 'discussion'. Just as in 'normal' ethics education, methods or generally acknowledged social concepts is the equipment. Whilst we are not able to explore each of the countless relevant Japanese social concepts in detail, the pages which follow contain a short summary of some of the most relevant concepts, together with an outline of their role in a postmodern society. In a Japanese context, they will be used ubiquitously to explain and 'analyse' situations and make a substantial contribution to the determination of possible courses of action. They are considered 'typically' Japanese, particularly by the Japanese themselves, and bear the halo of untranslatability and incommunicability, which, in turn, supports the Japanese claim to uniqueness.[101]

Haragei,[102] commonly described as 'using non-verbal, subtle and indirect communication[103] for the purpose of mutual influence, a visceral rapport; using experience to exert influence and formalia, rituals and accumulated mutual experience to provide courage of action'[104] or, more colloquially, 'subtly presenting the other guy the options', is one of the most important concepts involved in the transmission of value, in the context of communication within and between the groups in general. The word is derived from *hara*, the Japanese world for abdomen or belly as the centre of the human being, and literally means the art of feeling, analysing and acting on gut feeling.

Perceived in this way, *haragei* is the strategy to use, in correct proportions: (1) Machiavellian thinking, (2) *hara* (thinking from the abdomen) and (3) *amae* (a desire for solidarity).[105] This produces the right blend of competition and cooperation, which is effective initially (in the short term), subsequently creating *wa* (harmony) to ensure long-term performance.

The commonly used term *wa* is usually translated as harmony, balance or wavering. An amicable, intimate alliance between entities (persons, groups, institutions) which acknowledges individual peculiarities but has integration as its aim, is one element of this objective.[106] Deeply rooted in the psychologically profound dispositions known as *amae* is the struggle to attain *wa*, not just relative integration (intentional and maybe just situational subordination), but also (moderate) acceptance of contradictions. '[*Amae* is] the true essence of the Japanese psychology' which universally permeates Japanese society.[107] It is derived from the word *amaeru* (a desire for support and affection), and describes the positive sensation of mutual dependency which makes it an extremely complex sensory relationship rooted in the physical and emotional bond between mother and baby. Doi explains it as the desire to be loved passively, not yet fully recognizing subjects and objects or 'external' reality of any kind.[108] This fundamental relationship is subsequently transferred to the child's teacher and ultimately to its superiors. In a business environment, this represents more of a mentor–protégé relationship (an *oyabun-kobun* relationship, cf. Chapter 4, section III) but without the (negative) Western cannotations, for it implies reciprocity rather than unilateral dependency.[109]

This feeling of *amae* is not limited to just one relation but is a simultaneous feeling towards all relationships within the network of group affiliation defining the individual.[110] Nor does this imply nepotism, but rather a cohesive strength and communication-facilitating 'lubricant' in society, a society capable only of perceiving meaning and purpose in terms of the structural association which it still aims to create despite the pitfalls of ambiguities and differences. Thus, Japanese society is also confronted with (modern) alienation.[111] Via his strong sense of identification within the group and his conquest of alienation, the Japanese assumes membership of numerous similar groups, becoming an 'organization man', yearning for solidarity and being defined in terms of clubs, committees, guilds, circles, associations and posts. Self-invention occurs by means of the group: to *exist* means to *belong*.[112] In postmodern terms, this could be translated as *a belief in a web of minor 'narratives'* which form a world, or as the attempt to overcome the absence of universalia by means of loose, localized, frail cooperation and by the creation of common symbol worlds.

This cozy group feeling, the object of which is to protect against disorientation in a hypersaturated world, is operationalized on a tactical level by means of ethical concepts such as *on* and *giri*.[113] Based on the premise of integrative human comprehension, *giri* refers to minor commitments and friendly assistance given or received.[114] In a manner of speaking, this represents the tactical aspect of everyday life. On a strategic level, the more heavyweight notion *on* builds on the long-term and unconditional obligation *vis-à-vis* a person or a group (teachers, 'crisis counsellors', family members and colleagues in higher functions are typical examples of *'on/giri* targets'). Naturally, these commitments are not expressed verbally or even documented in writing. They are credited and debited just like funds in a bank account, with everyone aware of the balance, although the relationship never actually exists 'officially', or let alone in writing.[115]

For someone brought up in the West, the resultant network of individual responsibilities is totally invisible, remote and unfathomable; the Western maxims of *'quid pro quo'* or *'do ut des'* cover barely a small part of this relationship. It is impossible to use rational categories to describe the overall network to which a Japanese person belongs, thrown into its irreducible diversity with partial contradictions, combined with inherent pluralism and the compulsion to perform.

Group relationship structures

The result is an additional, informal 'invisible' group structure which is clearly more complex and frequently the opposite of the relevant *de jure* structure, in tandem with complex 'official', 'surface' relationships.[116] Consequently, the outsider who lacks reference information about the structural relationship, often sees paradoxical and 'illogical' constellations.

A brief résumé of typical group memberships serves to indicate the surface of this complexity. Ironically, a mental calculation of the relevant informal relationships makes it impossible – just due to the sheer variety – to perceive *multiple coding of the Japanese persona* as anything other than a euphemism. Typical affiliations might be: various alumni clubs, groups of contemporaries in companies and institutions; clan relationships, admission year groups in companies and institutions; *gakubatzu* (cliques at school and particularly at university); golf clubs and other sport clubs; parties, political splinter groups; smaller interest groups; family groups and the myriad of circles, committees or interest groups ('Friends of the home state of Kobe in Tokyo'; the firm's choral association; there is even a yodeling club in Tokyo). Not to forget the vast amount of tradition-based associations (usually around crafts and arts, ranging from sport (e.g. karate), to game (*igo*) and handicraft (woodcarving) The list excludes situation-dependent and short-term groupings which also have a defining effect.[117] Multiplying this by the vast amount of intensive Internet activities, and especially the myriad of Internet communities where the Japanese are usually hyperactive, then a human being cannot be defined other than in network terms.

By their very nature, these group affiliations do not serve purely to satisfy the quest for metaphysical definitions of identity. In a completely integrated society, connections, *kone*, are existential for all professional activities. During his lifetime, the Japanese is obliged to build up a permanent network of special, informal relationships or *jinmyaku*, for these relationships exert a special kind of overriding influence on all commercial and social decision-making.[118] These numerous group relationships make it harder to identify dividing lines, confines and boundaries in a rational context. Groups are mutually pervasive, limitless and diffuse and are best perceived as *diffuse foci* or 'strange attractors' in the cartography of the individual. Even here, the Japanese universe of categories provides pragmatic clues.

For the individual, concentrated groups exist around each of the individual group standpoints, with *miuchi* or the inner circle (not the ego) at their centre. This inner circle is the group of people with which strong *amae* relations are maintained. This is where the *uchi* or 'us' feeling is created. The rest of society, known as *soto*, *enryo* or *tanin* (the others), with whom (for the moment) no *amae* relationship exists, is the 'rest'. On top of this, a two-tier system is attributed to this network: on the one hand the private persona (*honne*), and on the other the public persona (*tatemae*, or, expressed rather negatively, *kao* (mask or face) if things are all too blatantly presented).[119] The terms *ura* (background) and *omote* (foreground) or, in an ethical context, *tatemae* (official opinion) and *hone* (personal opinion) are used analogously. The simplicity of the individual concepts is deceiving: '... the Japanese endeavored to infuse unlimited complexity into this simplicity'.[120]

These concepts demonstrate a highly-developed sensitivity to discrepancies and differences which adds a further dimension to group activities. In this connection, even the most minor of conflicts takes on strategic dimensions. For example, if in this context a conflict within a group is superficially (*uchi-omote*) perceived as non-existent, the aim is nonetheless to resolve it silently in the background (*uchi-ura*) or arrive at a workable consensus in respect of the dissent. However, these differing forms of action occur not only within groups. There is also a specific, equally complicated set of working parameters governing the horizontal links with other groups. Nakane makes a clear distinction between these horizontal relationships and the vertical links within the group. In the modern environment the simultaneity of group relationships becomes part of the level of complexity within a group, and of that between the groups in which the individual is inextricably involved. In early times he belonged to a single group (e.g. his clan), which provided him with security of values and actions. Today he is caught up in a maze of group allegiances which presents him not only with difficulties in terms of 'group management' (i.e. how he should play his part in the group), but also in terms of self-definition (how he should conceive or construct himself).[121]

The individual and the group

Just this short explanation serves to demonstrate how sensitively, contingently and provisionally an individual player must act in this society in order to be able to fulfil the general objectives expected of him. Any individualistic self-definition, any ego, can only be seen as a luxury, an impediment one cannot afford. 'Lack of individualism is common in feudal societies of all countries, but nowhere, it seems, is the sense of social affinity as predominant as in Japan.'[122] The group is perceived as self-magnification and also as the only self which exists. '[T]he Japanese choose to belong to the group even at the cost of temporary loss of the self.'[123] Individual autonomy is minimized, obliterating the dividing lines between private and public life, between 'I' and 'we'.[124] This does not, however, occur oppressively, against the will of the individual. '[T]he Japanese prefer to remain passive participants who are carried along in a comfortable emotional environment without having to do or decide anything by themselves.'[125]

Role definitions are largely dependent on actual context and given parameters. The ideal roles resemble cartoon characters, if one considers the ideal male roles (the honourable Samurai, the international businessman, the loyal subject, the for-bearing master of the house) and the ideal female roles (the tender Geisha, the devoted housewife and the caring mother). These symbols, which are entirely devoid of human substance, call to mind Barthes' 'kingdom of signs'.[126] Entirely different behavioural patterns are required depending on the group affiliation involved. However, personal integrity is not the overall objective but rather an ability to successfully play the roles demanded of one.[127]

These omnipresent, diverse role expectations and relationships open up, as it were, a postmodern topology in which references to reality (*qua* role expectations and values) are merged and altered to suit reality, resulting in an ambiguous decentralized area in which only the group reference creates security in terms of reality, thus allowing 'indifference towards concepts of reality' to prevail.[128] Japan is therefore a world without subject or objectivity. Individuals are *a priori* indif-ferent to every possible value and discourse. Only the flow within the community and group signs and symbols provide any bearing. 'And finally, so desubjec-tified and decentralized, citizens simply live – produce and consume, buy and sell – in the late stage capitalism, and [any fixed system] ... has been practically abolished.'[129]

The Special Features of Japanese Society

The pragmatic value system

Nonetheless, common basic values are too powerful to allow us to speak of a splintered society, despite the symptoms of dissolution described above. Nakamura describes the generally binding catalogue of fundamental values as a love of nature, honour, conformity, tolerance, prestige and loyalty.[130] But these are merely con-stants in the Japanese world of values. In the absence of a more radical and critical spirit of confrontation, due to the essential rule of tolerance applied to achieve 'harmony', the permanent rejection of an opinion would be impossible, unwise and simply hostile. The character of Japan, which is fundamentally pragmatic, prohibits a rigid scales of values:[131]

> Because of its eclectic tendencies and because of its non- or anti-intellectualistic attitude, Japanese thought and cultural values – the Japanese people and Japan, that is, the Japanese mind – have been variously described by authorities as 'enigmatic', 'paradoxical', 'ambiguous', 'flexible', etc. ...[132]

But this simplified view misjudges the Japanese axiomatic acceptance of life 'with all its confusions, incompatibilities and contradictions ... paradoxa, contradictions, and absurdities'.[133]

The *opportunistic pragmatism* and *worldliness* of the Japanese produces a relative morality which allows decisions to be reached from moment to moment, case by case.[134] But this should not be seen as an anomy. Concrete rules do exist, some unconscious, others unspoken; but for the Japanese it would be unthinkable to neglect the primacy of the 'human nexus'.[135] *One can assess morally correct behaviour only within its context.* Assessments cannot be made by individuals. Ethical standards are provisionally laid down in consultation with the surrounding group,[136] producing an acceptable truth to match the situation: '*uso mo hoben*'. However, this value-determination process within a group does not occur in a discursively rational way, but as a result of an intuitive understanding of values; a communication without direct signs (*ishin denshin*). Consequently, meaning is undefined and weak, conforming to the 'law of harmonious flow',[137] although understood not to be legal nor scientific, corresponding rather to the metaphysical concept of transitoriness (*mujokan*), and pragmatically perceived 'survival'.

Thus the dividing lines between law, customs, rules and convention, between 'order of nature and order of reason, natural inclination and social duty' are fluid and circumstance-dependent, and can be changed at any time and without notice.[138] It is almost impossible to translate these value principles into Western concepts, although the Japanese universe of products is very similar to our own in the West. 'The issue which moves the Japanese is whether something functions. He pays scant regard to concepts of good or evil; true or false.'[139] What is good or bad remains an issue of social consensus based on the relevant facts. Whatever social context demands is done, and to this extent one could even speak of a higher loyalty to values. And so, in this abstract sense, Japanese society is extremely homogeneous in its ethical methodology, even though it is definitely not monolithic, being divided into a sea of groups, subgroups and sub-subgroups.

A society without a reference system

In Japan, fixed systems have always played a subordinate role to symbolism. *Symbols* are all that *prevents Japan, as a structure, from disintegrating*, since they exist in the form of an amalgamous, coreless, centreless mass. 'Strip Japanese society of its rigid codes of individual submission, and there would be little left to hold it together.'[140] This is why Japan has traditionally had a 'legitimacy problem in terms of authority and power', since, apart from the imperial cult, there is no other external faculty (abstract laws, generally-applicable deity, etc.) which legitimizes the system. It is obliged to legitimize itself, self-referentially, by means of symbols.[141]

There is no dimension of 'Japan', as a system, in which it would possess a clearly distinguishable centre; it remains empty at the core.[142] The best example of this existential emptiness is the emperor and his court which symbolize extreme emptiness of core, and, in an immaterial sense, symbolic and unifying power.[143] Tokyo and Japan are grouped around this empty centre.[144] But even Tokyo's urban structure is deconstructive: no addresses, no street names for minor roads. The absence of any classification of Tokyo, in spatial terms, serves to remind us that rationality is just one of many systems.[145] Thus an area is the product of momentary events in which symbols and signs evaporate, 'before any kind of significat has time to "catch" [them]'.[146] When viewed from this perspective, Japan has something in common with the medium of television: primacy of the visual sense and the assortment of several situation-dependent interpretations. Its two-tier, dual-coded texts combining '*kanji* and *kana*' are not simply sensory and verbal notations, but independent communication aids of a visual nature.[147] The same applies to advertising, which is highly fragmented, high-speed and high-tech and, seen from a rational point of view, is a serial mass of independent images, words and pictures directly targeted, without any deviation, at wishes and longings in the context of the symbolic economy.[148]

Depth of meaning is substituted by surface, originals by reproductions, creativity by collages, thus allowing symbolism to act as the leading power.[149] Myths and signs are the language which moulds individuals and groups and actually constitutes their world.[150]

Japanese self-awareness or 'nihonron'

This modelling using myths can also be applied to the most interesting (and controversial) of all Japanese myths: the question of Japan's identity. In Chapter 1 we touched on the external effects of this phenomenon; here we explore the inner dimension, its meaning for the Japanese themselves.[151]

Nihonron (the question of Japan's identity) or *nihonjinron* (the question of Japanese identity) or *kokutai* (the sacred national entity) are themes running right across the disciplines from philosophical epistles and the uniqueness of the Japanese people to political, historic and cultural contributions. These themes proclaim the essential difference in quality, and therefore superiority, of the Japanese people. Even biology has something to say, claiming that the Japanese have a different brain structure; that Japan's snow is unique in the world and that the Japanese have longer intestinal tracts.[152] These claims are not just theoretical motions but are used, in a 'realpolitik' context, to erect non-tariff-compliant trade barriers for argumentation purposes.

All three concepts, usually translated as 'Japanism' in English, are based on the premise that Japanese ideology, culture and the Japanese persona are all unique and represent the highest level of human existence. In common with all concepts of 'a chosen race', this ideology is practically a religion, although *nihonjinron* is not confined to a single method or a canon of topics. It can include anything which serves the objectives of *nihonjinron*. To this extent, Wolferen's opinion seems plausible: 'Japanism is even more effective as a surrogate for religion than communism because it is less examined, more taken for granted and more inescapable.'[153] *Nihonjinron* is a broadly-based 'discussion', rich in tradition, concerning the personal identity and self-esteem of Japan and the Japanese. In this context, the word 'Japanese' is understood as a general classificatory term, not as an individual.[154]

This is where three dimensions merge, *language, culture* and *nation*, although they operate in an undefined meta-space. Here, in an endless circular argument, the case is put forward that Japanese culture is identified by reference to the Japanese language, which is, in turn, identified by means of its national identity. Ultimately the Japanese people are defined via the ensemble of language and culture. The *myth of natural homogeneity* has been reinforced by the *doctrine of national unity*, the family state and the Shinto religion, all of which have flowed and continue to flow into the *nihonjinron* debate and which accompany the Japanese through life, right from childhood.

To this is added a portion of self-exoticism, designed to uphold, *qua* myth, the sense of self-worth.[155] The Japanese have always been well-versed in this, capable of differentiated thought. Moreover, this self-regard as being 'exotic' has been enhanced by the increasing contact with the West.[156] Despite the fact that this self-comprehension was originally derived from metaphysical foundations, since the sixteenth century it has been 'intensively cultivated' to form a subservient mentality,[157] since it serves, in this form, a multitude of vital objectives. This conditioning provides stability in terms of domestic politics, helps to create an *esprit de corps*, and reinforces Japan's position *vis-à-vis* foreign countries.[158] The ruling elite has extended this 'debate' to such an extent that it has become a self-fulfilling prophecy. The image of a unique culture which, due to its biological and 'national' roots, is necessarily the 'top dog',[159] is one of the most important symbolic assets promoted by 'the ruling class'.[160]

So, the Japanese are united under one extremely blurred sign which, despite a hundred-year-old debate, has made no progress in terms of clarity, coherence or focus.[161]

One can determine from all these *nihonjinron* phenomena how a symbol, obscure by reason of its 'emptiness', can guide a country. This country is not dominated by either political principles or economic conditions, both of which are totally subservient to the symbolic vision of 'Japan'. Or, formulated in a different way, the symbol – the virtual – is more authentic than the reality.

Japan as a Social Network

In this context, some ethnologists and journalists describe 'Japan' as a *tense ethnic group*, a *tribal society* sharing with other prehistoric tribes to which this title is usually attributed some common features, insofar as they (a) were all split into small, closed, inhomogeneous groups; (b) had an aversion to outsiders; and (c) possessed mythical powers of integration.[162] However, the feature which distinguishes the 'Japanese tribe' from 'simpler tribes' is not so much the choice of category but the intensity or perfection with which Japan fulfils and utilizes these characteristics.[163] This method has been practiced for centuries and has consequently produced a complex, historical web of methods, strategies and relationships. This is why so many concepts are perceived in general terms and accepted as intrinsic objectives. This explains the conviction that relationships are balanced over the course of time by input and results (as a zero-sum game, a view only possible if society is essentially closed up from external 'players'), which accounts for the special significance placed on the historical dimension or internal 'track record'.[164]

Thus, to the Japanese, society is not a coherent monolith but an integral web of social relationships. This means that social interaction is more than just an economic interaction between rational commercial entities; social interaction is, in the true sense of the word, existence-defining. Whilst it is possible to add up the interaction between *homines economici* in monetary terms, intrinsic values, that is social assets (e.g. the standing of an employee *vis-à-vis* his colleagues), as well as symbolic assets (a diploma from Tokyo university; marriage to the daughter of an influential politician, and so forth), usually play a far more important role than extrinsic usefulness, although this is not ignored.[165] When expanding the analytical parameters, many 'typically Japanese' phenomena become explicable to the Western observer. For example, the lack of professional mobility and the rejection of financially more attractive positions in favour of the social capital accumulated in the present post, which would be wiped out (or even go into deficit) on changing firms (i.e. the social environment).[166]

When perceiving in the way in which a Japanese lives his life caught up in a thicket of groups and diverging roles and numerous stratified levels of action and assessment, one is immediately struck by that quality, the raw material which leads to success or failure – *information* (as a dynamic concept) or *knowledge* (as a static model).[167] The Japanese keep themselves *à jour* by means of an intensive flow of information and, in this respect, they are equally stern in their expectations of others (the proverbial 'telephonitis' of the Japanese and the current explosion in Internet use are a much discussed example of this). For this reason, Japan is on the list of 'high-context' countries, and therefore, in Japan, the consensus system rules. Nakane calls it a 'maximum consultation system', in which an information-based organization system, combined with highly-informed individuals, is capable of demonstrating, when necessary, an astonishing flexibility and efficacy not confined merely to speed.[168] The main characteristics of this information society are: widerspread and wider-ranging communicative interactions; the fast, free (within its own network), multichannel transmission of information; together with the most complex layers of activities, assessments and utilizations, the efficacy of which can be charted with the precise yardstick of economic success.[169] In consequence, this 'high-level, information society' bears the clear hallmarks of a postmodern society, if other indicators such as high consumption saturation, the over-availability of knowledge, the general overproduction of material goods and 'the corrosive solvent of multinational capitalism' are taken into account.[170]

Considering the immaterialism of the major building blocks, it is not surprising that instead of an 'architectural' perspective of Japanese, complete with foundations and pillars etc., a more abstract, undefined and non-systematic view should be adopted. Thus, the idea of a *sovereign state body* is pure fiction. Instead, it becomes clear how a *fragmented system of groups and subgroups* construct a polymorphous, fluid but nonetheless stable organism, to which traditional Western classifications such as the state, the economy and the individual cannot be validly applied.[171]

In this context, an organization is nothing more than a bundle of relationship links between 'enclaves of entities', in which groups and splinter groups create *local worlds* and communicate with other interfaces in order to create something resembling an outer skin, an 'official opinion' or voice.[172] In this connection, Wolferen differentiates between three levels of worlds of political contexts: 'beneath the outer political forms, there exists a semi-official reality of expected ritual behavior. Beneath this again, there is the true reality of power relations.' Reality and truth is formed and managed on these three levels.[173] The local worlds mentioned above, combined with these three levels, produce a diversity of *'spheres of reality'* which may, in certain circumstances, differ totally from one another although to the Western eye they appear to have common characteristics. Maruyama described this structure as *'takosubo shakai'* (a bunch of weir-baskets). Individuals are elevated within self-contained but interlocking weir-baskets (groups), which create a society that from the outside has a clearly perceptible structure. Everyone lives their life locked into their own environment and is able to communicate to a limited extent, although nourished by the same fluid (information, the 'Japanese' spirit, etc.).[174] In the economic sphere, this perspective coincides with new concepts involving the term 'network state', coined by Okimoto. In structural terms, Japan more closely resembles an organizational network than a traditional state: 'a societal network called Nihon'.[175]

'Zaibatsu', the major entrepreneurial conglomerates, come easily to mind as prime examples of the functional analysis of this network perspective, for they are relatively clearly comprehensible to the Western observer and can easily be distinguished from Western concepts. This viewpoint is accepted and also actively practiced by Japanese enterprise: for example, the company anthem of the Toyota Motor Company includes a stanza in which Toyota is perceived as an eternally expanding human network.[176] '[The] network view is a process view in which the basic unit is not the firm or any other economic agent acting in isolation but rather various economic agents acting in relation to another.'[177] This approach fits seamlessly into other aspects of Japanese society. These self-organizing links exist thanks to the application of typical concepts (general hyper-information exchange, *haragei, nemawashi*[178] etc.). Worlds (families or *ie*) exist and are either created contextually or simply quietly endured and accepted when being imposed.[179] This creates a 'paramarket', a market set apart from the normal market as an exchange of goods and services. This abstract marketplace consists of multilateral, reciprocal and simultaneous exchanges on many levels, in which the lines of communication between the individual acting entities, information flows and simulations of myths and symbols, in which to some extent they all participate, are the only links between the non-contemporary, heterogeneous worlds.[180]

Today, the Japanese belong to innumerable associations and communities, in its incoherence linked only by the necessity and intent to exchange. Social prestige is determined by their quantity and prestigious quality (e.g. which golf-club). This produces a *mosaic of cultural lifestyles* which are fragmented not only on the outside, as indeed has always been so. In postmodern times, dispersion and decentralization has penetrated the internal structure of the human being, who now has no other way of manifesting himself than by means of his structure of communicative relationships.[181] This multidimensionalism constitutes a social nexus from which human beings derive assurance and existence. The individual disappears into a maze of groups and his existence can subsequently be defined in terms of the relevant circumstances/contexts/groups. An autonomous ego can only be a hindrance in this maze of anticipations and expectations. The desired outcome is not *personal integrity* but pure *role performance* which *contributes to society*. In addition to a sensitivity to divergence and difference and the recognition that meaning and context is created only in a dynamic structural context, the primary prerequisite for successfully dealing with all these individual responsibilities is the ability to process information (speed, comprehensiveness, context identification, multichanneling, intensity, interpretation of vagueness, an ability to deal with contradictions, etc.). Via this process, truth and reality adopt situative, dynamic and multidimensional qualities. The fundamental issue of legitimacy thrives in such a society without core or centre, and can only be resolved self-referentially by means of symbols (group reference, imperialistic cult or *nihonron*).

> In short, one could use the following terms to describe Japan: a highly communicative network, without rational or permanent structure; multidimensional, partial interaction; mythical and symbolic simulations; the precedence of symbolic assets over material ones; individual groups with mutually-pervasive heterogeneous realities (broadly put, lifestyles); external and internal dispersion of the decentralized human being. In addition to conventional interpretations, one can interpret all these signs more effectively from a new, postmodern perspective.

V THIRD SUMMARY: THE SOCIAL PRINCIPLES ON WHICH JAPAN'S POSTMODERNITY IS FOUNDED

In spite of possible accusations concerning the arbitrary nature of the selections made in summarizing a few Japanese phenomena, this chapter serves to elucidate how social and cultural aspects, which exert an unusually strong influence on all commercial activities and Japan's economic structure, display certain features which can be called postmodern, based on the working definition of postmodern set out in Chapter 2. To this extent, it could be said that postmodernity is nothing new for Japan but merely a new name for a familiar mechanism of behaviour. Furthermore, it could be demonstrated clearly that Japan does not need to be enigmatic. When viewed from a postmodern perspective, many peculiarities are presented in a different, generally more comprehensible light. In a further step it can be maintained that exactly these postmodern qualities, though being deeply rooted in traditional practices, are precisely the capabilities that can be found on any wishlist of New Economy visionaries. The individual sub-topics conceal additional research themes but these would have to be the subject of special studies.

If we consider the Japanese language, it becomes clear how the intellectual and identifying cohesion of a group can consist of *myths* and *symbols*, without any need for a rational, bureaucratic, overorganized system. *Indeterminables* and *indifference*, as opposed to disorder and a *fundamental lack of solid footing*, form an existential part of all things Japanese and are enormously demanding, in terms of interpretative abilities, or more precisely the ability to sniff out differences within a 'high-context system'. This ambiguity produces a loosely defined, strongly relational language structure, rich in nuances and with a highly-refined symbolism, in which multiple objectives (realities, surfaces, worlds) are reliable concepts, dependent on the relevant circumstances and the near total, almost spineless flexibility of the individual. This non-existence of a strong-willed ego is also one of the pillars of Zen teaching whose relationship to the language we have examined. Ego and religious belief are subordinated to a pluralism in which nothing is fixed *a priori* and everything is accepted as *provisional* and *relative*.

The promotion of irrational discourse, contradictions and paradoxes (Zen, *No*-theatre) produces complete freedom from dogma which, when viewed in the context of the *abstract aim of pure performance*, allows the appropriate, optimal mode of performance (attitude, value system, role, etc.) to be quickly, easily and fluidly assimilated. In this context, the existence of multiple, situative realities (definitions of ego and goals of the subjects), each with their own inherent dynamics, is the coherent side-effect of the attitude of mind described as 'transcendental aloofness in the midst of multiplicities'. Adopting multiple personalities in the various chat rooms or expert groups seems to the Japanese like business as usual.

The interpersonal values of *solidarity* and *disinterested forbearance* flowing from this are derived not from unworldly ethics, but from the concrete radical pragmatism running through all areas of secular life. *Loyalty*[182] and *self-sacrifice*, in return for existential certainty and total insular comfort (cf. the concepts of *wa* and *amae*) render contradictions unimportant, since the Japanese find their intuitive and emotional basis within groups, families, clans and the nation, using the immediate context to provide role definitions. The diversity of these roles produces a postmodern reality in which references to reality (*qua* role expectations and values) are situatively merged and altered to create an ever-changing reality, resulting in an ambiguous decentralized state in which only group references and symbols represent the only valid reality. It is impossible to dream up a fixed set of ethical values by describing the truth in commonly-accepted, provisionally-determined, situation-oriented terms based on intuitive discussion. Amorality and a lack of principles are therefore inappropriate criteria for an extremely context- and group-dependent, local and flexible efficacy ethic. One could call this pragmatic *reality-management* (or *management of truth*).

Japan exists, *decentralized* and *without a power base*, in the form of a structure which is about (but not quite) to disintegrate; for the symbols and signs on which Japan is founded possess powerful centripetal forces. In spite of a deep-rooted problem of legitimacy, the 'metaécrit Japan' (an empty imperial cult; the empty centre of Tokyo; amorphous cities; superficiality rather than depth of meaning as far as signs are concerned; reproductions instead of originals; diffuse self-awareness) is overcome self-referentially by means of the cohesive power of the Japanese world of symbols. This is why the *main symbol of Japan*: 'Japan' (or *nihonron*) is eminently significant. This symbol encompasses all of Japan and is, as anticipated, not clear, illuminating and robust in structure but vague, ambiguous, empty and interpretation-dependent. Nevertheless, the 'symbol Japan' applies not only to Japan itself but also, in different form, to the rest of the world, and is from a postmodern perspective more genuine than the 'reality Japan'. Just as the 'symbol Japan' fails to represent any tangible concrete structure, the social apparatus from which it is created fails to fit snugly and securely. Rather than a monolith, it is a *rhizome*: a gigantic intertwined web of multi-channelled, separate relationships (economically; symbolically; officially and unofficially; formally and informally; privately and publicly; in the foreground and in the background; intra- and inter-group-specific, etc.).

The multiple pervasiveness of elementary groups and group relationships, the impossibility to define borders, the acceptance of contradictory values and partial responsibilities all form an integrated web which can no longer be managed by means of simple rational planning techniques, but which requires rituals, 'lubricants' and smooth management. This does not, however, exclude Machiavellian support strategies but rather assimilates them into the repertoire as major techniques.[183] In Japan, informal, intercommunicating networks (*kone*, *jinmyaku*) have achieved a level of competence without parallel in other societies. A prerequisite for the successful orchestration of these complex relationships is a sensitivity to divergence and difference and the recognition that a *dynamic structural correlation* is needed to appreciate meaning and context. The ability to transmit, evaluate and utilize a flood of sometimes contradictory and purely metaphorical information and knowledge quickly, comprehensively and on several channels at the same time can also be considered extraordinary. In this context, too, the concept of fragmented, overlapping and stratified *local worlds* proves itself.

This is why, if considered in the context of the hypotheses and working definitions used to describe the postmodern, it is possible to perceive Japan as a pure postmodern network without a physical tangible structure, a network state. All of these aspects of Japanese society would fit extremely well, irrespective of context, in a discussion concerning the 'ideal' economy for a postmodern society. One can draw parallel conclusions between the key points which constitute the image of Japan and the working definition of the postmodern and this strongly supports the hypothesis of the postmodernity of the Japanese economy (Chapter 1, section IV):

- the integrative effect of symbols and myths in a fragmented reality, characterized by decentralization and spectrality;
- sophisticated symbolism, multiple realities, a lack of strong self-conceptions, multiple role requirements, radical pluralism of values;
- external and internal dispersion and decentralization of the human being with smooth adaptation of new lifestyles and swift switches between identities;
- provisionally valid, situation-oriented truths based on intuitive discourse;
- non-rational discussions, contradictions and paradoxa, combined paratactically with rational logic aimed at the target of pure performance;
- uncertainty, indifference and contextuality of language, concepts and thoughts;
- the fundamental importance of interpretation, detection of differences and nuances;
- unprejudiced alertness, solidarity, sensitivity and tolerance towards difference;
- multiple pervasion of groups and group relationships, 'membership' of countless, indivisible groups, impossibility to discern exact dividing lines, multidimensional and partial interaction;
- primacy of information, knowledge and relationships above all else;
- a social rhizome structure without a rational or permanent framework, that can change its dynamics instantaneously;
- simulations of myths and symbols; the dominance of symbolic assets rather than the material.

4 The Structural Environment Surrounding Japan's Multinational Enterprises – a Driving Force for Change

Just how powerful will Japan be in the early twenty-first century?
Barring a large-scale war, or ecological disaster,
or a return to a 1930-style world slump and protectionism,
the consensus answer seems to be:
much more powerful.
        P. Kennedy, *The Rise and Fall of the Great Nations*, 1987, p. 467

I OVERVIEW

Having examined the cultural foundations of the postmodernity of Japan in the previous chapter, the main argument in this chapter focuses on fundamental economic strategies. Here, the framework of organization of production is applied as proposed by Best, whose analysis of future Japanese competitiveness was based on three basis elements: culture, strategy and production-organization.[1]

By applying the theory drawn from the conclusions reached in Chapter 3 that Japan is on its way to becoming a preeminent postmodern society, a major New Economy player, we can perceive its economy, structure, mechanisms and the prevailing behavioural patterns in a new light. This chapter focuses on macro-level strategies (in a general sense), without, however, neglecting the major components from which these strategies are generated and the anchorage in the dynamism inherent to decision-making.[2] Then, in Chapter 5, we discuss this argumentation analogously in the context of companies and conglomerates. Supported by a general literary consensus,[3] the argumentation is based on the premise that it applies in principle to any form of organization – political, large or small firms, as well as to the relationships between companies, nations and people.[4]

To round off the picture, we consider the inner dynamics of these economic strategies as mapped out by presenting the major principles of Japanese economic adjustment, whilst summarizing the relevant (economic) structural changes which have taken place. Using the most significant, identifiable 'change agent', the MITI

104

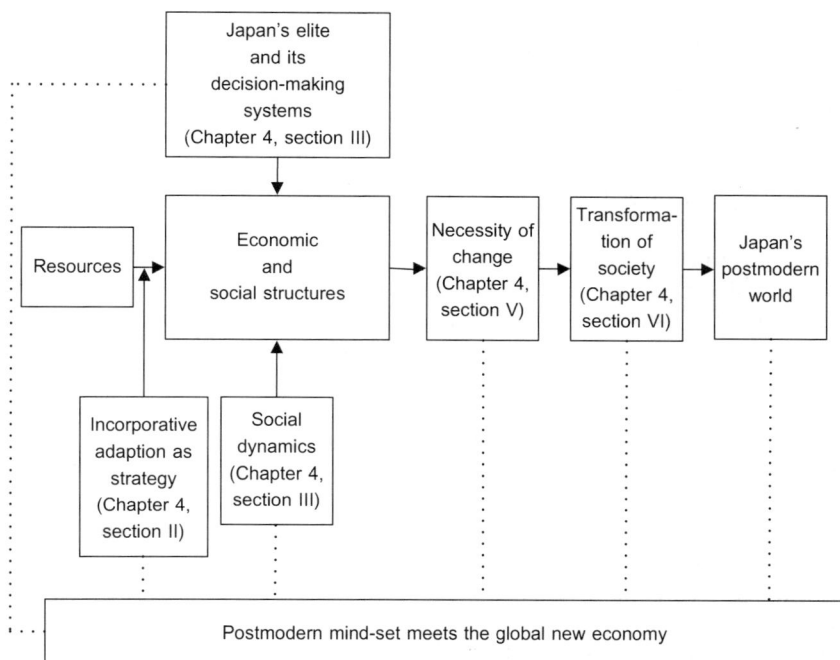

Figure 4.1 *Japan's dynamic energy – a bird's-eye perspective*

and the other surrounding important Ministries and agencies, to document industrial and economic policy, it will be demonstrated that these changes were not simple passive adjustments, but intentional future-anticipating measures. This chapter concludes with Japan's set of objectives for the global economy in the coming years.

The theory expounded in this chapter is that the Japanese, and particularly the economy of Japan, are determinedly preparing themselves for the postmodern role of 'paradigm leader' in the New Economy, for which extremely favourable conditions exist, the mechanisms of change[5] having already been tested and declared effective (see Figure 4.1).

II HOW JAPAN'S ABILITY TO ADAPT AFFECTS STRUCTURAL CHANGE

The most important basis of structural change in Japan is the ability and willingness to adapt flexibly and continually, in order to adjust rapidly and smoothly, to changing external structures and to unreservedly assimilate new approaches, applying them commensurately alongside the old in order to achieve practical objectives.[6]

Being open and acquisitive in nature, Japan's multiculturalism has always had little difficulty in assimilating diverse heterogeneous influences (from China, Korea, India, Europe and finally America). After the manner of scrap-metal dealers, the Japanese have dismantled (deconstructed) what they consider to be inferior civilization imports, sorting out useful individual components[7] and then incorporating them seamlessly, and rapidly, into the existing traditional cultural fabric. The partial ingestion of cultures postulated in Chapter 2 does not apply here in a consumer sense, but more on an aggregate level. Since the only guideline applicable here is performance-oriented pragmatism, the wholesale acceptance of complete systems and foreign turnkey solutions has been rejected in favour of functional units. Although national unity is the primary objective, an active coexistence of heterogeneous elements is desired at a subordinate level.[8]

The calculation used in the adaptation is reminiscent of the perception and unopposed acceptance of difference mentioned in Chapters 2 and 3, which is evidence of dogma-free interest. Model pluralism is actively created within the context of an almost Darwinian rivalry between paradigms. An *unconditional awareness of divergence* and a *sensitivity to the usefulness of foreign concepts* are among the most pronounced cultural features of the Japanese. This does, however, go hand in hand with an astonishing capacity for *assimilation*, which continually remodels useful elements and incorporates them into Japanese structure, leaving no trace of contrast whatsoever.

These innovations will later be perceived as genuinely Japanese (the most obvious success in this respect being the use of findings and methods derived from the natural sciences in the technological field).[9] In this process it is impossible to detect any impediment whatsoever, as far as morals and standards are concerned. Society accepts and 'digests' anything which is, in practical terms, of advantage to Japan.[10] The simulation of 'the West' is only skin-deep, and this simulation is incomplete since the West can always see an indefinable, 'mystical' Japan shining through from below. From a Japanese perspective, this is comparable with a submarinal sedimentation process, in which more and more layers of sands are deposited, forming first a diffuse mix of water and sea bed which, over the course of time, results initially in a sandy seabed, which is subsequently compressed into sandstone.

This system of enrichment worked so well that there has apparently been no need whatsoever for bilateral, reciprocal interaction between Japan and the rest of the world. Even in the Meiji period at the beginning of the twentieth century, large swathes of the population signalled their resistance to the too-wider 'opening up' of the country: '*fukoku kyohei*' (a rich country and a strong army) took precedence over learning. As in former times, knowledge, technology and 'progress' were merely devices employed to further the power-oriented, hegemonic concepts of dominant leading groups.[11] In 1857, Hotta, a government minister, wrote:

I am therefore convinced that our policy should be to stake everything on the present opportunity, to conclude friendly alliances, to send ships to foreign countries everywhere and conduct trade, to copy the foreigners where they are at their best and so repair our own shortcomings, to foster our national strengths and complete our armaments, and so gradually subject the foreigners to our influence until in the end all the countries of the world know the blessings of perfect tranquillity and our hegemony is acknowledged throughout the globe.[12]

Their behaviour mimicked the American idiom: 'if you lose – learn!' The humourist, Mikes, who is neither a Japanologist nor an economist, aptly uses the following terms to characterize the Japanese viewpoint:

> ... if the gaijin [the foreigner] can force us to do things we do not want to do then the gaijin is stronger than we are. The gaijin indeed must be better. So we must learn his ways, we must learn all he can teach us ... And then we can face the gaijin on his own chosen ground with his own weapons.[13]

There is simply no moral necessity whatsoever to cling to something old, that would be a mistake: 'they idolize success. What succeeds is good; what fails is worthless ... As soon as a better system is found, more suitable to the ages ahead, democracy[14] soon will be discarded. The Japanese will do it without blinking an eyelid ...'[15]

This serves to underline Japan's fanatical obsession with dimensions such as performance, efficacy and competence, which pay off in postmodern times too. In it, one can also identify here a fundamental lack of standpoint and total value-relativity, which permits the assimilation of any auxiliary device in the absence of any obligation to consider coherence, orthodoxy or logical consistency. In a sustained mood of emergence, intermediate and temporary objectives are acceptable on the basis of the concept of the fleeting moment, the 'perpetual now' or irreversible impetus which is deeply seated in Japanese thinking. The main objective is merely to achieve or maintain *total, long-term 'performance'*. This is the only relevant constant in Japan's growth, which has, until now, proved to be a successful basic strategy.[16] This is why Rohlen also attributes the economic success of Japan chiefly to knowledge-based factors: *'learning capacity'*, a highly-educated population, lifelong learning and social value concepts which place a high regard on knowledge and ability.[17] Other child-like aspects are an unconditional interest and a failure to observe fundamental differences and inconsistencies during the learning process. This is where the image of 'aloofness in the midst of multiplicities', used in Chapter 3 is again appropriate.[18] For this reason, the proverbial ability of the Japanese to copy should not be underestimated, for it produces skills which are significant for the future.[19] Rather than thinking in terms of copying, the verbs to emulate, adapt, imitate, improve and innovate should be used for describing these processes.[20,21] The method of 'learning from the best', absorbing and combining technology with domestic know-how, can only work insofar as the knowledge donors fail to attack the 'free-rider problem'.[22,23] In their study of international financial markets, Wright and Pauli perceive transfer of technology as

Table 4.1   *Innovation-intensive products as a percentage of exports*

	1965	1975	1985	1995	2005*
USA	27.5	24.5	25.2	25	60
J	7.3	11.6	20.2	35	50
F	7.3	11.6	20.2	22	30
D	16.9	16.8	14.5	20	35
UK	12.0	9.6	8.5	6	40

* Forecast
Source: Klenner, W., 'Grundzüge der wirtschaftspolitischen Entwicklung und Wirtschaftspolitik seit dem zweiter Weltkrieg', pp. 33, 45

the foundation stone of an 'acquisitive' hyperstrategy, ending, ultimately, in global Japanese dominance.[24] This expansionist strategy is based, in the main, on Japan's ability to progress technologically without any slow-down, a proficiency which also represents the general competitive edge which Japan has carved out for itself over a long period. This strategy is not easy to incorporate into the mechanics of the Heckscher–Ohlin model, which is why the West has failed to recognize the ongoing process (copying, adapting, 'riding the experience curve', expansion of production bases abroad, etc.) as strategic moves.[25] This Japanese strategy of *focusing on knowledge and information* as a *strategic factor in global competition* becomes evident when we compare the export share of innovation-intensive products (Table 4.1) and the overall increase in export productivity directly with that of other industrial nations.[26]

Within a long-range optic, the Japanese economy is enjoying a period of 'peak performance' in terms of technological structure. Stability of system performance continues to increase whilst the breadth of potential fields of implementation is decreasing (increased specialization with pure, application-oriented research is now routine). There are no longer any material barriers to economic growth (physically setting up production sites), only immaterial ones remain (licences, know-how; IT development). This success is not solely attributable to a strategy of imitation, which remained an optimal strategy only until all technologies capable of producing a large marginal change in productivity had been adapted. Lacking foreign role models to be copied, Japan had to display technological leadership: 'Readily available borrowable technology had been exhausted and many Japanese industries could no longer hope to increase their productive efficiency by adopting new foreign technology.'[27] Table 4.2 shows Japan's productivity and export growth and gross national product from 1870 to 1979 compared to other countries.

An analysis of technological progress over the last 100 years demonstrates that Japan's basic strategy, the acquisition of knowledge, represented a major competitive advantage.[28,29] The change in Japanese attitude towards the patent and license disputes with other countries, which were predominant in the 1980s, fits perfectly into this strategic framework. Instead of an obvious monodirectional technological

Table 4.2 *Productivity growth, gross national product (adj. for population growth) and growth of exports, 1870–1998*

	Real gross national product per working hour	Real GNP p.c.	Export volume (indexed: avg. export production in 1870 = 100)
GB	585	310	930
CH	830	471	4 400
NL	910	429	8 040
CDN	1 050	766	9 860
USA	1 080	693	9 240
AUS	1 270	643	4 740
D	1 510	824	3 730
F	1 590	924	4 140
J	2 480	1 661	293 060

Source: Klenner, W., 'Grundzüge der wirtschaftspolitischen Entwicklung und Wirtschaftspolitik seit dem zweiten Weltkrieg', pp. 33, 45

exchange, Japan now promotes a more open, inhibited dialogue, which must, however, be played by Japanese rules: a controlled outflow of information from Japan, accompanied if at all possible by application controls (in Japanese firms abroad), in return for which Japan is granted unrestricted access to all the research results of the Western world. Interpreted more positively, this represents 'selective technophilia in enlightened self-interest'[30] which Chapter 2 labelled as postmodern.

The *long-term nature of this knowledge strategy* was already documented in the Tokugawa period; a government office known as the 'Office for Checking Barbarian Writings' already existed in Nagasaki prior to 1800. During the Meiji period, feudalism adapted unbelievably effectively and in no time at all to the modern Western industrial system. Japan's basic predisposition to technology, coupled with an extraordinarily fast rate of adjustment has enabled it to achieve major technological advances, which are simultaneously philosophical advances, meaning an overhaul of its view of the world. We can discern three jumps in the field of technology and civilization. The first 'stride', which resulted from initial contacts with China, benefited the Japanese, particularly from a cultural point of view. This process probably began around 1000 BC and progressed only very slowly over a period lasting centuries due to the imperfect nature of transport and communications at that time, it was a lengthy advance rather than a revolution.[31] The next philosophical step, when the Western model of the world was examined, was made after 1868 as a result of contact with Western industrial nations. The emphasis here was on new technologies imported from abroad. The postmodern philosophical stride currently being made, as hypothesized in this work, is no longer imported from abroad but is perceived as globally diffuse to some extent, as an endogenous impetus in which Japan occupies a leadership role (Figure 4.2).

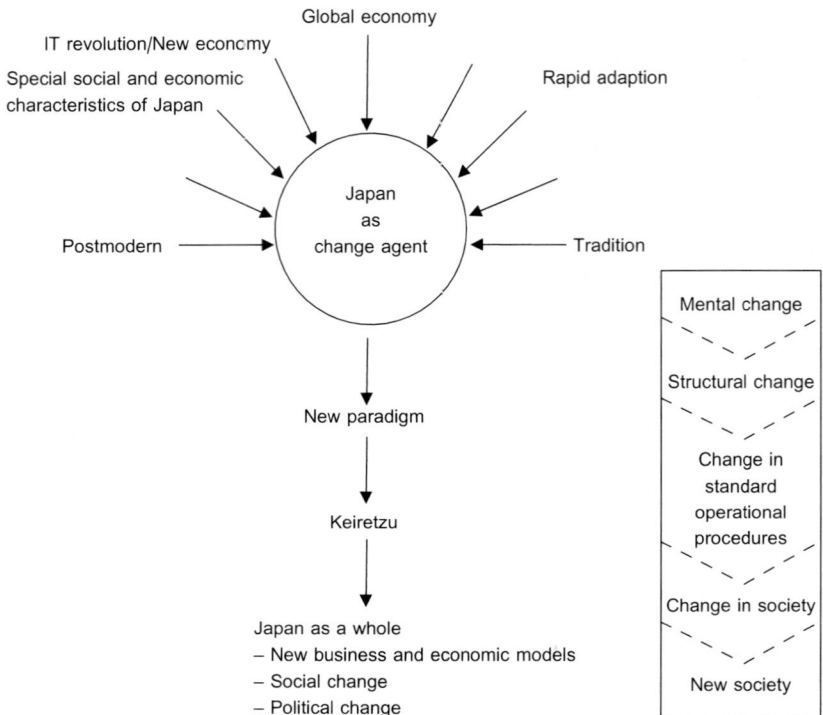

Figure 4.2 *Japan's mechanisms of transformation*

This is the reason why, especially today, the ability to adapt, to accumulate knowledge and to unconditionally and radically shift position are key elements in preparation for a postmodern environment. But it is not only the ability to adapt to the diffuse, changing corporate and industrial environment alone which is now a competitive factor, but the pace, smoothness and completeness of the adjustment to new economic framework parameters are also major factors yielding long-term growth.[32] Thus, Japan encompasses all the major strengths of a leading, post-modern society, and knowledge and information are seen as the most important and fundamental raw materials of the new era. Japan is clearly number one as far as the intensity and processing of information and communication is concerned. All things immaterial and symbolic takes precedence over the inflexible, the material or routine. Technology, as a basis for social change not only exists and is approved, but plays a leading role in the process of adjustment to a world in which a high level of technology is just a prerequisite.

III THE INITIATORS AND MECHANISMS OF CHANGE

Individual and Organizational Elements

Basic structural units

The basic attitude to knowledge, information, technology and future-oriented adaptability, described above, also affects the organizational and structural aspects of the national economy, leading one to assume that in these areas, too, Japan plays a prominent role in the preparations for a postmodern era. In the context of whether Japan has a fundamental strategy aimed at technological change, the second important aspect now becomes clear – that is its individual and organizational basis which can be described retrospectively as 'the (economic) wonder which is Japan' and, in anticipatory terms, as 'Japan's postmodern society of the future'. Specific Japanese organization principles can be perceived as the driving force behind this development, however not in this context on a sociographical level as in Chapter 3, section IV, but rather on an institutional level.

There can be no other country which has such a sophisticated, highly-developed network of associations, clubs and unions as Japan. This also has an impact on the economic and political environment, evidence of which can be found in all dimensions. There is historical evidence of unofficial neighbourhood committees (*chokai* or village councils), membership of which was automatically granted to every household and which were collectively responsible for crime, adult education, youth education, environmental programmes, public safety and cooperation with public institutions. During the Tokugawa period, these structures were promoted as organs of control and were, during the Second World War, subdivided into even smaller control units (*tonarigumi*). These structures still exist today, for example, in the form of *shotenkai* (Association of Traders in a Residential District).[33] From an external perspective, these groups and groupings are extremely industrious and successful and, from an internal perspective, frequently represent a community, the cohesive force of which cannot be underestimated. It is these factors which justify the view that precisely these background forces determine the formative processes which ensure success in the international, economic arena.[34] With the advent of the Internet it can be safely assumed that these processes of groupings and community building will take place in a similar fashion only on a much grander scale. Even now, it is already impossible to categorize this myriad of groups; our intention here is only to project those which play an important part in terms of the national economy and from the point of view of the Keiretsu.[35] These can be roughly divided into employer and employee associations, private or public clubs, and informal cliques.

1 *Employer and employee associations* The most important employer association is the Federation of Economic Organizations, *Keizai Dantai Rengokai* or in shortened form, *Keidanren*.[36] The primary task of Keidanren is to coordinate individual industries, study internal and external problems affecting the economy

and draft concrete proposals to overcome them for submission to parliament and
the public. When we look at the market shares of the industries to which the
corporate members of the Keidanren belong, we can see the economic and political
power which implicitly lies behind them:

Steel industry	93%	Chemical industry	100%
Electronics industry	73%	Oil processing industry	96%
Automobile industry	100%	Cement manufacturing	99%.[37]

A large, highly qualified workforce, a well-structured committee system and ongoing bilateral governmental contact make Keidanren one of the most important,
unofficial points of coordination for all Japan's economic processes. Naturally this
coordination does not occur on the surface. If a Keiretzu considers that a change
in policy is called for, no direct proposals or criticisms are made. The correct form
of expression might be a 'desire for a change in climate' which, according to the
rules, would warrant an invitation to the political authorities to attend a general
consultation.[38]

The second most important association is the *Nihonjeieisha Dantai Renmei* or
Nikkeiren in shortened form, the umbrella organization of Japanese employer associations. Keidanren and Nikkeiren complement one another. The leadership groups
of the two associations overlap in numerous places and they largely have an identical membership. Topics discussed within these organizations range from wages,
personnel, training and employment issues to social security, public relations and
regional coordination.

The third tier of firm- and Zaibatsu-related[39] commercial organizations is made
up of the respective industrial representatives. The following industries field the ten
most influential *lobby structures*: the electronics industry, the steel industry, the
automobile industry, chemical manufacturers, life insurance companies, cement
manufacturers, Hitachi, the banks, Toshiba, and Mitsubishi.[40,41] Within the ministries, they are complemented by a homologous organizational structure which
operates analogous systems. Figure 4.3 illustrates the fundamental structure of the
formal links between companies, associations and ministries. These formal links are
substantially reinforced and even further superimposed with the informal links.
Structurally, this ensures optimal fine-tuning of the intensive consultative processes
conducted between concerns, employer associations and governmental offices.

2   *Private and public clubs*   There are countless groups, cliques, discussion
societies and institutionalized gatherings in existence in Japan, apart from formally established, officially recognized associations. The basic character of these
informal groups can be described as either discrete, private or informal, depending
on which adjective one cares to use.[42] This is not significant in terms of the efficacy
and influence which these organizations exert, but they do have an important effect
on the professional careers of their members,[43] for it is here that they discuss
potential 'formal steps' (career moves) 'in confidence'. The Japanese dynamics discussed in the next chapter, such as the '*oyabun–kobun*' relationship and '*nemawashi*'

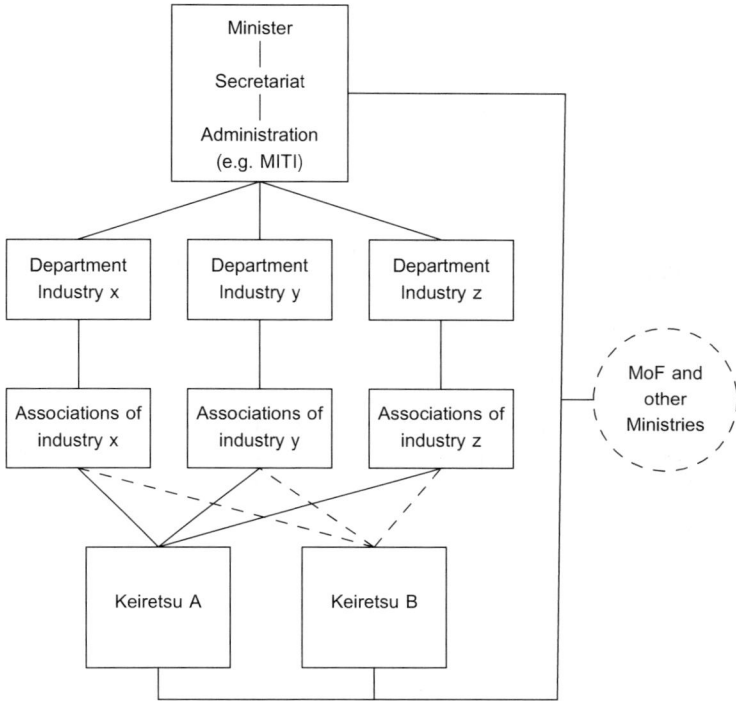

Figure 4.3 *Formal relations between business, (networking) associations and the political sphere*

(cf. Chapter 4, section III below) are also prevalent here. The following characteristics can be identified in the basic structure: (relative) informality, fluid group affiliations, intensive information exchange, hypothetical discussions on strategy and a desire for carefully honed public opinions of the group, all of which are subsequently presented individually to the 'outside world' and assimilated into other groups. Figure 4.4 illustrates this more clearly.

We can divide these clubs into *Keiretsu-oriented* and *politically-oriented* groups. Walkways have been constructed within the Keiretsu-oriented clubs to link up the separate hierarchical levels of the various companies which form each Keiretsu. Several hierarchical committees exist within a company; the Board, directors, senior departmental managers, heads of department and planning managers all socialize within their own committees – '*jomukai*', '*shachokai*', '*honbuchokai*', '*buchokai*', '*choki keikaku iinkai*'. This system is also applied throughout the company within the Keiretsu and even inter-Keiretsu clubs exist. The most famous examples are the club for the presidents of commercial enterprises (*torishimariyakukai*), or the Japanese Industrialists Club (*Nippon Kogyo Kurabu*). In a Keiretsu context, Figure 4.5 shows how some clubs are structured.

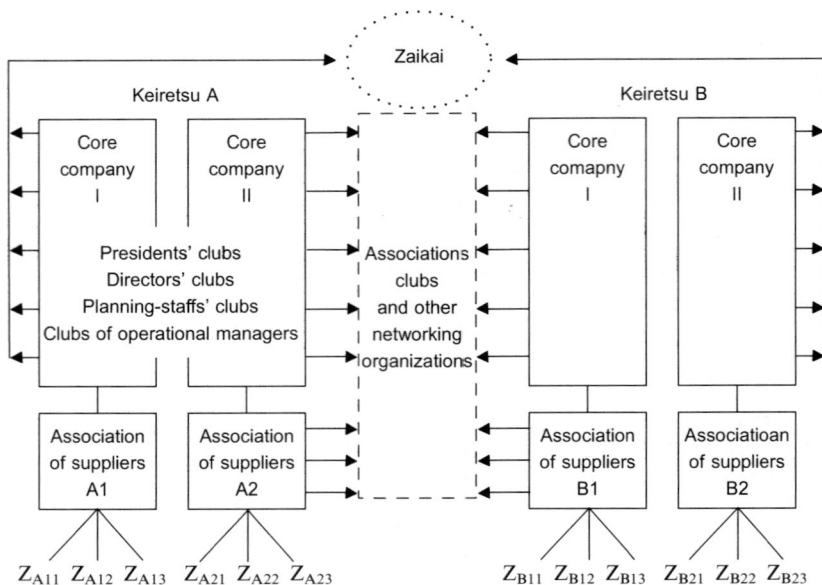

Figure 4.4   *Formation of a Zaikai*

In addition to these commercially-oriented clubs there are also clubs which are more politically-oriented and which sometimes merge to form an informal common interest group, the only organizational principle of which is that of intensive communication. Often they are clustered around symbolic political figures, like

Level / Keiretsu	Presidents	Directors	Department heads
Mitsubishi	Kinyo Kai (Friday Club)	Getsuyo Kai (Monday Club)	Kayo Kai (Tuesday Club)
Mitsui	Nimokku Club (Second Thursday Club)	Getsuyo Kai (Monday Club)	Sanmokku Kai (Third Thursday Club)
Sumitomo	Hakusui Kai (White Water Club)	Mokkuyobi Kai (Thursday Club)	Hakusen Kai (White Source Club)
Fuji	Fuyo Kai		
Dai Ichi Kangyo	Sankin Kai		
Sanwa	Sansu Kai		

Figure 4.5   *Selected clubs of the Keiretsu*

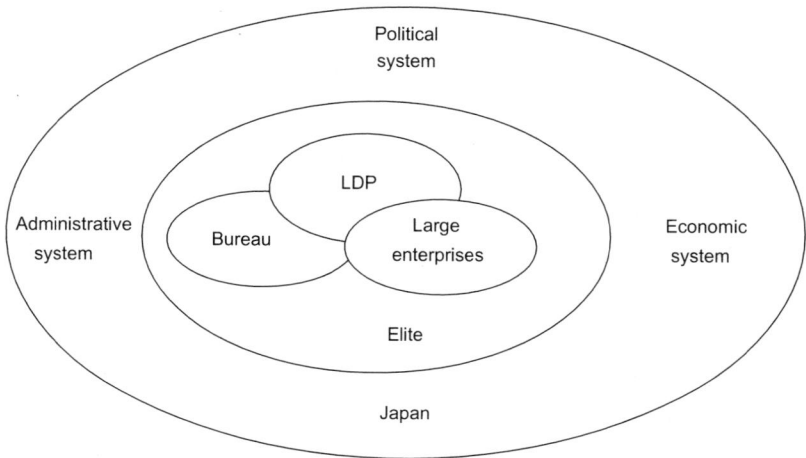

Figure 4.6   *Interlinkages between bureaucracy, parties and enterprises*

the Research Society for Creative Politics, associated with ex-Prime Minister K. Tanaka, or its 'opposite number', the New Liberal Club. The main clubs have names like Fan-Club (*Suehirokai*), Club for Tokyo University Graduates (*Nikoku-kai*), The Liberal-Democratic Party (LDP), the Hotel Okura-Club of the MoF (*Okura doyukai*) and the MITI's famous Tuesday Club (*Kayokai*) which, with a membership of approximately 600, is the largest club of its type. The diversity and impenetrability of these interrelationships determine official policy, which is of a ratifying symbolic nature rather than being active and implementational. Thus, Wolferen was forced to conclude that Japan is, in fact, ruled by three groups – elite bureaucracy, LDP and Keiretsu, despite its status as a parliamentary democracy[44] (see Figure 4.6).

3   *Informal cliques*   Cliques (*batzu*) and groupings (*zoku*, literally: tribes) are subordinate in terms of any official hierarchy, which cannot be exhaustively eluci-dated here due to space constraints.[45,46] We can, however, highlight one significant structural element: the collective term 'Zaikai' (business clique) covers a major grouping of cliques and is often perceived as Japan's major power centre. But, even this centre is strangely undefined; it must remain 'empty' because it permeates, like an amoebae, Japan's entire economic and political dimensions. Prior to 1945, this economic clique was indistinguishable from the Zaibatsu of the time; whereas, today, its significance is broader and more multilayered.[47] Thus, Yoshino perceives the Zaikai as 'a unique and elusive entity',[48] an unofficial organ without a distinct membership. Zaikai usually collectively describes the innumerable small groups which consist of the most powerful people in Japanese commercial life, who typi-cally occupy high positions in the enterprises, associations or bureaucracy.[49]

Thus the Zaikai fits perfectly into a picture of joint coordination, in which enhancements to Japan's competitiveness, as an ongoing process, are constantly pursued non-ideologically and without regard for logical constraints. This institutional arrangement of formal and informal, explicit and implicit social structures, in which the relevant 'elite' are mutually pervasive, can be seen as a determining factor in the Japanese 'economic miracle':

> The central institutions – that is, the bureaucracy, the LDP, and the larger Japanese Business concerns in turn maintain a kind of skewed triangular relationship with each other. [This is] ... a structure of double vision, by which [is meant] the tendency for subordinate, dependent or guiding parts to formulate their own policies as if the superior's policies were their own. It all looks like consensus to outsiders, but is, in fact, dictated by a calculation of the balance of forces and a sense of Japan's vulnerability ...[50]

It has proved impossible to identify a clear power centre or economic force, either on a formal or on an informal institutional level. Consequently, we need to examine the issue of whether this central role is occupied by those who represent the focus of power within the various organizational structures, that is an elite.

The centre: a Japanese elite?

It is not easy to determine a clearly-defined elite in a country where 90 per cent of the population sees itself as middle class. Other indicators point to a ruling class without, however, being able to define it clearly.[51] Many authors, for example, draw attention to the strong influence exerted by graduates of Tokyo University, in political and economic terms, who regularly make up more than 50 per cent of successful candidates sitting the senior civil service entrance examination. Most graduates join banks, life insurance companies, *Sogo Shosha* (trading companies) and steel companies, MITI, Ministry of Finance or other high-ranking Ministries. Members of the Zaikai and Keidanren are also regarded as the elite.[52]

But this elite is *not clearly definable*, it is constantly mutating, is interchanging and mutually pervasive, and impossible to grasp in any logical manner; which is why Wolferen sums it up as a 'system' and Sasaki-Smith as an 'elite-hegemony' with neither author concretely defining these terms.[53] To Wolferen, this elite is the sum total of all relationships and links ('*kone*', '*jinmyaku*', cf. Chapter 3, section IV on 'group relationship structures'), an 'informal network of special relationships'; the cohesive forces produced by numerous different structures such as common career paths, family relationships, corruption and friendship. According to Wolferen, these structures are the only observable parameters.[54]

'The Japanese elite hegemony thus continues to orient the nation's economic development in a way that would ensure its own cohesion, and that of the whole system, through continued growth without fundamentally altering the social and political structures on which the Japanese capitalist system has been built.'[55] Thus these overall objectives cannot be the agenda of one single grouping but the overall

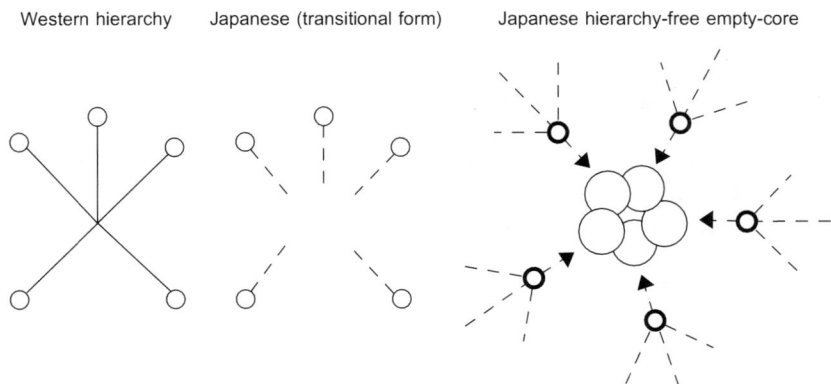

Figure 4.7 *Structures of leadership in Japan*
Source: Adapted from Dopfer, K., 'Elemente einer Evolutionsökonomik', p. 21

objective of the 'system', which has no centre, leadership or conceptual foundations. In Japan this is known as '*kuroi kiri*' or black fog, especially in the context of
scandals. This 'organized society' (*kumi shakai*) is held together not forcibly but by
means of a sophisticated combination of indirect control, shared symbols and close
communication, a combination which produces an extremely fragmented fluid network which is difficult to grasp.[56] Woronoff sees this governing organization (Zaikai)
or commercial organization (Keiretsu) '. . . as a rather loose grouping of companies,
meeting periodically with much goodwill but little institutional integration on an
operational level . . . and an even looser concept of government.'[57] Other authors use
comparable descriptive terms, such as a loose group structure or spiderless spider's
web, but the meaning is still the same: it is impossible to narrow down Japan's power
centre to a specific centre or elite.[58] The leadership structure cannot be determined by
applying external criteria, and it is not possible to identify those persons behind the
'things happening' (moves, activities). Instead, all the indicators point to primary
nodes in the form of processes rather than structures, a theory which could help us to
come closer to explaining the dynamics of Japan (see Figure 4.7).

*The Japanese approach to decision-making, or the art of
decision-making à la japonaise*

Japanese decision-making is seen as a unique process which foreigners cannot
understand, on the one hand, and if the doctrine of cultural relativism is then
used to defend one's own way of doing things, on the other hand, a tremendous
barrier is placed in the way of a foreigner's understanding of, and involvement
in, the activities of his or her Japanese counterparts. A mystique is created in
which Japan is hidden in mist. In such misty surroundings it is easier for
Japanese to parry the approaches of foreign negotiators.[59]

This conclusion shows how unclear the overall decision-making process is to the Western observer. This problem can be overcome by looking in a more abstract manner at the outcome of commercial decision-making processes as a whole, rather than in terms of a single process (the basic mechanism of which will be presented in Chapter 4, section III – 'interpersonal mechanisms' and 'links etc.').[60] Japanese organization, whether that of a company or macroeconomic coordination, is a *rhizome-like structure* in which all the components retain their own identity and interrelate. This structure consists of a complex network of human relationships which are intertwined like the roots of a tree. These interrelationships are not always apparent but are part of the more easier to comprehend bigger entities. The actual location of the power base is never entirely clear and, consequently, greater significance is attached to balance and harmony inside the organization.[61] To link this with the web world: this lack of tangible decision centres is comparable to how things happen on the Internet, where no polls or decision-making processes direct the evolution, but the network of communicative actions itself (cf. the concept of autopoiesis of Chapter 2) initiates developments.[62]

The nucleus of this fabric is the *work group* (*ka*), and its organizer (kacho or section leader). 'The ka is the basic work group of the company and is usually composed of fifteen workers of various ranks and skills plus Kacho, or chief.'[63] From several viewpoints, this group is the unit which supports the Japanese work structure. To the employee it is the central point as far as information, responsibility and work distribution are concerned.[64] Each *ka* is fundamentally a monad which, on the exterior, gives the impression of being the smallest hierarchical organism, despite the fact that it comprises a universe of relationships and meanings (Figure 4.8).

This is the mechanism which Vogel referred to concisely as 'central direction and local action'.[65] Although its backbone consists of local coordination activities, they

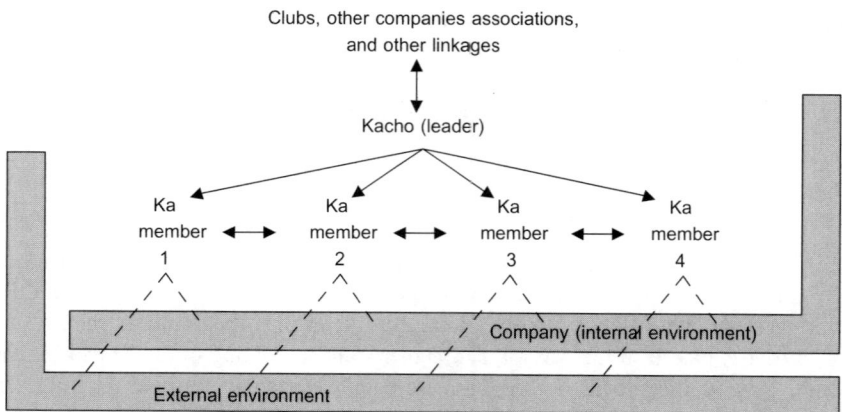

Figure 4.8   *The working team (ka) as the nucleus of company structure*

are not, as might appear on the surface, hierarchically determined by a dictatorial institution. Here again, the centre is strangely absent, and one can never pinpoint the true origin of a directive due to the lack of a focal point of orientation. It is always a committee, a general declaration on the part of several ministries or an announcement made by individuals who, although speaking as individuals, are in truth organs of their organization. This putative focus (similar to the image of the MITI portrayed in the foreign press in the 1980s) resembles in its composition a fairly fractal structure, rather than being one of Plato's ideal bodies. If one attempts to obtain a clearer view of its centre and later its subcentres, it dissolves into separate sub-elements which, in turn, form the rhizome-like composites on which Japanese society depends and which ultimately cause it to become indefinable and indistinct (see Figure 4.9). 'Japanese power in short is highly diffuse and, while it makes it particularly pervasive, it is not so immediately noticeable.'[66]

The degree of complexity of the power constellations and the *diffuseness of power itself*, which is persistently disputed or underplayed, prohibits opposition of any kind, which is why Wolferen does not see 'formal power' as a pragmatic power. Only informal or symbolic power is effective.[67] Since no-one is directly responsible, power is uncontrollable, with responsibility split up into numerous partial responsibilities. This generates a colossal system of rudderless non-responsibility, leaving aside for the moment the symbolic pro forma assumption of responsibility which often takes place.[68] In Japan, management or leadership (*jishu kai*) is practiced more as a form of self-organization, a voluntary set-up. The plan of action adopted

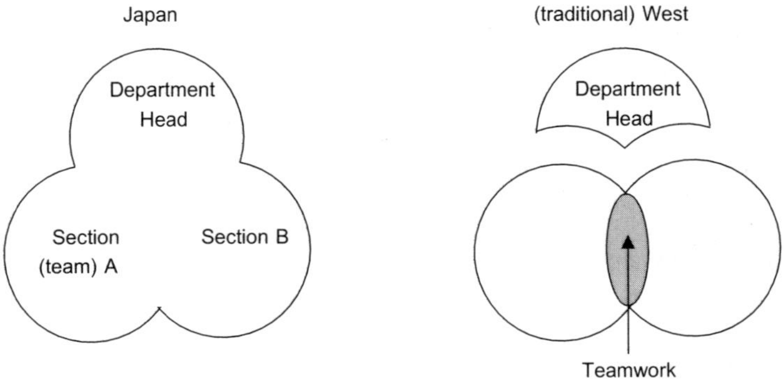

Japan   (traditional) West

- Unclear power structures
- Overlapping functions and roles
- Intensive cooperation and communication
- Shared (diffuse) responsibility

- Clear power-structures (chain of command)
- Defined functions and roles
- Communication only in complex/unclear situations
- Limited cooperation
- Insular responsibilities

Figure 4.9   *Principles of cooperation, responsibility and power*
Source: Adapted from Sazaki, N., *Management and Industrial Structure in Japan*, p. 78

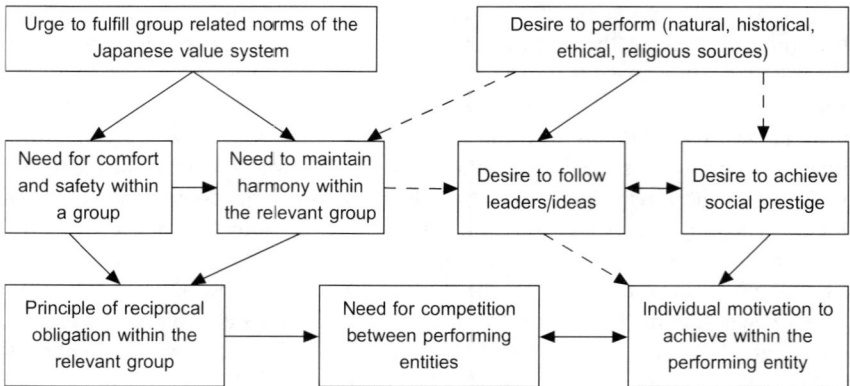

Figure 4.10   *Normative environment of decisions*
Source: Bierdümpel, E., *Japanisches Informationsverhalten*, p. 70

by the decision-making system is clearly defined, although the groups involved in it, together with its content, are constantly changing, overlapping and paratactic.[69]

As a result, the dialectic between contract and consensus is misunderstood in the West: to Japanese society, contracts are not diverse, they are simply declarations of intent.[70] In Japan contracts fundamentally serve only one main purpose: both parties declare their intent to discuss future possible differences of opinion in an honest atmosphere (see also Figure 4.10). Harmony, consensus and homogeneity are not the only aspects of decision-making; they are merely the result of intensive negotiations, carefully engineered and sensitively finalized within each structure and at all levels. Aoki characterizes this constellation, in concrete terms, as an Edgeworth-contract curve in a multidimensional space.[71]

Now, the main components of this analysis are visible: *interlocking decision-making*, a close symbiosis between party, administrators and the commercial world, blurred responsibilities and *fictitious familial ties* (virtual tribes) are for Johnson the primary elements which make up this Japanese decision-making system.[72] A short elucidation of this Japanese approach to decision-making is no more able to provide a clear answer to the question as to the forces behind Japanese dynamics than any theory of elitism. Therefore the next stage in the analysis will be to pinpoint the individual mechanisms which are significant for the maintenance and future development of this fragile system

Selected Interpersonal Mechanisms

Oyabun–kobun, the basic unit of the relationship network

This institutionalized relationship between *oyabun* and *kobun* flows through the whole of Japanese society. The meaning can be conveyed, somewhat inadequately, in English by the words: mentor, adoptive father, godfather or, in a more negative sense, nepotism or paternalism. This basic structure is apparent within every social group, not just bureaucracy, companies or, particularly, politics. It is not only the most important mechanism in the micro-organization but the *oyabun–kobun* principle is also a key element in simple day-to-day living (such as among Sumo wrestlers, doctors, taxi drivers – basically anywhere).[73] Gibney estimated that over 50 per cent of all companies practice a *strict system of seniority* (*nenko*), closely associated with the *oyabun–kobun* system. Due to the strictly limited role of women in Japanese society which still exerts a strong influence, even today, these *oyabun–kobun* relationships are purely a masculine domain.[74]

In linguistic terms the two words are formed from '*bun*', a fraction, piece, status or position, and '*oya*', parental or paternal (from *oyakata*: parental status, parenthood) and '*ko*', child, and are therefore imbued with unambiguously positive connotations. This enables us to identify two components: an emotional and almost familial relationship between the two persons concerned, and a clear implicit hierarchical status. The *oyabun–kobun* relationship is, in a manner of speaking, the smallest link in Japanese society, an interconnected social structure which further generates larger and increasingly complex sociograms. To some extent these relationships produce fictitious kinships which, in addition to the biological parent–child relationship, form a family which is more significant for the individual than his natural family.[75] In contrast to the rationalized, superior–subordinate relationship of the Western world, which is usually strongly influenced by hierarchical considerations, Japanese relationships depend on a sense of duty and personal loyalty, coupled with responsibility for the 'whole being'. 'A subordinate is characterized by his willingness to be flexible and obedient, a highly-regarded virtue in Japan, whilst the superior creates an emotionally charismatic authority, imbuing the relationship with qualities such as forbearance and patience.'[76] These multiple relationships, together with the duties associated with the function, force the individual to juggle a number of different roles, assuming fictitious simulated identities of relative validity between which he is compelled to make a smooth transition in order to discover firstly his significance, his structural context.[77]

Initiation rites, rituals, integrity ceremonies (*jingi*), rules of succession for retiring *oyabun*, together with the subsystem concept practiced within the larger networks, create the illusion of a formalist organization which proves to be false, as there are no permanent, fixed or rational systematic support structures within the organization. These purely immaterial entities of coordination which are not apparent or easy to identify but whose reconstruction requires sensitivity and intuition, prevent administrative principles from being unambiguously defined or clearly set forth. Leadership power is distributed diffusely over the entire system of overlapping and stratified local worlds, which present themselves merely as a self-supporting network of private (local) responsibilities, but fail to provide access to a 'whole'.[78] These networks are more important than formal systems (such as organizational structure, contracts of employment, commercial contracts, etc.) and can also be elucidated by means of proverbs, idioms and company mottos: 'aisha seishin' [love of the company or group]; 'jigyo ikkada' [the company is like a family]; 'kigyo ikka' (the company is an extended family); 'kigyo wa unmei kyodotai de aru' (the company is a community with a common destiny) are just some of the expressions frequently used. These slogans clarify the basic symbolic relationships and, for the Japanese, exert a primary influence which extends beyond all formal organizational parameters.[79]

Pursuant to Bierdümpel, these systems can be perceived as *communication systems*, in which the *oyabun* performs the role of a 'linking pin'[80] within the information chain.[81] The principle of a positive approach to information is totally valid within an *oyabun* group, whilst practiced to only a very limited extent externally.[82] It is here that the concepts of an internal and external world (*uchi-soto*), presented in Chapter 3, section IV ('group relationship structures') again come into play, creating a *multidimensional network of relationships* which symbolizes the network itself, making all superficial, legal, formal and official connections appear secondary and, sometimes, presenting them as obsolete. And indeed this is what these person-to-person relationships are, representing, in effect, the close link between groups, departments, ministries, parties, firms and companies, which should therefore be perceived as a prime explanatory model for 'Zaibatsu/Keiretsu', rather that large organizational charts.[83]

Bennet and Iwao see this *oyabun–kobun* relationship as the major factor in the mobilization and coordination of Japanese society. Perceived in this way, Japanese society is made up of innumerable Keiretsu (networks), with people rather than companies as the components.[84] In this context, Roberts advocates the theory that, after the Second World War, the Zaibatsu were only able to regain their constellations because the group network of people remained intact and was capable of cooperating outside and above the given legal constraints.[85] Critics arguing that this system bears no relevance anymore, should look for the casual day-to-day evidence presented by Japanese firms. Also it deserves mentioning that the analysts of Internet business models always stress the importance of 'buddy' or 'mentor' systems, especially in times of high complex problems, strong growth or fast change.

'Nemawashi', decisions but no visible decision-making process

Nemawashi can be defined as the pre-decision scenario behind procedural, preparatory and exploratory discussions, arrangements, negotiations and general information-exchange processes.

Originally, *nemawashi* was a collective term, used in a gardening context to describe the lengthy preparations which precede the transplantation of a mature tree. One needs to cut the roots and prepare the new soil before gently moving the tree. The foundations must be thoroughly prepared before action is taken at a higher level. Interpreted in a commercial context, *nemawashi* describes countless small meetings at a subordinate level, during which each interest is successively presented. Then at the next hierarchical level this eliminates any chance of a confrontation, perceived as an embarrassment or loss of face, which might arise if the issue were discussed openly within the framework of a formal discussion (cf. Chapter 3, section IV on group relationship structures).

To many authors, the *nemawashi* process is Japan's *primary, fundamental decision-making tool*.[86] On the one hand we could share the view of Reischauer, who describes the complete integration of all participants in the course of which all the relevant information and assessments flowing into the process are generated by means of extensive search actions, and, on the other, of Lu and Wolferen who argue that the development of these conflict-minimization strategies results from a failure on the part of the Japanese to recognize conflict situations and an inability to resolve them. According to these authors, the defect lies much deeper: lacking 'proper' decision-making tools, the decision itself remains strongly personalized in terms of '*éminences grises*', at worst someone hastily says something in the very last minute or the most powerful just carelessly decrees something. Following that, responsibility is distributed diffusely throughout the relevant network, which also adds to the lack of individual responsibility.[87]

Although these methods are extremely delocalized and undefined, they nevertheless form part of a *high-context system*, which depends on rapid, nuance-rich, intensive communication, within a multichannel relationship system which lacks a permanent, physical framework (such as a standing committee or staff organization). Here again, a 'transcendental aloofness in the midst of multiplities' is perceived as its fundamental quality, for, without this, the task of interpreting, of sensing variations in approach, background and multiple objectivity and of registering ambiguities and nuances would be impossible.

Thus, this negotiation process also superficially resembles the proverbial, conflict-free, consensus society, which is also fundamentally characterized by a common approach to objectives, by consensus, after the different interests have been weighed up within a homogeneous insider environment.[88] However, the nature of the '*nemawashi*' process is more reminiscent of the negotiations conducted with individual interest groups, which, in this instance, combine to form a temporary production network subsequently dispersing after the decision has been reached in order to make way for new constellations.[89] The argument that this type of decision-making process is too slow, isolated and uncontrollable can be countered by the argument that results, which are not optimum in Pareto-optimal terms, are excluded from the outset, thereby minimizing the cost of rectifying mistakes and also motivating participants to engage in its further evolution. This helps minimize the costs associated with major negotiations and allows compromises to be reached which would be unthinkable in an open, public debate.[90]

Consequently, in Japanese, this negotiation process is aptly described as '*suriawase*' (originally, the rubbing smooth or polishing of an earthenware pot) and '*kashi kari*' (give and take). This process removes any entrenched opposition which would render the further development of the decision-making process impossible. This mechanism can be described as transmoral with an ethos of flexible efficacy, since it fundamentally acknowledges the different aspects of each standpoint, approaching them with interest with the intention not of destruction or reversal, but of developing a pragmatic procedure for each decision. This method depends on a 'nose' for contradiction and a willingness and readiness to deal with it and then to create, in consultation, an acceptable reality to fit the situation, which makes sense of the fragmented worlds of groups, cliques, splinter and interest groups. The aim is pragmatic self-organization rather than optimum or maximum solutions, and the ability to remain focused on systematic, ideological thoughts.

In some form or other, *nemawashi* is used in all decision-making processes involving multiple groups or individuals (Figure 4.11). This is not necessarily followed by the bureaucratic '*ringi*' process, although informal decisions always have to be formalized,[91] either in the context of a formal discussion (*kaigi*) or by means of a 'decree' issued by a hierarchically superior authority, for example in the

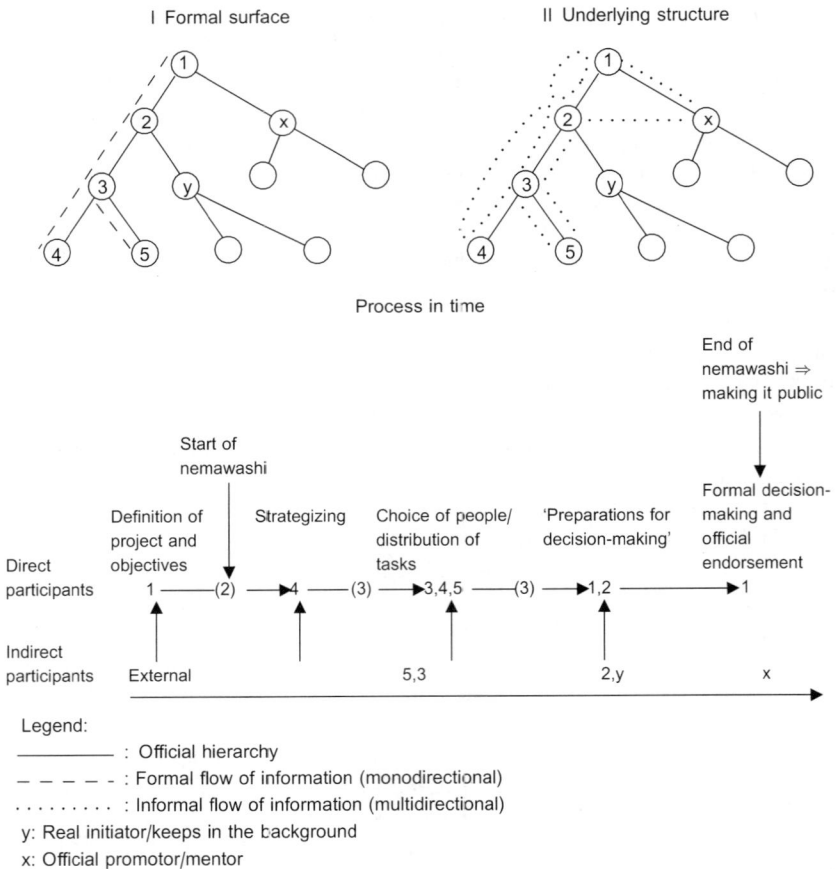

Figure 4.11   *The nemawashi decision-making process*
Source: Eli, M., *Sogo Shosha*, p 495

form of the notorious 'administrative guidance' (cf. Chapter 4, section III on Gyosei Shido). Hardly any decisions are, however, reached during these 'pseudo' discussions.[92,93]

The acknowledged organizational force is still reason, unless it appears too concentrated in a spatial, structural and personal context. Diffuse reason, incorporating non-rational psychological, strategic and historical logic, appears to be the only type of reason acceptable, specifically in Japan. This mastership in soft logic may be the factor why Japan is a market leader in the research and application of 'fuzzy logic' technologies and complex computer games.[94] In Japan, neither open, rational debate *à la* Habermas nor direct control meets with approval. The method implicitly linked with decision-making in Japan is simply *provisional, situation-contingent* and *flexible consensus*, stemming not from a harmony of desires but from targeted performance objectives which take account of contradictory positions.

Ringi-seido, the role of formal decisions in decision-making

As demonstrated in the last chapter, the search for consensus and harmony (*wa to hakaru*), for the purpose of achieving goal-oriented progress is transferred, via the *nemawashi* process, to the group, which implies that individual responsibility is transferred to a large number of people. The much-propagated euphoria of consensus produced by this should not, however, be exaggerated; the outcome of *nemawashi* can be pessimistically described as an ultimate state, resembling the 'living death' which is used in a cosmic context to describe the condition created when all the molecules of the universe come to a standstill for want of energy. This is poignantly summarized by Wolferen: 'What is mislabeled "consensus" in Japan, however, is a state of affairs in which no concerned party thinks it worthwhile to upset the apple-cart.'[95] After a provisional decision has been taken within the *nemawashi* system, the next step is to formalize it, affix it with an official stamp, thereby symbolically legitimizing the decision ready for implementation.

In etymological terms, the word '*ringi*' can be elucidated as follows: '*rin*' is considered untranslatable and means something like 'submitting a proposal to a superior for his approval', and '*gi*' corresponds approximately to the terms 'consultations' and 'decisions'. Thus, in this context it relates to a consultative proposal submitted to senior management; a proposal which so closely reflects senior management thinking that its ratification is automatic. The procedure on which the term is based certainly appears as lengthy and complex as the English translation of the term itself. The *ringi* system consists of the following individual stages:[96]

A plan or proposal (the so-called *ringisho* or *ringi* document) is drafted at lower or middle level, either at the request of a superior, or as the result of well-founded self-initiative. It may consist of a single decision proposal or several decision options together with their implications. The *ringisho* is then submitted to other organizational units involved, of the same hierarchical level, who are entitled to approve, amend, annotate or supplement the proposal with additional proposals, and so on. Before it is passed on, a departmental seal is affixed to the proposal, confirming both the *ringisho* and the fact that it has been brought (officially) to their attention. Since, in practice, not just one but many *ringi* are processed simultaneously, it is not unusual for a large number to pile up on the desk of a particular employee, who then practices the widespread custom of blind-stamping. This does not signify that he holds the material or the process in low esteem but represents, to some extent, a declaration of intent, based on an acceptance of collective responsibility, out of loyalty, without taking account of the circumstances. Reischauer correctly and pragmatically interpreted the value of a '*hanko*'[97] as: 'seen and not actively opposed'.[98,99]

After obtaining the affirmation or qualifying remarks, the originator of the *ringisho* places his stamp on it and forwards it to his superiors. After evaluation at senior level, during the course of which the *ringisho* also passes through each of the relevant lateral functions concerned, it arrives on the desk of the President, Director or Board member responsible. The *ringisho* now bears a dozen or more stamps, which prevents any localization of individual responsibility. 'The ringi system is a superb mechanism for diffusing and finally obfuscating all responsibility.'[100] The real, hidden function of the *ringi* procedure is to 'legitimize the narrative', and Takamiya empirically portrayed the function as shown in Figure 4.12.

Empirical research clearly validates the symbolic legitimization function, as well as communication and concept-assimilation functions.[101] The combination of *ringi* and *nemawashi* can also be described, in brief, as the Quality Circle of Middle Management in which a concept, the solution to a problem, is improved circularly and peripherally via a ritual which leads to its optimization as far as the relevant superior is concerned. This is particularly necessary as clear instructions are never given, only ever clues, hints and contextual innuendoes which refer to larger dimensions/strategies/visions within the Japanese management system in general. Only the skill of the employee determines how the task is interpreted.[102] The meaning of *nemawashi*, in this context, is the lateral exchange between employees in

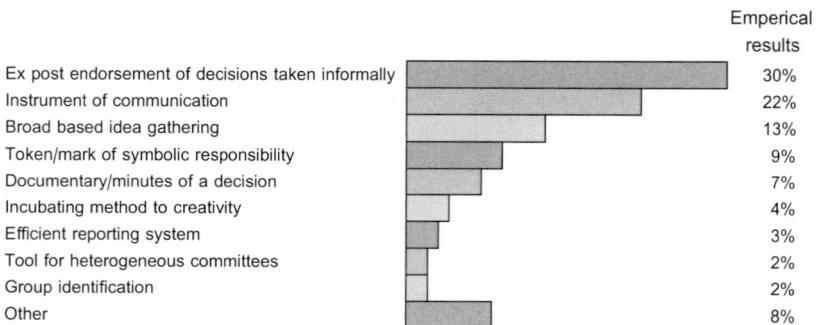

	Emperical results
Ex post endorsement of decisions taken informally	30%
Instrument of communication	22%
Broad based idea gathering	13%
Token/mark of symbolic responsibility	9%
Documentary/minutes of a decision	7%
Incubating method to creativity	4%
Efficient reporting system	3%
Tool for heterogeneous committees	2%
Group identification	2%
Other	8%

Figure 4.12   *Functions of the ringi process*
Source: Takamiya, S., 'Entwicklung des Management-Systems der japanischen Unternehmungen', p. 312

connection with the hidden intentions of management on the next highest rung of the ladder, and *ringi* is a vertical sounding out of these intentions:

> [T]he lower level man is not suggesting that things be done better or differently, he is just trying to get guidance from above as to what to do ... So this is what the magnificent system is there for: to find out what to do, not to propose any novel action.[103]

Sethi consistently defines the *ringi* system as 'a system of reverential inquiry about a superior's intentions'.[104]

The concept which dominates all group decisions is that of ultimate harmony (*wa*; cf. Chapter 3, section IV, 'the basic social context'). But here two dimensions, one represented by the abstract symbol of a close-knit group society and the other by the concrete desire to optimize goal-achievement, successfully overlap in a peculiarly Japanese fashion.[105] In this context, the special characteristics of the Japanese social structure ensure the optimum integration of human resources.[106] This can also be expounded as a reason for the extraordinary efficacy for which Japanese management is famous, both in terms of economic policy and enterprise. It is not only the decision-makers who actively participate in these processes; a broader spectrum of consultants, specialists, lobbyists and middlemen envelop this trend like a catalytic gaseous cloud.[107]

However, the communication process, which involves temporary decision-making groupings, is also important. The hierarchic structure of all Japanese companies and management systems is generally vertical, and combines in a unique way the responsibility of the group with that of the individual, involving all operational levels in the decision-making process. Although from the outside it appears to be the formalizing process of a homogeneous society, it is in fact a driving force, an underlying process of cooperation and *pragmatic consensus* over any *unopposed disagreement* which may exist.

If we again visualize the structure of a Japanese company or bureaucracy, we can see that within a company group or company sector the management elite is present in the form of a seemingly inextricable web, which is fractionally subdivided internally. Consequently, *responsibility for decision-making* extends *vertically* and *laterally*, in the form of a cumulative and collective decision-making process (*tsumiage hoshiki*). In this connection, Clark draws attention to the risk aspect of the decision-making mechanism, on which a different and interesting interpretation can be placed. Risk management is not achieved by means of control and centralization mechanisms, but by symbolic management of the group and group images. Clark reviews examples in which the superior in question assumes responsibility in a crisis, although he clearly had absolutely no involvement in the matter prior to the crisis.[108] Normally no-one is responsible, although everyone acts as if they were responsible. The *ringi* system minimizes the risks run by decision-makers: '... ringi as a mode of sharing responsibility ex post facto.'[109] The official aspect of the risk is pooled, spread and minimized to enable interests to interchange freely below the surface, thus ensuring that *risk management* always achieves the best possible results for the decision-maker. In an optimum situation, if the decision was a good one the author of the proposal is apparent, but when bad decisions are taken no-one can really establish the identity of the initiator. Despite the fact that all the interested parties are involved and informed and will also implement the decision, they are shielded.

The implementation of decisions is always perceived as an intrinsic part of the decision-making process. The fact that everyone, in theory at least, has been able to influence the decision, eliminates the possibility of any subsequent blatant contradiction. As a result, the *ringi* document or *ringisho* acquires a new dimension in terms of meaning: it indicates that a decision has been taken and that everyone has been immediately notified. Superficial symbols apply rather than profound standards. The symbols are more real than the reality, which is particularly appropriate when one considers the Machiavellian tactics permanently in the background.

In this section it has been demonstrated how, in both the economic and political arena, a temporary network which affects the formal official elements of decision-making is built up with the *nemawashi*. (Only) symbolic significance is attached to this temporary network, which appears in the guise of a structured decision-making process, legitimizing minor situation-dependent provisional 'histories'. In this context, managers are not perceived as leaders but as charismatic coaches, and employees as participants, in an intensive decentralized and delocalized communication network, rather than position fillers. Contingent understanding and pragmatic process thinking, as well as improvisation, clearly take priority over any 'metaécrit' of a systematic or rational nature. Furthermore, the example of the *ringi* shows how a document, decision or process is multicoded in quite definite terms. Multiple dimensions of interpretation (formal, symbolic, practically

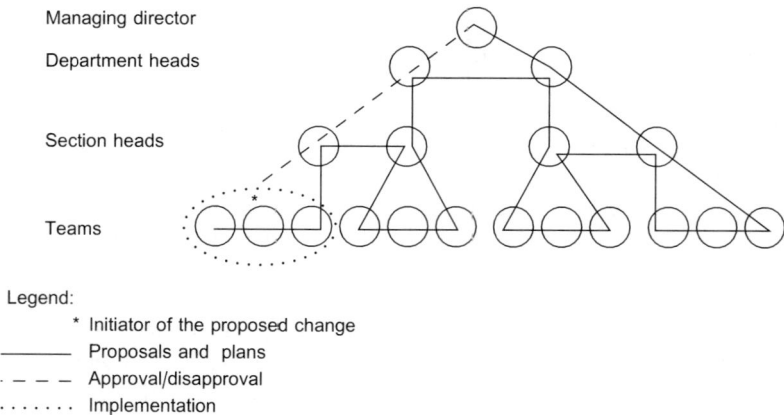

Legend:
        * Initiator of the proposed change
—————— Proposals and plans
· — — — Approval/disapproval
· · · · · · · Implementation

Figure 4.13   *Formal steps of a ringi process*
Source: Eli, M., *Sogo Shosha*, p. 556

realistic, Machiavellian) mutually permeate below the surface of a seemingly bureaucratic administrative process. Figure 4.13 elucidates the channels involved in a *ringi* process.

'Amakudari', the institutionalization of the informal network

At this juncture, we present a summary of the other special features of Japanese economic practice. *Amakudari* may be derived from the word *amaeru* (descending from heaven) and signifies the start of a new career on retirement from a company or official post for reasons of age. According to the last census, taken in 1980, 82 per cent of Japanese between the ages of 60 and 64, and 45 per cent of those aged 65 and over were still in employment.[110,111]

Amakudari is a widespread practice, at senior level, and denotes the *influence exerted indirectly, bilaterally and in the longer term* between the former employer and the new employer. The study undertaken by Johnson into the number of deputy ministers of the MITI remaining in post since the Second World War, discovered that all the most senior company positions (mainly in Zaibatsu companies) have been traditionally occupied by those of post-retirement age.[112]

To some extent, each ministry is also involved in the outplacement of executives approaching retirement, for this enhances the influence of the ministry; the more retirees it is able to place in prestigious companies the higher its status. These relationships are somewhat analogous to those between Japanese (and, to a far lesser extent, American) universities and their graduates.[113] Johnson highlights the trench warfare conducted between the ministries over senior positions within the government machine. The Japanese themselves refer to the gangster-like tactics applied during 'negotiations' (*'yakuza no nawabari arasoi'*) and talk about a 'fenced-off turf' (*'nawabari'*), which indicates the importance of these processes in terms of their subsequent influence on companies (and vice versa). Secondly, it clearly demonstrates how strongly considerations of power strategy dominate the Japanese economic and political world.[114] Certainly, this is an old and dated concept, but it is still valid as the number of *amakudari* cases is certainly not declining, just the strategic placing of key persons is taking on more modern forms and shapes.

This principle of personal interrelationships, which is consecutive rather than contemporary, nevertheless results in a level of interrelationships impossible to accurately measure using quantitative or legalistic analyses or a naïve tunnel view of 'interlocking-directorships'. For this reason, Wolferen refers to these inter-relationships as 'one grand amalgam' and presents striking examples of their 'ethereal' (or better: untraceable) nature. Often a bureaucrat who has enjoyed a certain degree of commercial influence during his tenure of a key function, receives, when he retires (that is in his capacity as a retired, private individual), a discrete but fully legal gift of money (known as *senbetzu*) from various companies, the reasons for which are open to speculation but understandable nonetheless.[115] The result of this custom is that the bureaucrat, anticipating a favourable 'retirement position', adopts a pro-business approach whilst still in office. This pro-business approach increases as he approaches retirement which, given the seniority system in operation, automatically signifies greater power, which places him in a better position to support commercial interests. This complex interaction demonstrates the closely linked network of multiple interrelationships and strategies which exists informally and invisibly, although this is presented by 'Japan' as 'a complete entity' or amoeba-like organism. This level, in addition to personal commitment relationships ('*giri*', '*oyabun–kobun*' etc.; cf. Chapter 3, section IV, 'the basic social concept', and Chapter 4, section III on *oyabun–kobun*) manifests itself in the form of a self-supporting network. This is interrelational in terms of interchangeability and competition and generally consists of a non-systematic plurality of heterogeneous systems, held together by symbolic elements and formal common characteristics of a interreferential and coordinatory nature.

'Gyosei shido', informal management practice, the most effective means of bilaterally communicating economic policy intentions

Gyosei shido commands great respect, especially within the 'most prominent' Japanese ministries, such as MITI and MoF, and represents, on the one hand, a special combination of indirect innuendo and *ad hoc* recommendations and, on the other, concrete strategic objectives in terms of the coordination between private commercial and official institutions. Wakayama defines this special tool used by the Japanese bureaucracy as 'an administrative action, without any coercive legal effects, which encourages related parties to act in a specific way in order to realize some administrative aim'.[116]

This is conveyed by phrases such as 'administrative guidance' or 'informal management practice' which, according to Foljanty-Jost, are auxiliary terms used by academics to describe an overall palette of concrete, informal management practices:

> The aim of stimulating individuals or organizations non-commitally and adopting a course of action designed to ensure the attainment of the management objectives desired, are common features which categorize the various ways in which management exerts influence.[117,118]

This versatile method is used in each of Japan's commercial sectors for coordination purposes. For this reason, Foljanty-Jost estimates that over 50 per cent of all management practices are of an informal, consultative nature.[119]

This '*infiltration of private commerce by official objectives*' does not fit into any of the traditional, academic management categories which apply to regulatory or deregulatory measures, but is a symbolic political tool unrivalled in terms of perfection and level of efficacy. These private, informal management measures, which are usually discussed over a cup of tea in a quiet corner of the office, consist primarily of verbal intimations of the proposed action which bureaucracy would prefer private enterprise to take. The justification behind 'advice' of this type is usually macroeconomic in nature, 'in the general interest of the executor'. *Gyosei shido*' is not preceded by any *ringi* or *nemawashi* technique. Provisional, situation-dependent 'mini-narratives' are generated pragmatically in a provisional, private and improvisational manner which, although initiated by a government official, is implemented (and possibly modified) by commercial protagonists and ultimately by everyone. Whilst adhering to official objectives, bureaucracy is extremely flexible, indirect, *ad hoc*, person-oriented and discrete in its dealings. This is why it can allow itself, in the name of efficacy, to be unprincipled, embracing a 'transmoral, concrete ethos' in which indifference to conventions, public structures and bureaucratic symbols provides greater room for manoeuvre: anything that works, goes. This is perhaps one reason why this management technique, which is highly regarded abroad, is successful. Rather than using regulations and legislation, it achieves flexible commercial management by using indicators, interpreting case histories and casually coordinating. To use a stylized term, one could speak of a 'management by symbols'.

Collectively, *gyosei shido* probably represent the most effective interaction between state and commercial enterprise. Their acceptance and efficacy is drawn from a social preference for the informal rather than the open formal approach. Informal consultations and conflict-avoidance are general features of Japanese coexistence, and *gyosei shido* pander to this inclination since they are situation-determined, flexible and practical, rather than definition-dependent, and possess the ability to smooth out conflicting interests without being forced to adopt a confrontational stance. In addition, a specific, authoritarian approach exists in Japan in which *giri* and *on*,[120] as well as other Japanese sociological concepts, plays an eminent part.[121]

The 'secluded' nature of these consultations precludes any form of public or parliamentary control. However, to the Japanese, this *limited transparency*[122] is not negative; on the contrary, they perceive it as a 'friendly' management tool which prevents abrupt changes, loss of face or harshness *vis-à-vis* the addressee. To some extent it provides management without the managers, politics without the politicians and the distribution of information without the disruption caused by the public media. Management is able to move around peripherally (in terms of legality and responsibility), since nothing is regulated as far as these informal management practices are concerned. No legal restrictions whatsoever exist, which implies an open relationship towards existing legislation; that is, laws can be circumvented, replaced or supplemented, anything is possible. Because each party conducts its activities without legal constraint and within an intentionally unregulated legal arena, no-one can take recourse in the event of problems and each participant can claim success in positive cases.[123] This creates, for all concerned, a scenario of interpretations and references which each participant builds up himself in the hope that it will correspond to that of the other participants. The application of the internal and external group concept structure, already presented in Chapter 3, section IV, provides a useful explanation of *gyosei shido* mechanisms of action. Superficially ('*tatemae*'; external effect) they are merely behavioural appeals, but in essence ('*honne*'; internal effect) they are quasi compulsory in nature.[124]

Although there was a noticeable decrease in the influence exerted by this tool in the late 1980s and 1990s, due to the fact that industrials, particularly new international firms, became more self-assured in their approach to officialdom, we must assume that periods of crisis result in its wider acceptance.[125]

However, it is not just officialdom which initiates *gyosei shido*; companies, too, often request, *ex ante*, the opinions of bureaucrats on forthcoming projects in order to cover themselves and create a favourable impression. This results, over the course of time, in an interactive common interest in an area marked by conflict and dialectic in Western national economies. This shared interest extends into a network of relationships linked to historic episodes, in which cooperation prevails in spite of contradiction, in the form of a cognitive difference. It is precisely these contradictions which, with the help of the informal spontaneous structure of this management policy, generate creative forces which tolerate lateral inconsistencies and logical contradictions, with the aim of implementing, together with dissent, the economic development objectives generally applicable. Section IV below, in describing the rule of the MITI, offers a concrete explanation of how this occurs.

The Links between Politics, Bureaucracy and the Economy from an Overall Perspective

As demonstrated, informal transactions are of fundamental significance in terms of the close cooperation which exists between private enterprise and public institutions, irrespective of whether these transactions are in the form of a confidential discussion between *oyabun* and *kobun*, a *nemawashi* process or administrative guidelines. We can usefully apply the commonly-used straightforward system of formal measures, such as legal reward and punishment (subventions, withholding of permits, etc.), to only a very limited extent for clarification purposes. Official assistance, communiqués, recommendations, statements, official requests, opinions and so on are the primary implementation tools used in business management, with the actual application of rules relegated to a subordinate role.[126] Nothing is concrete or tangible, and the purpose of communication is always orientation rather than permanent definition.

Thus the term *'madoguchi kisei'* (window guidance) is aptly used in a monetary policy context, when the Bank of Japan or the Ministry of Finance announces its growth target 'forecast', within the framework of monetary policy. Here, too, a fundamental difference to Western economic policy is evident; that is restrictive regulation versus *evolutionary 'co'-planning*.[127] In Japan, all conceivable forms of economic control are possible. The spectrum extends from a passive form of paternal reproach to the more aggressive device of official export guarantees, with nothing ruled out *a priori* as a matter of principle. This is where we have to debunk some Western myths which only serve to present a false picture of economic coordination in Japan. Firstly, there is the myth that Japan is a sovereign state with its own central autonomous government. The second myth is based on the belief that Japan can be categorized as a capitalist free market economy and, finally, we must correct the erroneous idea that it is possible to define the dividing line between state and the economy.[128] Japan is becoming a hyperpluralistic society and is also striving for national consensus on a symbolic level, without prejudicing its traditions. Critics, arguing superficially, perceive this as a clique economy, swindle or corruption, but they are, in effect, extremely efficient mechanisms which have evolved over the course of time.

Consequently, the support structures of this intense relationship between state and economy are not easy to demonstrate in an institutional context. In Chapter 3, section IV and Chapter 4, section III ('selected interpersonal mechanisms') we have been able to explain some of these mechanisms in a sociographic context, but we now concentrate on the overall nature of this relationship. In the following sections we focus on the practical effect of this relationship in historic terms. Furthermore, the relevant literature is extremely contradictory and impossible to narrow down to a common denominator, due to the random views or special perspectives adopted by many authors. For example, Kevenhörster identifies four main links between the economy and politics: the directors of the major company groups representing the main industries and the banks; trade association representatives; the proprietors of the major concerns (for example, K. Matsushita (Matsushita), S. Honda (Honda) or S. Ishibashi (Bridgestone)) and representatives from the various industry associations. Conversely, Murakami traces three major relationships: those between government and industry; the companies and the unions and the companies and their suppliers.[129] Japanese literature also explores hypotheses similar to those presented here: Murakami describes a para-political nexus leading to the creation of compartmentalized pluralism; Inoguchi sees it as a group-wide bureaucracy-run pluralism, radically different to normal concepts of pluralism.[130]

Japan is incapable of creating a clearly defined image which fits perfectly into a predefined category. Its existence depends on mutual permeation, a positive rivalry of paradigms which results not in a lack of interest and communication but in a networked, contingent co-evolution between economic protagonists. This evolution has been taking place since the concept of a macroeconomic policy was brought to Japan by traders from the West, and will constantly continue to evolve, improve and become more refined.[131] This link is not permanently reinforced in an organizational context, but is propagated heterarchically via formal 'public' hierarchic systems. It can also visualize, without major assistance from the changing (superficial) political constellations, the objectives of the 'developing nation' and improve the *performance 'tune-up' of the system*, which is why Japanese bureaucrats casually declare: 'Prime Ministers come and go, but we [ministry officials] are forever.'[132]

The Japanese government can take a more relaxed view of its national development role than a Western regulatory government. It perceives itself as less of a patron, policeman or patriarch, preferring to cast itself in the role of *trainer* or *'facilitator'*. 'Although Japanese bureaucracy is indeed omnipresent, in the industrial area, it has a co-ordinating effect, almost never working against the market but rather accelerating market processes.'[133] Whereas in Europe and North America the cooperation, opposition or juxtaposition of state and commerce is the subject of bitter and often ideological or idealized dispute when academics debate the economy,[134] Japan now has a structure in which cooperation between commerce and state is constantly evolving.[135] 'Often, the interrelationship between state and economy in Japan is characterized by the slogan "Japan Inc.", which refers to the close confidence enjoyed by these two elements of society, both of which represent the interests of the nation.'[136] The term 'Japan Inc.' or the European equivalents, Japan plc, Japan AG, fail to describe Japanese reality and demonstrate a lack of consideration of other traditions and developments.[137]

When this reflection is viewed from a distance it becomes clear that, in this context, informal interrelationships ('*kone*', '*jinmyaku*'; cf. Chapter 3, section IV on group relationship structures) produce an undefined division or deconcentration of power which cannot adequately be conveyed by unifying methods of interpretation. We can create an interpretation device which has none of the characteristics associated with a quest for or a discovery of meaning, by lining up smaller workable 'narratives' without being obliged to fall back on absolute universalia. Each protagonist lives within his perspective of the truth, in his section of the 'consensus', thereby maintaining a superficial symbolic harmony via the use of conventions (for example, the use of the vague symbol 'Japan Inc.'). For these reasons, the 'seductive idea' of an economic monolith must be rejected in favour of a much more dangerous, albeit nebulous 'hostile concept' – that of an invisible network.[138] All these monofactorial concepts can only serve as journalistic aids:

> The approach popularly labeled 'Japan Inc.' conceives Japan as closely knit and hierarchically ordered, with the government controlling the economy in a top-down fashion through regulation and other mechanisms.[139]

Other authors drawn on other factors: Japan's version of a 'Protestant ethic' as the driving force, Japan's unique composition of social values or Japan's well-known homogeneity are just some of the indicators.[140]

Although Wheeler forecasts a decline in the efficacy of industrial influence as a result of the increasing level of interrelationship between the Zaibatsu and the company-wide trend towards globalization,[141] one might assume that this network of economic coordination would undergo a dialectic process in order to adapt to new constellations.[142] In the future, too, Japan's special approach to industry, with its diffuse elite and indirect mechanisms of influence, will be perceived as effective, a marker for future development.

A Model Illustrating the Template on which Japanese Economic Coordination is Based

In the context of the conclusions reached earlier in this section in respect of the organizational and personal principles which apply to economic coordination, it is interesting to consider the models developed by American and Japanese political scientists to explain the relationship between trade associations and companies on the one hand, and government institutions on the other, in terms of the formulation of government policy. Four of the best-known models from the plethora of models studied are used here as examples:[143] (1) the model of a dominant state bureaucracy ('MITI-Super-managers etc.), (2) the model of a three-pronged power elite (politics, civil servants, banks; the tradition according to Galbraith of a bureaucratic–political–industrial complex), (3) the pluralistic model (diverse, conflicting power syndicates) and (4) the neocorporationalist model (joint economic decision-making by companies and policy-makers).

All these approaches are universal to the extent that they attempt to explain economic events in Japan quasi monofactorially. Based on the conclusions reached in previous chapters, we can, however, conclude that the only successful, basic model is the one which is open and iteratively definable. This model is based mainly on three dimensions: firstly, we can cite *economic coordination* which acts as the *nucleus* for the frequently documented interaction between *government, bureaucracy* and the *captains of industry* (see Figure 4.14). It is within this triumvirate that macro-economic political coordination and the creation of visions for society takes place.

From a second perspective, this coordination is split into *vertical and lateral lines of cooperation* between the *individual decision-makers* (Figure 4.15). This occurs on the one hand between state and commerce, and on the other within a specific sector and individual concerns as well. This is where the implementation strategies for major ideas and visions are conceived and prepared for implementation.

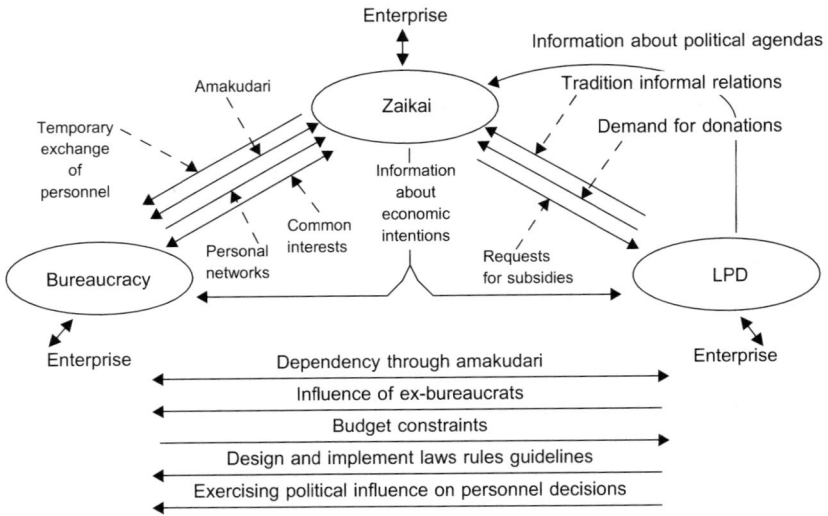

Figure 4.14   *The nucleus of economic coordination*
Source: Kevenhörster, P., *Wirtschaft und Politik in Japan*, p. 66

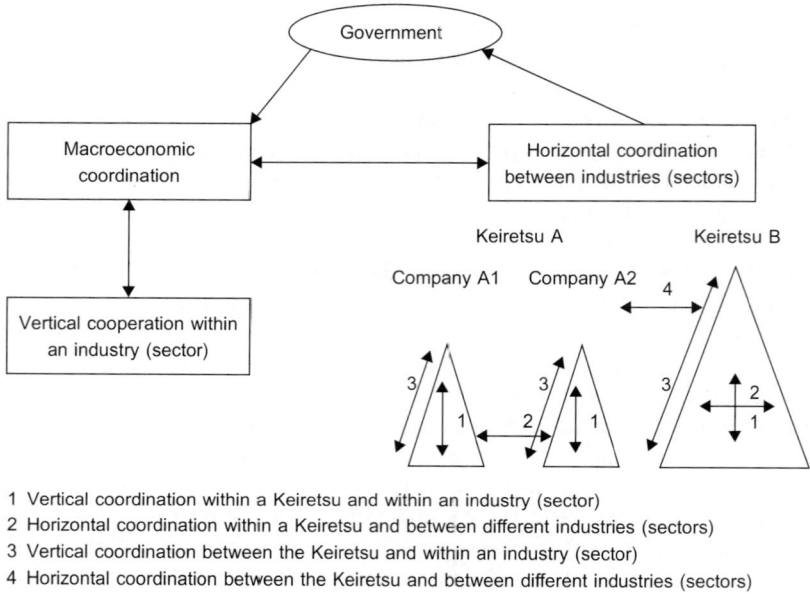

1 Vertical coordination within a Keiretsu and within an industry (sector)
2 Horizontal coordination within a Keiretsu and between different industries (sectors)
3 Vertical coordination between the Keiretsu and within an industry (sector)
4 Horizontal coordination between the Keiretsu and between different industries (sectors)

Figure 4.15 *Typical patterns of coordination in business and economic questions 'relevant' to politics*

Depending on their orientation in terms of company groups, sectors and hierarchies, these individual relationships can, in practice, be systematized as shown in Figure 4.16. The actual implementation of all major strategies, whether macroeconomic in nature or on the enterprise level, can take place at the *individual level within a group environment*. This involves the Japanese decision-making concepts (*ringi, nemawashi* and administrative guidance etc.) discussed earlier, which, even at this basic level, dispel any possibility of direct classification and clarity by creating a vagueness which to the outside observer represents an indeterminate situation, with the result that only an 'insider' can make sense of it using the interpretations at his disposal (see also Figure 4.17).

This illustrates the impossibility of simply and unambiguously identifying a core or fixed structure. No general principles apply, but only local (fractional) realities created within the appropriate environment (world).

One must revert to these basic models in their adapted form during an analysis of Japanese corporations, since these components can also be usefully applied here to

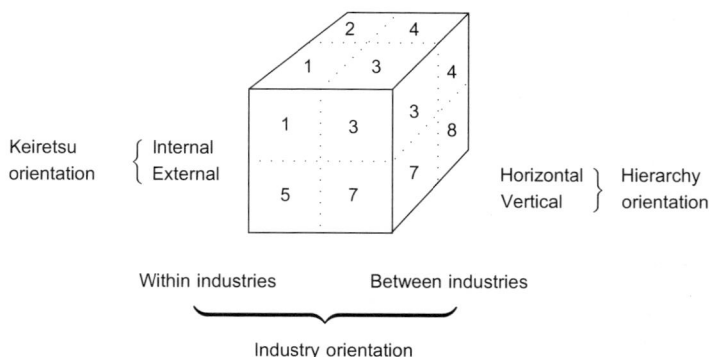

Figure 4.16 *Systematics of company networks*

Group	Industry	Hierarchy	Example	Function
1 Intern	Within	Vertical	Upstream downstream suppliers	Operational coordination
2 Intern	Within	Horizontal	Lateral coordination between affiliated/partner firms	Information exchange
3 Intern	Between	Vertical	Management of overall Keiretsu	Strategizing/coordination of overall behaviour
4 Intern	Between	Horizontal	Lateral coordination of Keiretsu	Implementation of strategy/ philosophy
5 External	Within	Vertical	Regional structures of associations	Lobbying
6 External	Within	Horizontal	Industrial organzation/associations	Steering of the association
7 External	Between	Vertical	Direct competition	Profit generation
8 External	Between	Horizontal	Direct competition	Coordination of alliances/cartels

clarify prevailing conditions.[144] The initial intention is, however, to illustrate the pragmatic deployment of fundamental Japanese concepts in the economic sector, in order to explain their characteristics more clearly in praxi.

IV   THE BASIC PRINCIPLES OF STRUCTURAL CHANGE IN JAPAN

The Role of the MITI in General Economic Policy

Inevitably, in any economic debate, one name crops up, the initials of which represent the embodiment of the entire mythology surrounding 'Japan's economic strategies': MITI, Japan's Ministry of Trade and Industry. As became clear in the previous chapter, this universal concept of a single national coordinator for all commercial activities cannot just be accepted *per se*.

As *The Economist* determined, the nature of economic structural control in Japan may well represent 'the most intelligently dirigiste system in the world today'. It is staffed by the best brains in the country[145] and, although multidirectional and

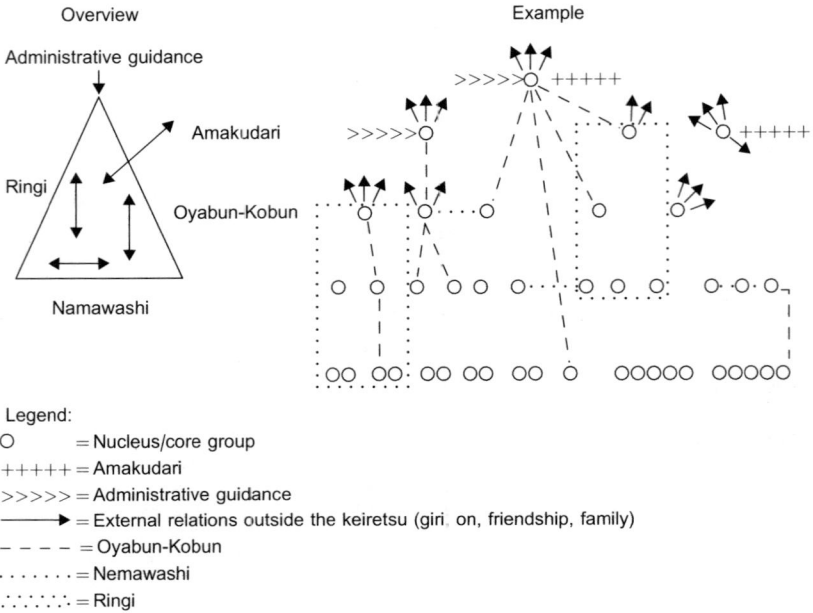

Figure 4.17   *General functional principles*

indirectly suggestive in effect, is never unidirectional and autocratic. Official organs have never been in overall charge in terms of the direct transfer of resources, and the influences affecting resources have only ever been induced by means of visions, recommendations and so on.[146] 'The government, therefore, has a direct and intimate involvement in the fortunes of the "strategic" industries (the term is widely used, but not in the military sense) that is much greater than a formal or legal comparison between the Japanese and other market systems would indicate.'[147] The foreign assessment of the MITI as the core or 'nerve centre' of Japanese economic power is certainly exaggerated when one considers that practically every Japanese ministry operates a similar system of industrial cooperation (*kyocho taisei*) within the scope of their activities, and that it is only coordination and communication mechanisms as a whole which make up the complex system which is Japanese economic strategy. Of equal importance to the MITI are the Ministry of Finance (MoF), which is responsible for all monetary and financial matters, and the Economic Planning Agency (EPA), whose 'policy guidelines' are implemented by all the ministries.

In the context of this analysis, it is impossible to draw a clear diagram which illustrates the distribution of power between the various governmental departments. Governmental structure is too variable and strangely undefined and its activities are, to the outsider, 'a maze of impenetrable government supports and subsidies'. Furthermore, the distribution of authority between the departments is apparently totally open to negotiation. Consequently, major disputes between the different departments create constantly changing power constellations.[148]

Even at intraministerial level it is impossible to identify a relevant structure. Although the superficial formalia of a sophisticated bureaucratic structure do exist – that is a minister, deputy minister, parliamentary secretary, secretariat and the various professional bodies (in the case of the MITI: commercial policy, commercial administration, industrial policy, regional industrial structure, core industries, and the engineering, information and consumer goods sectors), as well as subordinate authorities (in the case of the MITI: natural resources, the patent office, small and medium-sized companies and industrial technology) – the nature of this top layer is seldom unambiguous. Just like the old Chinese practice of dual occupancy, perfected during the Tokugawa period in Japan, higher bureaucratic positions, in particular, are held simultaneously by two people, the aim of which is to ensure that the two occupants check each other for compliance and performance.[149] This diagrammatic mode of expression fails to reveal the decision-makers or the decision-making processes themselves, which can be approximated only by conducting a more thorough analysis of the influential cultural aspects – cf. Chapter 3, section IV ('the special features of Japanese Society') and Chapter 4, section III ('basic structural units').

Consequently, the image of a monolithic, stable and omniscient 'big brother' MITI, which the West is only too ready to call upon, is no longer sustainable. Governmental departments are not solely responsible for paradigmatic change, although *long-term renaissance* could possibly be ascribed to them. Nor can private institutions (societies, lobby groups, informal clubs) be considered the sole initiators. Their role is more to provide *communication assistance* and to *process and disseminate information*. The role of *operational conceptualization* and *initial implementation* can be attributed to Japan's multinational corporations. Responsibility for Japan's successful performance does not rest solely with one institution or company, a single individual or group of individuals. The decade-long momentum towards future-oriented change can be attributed, first and foremost, to *flexible, concerted action*.[150]

This consistently raises the issue of whether defined methods or familiar political processes account for the success of Japan's economic strategy. One of the most important features of Japanese economic strategy is the combination of long-term social *designs for the future* – 'visions' (or '*bijon*') – and the concept of strategic industries, which are also known as key industries. These visions are generally created by governmental departments (including the EPA and MITI) and are vague, fluid images of the future, with the Japanese nation posing as the indistinct addressee. They should not be compared with the famous '5-year plan' associated with socialist countries. Contrary to a 5-year plan, which sets out the precise steps required to reach entirely economic objectives, these visions portray the future in anticipatory terms, an event for which preparatory measures must be taken. These visions and their formulation process stimulate a wide debate consisting of an intensive exchange of information whose coordination then acts as a platform for economic action.[151,152] This process, together with the 'pull factor' exerted by a highly imaginative presentation of ideals, generates strong dynamics, thanks to its flexibility of implementation in economic terms. In spite of all protectionist theories, this process opens up a window of opportunity which focuses purely on the future, rather than on the protectionism and traditionalism of the past and on the positive anticipatory policy of alignment founded upon it.[153]

Thus, the economy can be perceived as non-preferential, a *portfolio of sectors*, each with its own individual parameters (energy requirements, foreign links, technology, labour-intensity, etc.). On the one hand, this can lead to the infiltration of structural policy by theoretical financial concepts such as the investment portfolio, in terms of risk-spreading, risk/return ratios, etc. and, on the other, the creation of marketing-oriented approaches to product and market portfolios. These portfolios, together with relative production factors and production growth, enable us to identify the famous 'Stars, Dogs, Cash Cows and Question-marks' industries and anticipate opportunities and false trends.[154]

We list below some of the criteria included in the MITI and EPA analyses used to select target industries ('sunrise' or 'sunset' industries):

- major input/output links with the rest of the economy;
- a significant difference in domestic and foreign technological standards;
- long-term growth forecasts;
- elasticity in sector earnings;
- demand for Japanese goods dependent on real global income; and
- the relative benefit of technological advances to a business sector.[155]

A regrouping of this nature, in economic terms, produces *national projects* which are definitely comparable with major American projects like 'putting a man on the moon' or the 'Manhattan (atom bomb) project', the only difference being that the major endeavours of the Japanese ensure that the economy is permanently in a state of momentum, continually adapting to prevailing conditions. This is illustrated, quantitatively, by a variation coefficient of industrial structure which is almost twice as high as that of other G7-countries.[156]

As diverse as these basic models of *transformation induction* are, they can be demonstrated simply by listing some of the economic tools used over the last 20 years, although these cannot be fully enumerated. Equally, it is unhelpful to classify these measures rigidly since Japan has no tools which are distinct or 'pure' in form; generally speaking they are always used as combined or mixed forms.[157] A list of the measures applied includes the following examples:[158]

- Monetary policy measures (currency control, fixed exchange rates);
- Export measures (import restrictions, postponement of the liberalization of commercial markets, formal and specifically informal protectionist measures, etc.);

- Fiscal measures (taxation-induced changes in industrial structure);
- Anti-trust laws (and similar) measures (cartels, coordination of investments, 'industrial euthanasia');
- Capital market measures (postponement of the liberalization of capital markets, credits on the part of quasi-official financial institutions, preferential capital allocations);
- General measures (the promotion of R&D, flexible structural control by means of subsidies); and
- Informal measures (licenses, supervisory authorities ('*genkjoko*'), so-called closed public tenders etc.; cf. Chapter 4, section III ('selected interpersonal mechanisms').[159]

With the aid of these measures, the structure of the general planning system is that of a spiral-shaped self-referential process with constant 'controls' (checks and balances, 'reaffirmations', etc.), aimed in abstract terms at direct performance and the simultaneous optimization of information processing. Figure 4.18 schematically outlines the process of political planning in its role as a recurring, iterative process. But, in spite of all the vague diffuse images, assimilated in the context of economic modes of coordination, the scale of this 'coordination' is astonishing. McMillan[160] estimates that 35–40 per cent of trade is 'managed' in one form or another, that

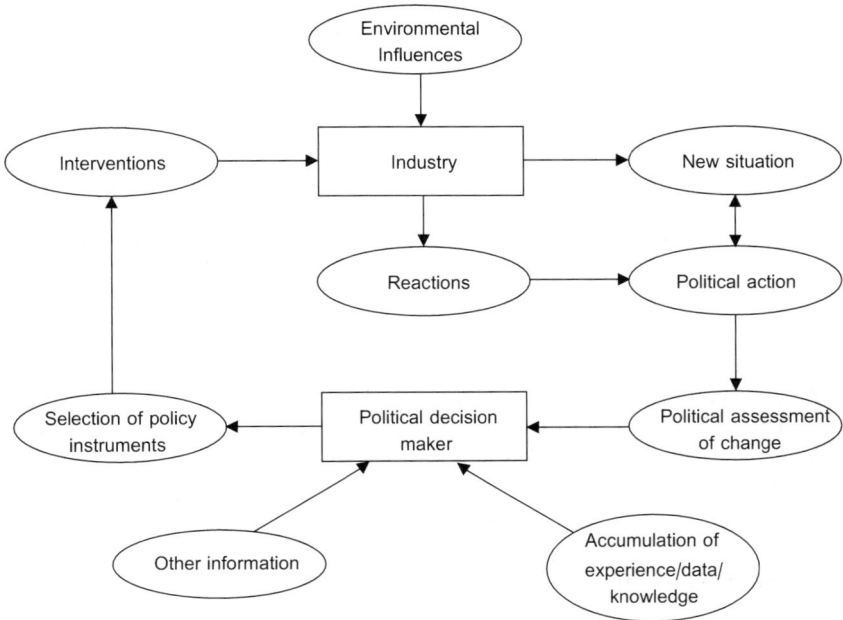

Figure 4.18 *Schematic overview of the political dynamics*
Source: Adapted from Yakushiji, T., 'The Government in a Spiral Dilemma', p. 267ff

is not determined by market structures but monitored by the bureaucratic system (in an international context, primarily by the MITI).[161]

The question of whether there are distinct analytical methods or isolable 'secret techniques' which ensure economic success must be answered negatively. Cultural principles (cf. Chapter 3) or fundamental sociological mechanisms (cf. Chapter 4, section III) are the main driving force behind development, rather than imposed 'management techniques' and rational procedures of a Western persuasion. Some of the factors which determine postmodernism serve here as helpful markers:

- Several, mutually applicable paradigmata of equal importance, producing paralogical contradiction; model pluralism and multidimensionalism exist and have a sensitizing effect in terms of divergence and difference.
- Diffuse hermeneutic reason, parataxis, learning in the midst of fundamental diversity, a high intensity of information, rapid information flow, mixing, permeating, ambiguities acting as classification criteria.
- Performance, efficiency, efficacy, pluralism and pragmatism act as target dimensions.
- Heterarchy (an interdependent network, free of hierarchy), provisional, contingent temporary relationship definitions, without power concentrations or centres, atomization of interests, a web of individual partial responsibilities, global (i.e. Japan-wide) total awareness determines individual decision-making, fundamental uncontrollability of organizational forms.
- Management by persuasion, proliferation instead of decreeing, imaginative and charismatic manager as a symbol, symbolic management, partial incompetence, entrepreneurialism, participation, flexibility as a general management principle.

These clues point more to the range of opportunities available in Japan in terms of economic coordination than to a one-dimensional, monocausal concept. In addition to the risk of trivialization, direct mechanical concepts such as 'the methods behind Japan's success' are always problematical due to their lack of transferability to other economic cultures. It is only at a higher level of abstraction, represented in this case by fundamental postmodern understanding, that general international trends can be easily identified without falling into the trap of emulating the copyist by 'learning from Japan's example'.

A new interpretation can be placed on Japan's experience in this form of economic coordination. Just how this postmodern economic constellation has been able, in reality, to achieve success in practical terms, is the subject addressed in the next chapter.

Economic Strategies from the Tokugawa Period to the Second World War

This period began in 1600 and restored peace and draconian regulation to the nation after centuries of war and chaos. A strict isolationist policy and a rigorous feudal and regulatory regime, which governed by a system of sophisticated checks and balances, produced a period of organized calm lasting more than 250 years. It was only with the advent of American 'black (steel-hulled) ships' in 1868 and their military superiority that this system disintegrated.[162] Webb characterized economic conditions at the end of the Tokugawa period as medieval feudalism, consisting solely of local economies which were poorly coordinated due to a deficient transport and communications infrastructure. Since everything in life was governed by traditions, customs, rules and laws, innovations were few and practically no coordination took place beyond the village. Leadership was usually local and *ad hoc* and lacked an active central power, in spite of the powerful political and military machine set up by the rulers which served *de facto* merely as a remote symbol which had none of the 'hands-on approach' needed to run the economy.[163]

During this period, the knights (samurai)[164] were purely a consumer class who, thanks to their leaseholds and fiefdoms, lived a carefree existence far removed from commercial activities. They had lost their role and authority when 'peace' came and had little respect for the commercial world. The (economically successful) merchant class enjoyed only limited social prestige, as at that time society in general held any kind of economic activity in poor esteem.[165] The external shock produced by the foreign offensive (from America), with its superiority in every commercial, technological and military sector, rocked this idyllic Orwellian society and opened up a gigantic technological chasm which led to the programmatic acquisition of new technologies.[166] But the fall of feudalism did not, in any sense, result in the abolition of feudal clan structures as some authors believe.[167] These structures merely shed their rigid, ritualistic outer layer to form a network of relationships which was more flexible, less visible and, consequently, less open to attack. The best indication of this is the fact that all of today's Keiretsu originate from precisely these erstwhile family clans. Although this 'restoration'[168] was not a political revolution, it represented a revolution in terms of Japan's attitude and its readoption of pugilistic, hegemonic, pre-Togukawa strategies.

As an emerging nation, Japan made strenuous efforts to catch up with the industrial developments of Western countries. The factors which were decisive, in terms of the initial steps towards the modernization of Japan's economy, were the concepts, processes and ideas which led to the development of a comprehensive production technology flexible enough to adapt to national conditions, rather than the latest machinery or physical assets.[169] Aptly, the 'war cries' of this period were '*wakon yosai*' (the Japanese spirit and foreign know-how) and '*sonno joi*' (honour the Emperor and resist the barbarians) and, especially, the visual image of the economic ideal: '*shikon shosai*' (the spirit of a warrior and the skill of a merchant). Consequently, the tasks of the subsequent Meiji period were defined: technological acquisition and modernization; industrial development which was strategically important to the nation; the rapid development of a domestic market for the economy; military build-up; centralization of state power; the abolition of feudal order and political equality with the West; automatic self-perpetuating partition into politically powerful cliques and elite groups; the intellectual assimilation of

Western culture; religious tolerance; and finally the cultural education of the masses.[170] Three slogans are predominant here: (1) '*bunmein kaika*': the development of a 'modern' state system with 'Western' institutional structures; (2) '*rekkyo*': the strength to become a world power; and (3) '*fukoku kyohei*': a rich country with powerful armed forces:

> [T]he history of the transition of Japan from Tokugawa feudalism to a modern bureaucratic state during the Meiji restoration period has often been traced but the central issue always remains the same: the astonishing speed of the transition from Shogun system to modern bureaucratic state; the absence of any charismatic leadership of any kind; the ease with which opposing groups were assimilated and, finally, Japan's sudden about-turn from complete isolation to a fanatical foreign abroad for 'better' solutions in almost every political and economic sector, whilst, simultaneously, maintaining its own social customs.[171]

Once again, we have to search for a connection, not in individuals or institutions but in the network actively used by some groups (known as: 'national hegemonic elite', the Samurai, the System etc. cf. Chapter 4, section III ('the centre: a Japanese elite?'), in structuring policies and the economy (in the form of the Zaibatsu). '[Japan's] statesmen judged that industrial development was too important to Japan to be entrusted to laws of supply and demand or to free enterprise.'[172] The purpose of these cartels and conglomerates; as far as the government and the groups behind it were concerned, was to keep imported know-how and the power associated with it in check.[173] This is how the typical configuration of the Zaibatsu gradually developed. This is when the concepts behind the Zaibatzu were first created, concepts which still apply even today. Using nation-centred entrepreneurs (Sakudo), also known as community-centred entrepreneurs (Ranis) as a starting point, state-supported diversification led to the formation of conglomerates which pursued a 'one-set strategy'. The aim was to turn each Zaibatsu group into a small, more or less self-contained and sector-wide national economy.[174,175]

Its function in this respect was two-dimensional; firstly, it would act as a window on the outside world (via the *sogo shosha* or general trading companies) and, secondly, as an internal coordination and financing machine for domestic markets (again, via the *sogo shosha* and the banks at the heart of the Zaibatsu). In this role it would be in a position to facilitate Japan's take-off. The results were not long in coming: by 1880 every Japanese town had a telephone system; in 1908 Mitsubishi was the first company in the world to introduce a product-related, divisional structure and, in 1920, Japan recorded a positive balance of trade. Within the first 50 years of this 'restoration', the production structure of the national economy shifted from tea and some other comestibles, silk and other textiles, to steel, ships, aircraft and other metal products.[176]

During the recession of the 1920s, the number of banks and companies drastically decreased in favour of the Zaibatsu, and the capital assets of the national economy were rigorously diverted into strategic industries. This is where

Japanese industrial policy started to focus on key industries and the active acceptance of 'cordial oligopolies' and cartels.[177] In 1936, the '*keiretzuka*' took place, that is the restructuring of the national economy into larger gigantic conglomerates which were regulated not by competition but by self-controls and state regulation. All economic activities were, in effect, controlled by the ministries of finance and trade who had two objectives: to increase production, and imports, although this was subject to foreign currency constraints. In 1939, the 'semi-nationalization' of companies started ('*kokyoka*' or making private companies publicly accessible). The first industries to undergo this transformation were those in the strategic sector (arms suppliers and other state suppliers), followed by the export industry and, finally, by the general consumer industry.[178] In 1941, these measures culminated in the general plan for the restructuring or closure of medium-sized and small companies,[179] which would have turned Japan into a single Zaibatsu system used by the military. During this period, capital-intensive industrialization, which was restricted in any case to the major companies, replaced the labour-intensive industrialization of the earlier Meiji period. This could be considered as Japan's initial economic miracle, if account is taken of the fact that production rose by more than 80 per cent during this prewar period.[180]

The concepts formulated during this period, which are still applicable today, are those of a technology-oriented, *structural strategy*; sustained *learning*; copying and improving; the use of 'courageous' *visions* to direct medium-term strategy; strategic *leadership on the part of Zaibatsu companies*; a clear preference for the industrial goods rather than consumer goods; the high level of political infiltration of politics by Zaibatsu managers; continuity of a management 'elite' despite changing structures; and a refocusing of hegemonic objectives from military policy to economic bureaucracy.

Economic Development up to the End of the 1970s

For Japan, total defeat in the Second World War was the greatest catastrophe of all times. They had never been conquered by 'foreigners' and the archipelago had never been occupied in the entire history of Japan. Doubts surrounding the uniqueness of the Japanese race surfaced but were softened into doubts about the military strategy adopted. Japan did not, however, degenerate into melancholic despair and apathy at the end of the war. Instead it viewed its situation as 'rock bottom', a point from which to develop new strategies. Former strategies had led to defeat and were consequently inferior and there was therefore no moral necessity whatsoever to hold on to them. Here, a decisive point in the 'history of Japan's postmodernity' again becomes apparent, for it was after this period that a state of absolute paralogism was achieved in respect of economic strategies. Emotional ties to long-established traditions no longer compulsorily prescribed specific courses of action. Equal validity is granted *a priori* to any method, even those deemed unethical from a Western viewpoint, the sole criterion being the extent to which it achieves the objective. In this context, a more radical interpretation, more akin to the 'anything that works, goes'[181] approach postulated by Feyerabend, was placed on the American proverb 'if you lose, learn'.

Whilst statements describing the customary setbacks to Japan's success as 'the fruit of conscious endeavor rather than the result of any adherence to a pre-existing cultural portfolio', meaning that Japan 'is not an exception in terms of Western social structure',[182] do in fact acknowledge the serious caesura of the war, they fail to take account of the aspects described in this work which pervade all of Japan's 'postmodern' structural elements. On the contrary, we can assume from the successes achieved by the Japanese economy after the Second World War that the combination of open social networks and symbolic intuitively shared ideals and specific unpredictable historic trends indicates a Japanese method which, precisely because of its flexibility, is ultimately able to prove its postmodernism and suitability as a post-industrial social ideal, provided there is understanding of its roots in terms of social history and it is applied in a purely logical and schematic manner.

The American occupation, led by the Supreme Command for the Allied Powers (SCAP) under General MacArthur, represents the starting point for this trend.[183] The objectives of SCAP, that is the break up of the Zaibatsu, land reforms, the restructuring of education, parliament and the legal system, were impossible to achieve unaided. Consequently, at administrative and senior management levels the Zaibatsu remained largely intact. Although these elements were fundamentally opposed to foreign intervention, they accepted America as the conqueror, a source of learning. In particular, the guiding principles behind American industry were of the greatest interest to Japan's commercial management, although anti-trust ideology was one undesirable side-effect which had to be confronted. MacArthur was acknowledged as a 'temporary Shogun' but his intentions were systematically adapted and perverted to suit Japanese objectives, using the trusted '*menjuku fukuhai*' strategy (superficially performing a task to the letter whilst placing a completely different interpretation on it below the surface).

The 'Holding Company Liquidation Commission' or self-elected *American 'trustbuster'* perceived the Zaibatsu, in particular, as the source of all evil. In this context, '*menjuku fukuhai*' became the focus of the most serious and also the most successful confrontations. Since holding companies became illegal, other groupings had to be found. The first steps taken to reintroduce industrial cooperatives were: share-block exchanges, interlocking directorates, verbal trade agreements and an impenetrable web of informal clubs and organizations. The former Zaibatsu were the very first companies to recover their sound commercial status following these postwar structural modifications, although they quickly outstripped their prewar competitiveness in terms of scale and power diversification. So the MacArthur plan to destroy the conglomerates ultimately resulted in the global dominance of these concerns. An outspoken way of interpreting this would be that General MacArthur was responsible for the dominant position now held by Japan and its superiority over America. On the two questions, firstly, of whether production should be increased or greater emphasis placed on achieving price stability and, secondly, as to whether light or heavy industry should be promoted, SCAP decided to increase production and focus on heavy industry, whilst concentrating economic development on a few key industries. The MITI was put in charge of foreign currency controls which represented, for the trade and industry ministry, 'the single most important instrument of industrial guidance and control that MITI ever possessed'. In 1949, the exchange rate was fixed at $1 = 360 yen until 1971, seriously undervaluing the yen, which indirectly boosted exports and actually fueled the export boom of the 1960s and 1970s.[184]

By the mid 1950s, the old Zaibatsu, which were by now called the Keiretsu (see Chapter 1, on 'the business revolution'), once again dominated economic activity and were therefore powerful enough to be the driving force behind the *modernization of the reconstruction process* and the *technological advances* needed to close the gap between Japan and Western industrial nations. The primary objective of the first postwar Prime Minister, Yoshida, was national independence (*waga kuni keizai no jiritsu ni tsuite*) and his 'economy first policies' became known as the 'Yoshida doctrine'. The economic boom produced by this doctrine was named the 'Jinmu boom' (after Jinmu, the legendary first ruler of Japan).[185]

Global economic conditions also favoured an *expansive economic strategy*, an opportunity immediately seized upon by Japan:

> the world economy following World War II offered Japan an extremely favorable environment ... Japan must strike out for the frontiers of the new industrial society on its own strength and initiative. Moreover, it is probably safe to say that the kind of new industrial society that Japan builds will have considerable impact on the whole world.[186]

Japan benefited to a greater extent than any other country from the global postwar situation: a liberalized US market, a strongly subsidized and isolated domestic market and an economy which favoured industrial production more than the consumer provided an ideal basis for the export growth of the 1960s.[187] Excessive competition between the various Keiretsu groupings, coupled with high rates of productivity, inevitably led to overproduction and the MITI introduced a quota system, channeling surpluses into exports. The theory was that the scalar effects on production would cut costs which would, in turn, enhance export opportunities.[188] Thus the slogan for the early 1960s was '*shuchugo teki yushutsu*', which translates roughly as 'a concentrated flood of exports'. The overall picture depicting this export strategy can be summarized as follows:[189]

The colonial periods of the 1930s in Manchuria were retrospectively perceived as 'the great proving ground' for Japanese industrialization. During this period, the Japanese regime exercised the rudiments of forced industrialization. After the Second World War, this industrialization process took place on the home front, shielded by strong protectionist measures (based on the 'infant industries' arguments expressed by List). Maximum use was made of a Darwinian-style rivalry between process, companies and products in order to ripen them for a promising global position. The third phase, which started in the mid-1980s, even went so far as to relocate production sites to foreign countries, creating space at home for major new projects. For twenty years, these enormous material efforts were supported by the Japanese without complaint, for the principle of production supremacy (*'seisan daiichi shugi'*) considers sacrifice to be an essential prerequisite for long-term growth and the attainment of a dominant global position. At the expense of domestic consumers, who were forced to accept short-term allocation deficiencies, Japan pursued long-term strategies designed to facilitate high growth rates due to higher rates of investment, which in the longer term 'overcame' the deficiencies.[190]

In principle, this strategy worked until the 1960s, when the Japanese pain threshold changed markedly. Global awareness of the limited nature of resources also started to filter through during the 1960s. The 1970s and 1980s brought increased uncertainty among buyers and sellers: the oil crises of 1973 and 1979, the US embargo of 1973, the stockmarket crashes of 1987 and 1989, the property crash of 1989 were only the tip of the iceberg. This is why the MITI promoted the so-called 'sunrise industries' (chiefly, the service industry, robotics, high-tech and the health and education sectors), in order to lessen dependency on raw materials. This is where the philosophy of growth changes course to take greater account of the utilitarian value of growth and is consequently able to pacify domestic consumers.[191]

The first stage of the *restructuring of industry into an information society* was a direct result of the above.[192] The intended objective was generally purported to be higher processing rates with the following industries promoted: R&D-intensive industries (e.g. computers, robotics, circuit boards and semi-conductors); 'high processing industries' (office communications, office automation, numerically controlled machinery, etc.); design-oriented industries (e.g. the fashion industry, electrical appliances and advertising) and genuine information industries (databases, software, systems, engineering, universities, etc.).[193] Just as with the advent of the black ships (the American steel-hulled ships in 1854), it took an external shock (in this case in the form of a shortage of resources) before Japan was able to convert its poor starting place into a strong competitive position. Although both oil crises had a greater negative impact on Japan than, for example, Germany, Japan was in a better position to use them to its advantage and also recovered from them more rapidly.[194] It is in this context that radical adaptability, unprejudiced learning and an unqualified desire for success,[195] can be perceived as postmodern success criteria in times of radical change.

Using the modernization or 'catch-up' phase as a starting point, an *export machine* was set in motion which offered import substitution and protection to the emerging industries and subsequently resulted in global power. This constituted Japan's main strategy until the end of the 1970s. The next phase was to move this export machine abroad in the form of Japanese production plants in foreign countries and, as a result of the economic crisis it had experienced, Japan began, at the end of the 1970s,[196,197] to restructure its economic base to resource-efficient, immaterial 'know-how industries'. The 1980s were a transitional period during which the purely economic target groups of 1950 to 1980 were balanced up with the comprehensive social plans of the 1980s and 1990s.

The 1980s and 1990s

In the past, the aim of Japanese industrial policy had been to catch up with the West. This involved the use of structuring measures, mainly of a protectionist nature, with the emphasis being on sectoral promotion and resource allocation. However, the catch-up process could be considered complete by the middle/end of the 1970s. The subsequent objective was not only to trump the West in actual economic terms, but also to achieve Western standards in the social sphere. The catalogue of objectives focused on the following: quality of life, increased high-tech activities, progressing the trend towards a tertiary sector and intensifying the transfer of mass production to foreign sites. In terms of structural policy, the 1980s is usually characterized in the following terms:

- the decade of the Ministry for International Trade and Industry (MITI);[198]
- [another] decade of intensified capital allocation within very narrow target sectors (growth imbalance);[199]
- the decade of intensified implementation of protectionist measures targeted at problem areas in the domestic market and new markets, in spite of international discussions on liberalization;[200]
- a reintensification of state planning parameters within the dynamics of the national economy;[201]
- concerted efforts on the part of state and the economy to coordinate purely economic aims with social objectives.[202]

Zysman *et al.* and Nijno present a synthetic view in which there is a gradual trend away from primary and secondary sectors in favour of information and know-how-based industries (high-tech, media, general intangibles and, to a lesser extent, the service industry in the narrower sense of the word) as the objective of Japanese industrial policy over the next 20 years.[203] This objective was concretely defined in the 1980s and Japan was caught up in the dilemma of whether to protect the status quo or change to a forward-looking structure. This conflict has gradually been resolved in favour of structural change.[204] The objective here is more ambitious than that of simply adapting economically to the growth curve pursued by the Japanese economy in terms of international competitiveness; it is an objective designed to economically, socially and intellectually prepare Japanese society for conditions in the next millennium. To this extent, the 1980s was a *transitional period*, during which exclusively *economic target structures were balanced with meta-economic ones*.

A résumé of the last 20 years shows that some sectors (electronics, robotics, automobiles, precision instruments etc.) were the clear winners, whilst others lost out (steel, mining, major chemical manufacturing and textiles). Of greater interest than a simple status review are the sectors which were intensively promoted during the 1980s. The palette of projects[205] involved was extremely diverse, and was related to the intensification of new product and materials development (semi-conductors, superconductivity, new ceramics) in order to create better methods and

brand images; the leisure industry; dilution of the dichotomy of banks/financial institutions; softening of the dividing lines between different sectors; expansion of bank activities; communication and information-processing industries; office technology; software; 'intelligent buildings', factory automation; information networks; realtors for overseas properties; transport systems and biotechnology. Despite this diversity, we can identify important basic trends: firstly, a sustained increase in human knowledge resources and, secondly, a *deliberate accumulation of human capital*.[206] The development of this knowledge bank followed a parallel course to that of technological progress: from energy-intensive, mass-production technology to energy conservation and highly value-added 'sophisticated' *information technology* products and their relevant networks. Accordingly, the MITI slogan for the decade has been 'the advanced information society'.

The third major trend of the 1980s was the exogenous force resulting from Japan's *internationalization*. Consequently, the direct protectionism which, together with import substitution, had constituted Japan's primary weapon of defence since 1868, now came under strong attack. Since many other companies, particularly those under the wing of the major trading houses, were becoming increasingly dependent on international markets, protectionism alone was of no further assistance. Thus, measures designed to stimulate international trade became more important that those aimed at national protectionism and, consequently, new basic strategies had to be developed.

The internationalization (or 'liberalization') of the domestic market was merely pro forma and was, in any event, only implemented fully in sectors in which foreign companies had no chance of success. Johnson cites the famous examples of motorbikes, sake and getas (traditional Japanese wooden sandals),[207] to which can be added the sectors in which the MITI strictly controls joint ventures and where the state is the only customer (e.g. railway products) or where a mass market simply does not exist (corn flakes, equestrian goods, etc.). In a counter move, Japan used the internationalization argument to go on the offensive, establishing production plants in foreign countries. This can be perceived as further example of '*menjuku fukuhei*', in which a 'naïve' perspective of global equality became an 'age of cosmopolitan nationalists'.[208] An analysis of the above must transcend geographical dimensions in order to reveal the cultural dominants, which are decisive in certain specific cases for success or failure, rather than becoming bogged down in 'triad-related' explanations. Japan is the only economic power to have advanced to these new competitive weapons and which can chalk up initial successes in the new era (a permanent trade imbalance, Japanese automobile production abroad to circumvent trade barriers).

Japan occupies a prime position in every economic sector. It has implemented capacity restrictions in global problem sectors (shipbuilding, mining, etc.) in a far more orderly manner and with less disruption than elsewhere. In addition, Japan is a leading medium and high-tech producer and also leads the field in advanced and future technologies. This has all been achieved by means of a far-sighted strategy: the route from import-substitution to an export strategy has led Japan to a phase of export substitution, in which exports are produced, under Japanese control, in the country of consumption. This frees up enormous capacity which will enable Japan to make its structural leap into the next millennium. In view of these preliminary measures, the prediction that Japan is set to achieve the highest growth rates in the world by the end of this millennium comes as no surprise. Although these rates are below those achieved during the exponential growth years of the late 1950s and 1960s, they nevertheless exceed those of the post-oil-crisis years from 1973 to 1985.[209]

But with all these high-flying goals, things went somewhat out of control through saturation and by the advent of the global Internet economy which spurred a new secular growth cycle, notably in the USA. Japanese companies did not react as hard as they should have to restructure, and the government likewise dragged its feet and Japanese leaders were not fast enough to understand the rapidity and gravity of the New Economy impact. Thus, Japan found itself sliding into a recession. As the government lost its talent to pick winners,[210] and the Japanese customer was drifting towards some kind of adapted 'Generation X' role model,[211] Japan needed about five years to fully reach the bottom, which was then (belatedly) properly addressed as a crisis.

The government concentrated on easy-money politics to stimulate ailing consumer demand, while companies started to approach the un-Japanese field of mergers and acquisitions. First they did some domestic deals, mainly in banking, then some international deals were made in order to keep these industries (mainly the car industry) afloat and to instill strategic and managerial knowledge that could serve as a change agent. This meta-strategy to respond slowly, to restructure internally and then to learn from the foreigner is the same as 130 years previously in the transition from the Tokugawa to the Meiji era, with Japan coming out stronger than anyone expected and even leapfrogging the (temporarily) superior foreign forces.

Overview of Japan's Economic Strategies

Even with the recent adjustments taken into consideration, we could characterize the focus of this economic development as *sectoral specialization*, which includes the major, intersectoral reallocation of production factors. In this context, purely protectionist and isolationist arguments are merely side issues, given the support for an anticipatory model capable of positive adaptation which incorporates a preventative and interventionist structural policy.[212]

Certain points are particularly noticeable when Japan's strategies are compared with those of the West (Table 4.3). Whereas Western strategies have always been born out of conflict, the Japanese system has always been able to pursue the basic strategy of a *never-ending road leading to increasingly higher added value*. This has been achieved by determinedly summoning up all the transformation forces it can muster.[213] The transformation achieved since the Second World War has, in fact,

Table 4.3   *Comparison of strategies and criteria for decision-making*

	Japan	The West
Philosophy of strategy	Relatively focused	Quite vague
Developer of strategy	Dynamic groups	State agencies intervene
Context	Open, broad	Rigid, defined
Methods	Constantly adaptive	Fixed set of tools
Industrial policies	Relatively free given high and clear expectations	Coordination by government
Autonomy	High and given	Low and of be achieved
External environment	Thoughts, finance and network driven	Structures, politics and rule-driven
Potential for conflict	Low, medium (but constant) pressure	High, on/off pressure
Stability	High, flexible adaptation as goal	Change and mobility as ideal
Power	Relatively little power for single players	Powerful single players (institutions)
Performance measurement	Overall economic growth	ROI of companies
Time horizon	Future	Now

been quite dramatic compared with the development of Western countries, and Table 4.4 shows some of the changes in the distribution of the Japanese workforce across sectors.

Even when compared longitudinally, the rise in Japan's production capacity has been extraordinary if somewhat inconsistent (Figure 4.19). The relative breakthrough of the 1970s was brought about by enormous technological advances, whereas production did in fact increase in absolute terms, the pace of technological

Table 4.4   *Distribution of the Japanese workforce*[a]

Sector	1955	1965	1975	1985	1995	2000*	2005*
Agriculture and forestry	40.2	23.5	13.4	8.9	7.0	4.8	4.0
Production of goods	19.5	24.9	25.3	25.8	20.7	19.1	16.9
Transport communication utilities	4.7	6.2	7.2	7.8	8.5	10.2	9.2
Trade and physical services	31.2	36.4	39.8	30.2	25.1	25.4	24.4
Knowledge sector[b]	4.4	4.5	14.3	28.1	38.7	40.5	44.5

[a] As percentage
[b] E.g. management and consulting, health care, public service, intellectual/virtual/IT related services)
* Forecast
Source: Compiled from Bureau of Statistics, *The Labor Force Survey 1991* and Robb, S., *Japan's New Imperialism*, p. 51f

	Index
1890	1 311
1937	17 320
1965	30 321
1980	15 866
1990	98 679
2005	310 800

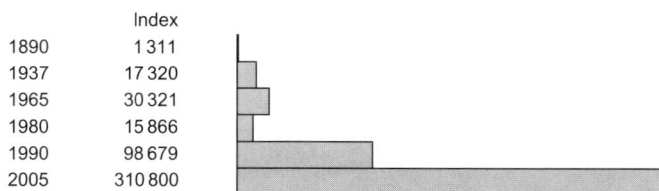

Figure 4.19 *Japanese factory production (physical and non-physical products combined) (indexed 100 = 1863 (start of modernization))*
Source: Okawa, K., Shinohara, M. and Meissner, L., *Patterns of Japanese Economic Development*, p. 37. Freeman, C., *Technology Policy and Economic Performance: Lessons from Japan*, p. 32ff

change was significantly faster. It was only in the 1980s and at the start of the 1990s that production could again increase at the same rate as technology. As discussed earlier, the mid- to end-1990s brought a damper which seems to have temporarily slowed the machine down, but, more importantly, motivated a redoubling of effort towards another jump in productivity in the coming years.

The continuous patterns radically and flexibly adapted to meet constantly changing environmental conditions are: a dogged adherence to long-term strategies (visions) such as modernization; the importation of the best technology available; and an enhancement of the standards of education among the population and intense cooperation between economic partners and the state. Five partly over-lapping value-added phases can be identified within this industrial policy:[214]

- *Phase 1* 1945–65: reconstruction. The defeat suffered at the end of the Second World War necessitated a fundamental reworking of previous plans. In addition to physical reconstruction, Japan needed to define its position and new direction strategically, whilst adopting an inconspicuous, apparently modest stance on the outside.
- *Phase 2* 1957–72: industrial modernization and preparations for the export boom.[215] After this industrial base had been established, an export production strategy was introduced and rapidly implemented.
- *Phase 3* 1967–90: development of higher value-added, 'sunrise' industries, on export boom.[216] During the export boom, the objective, in addition to profitability and achieving market-share targets, was a sustained increase in value-added rates.
- *Phase 4* 1990–?: complex and flexible production systems (CAD, CAM, CIM, Internet-based production planning) for a wide variety of different products; 'smart' factories and microproduction plants incorporating a complex network of multilevel supplier networks ('upstream' and 'downstream' concepts, JIT, TQC etc.).[217] This industrial structure is currently under development in Japan and will be 'exported' abroad once it has achieved its threshold value, again guaranteeing the availability of the space/freedom/flexibility required for the next step.[218]

154

Value added
Immaterial (non-physical) content of products and services
Knowledge content

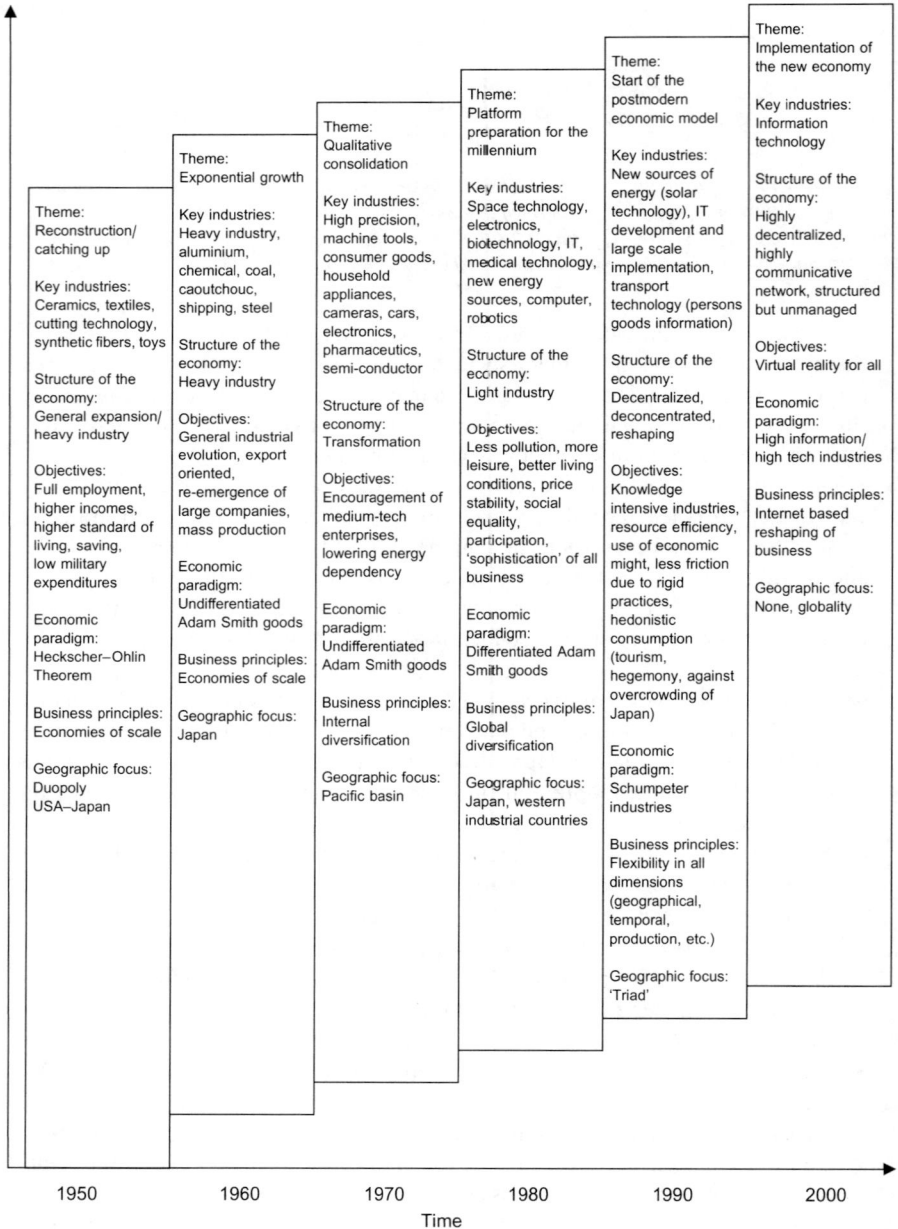

Theme:
Reconstruction/
catching up

Key industries:
Ceramics, textiles,
cutting technology,
synthetic fibers, toys

Structure of the
economy:
General expansion/
heavy industry

Objectives:
Full employment,
higher incomes,
higher standard of
living, saving,
low military
expenditures

Economic
paradigm:
Heckscher–Ohlin
Theorem

Business principles:
Economies of scale

Geographic focus:
Duopoly
USA–Japan

Theme:
Exponential growth

Key industries:
Heavy industry,
aluminium,
chemical, coal,
caoutchouc,
shipping, steel

Structure of the
economy:
Heavy industry

Objectives:
General industrial
evolution, export
oriented,
re-emergence of
large companies,
mass production

Economic
paradigm:
Undifferentiated
Adam Smith goods

Business principles:
Economies of scale

Geographic focus:
Japan

Theme:
Qualitative
consolidation

Key industries:
High precision,
machine tools,
consumer goods,
household
appliances,
cameras, cars,
electronics,
pharmaceutics,
semi-conductor

Structure of the
economy:
Transformation

Objectives:
Encouragement of
medium-tech
enterprises,
lowering energy
dependency

Economic
paradigm:
Undifferentiated
Adam Smith goods

Business principles:
Internal
diversification

Geographic focus:
Pacific basin

Theme:
Platform
preparation for the
millennium

Key industries:
Space technology,
electronics,
biotechnology, IT,
medical technology,
new energy
sources, computer,
robotics

Structure of the
economy:
Light industry

Objectives:
Less pollution, more
leisure, better living
conditions, price
stability, social
equality,
participation,
'sophistication' of all
business

Economic
paradigm:
Differentiated Adam
Smith goods

Business principles:
Global
diversification

Geographic focus:
Japan, western
industrial countries

Theme:
Start of the
postmodern
economic model

Key industries:
New sources of
energy (solar
technology), IT
development and
large scale
implementation,
transport
technology (persons
goods information)

Structure of the
economy:
Decentralized,
deconcentrated,
reshaping

Objectives:
Knowledge
intensive industries,
resource efficiency,
use of economic
might, less friction
due to rigid
practices,
hedonistic
consumption
(tourism,
hegemony, against
overcrowding of
Japan)

Economic
paradigm:
Schumpeter
industries

Business principles:
Flexibility in all
dimensions
(geographical,
temporal,
production, etc.)

Geographic focus:
'Triad'

Theme:
Implementation of
the new economy

Key industries:
Information
technology

Structure of the
economy:
Highly
decentralized,
highly
communicative
network, structured
but unmanaged

Objectives:
Virtual reality for all

Economic
paradigm:
High information/
high tech industries

Business principles:
Internet based
reshaping of
business

Geographic focus:
None, globality

1950   1960   1970   1980   1990   2000

Time

Figure 4.20   *Economic development of Japan, 1950–2000*

- *Phase 5* 2000–?: coming to terms with the postmodern world and the New Economy chiefly propelled by the Internet. Widespread application of sophisticated information technologies, and dramatically improved transportation systems (people, goods and, above all, information). A shift to a knowledge-based economy embracing entrepreneurial concepts. The recent recession is used as a chance to jump-start this new phase.[219]

The course of this integrated and complex process is examined in greater detail in Figures 4.20 and 4.21.

The change from a *mass economy*, via a *quality economy*, to a *knowledge economy*[220] (or New Economy; interlinked economy) is clearly perceptible which is in congruency to the life-cycle hypothesis. This cannot, however, be described as a meticulously planned procedure but rather as a fundamental lack of discrimination *vis-à-vis* mutually perceived visions, a procedure which corresponds to Moltke's dictum: 'the creation of a strategy involves the redevelopment of the original guiding concept to meet constantly changing conditions.'[221] This ties in with Johnson's concept of a growth-oriented, integrated economic policy (économie concertée, mixed economy, *kongo keizai*, Zaibatsu guidance model), a self-developing state. This concept is at odds with the traditional theories of the state based on religious, welfare, revolutionary or protectionist philosophies.[222]

Instead of coherent theoretical structures, a plethora of 'minor' theories – ranging from subsystem business microtheory and Schumpeter's dynamic theory of development to a free enterprise; the attractiveness of status as promoted by economic

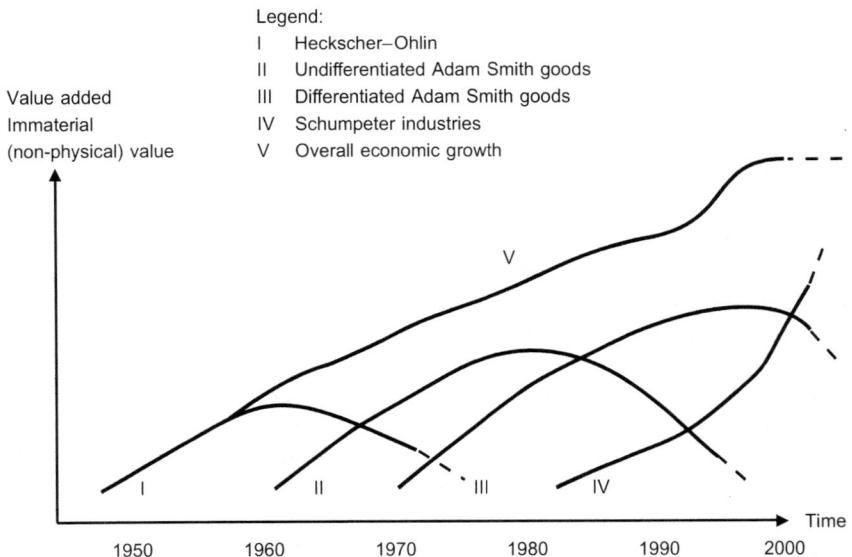

Figure 4.21   *Main paradigms of business in Japan, 1945–90*
Source: Adapted from Ozawa, T., 'Europe 1992', p. 7

policy and, consequently, enhanced international competitiveness – are pragmatically employed in an ideologically-remote manner, without any regard for consistency. The only dominant feature is the relevant benefit produced in each case.[223,224] These *meta symbols* changed from that of a *strong, united Japan* to a *Japan attempting to 'catch up' with and overrun the West* by *assimilating Western know-how* and *military imperialism*, to arrive currently at a vision of Japan making *preparations for the new era*. The conversion to a 'new Japan' (*shin nihon*) via 'growth as means to an end' (*seicho katsuyo gata*) had its roots in 'growth as the objective' (*seichi tsuikyu gata*). Structural adjustments have been the main theme of the past 40 years but the emphasis is now concentrated on adapting processes to meet the rapidly changing times and to bring the information (or 'knowledge', 'Internet', or 'new') society into reality.[225]

> Japan is no longer a leader simply in terms of economic paradigms, but also plays a leading role in the meta-economic implementation process for new postmodern paradigms.[226]

To some extent, the 1980s and 1990s were a transitional phase, in terms of new economic and meta-economic strategy, and also marked the end of a long period of development. The reason why this transformation took place more markedly in Japan than elsewhere cannot be explained in cultural terms alone. The direct economic relationships of recent years which have accelerated the momentum still further must be brought into the equation, and the following section deals with this aspect.

V THE QUEST FOR FUNDAMENTAL CHANGE

Japan, led by its economy, now faces a critical turning point which brings to a conclusion the 'catch-up' phase started in 1868, marking the beginning of a new phase. Industrialization has not been without its side-effects – environmental damage, urbanization, agricultural crisis etc. – and these need to be remedied. The industrial structure resulting from modernization has, due to inevitable over-reaction, resulted in instability due to an increased dependency on foreign raw materials. This dependency has already been drastically diminished but needs to be reduced even further, for example by the acquisition of foreign mines and production sites or even by relocating production to foreign countries. In addition, there is a need to enhance the quality of life in response to internal pressure. The social trends caused within Japan by modernization (oversaturation, exhaustion, social disintegration, criminality, a dangerous absence of ideals and objectives, hedonistic consumption, etc.) must be defused and must consequently be transplanted into a postmodern environment. These social problems are actually more diverse than these summary generic terms would lead us to believe, and represent a powerful force for change.[227]

But the perception is increasing that the *social costs* of the 1970s and 1980s must be reduced. The disintegration of traditionally high family solidarity is now bemoaned, alienation is becoming apparent everywhere, and the welfare system which has been on the political agenda since the 1960s has still not been fully implemented. Rebellion amongst the young and non-conformist microgroups hinders the creation of a 'homogeneous' society. The modern syndrome of the stomach ulcer, of 'working oneself to death' (*karoshi*)[228] and senile dementia are Japan's fastest growing diseases.[229]

These social symptoms are also reproduced in the economic sphere. An erosion of the work ethic is detectable; the social model of coordination in the workplace has been tarnished; the population is aging at a rapid pace with all its negative consequences; an individualistic hedonism is visibly spreading; and the united image of productive organization is now disappearing.[230] On another front, Japan is faced with serious urban problems, and rural flight is dramatic (a 45 per cent reduction in rural population between 1950 and 1980); urban property values are now out of the reach of the average citizen; and the collapsing road transport system counteracts any economic efficiency.[231] These are only the most important problems resulting from Japan's extreme economic and social concentration and from the economic distress of recent years.

One of the features of Japan's structural policy is the declared objective of dispersing this geographic concentration, but nevertheless 70 per cent of gross domestic product is still produced in the Osaka–Tokyo area and 30 per cent of the population continues to live on 1 per cent of Japan's surface area. Conversely, industrial relocation plans, high-speed trains every 10 minutes, rapid dispersion of Internet-based business models and general measures designed to deconcentrate the infrastructure are slowly being implemented.[232] Experts have calculated the costs of the current growth curve in environmental units and forecast that the environment, just like a commodity, will have to be imported in approximately 30 years' time; a process which *de facto* is already, indirectly, taking place today when one considers the environment consumed by Japanese tourists. These costs are now practically incalculable and would exceed Japan's total export revenue many times over.[233] This is another simple but compelling reason for Japan to bring the 'information society' into reality.

In addition to these problems relating to internal structure, exclusively economic problems also exist: saturated domestic (and in some cases also export) markets; slow restructuring and growing economic instability (the yen, the Nikkei, property and oil prices); budgetary problems; rising unemployment; and the threatened deprotectionism of the import market round off the crisis scenario. Material endeavours have for decades been supported by most Japanese; short-term sacrifice was perceived as essential to long-term growth ('*seisan daiichi shugi*' or the principle of the primacy of production). But this basic ideology is starting to fall apart;[234] it is caving in to pressure for change coming from all directions now that the structural adjustment plans of the 1970s and 1980s have lost their momentum.[235] Old symbols are worn out and have become unattractive, and the creation of a new set means not just copying other societies, as was necessary when Japan was forced to be a follower and others were the 'winners', but now, since Japan is in a forerunner role, requires a search to come up with a new paradigm. This is an unusual situation for Japan and hence the search is naturally longer and more painful than for example for America, where pioneering and entrepreneurial ingenuity have long been the core culture.[236]

Japan is being forced to adopt a different primary strategy since the existing strategy, which is more than 30 years old, has now turned in on itself. Although the national supply and demand structure has remained stable thanks to strong exports, with full utilization of all production capacity and possible economies of scale, this strategy has also intensified international tensions in terms of multilateral trade and incited a wave of protectionism against Japan both in the USA and in Europe.[237] But, since the mid-1970s Japan has also been increasingly compelled to abandon the role of the aggressive exporter, even in developing countries.[238] Although during the 1980s a more moderate version of the doctrine of growth was presented, the close focus of which was distributed over a few favoured industries, its target was only ever economic growth.[239] It was only at the end of the 1980s that meta-economic objectives noticeably played a more prominent role; 50 per cent of those who completed the last census form listed intellectual development as an objective. This rating, the highest in the postwar era, correlates to the lowest rating for the objective of material improvement of living conditions.[240] Following the longest period of growth in the history of the Japanese economy, society now wishes to reap some of its *meta-economic benefits* and is now prioritizing a social and intellectual set of objectives rather than the purely economic ones which have all been achieved to a greater or lesser extent.[241,242] Moreover, benefits, that is returns to knowledge, can be reaped more easier given the technological achievements that come with the information revolution, and as such it is an upwards-winding spiral.

Viewed from this perspective, the 1980s and 1990s can be perceived as an *interim stage between two technological cycles*.[243] The instabilities of the latter half of the 1980s have been attributed to ruts in the growth curve described by Kondratieff,[244] and for this reason the noteworthy *21st century project* concentrated on creating the favourable conditions required for an upturn following the lows experienced during these long troughs. Supported by Naumann,[245] the term '*postmodernization*' can be used to characterize this upturn which was achieved as a result of crisis management techniques (Americanization and internationalization).[246]

Many authors perceived this structural change as part of a global collective exchange of paradigms, whereby Japan initially anticipated future structures and then adjusted its own agenda accordingly.[247] These sections of the agenda focus on the pivotal role of mental capital; on its innovative effects in general (key words: ongoing improvements ('*kaizen*'), a rise in productivity on the part of the employee, the factory which serves as a laboratory, global exchange of information, etc.); on the importance of shared visions; on sustained, intensive, informal and mostly horizontal dialogue; on flexibility, speed, risk management, in its broadest sense; and, finally, on the ever-increasing information content of every product. On a more pragmatic level, companies had to learn to restructure themselves without governmental guidance, with capacity utilization at a 20-year low and seemingly everything going in the wrong direction.[248] But then public money (as subsidies or cheap loans) was made available against a 'commitment to restructuring'. The sheer size of the 10 trillion yen economic package shows how seriously the crisis was felt.

Analysts of the Japanese economy view the bankruptcy of the brokerage house Yamaichi in November 1999 as the symbolic apex of the crisis. It seemed that it became clear to every Japanese that before the Heisei era (achieving peace) can be completed, dramatic changes need to take place and any rigidity against change (*kochoku*) is to be eradicated. And as industrial growth has become positive again since mid-1999, it can be said that the combination of economic packages with a changed attitude towards a new openness and the recollection that rapid adaptation is one of the core competencies of Japan, changed the notion from crisis to solution.[249] Uekusa maintains that there is a serious change in the financial culture in Japan: more entrepreneurial moves and more risk-taking can be seen; hence, another dimension pointing towards the next evolutionary step of Japan. If corporate restructuring is again seen only through the eyes of Western book-keepers, this change is not fully noticed by the West. The vision of restructuring should be appreciated more to fully understand the importance of today's dynamics.[250] This is why Yoshihiko Senoo, director at the EPA, confidently said in a Bloomberg interview (6 October 1999) that: 'I think we can say that Japan's economy has finally gone into the full-scale recovery process.'[251] It may be premature to call this a rekindled spirit, but certainly the will to reposition is clearly visible.

This overview allows us to perceive the exact nature of the pressure emanating from several different directions for Japan to metamorphose into a postmodern society. The internal structural crises in Japan and the advent of the New Economy in the USA acted as *push factors* forcing the Japanese to stop prevaricating over the situation. The strategies pursued in terms of foreign trade and economic structures during the 1970s and 1980s no longer served any useful purpose and, finally, Japanese visions of the future acted as exceptionally powerful *pull factors* which encouraged and facilitated the transition to a postmodern Japan.

This is a process which is only delayed by the growth slump and the necessary exploratory search activities at the end of the 1990s; it is likely to soon show the first positive results as currently anticipated by all the economic analysts looking at Japan today.

VI   POSTMODERN SOCIETY, AN ABSTRACT PARADIGM AS A REALISTIC GOAL

Visions, acting as pull factors, play a dominant role in terms of the transformation ability of the Japanese social structure. The following section outlines how one of the fundamental visions perceives the 'turn of the millennium' concept and describes how the role of the Keiretsu, who now serve as the most influential generators of dynamism, evolved from this.

The 'Turn of the Millennium' Concept

The crisis factors presented in the previous chapter do not represent bottlenecks in the true sense of the word, but merely complement the successes achieved. They are, therefore, merely additional components contributing to Japanese dynamism. Now that the Japanese economy has experienced its longest period of growth, the next decade should bring meta-economic benefits. The economy has overcome the major conflicts of the period from 1975 to 1990, and no serious obstacles are anticipated in the coming years in the economic sector. In spite of fulminate growth, the newly-industrialized economies (NIEs) of Asia are still too small, the European Union needs firstly to resolve its internal problems, Russia is disintegrating, China shows only slow signs of progress and the USA will continue to be the 'major problem in the global economy':[252]

> Basically, greater importance should be attached to utilizing the existing strength of the economy rather than to increasing this strength ... [A]t present, determining the most effective way to utilize the current strength of the economy is considered to be the most important issue.[253]

The national Economic Planning Agency assesses Japan's approach to the next phase rationally and succinctly in the following terms: Japan is now a major international provider of capital and technology and it is high time that the importance of Japan's role was acknowledged, both in entrepreneurial terms and on a personal level. The basis of Japan's knowledge (education and values, the uniqueness of Japan, the 'Japanese way of life' etc.) should be used and exported in an active attempt to resolve global problems. Consequently, Japan is now entering a new phase, a phase which requires a new framework concept.[254] Japan enjoys the prestige required to lead this transition to a new phase, in a methodical and anticipatory manner, as opposed to the reactive and uncoordinated approach of all other nationals.[255] The transition to a new phase in a postmodern era has long since been prepared. The concentration on growth of the postwar era diminished little by little in the 1980s, and just as there was a need at the start of the 1980s to revise mass production and growth imbalance strategies, the strategy pursued at the beginning of the 1990s of pure high-technology production and balanced growth has now been upgraded to an international relocation of Japanese production and the comprehensive (economic and meta-economic) transformation of Japanese society.[256] The end of the 1990s seemed to have brought an end to these sometimes painful searches for new macroeconomic concepts and business strategies, leading now to correctly preparing for the anticipated postmodern society. According to the MITI, the three long-term objectives pursued over the last few years will continue to be pursued:

- ... to attain a dynamic society while improving the quality of life ...
- to ensure economic security by working toward a knowledge-based society, thereby reducing Japan's vulnerability to raw materials ...
- to make contributions to the world community as an economic power to earn the trust of other nations.[257]

These profound changes in terms of technology and industrial structure, which were already perceptible during the second half of the 1980s and the first half of the 1990s, have turned Japan into a leading nation in economic and technological terms. In addition to social objectives, for example improving the quality of life to complement the high standard of living now enjoyed, the present aim is also to achieve holistic objectives of readapting society as a whole to the conditions of the next millennium. Already the Economic Survey of Japan of 1989 cites some of the subordinate aims as: 'the sophistication of both industry and daily life', and the utilization of existing financial resources and globalization in a general context.[258] These generally held objectives are detailed in other MITI and EPA publications. Here we can present a short overview describing the scope of the concepts proposed for the end of the 1990s and the beginning of the new millennium,[259,260] with four dimensions can be drawn into the picture of the future:

- *International aspects*: raising the level of national competitiveness and decreasing exports by means of overseas production; globalization of corporate activities (particularly those of the Keiretsu); internationalization of the yen (international key currency) and the 'multistratification' of international trade.
- *National aspects*: the formulation of a new paradigm of economic behaviour; two-dimensional growth orientation, for example global and regional development (prefectures); the development of a 'multi-track pattern of resource allocation'; the 'state-led' demolition of one-dimensional patterns; the creation of 'micro-economies' within the national economy and transformation to a 'flexible' national economy.
- *Social aspects*: the promotion of new industries, new lifestyles, new cultural styles;[261] the 'marketing' of traditional Japanese values: altruism, national identity, group loyalty, the selfless use of creativity; networking the economy and culture; a trend towards a 'sophisticated information society' or 'knowledge-based society'; the acquisition of an exemplary social character in global terms; the integration of megatrends; labour shortages, women, satisfaction, age pyramids.

- *Technical visions*: technical expansion of the information society; the intensification of information in industry; technical target criteria: flexibility, speed, risk-management instead of risk-limitation and the highest know-how input possible to arrive at a truly and fully Internet-based society.

The motto '*Heisei era*' is used as a metaphor to link this conglomerate of objectives on a symbolic level. Just like the slogans: '*fukoku kyohei*' (a rich land with a strong army), used during the Meiji era; '*shokusan kogyo*' (industrial development and production expansion), which dates from 1950, '*shotoku baizo*' (a doubling of income) used from 1960; '*chishiki shuyakuka*' (intensification of high-tech) introduced in 1970 and '*joho shakai*' (information society) which originates from the 1980s, the slogan 'the Heisei economy' could be considered the principal slogan of the 1990s and the beginning of this new millennium. As such, simply but legitimately, the Heisei economy can be seen as the Japanese version of the *New Economy*. In accordance with tradition, this new period was named after the Heisei era (cf. Chapter 1, section II on 'Japan as the focus of attention'), which started with the enthronement of the Emperor Akihito (November 1990) and is generally translated as the 'final major endeavour before the new era of peace'. With the assistance of the government and official organs, the Keizai Doyuka (Committee for Economic Development) had already set up a high quality think tank in the mid-1970s, the Sogo Kenkyu Kaihatsu Kiko (National Institute for Research and Advancement), from private sector research institutions.

The so-called 'Twenty-First Century Project' was its main project, and it involved the conception of a long-term plan for Japan as a whole. Their interim report identified several clear focal points, in particular that *Japan must be transformed into a knowledge-based society*. Research and development in high technology; economic restructuring to create an information society; concentration on value-added products in Japan, and the production of low value products abroad (under Japanese management); lower energy consumption; lower material consumption and lower labour consumption (as a result of automation), are the objectives of domestic production restructuring. Less environmental damage (which also results from lower material and energy consumption) must be achieved; geographic concentration (at home, the Tokyo–Osaka Region; globally, the USA) of Japanese production must be dispersed; transportation and communication technology must be improved. These are the main points of this agenda.[262] The objective is no longer to restructure individual sectors but to *transform the whole economy* (including meta-economic values and sets of symbols) in the context of a knowledge and information-based social structure. This transformation encompasses all sectors of the economy and all social groups.[263]

The new plans of the Heisei economy are without parallel in other countries in terms of methodology, firstly because they allow *ad hoc* control of the economy but, secondly, because they prescribe an economic vision as well as a range of meta-economic objectives.[264] By concentrating on predefined sectors, this plan, in common with previous plans, covers the economy as a whole together with its economic subjects.[265]

> The attempt to move the economy and the society towards a greater knowledge intensity is nothing unique to Japan but is a universal trend ... to redirect, in a concerted manner, the entire structure of Japan as a whole into a more knowledge intensive system, particularly to deal with 'senescent' areas in the anticipatory adjustment manner – i.e. making adjustment in anticipation of where industries ought to be viable – is distinctive to Japanese policy ...[266]

The main objective of this unique Heisei economy is to prepare for a new *global 'phase'*[267] during which Japan will play a leading role by virtue of its position as one of the most powerful countries in the world (in Japan's eyes: economically, politically, militarily and 'intellectually and morally'). As a result '*Nihon ichiban*' (Japan is number 1 – cf. Chapter 1, section II) would once again become a reality.

When this interpretation is applied, the subordinate objectives which Japan strives for become extremely plausible. Having accumulated financial resources during the 1980s (the Nikkei share index boom, the property price boom, enormous profits from foreign financial transactions, the revaluation of the yen, the development of international competitive dominance on the part of the Japanese banks) and having secured a cutting-edge technological basis during the 1970s and 1980s (we refer here to the microchip industries, the production of high performance broadband technology and sustained successes in sectors of extreme relevance to the future, such as information technology and biotechnology), the aim was to use them as a launchpad for Japan's national and international transformation.[268] Having now lost ground during the crisis in the second half of the 1990s, strategies had to be readapted but the basic visions remained unchanged.

Just recently,[269] the Economic Planning Agency reiterated this meta-strategy seeing macroeconomic conditions favouring a swift recovery, with personal consumption fueled by demographic changes and tax breaks being one of the leading factors rendering the traditional classification of primary, secondary and tertiary sectors as irrelevant. The agency proposes a three-fold view: *production*, a *networking sector* (covering, for example, transport, communications, commerce, finance) and a *knowledge sector* (management, R&D, education, leisure and entertainment, public services).

Within the goods-producing sector, the weight of materials industries should continue to drop while that of the processing and assembly sector, particularly the electrical machinery industry, should rise, and the knowledge-intensity of the sector as a whole should increase. The moves towards offshore production and a horizontal international division of labour can also be expected to accelerate. In the networking sector, the activities of which are to form networks to transport and act as intermediaries for goods, people, money and information, new types of information and new communications technologies will make it possible to offer new services and to sophisticate and to speed up and enhance the sophistication of existing services, and competition will promote enhanced efficiency.

The knowledge-and-service-producing sector will continue to offer the largest share of new jobs. Demand should grow especially strongly for services that support corporate activities such as software design, information banks, building maintenance and engineering support; these services will make possible higher levels of productivity in manufacturing and financial services. Growth will also occur in services for final consumption, including medical care and health maintenance, education and leisure. And a variety of new services should appear on the scene in the area of housekeeping substitutes, currently represented by such businesses as dry cleaners and restaurants. As a result of these developments, by the end of the year 2000 each of the three sectors is likely to make up about one-third of GDP. International criticism is focusing mainly on the first and partially on the second category, neglecting to see the positive developments of the ensemble.

In national terms, the high material standards achieved would need to be maintained and the negative effects of modernization eradicated. Parallel to this would be a 'sophistication' of the country, which would constitute a preparatory measure for the new age involving not only a new environmental awareness and enhancement of information technology by the whole country, but also different value-structures.[270]

The aim is to (re-)consolidate Japan's international position but not only in terms of economic power. Japan is seeking greater political clout (as demonstrated by the fact that Japan has been accepted as a permanent member of the International Security Council) and is, quasi peripherally, consolidating its military 'front'.[271] To the Economic Planning Agency, globalization is a code word for '... the unification of the Japanese Economy and the global economy, and the development of world-wide corporations'.[272,273] However, this type of formulation cannot adequately describe basic concepts of a hegemonic nature. But, simply put, to embrace the world, Japan has first to embrace the new technologies that are so characteristic of the postmodern world.

The recent recession, in a way usefully, instilled a sense of urgency into the dynamics. Tokyo financial market analysts talk about a selective recovery – reshaping the industry landscape with a boom being around the corner. As the financial restructuring was done mainly in 1999, broad-based restructuring in other industries will now inevitably take place. Aggressive restructuring will lead to a sustained improvement in returns on capital, more efficient allocation of credit and meaningful restructuring. In this scenario, mere cost-cutting is just one variable in the transformation of the business models. Taking the German company Mannesmann, that changed from a steel company to a telecommunications company within five years as an example, a total metamorphosis of the corporate sector driven by a structural transformation of the economy is envisioned.[274]

One important factor will be the harmless-sounding postal savings system, where savings deposits of private investors reach maturity. In the next two years, 106 trillion yen (more than the GDP of China, Thailand and Malaysia together) will be invested outside the money market. According to an estimate by the Ministry of Posts and Telecommunications, nearly half of this is expected to flow out into the economy and possible mainly (directly and indirectly) into 'new Japan' businesses.[275]

After the bubble economy started to burst towards the end of the 1980s, ten years of decline and shock came. Now the digestion seems over and the discussion of a Project 'New Japan vs Old Japan' is fully underway.[276] Average IT spending is about 20 per cent of total expenses (USA 40 per cent), but growth rates are double the European and American figures with the Internet, the mobile phone (lagging) and further electronic applications being the external economic stimuli that will fundamentally change Japan.[277] According to McKinsey consultant Kentaro Aramaki, Internet and e-commerce will boom more strongly and faster in Japan than anything seen in the USA. First evidence is in the more than 200 Internet-related companies that go public in 2000. MITI estimates that 2.5 million Internet-related new jobs will be created in the next five years. This boom in such activities can be seen as the boost Japan needs to transform itself into a postmodern economy ready to strive again for leadership.

An interpretation of the term 'information and knowledge-based society', taking account of the prevailing conditions in the twenty-first century, provides a wider perspective, that of a postmodern society. In that sense the terms 'New Economy', 'New Japan', 'Heisei economy', 'pluralistic information society' and 'postmodern society' can be used synonymously and are mutually overlapping.

At this point we again revert to the notion that Japan 'has always' demonstrated postmodern traits.[278] Japan was 'postmodern' during the pre-Meiji period, when modernism was perceived an interim measure, 'Western knowledge superimposed upon Japan',[279] but emancipated itself from this and now combines traditional ways of thinking with Western concepts to create a postmodern alliance.[280] Consequently, it was only during the most torrid phase of modernization that Japan's postmodernism was temporarily suspended, that is from 1945 to 1980, and the country is now postmodern once again. In the 1930s, Nishida developed his theory of '*mu no basho*' (an empty place), a phrase 'which became the tacitly understood foundation of the postmodernism of the 1930s, or the so-called theory of "kindai no chokoku"' (away with modernism). Such Japanese theorists appeared then to be adopting the same stance as present-day Japan, to the extent that they supported the opinion: 'We must continue to pursue the Japanese path. It doesn't really matter if this is now called "postmodernism"',[281] and does it make sense to call this situation postmodern? Possibly. Yet, as we have noted, Japan's postmodern traits existed earlier in history, thus denying a temporal specificity.[282] The West has overcome modernism thanks to its postmodernism; Japan never experienced modernism in this sense, never believed in it as a paradigm but merely experimented with it. This is why Japan's postmodernism was also accompanied by another preconception, namely that of premodernism. '[T]he descriptions of postmodernism began to fit the Japanese conditions very well, as if the term were being coined specifically for the Japanese society.'[283]

This throws up an interesting perspective, one which perceives Japan's post-modernity as a *continuance of premodern modes of thought and behaviour*. We would not be able to recognize specifically this complex process were it not for an institutional concept in the contemporary form of the Keiretsu, which has played a fundamental role during each phase of more recent Japanese history. Other institutional concepts – for example parliamentary democracy, the aristocracy and, to some extent, the academic system – have not been flexible enough to accept the radical advancements of the times and consequently survive and absorb paradigmatic change.

> Thus the Keiretsu system plays a special part in Japan's paradigmatic change. It was not only during the modernization period before the turn of the century that these networks of a 'national elite', which manifested themselves in the Keiretsu (or respectively Zaibatsu) systems, took on exemplary and role-model functions. Even now, in the 'postmodernization period' at the turn of the millennium they have reverted to the same functions.

The Roles of the Zaibatsu and the Keiretsu

Since the start of modernization, Japan's economic development has been based on a series of *trickle-down effects*. During the Meiji period a small number of entrepreneurs were selected to implement paradigmatic change. The reason why industrial policy favoured the Zaibatsu of the 1950s was to allow them to rapidly consolidate production for the home market and also to become an aggressive low-cost competitor on the international market. The Zaibatsu are now, once again, the sole economic factors capable of generating the necessary dynamics, whilst weighing up the risks to be taken, in order to facilitate coherent change.[284]

During the Meiji period, the Zaibatsu were assigned core modernization functions: to acquire international technology; to set up industries of strategic importance to the nation; to rapidly develop the domestic market and transform family-oriented firms into 'modern' companies. This take-off would never have succeeded without the Zaibatsu. They had a dual role: firstly that of a coordination colossus in terms of foreign policy, and secondly to provide a domestic market if external markets were unavailable or undesirable. In this sense, the Zaibatsu have always acted as a *window on the world*, a window on the future. After the Second World War this process was repeated methodically in an almost identical manner, although the old Zaibatsu structures *per se* were no longer relevant.[285]

The dominance of the Keiretsu in postwar growth cannot be overestimated: the nine largest trading companies distribute more than 50 per cent of Japan's total exports. Mitsui, Mitsubishi, Sumitomo, Fuko, DKB and Sanwa together make up 650 large firms employing more than 2 million people. They control 20 per cent of total Japanese corporate profits and more than 2 per cent of world output.[286] Only the Keiretsu are existentially in a position to support drastic structural changes. For example, the privatization of the railways and general industrial restructuring resulted in 80 000 redundancies but the workers involved were re-employed in other (Keiretsu) companies. The same applies to Japan's burgeoning overseas production. It is forecast that 650 000 Japanese workers will lose their jobs by the year 2002, but their further employment is 'guaranteed', less now within the Keiretsu but more so in the emerging offsprings in the New Economy. 'The prime movers in developing this [new] structure have been larger firms who can expect favored treatment in times of expansion, and can transfer adjustment burdens along a chain of subcontractors in recessions.'[287] Again, the New Economy serves as an excellent buffer to absorb human capital, using it now more effectively in new ventures. This shift is actively managed by the Keiretsu not only from a cost-cutting point of view but also using the New Economy as a 'farming-out' or 'incubation lab' for themselves.[288]

Now, being again almost in a new Meiji period ('old systems that do not fit' coupled with the feeling of being left behind) the ever-changing Zaibatsu/Keiretsu are back on track and the objectives remain the same.

The restructuring in the car industry and, more importantly, in banking has generated some of the most spectacular combinations (e.g. the biggest ever deal between the USA and Japan: the 1999 transaction between Goodyear and Sumitomo Rubber was valued at 100 billion yen). Deregulation and the 'big bang' is slower than European and US experts had expected, but it has already changed the landscape completely with the mergers of DKB/IBJ/Fuji, Mitsubishi Bank/Bank of Tokyo, Mitsui Marine & Fire/Nippon Fire & Marine/Koa Fire & Marine, or Sumitomo Bank/Sakura Bank being the biggest. In 1999, combined deal values (total assets) amounted to 236.8 trillion yen, an unsurpassed figure, while merger activity doubled from 1993 to 1999. These mergers are seen as an eradication of cross-holdings, but it is overlooked that new Keiretsu formations are being created by this restructuring.[289]

After this serious restructuring, outsourcing (and network building) will be the main theme. This market will double in size in the next 5–10 years to over 30 billion yen employing 1.4 million people. IT spending is likewise expected to double to 15 per cent of GDP (from the present 8 per cent in 1999) and financial services will be rapidly rebuilt to cater to New Japan's equity/entrepreneurial culture and to digest the money flowing out of the traditional banking and savings system. Although reshaped, the 'old' Keiretsu are again at the centre of action, being the 'network managers' of even larger – albeit less tightly controlled – networks that have increased so much in complexity that rhizome would be a better description.[290] On their own, individual companies or polit-bureaucracies could not support the major tasks required of initiators of paradigmatic change and those buffering the cost of change. This requires an integrated structure, and the product of this integration, the Keiretsu, managing bureaucracy and leading policy-makers will 'control the central nervous system of the world'.[291]

Paradigmatic change to the postmodern is not chaotic but 'managed' by this 'internal elite structure' specific to Japan (cf. Chapter 4, section III on 'individual and organizational elements' and 'the links . . .'). This structure superbly produces an *optimum combination of Japanese strategy and Western economic concepts* within the (Keiretsu) companies, which makes Japan's competitive position in the battle for adaptability unassailable.[292]

> As organizations they [the Keiretsu] are superbly equipped to ride the next wave of economic change. They are highly adaptable, knowledge intensive enterprises, with no factories or line workers. All their personnel, in terms of education is the best that Japan can offer, are information workers . . .[293]

In this special form, the Keiretsu structure can be perceived as one of the primary factors in Japan's 'competitive advantage'.[294] However, in a global context, too, the MNEs generate the dynamics behind the transformation. 'Multinational corporations . . . were in the vanguard of the revolution in the world economic structure,'[295] and 'In "modern" industrial society the corporate group has become the standard form of business organization.'[296] The following is a short list of a few fundamental characteristics:

- a greater emphasis on 'soft', 'political' or 'strategic' points than on quantitative economic parameters;
- competing countries no longer see the MNE as a desirable object but as a superior unit ranking alongside the states;
- dichotomy between large mobile companies and immobile government interventions;
- intentionally impenetrable company-controlled 'markets', which leaves small 'non-Keiretsu' companies at a disadvantage;
- a fractal economy induced by the explosion in information technology (the Internet): network based (virtual Keiretsu) models of the firm might be better suited to follow this revolution than traditional theories of the firm.[297]

These are all successful traits adapted to forward-looking strategies and used by all MNEs in one form or another. 'The group enterprise increasingly bursts through the stays of traditional disciplinary-based, one-nation approaches to government, industrial relations and efficiency.'[298]

This results in the creation of an ideal, a cosmopolitan company the basic characteristics of which appear to be profoundly Japanese, since there is at its heart a fragmented and specialized mass of small units, an invisible and almost intangible mechanism which uses coordination as a management tool. All the slogans designed to achieve the competitive positions of the future, from 'just in time', 'lean production' to '*kaizen*', have been honed to perfection within the Japanese Keiretsu. These methods have to comply to general principles (such as the primacy of an open, hyperflexible network) which are totally unopposed by any national prejudices. This allows global localization in a postmodern context, in which small units combine autonomously but flexibly, demonstrating a level of performance which a modern monolithic corporation would never be capable of achieving.[299]

> The Zaibatsu has always been in overall charge during every structural collapse, but there is now another existential transformation to be expected, not only in Japan but throughout the world. Made possible by IT, 'virtual Keiretsu' and intensive vertical and horizontal information exchange will reinforce spaces/constructs earlier called 'Zaibatsu/Keiretsu', as the high information/high intensity nodes in the Japanese rhizome. These nodes will act (again) as crystallization points for new trends and evolutions. Again, all the signs point to the fact that the Zaibatsu/Keiretsu will assume a leading role in implementing the structural changes required during the next millennium.

VII FOURTH SUMMARY: JAPAN'S TRANSFORMATION TO A SOCIETY OF THE FUTURE

Building on the prevailing cultural conditions of a postmodern Japan, as elucidated in the previous chapter, this chapter has thoroughly examined the strategic aspects surrounding the Japanese MNE in an economic, political and structural context. The assimilation of the cultural dimension into the strategic economic statement has taken place in three main stages. Firstly, general *adaptability* and a sustained, unrestricted desire for improvement were isolated as the major forces behind Japan's dynamics. This endogenous transformation ability is now apparent not only in the unique intensity of information and communication and its processing, but also in the long-term development and implementation of economic (and meta-economic) strategies. We then considered the actual *operational units* and basic *mechanisms of structural change*, which have been embedded in their strategic role in 'tactical everyday life', on the basis of practical examples and examined for functionality in the general context of Japanese strategies. The plethora of organizations, associations, clubs and other informal societies, which act as determining factors in an economic and political sphere, combine to form the structural backbone of the power and knowledge conglomerate and are generally referred to as '*zaikai*' (big business). The driving force behind Japan is neither a centre nor an elite. This modality is particularly reminiscent, in terms of decision-making behaviour, of fractional processes since interminable and often similar processes take place at different levels, ranging from high-level macroeconomic decisions taken by the Board of Directors to the smallest workgroup at an operational level. When subjected to closer scrutiny, even these basic units dissolve into subcentres and then into vague structures, so that the overall decision-making processes and, consequently, the company remain, like a rhizome, indelimitable and difficult to define.

In this diffuse area of close symbiosis between the separate worlds (party, administration, commerce and individual company environments) with blurred responsibilities and personal structures, some mechanisms stand out: the *oyabun–kobun* (mentor) relationship, the *nemawashi* decision-making process (unofficial sounding out of opinions), the *ringi* mechanism (*ex post* symbolization and legitimization of decisions), *amakudari* (the targeted outplacement of bureaucrats for networking purposes), and administrative management practices (pragmatic, situation-dependent business coordination).

Together with the initiators of structural change, these individual mechanisms form a total picture, that of macroeconomic and political coordination and the generation of social visions in the form of self-reflexive decentralized growth. Coordination projects involving complex mechanisms are identifiable from every angle, but do not display any of the traits of a tightly-organized monolithic structure. The mechanics of this unique form of economic coordination can be explained only by the nature of their complex interaction. Here again it is clear that this is a Japanese tradition and that this skill is needed for success in the New Economy. The concrete implementation of these mechanisms in the context of a long-term economic strategy has been interpreted *ex post*, chronologically, from modernization up to present-day 'postmodernization'.

First of all, we considered the role of the MITI as a supreme, omniscient control centre in relation to a multidirectional and indirectly suggestive system of mutual influence between Japan's core groups. With increasing postmodernization, the power of one single guidance system diminishes in favour of a more open heterarchical process of instilling change. Governmental and economic departments are not the only structures underpinning paradigmatic change. Its basic nature consists primarily of dynamic, flexible and concentrated action (in the form of visions, general discussions, indirect support, etc.) which defies direct classification. From this it is quite apparent that clearly definable techniques used to induce this transformation are unexplainable. We can only demonstrate general, international trends at a higher level of abstraction. This total picture can be characterized as a postmodern economic composite.

In the temporal overview of Japan's economy strategies we have attempted to present a concise, plausible interpretation of global strategy. In the course of this overview, the transformation from a mass economy via a quality-based economy to a knowledge-based economy becomes clear. Despite the fact that this transformation has taken place within the growth-oriented, integral economic policy of a developing state, it represents nevertheless an autopoetic and evolutionary process of 'trial and error', as vividly shown at the end of the 1990s.

By digressing somewhat, it has been possible to demonstrate that Japan's structural transformation was not only a voluntary process of improvement from an already favourable position, but was decisively accelerated by the deficiencies caused by modern development. This conquest of modernism and its late effects were the result of a decrystallization which necessitated the reformation of certain internal components. This exerted pressure on Japan from various directions to transform the nation – the result of these internal crises acting as push factors was that Japan was no longer able to sit out the situation; the foreign trade and economic strategies of the 1970s and 1980s lost their momentum; and, finally, Japanese visions of the future acted as extraordinarily powerful pull factors to promote and facilitate the transition to a postmodern Japan.

The question as to the *guiding concepts* behind the *postmodernization* described above and the *role of the Zaibatsu* as a driving force might be answered as follows: the gradual transition to a postmodern era involves the comprehensive (economic and meta-economic) transformation of Japanese society. On a symbolic level, this transformed economy is underpinned by the new Imperial dynasty or 'Heisei era' which represents a coordinating metaphor. This Heisei economy (or Japanese form of the New Economy) can be distinguished from a pluralistic information society and a postmodern society by its set of objectives – information and knowledge intensity, sophisticated products, delocalized and deconcentrated production, classification of consumer preferences into atomic segments, the rapid stream of provisional market strategies, flexible cohesion in terms of company strategy, etc.

The Zaibatsu/Keiretsu networks play a special part in this process. During the modernization period, the Zaibatsu served as role models and, after the Second World War the Keiretsu assumed the task of reconstruction. Now in the postmodernization period around the turn of the millennium, these networks will undertake the complex tasks involved in the transformation. As initiators of paradigmatic change they must act as coordination and implementation structures (prime movers); information-generating and processing centres; and know-how disseminators (trickle-down). Since the MNEs are the first to implement these basic postmodern structures *anticipatorily*, they become *social role models* and, consequently, an example to follow.

In generalizing one could say that this anticipatory dynamics, which has set Japan apart even (and specifically) during postmodern times, has several sources – culture; the desire for a flexible, open transformation; and an imprecise relationship between elite, economy and administration. Those forces produce an abstract executive which impacts on overall economic policy, and also on the management of the Keiretsu. A characterization of this mechanism of economic and meta-economic structural policy (an appropriate term today for industrial structural policy) would, therefore, include the following attributes: 'vision-driven', flexible, inhomogeneous, inconsistent, *ad hoc*, networked, symbolic, with indirect vague connotations, economic primacy and Keiretsu-driven. Japan's economic evolution has retained its postmodern elements without ever having been labelled 'postmodern'. Nevertheless Japan is ideally equipped structurally to face the postmodern world.

During this realization process, several 'mythical images of Japan' have been consigned to the closet or weakened by factual comparisons. A network rather than a homogeneous unit; multilateral partial responsibilities rather than a vertical hierarchy; indifferent, provisional relationships rather than the conspiracy of a 'Japan Inc.'; an open, flexible network rather than monolithic dominance by the MITI, MoF, LDP etc.; local global interpretations rather than general consensus;

adaptive and anticipatory, long-term evolution rather than an export colossus; transrational and value-indifferent rather than irrational, illogical and mythical; the list goes on and on but the superiority of the basic nature of this postmodern interpretation cannot be disproved.

This reveals the postmodern as a latent variable within the Japanese economy and society and, consequently, Japan is also assigned the meta-economic role of paradigm-leader, in addition to its leading economic status. The conclusion which can be drawn from this chapter is that we have been able to identify a considerable number of indicators to support the primary theories of this work:

Postmodern ideas (in the context of the definition contained in Chapter 2) are clearly identifiable within Japan's economic structure, even if they are not, *per se*, explicitly postmodern but in fact bear conventional or traditional names. The real and long-term demonstration of Japanese economic power eloquently testifies to the the performance capabilities of this economic structure which, given the environmental changes involved in the current period of radical change, can undoubtedly be called postmodern.

In connection with the second hypothesis, which is fundamental to this work, that of the postmodern nature of Japan's economic structures and strategies, we have also been able to present convincing indicators through a macroeconomic argument. The specific issue of the 'postmodernity of Japan's multinational enterprises' follows seamlessly on from this and will be separately examined in the next chapter. The question of the Japanese role in the global New Economy is answered by stressing the fact that those postmodern qualities at which Japan excels are the prime value-drivers for success in the New Economy.

The argumentation put forward has also provided a substantial amount of material in support of the initial theory presented in this fourth chapter, that Japan, and particularly Japan's MNEs are preparing themselves steadfastly and actively for the role of global paradigm leader.

5 Keiretsu: Japanese Multinational Enterprises and the Postmodern

> Even in battle, focus on
> the true, inner strength
> of the opponent.
> The penetrating look signifies
> complete concentration
> on the soul of the opponent.
>
> M. Musashi, *Das Buch des fünf Ringe*, 1983, p. 128

I OVERVIEW

Chapter 3 concentrated on basic cultural principles, and Chapter 4 on basic Japanese economic strategies. In this chapter we look at the third dimension, which Best perceived as the basis for Japanese competitiveness: the production organization.[1] In this context, the term does not refer to management or production techniques, but has now been adapted in the postmodern context to mean a new type of business coordination and structure (particularly in the context of inter-company cooperation). Having described postmodern phenomena collectively in terms of mature social mechanisms and complex social structures, in an everyday economic setting as well as the role of the state and paragovernmental organizations in economic coordination, strategy-making and implementation, we can now examine the extent to which the conclusions reached can also be found at company and group level and then round them off to form a concise picture.

During this process we will present and interpret the *theoretical context of existing MNE paradigms* in greater detail. We will also demonstrate intrinsically how the theory of the classical paradigm of the firm developed into a postmodern economic definition. Special attention is devoted to the view that multinational enterprises are networked, since the numerous indicators provided by cultural (cf. Chapter 3) and macroeconomic factors (Chapter 4), which point to the 'network-like' nature of Japan, lead us to conclude that many parallels to Japanese structures can be found. Using these theoretical remarks as a starting point, we pursue the fundamental issue of whether all previous concepts are suboptimal, given the completely different environmental structure; whether they are outdated as procedural guidelines and, also, whether it is possible to build a platform for the future by using the building blocks provided by existing theories relating to multinational enterprises.

Following on from this, our attention turns to the Keiretsu structures which exist in Japan. We present a detailed description of their general features, structural background, contemporary presence and general functions, not only for the purpose of describing and specifically defining the Keiretsu, but also as a parallel method of describing MNE theories. The purpose of this interpretative description is to demonstrate the feasibility of presenting a coherent picture of the Keiretsu with postmodern traits. This generalized picture will then be tested in an attempt at a *postmodern interpretation*, based on the concrete example of the Mitsubishi group of companies. Here it is linked to a different interpretative project, which perceives the Keiretsu as a *'quasi-fractal structure'* which, based on the example of the Mitsubishi Keiretsu, indicates the possibility that the Keiretsu function as a forward-looking commercial organizational principle.

II THE CURRENT ECONOMIC THEORY'S EXPLANATION OF JAPANESE MULTINATIONAL ENTERPRISES

The Correlation between the Keiretsu and MNEs in Research Terms

We need to examine the extent to which the classical Western theory of multinational enterprises is of elucidatory assistance within the overall framework of Japanese companies, before we can analyse the Keiretsu in general (cf. Chapter 5, section III) using a specific practical example (cf. Chapter 5, section IV). Firstly, we examine the implicit similarity of the research objects (Keiretsu or MNEs). We then turn to major contemporary MNE theories, placing special emphasis on network theory. Finally, the findings will be assessed for explanatory content and comprehensiveness in the context of a special, postmodern, company concept study.

As already mentioned in Chapter 1, our analysis will include only paradigmatic Keiretsu structures; no explicit mention will be made, in this context, of multinational *kaisha* companies (Toyota, Honda,[2] etc.), although numerous hypotheses will equally apply to them. At this point we encounter a key problem area in terms of definition, which often diverts the Western observer from the issue at hand. Firstly, the fundamental homonomy of the major commercial groupings in Japan, which are permanently interchangeable, is generally underestimated.[3] In a historic context we could say that the Keiretsu have evolved from the Zaibatsu and, consequently, the latter have ceased to exist. However, even in the face of radically changing environmental conditions, the *sogo shosha* have always been capable of keeping the Zaibatsu successful, in functioning to a certain extent as the primordial cells of major Japanese companies and representing the sales and service centrepiece of these economic structures enabling them to retain the major elements of the Keiretsu even today.[4] Fundamental differences exist between the various strategic objectives, however. The aim of the *sogo shosha* was to be the heart, the powerhouse or family patriarch of an entrepreneurial society. Whereas the Zaibatsu had macroeconomic and political objectives, the Keiretsu concentrated mainly on basic economic values.[5,6]

The use of the collective term 'Japanese multinational enterprise' to describe the upper echelon is nevertheless totally justifiable, as it serves to provide a greater degree of argumentational clarity, when they are compared with other organizational forms in the context of modern-day global competition. A detailed differentiation, without (as yet) an independent 'generalized theory of Japanese international firms' usually produces a plethora of interesting details but no cohesive framework.

The second aspect of this problem is the obligatory attempt to force Japanese MNEs into Western categories such as 'concerns', 'cartels', 'conglomerates' or 'multinationals' (read: American-style MNE). This produces unimaginable problems in terms of comprehension, since many essential dimensions of a Japanese MNE (e.g. social, cultural or historic peculiarities)[7] are lost, in spite of technical congruence.

Interestingly, these approaches mostly produce negative definitions which endeavour to describe the Keiretsu as 'non-conglomerates' or 'non-concerns'.[8,9] Japanese authors frequently complain of the 'immaturity' of Japan's MNEs. This is the result of comparing the multiple dimensions (e.g. geographical and technical complexity, finance and controlling methods and economies of scale) of a standard model, based on American multinational companies, with the Japanese model, the characteristics of which are (almost inevitably) different from the American one.[10] Other literature generally postulates a *latent Japanese type of multinational company*,[11] one which in various phenotypes was the source of exponential economic growth. These companies were and still remain an 'indispensable means of facilitating the multinationalization of Japanese industrial firms'.[12] Abbeglen and Stalk summarize the problem as follows: although Japanese company structures (and Japanese management philosophy or *'nihonteki keiei'*) are not specific to Japan, precisely these structures must be labelled as 'non-nationally and philosophically dependent MNEs', due to the bond which exists between them and Japan. Nevertheless they can be considered system innovators for the MNE: 'In short, the "kaisha" [read: the Japanese companies] will be taking over a major new role as innovators, systems designers, and central contractors in a multinational system of manufacture and distribution.'[13]

In view of the difficulties experienced in the internal classification of Japanese companies, one should not attempt to fit them into American or European categories of classification when international comparisons are made.[14] On the contrary, a revolutionary comprehension is apposite, which postulates the adaptation of individual (Japanese, European, American) corporate models to a new type of environment. These models converge, in a diverse and open manner, to form a new image of a 'postmodern company'. This postmodern company is not, however, a purely Japanese phenomenon, the argumentation put forward is rather that many individual characteristics also apply to leading European and American companies.[15] It is therefore not surprising that, in many quarters, the structural principles of Japanese and Western MNEs are compared, on equal terms, with Japanese principles which are sometimes perceived as exemplary.

The French network of firms, in which parent companies surround themselves by a host of firms and subsequently loosen the liaison bit by bit as the subsidiary becomes more efficient, is regularly cited as an example of '*European quasi-Keiretsu*'. The financial and management networks on which the major German banks are based are also frequently quoted examples.[16] These direct comparisons can be perceived as problematic insofar as a structural feature in the form of a static company hierarchy is clearly apparent in the European examples.[17]

The single-product strategy typical in America (GM, DuPont, Exxon, IBM), which is incompatible with the complex role of the Keiretsu in terms of organization and product structure, provides only limited parallels with American global companies.[18] Eli's extensive analysis identified a few key firms of non-Japanese origin, which have evolved in a similar way to Japanese companies. These similarities range from a *sogo shosha* covering all product and services requirements, to a productive Keiretsu system. But Asia has also produced structures similar to those of the Keiretsu, for example the Korean groups of companies (*chaebol*) or the Chinese family dynasties which, in the Western world, are found primarily in Hong Kong or New York City.[19]

This is why empirical investigations are restricted in terms of methodology. International comparisons only consider Japanese company nuclei, which negatively distorts the international relevance of the Keiretsu and prevents the analysis from being extrapolated beyond the result. A uniform empirical analysis concludes that Japan is 'different', making national characteristics extremely significant. The methodological issues produced by this analysis or the hypotheses based on it, which apply specifically to Japan, are neither formulated explicitly nor expounded upon.[20] Equally, a structural descriptive analysis of the autonomy of individual elements within the companies (for example, aspects such as majority shareholdings or legal forms) is scarcely in a position to formulate any statement on the intensity of the given (formal and particularly informal) relationships existing between the individual corporate units.[21] In previous multinational research, special Japanese features have always been excluded *ex ante* or used *ex post* to explain why the findings differed from those produced by a Western model. In this context, Takamiya and Kobayashi can be seen as the exception:[22] Finance, production, purchasing and organization are the most strongly Japan-oriented functions. Globalization[23] is most pronounced in the areas of research and development, personnel and marketing. In American and European countries the pattern is different: globalization primarily affects personnel, organization, production, purchasing and planning, whereas finance, R&D and marketing are home-based functions. Japanese strategy becomes clear when a more profound interpretation is applied. Functions such as R&D, which are directly dependent on know-how, together with personnel and marketing which are indirect sources of know-how and experience, are relocated abroad in the expectation of discovering new sources of knowledge.

Areas which are subject to controls (strategic planning, general organization) remain in Japan. Equally, areas which can, by synergetic means, be targeted for other firms within the group – production and purchasing using direct methods, and finance, using the indirect method of centralizing financial requirements within the group's bank, which is then able to operate at a global level – are based in Japan.[24] Specific Japanese phenomena (e.g. company cooperation via status, rituals and clubs) cannot serve any useful purpose, in terms of elucidation and problem-solving, as long as purely Western categories are used to analyse Japanese multinational enterprises.[25] This methodology is also adopted by Negandhi who, in the context of international comparisons, promoted the notion that the stronger integration of informal networks could be used to explain Japanese success. The productivity of an MNE, in terms of individual goods and services, is evaluated separately in accordance with the prevailing global rationalization strategy prototype. This universal model must be expanded into a more flexible group of models which apply to all the phenomena exhibited by the multinational companies, without succumbing to a uniform global paradigm which is not only incapable of portraying contemporary reality but can only offer limited assistance in forecasting and meeting the (postmodern) global, competitive challenges which lie ahead.[26]

Thus, we can say that Japanese multinational enterprises are *more than typical of top flight MNEs*. Wolferen succinctly summed up this general fact: 'beneath the outer political forms, there exists a semi-official reality of expected ritual behavior. Beneath this again, there is the true reality of power relations . . .'[27,28] The inclusion of informal, 'meta-structural parameters' produces a more complex picture of the company, i.e. that of a conventional economic company model. Thus, we can say that Japan has *independently contributed to the future development of business organizations via the Keiretsu.*[29] In an analysis of Japan's competitive advantage, these additional parameters can be used for explanatory purposes. In this context they manifest themselves in the form of intense and yet flexible informal networks, comprising independent firms and groups; integrated oligopoly systems with effective entry barriers; interwoven interests, produced over many years by means of close cooperation and highly intensive communication; and as optimum economies of scale and vertical manufacturing ranges.[30] Already in 1974, Ozawa perceived the unique structure of the Keiretsu as Japan's *decisive, competitive advantage* in comparative terms.[31]

Although Western concepts, business practices and production technologies are intensively utilized and improved, the fundamental principles behind the 'Japanese miracle' have always been Japan's working hypotheses, strategies and social and physical structures, which have evolved historically, and these principles control the tools provided by the West.[32] There are primarily four features which set Japan apart in this context:

(a) *family* ideals (loyalty, the firm as a symbolic family, conservative principles);[33]
(b) *trust* (reciprocity within the confines of a rigid relationship);[34]
(c) *durability* in the form of a strategic requirement;[35] and
(d) a special genre of *competitive behaviour* (a fiercely competitive pseudo-oligopoly; closing ranks against outsiders).[36]

It is essential to avoid falling into the trap of dualism in which the Japanese model is compared with that of America. One can easily be seduced into folklorist opinions favouring a purely formal economic perspective, based on the premise that General Motors appears to be an American company and Mitsubishi a Japanese one. This geographical separation is less convincing than the view that the MNEs have developed away from a universal, monolithic and purely economic image[37] towards a new, more open one which portrays them as a *network* of (explicit but, above all, also implicit) *agreements, symbols and social relationships*.

Up to now, Japanese examples have been largely neglected or rejected as anomalies during the development of theories relating to multinational companies. This may also have weakened the explanatory function of these theories *vis-à-vis* the current evolution of global firms. However, a number of these examples provide a promising starting point and hold out prospects of rich results when applied to postmodern business organization.

This synthesis of network models, postmodern structural designs and Japanese social and cultural peculiarities provides us not only with a new interpretation method for the MNE, but also offers new starting points from which to extrapolate the general view of multinational firms[38] and their practical competitive strategies.[39] During the course of this integration of meta-economic dimensions (social, cultural and historical, psychological, political, etc.), new concepts such as the *fractal structure* of the MNE or the *rhizome economy* (cf. Chapter 4, section III ('a model illustrating . . .'), section IV ('overview of Japan's . . .') and section VI ('the turn of the millennium concept'), and Chapter 5, section IV on the 'role of the Mitsubishi Keiretsu') prove an effective tool which should be perceived in terms of the creation of business organizations. The Japanese MNEs, which serve as genuine, independent research subjects within the framework of MNE research, can produce a new impetus in their role as rich examples of new business structures.

Conventional MNE Theories

The origins and precursors of the MNE theory

Over the last 30 years, studies into the novel phenomenon of the MNE have, for inherent reasons, failed to produce a defined, concise, theoretical picture which could do justice to the complexity and dynamics of the MNE. 'The economic theory of the multinational enterprise lies at the interface of three separate specialisms: the theory of the firm, international trade theory and international finance.'[40] The Bain-style paradigm of structure–behaviour–market share,[41] used in the industrial economy, has been deemed inefficient from an MNE perspective since it serves only to depict static conditions in local markets and neglects to include parameters such as strategic policy, market entry barriers, foreign trade or technological progress.[42] This model could not provide the clarification needed to analyse the character of highly integrated, international firms and was consequently replaced by a perspective influenced by foreign trade theory.[43,44] Furthermore, the nature and function of the MNE could only partially be explained by reference to neo-classicism,[45] which concentrated on describing the allocative efficiency losses of major firms, which led to antitrust and regulatory policies aimed at counteracting ('countervailing power') an imperfect market.[46] But this theoretical and ahistoric abstract view not only fails to explain the complex internal relationships within the MNE; to a certain extent it has also created its own demons: Antitrust laws work primarily against flexible (horizontal) coordination of business activities. This has led to a wave of company mergers (particularly vertical mergers), precisely those phenomena which the regulators actually wanted to contain.[47]

Hymer was the first to reflect on this problematic issue in terms of the *special reasons for the existence of the MNE*, which extend beyond simple concepts of 'big business' and economies-of-scale arguments.[48] He postulated endogenous, non-marketable advantages (marketing, management skills, technical know-how, patents, etc.) which multinational companies possess, and which they use to cancel out the disadvantages (a lack of local knowledge, no connections in the administrative or political sector, etc.) involved in foreign expansion.[49] These advantages are (in contrast with national firms) greater than all the collective obstacles faced by the MNE in the relevant countries and generate a strong competitive position in the various national markets.[50]

The most important prerequisite for this theory is the assumption of imperfect markets.[51] Successful firms initially expand in the domestic market, and this commercial growth (via mergers and capital expansion) improves market share and profits. However, profits do not remain constant but reduce marginally, which is associated with stronger competition and more efficient markets. This explains the search for markets which are even less perfect so that the same process can be set in motion again. This is where the close link to the product life-cycle hypothesis becomes clear.

According to Casson, certain difficulties with Hymer's approach cannot be overcome. He failed to subdivide market imperfections into imperfections in market structure and transaction cost, and was unable to explain the existence of cartels and collusion. These are the starting points for the internalization theory (cf. Chapter 5, section II).[52] From the perspective of this work, the service performed by Hymer is that he developed the concept of the MNE as a *special* and *complex company structure* which, in an international context, replaces that of the 'conventional firm'. Hymer's understanding of an MNE is that of a firm with a *high degree of freedom*, in the advantageous position of being able to compare different environments and live successfully in them, without restriction in terms of form.[53]

Vernon developed his famous *product life-cycle theory* from the growth dynamics described above.[54] Technological know-how is assimilated (learning curve) and employed by competing nationally until it ceases to represent a competitive advantage because all the competitors have attained the same level. Subsequently, this know-how is used to compete in the foreign marketplace where know-how levels are inferior, and this know-how once again becomes a positive competitive advantage. However, Vernon's theory has now been sidelined due to the increasingly apparent implausibility of technological hegemony, increased cyclic rates and the greater fragmentation and volatility of consumer markets.[55] Consequently, according to Ozawa, Vernon's rigid model does not apply to Japan.[56] In one of his last books, the late Vernon emphasized the interlinkage between politics and economics. MNEs now generate about half of the world's foreign trade, so any change in the relatively benign climate in which they have operated during the 1990s will create serious tensions in international economic relations. As MNEs dominate globally, hence eroding national sovereignty, a retaliation by governments is tempting but should be avoided at all costs, rather a collaboration between governments and MNEs should be the model to follow.[57]

Vernon's image of an extremely *dynamically expanding international firm*, whose major assets (know-how, skills, corporate identity etc.) are *immaterial* and thus more *transportable* and competitively decisive in unstable markets, is still significant in terms of a contemporary understanding of Japanese MNEs.

Transaction cost economics

Picking up on the problems of Hymer, transaction cost economics attempts to explain the unanswered question of vertical organization, cartels and collusion.[58] Williamson, one of the main speakers on the theory of transaction costs, constructs a general economic theory based on the implicit and explicit costs of a contract and on 'realistic' behavioural assumptions (contracting man, bounded rationality etc.)[59] 'Transaction cost economics adopts a comparative contractual approach to the study of economic organization in which the transaction is made the basic unit of analysis and the details of governance structure and human actors are brought under review.'[60,61]

Thus transaction costs economics expands traditional economic theory, which *a priori* neglects transaction cost and other disruptive influences. But these transaction costs (or rather the need to reduce them by means of special organizational arrangements) are precisely the special motivation behind the creation of multinational companies in the first place.[62] 'Transaction cost takes the larger context. The social context in which transactions are embedded – the customs, mores, habits and so on – have a bearing, and therefore, need to be taken into account.'[63] Arrow defines transaction costs in this context as 'the costs of running the system'.[64] Simple maximization objectives become untenable when viewed in conjunction with Buchanan's view that emphasis should be placed not on both the explicit (and particularly the implicit) aspects of contracts between economic protagonists rather than on decisions,[65] and also that performative objectives which are more result-based should be developed, to which the maxim: 'organize transactions so as to economize on bounded rationality while simultaneously safeguarding them against the hazards of opportunism'[66] would apply.

This *extension of the narrow interpretation placed by homo economicus on rationality* allows us to perceive all economic activity as the contract of a '*contracting man*', who uses, for assessment purposes, a 'limited' organic, opportunistic, self-interest-based thinking which has to cope with uncertainty and the effects of social interactions.[67,68] Williamson refers to this type of economic behaviour as 'relational contracting',[69] since psychological and social categories strongly affect the result. Since contracts – particularly long-term, complex or implicit contracts – are neither perfect nor completely comprehensive, the essential and most important basis for a contract is trust.[70] Since responsibility fundamentally rests with a limited number of people, this produces an extremely lengthy, repetitive and complex interaction between the protagonists; individual recurring groups gradually form societies, 'religious sects' or 'brotherhoods' within which trust is built up, which in turn leads to lower transaction costs.[71] In this context, Japanese business culture exhibits astonishing parallels with the view (cf. Chapter 3, section IV, 'the web of individual relationships', and Chapter 4, section III on '*oyabun–kobun*') that personal relationships command great respect or are explicitly involved in decision-making parameters.[72]

Consequently, some Japanese authors perceive the Japanese MNEs also as *transaction costs-minimizing structures*, within which the important organizational functions involved in economic activities (information-processing, control, operational coordination, infrastructure provision, system management, etc.), durability, rapid adjustment flexibility, strategic efficacy and risk-minimization are achieved by means of increased stability and minimal (transaction) costs, via a network of long-term personal relationships which are the focus for implicit and explicit contracts.[73] But it is not only in Japan that pressure to increase efficiency in sectors ranging from *job organization* (Taylor, Fayol, scientific management) to *production organization* (mass production, continuous production) and *production system organization* (transaction cost minimization by means of cooperation and trust, symbol management, production system management, holistic organization concepts) continues to increase; this can be perceived as a general, if not always temporally parallel, trend.[74]

The new interpretation placed on the evolution of multinational companies, which is relevant from a postmodern perspective, involves the integration of meta-economic cost structures, that is ones which extend beyond the traditional economy and the relative approaches of the individual protagonists involved.[75] An additional mechanism exists, apart from the price and planning coordination mechanism, which is the knowledge-accumulating social production system, the main characteristics of which are *reciprocity*, high *information density*, behaviour (*trust*) designed to achieve long-term success, and open *sensitive environmental relationships*.[76] In this context the issue of peripheral interrelationships between the individual company sectors of a multinational company as well as between the MNEs and those around them constitutes an appropriate research object. Can these boundaries be clearly defined? Is it, in fact, desirable to do so? Does an optimum level of internalization exist within the structures in question? These issues represent the focal point of the theory of internalization.

The theory of internalization

The question of the optimum level of internalization becomes relevant when we consider the market imperfections which make non-market-oriented solutions attractive and the transaction cost economy which draws in not only monetary costs but also non-monetary costs into the equation:

> The process of internalization explains most (and probably all) of the reasons for foreign direct investment. Previous writers ... have noticed a response by the MNE to government induced market imperfections such as tariffs, taxes and capital controls. All of these types of market imperfections serve to stimulate one sort of MNE or another.[77]

The internalization of activities within existing company structures is an effective method of cutting transaction costs (market-making cost) and represents, according to Casson, one of the primary driving forces behind current company growth. Internal markets are created which generate intracompany activities, obviating the need to approach external market participants, and thus minimizing prospecting, control and know-how transfer costs.[78] The starting points here are issues such as: 'Why are plants in different countries brought under common ownership and control? The answer is: because the transaction costs incurred in intermediate product markets can be reduced by internalizing these markets within the firm.'[79]

Numerous phenomena within Japanese management practice lead to the conclusion that internalization objectives form the basis of the calculation. Thus, the absence of a Japanese takeover market points to the fact that monitoring, evaluation of company success and the controls resulting from it cannot be attributed to external market forces but are consciously internalized within the internal 'market' of a Keiretsu and thus implemented more efficiently. However, the aim of this assessment is not a mononomous structure. It takes account of flexible internalization, particularly in terms of 'soft factors' such as information, strategy and coordination and, to a lesser extent, 'hard factors' such as legal controls and official company relationships, desirable goals.[80]

This developing internalization can today be described as a major trend, which also generates overall structural and paradigmatic change:

The rapid growth of multinational companies signifies that international factor allocations, in the form of direct investments (tangible assets transfers), are leading to new legal and organizational structures, which influence the scope and nature of international business trends.[81]

These structures are now using this internalization as a concrete, global competitive advantage thanks to the trend towards multinationalism.[82]

However, these firms are not perceived as individual rigid entities, but rather as the *focus of economic activity*, the external and internal parameters of which are diffuse. In this connection, Coase quotes Sir A. Salter: 'The normal economic system works for itself. For its current operation it is under no central control, it needs no central survey ... [A] process that is automatic, elastic and responsive.'[83] When interpreted in this way, a 'firm's parameters' can only be defined diffusely or randomly. Key abilities, internally assimilated know-know and the system of trust existing within the company, with its numerous gravitational centres, around which all the concentrically decreasing substructures gather, becomes more significant in existential terms. Here, the resulting company structures cannot successfully confront this complexity of objectives, possible options, structures, networks, temporal preferences, environmental dependency, personal dynamics and strategies with universal hierarchically-oriented logic. The company therefore has to adopt a *comprehensive, flexible* and *open dynamics* approach.[84]

Boundaries of the firm become meaningless, as evidenced in the growing trend towards extranets and freelancing employees. In that sense a company is even less than a bundle of contracts but a 'market of conversations' where the question of being inside or outside becomes irrelevant or at least very relative. The network called 'company' is so much linked to its surroundings that there are no clear definitorial rules to determine the extent, the reach of a company. As little as necessary is incorporated into the core nucleus of the company in order to be ultra-flexible and swift. But, at the same time as much knowledge as manageable is attracted into an outer sphere around the nucelus. Therefore, internationalization does not mean that a monolithic company is the ultimate result, but a hard to define arrangement of management, employees, partners and suppliers that are in an open, dynamic, but intense exchange.[85]

On a theoretical level, this plethora of problems does not constitute a standardization concept. It actually requires fundamental openness towards the individual theories when the contemporary features of a multinational company are considered. In this connection it may prove helpful to take a holistic, macroeconomic view. Kojima examines this approach, whereas Dunning chooses a different modus operandi, that of the eclectic theory of the multinational company.

The macroeconomic explanation

Based on Heckscher and Ohlin's foreign trade theory and supported by the international asset arbitration hypothesis, Kojima bases his attempt to elucidate multinational companies specifically on the special features of Japan's development.[86] According to Kojima, the *relative factors endowments* of a region are the driving influences behind the medium- and long-term development of multinational companies and directly affect their strategies. The standard approach of asset arbitration closely associated with it, predicts that actual marginal capital productivity (or in more general terms factor productivity) is becoming more closely aligned in different (global) regions. This is primarily the result of the activities of the MNEs (as well as global financial institutions), which profitably utilize and equalize any productivity (interest rate) differences which existed *ex ante*.[87]

The irreversible shortage of resources and space is a limiting factor in terms of domestic industrial growth (the Ricardo–Hicksian trap of industrialism) and necessitates the use of relatively cheaper input markets to provide labour and land outside Japan. By minimizing risks, via group investments and state cooperation, Japan has been able to become an outward-looking, genuinely trade-oriented nation. This situation of an uncertain supply base in terms of (foreign) raw material and a (culturally) indiminishable over-demand for labour and ground does justice to a classic macroeconomic theory in which Japan accumulates commercially-oriented know-how, experience and management techniques in order to improve its domestic industrial structure. The outdated industrial/production methods which this produces are relocated to countries which have not yet progressed beyond that lower level of complexity.[88]

According to this theory, the result of this development process, described by Lewis-Fei-Ranis, is that all industrial nations become more and more alike.[89] The same critique applied to the product life-cycle hypothesis is also useful here. The impetus behind the exportation of outdated industries and innovation decreases in direct relation to the differences between trading regions.[90] Furthermore, the direct synthesis between MNE theories and orthodox foreign trade theories is associated with conceptional problems: a lack of transaction cost estimates, a lack of differentiation between direct and indirect investments or formal and informal controls.[91] The concept of different factor endowments is equally not undisputed, since a number of research findings perceive different inputs apart from traditional ones such as the major competitive advantages.[92,93] On the other hand, empirical findings argue in favour of the fundamental viability of the Heckscher–Ohlin approach which is subject to modification, in Japan's case, by the phenomenon of intra-company (or intra-industry[94]) transactions.[95]

Abstractly, we could say that this approach is based on competitive advantages which are relevant for the future: trade (external or intra-company or groups) and *know-how* and *information transfer management* represents a decisive criteria in competitive terms. An interesting question in this connection is also what will happen once the existing input supply variations have been dismantled. Will this lead to the creation of new supply variations interregionally? (The following could be conceivable: symbols, reputation, status, know-how, a creative climate or Dunning's 'created assets' etc.) Will the trading regions, closely linked due to the activities of the MNEs in a fragile balance of fundamental equality, be distinguishable only by dint of certain rapidly-changing differences? Will the structural and regulatory differences between the regions become more pronounced, forcing multinational firms to become useless jugglers complying with all requirements and values and processing all the contradictions which arise internally without negatively affecting local efficiency? The relevance of the macroeconomic approach in terms of the nature of the distinctive features of future multinational companies is based on these issues, specifically when viewed from a postmodern viewpoint.

By choosing these 'conventional' theories, we have identified a general loosening and expansion of the image of MNEs. In this connection, four points are worthy of note and these points are demonstrated in sections III and IV below by means of real examples which fit seamlessly into a postmodern image of the MNEs:

- The relevance of know-how and information (or its management) crops up repeatedly as a competitive factor in all studies (Hymer, Vernon, Kojima *et al.*);
- Company parameters become diffuse, and the picture changes from a dinosaurian colossus to an agile, dynamic network (internalization hypothesis);
- The symbolic and immaterial gains (economic) ground with the rational relegated to the sidelines (transaction cost economics);
- A trend towards more complex viewpoints (from the labour organization, via the production organization to the production system organization).[96]

'Unorthodox' MNE Perspectives

The eclectic approach

Based on the two theories: firstly that monocausal maximization objectives no longer exist but have now been replaced by multifactorial and multidisciplinary options, and secondly that in the modern world it is impossible to make generalizations about the optimum structural relationship between the state and the MNE, or in relation to the optimum competitive strategies of the MNE,[97.98] Dunning constructs a target-driven conglomerate consisting of an overabundance of theories concerning MNEs, which is designed to serve as a template for methodological interpretation.[99] The eclectic paradigm attempts to be an *open synthesis* combining all approaches and explicitly opposes a 'new general theory'. Its objective is not to serve as the ultimately valid explanation but as the overall starting point (which is why it is a paradigm and not a theory):[100] 'it offers a general framework for theorizing about all kinds of international involvement'.[101] Consequently the eclectic paradigm is able to successfully combine the significant advantages of macroeconomic findings, foreign trade theory, the internalization theory and other approaches.[102]

Based on the general issue of the position of multinational companies, an analytical concept has been developed based on three basic principles which are decisive in terms of the success or failure of an MNE.[103] These three basic principles are abbreviated into the letters OLI (ownership advantages, location, internalization).[104] The combination and interaction of these parameters within a framework of technology, competitive position and state influence, as well as their effective use in deciding what will be produced where and how and the nature of the production system involved ('knowledge of asset creation … knowledge of organizing economic activity'[105]), are decisive for the global success of a company. In this interpretation, the MNEs are essentially different from mononational companies primarily as a result of their ownership advantages, since they are capable of manufacturing and marketing in the most diverse of environments and political systems. Their ability to combine numerous different production opportunities gives them an added advantage.[106]

In conditions of *growing uncertainty* and *rising economic interdependence*, in which costs and benefits unanticipated either by the seller or by the consumer continually crop up, large batch production is declining and small batch production within the (MNE-) networks is continuing to grow. Optimum forecasting of economies of scale, control of undetermined cost situations, know-how accumulation and learning, together with multidimensional (economic and meta-economic) transaction cost monitoring and optimum integration, are important abilities in adapting to the lightning pace of global competition.[107] This eclectic paradigm is opposed by a clear but constructive critique. The structure of the OLI paradigm is open to the criticism that the relationship between the parameters is unclear, the three parameters are adequate, although not intrinsic in terms of an explanation of multinational phenomena, and ownership advantage is redundant, since the explanatory potential of the internalization theory has been underestimated.[108,109,110]

In summary, we can identify the following correlates for a postmodern perspective of the MNEs. The method does not depend on a rigid but on a contingent optimum, in order to do justice to a *modular, multimethod approach*. The pragmatic description predominates; no universal model of an MNE or prediction of its behaviour is envisaged.[111] *Knowledge and coordination* which exceed all traditional boundaries (geographical, organizational, social) and *increased flexibility* which allows the environments to adjust to one another (customers, state regulatory institutions, procurement markets) are the fundamental abilities which a successful MNE must demonstrate according to eclectic and postmodern paradigms.

The systems perspective

The systems view or systems approach of Casson follows on from the concepts of an eclectic theory. In it, the *cultural* and *psychological components* of an economic network are more highly developed in the context of both small firms and multinational companies:

The central thesis ... is, that new economic environment challenges the long-held belief that economics is a discipline that can be adequately pursued in isolation from other social sciences.[112]

Therefore, in terms of the analysis, pure rationale or logic are not the only tools used within the interdependent environments. Values and psychological structures (trust, sympathy, network) again provide new interest from this perspective.[113] The complexity thus produced[114] represents the most important competitive advantage and takes precedence over commonly cited national, industrial, regional or production-specific advantages. It has the ability to structure and make use of complexity: knowledge (or rather the transfer of knowledge) has now become the most important global competitive advantage.[115]

The *competitive advantage* derived from *complexity*, *information* and *network management* is primarily determined by the culture on which it is based. One of the major distinguishing features of this type of management, which is present in all economic transactions, is the concept of *trust*. Trust, defined as integrity and a lower level of opportunist behaviour,[116] reduces the risks and side-effects, which cannot be explicitly defined contractually. This investment in mutual emotional ties reduces transaction costs by decreasing control costs and minimizing prospecting costs. Casson differentiates (as do Hall and Reed-Hall)[117] between 'high trust-economies' (e.g. families, small clubs, or Japan,) and 'low trust economies' (provisional groups, large heterogeneous societies, or America).[118] In the first, the coordination of the social group is controlled by means of reciprocity. The information flow is higher and denser, creating an educational and social system and a valid alternative to a planning system or price (contract) system.[119] Tendentially, these economic structures are immobile and exhibit clear stratification in terms of status, reputation, symbols and image, in which moral homogeneity and personal identity dominate. Although sustained long-term (business) relationships are prioritized, effective flexibility is also extremely high.[120] Within these commercial relationships of trust, informal personal contact is the key component in confidence-building. Within an environment of trust, a formal ownership structure and external formal contracts are rejected in favour of implicit agreements, emotional assessments and values, even though, superficially, formalia still appears to be the common language.

We can perceive that a system of trust consists of this type of quasi-integration and internalization. In today's world, the material assessment of a deed or decision is less important than emotional, symbolic or 'moral' evaluations.[121,122] Thus, Casson speaks of the superiority of the moral/psychological mechanism of coordination, as opposed to a system of control and pricing.[123] Consequently, the non-quantitative, non-technical aspects of a commercial transaction assume new significance: '[N]ational culture can have a significant impact on performance of the firm, since it reduces transaction cost within the economy'. Trust, perceptions, information flow, decision-making mechanisms and cooperation efficiency are all variables influenced by this basic culture, which are, for their part, decisive in terms of overall commercial performance. However, these variables evolve over a period of time and cannot be adapted quickly or learnt.[124]

For this reason we can say that a *basic common culture* is one of the most important competitive advantages and is rapidly assuming greater significance. Cultures in which reciprocity, close personal relationships, high levels of trust, faster information flow and entrepreneurial spirit are dominant, positively affect competitiveness.[125]

On the basis of these criteria, Casson concludes, within the framework of a general analysis, that Japan is the nation with the greatest cultural (entrepreneurial) competitive advantage, followed by the USA, Sweden and France.[126] This perspective sees Japan as nothing other than a plethora of small interdependent units which form a highly complex network of reciprocal favours and tokens of trust, with restricted intergroup mobility, which allows each group to react quickly, adaptively and flexibly due to the lack of rigid control mechanisms and stiff formalities. 'Success' can also be attributed to a highly-trained workforce which, in addition to technical training, boasts the following features: homogeneously internalized ethical and moral values;[127] a combination of strategic action and Confucian values; seamless cooperation between individual economic supporters (state, companies, workforce); and special working procedures (quality circle, JIT) generated by trust-based organization.[128] Trust (*shiyo*), 'belly to belly friendship' (*haragei*) and a 'conspiracy of silence' can be perceived as fundamental decision-making factors.[129]

A group is transformed into a *symbolic family within a network* by means of a method involving 'behind the curtain rules' and '*maihai*' (teahouse politics). This method is based on trust, personal loyalties, image, prestige, status and '*giri*' and the network can, therefore, include many different phenotypic characteristics. Family, state, firm and multinational company support each other componentially and, in so doing, resort to the same principles.[130,131] Conventional clarification approaches which attempt to interpret the success of Japanese multinational companies are always structurally inadequate since they have, regrettably, largely failed, thus far, to provide anything other than monofactorial partial explanations (the interrelationship between state and economy, employee–employer relationships, production organization, or strategic foreign trade policy). Only an approach which comprehensively perceives each subsystem and its economic and meta-economic dimensions can effectively tackle a topic as complex as that presented by Japan's multinational companies.[132] The bridge between this systemic approach and postmodern thought patterns is easy to construct in Japan's case.[133] Trust, durability and personal relationships acquire greater explanatory strength in a world of increasing complexity in which rigid formalia are rejected in favour of informalia, imprecision, ambiguity, differences and flexibility, when based on a fundamental multidisciplinarianism which specifically casts aside the psychological and sociological ramifications of rationalism.

Nevertheless one should not lose sight of the fact that only performance and success are decisive in terms of long-term existence. The resultant success criterion is the *ability to manage complex systems, their subsystems and interdependence.* When considered from this stance, ability is almost the same as cultural orientation. Culture is a global competitive factor which the multinational companies possess. It should not be perceived, in this context, as the local national culture of a national firm but as pan-national splinter cultures, manifested within complex subsystems and, in turn, within larger networks.[134,135] In a special way, this perspective takes account of both views: that of the multinational company as the currently most effective complexity management method and that of a Japanese economic structure with strong cultural undercurrents.[136]

International competitiveness of industries

This research area is based on the globalization trend which is now omnipresent and examines, more closely, its effects on companies, industries and nations. The theory that national markets are dissolving into a global market has been postulated for some time now; the survival of the majority of larger companies depends on the globalization of all activities. This is accompanied by constantly intensifying competition, and competitiveness is the supreme goal.[137] At its most fundamental, this can be defined according to Orlowski as the 'ability to sell'[138] which, for Porter, is just as important as productivity.[139] Blattner perceives the relationship between per capita income, labour productivity, gross value added, return on capital and market share as an indicator of competitiveness;[140] however, there is general agreement that conventional theories cannot adequately convey the phenomena of international competitiveness.[141]

The old approach was that the industrial economy is formed from an aggregate of sectors and industries. Unfortunately this abstractive perspective fails to explain the success of individual firms, certain subsectors or industrial groups.[142] According to Porter, these successes can be explained more plausibly by a bottom-up approach, which postulates that individual successes should be examined in the broader context of holistic competitiveness.[143] Using this principle, Porter subdivides branches of industry into '*strategic groups*' (clusters or industries),[144] comprising firms which together form a relatively homogeneous unit in terms of their actions and reactions. These clusters compete on a global level with analogous groups and are embedded in a complex sphere of subclusters, input markets and regulatory effects.[145] Some of the basic premises are worthy of mention here: a competitive nation (region, continent) is not an isolated fixed physical entity, but a portfolio of industries clustered around a few (excellent) key companies which are either stimulated or hindered by the surrounding framework. For this reason, competitiveness can ultimately be whittled down to *productivity, cooperation* and *flexibility.*[146]

As time goes by and the importance of information and transport costs, comparative cost advantages, factor endowment advantages or differences in infrastructure declines,[147] the classic theory of international trade is becoming weaker and less appropriate.[148] However, Porter simultaneously identifies a new trend in which nations and public assets are seen as optional resources and assessed in the context of dynamic strategies[149] in a global context. Thus, *dynamic competitive factors* such as know-how, experience, innovation, anticipation/forecasting, flexible long-term strategies and network performance become more important than traditional, static factors such as geography, economies of scale, rights or competitive climate.[150,151]

This new competitive company dimension runs parallel to a new stage in national (regional) development. The evolution of a nation (region)[152] is perceived by Porter[153] in terms of the Rostow theory of stages.[154] The course of evolution proceeds from a factor-induced stage (factors of production are taken for granted), via an investment-induced stage (concentration on a few industries and their growth via economies of scale) and an innovation-induced stage (competition *à la* Schumpeter) to a prosperity-induced stage (in which money is the most important economic commodity, sophisticated requirements and risk-aversion increase, dynamic momentum grows weaker and weaker and global competitiveness falls).[155] Globally, the majority of economically relevant countries are on the threshold of a new stage. The NIEs (newly-industrializing economies) (e.g. Korea and Taiwan) are on the threshold of an investment-induced stage, leading to an innovation-induced stage (computer production for example). In many cases, 'former industrial countries' (Germany and England) were only able to maintain this stage for a very short period of time and have now progressed to a prosperity-induced stage. It is here that the loss of dynamics manifests itself most painfully and generates a momentum which drives society towards new dimensions.[156]

Over the last 30 years the trend of corporate development continued from internationalization to globalization to globality, with globality being understood as 'global interconnectivity'[157] of individual entities associated with each other in a company environment. ABB's slogan of the art of being local everywhere captures this phenomenon well, although it leaves out the open network idea of the New Economy (cf. the following section).

With the full force of the Internet, the question of sovereignty of nations and the debate about the 'rightfulness' of globalization becomes a historical sidetrack.[158] The question whether globalization should be allowed or fought is irrelevant as this was just a transient intermediate stage of development. As an aside it may be noted that the arguments to actively support globalization activities are convincing: globalization brings more efficiency and more 'context-richness' across the world and even creates more jobs in industrialized countries as well as in lesser developed countries, as it is not a zero-sum game but a windfall profit for any nation and individual.[159]

As it becomes clear that the architects of the global society are not the countries or nations, but the companies,[160] the focus now shifts back again to the proactive parts of business: structures and processes inside and around companies and entrepreneurs. Hence, rather than static geographical concepts, more abstract ones based on new forms of cooperation and technology are currently needed.[161] Accordingly, the overall medium-term fate of a region (nation, group of states) is chiefly determined by the success of the clusters of firms working within it and its sustained efforts to do justice to the challenges of the new strategic dimensions.[162] This also explains the paradox generally apparent in recent times for which Japan has always been criticized. National governments are increasingly pursuing a dual strategy: on the one hand they are promoting global competition, whilst erecting protectionist barriers on the other.[163] Regions are competing, on the one hand, at intercompany level, and groups are competing at an interregional level on the other. Japan is a typical example of this. The features which characterize this nationally protectionist type of structure are excessive competition between groups and intensive cooperation within them. According to Porter, Japan has the ideal prerequisites for (further, possibly global) cluster formations, since numerous horizontal and vertical information social networks already promote group formation.[164,165] Parallel to this opinion, Borner also favours, in an abstract manner, the *intra-company group-specific use of competitive advantages*, with the exclusion of 'non-members' in order to minimize gratuitous losses and utilization by outsiders.[166] Fundamentally, in Japan's case, we can use the highly competitive climate which exists between the Keiretsu as a starting point although, in terms of the categories mentioned, they all appear to correspond. The interpretation placed on 'excessive competition' (*kato kyoso*),[167] which nonetheless exists, necessarily transcends the usual definition of competition as a sporting term.[168] This competition becomes an embittered 'metaphysical' conflict in terms of symbols and prestige, in which pure profit motives are only one, technical, component.[169]

In the midst of these target dimensions, the focus of group strategy must be to balance specific national strategy, whose objectives are inherent to a globally integrated group system, with conflicting needs. Just as one might say that multinational companies are determining international economic policy, one could also say that neither a uniform international competitive structure nor a single global company strategy can possibly exist; that is it is impossible to create universal monopolizing forces.[170] Coalitions, intensive coordination and broad (geographical) dissemination are the main trajectories involved in strategy-making. As a result, multinational firms have to pursue *dual and multiple strategies at the same time* in order to treat the 'host country' (each country) with sensitivity, whilst, at the same time being obliged to apply the same dynamics to the company as a whole.[171] Forward-looking companies are forced to deal with constantly changing factors affecting strategy and to confront numerous, frequently conflicting, opportunities, restrictions and demands. The prerequisites here are *decentralized, federal organization models*, capable of performing numerous holistic functions (a multidimensional matrix).[172] Similarities between the cluster concept and Japan's actual structures, in the form of the Keiretsu, are also apparent:[173] the Keiretsu can be perceived as the *most intensive type of 'cluster'* around today. From a theoretical perspective this may be accompanied by an (unanticipated) convergence. The series of 'economic stages' in terms of a national economy can be seamlessly extended by follow-up stages, if Baudrillard's indicators relating to a symbolic economy as the next stage are incorporated as well.[174]

These three basic principles – that is the *dissolution of national concepts*, the *coagulation of companies* and the *restructuring of organization and strategy to form open networks* – can also be applied to the concrete example of Japan as a paradigm[175] for the development of multinational companies. The most pronounced representative of this, from this perspective,[176] is Ohmae, a nuclear physicist and party founder[177] who is also McKinsey's top man in Japan.

Despite the hypothesized standardization of consumer preference within OECD countries, nations still compete as separate entities.[178] Multinational companies attempt to play nations off against each other and to optimize their own global needs. Each country needs its own management philosophy which prevents the creation of any genuine, global, indistinguishable, comparable mentality among the multinational enterprises.[179] Using Japan as an example, Ohmae generates an outward-looking view of Japanese multinational enterprises, for whom the role model is that of the *Swiss multinationals*. Lacking natural resources but equipped with well-trained staff, they are heavily involved in business activities outside Switzerland. In general terms, they are reserved, prestige and symbol-ridden, although effective, alert and successful.[180] Nation states are beginning to become unimportant for the *companies without countries*, as well as for consumers whose buying habits are determined by preference rather than national emotions.[181] This is why attempts in the United States and the United Kingdom to stimulate demand for domestic products by using slogans like 'Buy British!' or 'Be American – Buy American!' are never successful:

National borders are virtually meaningless today. In our new economic system, co-operation and interdependence are prerequisites for survival. If only we can dispel our illusions, wake up to the truth, and broaden our perspective, we'll see a whole new world before us.[182]

This thinking is expanded by the *total globalization* of all economic dimensions. Instead of a combination of states, Ohmae sees the triad as an '*interlinked economy*', a global economic union. It forms an economy without borders or differences, a diverse and multilayered economy, comprising Europe, Japan and America as well as a few aggressive developing countries such as Taiwan, Hong Kong and Singapore.[183] Japan, ahistorically being more an introverted country has more to overcome. The prevailing '*sakoku*' mentality (secluded nation), described by critics as 'parochialism and exclusiveness', is still to be overcome, although this limiting habit is clearly waning.[184] In general, it can safely be said that global companies produce global goods for global consumers. Although these goods are adapted to suit local requirements, or cater to the myriad of fractal consumer markets as well as market and production structures, once the marketing and symbolic 'packaging' has been peeled off, their complicated form of existence precludes any national flag being pinned to them. The multinational companies have an *amoebae-like character*.[185] They are flexible and diffusely spread, and appear superficially to be undifferentiated. They are also strangely decentralized, without a power centre or detectable control centre. Thus Ohmae comes close to postmodern concepts.[186] Europe, America and Japan are, in many ways, united (industrialization, consumerism, international politics and all other possible forms of discussion); but at the same time, juxtaposed local cultures of equal importance do exist. Foucault calls this a cultural transgression: two (or more) cultures simply do not oppose one another, they are not opponents in a 0–0 draw but coexist separately and interrelate.[187] Even from other viewpoints, the findings of 'unorthodox theories' can be interpreted in parallel with basic postmodern approaches:

- All methods of clarification are acceptable, the intention being to pragmatically achieve a description via unbiased combination;
- The endogenization of cultural and psychological components (e.g. trust or the influences created by sociological relationships) offers greater opportunities in terms of the comprehension of postmodern economic phenomena;
- The management of complexity, knowledge and flexibility is an abstract survival maxim; the utilization of existing cultural forces as competitive factors is becoming more significant;
- The global economy is perceived both in terms of increasing interdependency and simultaneously rising instability, embracing fragmention, globalization, differentiation and general acceleration;
- Situative or loosely defined networks and clusters are being emancipated as independent units, in contrast to second-hand concepts (such as the state, hierarchic economic structures, etc.); symbolic group orientation instead of monadic rationality, greater (intensity, scope of) environmental sensitivity.

The Network Approach

Network definitions

Network theory, which is a creative new development, can provide a new alternative in explanatory terms and make a significant contribution to our understanding of multinational conduct and the search for new competitive advantages.[188] The view that companies and other complex social structures should be perceived as networks is based on the relevant technical disciplines of all general communication sciences (logic, computer networks, human interaction-psychology).[189] Lipnack and Stamps provide the first non-technical definitions:

> Networks, ... are informal systems, where dissonance is encouraged and consensus is a common goal [or prescribed output]. The nature of [actual]

networks is that they are short-lived, self-camouflaging and adisciplinary ...
Networks are invisible, uncountable, unpollable, and may be active or
inactive.[190]

In this context, networks are perceived as the *lines of communication*, in terms of
information and power, between a plethora of protagonists (groups/individuals/
institutions) *within a communal setting*.[191]

The perception that companies are networks is an extremely holistic ('eclectic')
approach in which existing knowledge is used to produce a new, more productive
perspective. The coordination costs incurred within these complex systems form the
nexus to the transaction cost hypothesis.[192] Complex organizations which operate
in a turbulent environment, using evaluation-dependent and imprecise/incomplete
data, can no longer process information optimally or make sound decisions, due to
their rigid hierarchies. It is precisely these companies which profit to a propor-
tionally greater extent from the existence and efficiency of internal and external
networks.[193] From the perspective of internalization theory, the view that companies are in fact networks can be perceived as an evolutionary stage which begins
with external markets, continues with their internalization into domestic markets
and, ultimately, ends with (internal) networks.[194] The systemic approach is an ideal
complement to the network view, since the former examines internal prerequisites
(the formal/informal sociogram between information- and decision-makers and
their trust basis) more closely. Finally, companies, in the form of networks, can be
integrated seamlessly into the Porter/Ohmae theory of global competition, since in
this theory the firm is presented rather cryptically as a translocal, diffuse, sensitive,
flexible and reactive entity. Networks are the evolutionary answer to a new,
information-oriented world in which greater uncertainty, the revised basic values of
all societies, the dismantling of organization structures, the replacement of people
by hierarchies and sensitivity, of informal and symbolic power by rational, hierarchic and physical might, are the decisive factors.[195]

The major, general characteristics of all networks are that:[196]

- their key element is information processing, information control and
  dissemination;
- they have independent autonomous separate units which interchange during
  'voluntary' communication;
- their creation is always unplanned and need-driven;
- they represent a perpetuating process without beginning and end;
- as a rule, they act as an overlay ('power structures') or underlay ('gossip
  factory') in conjunction with more formal structures;
- the number of juxtaposed network layers is constantly increasing;
- power distribution is not vertical/pyramidal but rather horizontal or diffuse;
- many different forms of the relationship between parts of the network
  (individuals, casual or formal groups) exist and are of equal importance;
- they are generally 'fuzzy' with hardly any clear, identifiable boundaries;
- a 'them' and 'us' attitude prevails.

Apart from the direct objectives of a network, the more profound purposes of network activities are wide-ranging:

- to provide the necessary influence and power to control via targeted information flow management;
- to represent common interests, ideologies, rituals, symbols and social positions;
- to nurture friendship, kinship and relationships of indebtedness and gratitude;
- to use communication opportunities (information dissemination, risk spread, etc.);
- to promote the network as a 'corporate culture', as the preserver and architect of psychological ties;
- as a total business activities structure;
- to use the network as an anonymous change agent (organizational change without overt conflicts);
- to facilitate interinstitutional (intergroup) coalitions.

At the moment, this type of organizational form is asserting itself as the most efficient, in all sectors and areas of 'highly developed societies'. Political, religious, economic, ideological and social groupings of all persuasions can be analysed effectively by adopting this view.[197,198] This broad base is particularly appropriate when analysing complex company structures like multinational companies and, particularly, the Japanese MNEs.[199]

Company networks

We can also raise the same question of raison d'être posed by Coase in relation to companies *per se*, and Hymer in the context of the MNEs, in connection with company networks. Why is this new type of structure formed? What are its distinguishing features? Is it a radical departure, a revolution or merely a gradual change? Are networks an inevitable development? Will they be perceived as a forward-looking success structure?

The arguments of Chandler, Williamson and Auerbach are based on these issues.[200] According to these authors, the fundamental driving force for structural change has always been variations in managerial competence. Technical advances leading to better methods of control have facilitated company expansion. The graduation from a Williamsonian U-form (functionally organized) to an M-form (multidivisional form) has ultimately been achieved by enhancing the image of the *homo economicus*. Limited rationality and opportunism as well as specific long-term investments in transaction channels have allowed company understanding to expand into a multidivisional form.[201] Parallel to this development, the MNEs, in general, have restructured themselves from a portfolio of foreign investments (capital investment in production plants close to the company), via a decentralized federal model (more flexible, simple, direct (financial) controls and highly-decentralized strategic decisions) and a centralized hub and spoke model (in which close, direct controls, strategic decisions remain highly-centralized, with mono-directional information, product and cash flows towards the holding company (headquarters)), to a dynamic, integrated network with complex controls and comprehensive coordination, as well as close cooperation on strategic issues and the densest flow of all company resources (information, products, finances, services).[202]

In empirical studies of American and European MNEs, Ghoshal and Nohriah were able to demonstrate four types of this new organizational profile, which are inhomogeneous and contingent in terms of the relevant environment they portray.[203] We can make a distinction between the four forms – that is, hierarchy, federalism, clan and a holistic form of organization – based on dimensions such as centralization, formalization and socialization (common values), complexity and resource availability.[204] A general trend, which crystallizes in respect of all categories, is an *increasing complexity and symbolization*, the purpose of which is to use resources more efficiently by means of flexible operationalization.[205] The greater complexity resulting from departmental autonomy should be perceived as an evolutionary chain leading to ever more pronounced *self-organization* (autopoeicism), as well as more complex structures and relationships. Company structure becomes less tangible once the physical framework (based on Marshall's criterion of the long-term average costs curves) forming the company's boundaries[206] has disintegrated, and Penrose's theory that company size is a function of managerial competence[207] has been widened to create the image of a company as 'the nexus of individual contracts'.[208] This transforms the bilateral contracts into a network which explodes both the neo-classical view of the company as a monad and the strict theoretical view that a contract[209] is a dyadic relationship, in favour of a pleiade of multilayered relationship bundles.[210]

For its part, this contractual view of the company extends from a strict legal interpretation to a psychological/strategy overall understanding of contracts, cooperations and economic coordination.[211] The company becomes a *network* made up of a plethora of sometimes *overlapping or contradictory contracts*, which, because it is multichannelled, can no longer be viewed in terms of simple interests but rather in the context of perceptions, evaluations and expectations. Thus, the company framework finally becomes arbitrary, with the consequence that only internal and external (contractual) networks can be extemporized. 'The network is the firm's frame of operation ... [i]t constitutes the arena in which the struggle for survival takes place, but is also an important tool in that struggle.'[212] A company is no longer perceived as a structure but rather as a (permanent) process. This level of perception shifts away from the individual 'unit' and focuses simultaneously on numerous 'individual components' (groups, departments, companies, company associations); the resulting market is no longer a balance between supply and demand, but is rather an administrative coordination process. Competition is no longer restricted to price, but is functional and strategic instead. A company is no longer accepted *a priori* as a fact, but is defined by means of contractual relations and, particularly, by non-contractual correlations.[213,214] As a result, the congruence of the company, the network and postmodern environment, in terms of prerequisites, values, structures and functions, becomes apparent.[215] The company is thus perceived as a cumulative process in which the individual protagonists occupy complementary and reciprocal positions and control the company by means of experimental trial-and-error experience and by entering into commitments which are debated from all angles.[216]

According to Chandler's doctrine ('structure follows strategy'), the incorporation of immaterial, psychological, historical and strategic dimensions also changes the organizational principles and promotes new forms of company structure.[217] In order to guarantee efficiency and efficacy, 'soft' rules, symbols, visions and trust are included in the equation rather than an optimization potential. This equation promises higher productivity in a fast and uncertain environment which is too complex to allow the creation of rational optimum solutions.[218]

This management form is no longer applied just internally within the company, but also externally in terms of its links with the outside world:

> Enterprises embedded in networks through the new forms of internationalization obtain the best of both worlds: the co-ordination and scale associated with size and the flexibility, creativity and low overhead associated with smallness.[219]

This is where the company network, which acts as a protagonist in terms of its environmental links, follows seamlessly on from the network of the individual protagonist via the internal network within a company.

Macroeconomic networks

In addition to perceiving companies as networks, the same method can also be usefully applied at a higher level of aggregation.[220] On the one hand this can occur when the macroeconomic coordination of the economy and economic (structural) policy is interpreted as the product of network processes (cf. Chapter 4, sections III and IV). On the other hand the networks formed as the result of concepts of flexible production or regional economic coordination could help to interpret the Keiretsu and their sphere. By combining all three perspectives – that is companies, business and political relationships and regional coordination – we hope, in Japan's case, to come up with some interesting findings.[221]

From this standpoint an MNE can be perceived as the unifying quantum of all internal and external contracts.[222] Thus the company is made up of a basic strategic body[223] (cf. the previous subsection), and a shell consisting of 'strategic alliances' with other companies on the one hand, but also with non-economic (e.g. political) dimensions on the other. This is where the theories of vertical and horizontal integration bear fruit. According to these theories, it is possible to generate economies of scale in all sectors by means of integration and also to implement long-term trust-based strategies efficiently when competing (locally and globally) with competitors.[224] It is not our aim at this juncture to delve deeper into the divergent discussion on the extent of the preference given to horizontal or vertical strategies or the strategies which predominate within Japan's MNEs,[225] but by combining all the positions we obtain a clue as to the intensity and diversity of the relationships.[226] In general, this type of alliance can be seen as a 'hybrid form of organization that is located between coalitions and mergers'.[227] The aim is to strive for alliances that are not self-limiting but are flexible enough to procedurally discuss, revise and, if necessary, even redefine the objective whilst safeguarding cultural differences.[228]

The sum of all the external contracts produces a network of alliances for the company which is not only decisive in terms of relative strategic positioning, but is directly instrumental in determining success or failure.[229,230] Ronne sees this network of strategic alliances as a trend towards increasingly open systems on which an asymmetric network of external company relationships, rather than symmetrical dyads, is formed.[231] Endogenous variable objectives, such as company growth and profit margin, are no longer *a priori* relevant, whereas exogenous relative objectives like competitive position, intensity of affiliation or efficacy of the network become critical dimensions.[232] The direct entrepreneurial sphere grows and is transformed into an organic network, the structure of which is the product of a self-organizing, unpredictable process.[233,234] Perception, experience and flexibility thus become the primary characteristics of a successful company, which sees itself as a 'loosely coupled system'.[235,236]

Since pure mass production can be perceived as an outdated paradigm, new forms of flexible specialization – for example in the form of regional concentrations, federalized companies or solar company structures or grass-root, Internet-based cooperation – now occupy the limelight, on an experimental basis.[237] The resulting network of a 'quasi-market system of cooperation' is ideal for making use of these technological innovations and also for countering increased general instability.[238] Consequently, the markets are no longer perceived as *goods exchanges*, but as *relational interfaces*. 'A market is not a thing, but a behavioral relation.'[239] Cooperation and competition are no longer seen as mutually exclusive polarities; direct competition is now being replaced by relative positioning in some sectors and future environment (market) conditions are now being influenced.[240] Consequently, both sides (the company and the market) could claim that the network system is superior to all other cooperative, market and planning systems.[241]

Macroeconomic control within the network paradigm is taking place analogously, outside company environs. Administrative and political networks enjoy the closest of links with the economy and thus form a 'network state' in which the same principles apply as those used in our internal perspective of company networks (see the previous sub-section).[242] These principles consequently result in a new form of macroeconomic management. These *evolutionary lines from state to network* are not only present in a specific nation; the situation in Japan is a cliché (cf. Chapter 4, section III ('the links between ...')), but some constellations in the USA (Washington's 'iron triangle': lobbies, authorities and congress committees) and in England ('Whitehall village') are also famous for it.[243] In this context, Wilks and Wright contrast 'interventionist' states (Japan, France) with 'non-interventionist states' (UK, USA) and reach the conclusion that the former greatly facilitate the development of a network state by dint of proactive government, the cooperation which exists between representatives of the economic sector, as well as regular and robust contacts and informal consultations. Both perceive the 'corporatistic state' as an earlier form of network state, one of the most effective macroeconomic organizational forms.[244,245]

Japan: the networks in practice

This interpretation of all institutions – that is, state, companies, society – as a network is also one of the basic concepts in Japan's theoretical self-perception.[246] At a lower social level, the informal multidirectional and vague composition of all relationships is stressed. These relationships define themselves 'somewhat hierarchically and semi-autonomously' as a network,[247] an opinion which reappears in a political context. Kumon is of the opinion that only the network approach can do justice to these complex interrelationships, and consequently he describes *the network state Japan*, which is made up of administrative, political and economic sub-networks.[248] By concentrating on economic sectors, this portrayal corresponds to that of Imai. The most comprehensive explanation which can be used to describe economic relationships is that they are networks in which communication, openness, negotiations to reach consensus, trust and loyalty, strategic and psychological considerations and all other invisible assets are major components.[249] Pure (neoclassical or Keynsian) market perspectives can only serve to mislead.[250] A network consisting of an (almost) endless number of flexible, undefined relationships is consequently the sphere of action, both for individuals and the company itself.[251]

'The evolutionary process of Japan's industrial organization is characterized by a process of a gradual loosening of the intercorporate linkages and a gradual fuzzying of corporate boundaries.'[252] A frequently quoted example is the completely open but nevertheless intensive relationship between the automobile manufacturer, Toyota, and its suppliers,[253] although this technique can also be considered general practice in Japan. Between the twin poles of autonomy and total internalization, an interim stage is employed which guarantees maximum flexibility and maximum utilization of resources.[254] This concentration on the system, on the network of individual components, is therefore also the dominant feature of Japanese companies. Even Western authors interpret 'Japan's advantage' in this way:[255]

The systems approach to production, the implementation of a rational 'division of thought' and the use of social mechanisms to establish networks of trust are all features ... that distinguish Japanese multinationals from their US and European counterparts.[256]

'We are of the opinion that the Keiretsu and industrial groups represent the most dynamic and efficient industrial system [industrial structure] ... although it is not regarded in the West with the respect it deserves.'[257] In Porter's concept of the industrial cluster as the most successful strategy for the future, Japan also comes out on top. Japan is ideally equipped for cluster formations since it has numerous informal social networks both horizontally and vertically between small, national and international firms.[258] Vernon sees the Japanese networks as a global escape route through which to overcome existing obstacles to the development of the MNEs. This involves the simultaneous creation of a production zone in East Asia under Japanese management and Japanese 'islands' on other continents.[259,260]

After this geographical movement, the current frenzy to embrace the Internet in all its forms is the next level of Japanese network building. Being curious, information-maximizers and gadget happy, the possibility of intensified communication without the psychological and ritual complexities of a direct physical meeting will greatly enhance Japanese performance. *Fractal organization* is in Japan not a buzzword but a *living experience*.[261] Postmodern marketing strategies and the counterpart of the economy of signs[262] are applied in a complex communication network, now exponentially powered by the technological change.[263] This will allow new concepts of work and strategy based on the resources given – that is, the current structure, tradition and experience.[264]

In the light of these considerations, many authors perceive the terms 'Japanese networks' and 'Keiretsu' as identical in terms of their framework conditions, motives, objectives and methods.[265] Japan, characterized in the form of a network and also by the Keiretsu, is perceived as a complex network based on trust, repetitious negotiations and flexible, mainly informal (and sometimes very indirect) target attainment:[266,267]

> The Japanese company is perceived externally as an integral component of Japanese society and the national economy and, inwardly, by its members, as a community in which everyone shares a common fate. This defines its national and social characteristics and explains its determined approach towards market action.[268]

However, this behaviour is not a recently developed trend but a cultural constant: 'Japan has no native concept of "organization" or "network" abstracted or divorced from actual man; "organization" is perceived as a kind of succession of direct and concrete relationships between man and man.'[269] The fractal view of relationships between (economic) protagonists covers all levels, from the dyadic two-person relationship to the diverse network of the Keiretsu.[270] The development trend is clearly demonstrated in the evolution of the MNEs, which have developed from rigid, family-oriented firms, via industrial concerns with Western traits, to a new paradigmatic form of global network made up of Japanese companies.

Interpreting *Japan as a single network* is just as bold and succinct as perceiving the whole of Japan as a single Keiretsu. In doing so, we reject all mono-lithic universal interpretations of the economic reality of Japan in favour of a

Table 5.1 *Evolution of Japanese economic and business networks*

	Zaibatsu	*Keiretsu*	*New economy-networks*
Time frame	1870–1940	1950–1995	1995–
Technology	Import of innovations economies of scale,	Mass production	Small scale, small batch, high tech, real time
Information	Exogenous, special channels	Endogenous, arbitrage, multichannel	Endogenous & exogenous, interactive, open community
Linkages	Shareholding, directors (close control)	Clubs, directors, multidimensional network	Cooperation, rhizome, instant but loose interaction
Organization	Hierarchy	Lateral organization	Open quasi-market
Management	Control, ritual	Formal and informal authority	'Leadership & rules', symbols, mild anarchy
Vision	Family	Group	Community, rhizome
Target level	National	Group	Global
Advantages	Swift decision Strategy Coherence	Strong growth Flexible Hard to attack	Maximal information Ultraflexible Quick reaction
Disadvantages	Rigid financial control Vulnerable Little entrepreneurialism	Need to orchestrate 'Inbreeding' Excessive competition	Unstable Inconsistent Permanent 'crises of identity'

Source: Based on Imai, K., 'Evolution of Japans Corporate and Industrial Networks', p. 143

new image of multinational companies, one based on an integrated network (see also Table 5.1). Generally-speaking, we might expect this research direction to yield long-range momentum, both in terms of Japan as a research area and the MNE theory.

This new view of a company as the sum total of all (contractual, psychological, strategic, implicit, formal etc.) relationship allows maximum flexibility and adaptability in the face of unstable business climates without, however, diverting attention from the main and secondary objectives of the individual 'protagonists'. Network theory, which used existing models of a multinational company as a starting point, generates a new level of understanding of the structures, strategies, actions and future plans of modern MNEs.

This model should not only be considered as the 'leading' model, in terms of microeconomic theory, but also promises relevant results in an analysis of the business climate, the cooperation between companies and the interaction between the state and the economy.

III 'KEIRETSU' STRUCTURES IN THE JAPANESE ECONOMY

Phenotypes of the Keiretsu

Just as multinational companies, in general, defy all reliable definitions, Japanese MNEs in particular cannot be adequately described using simple standard definitions or descriptive endeavours, due to their multidimensionalism and the complexity of their structure. In spite of all their inclinations towards international convergence,[271] 'Japanese firms' must be evaluated as uniquely Japanese, in terms of structure and evolutionary trends, in the same way as we perceive 'Japanese management' as a product of its fundamental culture.

Contrary to Western industrial nations, the Japanese do not usually separate the two terms 'national economy' and 'business administration', or 'macro-' and 'micro-economy'. Companies are not perceived in the context of static, economic and juridical categories, but are more an expression of social groupings which cannot, *a priori*, be divided into any systematic classification scheme. '[W]hat may be quite specific in sociological terms, is, however, not so clear in economic terms. "Related companies" is a popular expression, rarely defined and most loosely used.'[272] This navel-gazing produces systematic catalogues of terms which attempt to describe the diversity of Japanese MNEs, but which leave behind only a confusing lack of clarity. Organizational complexity worsens this situation to such an extent that we are forced to accept methodological aporia:

> Within the so-called company groups ... the mutual shareholdings are so complicated that it is impossible to define, in legal terms, how a concern has been established ... In our opinion it is impossible to legally regulate companies of this type as a company group.[273]

These are the findings of an exemplary analysis of the Sumitomo group in which the individual aspects (the whole consisting of marginal joint shareholdings which, nevertheless, form a tight web in which no one company is dominant) can indeed be analysed, but this very contradictory diversity obstructs the total perspective.

In a Japanese context, the company groups created can cover a plethora of descriptions: '*bekkeren*' (a group of subsidiaries), '*kigyo Keiretsu*' (amalgamated companies), '*kontserun*' (Western-style concerns), '*kigyo gurupu*' (a group of firms), '*kinyi Keiretsu*' (share group) etc.[274] Interestingly and historically explicable, the term 'multinational company' is used in Japanese literature either to describe non-Japanese companies or in superficial translations of texts aimed at a Western readership. The taxonomy provided in the literature is based on the unambiguous and one-dimensional relationship between companies and represents the fundamental building blocks.[275] In terms of contemporary Japanese company groupings, the resulting classifications inferentially describe the available group options, of which the following is an arbitrary selection.[276]

One of the first classification proposals came from Hadley,[277] who defined four groups:

- the 'combine', a network of companies grouped around a raw material (e.g. oil or steel);
- the Zaibatsu (a cluster of family-owned companies or trading houses);
- a bank-centred group (a group of companies with a bank at its centre); and
- a supplier system (a supplier universe surrounding a major production company).

Komiya[278] differentiates between three types of company groupings:

- traditional, evolved from the 'old' Zaibatsu (Mitsubishi, Mitsui,[279] Sumitomo);
- bank-centred groups (Daiichi-Kangyo, Fuji, Sanwa); and
- industrial groups draped around a major production company (Matsushita, Toyota, Hitachi).

Clark[280] and others differentiate between two types:

- former 'Zaibatsu' with quasi-holding companies; and
- the younger 'non-Zaibatsu' groups which form looser, coordinated groups around the banks.

Imai[281] postulates the most comprehensive typology which contains five types of Keiretsu, apart from the Zaibatsu:

- Zaibatsu ('loosely affiliated and highly diversified'; e.g. Mitsubishi[282]);
- single-manufacturer Keiretsu (based on a strong key company; e.g. Hitachi);
- spin-off Keiretsu (successful departments become separate companies with the main company acting as the centre of innovation; e.g. Matsushita);
- supplier-Keiretsu (a pyramid-shaped structure consisting of suppliers, sub-suppliers etc.; e.g. Toyota);
- regional-Keiretsu (regional departments expand into subsidiaries; e.g. NEC); and
- person-oriented Keiretsu (the group is held together by a charismatic owner; e.g. Seibu, Softbank).

The following dichotomy is based on the extensive empirical analysis conducted by Dodwell:[283]

- horizontal groups, divided into:

  (1) Zaibatsu-oriented (Mitsubishi, Mitsui, Sumitomo) and
  (2) bank-oriented (Fuyo, Daiichi-Kangyo, Sanwa, Tokai, Industrial Bank of Japan); and

- vertically integrated groups (Toyota, Daiei, Ito, Taisei, Kajima, Shimizu, Kirin, Nippon Oil, Showa Shell, Sekiyu, Cosmo Oil, Nippon Steel, NKK, Kobe Steel, Sumitomo Metall, MHI, Matsushita, Hitachi, Toshiba, Mitsubishi Electric, NEC, Fujitsu, Sanyo, Sony, Sharp, Nissan, Honda, Mitsubishi Motors, Isutzu, NTT and Nippon Express).[284]

To the Western observer, this vast number of specifically Japanese descriptions and historically evolved terms appears to be an inextricable turmoil of definitions, the indistinctiveness of which seems to have been created intentionally. For example, the Chairman of the Board of the Mitsubishi Corporation, M. Makihara, prefers to describe Mitsubishi as a 'series of independent companies', rather than 'the Mitsubishi group' or 'the Mitsubishi family', for reasons relating to the anti-trust laws.[285,286] In general, vague concepts of definition also prevail in Japanese scientific literature. Reference is made to 'soft groups', which denotes a 'loose structure of business groups',[287] based on the premise that the generalization produced by concrete terminology is unacceptable, ergo only vague blunt terms are capable of describing all the manifest forms.[288,289]

Nevertheless, it is possible to identify three frequently used definitions which are of fundamental relevance, in terms of a basic concept. On the other hand, when these definitions are translated in Western literature, they are more often than not inaccurately interpreted. They are the terms *sogo shosha*, *Zaibatsu* and *Keiretsu*. The first (chronologically-speaking) term, *sogo shosha*, is variously translated in English as 'General Trading Companies' or 'All-Around Trading Companies'.[290] Young defines the *sogo shosha* simply as 'huge, highly diversified trading companies', most of which have evolved, from a family tradition spanning several centuries, into dominant, multinational service companies.[291,292] In their role as intermediary between the companies of a group, these *sogo shosha* shared the following common characteristics:

- similar resources
- comparable production technologies
- similar recruitment practices
- exclusively male-managed
- extensive *amakudari* (cf. Chapter 4, section III on *amakudari*)
- guaranteed employment up to retirement age[293]

- a common base in terms of cultural history
- formerly in family ownership
- comparable company objectives
- extremely intense internal competition
- numerous subsidiaries and affiliated companies

But the Japanese *sogo shosha* is more than a 'general trading company' comparable to the English company, Jardine Matheson, or the American company, Sears. 'The Sogo Shosha is an institutional innovation for economic growth', whose main competence is organizational in nature. The main tasks of the *sogo shosha*[294] are gathering and processing information; coordinating activities, expanding the company group and strengthening the cohesion of the group. As we shall demonstrate in Chapter 5, section IV, using Mitsubishi as an example, this trading company constitutes the core firm in a typical company group, together with a bank and a manufacturing company.

The first clearly identifiable company group in the modern understanding, the Zaibatsu appeared during the Meiji modernization (cf. Chapter 4, section IV ('economic stages from . . .') and the following section of this chapter). Standard Western definitions of the Zaibatsu are:

- privately-owned industrial empires;[295]
- a group of companies with historical connections;[296]
- financial agglomerates stemming from keibatsu or family cliques; or[297]
- as 'a merger of about a dozen large companies – trading, insurance and fiduciary companies, under family ownership, and at their center, the bank and holding company which had established the joint concern'.[298]

These can now be assessed as too historically-oriented since they fail to highlight the dynamic, forward-looking aspect of the structure involved. Piore and Sabel[299] convey the basic characteristics extremely well:

- centralization around one or two key companies;
- key companies under family ownership;
- extremely long-term (often centuries old) company relationships;
- the closest personal links between firms, key companies and founder families; and
- conglomerate-style diversification.

The most important feature of the Zaibatsu was the family connection. The prewar Zaibatsu may well have been under family ownership, but the relationship between property and management was tradition-oriented too. From as long ago as the seventeenth century, business management has often been transferred by the old merchant families to the most capable and trustworthy manager (*banto*). The basis for this was the concept of family. A powerful symbolic wealth facilitated (see Chapter 2, section III on 'the symbolism of postmodern change') the transfer of company management to an outsider, who could only become an integral part of the family through his activities and whose loyalty was never questioned.[300] Simultaneously, the Japanese Zaibatsu can be perceived as a prototype for rapid industrialization of a developing country. This does not involve structural evolution but rather the assimilation of production forms and techniques from Western European countries which have then been combined with effective, endogenous organizational forms. The structure of the multiple company group[301] has evolved from the government's desire to implement industrialization quickly, in a show of strength, and the willingness of some entrepreneurs to go along with it.

These processes have made the Zaibatsu the prototype for the Japanese economy: uncontrolled and lacking one-dimensional focus, they continue to expand until their identity and that of the Japanese national practically almost merged; a merger which was torn apart only by defeat in the Second World War. Officially (i.e. legally and linguistically), the Zaibatsu were dissolved and declared defunct by the American occupiers. The existence of structures resembling the Zaibatsu were denied with almost ideological stubbornness in the postwar period, and persistent reference was made to the prevailing Keiretsu company group structures.[302] Only in recent times have a few analyses resurfaced which speak of the reconstruction of the Zaibatsu: 'Although holding companies are still illegal in Japan, the so-called groups preserve the spirit, if not the letter of the Zaibatsu organization.'[303] New descriptions of this phenomenon refer to the 'post-war industrial Zaibatsu', which can be subdivided into old Zaibatsu (*kyu Zaibatsu*), that is Mitsui, Mitsubishi, Sumitomo, Fuyo, Daiichi-Kangyo, Sanwa; and new Zaibatsu (*shinko Zaibatsu*), that is Sony, Toyota, Nissan, Hitachi, Matsushita, Honda, Ricoh, Sharp.[304]

Consequently, contemporary Zaibatsu descriptions differ only marginally from those of the Keiretsu.[305] Nevertheless, many authors perceived the Keiretsu as a completely different type of successor to the Zaibatsu, due to the fact that the family concerns (Zaibatsu) formed themselves into company groups (*kigyo shudan, gurupu*, Keiretsu).[306] However, this differentiation between the Zaibatsu and Keiretsu has led to confusion in terms of semantics. For this reason we attempt, at this juncture, to extract some clarification from the various positions as to whether or not the Keiretsu and Zaibatsu are identical.[307]

Although the main difference between the Zaibatsu and the '*kigyo Keiretsu*' is indeed based on the one hand on the relevant shareholding situation, and on the other on the different structures which link together the individual members, there has been no change in the informal style of management used or the principle of a loose network of firms, despite all cosmetic attempts to gloss over the fact.[308] The difference is that the individual components are not centrally controlled by one family but assume the structure of a network characterized by its mutual, sublime dependencies. To the outsider, there appears to be no reason to believe in a closer correlation between the firms.[309] The great extent to which the old Zaibatsu and the new '*kigyo shudan*' are similar in appearance to company groups is demonstrated by the following attempt to define the Keiretsu system (*kigyo Keiretsu*):

> The term 'kigyo' corresponds, in its role, to a German company and the term 'Keiretsu' refers to a systematic order based on uniform principles. The word 'Keiretsu' expresses the integration or composition of previously individual elements into a whole ... In a wider context this means that firms are joined together loosely.[310]

These cautious Keiretsu definitions could also be used without any problem to define the Zaibatsu. The link between the two terms represents the symbolic capital and the shared information within the network, irrespective of whether it is called Zaibatsu or Keiretsu. Together they represent the stratification of coordinated firms which are juxtaposed in a quasi-permanent but flexible network relationship.[311,312] For all their independence, we can still identify the 'old' Zaibatsu principle of *wan setto shugi* (one set principle). This principle is prominently displayed in Keiretsus' strategy to be represented in all key economic sectors.

The relevance of share and director swaps, presidential meetings and the subdivision of key firms and member firms is reemerging.[313] The starting point for interpretation purposes is, once again, the *oyabun–kobun* concept and the parent–child (*amae*) relationship. These relationships can be used to explain the dyadic relationships between the complex company networks.[314] Despite the fact that the *company networks* are totally cohesive and tradition-oriented, they are not rigidly fixed or perceived as 'set in stone' but, in a significantly more open interpretation, as a 'society of long-term relationships'.[315] To this extent, the Keiretsu can be perceived as a deliberate but indirect progression from the old Zaibatsu since, albeit from a superficial (in quantitative, formal, juridical, auditing and 'public') perspective, the relationships between the individual companies are becoming looser, vaguer and interconnected,[316] whilst on an existential (real, informal, psychological, symbolic, abstract and sociological) level they are becoming increasingly inextricably linked. The definition which describes the Keiretsu as a 'society of businesses', or the view that '*the whole of Japan is a single Keiretsu*' fits in very appropriately here, since it takes account of the links which exist between sociological and traditional aspects.[317]

Thus, in terms of an economic structure, the Keiretsu are nothing unusual in Japan since they correspond exactly to Japanese cultural and sociological modes of thought and should therefore be perceived as company groups; as '(company) groups consisting of (departmental) groups consisting of groups (of people)'.[318] It is at this point that an important aspect of a new understanding of modern company configurations becomes apparent, which has not previously been extrapolated. A homogeneous line of relational patterns is detectable within the entire Japanese (economic and non-economic) living environment. On all levels (macroeconomic coordination, inter-Zaibatsu cooperation, company group organization, and the sociology of the work groups),[319] one can detect homologous processes and structures which display two fundamental 'postmodern' characteristics.

Firstly, we can always detect a heterarchical (self-) organized network structure, which in each case and from many perspectives constantly gives rise to different clusters and which cannot be subsumed in their escalating entirety in a single classificatory structural principle. The second postmodern attribute which becomes apparent when the Keiretsu are considered is the fractal composition. Arbitrary dividing lines remain (the separation of state and the economy, the exact definition of Keiretsu components, an unambiguous 'border of the firm', the clear distribution of competence), but nevertheless, at every level of analysis, the same methods, processes and structures crop up.

Based on these considerations, we now propose the use of two new terms which extend beyond partial analyses, which will on the one hand serve to bridge typological and semantic difficulties, and on the other bring in a new perspective, one which points to a postmodern reporting pattern. These terms are *fractal economy*[320] and *rhizome economy*. We are interested in the extent to which these terms can be used as general terminological tools of efficacy, to describe appropriately the specific features of Japanese business models and commercial structures.[321] In addition, these concepts may also offer new reference points in the search for new paradigms to help us understand multinational companies (or trend-setting companies in general). However, the task of elaborating on the specifics of these concepts is reserved for future studies.[322]

Thus, the practice is continued to use the terms Zaibatsu, Keiretsu and 'the Japanese multinational company' which are for these purposes synonymous in meaning (reflecting a 'fractal economy', 'rhizome economy' and 'postmodern economy'), since terminological diversity can only, at best, have a palliative effect, without clarifying the basic model.

Structural History[323]

After the First World War, the major Japanese concerns became familiar, in name, all over the world and then ubiquitous during the 1980s. However, they are not a phenomenon of the postwar or modern era, but rather a category which transcends many historic periods.[324] Although the origins of the Keiretsu as Japan's leading economic force can be traced back to early (16th and 17th century) family roots and family concerns, the starting point selected by literature, in terms of the evolution of the Zaibatsu, was the beginning of the Meiji period around 1868.[325]

In this context, the focus of the analysis is either the entrepreneur, who used the opportunities afforded to him by the state,[326] or alternatively the perception of government impulses as the nucleus from which the major concerns evolved.[327] In either case, personnel build-up and structural integration were monitored and both poles connected, which at the end of the Tokugawa period[328] facilitated the transformation of the Meiji restoration into a political power and the Zaibatsu into an economic power for paradigmatic change. The basic framework for company philosophy and organization can be traced back historically to the very roots of family traditions. The absolute supremacy of the family; thrifty reinvestment rather than consumption; close cohesion, underpinned by signs and symbols; the perception of the family (group) as the smallest, social unit; permanence and flexibility – were all qualities and goals directly adopted from the traditional model, which portrayed the Japanese extended family as surrounded by a voluntary economic commune.[329]

When, after two centuries of self-imposed isolation Japan made its debut on the international stage under the leadership of the new Meiji government, it lacked economic structure, particularly in terms of foreign interaction. The government

was quick to perceive that the country had been left behind not only in technological terms but was also consistently at a disadvantage in terms of the know-how
needed to conduct foreign trade, due to a lack of many simple skills, for example,
the ability to process English-language documents. Very few competent business
people were available to manage the required and desired transfer of know-how.
Consequently, Japan pinned all its hopes on this small group and gave its total
and sustained support to a 'knowledge-elite'.[330,331] It was essential to create a new
economic structure based on this small group of people, and this cluster provided
the stimulus needed to form the Zaibatsu:

> Within the breathing space afforded by the peasants, modern industries were
> created, largely by the state. The establishments inherited from 'Tokugawa
> government' – mines, shipyards and engineering workshops – were expanded.
> New ventures were attempted not only in heavy industry but also in light
> industries such as cotton spinning, silk filature, cement and glass. Modern
> communications were established. A post and telegraph service was set up and a
> railway was built between Tokyo and Yokohama in 1870–1872.[332]

Thus the Meiji government not only created the initial infrastructure for industrialization, but was also actively involved in establishing and expanding companies.
Here it faced two problems: firstly, its success was hampered by a lack of managerial
talent, and secondly, competent managers and entrepreneurs were ready and waiting
in the old Samurai family companies to assume leadership and power.[333] In terms
of personnel and institutions, the government bet heavily on the old commercial
families (and, consequently, less on the higher-ranked nobility). Their task was to
explore new business methods and the profit opportunities available in foreign countries. For this reason, it is also not surprising that initial sorties closely resembled
foreign models. The kick-off mentors[334] were, specifically, successful British trading
companies and the French concept of a central, planned market economy. These
were later reinforced by the German concept of a (heavy industry) concern.[335]

The result of these projects was the creation of the Zaibatsu. 'The Zaibatsu
was indeed an ingenious invention for a society that had limited resources but was
anxious to industrialize rapidly.'[336] In historical terms, two processes led to the
creation of today's key firms: (1) the transition from small general trading house to
large, globally-based organizations (Sumitomo, Mitsui and Mitsubishi are all
examples of this), and (2) the diversification of a specialized trading and production
company into a 'general trading firm' (in this context the names Itoh, Marubeni
and Nissho-Iwai spring to mind).

The first *sogo shosha* to be created was Mitsui, which evolved in 1876 from the
noble Mitsui family. Initially, Mitsui traded mainly in coal, cotton and spinning
machines and consistently concentrated on developing products with guaranteed
sales outlets. In 1911, Mitsui alone exported almost one-third of Japan's silk
exports and 96 per cent of its coal exports. After the First World War, trade and
production made equal contributions to Japan's success. Mitsubishi was the second

Zaibatsu nucleus to be created: the Mitsubishi Corporation was founded in 1889 as the marketing hub of the Mitsubishi family. Initially, Mitsubishi also concentrated on non-food products such as paper, glass and coal, a range which was later supplemented by practically every agricultural trading commodity. The individual Zaibatsu had a total monopoly in one or two industries and, consequently, divided up the whole of the national economy between them. This hardly ever resulted in fierce competition, which meant that all their energy could be devoted to company expansion.[337]

The major task of the Zaibatsu was firstly to attain supremacy in foreign trade, which was dominated by foreigners,[338] because the young Japanese firms had little marketing information, hardly any linguistic abilities and no business experience whatsoever.[339] This was an additional reason why the government of the time gave their unqualified support to the young companies. The three main objectives of the state were to break the export trade monopoly of foreign countries; to promote the import of raw materials and technology; and, thirdly, to set up a vertical labour structure which would allow a few firms to concentrate solely on foreign trade and others on export production, and so on. Prerequisites for this were close cooperation and an active exchange of information, which resulted in closer intracompany relationships and the creation of individual firms from the parent company. This slowly produced a web of companies.

The system had been established centuries earlier (for example, the date given by Mitsui for the establishment of the family company is 1683),[340] but it was only with the meeting of two fortuitous paths – that is, the chance to close the modernization gap and the opportunity provided by total state sponsorship – that the Zaibatsu were created from an agglomeration of companies.[341] Thus the nation gained an efficient economy and the family businesses were able to expand to an extent which would otherwise have been impossible. By the end of the First World War, each Zaibatsu had launched at least one major manufacturing company in each sector and controlled, respectively, a bank, an insurance company, a shipping line and a trading company. The years between the world wars were golden years for the Zaibatsu, since they dominated and controlled practically all of Japan's economy and politics. Intra-Zaibatsu trade increased sharply and was used to maximize and stabilize group profits (by optimizing transfer prices), a situation which would ultimately lead to greater independence and constantly increasing oligopolistic market power.[342]

Table 5.2 illustrates Japan's foreign trade concentration. Of the 4850 firms engaged in foreign trade before the Second World War, just ten Zaibatsu general trading companies were responsible for a share of over 50 per cent. The vast majority of both foreign and internal trade was channeled through these ten firms and the Nihon Kogyo Kurabu (the Industrial Club of Japan) (cf. also Chapter 4, section III ('individual and organizational elements') and section IV ('economic strategies from the Tokugawa period')).

In 1930, an estimated 75 per cent of Japan's GDP was directly or indirectly controlled by the 15 largest Zaibatsu, a percentage which hardened massively due

Table 5.2 *Japanese export concentration pre-1950 (average 1930–43)*

Sogo shosha	Foreign trade	Percentage share	
Mitsui	1.010	18.3	
Mitsubishi	568	10.3	
Tovo-Menka	358	6.5	
Nichiren-Jitsugyo	273	5.0	
Gosho	219	4.0	51.8%
Iwai-Sangyo	118	2.1	
Kanematzu	106	1.9	
Ataka	73	1.3	
Nissho	65	1.2	
Naigai-Tsusho	65	1.2	
Other (non Sogo shosha)	2.654		48.2%
			100%

Source: Eli, M., *Sogo Shosha*, p. 11

to the 1000 or so company mergers which took place between 1941 and 1943. Until the end of the war, the ten largest Zaibatsu directly controlled some 35 per cent of share capital and indirectly controlled an estimated 30 per cent of smaller companies; and 71 per cent of all public loans and approximately 60 per cent of all bank assets and deposits were in the hands of the Zaibatsu banks. *During this period, Mitsui and Mitsubishi were the largest companies in the world by any criteria.*[343]

Since 1868, the political power of the Zaibatsu has also continued to grow parallel to its economic might. Whereas in the nineteenth century high politics was the domain of the respective regional cliques (Mitsubishi: the Satsuma clique; Mitsui: the Choshu clique), at the beginning of the twentieth century, the major parties were in the hands of the Zaibatsu (e.g.: Mitsubishi: the Minseito party). Thus, the terms 'Mitsubishi cabinet' and 'Mitsui cabinet' were unofficially adopted during the formation of governments.[344] Although the military regime, which replaced the elected government in 1932, did not initially enlist economic support for its military invasion of China from the Zaibatsu which, by this time, had grown extremely powerful, they ultimately became involved and these colonies acted as an economic testing ground for industrial development methods and strategies which they were later able to employ successfully at home.[345]

After Japan's collapse at the end of the Second World War, the American occupation force attempted to dissolve the Zaibatsu (*Zaibatsu kaitai*). Due to their incompatibility with the anti-trust ideology of the Americans, they were broken up and dissolved into countless smaller firms by General MacArthur's Supreme Command for the Allied Powers. In retrospect, this is now perceived purely as a (rather ineffective) formality, designed to achieve legal disintegration, without changing anything, *de facto*, in terms of the (more informal) company networks which existed.[346] According to Shibagaki,[347] the occupation force had two ideological objectives: one was to destroy the economic base of Japanese military might, perceived as the Zaibatsu, and the other was to prevent monopolistic market concentrations. But what happened in reality could not be perceived as the simple and determined implementation of American plans. Thanks, on the one hand, to the dialectic strength of the Allies who at that time fully ascribed to the views of the fashionable antitrust movement and did not wish to tolerate concerns of any kind, and the national elite of Japan whose aim was to reconstitute the Zaibatsu, on the other, a new system was created which, despite its new name, assumed almost all the same, albeit cosmetically modified, characteristics as the old. From 1946 to 1951, the Holding Company Liquidation Commission supervised the dissolution of the old holding companies with only sporadic success, which was merely a formal, legal accommodation *vis-à-vis* the occupiers.[348]

A few examples clearly demonstrate the cosmetic nature of this operation. Unaware of the background, the American occupier tolerated a 'government of Zaibatsu sympathizers'. Due to linguistic problems and the enormous complexity of the task in accounting terms, these firms were allowed to appoint their own liquidators and accountants to oversee the deconstruction of the Zaibatsu, although the Zaibatsu banks were not 'deconcentrated' for reasons related to the national economy.[349] Nevertheless, the rhetoric of the occupier was elated and naively victorious: 'Excessive concentration of economic power had been completely broken.'[350] In fact, very little had changed as far as the real power clusters and concentrations were concerned:[351]

[A]fter the Allied troops left and Japan regained her independence, some of the companies of the prewar Zaibatsu began to knit themselves together. They exchanged shares with other firms which bore the common 'Zaibatsu' name, deliberately relied on the group banks, trust banks and insurance companies, and did business with each other through the trading companies. They also exchanged directors and set up clubs where the presidents of the companies could meet. In this way there took place between 1952–1965 a revival of the prewar Zaibatsu, and the word is commonly used for the collections of companies with the name of Mitsubishi, Mitsui or Sumitomo, which were all once divisions of giant companies.[352]

Thus, by the middle of the 1950s the process of reorganizing the company groups was considered complete,[353] since the old company clusters had been rebuilt in a new form but still retained their former power, 'on a much larger scale and with more diversified product lines'.[354,355]

As well as the classic Zaibatsu companies,[356] a small number of, up to that point, relatively insignificant firms now saw their opportunity. The so-called 'bank-centred conglomerate groups',[357] clustered around the powerful and influential banks, quickly achieved economic parity with the classic Zaibatsu. The three most successful were the Fuji Bank, the Daiichi Kangyo Bank and the Sanwa Bank. The contemporary phenotype was rounded off by a few pioneering companies who were able to achieve a dominant (international) market presence after the Second World

War and who, for their part, have been able to build the foundations of Keiretsu structures around themselves. The best-known representatives of this trend are Honda, Toyota and Matsushita; although they do not (yet) fulfill the criteria usually applied to the 'classic' Zaibatsu and Keiretsu, they should be seen as 'youngsters', or the third group of Japanese MNEs.

'This Japan ... is adroitly capitalizing on the present global trend of this particular form of economic integration in the factor market, a trend called multi-nationalism.'[358] The Zaibatsu form the tip of the evolutionary spear within this long-term trend, which is designed to turn Japan into a leading nation – and this not just in an economic context, but in a broad sense (cf. especially Chapter 4, section VI on the role of the Zaibatsu and Keiretsu).[359]

Their Contemporary Presence as Multinational Enterprises

The contemporary phenotype of Japan's multinational enterprises is based on almost 100 years of experience in specialized foreign trade between Japan and the Western world. Since 1868 the Zaibatsu have enjoyed an almost total monopoly and have been able to use this as the basis on which to develop an international colossus (see Table 5.3). The actual process of internationalization beyond the boundaries of foreign trade administration started in the 1970s, when so-called Overseas Enterprise Departments were formed, which pursued an active direct investment strategy.

Starting with minor joint venture projects, these in turn by the beginning of the 1980s grew into larger independent projects. During this period, internal global communications and trade networks were extended, which resulted in a wide network of foreign subsidiaries, branches, representations and offices. At the same time, the communication flow between stations abroad intensified. Typically, information was transmitted only between foreign stations and the parent company and communication between stations was a rarity. However, the multipolarization of information flow increased trade between Japanese companies outside Japan as well. Mitsubishi took the greatest step forward in 1972 when it doubled this type of trade to 7 per cent within one year.[360] Whether this foreign investment strategy has been designed for trading purposes (the comparative national advantage expounded in Japanese analyses),[361] or for political reasons (to circumvent trade

Table 5.3 *Share of foreign trade captured by the big trading companies/Keiretsu/networks*

	1868	1873	1910	1935	1945	1966	1970	1980	1990	2000*	2010*
Foreign trade share (%)	<5	40	50	55	60	58	48	45	55	65	50

* Forecast

Source: Takamiya, S., 'Organisation des Japanischen Aussenhandels'; Eli, M., *Sogo Shosha*, p. 116ff

barriers which is the argument put forward by the Europeans),[362] is of secondary importance, only the important structural changes influencing this strategy in the 'host country' as well as in Japan are of major significance and demonstrate just how impossible it would be to eliminate the global competition presented by major Japanese companies.

Since the middle of the 1980s, Japanese foreign investment has been boosted: '. . . in 1989 alone, Japan invested more than in all of the 33 years from 1950 to 1983. The US\$68 billion spent in direct investments actually exceeded its total current account surplus (US\$57 billion). Japan invested this surplus in tangible assets rather than promissory notes.'[363] In the 1980s, this process could only be described as exponential. Direct Japanese investments in Europe rose from under US\$5 billion in 1980 to more than US\$20 billion by 1989.[364] Whereas the American economy was still the dominant foreign investor during the 1960s, Japan has now taken over the lead from America. 'In 1989, Japan invested four and a half times as much abroad as the German Federal Republic in 1988: US\$68 billion compared with US\$15 billion.'[365,366] The Keiretsu played a decisive part in this trend.

In this connection, a division of labour emerged which reflected Japan's overall strategy. The old Zaibatsu (chiefly the large trading companies) concentrated their activities on intensified globalization via their economies of scale,[367] whilst the objective of the new Keiretsu (primarily the electronics giants Toshiba, Hitachi etc.) was to extend their lead in the new high-tech markets. Sony was to reconnoitre the consumer electronics sector; Toshiba had the same role in the industrial electronics sector; Matsushita in the overall industrial automation sector; and Toyota in the automobile production sector. Research companies (comparable with R&D spin-off companies) were to explore risky markets, in order to limit the risks for Japan.[368]

The newer Keiretsu groups like Canon, Sony or Honda now earn some 70 per cent of their turnover abroad, and approximately 30 per cent of their production takes places overseas. This trend is ongoing and is taking hold further and further up the net product ladder from simple 'assembled products' (transistor radios) to more complex products (microchips). During the next phase, Japanese cars and highly complex electronics will also be produced by Japanese companies abroad. This transfer of production will result in about 650 000 job losses in Japan by the year 2000, and the Japanese government is counting entirely on the major company groups to resolve this situation.[369] Public sector projects or other company clusters cannot possibly perform the dual roles of initiating, supporting and progressing economic restructuring at home and 'globalizing'[370] the Japanese economy simultaneously.

Japan's advantages in terms of this general trend toward internationalization are indisputable. The characteristics which contribute to the strong competitiveness of Japanese multinationals are: reduced individual risks as a result of their group-like company structure; a low level of receiverships among their foreign companies; and very little pressure to show a profit. Apart from this, the Japanese have been totally unencumbered by old, inefficient, foreign organizations, compared with British companies for example, and have consequently been in a position to benefit from the latest organizational and technological concepts.[371,372] The globalization taking place is accompanied by a new relationship between capital, labour and information. In terms of the experience required to generate all three, Japan's large companies are at a significant advantage over their American and European competitors, who have chosen Japan as their role model. Japan, on the other hand, is extremely eager for the Japanese system to be used as a global reference standard, with the consequence that the '*Keiretsuka project*', which dates back to 1936 and involves the 'Keiretsufication' of the Japanese economy, is now being revived in the form of a *global strategy*.[373] This Keiretsufication of the world as well as the relevant international activities of the Japanese MNEs should be perceived as an essential feature, in terms of the global implementation of the 'domestic' competitive situation, industrial restructuring and flexible adaptation to the next millennium.[374]

In order to advance this 'Keiretsufication' of the world, Japan is also striving to fulfill its role in terms of domestic paradigms.[375] 'At any rate the Japanese economy and Japanese management are now in a transition period.'[376] This desire for change is not limited merely to theoretical considerations; in a survey of all companies listed in the first and second sections of the Tokyo stockmarket, 73.3 per cent admitted that their main business sector was established in a mature or aging market and that, in order to maintain their leading position, higher priority must be given to a strategy of diversifying business activities into new areas and increasing global market share rather than any other strategy.[377,378] During the 1980s, the Keiretsu emerged complete and reorganized, from the crisis of the 1970s, in the form of *multinational enterprises*. During this period the major companies had grown at a slower rate than gross national product and, consequently, had run the risk of becoming the ball and chain around the neck of the national economy. These MNEs used their main assets, including permanence, flexibility and *an ability to function as Japan's central nervous system* to secure further global and domestic advantage.[379] Precedents for success are not difficult to find: after each crisis or period of change, the Zaibatsu become more powerful and successful as a result of crisis reforms. Even in 1924, major Japanese companies were successful in exerting their influence on Senate and Congress. In 1936, warnings were already rife in both Asia and Europe about 'the yellow peril', and the theory that '*Japan was a global shogun and the Zaibatsu were daimyo*' was propagated right up to the end of the Second World War.[380]

The Zaibatsu groups were responsible for every one of Japan's evolutionary advances, including the 'upstream'-trend (diversification into primary areas such as steel production) started by the general trading houses and the subsequent 'downstream' expansion into distribution and marketing systems, as well as the fulminate development of the Japanese financial system.[381] In the course of this ongoing process, the Zaibatsu/Keiretsu groups have always been fundamentally responsible for Japan's leading position.[382] Today the Keiretsu are reconciled to achieving their aim 'of restoring the glory of earlier years' in a comprehensive and unobtrusive manner.[383] Thanks to enormous foreign investments, the precursors of a possible 'nipponized world' are being created in target or 'mini-Japan' areas.[384]

Almost 70 per cent of Japanese investments in US high-tech sectors have been made by Keiretsu companies. Whereas direct foreign investment was the main tactic of the 1970s and 1980s, more indirect forms such as joint ventures, strategic alliances or informal cooperations within the networks of independent firms are emerging as the evolutionary forms of the late 1980s and 1990s. The Keiretsu have uprooted their supply systems for automobile manufacture to the United States, with the result that about 90 per cent of the components for Japanese cars manufactured in the USA are supplied by firms under Japanese control. For this reason, the term 'Keiretsu syndrome'[385] is also used by the Americans, who are consequently now submerged in a veritable wave of 'Japanese studies'. Their current aim is to create American-style Keiretsu, with the aim of inspiring new cooperative structures in America based on long-term strategies and mutual trust.[386]

All American companies are searching for strategic responses to the Japanese Keiretsu. However, in most cases these projects must be described as half-hearted, since they usually only pay lip-service to the issue (as if a smooth transition from 'competitive and individualistic American ideals' to 'greater trust' could be achieved quickly) or fail to take the matter seriously – proposals regularly fail to take account of essential links with a trading house and an international bank or, more specifically, fail to properly consider the relationship with the public sector. The scope of these projects should be widened comprehensively and underpinned by a new entrepreneurial paradigm.[387] Companies like Ford are the furthest advanced with their Keiretsufication, insofar as they are forming close cooperations with their suppliers and sales partners in the areas of finance, marketing and research and see themselves as the key company supplying experience, know-how and expertise to the network around them, which it is also managing and coordinating.[388] Even developing countries like Korea[389] and Brazil are involved in ventures (some of them with Japanese assistance) aimed at the creation of their own *sogo shosha* and Keiretsu groups.[390] In a global context, one of the most spectacular forward-looking ventures, in terms of strategic alliances, is the cooperation between the Mitsubishi group and Daimler Benz.[391] Although caught by the dynamic German strategy executioners in a weak moment, Mitsubishi Motors negotiated successfully to avoid the fate of Nissan, thus reemerging as a 'junior partner' in a pathbreaking business model of MNEs that will dominate the global sector. As a result of these new models, the Keiretsu (no matter whether specifically Japanese, global or of any other nation) are able to take a further step towards becoming a global exchange of knowledge and are widening the gap between themselves and other companies.[392]

This chasm, in terms of know-how, experience, performance and future competitiveness, between Keiretsu companies and the rest of the national economy (or between 'New Economy'/rhizome economy/knowledge economy/postmodern economy and 'old economy') is becoming increasingly apparent, particularly in Japan. Although already outdated but nevertheless instructive, extensive empirical studies of 112 firms listed in the first section[393] of the Tokyo stockmarket[394] produced the following findings in respect of the scale and influence of the Keiretsu:

- Japan's economy is dualistic in nature: in each sector there are a few large (Keiretsu) companies which control the major technologies, and a peripheral area in which numerous small firms, whose methods are second-rate, fight for survival, primarily in the form of subcontractors or semi-finished goods manufacturers.
- The largest companies have merged to form approximately ten interest groups, which have split the entire economy between them. They play a more dominant role than is apparent from official statistics.
- The most influential of these, apart from the banks, is the Mitsubishi group, followed by Mitsui and Sumitomo.
- Sumitomo has the strongest group cohesion and Mitsui the weakest.
- The official financial complex (the Japanese Development Bank, the Export and Import Bank of Japan, the Central Farmers and Fishermen's Cooperative), the former 'Zaibatsu banks (Mitsubishi Bank, Mitsui Bank and the Sumitomo Bank) and the groupings with the long-term credit banks (the Japanese Industrial Bank and the Long Term Credit Bank) at their heart exert the greatest influence of all the credit institutions.
- The Keiretsu exert a powerful influence not only on the economy but also on Japanese politics.
- They even affect social and cultural life, in general. 'Not one single soul in Japan can escape the influence of the Keiretsu.'[395]

The Mitsubishi Research Institute summarizes this situation succinctly: 'the image of the Japanese economy is now dominated by 6 commercial groups and 10 large concerns which largely influence commercial life either directly or indirectly.' The aggregate sales share of the six commercial groups, taking into account 'all' interdependencies within the Japanese industrial structure, amounts to 59 per cent (i.e. around 2 per cent of the global economy), is produced by 0.1 per cent of total companies and 20 per cent of the workforce (excluding the self-employed).[396]

This concentration also becomes apparent when we consider the example of Mitsubishi. In 1989, core Mitsubishi companies (cf. Chapter 5, section IV) held over 4 per cent of all issued shares in Japan and thus together represented one of the largest shareholders in Japan, and one of these companies (the securities deposit bank for the Keiretsu: Mitsubishi Trust & Banking) has the lowest percentage of private individual shareholders of all Japanese joint-stock companies (4 per cent).[397] General statistics on company structure prove that Mitsubishi is not an isolated case. Of the 1612 companies traded on the Tokyo stockmarket in 1990, 78 per cent (1100) can be described as members of Keiretsu groupings; of these, 846 firms (61 per cent) can be classified as Keiretsu banks or Zaibatsu successors, whereas the remaining 254 firms (17 per cent) belong to the younger, industrial Keiretsu.[398] The relevance of the six Zaibatsu units, in terms of the national economy, is shown in Figure 5.1.

By considering the structural interdependence of the six large 'Keiretsu' nuclei, we obtain a clearer picture of a conglomeration of colossal economic giants, as depicted in Table 5.4 and Figure 5.2.

	1981	1987	1995	2000*
Shareholders' equity	30.8	32.0	31.7	33.0
Assets	23.2	27.0	25.9	28.5
Turnover	27.6	25.2	26.2	30.0
Cross holdings	25.5	22.7	20.8	17.0
Interlocking directorates	8.7	7.1	6.1	4.0

*Forecast

Figure 5.1   *Relative importance of the top 6 Keiretsu in the Japanese economy*
Source: Imai, K., 'The Legitimacy of Japan's Corporate Groups', p. 22

The size of this network creates the overall impression that 'the whole of Japan is one big Keiretsu',[399] in which a few indefinable, apparently boundless edifices have the capability to directly influence Japan's economy and even to indirectly influence society, while the 'traditional sector' of the national economy described by general theories of clearly identifiable definable legal rights, price paradigms, identical organizational structures and power hierarchies becomes less and less significant.

Table 5.4   *Relative sizes of the Keiretsu 1990–1995 (average) and trend (2000)*

	Mitsubishi		Mitsui		Fuyo		Sumitomo	
	Average	Trend	Average	Trend	Average	Trend	Average	Trend
Capital base[1]	100	Up	14	Down	67	Down	77	Down
Turnover[1]	100	Same	18	Down	81	Down	72	Down
Profit[1]	100	Up	50	Down	56	Down	92	Down
Loan outstanding[1]	100	Down	15	Up	83	Same	90	Down
Cross holdings[2]	25.6	Up	14.3	Down	16.7	Up	20.5	Up

	DKB		Sanwa		Tokai		IBJ		All 8 as %
	Average	Trend	Average	Trend	Average	Trend	Average	Trend	
Capital base[1]	73	Up							
Turnover[1]	46	Down							
Profit[1]	68	Down							
Loan outstanding[1]	88	Up							
Cross holdings[2]	13.8	Same							

[1] Billion yen
[2] In % of all Keiretsu shares
IBJ = Industrial Bank of Japan
DKB = Dai Ichi Kangyo Bank
Note: Adjustments for mergers & acquisitions have been made
Source: Dodwell, *Industrial Groupings in Japan*, p. 8ff

Mitsubishi

Tokai

Toshiba

Nippon Steel

Toyota

Mitsui

IBJ

Sumitomo

Seibu Saison

Fuyo

Nissan

Nippon Express

DKB

Hitachi

Hakyu/Toho

Sanwa

Kobe Steel

IBJ = Industrial Bank of Japan
DKB = Dai Ichi Kangyo Bank

The top 6 Keiretsu
Bank-centred Keiretsu
Vertical integrated groups

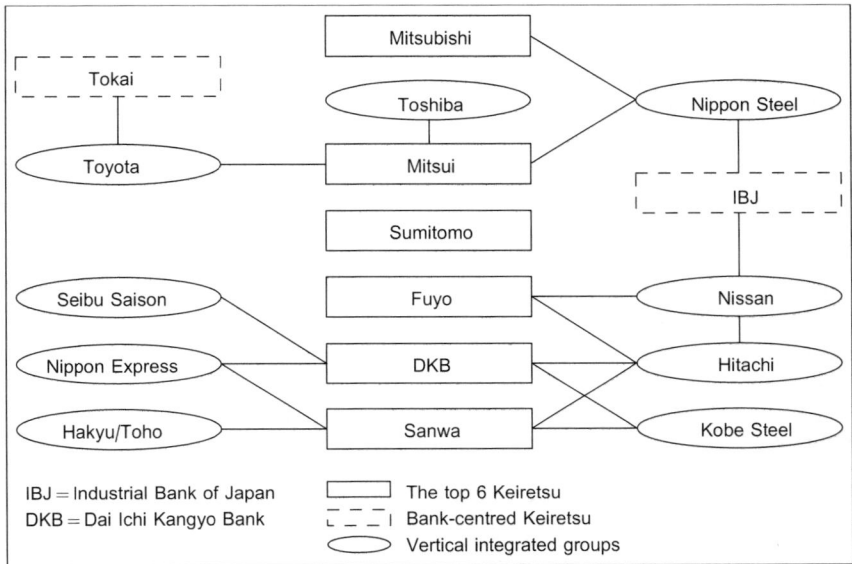

Figure 5.2   *Networks between the Keiretsu, pre-crisis, 1998*
Source: Dodwell, *Industrial Groupings in Japan*, p. 9

However, this knowledge-based dualism in industrial structure between the closely interrelated MNEs and the undefined peripheral firms is not uniquely Japanese, but is endemic to all industrial nations which possess sophisticated MNEs.[400] The next logical step is the 'globalization' of this dualism, that is the creation of a global dualism consisting of the individual top-performing groups of various countries. One indicator for this might be intra-company trade which is increasing in leaps and bounds,[401] and this is an area in which the Japanese MNEs have been able to achieve an above-average upturn. In 1980, their share was still around 15 per cent, but by 1986 it had risen to over 20 per cent.[402]

The developments at the turn of the millenium prove to be particularly interesting as two crass statements clash at this point: 'Keiretsu are dead' vs 'new Keiretsu are formed'. Currently, there is – after the Keiretsu bashing in the last decade – an attempt to declare the Keiretsu extinct. But just the simple fact that banks rid themselves of cross-shareholdings should not lead to the erroneous conclusion that Keiretsu are dead.[403] Also, the fact that though the cooling of foreign trade dampened the trading companies' 1999 results, it is noticeable that the companies not embedded into any Keiretsu system (e.g. Itochu, Marubeni or Nissho Iwai) have suffered significantly more than those within a Keiretsu (Mitsubishi, Mitsui and Sumitomo could pose the best results of about 35 billion yen on average). This serves well as an argument for the functioning of Keiretsu especially in downmarkets.[404] So, it seems that the restructuring can be sometimes seen as a discontinuing of old models and as the 'new' models are not yet in place, extinction is declared.

On the other hand, new (and New Economy-based) Keiretsu seem to be emerging. The most oft-cited example is the new giant Softbank that has been rising from nothingness to an acclaimed global status in just months during 1999. As one of the world's largest investors in the Internet, its strategy of developing a global Internet Zaibatsu called 'Net Clique' is expected to hit full stride from 2000.[405] Critics of this company, however, see the corporate strategy rather as fantasies or 'visions that sell', where 300-year business plans are peddled by finance artists to the beguiling global audience. Softbank's founder, Masayoshi Son, incessantly likes to talk about Internet-Zaibatsu and his role in defining new standards for the global economy.[406] Be it reality or (rather) not, monolithic dominance is unlikely to play the role model for new business models (cf. also the Microsoft antitrust case), but it shows the New Economy paradigm is shaped along the lines of the 'old' Keiretsu.

One should also not forget that any Keiretsufication needs strong external stimulus and help. The immense amounts of capital needed would bring any capital market to its knees, and access to vast new markets seems currently impossible or too aggressive a strategy; also, bold enlightened management (which would have to be trained over some considerable time) is not readily available in the desired quantities. Hence a completely new birth of a Keiretsu seems very implausible. But, as the existing system was and is performing, all it needs to do is to continue to increase its system performance. And, as in Tokugawa times, it is helped by external pressure. Simply put, the process is twofold: (a) get the scouts out and see what useful knowledge is available, and (b) get the knowledge in and implement it to perform better and be reborn. In 1880 the scouting was called 'opening of the country', and in 1980 it was 'globalization'. The second part, knowledge application, was in 1890 the 'industrialization' that took place after some (but still quite swift) learning and adaptation and is now in 2000 – after some introversion and contemplation of problems – the preparation for the 'next level' of economic complexity which is fully underway (see Tables 5.5, 5.6 and 5.7).

Table 5.5   *Financial relations between banks and trading companies at the beginning of the 1990s*

	Banks *(loans outstanding im million yen)*					
Sogo shosha	*Mitsubishi*	*Mitsui*	*Sumitomo*	*Fuji*	*Sanwa*	*DKB*
Mitsubishi	**158 541** ⇑	39 460 ⇒	84 625 ⇓	81 638 ⇒	110 404 ⇓	128 836 ⇒
Mitsui	47 048 ⇓	**107 962** ⇒	63 568 ⇓	91 943 ⇓	27 865 ⇒	33 828 ⇑
Sumitomo	23 033 ⇓	5 326 ⇒	**93 108** ⇓	10 550 ⇓	6 068 ⇓	1 357 ⇓
Marubeni	56 645 ⇓	5 443 ⇒	38 422 ⇓	**142 274** ⇒	44 313 ⇓	27 147 ⇒
Nissho Iwai	36 454 ⇒	18 145 ⇓	30 568 ⇓	12 540 ⇒	**92 519** ⇑	86 262 ⇑
Itoh	23 445 ⇓	38 710 ⇓	102 583 ⇓	61 206 ⇓	12 557 ⇓	**107 963** ⇒

Source: Sazaki, N., *Management and Industrial Structure in Japan*, p. 17

Table 5.6   *Share of Keiretsu-owned equity holdings in the Keiretsu*

	Mitsubishi	Mitsui	Sumitomo	Fuji	Dai Ichi Kangyo bank	Sanwa	Total percentage of this Keiretsu's shares owned by Keiretsu firms
Mitsubishi-group	**25.01**	1.02	0.44	2.30	2.59	2.07	27.80
Mitsui-group	0.79	**18.92**	1.16	1.60	2.35	2.98	33.43
Sumitomo-group	0.17	1.06	**28.24**	1.24	0.98	1.03	32.72
Fuyo-group	1.02	0.96	1.00	**16.59**	2.92	8.36	30.85
Dai Ichi Kangyo-group }	1.96	1.47	0.68	2.27	**13.73**	10.21	30.32
Sanwa	0.63	0.72	1.06	1.39	2.10	**17.35**	23.25
Total percentage of all Keiretsu shares owned by Keiretsu firms	29.58	23.65	32.58	25.39	24.77	42.00	

Source: Imai, K., 'Japan's Industrial Structure', p. 131

Table 5.7   *Composition of banks' and insurance companies' cross holding portfolios, 1999*

Invested in sector	Investment level relative to Topix index (%)	Trend 1995–99	Comment
Banks	100	⇒	Still overly
Pharms	80	⇒	invested, as a
Machinery	60	⇓	remanent of the 1980s
Electrical	100	⇓	but declining
Steel	30	⇓	in importance
Cars	80	⇓	
Retail	30	⇒	Already out,
Real estate	20	⇒	as this represents
Construction	50	⇒	the economy of 1960/70
Services	120	⇑	Not yet overweighted
Communication	150	⇑	enough, as investment
High tech	150	⇑	process is (too) slow

Source: Adapted from Matsui, K. *et al.*, *Millennium Metamorphosis*, p. 21ff

As Table 5.7 shows, there is a third way between the two statements 'dead' or 'new': the 'old guard' is now reshaping itself to be reborn in a new, more open and more flexible form.[407] In that sense, Japan's multinational enterprises are in the middle of their most expansive phase, during which they intend to realize their ambition to make their system the standard against which the whole world is measured. However, these ambitious aims should not, *a priori*, be considered as entirely negative. If we conduct an unbiased analysis of the general functions of a Keiretsu, we can identify some major economic tasks which can optimally be assumed by it.

The Functions of the Keiretsu

Having analysed the phenotypes and history of the Keiretsu to clarify their indirect influence and relevance within the Japanese national economy, the aim of this section is to explicitly delve into the functions of the company groups.

Apart from the purely business administration which takes place in a cluster of companies, there are a number of specific functions which ensure the success of a group such as a Keiretsu network.[408] The following list shows the seven primary tasks performed by a Keiretsu on behalf of the members of its group:

- organization of overall business procedures
- information function
- risk-distribution function
- forward-looking structural changes function

- strategic group coordination function
- symbolic function
- internal financial market function

Organization of overall business procedures

The most obvious function of a Keiretsu is to organize the operational activities of all group members, which primarily involves the provision of infrastructure-related services. This mediating function encompasses all sectors from goods procurement and marketing, logistics, transport, warehousing, insurance, distribution and outlet management to ancillary administrative services and other general organizational functions.[409] The joint deployment of special capabilities (which may be hived off in the form of separate firms) prevents redundant procedures and multiple overheads.

The trading companies (*sogo shosha*) undertake the major portion of this comprehensive organization function. They are not solely engaged in trade, egoistically pursuing profit-maximization, but serve to coordinate and generate supply and demand on the home market within a Keiretsu. Their secondary role, as supplier and customer, is to balance out all possible intra-Keiretsu transactions on the external goods and services market. This role is similar to that of a market-maker on the stock exchange.[410]

This organization function cannot be assigned to any particular firm but is one of the most important principles affecting the structure of the Keiretsu itself.[411] Apart from long-term stability, this coordination produces economies of scale which can result in considerable cost savings. When combined with lower fluctuation levels, they can also produce projectable development trends, consequently minimizing risk-management costs and increasing strategic efficiency.[412] The aim of these measures is to increase overall efficiency within the group which, in turn, improves its chances of prevailing in the struggle for market shares, growth rates and new markets.[413]

Information function

Within Japan's industrial structure, the company groups (particularly the former Zaibatsu' trading companies) have traditionally performed the role of information agencies and 'matchmakers'.[414] Companies specializing in foreign trade have historically acted as the information window on the rest of the world and, consequently, as major information generators, gatherers, processors and distributors within Japan's economic system. This specific competence is still second to none. Better access to relevant key information, increased information turnover, as well as improved analysis and evaluation methods are the key features of this capability and should be considered one of the major benefits of a Keiretsu system.[415] For this reason, the primary features of every Keiretsu should be seen as intense, rapid and comprehensive information flows via a multidimensional information network.[416] Market data and, specifically, foreign data are fed into the network from the sales-oriented firms and trading houses; financial information from financial and trading links which is coordinated by the main bank. Finally, the clubs, company-wide committees and councils disseminate informal and strategic information.

In this context, the plethora of participating firms can be assessed as a positive factor, guaranteeing the availability of detailed information on diverse consumer requirements and providing increasingly stratified markets for the Keiretsu as a whole. In a similar way, the multiplicator effect offers an all-round opportunity to utilize relevant know-how.[417] These information mechanisms are regularly assessed as particularly effective:

> A study by the Japan Socialist Party concluded that Mitsubishi Corporation was the most effective information gathering organization in Japan, well ahead of the media and governmental bodies. Information equivalent to 7000 pages of the *New York Times* is transmitted within the company every day.[418]

In this context, Mitsubishi proudly perceives itself as Japan's 'informational gatekeeper': 'We discover, transmit, and organize the latest developments coming into and going out from Japan.'[419] The successful information strategy adopted by Japanese companies leads Bierdümpel back to the special, open manner in which the Japanese handle information, the high availability of information and intense demand for it, as well as the general assessment that knowledge is the most influential of all resources.[420] The global scale of direct communication and computer systems is no novelty to the Keiretsu. During the 1970s, Mitsui was one of the first companies in the world to boast a truly global computer network and the Japanese Keiretsu were the first to own satellites: Mitsubishi was the first company to launch a dedicated satellite into space, exclusively for internal purposes. The Japanese have regularly been the first to develop and use state-of-the-art communication technologies.[421] The information sector has been purposefully developed into a major strategic resource and, for Keiretsu enterprises, is a fundamental component in terms of company success, although it does not represent an identifiable company division in an organizational or legal sense but is rather a capacity possessed by the entire Keiretsu organism and, as such, is not directly classifiable. This is not only significant in an abstract strategic sense but leads to real success, especially when applied practically.[422]

Risk distribution function

But information and organizational management are only the most obvious way of reducing risks within the Keiretsu.[423] Of greater significance are the secondary risk distribution effects. Whilst the prewar Zaibatsu maximized mutual profits, the primary objective of today's Keiretsu is risk-optimization.

Their fundamental procedural principle of this risk management is the creation and maintenance of long-term, implicit arrangements between members, leading to shared risk and reduced risks for individual members.[424] Large, difficult to assess, long-term risks are more readily acceptable due to the cumulative risk capacity of the Keiretsu, and this results in enhanced competitiveness, particularly in a global context. Nakatani confirmed the stabilization and risk limitation function of the Keiretsu in his empirical work. The nine Keiretsu studied had significantly lower relative volatility in profit and growth rates and dividend pay-out ratios, while the ratio of debt to equity was constantly lower than in the case of non-Keiretsu firms. Conversely, internal return on assets, internal credit default rates and growth rates were significantly more stable than in the case of non-Keiretsu companies and their workforce was better paid.[425] Additional stabilization factors are high levels of non-distributed profits,[426] minimal transaction cost sensitivity due to internal markets, and lower distribution costs resulting from stable distribution channels. Another stabilization factor stems from the relative market strength of a Keiretsu, which is used, not to maximize profits by raising prices, but to control risk. Other financial relationships also have a stabilizing effect. At-risk banks always have 'tame' borrowers who will request large sums just to oblige, even if hardly any need exists. And companies in crisis can always expect to obtain credit with the Keiretsu. These individual effects have a positive influence on the continuity of the overall performance capability of the Keiretsu.[427]

In addition, the overabundance of mutual business relationships acts as a natural hedge or offsetting risk, since, in principle, only external risks have to be secured, not intra-company group risks. When we perceive the company group as a unit and consider the extent of sales diversification, the creation of this portfolio can be described as a risk-optimization exercise, an option unavailable to a one-product firm. The extent to which these two principles, that of an internal natural hedge and the other of external diversification, have contributed to the risk-limitation objective becomes clear when the preference given to intra-group trade is interpreted not simply as a transaction-cost limitation measure but also as a risk-limitation strategy.[428] In Japan, contrary to Europe and the United States, this risk-management technique is a firmly established feature of industrial structure. The structure of the Keiretsu demands that business transactions between group members are conducted on the basis of transfer prices which differ significantly from hypothetical market prices. The implicit objective is to even out the aggregate profits of the group as a whole. These transfer prices represent the average marginal costs of the whole group, and contra payments are made to those Keiretsu members who fail to profit. Although this, in fact, contradicts the egoism principle of the market economy, rooted in Hobbes' tradition, it represents from an 'eastern' or Japanese perspective the rational strategy of maximizing the success of the company group as a whole.[429]

The internal financial market function

This task is easier to exemplify as an institutional structure, since the bank forming its nucleus[430] naturally plays an important role.[431] In this connection, we can identify two fundamental tasks. On the one hand, differing credit and investment requirements can be coordinated internally (offsetting), which reduces total risk and frees up more financial resources for the nucleus bank, which can then provide a powerful safety cushion or risk-management tool during periods of crisis. The second task is to provide access to international money and capital markets which is barred to individual, smaller and lesser-known member companies. The bank bundles these individual capital requirements together and endeavours to satisfy them efficiently, either from its own funds or via the global capital market. This reduces interest charges to smaller companies. The extraordinary strength of the Keiretsu house banks guarantees the availability of cheap, almost unlimited financial resources for expansion purposes.[432] Even though severely tested, the general principle will hold also for the future. The financing function will still be mainly internal though maybe not centralized at the bank.

To this extent, the financial aspect of the existential justification for the Keiretsu, apart from its above-mentioned stabilization function, should be perceived as the provision of risk capital at minimal capital cost at any given point in time (i.e. not just at opportune and favourable moments). However, this responsibility does not rest with the nucleus bank alone. The second core company, the trading house, also performs an important role in this respect.[433] While the bank pursues financial resources externally, the aim of the trading house is to expand Keiretsu markets.[434] However, these core Keiretsu companies are not antagonistically interdependent but are, in fact, mutually complementary. For the bank, the trading house is an optimum borrower (low risk, minimal supervisory costs associated with a single loan); the *sogo shosha*, in general, make attractive customers (foreign currency, export finance and monetary transactions).

From the point of view of the trading house, the central Keiretsu bank is the optimum partner since its concentrated market strength ensures that it can always offer optimum terms and is inclined to arrange special terms.[435] The financial relationships of the trading house are diverse. They range from favourable terms for other group members, to loan and guarantee provisions when available funds are invested in new major projects, new products and the R&D required by most of the numerous small Keiretsu firms. Just as the bank acts as the leading financier during periods of expansion, the trading company is able to ameliorate recessionary effects via intra-group trade,[436] for example by granting loans to suppliers, providing extended payment terms or credit to the members of the Keiretsu for material purchasing. This 'quasi-banking function'[437] is one of the major features of a Keiretsu and thus serves to explain, more precisely, why the definition 'financial conglomerate' is used to define them (*kinyu Keiretsu*; cf. the earlier section on 'phenotypes of the Keiretsu').

Lichtenberg and Pushner quantitatively demonstrate the positive links between Keiretsu control and the commercial performance of the company group. In this context, inside ownership (either by the directors, affiliated companies or strategic partner) clearly has a positive effect, since it serves to minimize the frequency and severity of performance losses.[438] Nakatani assesses these financial relationships more critically for two reasons: firstly, capital is blocked unnecessarily as a result of these mutual shareholdings and more expensive loans (obligatory borrowing) are then needed to compensate for this loss; and, secondly, on a macroeconomic level we can identify a 'Balkanization' of capital markets[439] since each company group generates its own internal 'mini-capital market', which can lead only to a significant fall in macroeconomic performance.[440] Therefore, the Keiretsu structure must be viewed somewhat ambivalently from a financial perspective. We must leave the task of clarifying these points to future empirical and analytical studies. If a wider perception, which includes group coordination, is applied to the structure of this financial market function, other effects emerge (strategic coordination, homogenization, risk distribution, etc.), which can form a powerful counterbalance to a perspective relating purely to price and efficiency.

The strategic group coordination function

The complex structure of a Keiretsu in terms of cooperation and communication, has led to the creation of a new type of 'quasi-market'[441] between the two markers represented by the market economy and management planning, a market which is used to calculate invisible prices on the domestic market and relative marginal gain. The more effective the linkage mechanisms and the more extensive the network, the better the internal market performs. This is why Yoshino perceives the Keiretsu as 'linkage mechanisms', the supreme aim of which is to extend the network. Thus, the primary duty of companies within a Keiretsu is to expand and manage the network,[442] a basic function traditionally associated with these firms since the Japanese perceive the ability to forge relationships as a primary skill of the old trading companies.[443]

The numerous service companies within the Keiretsu perform the special associated functions, which are placed at the disposal of the Keiretsu as a whole (banking, commerce, insurance, shipping, warehousing, property). The provision of clear internal functions is also apparent when one considers the particularly small proportion of non-Keiretsu business transacted. These factors produce an internal system equivalent to a vertical distribution of labour, within the framework of which each link in the production chain can be supplied with the correct level of input, and optimum input prices.

This can, however, be achieved more efficiently than by a fully integrated monolithic company, as system openness produces an otherwise unachievable flexibility.[444] The umbrella of the company group shields smaller firms from excessive risks. As its management and product efficiency grows, the firm attains greater independence and becomes more flexible and dynamic. This constitutes another advance for the Keiretsu in their role as a highly diversified network of products and markets, since both these parameters are currently undergoing a massive period of splintering, stratification and 'decommodification'. Economies of scale are reducing in size, optimum company sizes are decreasing rapidly, the proportion of product know-how is rising. The Keiretsu system is ideally equipped to face these challenges, which, in fact, constitute an opportunity as far as Japanese company groups are concerned due to the importance placed on input–output relationships, their orientation on anticipated long-term growth and the sustained transfer of know-how.[445]

In order to prevent any unwanted externalization of the positive effects to outsiders, it is of paramount importance to keep the network 'introverted'. The Keiretsu provide environment protection against the intense competitive pressures prevailing in Japan, and also against foreign market players. Although precedence is usually given to group members as far as business is concerned, empirical analyses prove that the formation of cartels and intra-company trade tends to optimize the use of resources, rather than reduce competitiveness as many theorists assume.[446]

The Keiretsu have an additional part to play in their role as a company group. Apart from their role as an introverted cooperative network and general protector, they also protect members from voluntary or 'enforced' departures from the group. The network of company interrelationships[447] basically prevents speculators, corporate raiders and hostile take-over. These are all familiar side-effects in the USA of an open, efficient capital market. The absence of a large merger and acquisitions market does not imply that the company market is inefficient or that company controls are ineffective. These duties are performed internally within a Keiretsu by their financial institutions, who perform management control and monitor company performance.[448] Thus the efficiency-enhancing pressure to perform is generated not by means of Western mechanisms (earnings per share, growth rates, market prices) but by using specific Japanese methods (endogenization, informalization and diffusion).

The symbolic focus

This type of group control relates indirectly to a further sphere of activity, from which perspective the Keiretsu are not only closely intertwined on a contractual, financial or control level, but their cohesive strength is especially evident on a symbolic level. By looking at the symbolic function of Keiretsu company associations, we can perceive all the indirect and subtle signs indicating the tightness of group cohesion: membership of a president's club (or other club-like societies), permanent (i.e. non-commercial) credit relationships, share lock-ups, the awarding of directorships, shared foreign organizations, joint corporate images (logo, house style, brand names) and corporate identities, and symbolic gestures (donations, crisis aid, measures to support government policy) coordinated group-wide, and many more.

The symbolic, flexible partnership presented by company associations has led to superordinate cohesion aimed at preventing a decline into excessive flexibility, fashionable chaos management and 'speed management'. On the one hand, the role of these associations is to act as a vague benchmark in terms of company policy and, on the other hand, to robustly present heightened brand awareness and a coordinated public image, which also positively enhances the commercial success of its members.[449,450]

The bond between individual companies, which stretches from routine coordination to strategy cooperation and culminates in the comprehensive integration of the social clubs, is becoming ever tighter.[451] In addition to the previously mentioned assimilation of the symbol of the family by Japanese firms,[452] particularly strong community-building measures have been encouraged over the centuries, particularly among the Zaibatsu company groupings, and these measures continue to produce a proverbial 'Zaibatsu sense of community' even today.[453,454] This symbolic cohesion can be considered the most important asset of the Keiretsu in terms of structural content. It is the only element which does not form part of the relevant environmental adjustments required, but manages them instead. The aim of this approach is to manage and lead the eco-system of a company or company association – that is, the overall political, commercial, social and cultural links between a firm and its workforce – that is, both inside and outside the confines of the company.[455] The vagueness and openness of these indicators is seen as a strength, since it basically permits a collective sharing of long-term visions without the danger of being side-tracked by short-term contradictions which may arise during their actual implementation. The symbolic and long-term coordination of group members also reinforces the final role of the Keiretsu, since management by symbols, whilst making use of traditional symbols, is always forward-looking in nature.

The future-oriented structural development function

As we have perceived in other chapters (for example Chapter 4, section VI, and Chapter 5, section III on 'structural history'), no rigid development plans ever existed but only future-related concepts in terms of economic and entrepreneurial development:

> The evolution of the 'sogo shosha' [and the Zaibatsu which evolved from them, the Keiretsu and the Japanese MNEs] is not based on any preplanned, fixed concept. Environmental conditions and the Japanese mentality have, in fact, been responsible to a far greater extent for long-term development.[456]

Whilst many authors[457] acknowledge the role of the Keiretsu in terms of the structural definition of the national economy, they fail to address the 'futuristic' aspect, their visionary or active role in its reconstruction. The responsibilities which should be perceived as specific to the Keiretsu[458] are not limited solely to researching the future, trend analyses or planning capacity alone. Their active role in the formulation and particularly the implementation of overall economic and meta-economic visions is also of special significance in terms of understanding the efficiency of the Keiretsu.[459]

Thus, the role of the Keiretsu may also be perceived as that of an information generator for the future and a relevant information clearing point, processing a hitherto unattained volume of know-how about the future for subsequent integration into current activities. This capability is increasingly becoming one of the most important assets of a competitive organization. From this perspective, Japan's MNEs are excellently equipped to face competition in global markets, where information and accurate forecasting deliver major competitive advantages (Figure 5.3).[460] In the course of time, we shall be able to align development trends for Zaibatsu and Keiretsu structures with those of Western structural dynamics. Consequently, the current situation is clearly emerging as a springboard which will entirely encompass economic cultures in the new millennium.

The current gyrations in business structures are felt most by the Keiretsu. Hence they represent the cutting edge of developments, even if these changes are cutting to the bones of the old economy, forcing the Keiretsu to reshape and regain their accustomed position as role models.

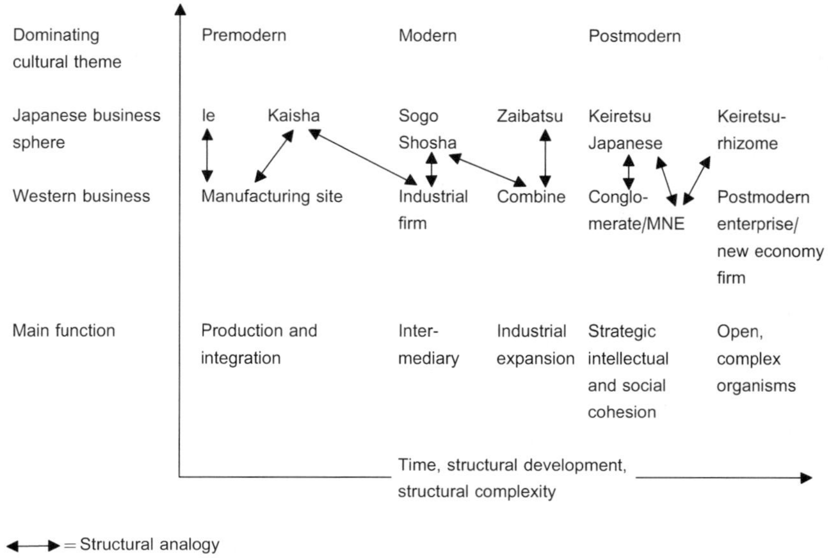

	Premodern	Modern		Postmodern	
Dominating cultural theme					
Japanese business sphere	Ie Kaisha	Sogo Shosha	Zaibatsu	Keiretsu Japanese	Keiretsu-rhizome
Western business	Manufacturing site	Industrial firm	Combine	Conglomerate/MNE	Postmodern enterprise/ new economy firm
Main function	Production and integration	Inter-mediary	Industrial expansion	Strategic intellectual and social cohesion	Open, complex organisms

Time, structural development, structural complexity

◄——► = Structural analogy

Figure 5.3 *Integration of enterprises across time, Japan vs West*

The Keiretsu have taken the lead in so many areas of Japanese development that they will continue to play a leading role in moulding the future. By transforming their companies internally from industrial to postindustrial and subsequently to postmodern, they are not only restructuring the entire Japanese industrial landscape but have also assumed the power and responsibility to predetermine future social and cultural objectives.

In a concept which sees Japan as the future nerve centre for global investment, production and market strategy, the Keiretsu, in its role as the largest and most relevant institution,[461] will make a substantial contribution to the realization of that project. Thus the functions of the Keiretsu, ranging from effective organizational tasks (overall business procedures, information, risk, financial resources) to group-merger projects (overall strategy, symbols, structural changes), have now come full circle.

IV   THE MITSUBISHI KEIRETSU AS A CASE STUDY OF A KEIRETSU'S BASIC STRUCTURE

Historical Overview[462]

The Mitsubishi group can be seen as the prototype for the Japanese Keiretsu, which is why they are described by Johnson as 'the largest and most distinguished Keiretsu'.[463] In Japan they are considered, together with the Mitsui group, as the general benchmark. In a head-to-head race with Mitsui, lasting a century, Mitsubishi has become the oldest and largest Keiretsu in the world.[464] Mitsubishi is considered the most tradition-oriented of the Keiretsu[465] and has, throughout the ages, consistently demonstrated more clearly than all the others the basic structure of a Japanese multinational enterprise. Together with Mitsui, it is also the most significant in terms of political power. The most often quoted, outstanding capabilities of Mitsubishi are, in particular, organizational efficiency and internal cohesion, its 'esprit de corps'.[466]

The main company in the group, the Mitsubishi Corporation, can trace its origins back to 1870 when Iwasaki Yataro established a company called Tosa Kaisai Shosha.[467] In 1873, it was renamed Mitsubishi Shokai and specialized, at that time, in trading and shipping. Officially, this can be considered as the foundation of the Mitsubishi concern.[468] Thanks to its close links with the new Meiji government,[469] this shipping company was extremely successful right from the outset, and within four years already controlled approximately 80 per cent of Japan's shipping. Mitsubishi thus became the main business partner of the emerging state, particularly during the military campaigns against Taiwan and Satsuma. As a result of this highly profitable sinecure, shipping became increasingly competitive from 1885, since the aim of the other companies (especially Mitsui) was to break the monopoly. This provided Mitsubishi with the incentive to continually expand its commercial activities and diversify into other sectors. During this process it evolved into a small conglomerate, and split into an increasing number of product divisions.[470]

Further developmental stages were the foundation of Mitsubishi Kaisha in 1886, which was engaged in finance and foreign exchange, mining and ship repairs, and Mitsubishi's take-over in 1887 of the publicly-managed Nagasaki shipyard. In 1885, Mitsubishi was converted from an autocratic one-man firm into a limited partnership and extensive powers were delegated to managerial staff (*banto*).[471] A major step was taken in 1908 when the company was initially decentralized worldwide into divisional product groups to form a concern structure, which was subsequently used by DuPont and General Motors in an adapted form.[472] These six divisions (banking, mining, coal, shipping, property and logistics) continued to grow exponentially. Thus it seemed sensible from 1918 to convert core company departments into independent companies ('*bunkei kaisha*', branch firms) which resulted, *de facto*, in a holding structure. All the companies of global relevance today – Mitsubishi Heavy Industries, Mitsubishi Bank, Mitsubishi Electric, Mitsubishi Oil etc. – already existed at the start of the 1930s. In 1937, the holding company, Mitsubishi Honsha, was converted into a public company, the management of which was completely in tune with national objectives: 'Mitsubishi is not the exclusive property of the Iwasaki family ... We must perform our duty with a clear-cut resolve to serve, above all things, the interest of the state.'[473,474]

At this time, the state and Mitsubishi were ideologically and personally at one.[475] At the end of the war the Mitsubishi Keiretsu comprised 75 core companies under direct control and another 166 indirectly controlled companies. It also contributed approximately 10 per cent of the Japanese gross national product.[476] In 1945, the Mitsubishi Honsha was smashed by the Americans after Mitsubishi had refused to accede to the request to disband voluntarily. Mitsubishi Shoji, which as a *sogo shosha* was one of the core companies in the concern, was split into 140 companies, and each of the others into at least two or three independent companies. Only Mitsubishi Heavy Industries was able to evade this fate, since the Americans planned that the armaments giant would play a supporting role in the Cold War (with China and Russia).[477] However, the links between the individual companies remained intact, with the unshakable aim of the Mitsubishi group to rebuild a fully integrated concern which would nevertheless do justice to official requirements: no holding company, no common management and no controlling shareholders.[478]

At no time during this transformation period has it ever been possible to distinguish between information flow and informal coordination flow, due to the personal relationships of management; only the methods have changed. A more open, more subtle system of '*collective guidance*' has evolved from the prewar system, in which the Iwasaki family and the '*honsha*' acted as the masters of strategy, primarily via the various 'clubs' and other informal contacts maintained at all levels between the individual firms (in this connection cf. Chapter 3, section IV ('the web ...') and Chapter IV, section III ('individual and organizational elements')). The explicit objectives of this system are strategic planning, control and management of the entire Mitsubishi world. Its organizational skills, the envy of the whole of Japan, and the closer mutual business relationships currently existing within the Keiretsu, as well as a high degree of congruence between the state's national economic development goals and those of Mitsubishi, have led to the creation of an MNE whose role remains unchallenged in Japan and who has occupied one of the pole positions in global markets since the 1980s.

In Japan, the influence of the Mitsubishi Keiretsu on everyday life is impressive. The group comprises 44 main companies employing a total workforce of 480 000. If we consider the capital investments which this 'Keiretsu' has in approximately 1300 Japanese companies and their other shareholdings in at least another 650 group-affiliated firms, we can assume that approximately *a quarter of the Japanese population is directly dependent economically on the Mitsubishi group.* For decades, Mitsubishi has held an unbroken, dominant integrative position within Japan in many sectors, in the face of extremely intense competition. The major sectors in this context[479] are beer, sheet-glass, ceramics, non-ferrous metals, heavy engineering, banking, insurance and foodstuffs. Even when compared with other Keiretsu, Mitsubishi is seen as a role model, particularly in terms of the level of integration and the future-oriented dynamics of the company, which caused Makihara, the Chairman of the Board of the Mitsubishi Corporation, to proudly proclaim: 'Our people – among the best anywhere.'[480]

Mitsubishi has always been considered the trendsetter in terms of the evolutionary history of the conglomerates. It played a leading role in modernization, and was never beaten by any Japanese company in growth rate and dynamics during the period of intense industrialization in the first three decades of the twentieth century. Even during the new transformation phase, Mitsubishi has prepared itself for the role of trendsetter, and in this context the traditional basic virtues of balanced growth, constant demonstration of flexibility by means of diversification and commercial dynamism, extolled on all sides, can again be considered primary qualities.[481] Echoing Johnson's theory of the 'Keiretsufication of the world', Okumura refers to a 'Mitsubishification of the world'[482] which reflects how successful Mitsubishi has been, in recent years, in building strategic positions for the future.[483]

Japan and Mitsubishi are in a new transformation phase that will have a major impact on all aspects of business activities worldwide. Precedents for success are not difficult to find: after each crisis or period of change, the Zaibatsu have become more powerful and successful as a result of crisis reforms. Already in 1924, major Japanese companies were successful in exerting their influence on US Senate and Congress. In 1936, warnings were already rife in both Asia and Europe about 'the yellow peril' and the theory that 'Japan was a global shogun and the Zaibatsu were daimyo was propagated right up to the end of the Second World War.[484] Now the cycle is again at such a stage. As the Zaibatsu groups were responsible for every one of Japan's evolutionary advances, including the 'upstream'-trend (diversification into primary areas such as steel production) started by the general trading houses and the subsequent 'downstream' expansion into distribution and marketing systems and the fulminate development of the Japanese financial system, the successors of the Zaibatsu are exerting their skills again.[485] To cite one example: Mitsubishi launched a 'Mitsubishi Heartbeat 21' campaign that has as its aim to reinvigorate and reenergize the group as a whole, with the aim of being a role model for every company on earth. The case study following will show that Mitsubishi's development mirrors the demands that are shaped both in the postmodern discussion as well as in the business and economic literature on the New Economy.

The Composition of the Core Structure

In our analysis of the Mitsubishi structure, we briefly consider three structural levels: firstly, we identify the *nucleus of the Keiretsu*, the area responsible for coordination, integration and development. This is the hub to which the actual *network of Keiretsu firms* is connected and, in a third phase, we use examples to demonstrate the similarity of this network to a '*sub-Keiretsu*', a mini-Keiretsu within the bigger Keiretsu structure in the context of the sphere surrounding each of these firms.

The nucleus consists of three elements: a *bank* (commercial bank: Mitsubishi Bank[486]), a *trading company* (*sogo shosha*: Mitsubishi Corporation) and a *manufacturing base* (heavy industry: Mitsubishi Heavy Industries). This basic structure is self-evident from the company name and logo, which are derived from the Samurai crest of the founding family: the direct translation of Mitsubishi being 'three precious stones/diamonds'.

The *Mitsubishi Corporation*,[487] officially the 'primary core' of the Mitsubishi group,[488] and a world leader in many sectors, is Japan's largest trading company. The energy sector, research and development facilities, heavy industrial product sales and satellite communications represent merely the key sectors in which the might of the Mitsubishi Corporation is apparent. The Mitsubishi Corporation can be perceived as the entrepreneurial core of the Mitsubishi group, since it generates all-important coordination and integration dynamics and also produces the momentum which, for the 'Keiretsu' companies,[489] is decisive for the implementation of expansive global strategies.[490]

If we look at a list of shareholders, which by Western standards is extremely constant, we can perceive the level of homogeneity of this Keiretsu core. The ten largest shareholders of the Mitsubishi Corporation hold more than 42 per cent of the total shares, five being members of the Mitsubishi Keiretsu, while the other five are from other Keiretsu groups. No other major (>5 per cent) shareholdings exist, and no non-Keiretsu company holds more than a 1 per cent share in the Mitsubishi Corporation.[491] In 1975, and in 1995, the major shareholders were: Mitsubishi Bank, Tokyo Marine & Fire, Mitsubishi Heavy Industries, Meiji Life Insurance and the Mitsubishi Trust Bank, each with a shareholding in excess of 5 per cent. The percentage of shares held by foreigners rose simultaneously from 0.7 to 4.6 per cent and to 6.3 per cent, which, in international terms, is still an extremely low figure.[492]

Consequently, at least 31 per cent (in total) of shares are held by companies within the same Keiretsu. To this we can add about another 15 per cent, which are held by other Keiretsu. This means that more than half the shares are secured within so-called 'friendly cross-holdings'. Even the majority of private shareholders are Mitsubishi members: 87 per cent of Mitsubishi shareholders (about 30 000) own just 6.5 per cent of the shares. Although these statistics are based on the last detailed analysis undertaken in 1974, this ratio has remained constant until today. 'The major owners of the large trading companies today are not private citizens, but Japan's giant corporations [themselves].'[493]

Sectoral sales trends after the Second World War rose in line with the growth curve presented in Chapter 4, section IV. In the 1950s and 1960s, the main sales sector was heavy and chemical industry, whereas information systems, information services and high-tech machinery accounted for the major proportion of turnover during the 1980s and 1990s. By preemptively expanding the scope of its business from that of a trading company to that of a complex service provider (finance, industrial research, the development of raw material sources, the planning and organization of major projects, etc.), the Mitsubishi Corporation has assumed an increasingly key role within the Keiretsu. This particularly applies to its role as the knowledge centre for the Keiretsu. The Mitsubishi Corporation has set itself the ambitious goal of becoming a 'global database for information technology'[494] and of being able to provide its own Keiretsu (and, in a diluted form, other business partners as well), with comprehensive and sensitive competitive information in all areas of high technology.

Alongside the trading company, the bank – *Mitsubishi Bank* – Mitsubishi Ginko – also plays a decisive role in its basic function as group financier. Together with Mitsubishi Trust and Banking, it represents the financial pillar of the group.[495] Its role in ensuring the financial stability of the group becomes very clear when we consider its assets and liabilities. Between 1990 and 1995, 75 per cent of loans were granted to companies, and only 21 per cent to private clients and investments were predominantly in the short-term money market (71 per cent). This allowed cash-flow to pour back into Keiretsu firms in need of funds, whilst the loans provided 'associate' companies with the finance required to support their plans.[496] This role as the 'war chest' of the Keiretsu is the reason for the 'typically Japanese' phenom-enon of high debt finance among the companies. The main bank favours financing via debt above equity funding, since these terms are strangely perverse in a Japanese context. In a Japanese context, debt funding is not, in general terms, third-party capital but group capital, that is 'proprietary capital' in a strategic sense. Thus, to confuse European definitorial terms, Japanese equity, excluding share cross-holdings, is in fact third-party capital of 'outside' shareholders, while debt is more an internal resource of capital. Particularly during a growth phase, the core bank has the task of promoting expansion by increased lending to sectors and projects strategically desirable to the Keiretsu.[497]

But it is not only during periods of growth that the core bank is active. Specifically during times of recession the bank is also responsible for expanding the

Keiretsu by lending to companies which are basically sound but temporarily in trouble. These loans are used to draw companies into the Keiretsu network or to tighten their links with the Keiretsu. The core bank can also be perceived as the 'lender of last resort' within the existing Keiretsu. In this way, the bank controls the financial affairs of other Keiretsu member companies who may be showing signs of weakness. It is able to provide an almost impregnable line of defence against (enforced) insolvency by offering extremely cheap capital and practically unconditional guarantees, as well as symbolic 'cohesion' between the Mitsubishi firms.[498] This is why the president of the Mitsubishi Research Institute, Makino, can claim with confidence that: 'a Mitsubishi company never goes bankrupt.'[499] But recent times showed that it can shake it down to its foundations, thus forcing it to reshape in a major fashion.

The shareholding structure of Mitsubishi Ginko, like that of the Mitsubishi Corporation, is extremely introverted in favour of its own Keiretsu, which accounts for its extremely independent image. Furthermore, foreign investors account for only about 1 per cent of its shareholders, which represents the lowest foreign shareholding of the bigger listed companies. In its role as one of the largest 'city banks' in Tokyo and one of the five largest banks in the world, it heads the field in terms of the globalization trend pursued by the Mitsubishi Keiretsu and occupies a dominant position in every global financial market.

Literature contains many clues, most of which indicate that the banks (and less frequently the *sogo shosha*) are the main hub of the Keiretsu.[500] But, particularly in the case of Mitsubishi, one can perceive the supplementary role played by both nucleus companies, that is the bank and the trading house. Although each of them individually represents a major international economic force, they are optimally used by the Mitsubishi Keiretsu in a mutually complementary way. If we are to pursue a historic perspective, we can speak in terms of a power transference. Until Japan started to prepare itself for the Second World War, the Keiretsu was dominated by the trading companies. Once these preparations were underway, manufacturing companies like Mitsubishi Heavy Industries assumed the leading role. After the war was over, the Mitsubishi Bank was given the task of recreating the original character of the group.[501] As a consequence of the export boom,[502] the spotlight during the 1960s and 1970s reverted to the trading company. By 1990, the cluster forming the leadership of the Mitsubishi Keiretsu[503] consisted of two nuclei (the banks and the trading company) and the leader of the company group (Mitsubishi Heavy Industries). Today, the cluster is no longer delineated clearly, as it is in flux, scrambling to readapt to the changes which have come from the outside faster than anticipated, and in a quite negative form, as a threat rather than being a positive self-induced form or remodelling. Hence it can be expected that this transition will continue for some time until a new constellation can be discerned. One trend is clearly the 'blurring' of the nuclei, in the sense that instead of one company representing that nucleus, for example the finance function, several companies fill this role. Instead of having one giant bank at the core, four (still relatively big) institutions (Bank of Tokyo–Mitsubishi Bank, Mitsubishi Trust and

Banking, Tokyo Marine and Meiji Life)[504] now share the work once done by Mitsubishi Bank alone, thus rendering the structure more intangible and defensible.

Of the three companies in this cluster, the history of Mitsubishi Heavy Industries (MHI) is probably the most capricious. It expanded explosively during the general industrialization wave of the last century, was fêted as the nation's largest war machine, and later completely destroyed by the effects of war. Today MHI is again one of the largest individual employers within the Mitsubishi group, with a workforce totaling 44 000.[505]

Through all its periods of instability, Mitsubishi Heavy Industries has remained a broadly-based colossus. Since 1929, it has been the only company in Japan consistently included in the list of Japan's 10 largest manufacturing companies.[506] Traditionally, MHI had always been the king of the Mitsubishi giants and maintained this decades-long position right up to the end of the war, which explains why Mitsubishi's clan chieftain, Iwasaki Koyata, was glorified as the 'Krupp of the Orient' during the prewar era.[507] Despite its militaristic connotations (MHI was the largest armaments manufacturer in the world), Mitsubishi Heavy Industries managed to survive relatively unscathed due to the American occupiers' fear of communism. After the war, the state supported the reconstruction of MHI, which was designed to be a testing group for the 'scrap and build' strategy of the MITI: 'scrap medium and smaller enterprises and build Mitsubishi Heavy Industries'.[508] MHI is today considered the largest heavy machinery manufacturer in Japan, and holds a dominant position in many sectors from shipbuilding, power station construction and aircraft manufacture to printing machines, construction vehicles and environmental technology. MHI is now also able to build on its past experience as the largest military manufacturer in the world in its role as the largest supplier, by far, of the Japanese Ministry of Defense.[509] When one compares MHI with its rivals, its competitive position appears unassailable (see Figure 5.4).

In addition to its visible role as a commodities manufacturer and its symbolic role as the leading industrial coordinator within the Mitsubishi group, Mitsubishi Heavy Industries is also playing a leading role in opening up foreign markets and effecting direct investments. Of all three core companies, MHI also displays the highest degree of linkage: its two subsidiaries with the highest international profile being Mitsubishi Electric and Mitsubishi Motors.[510] The precise number of companies economically dependent on MHI is difficult to determine. MHI itself lists 120 affiliated companies, although Dodwell estimates the figure at 150 and according to the estimates produced by Japanese analysts the number is significantly higher: '... the combined total of its subsidiaries and subaffiliated companies is said to exceed 300'.[511]

In abstraction, none of these three core firms can be identified as the clear leader, but all three appear to be on a par with each other. The task of managing the Mitsubishi Keiretsu is divided between all of them, although this responsibility is implicit and never mentioned. For example, the annual report consistently fails to mention the overall links which form the Keiretsu. Only isolated, accidental information is ever presented. The aim of this omission is to sustain the fictitious

Name	Group affiliation	¥ bn turnover 1999	Index	Relative trend 1990–2000
1 Mitsubishi Heavy Industries	Mitsubishi	2970	100	Reference
2 Kawasaki Heavy Industries	DKB Kawasaki	1190	40.1	Down
3 Kubota Ltd	Fuyo	970	32.7	Down
4 Ishikawajina Harinma Heavy Industries	Mitsui	1030	34.7	Same
5 Komatsu Ltd	–	1060	35.7	Up
6 Daikin Industries	Sumitomo	456	15.4	Same
7 Sumitomo Heavy Industries	Sumitomo	560	18.9	Up
8 Hitachi Zosen Corp	Sanwa	520	17.5	Up
9 Hitachi Construction Machinery	Sanwa	315	10.6	Down
10 Niigata Engineering	–	204	6.87	Same

Name	Group affiliation	Total assets 1999	Index	Trend 1990–2000
1 Mitsubishi Heavy Industries	Mitsubishi	4110	100	Reference
2 Kawasaki Heavy Industries	DKB Kawasaki	986	24	Down
3 Kubota Ltd	Fuyo	874	21.3	Down
4 Ishikawajina Harinma Heavy Industries	Mitsui	1055	25.7	Down
5 Komatsu Ltd	–	746	18.2	Down
6 Daikin Industries	Sumitomo	321	7.81	Down
7 Sumitomo Heavy Industries	Sumitomo	432	10.5	Down
8 Hitachi Zosen Corp	Sanwa	527	12.8	Down
9 Hitachi Construction Machinery	Sanwa	281	6.84	Down
10 Niigata Engineering	–	233	5.87	Down

Figure 5.4   *Mitsubishi Heavy Industries – relative size*
Source: Dodwell, *Industrial Groupings in Japan*, p. 599

impression that each company is an independent entity. Holstein sums this up succinctly: 'Despite these links, there is no evidence of a comprehensive central strategic plan, and Mitsubishi executives insist that each of their companies pursues its own particular goal.'[512]

This impression of independence, which was created after the public burial of feudal structures and the Zaibatsu, can be considered a major feature of Japan's old strategy. The purpose of this strategy is to consistently keep Japan's real intentions and true rulers out of the limelight:[513]

In the old days the president of any subordinate company was like a feudal lord, loyal to the grand lord of the main castles. The relationship was that of master–servant. The family was destroyed after the war, leaving only the servants behind. Then the servants got together and tried to revive the family even though there was no master.[514]

But, in spite of all the protestations that Japan lacks a hierarchy and coordination and is apparently helpless, it is impossible to overlook a strategy-oriented, concerted *modus operandi* if we consider the indicators. Consequently, the failure of Keiretsu managers to officially acknowledge the existence of Keiretsu power smacks of a compulsory exercise, designed to underplay the powerful punch which the organization packs.

The founding families are no longer the central focus but part of a highly elusive management elite (cf. Chapter 4, section III, 'the centre: a Japanese elite?'), and the old principal company (*honsha*) together with its holding structure have disappeared, but the basic principles of indirect strategic planning, circular control and an empty core have survived this transformation.[515] Thus the generally admired, intense integration of the Mitsubishi Keiretsu is even more astonishing.[516] A superficial approach fails to reveal any concrete clues pointing to a strict dirigiste management:

> The group does share a research center and an exhibition hall, but there is no over-all boss, no controlling stockholder and no formal organization framework. Most actual business deals between Mitsubishi firms are worked out and signed by the individual corporate officers. But this vague organization suits Japan, where personal relationships and group loyalties are far more important than legal documents.[517]

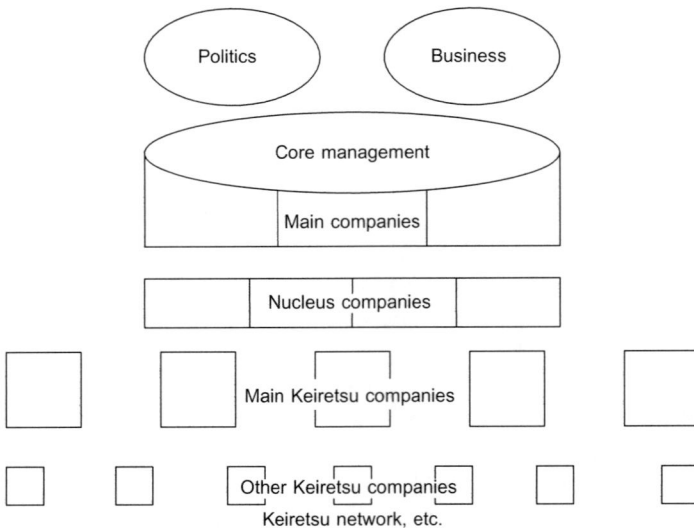

Figure 5.5   *Typical structure of a Keiretsu*
Source: Adapted from Eli, M., *Sogo Shosha*, p. 9

Even a more formal view of the organization reveals once again the 'old' Zaibatsu structure, although this time one which is less ideological and more diffuse, as Figures 5.5 and 5.6 show.

These three core companies (or, respectively, their top management) manage an extensive conglomerate of other firms using an arsenal of indirect and subtle techniques, without ever having to resort to official or public influence. Influence is exerted layer by layer and in coordination with companies included in its inner circle.

Despite the minimal amounts involved, share capital tie-ups between the nucleus companies are not merely of symbolic value. Share tie-ups at core company level (average 3 per cent) cannot be compared with tie-ups on other levels. At a *Kinyokai* level[518] the share tie-up with core companies and other *Kinyokai* firms is often in excess of 30 per cent. On the next layer up, there is an even higher capital tie-up (potentially in excess of 50 per cent).[519] Market data can shed a far clearer light on the global power exerted by these three companies than any mathematical calculations based on equity shareholdings. To clarify the (economic) power involved here, we can use comparative dimensions based on Sazaki's[520] calculations to roughly relativize the economic potency of the nucleus companies. Between 1986 and 1988, the three core Mitsubishi firms (excluding the Keiretsu), posted sales of almost US$120 billion per annum. This put them in nineteenth place in world rankings, behind the gross national product of Switzerland (approx. US$142 billion) and in front of Belgium (approx. US$114 billion), General Motors (US$101 billion) and Sweden (US$97 billion). Today, the total Keiretsu, though not the core, could still be ranked in the global top twenty.

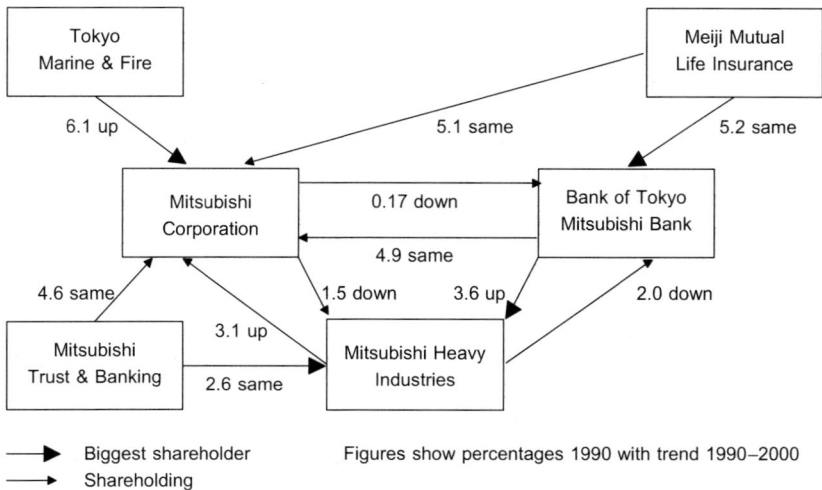

Figure 5.6 *Equity cross holdings in the nucleus*
Source: Compiled from *Japan Company Handbook 1990*

This triumvirate is closely interrelated and, in operational terms, constitutes a coherent block which, from an external perspective, is able to perform tasks flexibly. Thus the nucleus firms are mutually interchangeable, eliminating the need for a clear centre, each respectively as a principal. They can only jointly perform all the tasks required of them by the circle of Keiretsu firms around them. Only in combination are they able to fulfil the role of symbolic and visionary leadership and loose, integrative control. In this way individual companies are protected from intense external criticism.[521]

Within this web of functions, three companies form the management elite. This extremely influential elite is and aims to remain extremely elusive in terms of actual procedures, in order to avoid being labelled, *a priori*, a fixed structure, a fixed strategy or a clear set of objectives. The aim of this diffuse structural leadership is to be free, flexible and contingent; able to adapt pragmatically to the constantly increasing pace of environmental change. Since this does not generate solid organizational bodies based on rational patterns, environmental 'assaults' cannot be selective but merely diffuse and broad in focus and effect, converted to self-advantage, according to *aikido* and *judo* principles. The management thus formed can be considered effective in terms of strategy and performance, in spite of all the complexity involved. Figure 5.7 schematically explains the interaction and coordinated functions of these three core companies.

The Relationship Network of the Keiretsu Firms

The three nucleus firms are easy to identify and their functions are fundamentally also comprehensible, whereas the overall structure of the group of subsidiary companies remains unclear. The complex network of firms referred to, in general terms, as the Keiretsu encircles these three nuclei. In addition, several non-profit organizations are directly linked to the nucleus, whose primarily tasks can be seen as coordination, top management training and research on behalf of all the companies within the Keiretsu. For example, the most significant of these organizations are: the Public Affairs Committee, whose task it is to optimize all public contacts and communications; the Mitsubishi Bank Forum, which is the international discussion forum grooming the group's top young executives; and the Mitsubishi Research Institute, whose primary task is to provide fundamental economic research on behalf of the group.[522] The fundamental structure of the Mitsubishi world most commonly used as a starting point is that of a core group, encircled by a group of companies, whose presidents are represented in the *Kinyo-kai*.[523] These two groups, the nucleus group and the *Kinyo-kai*, together form the core of the Keiretsu.

The *Kinyokai* (literally 'the Friday Club') is a place where the presidents and board members of the major Mitsubishi companies regularly meet every second

241

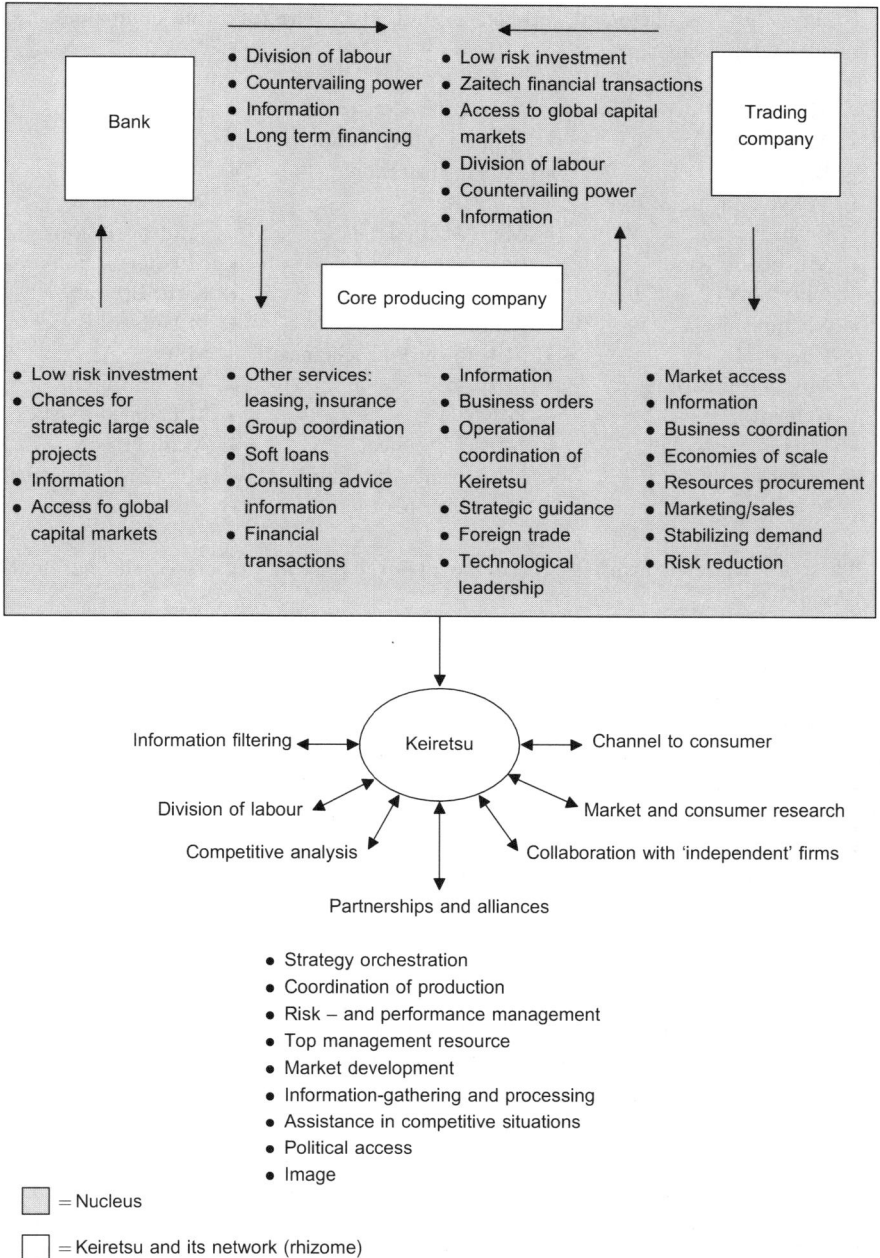

Figure 5.7 *Function and coordination of the Keiretsu nucleus companies*

Friday in the month. Over the years, the exact number of member companies in the Friday Club has fluctuated between 25 and 30.[524] The following companies are regularly represented:

- Mitsubishi Corporation
- Mitsubishi Trust & Banking
- Tokyo Marine & Fire (insurance)
- Mitsubishi Kasei (chemicals)
- Mitsubishi Gas Chemical
- Mitsubishi Mining & Cement
- Mitsubishi Metal
- Mitsubishi Kaoki (mech. engineering)

- Mitsubishi Construction
- Nippon Yusen (shipping)
- Mitsubishi Heavy Industries
- Meiji Mutual Life (insurance)
- Mitsubishi Rayon (textiles)
- Mitsubishi Petrochemical
- Mitsubishi Kesei Polytech
- Mitsubishi Steel
- Mitsubishi Aluminium
- Mitsubish Motors

- Mitsubishi Real Estate
- Mitsubishi Warehouse & Transportation
- Mitsubishi Bank
- Kirin Brewery
- Mitsubishi Paper Mills
- Mitsubishi Oil
- Mitsubishi Plastics
- Asahi Glass
- Mitsubishi Electric
- Nikon (cameras)

These 28 Keiretsu firms cover all the major industrial sectors of the national economy:

- banking and insurance (4 companies)
- wholesale and international trade (1)
- chemicals (5)
- glass/cement/ceramics (2)
- the retail trade (1)
- foodstuffs (1)
- paper (1)
- iron/steel (1)
- electronics (1)
- precision machinery (1)
- warehousing (1)

- non-ferrous metals (2)
- the construction industry (1)
- textiles (1)
- the energy sector (1)
- mechanical engineering (1)
- transport (1)
- property (1)
- shipping (1)

The permutation of equity ratios would produce extreme intransparency were we to attempt to portray graphically the links between the *Kinyokai*. It is, however, possible to highlight some important points. The three nucleus firms are striking not only because of their size but also in terms of their somewhat unilateral links. In total, they regularly hold over 10 per cent of their own equity, and the banks and the insurance companies are the only shareholders with a significantly larger stake. The shares held by the three nuclei in the other banks and insurance companies can be perceived as a relocation of stock into other *Kinyokai* firms, since Mitsubishi Trust & Banking, Meiji Mutual Life and the Tokyo Marine & Fire Insurance Company each maintain strategic shareholdings in all the other *Kinyokai*

Kinki Coca-Cola

Iwaki Glas

Nippon Carbide Industries

Paper — Mitsubishi Papermills

Food — Kirin-Brauerei

Energy — Mitsubishi-Oil

Real estate & construction — Mitsubishi Estate — Mitsubishi Const.

Nihon Nosan Kogyo

Fudow Co. JSP Corp.

Chemical — Mitsubishi Gas Chemical — Mitsubishi Petrochemical — Mitsubishi Kasei Polytee — Mitsubishi Plastic Inds. — Mitsubishi Kasei

Finance & Insurance — Mitsubishi Trust & Banking — Meiji Mutual Life Insurance — Tokio M. & F. Insurance — DC Card

Glass — Asahi Glass

Meiwa Trading

Diomond City

Chukyo Coca-Cola Bottling

Nitto Kako

Taiyu Sanso

Toyo Carbon

Nippon Synthetic Chemical Ind.

Nippon Kasei Cehmicals

Kawasaki Kasei Chemicals

Tayca Corp.

Nikko Sanso

Kodama Chemical Ind.

Steel & Metal — Mitsubishi Alu — Mitsubishi Metal — Mitsubishi Cable Inds. — Mitsubishi Steel mfg.

Top 3 Leaders

Mitsubishi Corp.

Mitsubishi Bank

Mitsubishi Heavy Inds.

Textile & fiber — Mitsubishi Rayon

Electronics and machinery — Mitsubishi Electric — Mitsubishi Kakoki — Nikon Corp. — Mitsubishi Motors

Shipping & Storage — Nippon Yusen — Mitsubishi Warehouse & Transport

Nitto Flour Milling

Pasco Corp.

Nitto Chemical Ind.

Ryoden Trading

Nihon Kentetsu

Kodensha Co.

Kanagawa Electric

SPC Electronics

Tokyo Takasago Dry Battery

Optec Dai-Ichi Denko

Mining and Cement — Mitsubishi Mining & Cement

Mitsubishi Shindoh

Sakai Chemical Ind.

Tokyo Engineering Works

Tokyo Sangyo

Z.R. Concrete

P.S. Concrete

Intra-group Joint Ventures

Mitsubishi Petroleum Dev.*   Mitsubishi Atomic Power Inds.*

Mitsubishi Research Inst.*   Diamond Lease

Tokyo Senpaku

Taiheiyo Kaiun

☐ Kinyokai members   ▨ Nucleus   * Unlisted companies

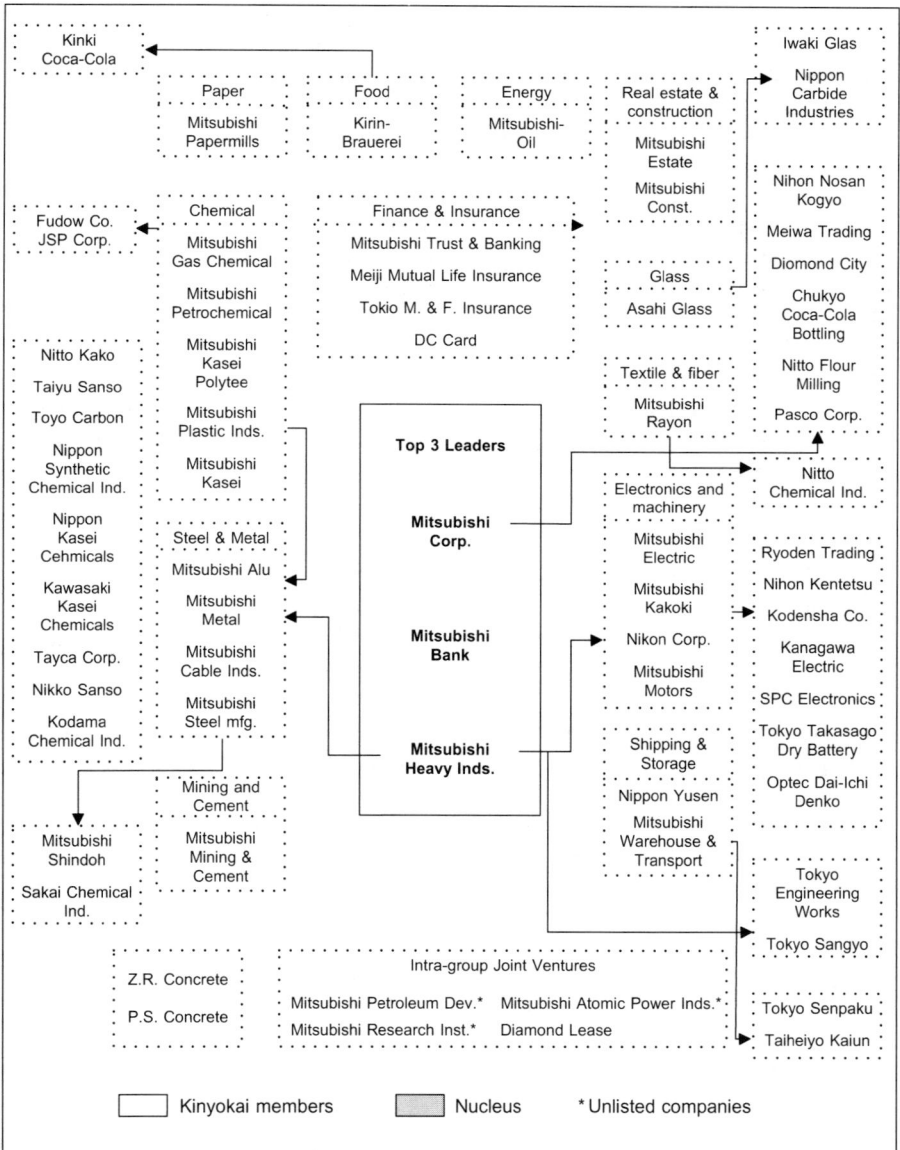

Figure 5.8   *The Mitsubishi Kinyokai in the 1990s*
Source: Dodwell, *Industrial Groupings in Japan*, p. 52

companies. All other links between the companies are homogeneous and bilateral. In addition, the two groups, that is the nuclei and the remaining *Kinyokai*, both have extensive shareholdings in the companies on the third layer of the structure (Figure 5.8).

Each of these *Kinyokai* firms is one of the top companies in their sector in Japan, which is why the Mitsubishi *Kinyokai* can also post such imposing figures overall, as shown in Table 5.8. However, these quantitative dimensional aids can only roughly illustrate the overall influence of these 28 companies. The fact that, in terms of Keiretsu management, significantly greater importance is attached to informal and indirect mechanisms of influence downgrades quantitative or formal indicators to self-evident, *ex post factum*, symbols.

The *Kinyokai* functions as an extended power base, free of all clearly definable hierarchies, without taking recourse to formal and juridical measures. The objectives of this consortium include new projects, foreign investment, major lending, support measures for companies in crisis, in addition to its role as a 'general' information forum.[525] This is the primary area of application for the aforementioned Mitsubishi principle of collective guidance:

Collective guidance as a supreme law of the Mitsubishi Group is most aptly exemplified by the function of the Kinyokai (Friday Conference), composed by specially important Mitsubishi organizations [one fact which is remarkable is that, despite the maxim of optimum vagueness, organizations rather than individuals are appointed as members], each of which sends its president or board chairman to the meeting, and is virtually the supreme decision making organ. Doubt remains as to whether, and how far, Kinyokai is a success as a high command to study and determine the strategy of the whole Mitsubishi Group and to exercise control and guidance of the member organizations in their respective business management. There is no doubt, however, as far it is concerned that, with Kinyokai at the top of hierarchy, the Mitsubishi Group is proving its power as a business group.[526]

Table 5.8   *General data of the Mitsubishi Keiretsu in the 1990s*

	Nucleus companies	Companies in the Kinyo-Kai
Net profit*	176 000	668 000
Shareholders' equity*	4 699 551	13 291 783
Employees	66 202	278 641

* In million yen
Source: Compiled from Dodwell, *Industrial Groupings in Japan*, p. 53ff; *Japan Company Handbook 1991*

Despite the visible presence of 'typically' Japanese argumentation techniques, the significance of the *Kinyokai* in the integration and long-term strategic implementation of the Keiretsu is perceptible.

Although it is a well-known fact that Mitsubishi has the best organized, comprehensive decision-making structure of all the Keiretsu,[527] only a few, extremely indirect analysis options are available to the outsider in terms of the areas of activities, division of responsibility, powers, etc. which apply to this diffuse focal point within the Mitsubishi universe, and these usually only produce generalizations.[528]

The Mitsubishi managers themselves do not attempt to change this overall impression of vagueness. Yoshino and Lifson cite a Mitsubishi manager who commented as follows on the structure of the group: '. . . while we look like a profit center organization on paper, in fact we're closer to an informal qualitative evaluation system in practice.'[529] Thus, it is impossible to find any clearly defined concern structure.[530] In this context we could again compare it to an undifferentiated root network. Mitsubishi itself sees its organizational structure in a similar way: '. . . we are like the air, invisible but pervasive, providing essential things to sustain life'.[531] This basic stance naturally impedes any formal structural analysis, and thus a qualitative evaluative perspective would do greater justice to the research object:

> The Mitsubishi group is not a single corporate entity with a central brain. These cross-shareholdings, interlocking directorates, joint ventures, and long-term business relationships – all underpinned by shared educational and historical links – create a family of companies, dependent not on formal controls but on acknowledged mutual interest.[532]

This open structure is maintained by means of a few direct controls, although the informal links are far more significant. The formal controls consist primarily of the mutual shareholdings mentioned above, intragroup trade and the network of directorships.

On both these structural levels, Mitsubishi perceives the channelling of a minimum sales percentage to members of the family firm as the primary objective of group coordination in addition, more pragmatically,[533] to fundamental functions such as strategy implementation, the exchange of information, and so on. However, the term 'Profit Club',[534] used to describe these intragroup preferences, appears too polemic. The Mitsubishi Corporation formulates one of its aims as 'the constant enhancement of profits for its business partners'.[535] Tasker estimates that, on average, up to 25 per cent of sales are generated from intragroup trading:

> Mitsubishi companies pay their wages through Mitsubishi Bank, rent their head offices from Mitsubishi Real Estate, and their storage space from Mitsubishi Warehouse. By choice they are using air-conditioning systems made by Mitsubishi Electric, machinery made by Mitsubishi Heavy, trucks made by Mitsubishi

Motor, and fuel supplied by Mitsubishi Oil. Their factories are insured by Tokyo Marine and Fire, the group insurance company, and the beer for their 'forget-the-year-parties' is supplied by Kirin, the group brewer.[536]

Intragroup trade is conducted primarily for stabilization purposes but is also conducted with the aim of improving intercompany integration. Trust, a more solid information base and cumulatively high positive experiences are further contributory factors. However, this preferential treatment between family members is totally unstructured, is only ever totally informal and has evolved as a result of the personal relationships existing between employees and a high degree of interlinkage at director level.[537,538] To the Japanese, mutual directorships are a tried and trusted device used to bind companies together loosely (in this context, cf. our comments on long-term employee networks in Chapters 4, section III on *oyabun–kobun* and *amakudari*).

More than one-third of all executives simultaneously hold at least two positions in different firms,[539] the intention of which is to maximize information, intensify communication flow and coordinate strategy. For example, the insurance company, Tokyo Marine & Fire at Mitsubishi, is one of the most frequent users of this method; its president holds more than 20 directorships within other Mitsubishi companies. Prior to the Second World War, this was the most common device used by holding companies to control members of their group. This unilateral process has now been split open to form an almost hierarchy-free network of mutual directorships, within the framework of a multilateral linkage structure:

In 1937 the seventeen holding company directors held between them ninety-six directorships in nineteen major core companies. In 1976, however, no Mitsubishi company appeared to share directors with more than four other companies, most companies shared only one or two directors.[540]

This allows us to speak of a *rhizome economy* (cf. Chapter 5, section III ('phenotypes …')) in terms of a meso-economic company network, analogous to the linkage processes which occur on a macroeconomic level (e.g. cf. Chapter 4, section III ('individual and organizational elements', 'the links between …' and 'a model illustrating …')). The current situation can be depicted schematically as shown in Figure 5.9.

This dovetailing of capital, personnel and business opportunities generates trust and symbolic capital (cf. Chapter 2, section III, 'the symbolism of postmodern change'), which subsequently feeds back as one of the primary motivations behind the Mitsubishi-oriented activities of the Keiretsu firms.[541] This closely interwoven network of large companies leads to the creation of a 'fractal mini-economy',[542,543] the scope of which is generally vastly underestimated since purely formal points of view produce a false picture of its scope and degree of integration.

It is opportune to compare this inner Keiretsu group to the Swiss economy, in order to clarify its economic power. Only a mega-concern made up of the 100

Mitsubishi Zaibatsu

Iwasaki family

Top manager
(banto)

Holding

Directors

Extended network

Mitsubishi Keiretsu

Nucleus companies

Kinyokai companies

Mitsubishi companies
Mitsubishi group companies

Mitsubishi Rhizome

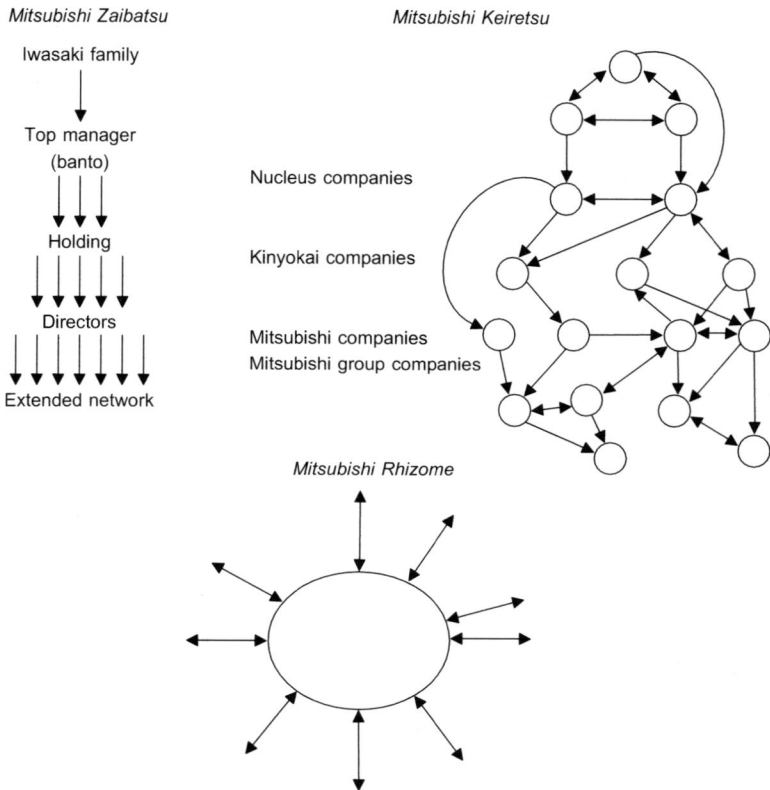

Figure 5.9   *The directors' network: a structural comparison, Zaibatsu–Keiretsu*

largest Swiss companies achieves the same turnover as the Mitsubishi Kinyokai group.[544] But this is purely an economic dimension. Without wishing to go into the broader 'world creation' dimension which involves a large proportion of the Japanese population, we can nevertheless point to the extensive influence exerted by Mitsubishi (and every other Keiretsu) on the everyday life, ambitions and values of the Japanese people:

What counts is that he works for Mitsubishi. If he works for Mitsubishi, he is a Mitsubishi man. Most of his friends come from Mitsubishi ... He competes with them, surely, but like siblings competing within a family which no one would think of leaving. With the exception of his relatives, and possibly a few school friends, most of his associations – and often those of his family's – go on within the framework of the company.[545,546]

Research on the complex issue of whether these *firm cultures and structures* lead to the *creation of worlds* is promising. Johnson sees the Keiretsu as one of the most significant research subjects of our time. '[T]he Keiretsu is one of the main intellectual challenges of our time. Mitsubishi's march is bound to help force this issue.'[547] This global effect is consistent with the interpretation that the Keiretsu act as 'change agents', as far as economic structure is concerned (Chapter 4, section VI, 'the roles . . .'). If we, in turn, perceive the member companies of the *Kinyokai*, on the third layer of the structure, as the core firms in a sub-Keiretsu, this produces a linkage which defies detailed, precise definition. It can however be used to illustrate the scope of Mitsubishi's commercial world and the renewed appearance of the mechanisms which determine the *Kinyokai*.

The Keiretsu Enterprise as a Fractal Structure

On another level, we can demonstrate the extent to which formal structures have been completely destroyed, by looking at how they are counteracted within the relationship network. A hierarchical structure is totally out of the question when we consider the company ties on the 'periphery of the internal core'; that is, the relationship structures of the *Kinyokai* firms upstream. Here again, we are confronted with quasi-fractal structures since, at this level, we can assign each *kinyokai* firm to its own 'mini-Keiretsu'. The structure of this hypothetical, secondary *Keiretsu* disintegrates again in its relationship to smaller, secondary and tertiary suppliers.

Dodwell Marketing Consultants estimates the number of main companies, comprising the third layer of this Keiretsu structure, as 184.[548,549] These firms, under 200 in number and operating under the Mitsubishi banner, wield considerable influence and control over Japan's national economy, although this assessment fails to take account of the impressive multiplicator effect which would be produced were we to include the subsidiaries and suppliers subordinated to these Keiretsu firms. By way of comparison, the Mitsui Keiretsu (152 firms) achieved net receipts of around 580 000 million yen during the same period (1991), with a workforce of approximately 280 000[550] (Table 5.9).

Table 5.9 *Economic top-line figures for Mitsubishi Keiretsu in the 1990s v. today*

	Nucleus companies	Companies in the Kinyo-Kai	Keiretsu companies
Net profit*	176 000 ⇓	668 000 ⇒	751 000 ⇒
Shareholders' equity*	4 699 551 ⇑	13 291 783 ⇑	20 153 249 ⇑
Employees	66 202 ⇒	278 641 ⇓	482 187 ⇒

* In million yen
Source: Dodwell, *Industrial Groupings in Japan*, p. 53ff

At this juncture, we single out two examples which we use to define, more precisely, the characteristics of the subgroups in question. The example selected from the nucleus group is Mitsubishi Heavy Industries, which we use to illustrate the *cascade-like distribution of the group*. We will also use Mitsubishi Electric, a member of the *Kinyokai*, to demonstrate the *structure of a sub-Keiretsu*.[551]

As a first example: for more than 100 years, Mitsubishi Heavy Industries (MHI) has been considered the largest integrated manufacturer of industrial machinery in Japan. In 1990, MHI posted consolidated sales of 2.4 trillion yen and, if we include its dependent companies, this figure increases to approximately 8 trillion yen (around US$615 billion).[552] With over 300 subsidiaries and directly dependent firms, MHI is surrounded by the largest number of Mitsubishi affiliates. Despite this number, the interrelationships are considered universally intense and highly integrative.[553] It has major stockholdings and controls in the area of mechanical engineering, car production, trade, industrial plant engineering and industrial property. Mitsubishi Motors is the most important firm under the MHI umbrella, which is why we have chosen it to represent the other major companies in Figure 5.10.

As one of the 150 'child-companies' belonging to the Mitsubishi Heavy Industries giant, Mitsubishi Motors has its own network of 213 directly dependent companies and consequently constitutes a Keiretsu within a Keiretsu, or sub-Keiretsu for short. The significance of Mitsubishi Motors within the overall Keiretsu becomes apparent when we consider that it has individual membership of the *Kinyokai*, rather than as part of MHI. In a market context, Mitsubishi Motors is Japan's third largest car manufacturer, with a turnover of 2.6 trillion yen (1990), spanning the entire product range from a 600cc Minimobil right up to a 35 ton truck.[554] Admittedly, the recent recession temporarily tainted this success story, but the relatively quick reemergence with perhaps the strongest car company of the world – Daimler Benz – as a strategic partner shows the ingenious strategy mechanisms at play turning a threat into a comfortable position with potential.[555]

Mitsubishi Motors frequently flexes its economic muscles in the Mitsubishi world, since it is famous for the preference which its semi-finished products and services procurement policy gives to group members. Using Mitsubishi Motors as a link, Figure 5.11 illustrates how the extended Heavy Industries sector of the Mitsubishi 'Keiretsu' forms part of the total picture.

Thus the scope of the MHI world is remarkably extensive at a lower level; the first signs of the fractal structure of a Japanese MNE becomes apparent in this diagram. The same basic structural principles, which we have been able to identify in the relationship between nucleus and *Kinyokai* firms are exactly the same as those which now reappear on a lower level. A practical analysis discovers once more the concept of a *fractal economy*, as presented earlier (Chapter 5, III). This principle can be extrapolated step by step until it reaches the larger satellite companies (Mitsubishi Electric, for example) and, on the subsequent level, the suppliers.

The second example is Mitsubishi Electric, the fifth largest electronics and electrical appliances manufacturer in Japan. Dodwell lists the number of subsidiaries under the control of the parent company as 163, although there are a further

```
                                    Meiji
        Bank of Tokyo      Mutual Life-Insurance    Tokyo Marine &
       Mitsubishi Bank  \          |         /      Fire-Insurance
                         \         |        /
                          ┌─ ─ ─ ─ ┼ ─ ─ ─ ─┐
       Mitsubishi Trust   |     Mitsubishi   |      Mitsubishi
         & Banking  ─────▶ | Heavy Industries | ◀────  Corporation
                          └─ ─ ─ ─ ┼ ─ ─ ─ ─┘
                                    |
                                    ▼
```

Machinery-General	Construction	Real Estate
Mitsubishi Agricultural Machinery*	Mitsubishi Juko Construction	Tamachi Building
	Mitsubishi Juko Plant Construction	Kanto Ryoju Estate
Shin Caterpillar Mitsubishi*		Kinki Ryoju Estate
Toyo Engineering Works	Shinryo High Technology & Control	Nagoya Ryoju Estate
Dai Kikai*		Nishi-Nihon Ryoju Estate
	Mitsubushi Atomic Power Industries	

Transportation Machinery		Land Transportation
Mitsubishi Motors	Nuclear Plant Service Engineering	Shonan Monorail

Trading & Commerce	Nihon Kensetsu Kogyo	
Toryo Kiki Kogyo*	Mitsubishi Juko Environment Engineering	Service Industry
Tobu Ryoju Engine Hanbai*		Ryosen Engineers
Mitsubishi Juko Air Conditioner Hanbai*		Ryonichi Engineering
Mitsubishi Juko Reinetsu Service*		Churyo Engineering
Ryoju Cold Chain Service		
Mitsubishi Heavy Industries Air-Conditioning & Refrigeration Systems		
R.S.E. Ltd.		

* = unlisted companies

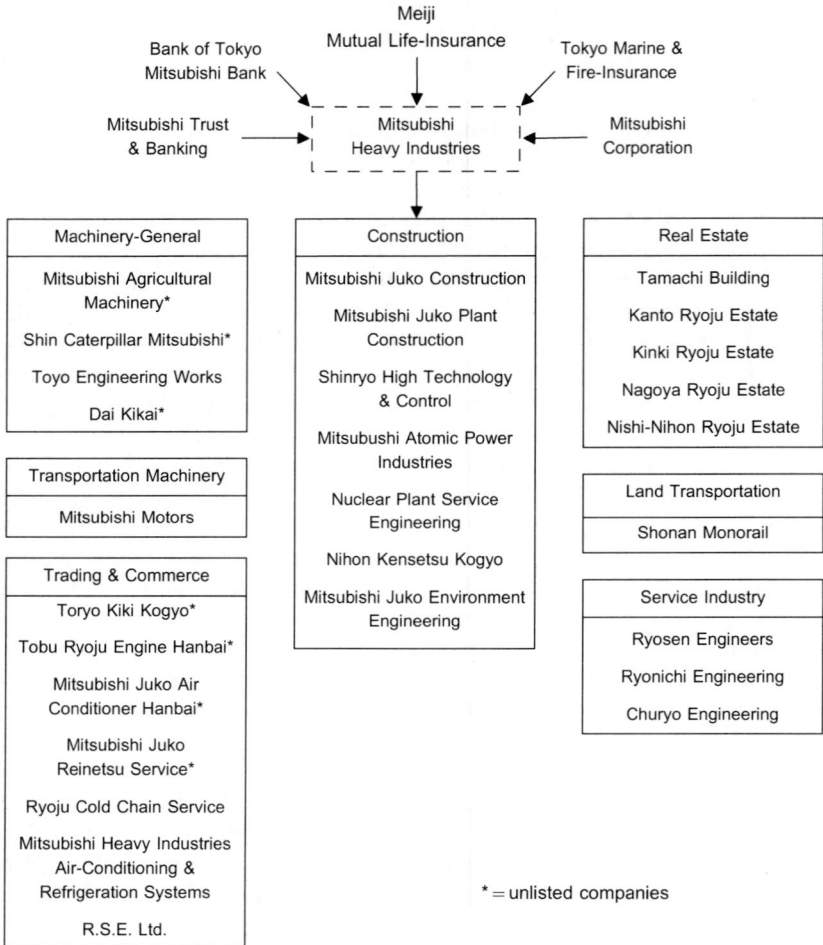

Figure 5.10   *Mitsubishi Heavy Industries as a sub-Keiretsu in the 1990s*
Source: Dodwell, *Industrial Groupings in Japan*, p. 201

96 firms outside its immediate sphere which should also be included. Of these, only eight are publicly, stockmarket-listed companies. The overall scope (Table 5.10) of the Mitsubishi Electric Group explains the meaning of the term 'sub-Keiretsu'. We can therefore perceive Mitsubishi Electric as an extremely important, strategic building block within the Mitsubishi group.[556] Using the basic structure of a Keiretsu to support this view, we can also attribute a trading company function to Mitsubishi Electric (achieved via numerous smaller trading firms). This, together with its role as group bank/financier (Mitsubishi Electric Credit), transforms it into a nucleus within its own sub-Keiretsu.

MHI

Machinery	Service	Trade		Transport

Strategic Alliances
First with Chrysler and
Mercedes Benz
Now with DaimlerChrysler

Mitsubishi Motors

Mitsubishi Corporation
Bank of Tokyo Mitsubishi Bank
Mitsubishi Trust & Banking
Meiji Mutual Life Insurance
Tokyo Marine & Fire Insurance

Auto Parts

Kato Body Mfg.
Kureha Motors
Ryowa Sheet Metal Processing
Tohoku Mitsubishi Automotive Components
Suiryo Plastics
Meiji Rubber & Chemical
Namba Press Works

Sankei Kogyo
Wako Industrial
Yasunaga Corp.
Toyo Koki
Nagoya Screw Manufacturing

Finance & Insurance

Mitsubishi Auto Credit Lease

Designing

Stuttgart Auto Service
Mitsubishi Automotive Engineering

Trading & Commerce

Tokyo Mitsubishi Fuso Hambai
Kyushu Mitsubishi Fuso Hambai

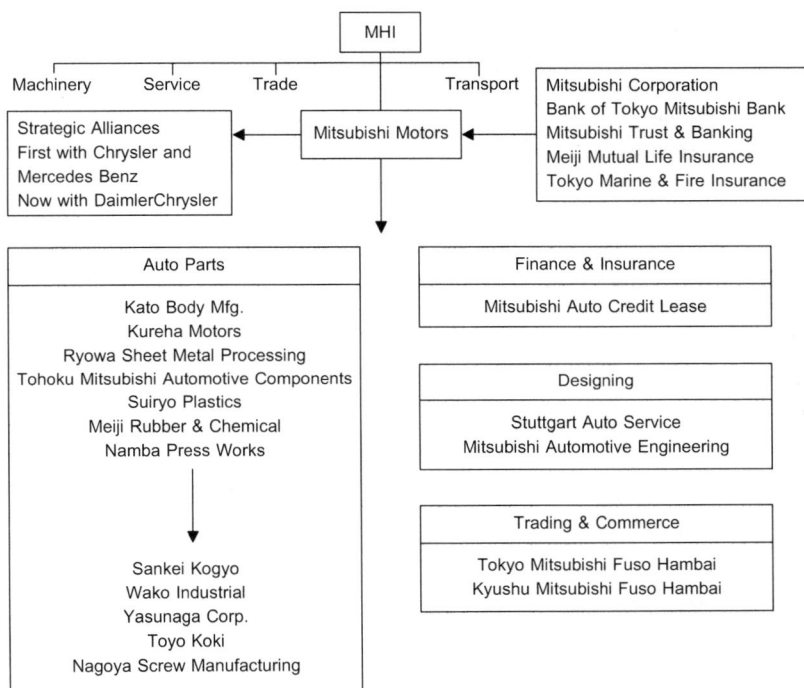

Figure 5.11   *The Mitsubishi Motors sub-Keiretsu in the 1990s*
Source: Dodwell, *Industrial Groupings in Japan*, p. 226

Table 5.10   *General business data of the Mitsubishi Keiretsu in the 1990s vs today*

	The 28 companies in the Kinyo-Kai	MHI sub-Keiretsu pre alliance with DaimlerBenz-Chrysler	ME sub-sub-Keiretsu	For comparison: Industrial Bank of Japan Keiretsu
Net profit*	886 411 ⇒	77 392 ⇓	48 446 ⇑	189 499 ⇑
Shareholders' equity*	2 158 698 ⇑	415 618 ⇓	213 481 ⇑	417 125 ⇑
Employees	282 122 ⇓	89 592 ⇓	75 386 ⇒	70 471 ⇒

* In million yen
Source: Dodwell, *Industrial Groupings in Japan*, p. 133ff; 226ff; *Japan Company Handbook 1991*

The influence of this type of sub-Keiretsu on its national economical environment should not be underestimated, a fact which becomes clear when we adopt a speculative approach. If 10 suppliers, each with an average workforce of 50, are dependent on each of the 259 sub-Keiretsu companies and, in turn, these 10 suppliers are supplied by five dependent upstream firms on the second level, each with 10 employees, this produces a small mini-national economy consisting of 15 540 firms and 259 000 employees. Based on an average family of four, this means that in excess of one million people have some form of link with just one (!) of the 28 *Kinyokai* firms. If one then adds the number of employees and their households who are dependent on the main companies, this sum total rises to approximately 31 million people who are, in some way, directly associated with the Mitsubishi Keiretsu. This calculation provides empirical evidence that around a quarter of the Japanese population is dependent on Mitsubishi. If we also include other (smaller) Keiretsu, we can roughly estimate that almost the entire Japanese national economy is directly or indirectly linked to the Keiretsu. The group structure of Mitsubishi Electric showing the major companies is shown in Figure 5.12.

Due to the difficult data situation and the problem of creating transparency, we have not attempted to illustrate the Mitsubishi supplier network graphically, but

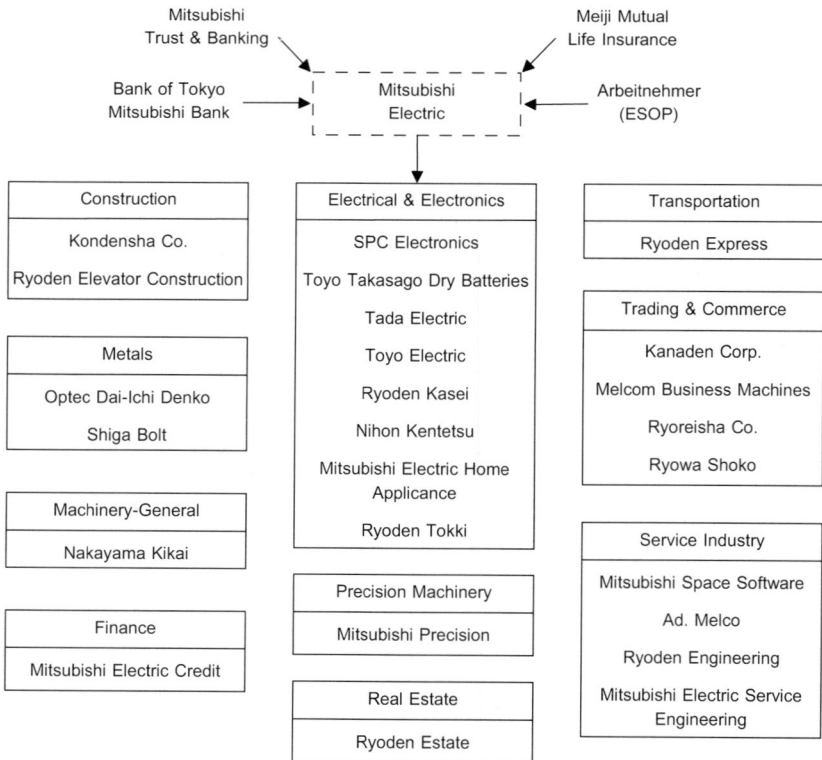

Mitsubishi Trust & Banking		Meiji Mutual Life Insurance
Bank of Tokyo Mitsubishi Bank →	**Mitsubishi Electric**	← Arbeitnehmer (ESOP)

Construction	Electrical & Electronics	Transportation
Kondensha Co.	SPC Electronics	Ryoden Express
Ryoden Elevator Construction	Toyo Takasago Dry Batteries	
	Tada Electric	**Trading & Commerce**
Metals	Toyo Electric	Kanaden Corp.
Optec Dai-Ichi Denko	Ryoden Kasei	Melcom Business Machines
Shiga Bolt	Nihon Kentetsu	Ryoreisha Co.
	Mitsubishi Electric Home Applicance	Ryowa Shoko
Machinery-General	Ryoden Tokki	
Nakayama Kikai		**Service Industry**
	Precision Machinery	Mitsubishi Space Software
Finance	Mitsubishi Precision	Ad. Melco
Mitsubishi Electric Credit		Ryoden Engineering
	Real Estate	Mitsubishi Electric Service Engineering
	Ryoden Estate	

Figure 5.12   *The Mitsubishi Electric sub-Keiretsu in the 1990s*
Source: Dodwell, *Industrial Groupings in Japan*, p. 228

the basic principles developed in Chapters 3, section IV, Chapter 4, section III, and Chapter 5, section IV, equally apply *cum grano salis* in concrete terms to this third layer.

Nevertheless, the disintegration of the concern as we now understand it (i.e. in its modern interpretation) becomes clearly apparent even from these examples. A broadly based rhizome (or root ball) is fanning out, from a diffuse core, into the surrounding national economy and social system. This rhizome becomes increasingly fragmented and its relationships increasingly entangled, which obliterates any possibility of a comprehensive uniform perspective, allowing only a partial perspective-dependent temporary view of the individual subsystems. Influenced by Silicon Valley, this fractal economy is usually seen as the Internet centred New Economy, but this example clearly shows that, enriched by postmodern perspectives, this can be broadened to a well-founded new paradigm that affects all industrial sectors. It also shows how deeply rooted these 'path-breaking' developments are in the traditional – if seen from a postmodern point of view. As Japan is the most clear example of this, Mitsubishi is it within the context of Japan. The potential impact of such a transforming company on the whole is summarized in the following section.

The Role of the Mitsubishi Keiretsu as a Futurizing Organization

First a brief definition of futurizing may be necessary: it is understood as actively anticipating the future and preemptively implementing it in a dynamic process.[557] Current literature operationalized this in the imperative of 'intense and intelligent communications', 'the power of decentralization of decisions', the need to 'seek sustainable disequilibrium' and to 'transgress organically the dicotomy of partner and competitor' in a kind of 'constructive ambiguity'.[558]

Seen from that angle, Mitsubishi in its adaptive and knowledge-increasing way can be seen as a paradigm-leader, or futurizing enterprize. It seems that the concept of networks has now won the race with the market paradigm, both leaving behind the communistic/socialistic failure. Here again an enterprise with over 200 years of network experience has the odds in its favour.[559] On a more topical level, it is noticeable that the three core companies are now reaching out into the global economy and into the new Internet-based world in order to become revitalized. Mitsubishi Heavy Industries gets globality via the Mitsubishi Motors–Daimler Chrysler deal,[560] Mitsubishi Bank reforms itself with the integration of a major city bank and insurance house, and Mitsubishi Corporation embraces all kind of communication/Internet-based strategies to adapt its function as the Keiretsu intermediary to (post)modern standards of the New Economy.

In terms of the inner structure (nucleus–surrounding companies), a shift from 'identified' core companies to a small group of companies that provide the functions of the core company is noticeable (for example, in the finance area at least four companies now play the role that formerly was given to Mitsubishi Bank alone). The nucleus as a whole becomes more diffuse in itself. As communication technology (from mobile phones to Internet application to sheer bandwidth) explodes, the need to centralize becomes smaller. Decisions still rest at the nodes that remain in power, but those nodes (people, committees, procedural structures) need not be closely knitted in the 'physical world' but rather tightly connected in a virtual manner yet seemingly distanced on the surface. *The rhizome becomes virtual and the core empties itself.* This represents yet another level of complexity where tangible targets become harder to find, and the rhizome is now bonded not by crossholdings and ritual meetings but by hyperactive communication via technology. This represents a leap in flexibility but also in vagueness and lack of structure to the outsider. Clearly, this is a situation very familiar when turning back to postmodern concepts.

This structural analysis of Mitsubishi allows us to highlight three interesting viewpoints:

- The first is the strange absence of a head, a lack of clear predetermined leadership; an empty centre, without an undisputed leader, the diffuse emphasis of which appears out of focus. The all-important integrating factor is symbolic management. This management can handle all the overlaps and mutual permeations without any risk of plunging the structure into chaos. But, equally, this management does not depend on rigid, narrow or dirigiste controls. We could perhaps refer to this as 'low management intensity', which is comparable with 'soft thought' concepts of postmodern philosophers,[561] although this should on no account be interpreted as imprecision or muddled thinking. Its aim is to achieve the status of an alternative mode of thinking as opposed to powerful (in terms of quantity and formal, logical) thought, the efficacy of which has been overtaken by new analyses and methods.[562]

- Following on from this, we can detect a clear lack of rigid structures. A complex consisting of individual firms can no longer be perceived as a single structure with defined parameters, but rather as an extremely elusive creation, without centre, exterior or dimensional scale. The Keiretsu is fragmented into a highly diversified, differentiated, interdependent network of multiple relationships. The Keiretsu, *per se*, is only discernible via its diverse subgroups and sub-subgroups, each of which uses minor structural correlations to convey sense and meaning to outsiders. This deconcentrated market force is created and coordinated by means of a kind of autopoeticism, self-referentially and without direct causal relationship to a universal, hierarchic, superior 'concern'. Its coordination and combination is effected more by means of informal, local and contingently-changing partial forces and the latent strength (characterized by the vagueness tolerated by dissent) provided by superior symbols, values and visions.[563,564]

• The product of this structure is an extremely flexible and dynamic overall structure which, in spite of all its loyalties and obligations, is extremely open but which should nevertheless not be perceived as an integrated unit. Its radical pragmatism and performance-orientation allows it to adapt to the forces of rigorous competition and the visionary and cooperational models of state bureaucracy. It has proved its success in its decade-long role as 'number one', as well as by means of its ambitious plans for the future. This can be seen as the best proof that Mitsubishi is not only prepared for the future but also that this Keiretsu will play a leading role in the global transformation to a post-modern world.

V   FIFTH SUMMARY: ARE JAPAN'S Mnes POSTMODERN? AND WHAT ABOUT THE 'NEW ECONOMY'?

This chapter, which deals with the theory and empiricism of (Japanese) multinational companies, has concentrated on the *peculiarities of the Japanese production organization* (and *production system organization*), as well as its international relevance and in this way has combined the two hypotheses taken as a starting point for this study (the hypothesis of a postmodern economic model and that of Japan's postmodernity). By analysing the terminology, we have been able firstly to establish that Japanese multinational enterprises, in the form of the Keiretsu, definitely represent an independent category among the multinationals, although in many respects (complexity; active environmental management; 'world creation'; symbolic management; the assimilation of specific Japanese thought and value patterns; and 'familial', long-term, trust-based, strategic thinking, etc.) they are *more than 'just' blurred images of a universal MNE model*. It is impossible to entirely explain specific, Japanese phenomena (such as 'company cooperation via status, rituals and clubs', or social group phenomena) by using conventional elucidatory approaches exclusive to the West, since significant, informal, 'metastructural' parameters should not form part of any attempt to understand the Japanese (and postmodern) MNEs. This creates a more complex company image than that of a conventional economic entrepreneurial model, in the context of which the Japanese MNEs must be considered role models and forerunners in terms of the evolutionary dynamics of the MNE.

For this reason, most established MNE theories (we have dealt with transaction costs economics, the internalization theory and the macroeconomic approach) must be considered redundant. Only isolated core statements retain their validity – that is, Hymer's and Vernon's observation that the endogenous non-market capability and immaterial competitive advantages of a company are the most important assets in its struggle for competitiveness; Williamson's inclusion of meta-economic psychological elements, and Casson's and Buckley's questioning of the rigid definition parameters used to describe companies). On the other hand, perspectives classified as unorthodox (the eclectic approach taken by Dunning; the systemic view taken by Casson and the internationally-oriented competition analysis of Porter and Ohmae) contribute major new aspects and additions to the debate. In this context, we can highlight the following findings: the totally pragmatic openness and modular multimethodology of the research study and practice; the inclusion in the analysis of cultural and psychological factors, such as trust or people-oriented strategies; a performative success criterion in the form of the skills needed to manage highly complex systems and subsystems and their interdependencies; and, finally, the disintegration of the national and defining framework comprising strategies, markets and companies in favour of open, amoeba-like network structures within an interlinked economy.

The most promising explanatory approach as far as contemporary MNE structures are concerned, is the portrayal of the network theory which follows this comprehension of 'unorthodox' theories. Following on from the basic definition of the networks as an *active form of complexity management via implicit or explicit contracts, common symbols and communication/information and power links*, to form a *self-organizational (autopoetic) web of multidimensional relations*, the application of the theory both on the commercial and the macroeconomic level has also been investigated using Japan as the concrete case. Using the perspective presented by these networks, we have been able to identify the structural generators of momentum (the abundance of loose links; the breaking open of structural frontiers; the maintenance of the network, with communication and performance as the supreme goals) which provide the companies with maximum flexibility and adaptability in the face of erratic and unstable environments. Thus, this approach also combines, for the first time, all levels of perception (the individual, labour groups, the company, the economy and politics) into a harmonious picture. Based on these facts, network theory is not only able to stand as the *best model of an MNE currently available* but is also particularly appropriate in the case of the Japanese MNEs which almost everyone complains are a 'special case', since this approach serves to bring an explanation of the many research problems (the formation of cartels and competitive behaviour, people-related, long-term strategies, structural ambiguities, etc.) closer.

In a second phase, we have explained the principles behind the general structural parameters of the Keiretsu. In this context, we described the Keiretsu as a *heterarchical, self-organizing network of firms* and as '*societies of long-term relationships*'. The fractal nature of the Keiretsu structure was of special interest: without a centre or clear structure, in organizational terms, with a set of logically allocated tasks at each level of consideration (labour group, individual company, Keiretsu, industrial sector, national economy), we have been able to perceive a repetition of the structural and procedural mechanisms. For this reason, the introduction of the terms *fractal economy* to define the micro-economy, and *rhizome economy* in the context of the meso- and macro-economy, have proved helpful.

It is evident from the structural history of the Keiretsu that they are inextricably linked to the national economy as well as Japan's social trends and objectives. Of special significance are their long-term, basic functions in relation to group coordination strategy, identity, integration and coordination management, and proactive forward-looking structural change as well as their *primary functions* which include a superior organizational role, a role which is analogous to that performed by the central nervous system in biological terms (the organization of all business procedures, information gathering, distribution and processing), and operational tasks in terms of risk management, the provision of an internal quasi-market within the Keiretsu and, finally, the role as a general network engineer and manager and internal market financier. Thus, the Keiretsu can also be seen in practice as *the major force behind the transformation of Japanese society from a postindustrial into a postmodern society, in close cooperation with powerful political and social influences.*

In the third phase, we have examined the basic structure of a company network based on the largest and most complex of the Keiretsu, the Mitsubishi Keiretsu (on which approximately 25 per cent of the Japanese population depend economically). The structure of this colossus has been examined in three analytical stages: the *three core firms* operate within a *nucleus area* (Mitsubishi Corporation – trade; Mitsubishi Bank – financial services; and Mitsubishi Heavy Industries – basic production operation) in their role as *initiators and coordinators of total strategy*, which involves symbolic and visionary leadership whereby Japan's general Keiretsu principles (non-hierarchic structure, despite its superficially unstructured appearance; diffuse distribution of power, fulfilling multiple tasks, etc.) are again predominant. And, although the centres of gravity are changing and reshaping, the principles remain valid.

These three firms are surrounded by *28 other main firms*, which are loosely linked within the so-called Friday Club (*Kinyokai*), and represent the main economic might of the Mitsubishi 'Keiretsu'. The integration of all the Keiretsu firms and their coordination ('collective guidance') within this rhizome economy are the main tasks of the *Kinyokai* firms, in addition to their role as an actual production organization for the 'Keiretsu'. The definition of the term 'Keiretsu' usually includes the following companies.

In the course of a further analytical procedure, we have demonstrated *how this Keiretsu structure has penetrated right through to the deepest layers of Japan's national economy.* Using the example of the nucleus company, Mitsubishi Heavy Industries, we have shown how the Keiretsu, in association with small firms, has fanned out, like an avalanche, to include specialist handicraft businesses to form a national economy within a national economy, whilst maintaining the principles of structure and function already valid for the nucleus area. These structural principles, referred to as a *sub-Keiretsu* have been explicitly explained by using a *Kinyokai* member, Mitsubishi Electric, as an example. Within its own sub-Keiretsu, Mitsubishi Electric assumes responsibility for nucleus functions (trade, banking, primary production) by means of which it controls its innumerable, dependent companies. This structure applies equally to all other primary firms and, therefore, the use of the phrase *Keiretsufication of the world* to describe the strategy of the Keiretsu, provides us with further arguments.

The parallel between postmodern concepts (according to the definition of the post-modern presented in Chapter 2) and the theory of the MNE, respectively the practices of the Keiretsu, can be outlined as follows. Postmodern characteristics bear fruit when *multinational enterprise theories* are expanded. In addition to postmodern attitudes, some of the major characteristics which have been incorporated into economic theories concerning the MNE are knowledge, cooperation and flexibility, in the form of basic values; autopoetic organizational principles without a central, hierarchical authority; and a 'boundless' company, without exterior, centre or rigid structures. For this reason, in the context of the theory of multi-national enterprises, we can consider the Japanese MNEs as the currently most effective form of complexity management in terms of global operations and strategies aimed at a postmodern future.[565]

The application of *network theory* leads, on a business level, to a fractal economy; on an intercompany relationship level, to the Keiretsu (in its role as a coordinating mass consisting of the fractured economy and the rhizome economy); and, on the level of inter-Keiretsu links, to a rhizome economy which acts as a model in terms of national economic activities. The creation of decentralized, local ontologies; deconstruction and atomization; multiple coding and paralogical, socially- and historically-determined heterarchies are also postmodern structures which can be seamlessly and profitably be drawn into the network analysis.

The focus of the postmodern within the Keiretsu is Japanese culture (tradition and transformation, cf. Chapter 3); the postmodern in terms of economic coordination (competition and industrial structure management, cf. Chapter 4); and a postmodern organization (postmodern products, markets and production, cf. Chapter 5). The two worlds of the Keiretsu and the postmodern may speak different languages, but the predominant concepts of both are loose, local cohesion in the form of the coordinating principle. The interpretation of markets as networks, the acceptance of blurred, highly-dynamic production and information systems rather than inflexible, rigidly divided companies and the perception of the Keiretsu as fractals (with an inward-looking business perspective) or as rhizomes (from the external economic perspective) applies equally well to both objects.

The interpretation of these theories and the concept of the Keiretsu have produced clear parallels to postmodern approaches in terms of basic *management and structuring principles*. In the lower structural sections of a company or a Keiretsu, informal, local and contingently-adapting, temporary and partial forces merge to form highly differentiated and interdependent units which cooperate intensively with one another in the midst of diversity. Cohesion is achieved not by using rational standards or rules, but by means of the latent strength provided by blurred visions and implicit (psychological and socially motivated) contracts and symbols, the significance of which is produced only by way of its structure and temporary context. The abstract objectives of pragmatic, performative orientation and dynamic, strategic procedural thinking provide the additional cohesion for this management direction.

However, a *postmodern company paradigm* has yet to be identified in the present theoretical debate; on the other hand we can claim to have come closer, congruently, to a theory (especially in respect of the network theory) and practice (especially in respect of the Japanese MNEs) in terms of a future multinational companies theory which might be called postmodern. We have been able to find indicators to support the hypotheses formulated in Chapter 1, in Chapter 3 on the cultural bases of Japanese postmodernity; in Chapter 4 on the macroeconomic spheres surrounding Japanese multinational enterprises in the postmodern era as well as in Chapter 5 on the Keiretsu as a postmodern company type.

The first hypothesis, that of a *postmodern reading of business*, is supported by the arguments contained in Chapter 5. We have been able to demonstrate parallels between contemporary undercurrents, within the theory of the multinational company, and postmodern concepts which we were able to apply profitably to elucidate the most recent, long and medium-term course of development of the Japanese MNE. In theory and in practice, the origins of a postmodern economy are demonstrable, an economy which is rooted in a radical new understanding of economic correlations and which perceives its objective as preparing for a new (postmodern) era.

In this chapter we have also found support for the second hypothesis following on from this – that of *Japan's postmodernity*. A new interpretation, based on a postmodern perspective, can be placed on numerous historically-dependent correlations within the structure of the Keiretsu and the production system organization in general. Equally postmodern constituents can be found in the strategies and (implicit) visions for the future of the Japanese MNEs.

Thus our study has reached a point where we can, in conclusion, propose a few theories based on what has been reported, whilst leaving ample scope for future research projects:

1 The *postmodern debate* should not only be seen as negative, destructive, chaotic and pointless, but as capable of generating a social plan which outlines a new model for society, based, in open pragmatism, on limited trust and tolerated dissent, particularly in considering the prevailing circumstances.

2 Taking the historic origins of the *Japanese culture* as a starting point, Japan appears to be a nation of culture which is optimally prepared for a postmodern future with all its complexities, ambiguities and paradoxes.

3 A future, practice-relevant *theory of multinational companies* can clearly be extrapolated using Japanese examples and bears the postmodern stamp.

4 The *theory of networks* is, from two points of view, the currently most appropriate explanatory approach, since on the one hand it has no difficulty in absorbing a postmodern scenario, and on the other appears to be particularly well-suited to the 'special case' presented by the Japanese multinational enterprises.

5   The *Keiretsu* are Japan's economic 'leaders'. In particular, the environment of fractal structures and the rhizome economy in which they operate has given them the special ability to achieve the transition to a postmodern economy, not only in Japan but also in Western industrial nations.

6   Thus, we can consider *Japan* overall as a pioneer and paradigmatic model within the global trend towards the postmodern – and this with all the far-reaching consequences which result from Japan's (hegemonic) global strategy.

To 'answer' laconically the question of Japan's Postmodernity and its role in the New Economy: Yes. In the view presented here, the Keiretsu and their fertile environment are the delegates of the New Economy in Japan. One should not forget that the label 'New Economy' is a California-based business model after all, and, seen from that Californian angle, the answer would be 'no' as Japan has emancipated itself from the level of simply copying, but adaptations and improvements of that model are and will be made by the Keiretsu. Therefore, one can expect to see a Japanese form of New Economy. Japan has more experience in designing and managing networks and complex systems and is embedded into a richer historical context than America. And, as Europe scrambles to fit itself into the Californian model and is adapting it to the particular systems in Europe, Japan and the Keiretsu will do it differently leveraging their ample resources to succeed in the future.

As the postmodern literature[566] starts now to stress the economic nucleus of postmodern spaces, or sees the postmodern as the ontology of the economy, students of Japan and of business should learn to understand that 'postmodern' is not at all a passive description or a flaky attribute, but rather an active verb, a project. And Japan is well-underway in this project to shape our new and postmodern world.

6 Postscript: Bringing it all Together – Postmodern–New Economy Japan–MNE

> It wasn't time for panic,
> but it was dammed sure time for action.
>
> T. Clancy, *Rainbow Six*, 1998, p. 653

During the ten years of research that have been the basis of this book, incredible dynamic forces have been reshaping our economic system and even the daily life of nearly everyone. Yet all these various and sometimes confusing elements of energy flow more or less in one direction. Concurrent with the 'fall' of the old economy and the necessary deconstruction and regrouping, the postmodern position was the intellectual equivalent (though a bit ahead) to the economic changes. Seen from that perspective, the emergence of a New Economy was the result of three elements: the slowing innovative stride of the old economy; the IT revolution; and the postmodern atmosphere.

It is hoped that the flow of arguments and illustrations presented goes to show that postmodernity is not just 'dead' or the 'ultimate intellectual bankruptcy',[1] but is a useful stepping stone. Understood as an activity, postmodern concepts have helped to define 'survival tactics' to cope in (and to shape) our turbulent times. Understood as an abstract guidance, they help to better understand the current changes of all aspects of economic and business life.

In that sense, Japan can be understood as the application of postmodern thoughts. The recent recession in Japan has dampened and extended the time frame of the Japanese advance, but has not altered it. Reform in Japan is not (like it is in Korea) a destructive tour de force, but a deconstruction, an adaptation, and a reassembling. In the USA and in Europe, the major forces of the 1980s, the MNEs, were somewhat exhausted, and a myriad of grassroots entrepreneurial companies, heavy on technology[2] but without abstract organizational or strategic concepts, took over the lead. In Japan, however, the bigger associations of firms, the Keiretsu, were always the driving force. Once they stood still in the 1990s the country came to a halt. The currently emerging Japanese grassroots-level economy (venture capital based entrepreneurialism) is just the 'farming-out area' where 'creative and risky ideas' are tested. Successful concepts, models and strategies will then be integrated swiftly. There will be new ways of functioning as a Keiretsu, and the model of a nucleus with companies surrounding it will be too rigid. Because now, by means of IT and the Internet, a total rhizome/fractal economy is possible where all are interlinked and more loosely connected, but with higher communicative intensity.

And, the best communicator, the one that can deal with all this postmodernity, will win.[3] As Thurow points out in his recent book,[4] success in the twenty-first century depends upon how effectively the lower levels – fundamental knowledge, human skills, entrepreneurial and organizational abilities, natural resources and capital investments – have been put together. But in order to do this, abstract strategies are vital. Today, values and concepts ('business models') matter more than number crunching and display of muscle ('rationality' and 'simple economies of scale'). Abstract thoughts guide the 'real' world by virtue of shaping the 'virtual' world of the New Economy.[5]

Japan, known for its dexterity with abstract concepts, is well-adapted for complex strategies, intense communication contexts, unstable and unclear situations with ever-changing alliances and partners, and is able to deal with alogical, rapid change allowing multiple meanings. In this sense, Japan is currently adapting its systems to the postmodern/New Economy world, accompanied by a reinvigorated vision of Japan.

It is hoped that this book succeeds in showing that there is an inner meaning, a long-term sense to Japanese development. Simply said, Japan is the 'best fit for postmodern times'. Or, to say it more poignantly: there is mind in the madness – a Japanese mind in the global frenetic madness. In our times, 'new' competencies are in dire need; a new mind-set is needed in the new millennium. But, if one reads the description of these new competencies and compares it with Japanese characteristics, the congruence is striking. Japan, or the Japanese model, or characteristics that are predominant in Japan, will be best adapted to this New Economy. Currently, the Silicon Valley mind-set is propagated as the unique dogma, but one can bet that in the next five years Japan will create a counter-vision as the 'Japanese way' to deal with the new world, as the New Economy is just the entry into a new world. And, for the Japanese psychology, the New Economy/information revolution is just another revolution, as in 1868 and 1945. One should not forget that Japan has always had a 'we try harder' syndrome that propels it more than any other motivational factor.

This fertile energy inside Japan, inside the whole economic structure, and inside the Keiretsu, nurtures the rhizome/network approach that is needed for current 'postmodern times'.[6] Thus, Japan is best prepared to be among the leaders of this new phase of the global economy. In that sense it is conclusive to answer the question of the title of this book, laconically, with 'yes, but it is not as simple as that', meaning that Keiretsu-rhizome-network structures are currently the best 'practice model'; but a simple equation 'New Economy = Keiretsu' is overly simple. The qualities fostered by Keiretsu structures as elucidated throughout this book will prove winning in the New Economy no matter whether in a Keiretsu structure or in any other organizational form.

As they are not unique to Japan, other clusters/locations/associations may also succeed. Yet, as illustrated in nearly all chapters, Japan has a long 'postmodern tradition', for the character traits and skills needed today have been used and trained over centuries. Hence success in our amorphous and dynamic times is very likely, to say the least. In the Western world the word 'futurizing' is buzzword *à la mode*.[7] In the sense of this book, Japan and its Keiretsu have been 'futurizing' over centuries. So, do not expect miraculous solutions, but do expect the unexpected.

Notes

1 Introduction

1 Lash, S., *Sociology of Postmodernism*, p. 1.
2 McHale, B., *Writing about Postmodern Writing*, p. 212.
3 Küster, R., 'Richard Wagner – oder die Geschwätzigkeit der Postmoderne', p. 91.
4 Welsch, W., 'Vielheit ohne Einheit?', p. 114.
5 For an introduction to postmodernism see: Lee, J. and Powell, J. N., *Postmodernism for Beginners*.
6 Frank, M., *Was ist Neostrukturalismus?*, p. 109 and p. 201f.
7 Cho, H. T., *Postmodern Philosophy, Relativism, and a Renewed Vision of Education*, p. 3.
8 Feyerabend, P., *Wider den Methodenzwang*, p. 32 and Feyerabend, P., *Erkenntnis für freie Menschen*, p. 97.
9 Salanti, A., *Falsificationism and Fallibilism as Epistemic Foundations of Economics*; see also Musgrave, A., *'Unreal Assumptions' in Economic Theory*. Quotation: Arbeitsgruppe Soziologie: *Denkweisen and Grundbegriffe der Soziologie*, p. 128.
10 Bateson, G., *Mind and Nature*, p. 3; Lorenzen, P., *Lehrbuch der konstruktiven Wissenschaftstheorie*, p. 178. Rigid postmodern writers see as a stringent consequence of the denial of the 'written', the existence of meaning in texts, necessarily the impossiblility of meaningful statements about reality. (Angermüller, J., *Derrida vs. Bourdieu: Sociologizing Deconstruction, Deconstructing the Social*). As demonstrated earlier here, a more pragmatic use of the term 'postmodern' is advocated as it helps to bridge the gap between theory and reality, between philosophy and the New Economy.
11 Armin, H. H., *Volkswirtschaftspolitik*, p. 116; Joswig-Kühl, G. and Hölzel, K., *Gablers Wirtschaftslexikon*, vol. 6, p. 2323f.
12 Often cited examples of fruitful analyses are: (a) on the political economy: Johnson, C., *MITI and the Japanese Miracle*; Higashi, C. and Lauter, G. P., *The Internationalization of the Japanese Economy*; (b) on the level of families and individuals: Nakane, C., *The Japanese Society*, and Benedict, R., *The Chrysanthemum and the Sword*.
13 Hamel, G. and Prahalad. C. K., *Managing Strategic Responsibility in the Multinational Corporation*.
14 Good overviews are provided by: Buckley P. J., *A Critical Review of Theories of the Multinational Enterprise*; Casson, M., *General Theory of the Multinational Enterprise*; Williamson, O., *The Modern Corporation: Origins, Evolution, Attributes*; Dunning, J. H., *Trade, Location of Economic Activity and the MNE: A Search for an Eclectic Approach*; Hirsch, S., *An International Trade and Investment Theory of the Firm*; and Vernon, R., *International Investment and International Trade in the Product Cycle*.
15 Cf. Wilkins, M., *European and North American Multinationals, 1870–1914: Comparisons and Contrasts*.
16 Dunning, J. H., *Economic Analysis and the Multinational Enterprise*, p. 13; Casson, M., *Transaction Cost and the Theory of the Multinational Enterprise*, p. 31.
17 Hilb, M., *Personalpolitik für multinationale Unternehmen*, p. 17f.
18 Buckley, P. J., *A Critical View of Multinational Enterprise*, p. 1f.
19 Stopford, J. M. and Dunning, J. H., *The World Directory of Multinational Enterprises*, p. xxi.

20 Yoshino, M. Y., *Japan's Multinational Enterprises*, p. 24ff. and Yoshino, M. Y., *Emerging Japanese Multinational Enterprises*, p. 157f.
21 Kobayashi, N., *The Patterns of Management Style Developing in Japanese Multinationals in the 1980s* in Takamayi, S. and Thurley, K. (eds), *Japan's Emerging Multinationals: An International Comparison*, p. 234ff.; Abegglen, J. C. and Stalk, G., *Kaisha: The Japanese Corporation*, p. 254ff.
22 Kobayashi, N., *The Patterns of Management Style Developing in Japanese Multinationals in the 1980s*, p. 230.
23 Clark, R., *The Japanese Company*, p. 29f.; Abegglen, J. C. and Stalk, G., *Kaisha: The Japanese Corporation*, p. 271ff.
24 Some examples: (a) the beer industry: Asahi Breweries, Kirin, Sapporo, or (b) the paint & coatings industry: Nippon Paint, Shinto Paint, Dai Nippon Toryo. Both groups comprise of the industry leaders in terms of sales and management capability while having practically no exports! *Japan Company Handbook*, First section, passim.
25 Cf. Nester, W. R., *The Foundation of Japanese Power*, p. 180ff. Another reading of these terms is more aimed at a 'financial gang', in contrast to the 'gang of bureaucrats' (Mombatzu) or to the 'old school-tie' (Gakkubatzu). Hall, J. W., *Japan*, p. 310.
26 Beasley, W. G., *The Modern History of Japan*, p. 227.
27 Yoshino, M. Y., *Japan's Multinational Enterprises*, p. 5.
28 Further explanations are to be found in Chapter 5.
29 To put it more succinctly: New Economy is Postmodern Philosophy put into action by IT and network concepts. Thus, one should look first at the foundations and the building blocks rather than beginning with the end and praise the finished glittering palace for its splendour.
30 In any event, one can claim a 'Japanization of the West', though without (!) an active participation of Japan herself. Evidence for this is the (sub-) urban traffic chaos, the increasing scarcity of space in the city, the growing complexity of everyday life, the communication and information craze (given a rather constant amount of 'real' information, hence an explosion of informational noise) or the 'global' urbanization to shape every rural hamlet according to the nondescript international mould. Should these trends continue, then 'average' Europeans will face a socioeconomic environment that the Japanese have already long endured.
31 For more on this subject see Bricmont, J. and Sokal, A., *Fashionable Nonsense: Postmodern Intellectuals' Abuse of Science*.
32 Rorty, R., *Philosophy and the Mirror of Nature*, p. 3 and p. 369f. See also Rorty, R., *Contingency, Irony and Solidarity*, p. 19.
33 Rorty, R., *Consequences of Pragmatism*, p. 165; and also Sardar, Z., *Total Recall: Aliens, 'Others', and Amnesia in Postmodernist Thought*.
34 Habermas, J., *Der philosophische Diskurs der Moderne*, p. 16.
35 Cf. Sakaiya, T., *The Knowledge-Value Revolution: A History of the Future*.
36 Prime examples are: Capra, F., *The Tao of Physics*; Ferguson, M., *The Aquarian Conspiracy* and Lutz, R., *Pläne für eine menschliche Zukunft*.
37 The term 'ecclectic' is used here in its general sense. For its usage within the theory of the multinational company cf. Chapter 5.2.3.1.
38 McGuigan, J., *Modernity and Postmodern Culture*, p. 67 and Allan, S., *Modernity and Postmodern Culture. News Culture*, p. 85.
39 See Chapter 2, III.
40 Cf. Gebhardt, E., *Abschied von der Autorität: Die Manager der Postmoderne*; Koslowski, P., *Wirtschaft als Kultur* and Brown, D., *An Institutionalist Look at Postmodernism*.
41 Wagstyl, S., *Sensitivity over Surplus*, p. 3; Rowley, A., *Odd Man Out*, p. 57; Smith, L., *Why Japan's Surplus is Rising*; Anonymous, *Japan may be the Last Economic Power*;

Tran, D., *Securities Markets in Asia and Oceania*; Zengage, T. R. and Ratcliffe, C. T., *The Japanese Century*.

42 Vogel, E. F., *Japan as Number One: Lessons for America.*

43 Galbraith, J. K., *Die Entmythologisierung der Wirtschaft*, p. 349. Already in 1968 J. J. Servan-Schreiber, who was more concerned about the cultural invasion of Europe (read: France) by the USA, warned in his notes on the Japanese experiment about the next wave of problems: 'Japan will surpass Europe and the United States earlier than any other country possibly could.' Servan-Schreiber, J. J., *Die amerikanische Herausforderung*, p. 284.

44 Quoted from Benedict, R., *The Chrysanthemum and the Sword: Patterns of Japanese Culture*, p. 22f.

45 Wright, R. W. and Pauli, G. A., *The Second Wave – Japan's Global Assault on Financial Services*, p. 1; Baranson, J., *The Japanese Challenge to the U.S. Industry*; Kraus, W., *Die japanische Herausforderung*; Burstein, D., *Yen!*; Zengage, T. and Ratcliffe, C. T., *The Japanese Century*, especially p. 191ff.

46 Wolf, M. J., *The Japanese Conspiracy: Their Plot to dominate Industry Worldwide*, p. 5. Further support for the hypothesis of hegemonial interests is the renewed interest of Japan in her military powers. After having achieved a strong level of economic might, support from the military would come in handy to complement the spearheading of economic, trade and political strategies. Further developments of this hypothesis are Awanohara, S., 'Paradigm Paranoia', p. 15; Droughty, A., *Japan 2000*; Friedman, G. and LeBard, M., *The Coming War with Japan*; Manegold, C. S., *A Military Power, too?*, p. 22f.

47 Interestingly enough, Ishihara's book: *'No' to ieru Nihon* (Japan says 'No') was published in an authorized version only after a considerable delay (Ishihara, S., *The Japan that can say 'No'*).

48 Anonymous., *Pornographie für US-Handelspolitiker*; Reid, T. R., *Tokyo Officials call U.S. 'Subcontractor' to Japanese Economy*, p. 1; Hiraiwa, G., *Rethinking Japanese Culture*, p. 2.

49 The basic concepts of this booklet are laid out by A. Morita, the late Sony Chairman, undoubtedly a leading figure in Japan comparable to the old role of a Daimyo (second in power to the king). Morita was also in the international limelight as Japan's voice concerning topics relating to the international economy. Morita gave his approval for publication only with the stipulation that his ideas will be published only (!) in Japanese. By way of an unauthorized, private translation into English, the book was made known to Washington's power circles, where immediately vigorous protests were voiced. Morita tried to distance himself from the content wanting to play down its role as contributor. Despite all the smokescreen, some strong undercurrents of the Japanese self-regard are clearly visible, for worlds like: 'supremacy', 'superiority' and 'national awakening' are found all too often throughout this book. Ishihara, S., *The Japan that can say 'No'*, cf. p. 23, p. 24, p. 38.

50 Anonymous, *1992: Europe's Counterattack: Japanese Industry will be Shut Out*, p. 6f.

51 *Ibid.*, p. 8.

52 For a broader explanation see Chapter 4, section VII.

53 Ohmae, K., *Triad Power: The Coming Shape of Global Competition.*

54 Kahn, H., *Bald werden sie die ersten sein.: Japan 2000 – Zukunftsmodell der Herren der Welt*, p. 18; Kahn, H., *Vor uns die guten Jahre*, p. 259; Droughty, A., *Japan 2000*, p. 34ff. EC Commission on International Trade, *The Group of Thirty: 1992: The External Dimension*, p. 15; see also Dunning, J. H. and Cantwell, J. A., *Japanese Manufacturing Direct Investment in the EEC, Post-1992: Some Alternative Scenarios.*

55 Keidanren, 'Brief an die Staatsoberhäupter der EG-Mitglieder v. 05.03.1987. 1987'. For the underlying strategies see Mann, C. L., *Determinants of Japanese Direct Investment in*

US Manufacturing Industries. The mega mergers in the Japanese banking sectors (Mitsubishi Bank with Bank of Tokyo, April 1995; see more in Chapter 4, section V) might have had not only economies of scale as objectives, but also economies of scope as an economic power are thus achieved by Japan in a deceivingly Western manner.

56 James, B. G., *Wirtschaftsmacht Japan: Das Trojanische Pferd*, p. 365; see also Ozawa, T., *Japanese Multinationals and 1992.*

57 Kendrick, D. M., *Where Communism Works.*

58 *Ibid.*, p. 197.

59 Cf. Frischkorn, T., *Zazen für Arbeitnehmer. Zur Symptomatologie zen-buddhistischer Rituale in Japans Wirtschaft.*

60 Kuroda, M. (Vice-Minister, MITI), *Japan in a Changing World.*

61 This divide can be traced throughout the Japanese language: earlier – but also sometimes today – Western items have the attribute '*bata-kusai*' which means on the one hand 'stench like rancid butter', but is today, on the other hand, considered as an outdated idiomatic expression for 'foreign'. See also Chapter 3, section IV.

62 Reischauer, E. O., *The Japanese Today*, p. 396 and p. 397.

63 Wolf, M. J., *The Japanese Conspiracy: Their Plot to Dominate Industry Worldwide*, p. 3.

64 'The West is lacking a realistic perspective on the underlying motives that drive Japanese economic policies [and the resulting economic reality].' James, B. G., *Wirtschaftsmacht Japan: Das Trojanische Pferd*, p. 57.

65 The first analyses in the German-speaking world were Sartorius v.Waltershausen, A., *Das volkswirtschaftliche System der Kapitalanlage im Auslande*; Ertel, E., *Internationale Kartelle und Konzerne der Industrie* and Birkenkamp, F., *Deutsche Industrieanlagen im Ausland.* More recent studies include Ramonet, I., *Die neuen Herren der Welt. Globale Politik an der Jahrtausendwende*; Feketekuty, G. and Stokes, B., *Trade Strategies for a New Era: Ensuring U.S. Leadership in a Global Economy.*

66 Good conceptual overviews are Kindleberger, C. P., *American Business Abroad: Six Lessons on Direct Investment*; Lall, S. and Streeten, P., *Foreign Investment, Transnationals, and Developing Countries* and Buckley, P. J. and Casson, M. C., *The Future of Multinational Enterprise.* Concise historiographics of the development of multinational enterprises are Williamson, O. E., *Industrial Organization* and Wilkinson, M., *The Growth of Multinationals.*

67 Welge, M. K., *Multinational Corporations*, p. 1501.

68 *Ibid.*, p. 1502.

69 Best, M., *The New Competition*, p. 7; see also Gilroy, B. M., *Networking in Multinational Enterprises*; Deresky, H., *International Management: Managing Across Borders and Cultures.*

70 Best, M., *The New Competition: Institutions of Industrial Restructuring*, p. 147ff.; see also Cantwell, J. A. and Randaccio, F. S., *Growth and Multinationality amongst the World's Largest Firms*; Ouchi, W., *Theory Z*, p. 225; Ohmae, K., *The Borderless World: Power and Strategy in the Interlinked Economy*, p. 22, p. 122 and p. 131; Waterman, R. H., *Leistung durch Innovation: Strategien zur unternehmerischen Zukunftssicherung*, p. 61.

71 Matsushita, K., *The Secret is Shared*, p. 19.

72 Grilliches, Z., *Data and Econometricians – The Uneasy Alliance*, p. 198; Morgenstern, O., *On the Accuracy of Economic Observations.*

73 This approach can be found in Sapelli, G., *A Historical Typology of Group Enterprises*; Tirole, J., *Hierarchies and Bureaucracies*, p. 181f.; indirectly also in Porter, M. E., *The Competitive Advantage of Nations*; and Borner, S. and Porter, M. E., *Internationale Wettbewerbsvorteile: Ein strategisches Konzept für die Schweiz.*

74 Representative literature: Lu, D. J., *Inside Corporate Japan*; Hayashi, S., *Culture and Management in Japan*; Chandler, A. D., *The Growth of the Transnational Firm in the*

United States and the United Kingdom: A Comparative Analysis; Wilkins, M., *Japanese Multinational Enterprises before 1914*.

75 Doz, Y. and Prahalad, C. K., *Quality of Management: An Emerging Source of Global Advantage?*; Knipes, B. J., *Corporate Reputation and Strategic Performance*; Macharzina, K., *Diskontinuitätenmanagement*; Negandhi, A. and Welge, M. K., *Beyond Theory Z: Global Rationalization Strategies of American, German and Japanese Multinational Companies*.

76 For example, Clark, R., *The Japanese Company*; Bennett, J. W. and Ishino, I., *Paternalism in the Japanese Economy*; Murakami,Y. and Kosai, Y., *Japan in the Global Community*; Mouer, R. and Sugimoto, Y., *Images of Japanese Society*.

77 For example Fujimoto, K., *Working their Way to a Sudden Death;* Anonymous, *Japan's Working Woman the Most Dissatisfied*; Japan Travel Bureau, *Salaryman in Japan*; Mori, S., *Yet Again, there is Reverse Culture Shock*; De Mente, B., *Bachelor's Japan*; Danger, M., *Adventures of a Gaijin*.

78 See Ballon, R. J. and Tomita, I., *The Financial Behavior of Japanese Corporations*; Reddies, B., *Der Recruit Skandal in Japan: Modernisierungskrise einer Wirtschaftsmacht*; Sasaki-Smith, M., *Japan's Leasing Industry*; Schaede, U., *Der neue japanische Kapitalmarkt*.

79 Ichihara, K. and Takamiya, S., *Die japanische Unternehmung*; Komiya, R., *The Japanese Economy: Trade, Industry, and Government*; Choate, P., *Agents of Influence*; Johnson, C., *MITI and the Japanese Miracle*.

80 Lu, D. J., *Inside Corporate Japan*; Pascale, R. T. and Athos, A. G., *The Art of Japanese Management*; Maury, R., *Die japanischen Manager*.

81 Shimizu, R., *The Japanese Business Success Factors*; Ishihara, S., *The Japan that can say 'No'*.

82 Schwarz, S., *Wettbewerbspotentiale politischer Kulturen am Beispiel der Vereinigten Staaten und Japan*; Hagiwara, S., *Doing Business in Japan*.

83 Tasker, P., *Inside Japan*; Gibney, F., *Japan: The Fragile Superpower*; Glazer, N., *Social and Cultural Factors in Japanese Economic Growth*.

84 Nuyen, A. T., *Postmodern Theology and Postmodern Philosophy*, p. 65f.; Heartney, E., *Mixed Messages: Western Influence in Postmodern Japanese Art*, p. 212f.; Vondereau, R., *Cultural Gap Experienced by a Gajin Engineer*, p. 70f.; Sim, S., *The Routledge Critical Dictionary of Postmodern Thought*; Barker, S., *Signs of Change: Premodern – Modern Postmodern*.

85 Miyoshi, M. and Harootunian, H. D., *Postmodernism and Japan*; Pfeiffer, K. L., *Schwebende Referenzen und Verhaltenskultur: Japan und die Praxis permanenter Postmoderne*, p. 344f.; Yamamoto, C. and Blume, G., *Keine andere Stadt ist wie Tama: Tokyo's postmoderne Vorstadt*; Wie-Hsun-Fu, C. and Heine, S., *Japan in Traditional and Postmodern Perspectives*.

86 Exceptions are Gebhardt, E., *Abschied von der Autorität: Die Manager der Postmoderne*; Horvitch, M., *Postmodern Strategic Management*; Koslowski, P., *Wirtschaft als Kultur: Wirtschaftskultur und Wirtschaftsethik in der Postmoderne*.

87 L. Gronlund was the first to expand economics into postmodern territory: Gronlund, L., *New Economy*.

88 At least the postmodern language invades economist's academia: Evans and Wurster talk about 'deconstructing industries' and disappearing structures ('the glue that holds today's value chains and supply chains together is melting'), though a systematic use of postmodern philosophy is still unseen. Evans, P. and Wurster, T. S., *Blown to Bits*.

89 For example Magretta, Ormerod or Hollstein point to the impact of hyper-information on strategy and the decline of rational man favouring more unstructured networks of cooperation and planning: Magretta, J., *Managing in the New Economy*; Ormerod, P., *The*

Death of Economics; Ormerod, P. *Butterfly Economics*; Hollstein, B., *Der Arbeitsbegriff in der ökonomischen Theorie und das Ehrenamt*. Or, the treatment remains descriptive and has invariably only American empirical observations: Japan is overlooked. Inglehart, R., *Modernization and Postmodernization: Cultural Economic and Political Change*; Kelly, K., *New Rules for the New Economy*.

90 Kiuchi, T., *New Economy*, **4**.

91 A nice account of the fragility ('elegant nonsense') of the term postmodern is given by Sokal and Bricmont in *Intellectual Impostures*. In 1996, their article entitled 'Transgressing the Boundaries: Toward a Transformative Hermeneutics of Quantum Gravity' was published in the cultural studies journal *Social Text*. Packed with recherché quotations from 'postmodern' literary theorists and sociologists of science, and bristling with imposing theorems of mathematical physics, the article addressed the cultural and political implications of the theory of quantum gravity. Later, to the embarrassment of the editors, the author revealed that the essay was a hoax, interweaving absurd pronouncements from eminent intellectuals about mathematics and physics with laudatory – but fatuous – prose. In *Intellectual Impostures*, Alan Sokal, the author of the hoax, and Jean Bricmont contend that abuse of science is rampant in postmodernist circles, both in the form of inaccurate and pretentious invocation of scientific and mathematical terminology and in the more insidious form of epistemic relativism. Nonetheless, one of the most basic axioms of this book is the usefulness of this theoretical term as it reflects on the theoretical level the practical world of the New Economy.

92 Quoted from Cho, H. T., *Postmodern Philosophy, Relativism, and a Renewed Vision of Education*, p. 55. Cho recurs in this passage on Rorty, R., *Philosophy and the Mirror of Nature*, p. 10.

93 Here, Rorty is grounded on concepts developed earlier by Dewey, *The Quest for Certainty: A Study of the Relation of Knowledge and Action*, p. 176.

94 Dewey, J., *Logic: The Theory of Inquiry*, p. 345.

95 The most promising area where this nexus might be established first is the area of knowledge. As it was the initial problem Lyotard (cf. Chapter 2, II) tackled to start the postmodern debate, the strategic impact of knowledge and its management might point to postmodern sources: e.g. Neef, D., Siesfield, T. and Cefola, J., *The Economic Impact of Knowledge*. See also MacDonald, W., *Postmodern Management* or Inamori, K. and Reid, T. R., *For People – And for Profit: A Business Philosophy for the 21st Century*; Jameson, F., *Cultural Turn: Selected Writings on the Postmodern*.

96 An interesting bridge between postmodern concepts and economic designs is provided by Kotkin, arguing that tribes (groups around symbols, ethnic networks) will guide into the future, Krotkin sees Japan as the prototypical tribe in *Tribes: How Race, Religion, and Identity Determine Success in the New Global Economy*.

97 Miyoshi, M., *Against the Native Grain: The Japanese Novel and the 'Postmodern' West*, p. 221f.; Arata, I., 'Of City, Nation, and Style'; Pfeiffer, L. K., *Schwebende Referenzen und Verhaltenskultur: Japan und die Praxis permanenter Postmoderne*, p. 344f.

98 Classical accounts of Japan's (economic) history are Yoshihara, K., *Japanese Economic Development: A Shorter Introduction*; Beasley, G. B., *The Modern History of Japan*; and Hall, J. W., *Japan*.

99 Klenner, W., *Administrative Guidance*, p. 57f.; Reddies, B., *Der Recruit Skandal in Japan*; Johnson, C., *MITI and the Japanese Miracle*; Wolferen, K.v., *The Enigma of Japanese Power*.

100 Tasker, P., *Inside Japan*, p. 148–85; Pohl, M., *Japan 1989 and 90: Politik und Wirtschaft*; Richardson, B. M. and Flanagan, S. C., *Politics in Japan*; Gibney, F., *Japan: The Fragile Superpower*, p. 264–96.

101 Representative for the legion of pertinent literature (a) on the topic of the Japanese psyche: Nakamura, H., *Ways of Thinking of Eastern People*; Singer, K., *Mirror, Sword and Jewel: The Geometry of Japanese Life*; Doi, T., *The Anatomy of Dependence*; (b) on dynamics in groups: Benedict, R., *The Chrysanthemum and the Sword: Patterns of Japanese Culture*; Nakane, C., *Japanese Society* and Matsumoto, M., *The Unspoken Way – Haragei: Silence in Japanese Business and Society*.

102 Heller, F. A., *Some Problems in Multinational Research on Organizations*, p. 22ff.; Holesovsky, V., *Economic Systems: Analysis and Comparison*, p. 11; Haitani, K., *Comparative Economic Systems*, p. 1f.

103 Hilb, M., *Personalpolitik für Multinationale Unternehmen*, p. 257f.; Schwalbe, H., *Japan*, p. 22ff; Heller, F. A., *Some Problems in Multinational Research on Organizations*, p. 24. Ever since the sixties this demand has been voiced: North, R. and Holsti, O., *Content Analysis: A Handbook with Applications for the Study of International Crisis* or Rokkan, S., *Comparative Research across Cultures and Nations*.

104 Semsch talks about a baroque richness of symbols surrounding the term postmodern: Semsch, K., *Prolegomena zu einer texttheoretischen Diskurslogik zwischen Moderne und Postmoderne*.

105 Collins, J., *Uncommon Cultures*, p. 112; see also Portoghesi, P., *After Modern Architecture*, p. 26f.

106 Lyotard, J. F., *La condition postmoderne*, p. 36.

107 See Simon, H. A., *The Failure of Armchair Economics*, p. 18f.

108 See Brandes, W., *Über die Grenzen der Schreibtischökonomie*.

109 Schopenhauer, A., *Gesammelte Werke*, Bd. IV, pp. 118, 241.

110 Rorty, R., *Philosophy and the Mirror of Nature*, p. 36f.; see also Feyerabend, P., *Wider den Methodenzwang*, p. 121

111 The term 'eclectic' is used here in a general sense. For its usage within the theory of MNE cf. Chapter 5, section II.

112 Friedman, M., *Essays in Positive Economics*, pp. 4, 39.

113 Johnson, G. L., *Philosophic Foundations of Agricultural Economics Thought*, p. 3. See also Wilber, C. K. and Harrison, R. S., *The Methodological Basis of Institutional Economics: Pattern Model Storytelling, and Holism*, p. 74f.; Dopfer, K., *Mechanistisches Denken und seine Überwindung in der Ökonomie*, p. 401.

114 Frank, M., *Was ist Neostrukturalismus*, p. 39; see also Feyerabend, P., *Erkenntnis für freie Menschen*, p. 44.

115 Kaplan, A., *The Conduct of Inquiry*, p. 54ff. and Gergen, K. J., *The Social Constructionist Movement in Modern Psychology*, p. 266f.

116 Maturana, H. and Varela, F., *Der Baum der Erkenntnis: Die biologischen Wurzeln des menschlichen Erkennens*, p. 7 and also Munéva, G., *Radical Knowledge*.

117 A homologue simile in the realm of biology would be the co-evolution between the beak of a hummingbird and the petals it feeds upon. H. Maturana and F. Varela call this phenomenon 'structural coupling'; Maturana, H. and Varela, F., *Der Baum der Erkenntnis: Die biologischen Wurzeln des menschlichen Erkennens*, p. 85.

118 I. Hassan refers to hybridization of methods and to constructed meta-morphologies (constructionism); M. Sarup (quoting F. Jameson) talks about pastiche and schizophrenia; W. Welsch's concession that, when trying to see pluralism in a postmodern context, one has to see it as a 'complex helter skelter' especially in methodological questions. Hassan, I., *Pluralism in Postmodern Perspective*, p. 20ff.; Sarup, M., *An Introductory Guide to Poststructuralism and Postmodernism*, p. 133; Welsch, W., *Rückblickend auf einen Streit, der ein Widerstreit bleibt*, p. 9.

119 Popper, K. R., *Die Logik der Forschung*, p. 13.

120 Arbeitsgruppe Soziologie, *Denkweisen und Grundbegriffe der Soziologie*, p. 78.

121   In the interpretation according to Weber, M., *Gesammelte Aufsätze zur Wissenschafts-lehre*, p. 154.
122   On the taxonomy of explorative, explanative and functional definitions in economics and business administration see Ulrich, P. and Hill, W., *Wissenschaftstheoretische Grundlagen der Betriebswirtschaftslehre*, pp. 345–50.
123   Hohmann, W. L., *Einige Überlegungen zur Einführung*, p. 9.
124   Menzel, U., *Im Schatten des Siegers: Kultur und Gesellschaft*, p. 12. Hall and Reed-Hall talk about a 'morass of conflicting statements': Hall, E. T. and Reed-Hall, M., *Hidden Differences*, p. xx.
125   Schwalbe, H., *Japan*, p. 15.
126   Barthes, R., *Das Reich der Zeichen*, p. 131 and p. 143.
127   *Ibid.*, pp. 17, 147; quotation p. 51.
128   Reischauer, E. O., *The Japanese Today*, p. 127.
129   Snyder, J. R., *A Study in Canadian Postmodernism*; Jameson, F., *Postmoderne und Utopie*, p. 83; Flierl, B., *Postmoderne Architektur*, p. 213.
130   Sombart, W., *Die Ordnung des Wirtschaftslebens*, p. 14.
131   The interested reader can refer to the discussions on 'Wirtschaftsstils' (economic style), for example in Spiethoff, A., *Die allgemeine Volkswirtschaftslehre als geschichtliche Theorie*, p. 916.
132   Dopfer, K., *Ost–West Konvergenz*, p. 43.
133   Haitani, K., *Comparative Economic Systems*, p. 4.
134   Gernalzick, among many others, stresses the economic nucleus of postmodern spaces no matter where applied. More generally, the postmodern approach is often seen as the ontology, as the tool to analyse the underlying construction of the economy. Gernalzick, N., *Gegen eine Metaphysik der Arbeit: Der Ökonomiebegriff der Dekonstruktion und im Poststrukturalismus*; and also Martens, G., *Broch, Musil und die Grenzen der Moderne*.
135   This approach was successfully developed by Reischauer, E. O., *The Japanese Today: Change and Continuity*, p. 15ff.; Schwalbe, H., *Japan*, p. 33ff.; Tasker, P., *Inside Japan*, p. 5ff.
136   Lakatos, I., *History of Science and its Rational Reconstructions*.
137   Best, M., *The New Competition*, p. 137f.
138   Ulrich, P. and Hill, W., *Wissenschaftstheoretische Grundlagen der Betriebswirtschaftslehre*.

2   Postmodern Principles

1   As for taxonomy, the terms 'postmodern', 'postmodernity', 'postmodernism' are used somewhat loosely and sometimes interchangeable; 'post-modern' and 'postmodern' is treated as equivalent, although strictly speaking 'post-modern' directly refers to the modern, while 'postmodern' can be seen as autonomous.
2   For this, see Chapter 2, section II.
3   Whitehouse, I., *A Reading of the Postmodern*, p. 5.
4   See especially Chapter 5, section II.
5   For the genealogy of the term 'postmodern' and its evolution: Welsch, W., *Unsere postmoderne Moderne*, p. 12ff.; also Willms, B., *Postmoderne und Politik*, p. 324ff. More expansive accounts give: Kermode, F., *Continuities*, p. 55ff.; McKinney, R. H., *The Origins of Postmodernism* and Agger, B., *The Discourse of Domination: From the Frankfurt School to Postmodernism*. U. Eco states ironically that, due to the imminent discord

between postmodern writers, the presumed first use of the term postmodern will be antedated more and more, so that soon Homer will be claimed as the first postmodern writer. Eco, U., *Postscriptum to 'In the Name of the Rose'*, p. 77.

6   Köhler, M., *Postmodernismus: ein begriffsgeschichtlicher Überblick*, p. 16. Semsch speaks of a 'baroque richnes of symbols' that characterized the postmodern. Semsch, K., *Prolegomena zu einer texttheoretischen Diskurslogik zwischen Moderne und Postmoderne.*

7   Quotation: Hassan, I., *Ideas of Cultural Change*, p. 25. See also Chapter 1, section II.

8   Howe, I., *Mass Society and Post-Modern Fiction*, p. 428 and p. 433; see also Levin, H., *What was Modernism?*; Bertens, H., 'The Postmodern Weltanschauung and its Relations with Modernism', in Fokkema, D. and Bertens, H. (Eds.), *Approaching Postmodernism*, pp. 9–51; Kamper, D. and Reijen, W. v., *Die unvollendete Vernunft*, p. 47ff. and Lyotard, J. F., *La condition postmoderne*, p. 11.

9   Köhler, M., *Postmodernismus: ein begriffsgeschichtlicher Überblick*, p. 12.

10 'The postmodern harbored the promise of a post-white, post-male, post-humanist, post-puritan world.' Huyssen, A., *Mapping the Postmodern*, p. 18ff. One might get the wrong impression that there was some kind of (unwanted and unintended) unity among postmodern writers. Already when trying to formulate goals for the postmodern movement any unity was immediately dissolved.

11 Sonntag, S., *Against Interpretation*, p. 19ff.; Fiedler, L., *The New Mutants*; Graff, G., *Literature Against Itself: Literary Ideas in Modern Society*, p. 55.

12 For a critique on the underlying concepts of Habermas see: Dews, P., *Habermas: A Critical Reader.*

13 For more on Lyotard's thoughts see: Williams, J., *Lyotard: Towards a Modern Philosophy* and Sim, S., *Jean-Francois Lyotard.*

14 Quoted after: Huyssen, A., *Mapping the Postmodern*, p. 30. An overview of this debate give: Lash, S., *Sociology of Postmodernism*, p. 122; Rorty, R., *Habermas and Lyotard on Postmodernity*, p. 161; Jay, M., *Habermas and Modernism*, p. 1f. There is a potential to mistake the debate as a local conflict at the German–French border. On closer look, it is obvious that participants of all Western industrial nations involve themselves, so that – like modernism was – a 'truly international movement' developed. This argument is proposed in: Bertens, H., *The Postmodern Weltanschauung and its Relations with Modernism*, p. 21.

15 Huyssen, A., *Mapping the Postmodern*, p. 50; see also Lyotard: *Postmoderne für Kinder*, p. 100.

16 Schwengel, H., *Nach dem Subjekt oder nach der Politik fragen*, p. 375. see also Lyotard, J. F., *Postmoderne für Kinder*, p. 38.

17 Many authors consistently declare the dualism modern and postmodern as antiquated. Opposing this, F. Jameson regards this essential pairing Anti-modern = Pro-postmodern and Pro-modern = Anti-postmodern as insurmountable. He proposes somewhat weakly a bridging by 'Realism' 'for the moment and for want of something better', but Jameson agrees that eventually the modern will be dissolved in the postmodern. See Jameson, F., *Postmodernism, or the Cultural Logic of Late Capitalism*, p. 65 and p. 202.

18 Safdie, M., *Architectural Trends*; Slemon, S., *Modernism's Last Post*; Howe, S., *Dead Ends New*; Li, V., *Naming the System: Fredric Jameson's Postmodernism*; Brock, B., *Selbstanmache.*

19 Much has been written on postmodern times as a fin de siècle. For example, Hofmann, W., *Emanzipation der Dissonanzen*; Newman, C., *The Post-Modern Aura*; Lyotard, J. F., *Postmoderne für Kinder*, p. 108f.; Eco, U., *Postscriptum to 'In the Name of the Rose'*, p. 77. Cf. Chapter 2, section III (first sub-section). On the other hand, some writers see the 1990 as the late postmodernity that is just a door to something new: Christensen, P., *Minding the Underworld: Clayton Eshleman and Late Postmodernism.*

20 See Soper, K., *Postmodern and its Discontents*; Swirski, P., *Playing a Game of Ontology: a Postmodern Reading of the Futurological Congress*; Sarder, Z., *Total Recall: Aliens, Others and Amnesia in Postmodernist Thought*.

21 See Köhler, M., *Postmodernismus: ein begriffsgeschichtlicher Überblick*, p. 8.

22 In this sense C. Newman can state that '[t]he Apocalypse is over. Not because it didn't happen but because it happens every day'. Newman, C., *The Post-Modern Aura*, p. 56; F. Kermode echoes this in talking of a 'routinized apocalypse'. Kermode, F., *History and Value*.

23 '...architecture, where postmodernism has achieved its highest profile'. Callinicos, A., *Against Postmodernism*, p. 138. See also Sim, S., *The Routledge Critical Dictionary of Postmodern Thought*.

24 'At present, postmodern architecture offers one of the most coherent and best articulated expressions of the postmodern tendencies in the arts and sciences...' Whitehouse, I., *A Reading of the Postmodern*, p. 3; also Welsch, W., *Unsere postmoderne Moderne*, p. 87ff. and also Miller, R., *Putting on the Glitz: Architecture After Postmodernism*.

25 Portoghesi, P., *The Postmodern*, p. 3. 'Postmodernity is a stage of development not just a reaction to modernity.' Jencks, C., *Was ist Postmoderne?*, p. 59.

26 Grabow, S., *The Search for a new Paradigm in Architecture*, p. 23f.; Portoghesi, P., *The Postmodern*, p. 14. For private homes A. Erickson's designs combine postmodern elements with the natural, even rustic surroundings of the building. For more, see Gantenbein, D., *Architecture: Arthur Erickson*.

27 In Japan, interestingly, not only architecture but all other creative areas as well made it their goal to interpret progress as a dialogue with tradition, and stressed the necessity of carefully fitting and blending the progressive elements into the existing delicate structural body. See Singer, K., *Mirror, Sword and Jewel*, p. 92ff.

28 C. Jencks architecture is always looking for sensible, thoughtful combinations, rather than falling for effects. 'Architectural borrowings' preclude not symbolism or intelligent irony. Here architecture becomes a metaphor for biology, knowledge and meaning. Jencks, C. and Anderson, K., *Architectural Dialogue*, p. 31f.

29 As an early example serves J. Stirling's *Neue Würtembergische Staatsgalerie* in Stuttgart (1984). But, there is not a more brutal way to display clashes of styles as in Japan's newest hotel designs: Italian atmospheres, 'cool design', Op-Art, traditional Japanese interior design are thrown helter skelter in the midst of small industrial towns. Thakara, J., *Japanische Designer Hotelarchitektur*. This phenomenon is however visible in the last 100 years of Japanese architectural design: western construction techniques and western style was always used in any combination that was opportune for the moment. Schwalbe, H., *Japan*, p. 294f.

30 Deleuze, G., *Différence et répétition*, p. 7f.; see also Klotz, H., *Moderne und Postmoderne*, p. 101.

31 Cf. Portoghesi, P., *The Postmodern*, p. 82. A famous example is C. Moore's Piazza d'Italia in New Orleans, where picturesque Italian elements play ironically with the surrounding dull commercial buildings. Interpretations offer: Hutcheon, L., *A Poetics of Postmodernism*, p. 31ff. and Jameson, F., *Postmodernism, or the Cultural Logic of Late Capitalism*, p. 100; Portoghesi, P., *After Modern Architecture*, p. 26f.; Martland, T. R., *Post-Modernism – or what's become of us, Tarzan?*, p. 587f. Compare also B. Flierl's, view that postmodern construction creates 'inhabitable quotations'. Flierl, B., *Postmoderne Architektur*, p. 234.

32 Venturi, R., *Komplexität und Widerspruch in der Architektur*, p. 80f. Several ways can be chosen in reality: be it the hard, deconstructive design like E. Becket and his Northwest Airlines terminal, or soft and transparent as T. Ito did with his Center for Japanese Culture in Paris. Cf. Thomsen, C. W., *Die Utopie der Städte*.

33   P. Blake quoted in Portoghesi, P., *The Postmodern*, p. 25.
34   See e.g., Ellin, N., *Postmodern Urbanism*; Colquhoun, A., *Modernity and the Classical Tradition: Architectual Essays 1980–1987*; Girardo, D., *Architecture After Modernism*.
35   For a provoking explanation of this phenomenon see Hannigan, J., *Fantasy City: Pleasure and Profit in the Postmodern Metropolis*.
36   Figlestahler, P., *Zwischen Ghetto und Metropolis*. Ironically all firms mentioned are either bankrupt, restructured, merged or otherwise in trouble.
37   Cf. Barsky, N., *What will become of Skylines without Edifice Complexes*; Mills, C. A., *Creating a Disney World*, p. 40f. A critique of the architecture in New York offers: Baudrillard, J., *Simulacra and Simulations*, p. 135.
38   Here, the expression 'a new reading' is very useful: more and more indicators creep into the vision and all of a sudden even modern signs bear postmodern meanings. Though there is not a fully fledged methodology behind it, this evolutionary and subversive process is typical for postmodern thought and can be found in all postmodern areas of debate. For more see Jencks, C., *The Language of Postmodern Architecture*, p. 46.
39   Lash, S., *Sociology of Postmodernism*, p. 129.
40   Cf. Foucault, M., *The Order of Things*, p. 244 and p. 349.
41   Good overviews of these new concepts and their cartography are Schuster, H. G., *Deterministic Chaos*, Esposito, E., *Paradoxien als Unterscheidungen von Unterscheidungen*, p. 35f.; Nash, C., *World Games*, p. 37f.
42   Welsch, W., *Rückblickend auf einen Streit, der ein Widerstreit bleibt*, p. 9.
43   Capra, F., *Das neue Denken*, p. 63 and Capra, F., *Wendezeit*, p. 98; also: Wilson, R. A., *Die neue Inquisition*, p. 228.
44   For the full account, read Sokal, A. and Bricmont J., *Intellectual Impostures*.
45   The responsibility that the postmodern has with respect to intellectual sincerity and dillegence in Popper's tradition is stressed by Sassower. Sassower, R., *Cultural Collisions: Postmodern Technoscience*.
46   Spaemann, R., *Philosophische Essays*, p. 147f.; Kray, R. and Pfeiffer, K. L., *Vom Ende und Fortgang der Provokationen*, p. 14.
47   Kunneman, H., *Der Wahrheitstrichter*, p. 202.
48   Even in the economic analysis of competitive structures, fragmented (fractal) industries are used as conceptual tools. Porter, M. E., *Competitive Strategy*, p. 196ff.
49   Kunneman, H., *Der Wahrheitstrichter*, p. 92 and p. 97.
50   Capra, F., *Das neue Denken*, p. 55 and Hassan, I., *The Postmodern Turn*, p. 136.
51   This new overlap between current theory of science and postmodern conceptual thinking is documented by many: Fokkema, D., *Semantic and Syntactic Organization of Postmodern Texts*, p. 81f. and especially Sobchack, V., *All-Theorien: Reflexion über Chaos, Fraktale und die Differenz, die zu Indifferenz führt*, p. 809f.
52   See Frank, M., *Die Grenzen der Verständigung*, p. 12; Lyotard, J. F., *La condition postmoderne*, p. 97; Jantsch, E., *Die Grenzen westlicher Rationalität*, p. 48; Lutz, R., *Das Paradigma als Weltanschauung der Wissenschaften*, p. 207f. Critical of Lyotard's interpretation of science's dynamics: Rorty, R., *Habermas and Lyotard on Postmodernity*.
53   The argument that these three writers encompass the breadth of postmodern positions is proposed in detail in Reijen, W. v., *Miss Marx, Terminals und Grands Récits oder: Kratzt Habermas, wo es nicht juckt?*, p. 546ff.
54   Habermas, J., *Strukturwandel der Öffentlichkeit*; Habermas, J., *Theorie des kommunikativen Handelns*; Habermas, J., *Faktizität und Geltung*.
55   Habermas, J., *Theorie des kommunikativen Handelns*, vol. 1, p. 16f.
56   Habermas, J., *ibid.*, vol. 1, p. 48; see also Toulmin, S., *Human Understanding*.
57   Habermas, J., *ibid.*, vol. 1, p. 410.
58   Habermas, J., *ibid.*, vol. 2, p. 579.

59 Habermas, J., *ibid.*, vol. 2, p. 65.
60 Habermas, J., *ibid.*, vol. 2, p. 238.
61 Habermas, J., *Faktizität und Geltung.* See also Arato A. and Rosenfeld, M., *Habermas on Law and Democracy: Critical Exchanges.*
62 Habermas, J., *Faktizität und Geltung*, p. 245f. and p. 378ff.
63 Habermas, J., *Theorie des kommunikativen Handelns*, vol. 1, p. 9.
64 Habermas, J., *Theorie und Praxis*, p. 328; cf. also Habermas, J., *Modernity – an Incomplete Project*, p. 64ff.; Koslowski, P., *Prüfungen der Neuzeit*, p. 32 and also Habermas, J., *Die Zweite Lebenslüge der Bundesrepublik: wir sind wieder normal geworden.* See also Cooke, M. and Habermas, J., *On the Pragmatics of Communication.*
65 Habermas, J., *Theorie des kommunikativen Handelns*, vol. 1, p. 72f., p. 225, p. 240, p. 275, p. 294, p. 381 and p. 501.
66 Habermas, J., *Legitimationsprobleme im Spätkapitalismus*, p. 108. Quote: Bernstein, R. J., *'Introduction' to Habermas and Modernity*, p.18.
67 Rorty, R., *Habermas and Lyotard on Postmodernity*, p. 166.
68 Habermas, J., *Theorie des kommunikativen Handelns*, vol. 1, p. 130 ff. Rorty, R., *Habermas and Lyotard on Postmodernity*, p. 166. See also Habermas, J., *Die Zweite Lebenslüge der Bundesrepublik: wir sind wieder normal geworden.*
69 In further studies it could be interesting to explore the relevance of such a concept to the activities on the Internet where power and truth are hardly existing in the communication in the virtual communities.
70 Lyotard, J. F., *L'inhumain: causeries sur le temps*, p. 57ff.; cf. Habermas, J., *Der philosophische Diskurs der Moderne*, Preface.
71 Habermas, J., *Theorie des kommunikativen Handelns*, vol. 2, p. 549f.
72 Habermas, J., *Theorie des kommunikativen Handelns*, vol. 2, p. 580 and Habermas, J., *Theorie des kommunikativen Handelns*, vol. 1, p. 226. This chain of arguments goes back to Weber, M., *Gesammelte Aufsätze zur Wissenschaftslehre*, p. 661. For a summary see Seidman, S., *Contested Knowledge: Social Theory in the Postmodern Era.*
73 Foucault, M. and Raulet, G., *Um welchen Preis sagt die Vernunft die Wahrheit?*, p. 2; Huyssen, A., *After the Great Divide*; Huyssen, A., *Mapping the Postmodern*, p. 16 and p. 23.
74 Habermas, J., *Theorie des kommunikativen Handelns*, vol. 1, p. 334. Refer also to Habermas, J., *Theorie des kommunikativen Handelns*, vol. 2, p. 232f.
75 Habermas, J., *Theorie des kommunikativen Handelns*, vol. 2, p. 464.
76 G. Vattimo brings it to the point: 'Modernity characterizes itself as the era of worldliness, abandoning all spiritual views of life in favor of profane surfaces, in short the era of secularization.' Vattimo, G., *La fin de la modernité*, p. 106.
77 Habermas, J., *Der philosophische Diskurs der Moderne*, p. 139; Adorno, T. and Horkheimer, M., *Dialektik der Aufklärung*, p. 3.
78 Jameson, F., *Postmoderne und Utopie* p. 73ff.; see also Porter, M. E., *Competitive Strategy*, p. 206ff.
79 Baudrillard, J., *Les stratégies fatales*, p. 79f.
80 Baudrillard, J., *ibid.*, p. 85f.
81 Gumbrecht, H. U., *nach MODERNE ZEITENräume*, p. 64f.; see also Seitz, B., *The Identity of the Subject, after Sartre: An Identity marked by the Denial of Identity*; and Hawthorn, G., *The Impossible Sociology of Postmodern Persons.*
82 Cf. Habermas, J., *Theorie des kommunikativen Handelns*, vol. 2, p. 574 and Lyotard, J. F., *Economie libidinale*, p. 27f.
83 Habermas, J., *Modernity – an Incomplete Project*, p. 59.
84 Giddens, A., *Reason without Revolution*, p. 99.
85 Rorty, R., *Habermas and Lyotard on Postmodernity*, p. 166.

86   Schönherr, H. M., *Die Technik und die Schwäche*, p. 13; Bernstein, R., *Habermas and Modernity*, p. 11; Gadamer, H.-G., *Wahrheit und Methode*, e.g. p. 399ff. and 432ff.

87   Lyotard opposes this view as explained by Schönherr, H. M., *Die Technik und die Schwäche*, p. 13.

88   Lyotard disapproves: Lyotard, J. F., *La condition postmoderne*, p. 102ff. Examples for infinite discussions without hope for consensus à la Lyotard are fractals or paradoxa. For more refer to Seifritz, W., *Wachstum, Rückkoppelung und Chaos*, p. 155ff. and Hofstädter, D., *Gödel, Escher, Bach*; or Krohn, W. and Küppers, G., *Rekursives Durcheinander*.

89   Rorty, R., *Habermas and Lyotard on Postmodernity*, p. 167 and p. 170; Raulet, G., *From Modernity as a One-Way Street to Postmodernity as a Dead End*, p. 68; Koslowski, P., *Prüfungen der Neuzeit*, p. 68ff.; Bernstein, R., *Habermas and Modernity*, p.10.

90   Rorty, R., *Habermas and Lyotard on Postmodernity*, p. 170.

91   Foucault, M. and Raulet, G., *Um welchen Preis sagt die Vernunft die Wahrheit?*, p. 18.

92   Lyotard, J. F., *Le différend*. Use also Chapter 2, III.

93   Lash, S., *Sociology of Postmodernism*, p. 108f. The exact structure of the argument is detailed in Lyotard, J. F., *Réponse à la question: Qu'est-ce que le Postmoderne?*, p. 358.

94   Bernstein, R., *Habermas and Modernity*, p. 5.

95   Lash, S., *Sociology of Postmodernism*, p. 260 and p. 272.

96   Lash, S., *Sociology of Postmodernism*, p. 272f.

97   Kamper, D. and Reijen, W. v., *Die unvollendete Vernunft*.

98   Wolfe, T., *The Bonfire of Vanities*, p. 283.

99   Najita, T., *Culture and Technology*, p. 11.

100 Habermas, J., *Der philosophische Diskurs der Moderne*, p. 111.

101 More on the postmodern view of Marx see: Carver T., *The Postmodern Marx*.

102 ''Tis all in pieces, all coherence gone.' Donne, J., *Anatomy of the World* [written in 1611]; see also Berman, M., *All that is Solid Melts into Air*, p. 15.

103 U. Eco: *Postscriptum to 'In the Name of the Rose'*, p. 77. Haft, A. J., White J. G., White, R. J. and Haft, A. T., *The Key to the Name of the Rose: Including Translations of all Non-English Passages*. See also Lyotard, J. F., *L'inhumain: causeries sur le temps*, p. 13: 'The term postmodern has served, more or less well if judged by the results, to commence this transformation.'

104 Lyotard, J. F., *Postmoderne für Kinder*, p. 33 and p. 73.

105 Lyotard, J. F., *L'inhumain*, p. 43: 'The postmodern is not a new age, that would be just a rewriting of some pre-used concepts of modernity; it is an overhauling of modernity's pretension to ground itself – assisted by science and technology – on the emancipatory project of humanism.' Further explanation is found in Deleuze, G. and Guattari, F., *L'Anti-Oedipe*.

106 Koslowski, P., *Prüfungen der Neuzeit*, p. 41; Raulet, G., *Singuläre Geschichten und pluralistische Ratio*, p. 281.

107 Critics like S. Sonntag argue vehemently against 'the hypertrophy of the intellect at the expense of energy and sensual capability.' Sonntag, S., *Against Interpretation*, p. 7. In economics T. Roszak was one of the voices. Roszak, T., *The Making of a Counter Culture: Reflections on the Technocratic Society and its Youthful Opposition*, p. 232.

108 Habermas, J., *Der philosophische Diskurs der Moderne*, p. 4.

109 Welsch, W., *Postmoderne – Zwischen Indifferenz und Pluralität*, p. 24.

110 Vester, H. G., *Moderne-Postmoderne und Retour*, p. 19. Barker, S., *Signs of Change: Premodern–Modern–Postmodern*; Foster, H., *The Anti-Aesthetic: Essays on Postmodern Culture*, p. 35.

111 Newman, C., *The Post-Modern Aura*, p. 10.

112 Frank, M., *Was ist Neostrukturalismus?*, p. 30.

113 Lima, L. C., *Tropischer Kontrapunkt der Postmoderne?*, p. 571.

114 Harvey, D., *The Condition of Postmodernity*, p. 5.

115 Connoly, W., *The Terms of Political Discourse*, p. 10f.

116 Derrida, J., *Disseminations*, p. 147. Hassan, I., *POSTmodernISM*, p. 6; Hassan, I., *Paracriticisms*, p. 39ff.; Sim, S., *Derrida and the End of History*.

117 Vattimo, G., *La fin de la modernité*, p. 10.

118 Many writers agree to this: Raulet, G., *Singuläre Geschichten und pluralistische Ratio*; Raulet, G., *Modernes et postmodernes*; Raulet, G., *La fin de la raison dans l'histoire*; Ruhloff, J., *Widerstreitende statt harmonische Bildung – Grundzüge eines postmodernen pädagogischen Konzepts*; Engelmann, P., *Zur Ambivalenz von Moderne und Postmoderne*, p. 22. See also Welsch, W., *Die Geburt der postmodernen Philosophie aus dem Geist der modernen Kunst*, p. 15.

119 Scobel, G., *Chaos, Selbstorganisation und das Erhabene*, p. 285 and Welsch, W., *Nach welcher Moderne*, p. 255.

120 Graff, G., *Literature Against Itself: Literary Ideas in Modern Society*, p. 208; Mellard, J. M., *The Exploded Form: The Modernist Novel in America*, p. 140; Bell, D., *The Cultural Contradictions of Capitalism*, p. 51.

121 This figure is analogue Nietzsche's proposal to see nihilism as an unavoidable consequence of the 'old values': 'But why is the dawning on nihilism necessary now? Because the very values we had until now are drawing their logical consequence; because nihilism is the logical finalization of our grand values and ideals; because we have to live nihilism to realize the true value of our values. ... Sooner or later we need new values ...' Nietzsche, F., *Aus dem Nachlass der Achtziger Jahre, Gesammelte Werke*, vol. 3, p. 635.

122 Vattimo, G., *La fin de la modernité*, p. 8f. Later, Vattimo draws a more exact border between 'post-something' and 'postsomething' in contrasting Heidegger's terms 'Verwindung' and 'Überwindung' (getting over with something vs. conquering something). Vattimo, G., *La fin de la modernité*, p. 169.

123 Welsch, W., *Postmoderne – Pluralität als ethischer und politischer Wert*, p. 35; Lyotard, J. F., *Postmoderne für Kinder*, cover text.

124 Huyssen, A., *Mapping the Postmodern*, p. 44.

125 Newman, C., *The Post-Modern Aura*, p. 5.

126 Lyotard, J. F., *Le différend*, p. 262. It may be interesting in the area of language theory to look at the attempts that try to overcome this crisis modernity by creating a Neo-Modernity in response to postmodernity. Zweigle, F., *Topoi der Rotationslyrik – Ein kritischer Beitrag zur Analyse überstrukturierter Texte*, p. 148ff.

127 Welsch, W., *Rückblickend auf einen Streit, der ein Widerstreit bleibt*, p. 7f.; Kamper, D., *Aufklärung – Was sonst?*, p. 44.

128 Kamper, D., *Aufklärung – Was sonst?*, p. 42ff.; Weimann, R., *Ende der Moderne*, p. 51.

129 Writers that see postmodernity as a clear separation from modernity: Lima, L. C., *Tropischer Kontrapunkt der Postmoderne?*; Hassan, I., *POSTmodernISM*; Harvey, D., *The Condition of Postmodernity*, p. 7; Huyssens, A., *Mapping the Postmodern*.

130 Foucault, M., *Of other Spaces*, p. 24.

131 Jameson, F., *Postmoderne und Utopie*, p. 82.

132 Engelmann, P., *Zur Ambivalenz von Moderne und Postmoderne*, p. 22 or Hudson, W., *Zur Frage postmoderner Philosophie*, p. 128.

133 McHale, B., *Postmodern Fiction*, p. 219. See also Harper, P. B., *Framing the Margins: The Social Logic of Postmodern Culture*.

134 Quasi-empirical proofs of the autonomous existence of postmodernity suggest: Vester, H. G., *Moderne-Postmoderne und Retour*, p. 21f.; Naisbitt, J. and Aburdene, P., *Megatrends: Frauen*; Naisbitt, J. and Aburdene, P., *Megatrends 2000*; Popcorn, F., *The Popcorn Report*; Siegel, D., *Futurize your Enterprise*.

135 Spiegel, H., *Revue der alten Republik*.

136   Harvey, D., *The Condition of Postmodernity*, p. 356; Safdie, M., *Architectural Trends*.
137   N. Postman argues against discontinuity and the sense of being lost to reorientate our-
      selves to the Enlightenment's philosophers as a positioning system. The age of reason as
      an antidote to the hazy values of postmodernism. Postman, N., *Building a Bridge to the
      18th Century: How the Past can Improve our Future*. See likewise Vladislav, L. and
      Inozemtsev, V. L., *The Constitution of the Post-Economic State: Post Industrial Theories
      and Post-Economic Trends in the Contemporary World*.
138   Whitehouse, I., *A Reading of the Postmodern*, p. 140; Cloyd, J. T., *Postmodern Praxis
      in Politics*.
139   Levin, C., *Art and the Sociological Ego*, p. 44.
140   Gardbaum, S. A., *Liberalism, Postmodernism, Antimodernism*; Rothleder, D., *The
      Work of Friendship: Rorty, His Critics, and the Project of Solidarity*. For an overview
      by Rorty himself, take Rorty, R., *Achieving Our Country: Leftist Thought in Twentieth
      Century America*.
141   Rorty, R., *Philosophy and the Mirror of Nature*.
142   For a critical view of Rorty's political philosophy see Gander, E., *The Last Conceptual
      Revolution: a Critique of Richard Rorty's Political Philosophy*; Rothleder, D., *The Work
      of Friendship: Rorty, His Critics, and the Project of Solidarity*; Melkonian, M., *Richard
      Rorty's Politics: Liberalism at the End of the American Century*.
143   Cho, H. T., *Postmodern Philosophy, Relativism, and a Renewed Vision of Education*,
      S. 28; Carr, D., *Education, Knowledge, and Truth: Beyond the Postmodern Impasse*.
144   Habermas, J., *Modernity – An Incomplete Project*, p. 9; Rorty, R., *Habermas and
      Lyotard on Postmodernity*, p. 167.
145   Schrag, C. O., *Communicative Praxis and the Space of Activity*, p. 94f.; more explications
      can be found in Wildermuth, A., *Postmoderne Aufklärung*, p. 35.
146   Rorty, R., *Hermeneutics, General Studies, and Teaching*, p. 2. Vehemently opposing
      from a spirutal view argues: McCallum, D., *The Death of Truth*.
147   Rorty, R., *Consequences of Pragmatism*, p. 161; Gutting, G., *Pragmatic Liberalism and
      the Critique of Modernity*; Critchley, S., Derrida, J., Laclau, E. and Rorty, R., *Decon-
      struction and Pragmatism*; Festenstein, M., *Pragmatism and Political Theory: From
      Dewey to Rorty* and King, U., *Faith and Praxis in a Postmodern Age*, p. 60.
148   Rorty, R., *Contingency, Irony, and Solidarity*, p. 5.
149   Maturana, H. and Varela, F., *Der Baum der Erkenntnis*.
150   Autopoiese: gr., aùtopoietikós developed, created by itself, from within.
151   Maturana, H. and Varela, F., *Der Baum der Erkenntnis*, p. 50 and p. 54.
152   Maturana, H. and Varela, F., *Der Baum der Erkenntnis*, p. 185.
153   Jameson, F., *Postmoderne und Utopie*, p. 89. The interested reader refers to: Whorf,
      B. L., *Sprache – Denken – Wirklichkeit*, p. 12. Earlier, Gadamer mentions similar ideas:
      '...all forms of human community are necessarily forms of language communities'.
      Gadamer, H.-G., *Wahrheit und Methode*; Quote p. 422. See also p. 450 and Gadamer,
      H.-G., *Begriffsgeschichte und die Sprache der Philosophie*, p. 10.
154   Frank, M., *Was ist Neostrukturalismus?*, p. 201f.; see also generally: Wildermuth, A.,
      Postmoderne Aufklärung, p. 8.
155   According to this view, no common language exists, on which orchestrated social
      behaviour or sensible individual action can be founded. Cf. Lyotard, J. F., *La condition
      postmoderne*, p. 11; Lyotard, J. F., *Le différend*, p. 231 and p. 263.
156   Harvey, D., *The Condition of Postmodernity*, p. 46.
157   Quote: Foucault, M., *Languages, Counter Memory, Practice*, p. 54; Zweigle, F., *Topoi
      der Rotationslyrik: Ein kritischer Beitrag zur Analyse überstrukturierter Texte*, p. 69f.
158   Rorty, R., *Philosophy and the Mirror of Nature*, p. 36f. Quote: Whitehouse, I., *A Reading
      of the Postmodern*, p. 87.

159 Nietzsche, F., *Aus dem Nachlass der Achtziger Jahre, Gesammelte Werke*, vol. 4, p. 769. Refer also to Friedman, M., *Essays in Positive Economics*, p. 55ff.

160 Rorty, R., *Philosophy and the Mirror of Nature*, p. 316 and p. 377; Cloyd, J. T., *Introduction: Postmodern Praxis in Politics*; Dwight, T. H., *Quotation: Tracing Postmodernism in Washington*.

161 Rorty, R., *Philosophy and the Mirror of Nature*, p. 377; Gibbons, M. T., *The Ethic of Postmodernism*.

162 Quote: Rorty, R., *Philosophy as a Kind of Writing*, p. 90. Rorty elaborates this further in Rorty, R., *Truth and Progress*. See also Mounce, H. O., *The Two Pragmatisms: From Peirce to Rorty*.

163 McCallum, D., *The Death of Truth: What's Wrong with Multiculturalism: the Rejection of Reason and the New Postmodern Diversity*, p. 75.

164 Jäger, M., *Das Problem der Namen bei Lyotard*, p. 104.

165 Schmid, G., *Geschichtsbilder und die unendliche Schreibbarkeit*, p. 301. Schmid attempts to reinterpret the elements of modern crisis (Chapter 2, section III – knowledge as the powerhouse) constructively as positive points of departure.

166 For more on the loss of identity see Anderson, W., *The Future of the Self: Inventing the Postmodern Person*.

167 Weizenbaum, J., *Die Mucht der Computer und die Ohnmucht der Vernuft*.

168 Huyssen, A., *Mapping the Postmodern*, p. 191f.

169 See Anonymous, *Acht für eine bessere Welt* and Amato, J., *Bookend: Anatomies of a Virtual Self*.

170 Baudrillard, J., *L'échange symbolique et la mort*.

171 Harvey, D., *The Condition of Postmodernity*, p. 113 and Raja, T. and Sarup, M., *Identity, Culture and the Postmodern World*, p. 60.

172 Anders, G., *Die Antiquiertheit des Menschen*.

173 Lash, S., *Sociology of Postmodernism*, p. 22.

174 Greiner, B., *Die Hamletmaschine*, p. 76f.; see also Wildermuth, A., *Multikulturelle Gesellschaft*, p. 5.

175 Lash, S., *Sociology of Postmodernism*, p. 25 and p. 112; see also Chapter 2, section III (postmodernism).

176 Bourdieu, P., *Champs intellectuels et projet créateur*, p. 867ff.; Bourdieu P., *La distinction*, p. 70ff. and p. 255ff.

177 Guillaume, M., *Post-Moderne Effekte der Moderne*, p. 75.

178 Baudrillard, J., *Les strategies fatales*, p. 51ff.; Lyotard, J. F., *Histoire universelle et différences culturelles*, p. 564; Schmid, G., *Geschichtsbilder und die unendliche Schreibbarkeit*.

179 Malraux, A., *Liberation*, p. 208. What happens in Beirut today will be happening in Marseille tomorrow. Scholl Latour, P., *Leben mit Frankreich*, quote p. 262; see also p. 371 and p. 636.

180 To detect and map these convolutions and conflicts is one of the tasks of philosophy and of writing. Anonymous: *Témoigner du différend – quand phraser ne se peut. Autour de Jean-François Lyotard*, p. 119.

181 Wellmer, A., *Zur Dialektik von Moderne und Postmoderne: Vernunftkritik nach Adorno*, p. 109.

182 Kunneman, H., *Der Wahrheitstrichter*, p. 304ff.; Lyotard, J. F., *Le différend*, p. 309; Wildermuth, A., *Multikulturelle Gesellschaft*, p. 5.

183 Lyotard, J. F., *Eine post-moderne Fabel über die Postmoderne*, p. 296f.

184 Derrida, J., *Gammatologie*, p. 45; see also Wilke, S., *Adorno and Derrida as Readers of Husserl: Some Reflections on the Historical Context of Modernism and Postmodernism*.

185 Derrida, J., *Die Schrift und die Differenz*, p. 446; Shapiro, S. G., *Teaching Postmodernism in a Values Elective*.

186 Newman, C., *The Post-Modern Aura*, p. 34 and p. 135.
187 Gasché, R., *Infrastructures and Systematicity*, p. 7f.
188 Derrida, J., *Disseminations*, p. 220.
189 Stam, R., *Mikhail Bakthin and the Left Cultural Critique*, p. 128; Jameson, F., *Post-modernism and Consumer Society*, p. 8ff.
190 Bell, D., *The Cultural Contradictions of Capitalism*, p. 51.
191 Welsch, W., *Postmoderne – Pluralität als ethischer und politischer Wert*, p. 43.
192 In real life, it is practically impossible to herald any part of society as being the torch-bearers of emancipation and social development. The elite is resocialized, the bourgeois and the proletariate has succumbed to the debility of consumer society, aesthetics is degraded to a lifestyle. Any real avant-garde is submerged into thousands of sub-avant-gardes and would-be avant-gardes. There is no grand social movement, but only a loud cacophony of singular interests. This is pointed out in Feyerabend, P., *Erkenntnis für freie Menschen*, p. 38 and p. 73.
193 Lyotard, J. F., *Postmoderne für Kinder*, p. 110. Related views in Habermas, J., *Theorie des kommunikativen Handelns*, vol. 2, p. 533.
194 Welsch, W., *Unsere postmoderne Moderne*, p. 194; see also Habermas, J., *Theorie des kommunikativen Handelns*, vol. 1, p. 232f.; Hawthorn, G., *The Impossible Sociology of Postmodern Persons*.
195 A conceptual analysis gives Bourdieu, P., *La Distinction*, p. 191; it is further developed by Munéva, G., *Radical Knowledge*; critical: Kuntz-Brenner, R., *Ästhetik verkommt zum Lebensstil*.
196 Goodman, N., *The Structure of Appearance*, p. xxvii and p. 16ff.; Goodman, N., *The Way the World is; Rorty, R., The World well lost*.
197 Goodman, N., *Of Mind and Other Matters*, p. 33.
198 Habermas, J., *Theorie des kommunikativen Handelns*, 2 vols, p. 587.
199 Lutz, R., *Die unbewusste Revolution*, p. 74.
200 Henderson, H., *Global Denken, lokal Handeln*, p. 281; Johnson-Lenz, P. and Johnson-Lenz, T., *Soziale Vernetzung*, p. 342.
201 Deleuze, G. and Guattari, F., *Rhizom*. This term will be used extensively in Chapters 4 and 5. See also Bogue, R., *Gilles Deleuze: Postmodern Philosopher?* And, by the way, what else is the Internet but a rhizome?
202 See also the text on graphs, cliques and *batzm* in Chapter 3, IV, and 1, I. Cf. Blom, A. 'The Closing of the American Mind', p. 374ff.
203 Bernstein, R., *Beyond Objectivism and Relativism: Science Hermeneutics and Praxis*, p. 18.
204 Rorty, R., *Consequences of Pragmatism*, p. 166.
205 Cf. Smith, B., *Value without Truth-Value*.
206 Goodman, N., *Ways of Worldmaking*.
207 Cf. Popper, K. R., *Die Logik der Forschung*.
208 Cronin, C., De Greif, P. and Habermas, J., *The Inclusion of the Other: Studies in Political Theory*, p. 87.
209 Bernstein, R., *Beyond Objectivism and Relativism: Science Hermeneutics and Praxis*, p. 168.
210 Rorty, R., *Consequences of Pragmatism*, p. 166; Rorty, R., *Hermeneutics, General Studies, and Teaching*, p. 5 and Rorty, R., *Philosophy and Social Hope*, p. 55.
211 Rorty, R., *Consequences of Pragmatism*, p. xxxviii.
212 Rorty, R., *Consequences of Pragmatism*, p. 166.
213 Cf. Taylor, C., *Human Agency and Language*, p. 8. 'Worldmaking as we know it always starts from worlds already on hand; the making is a remaking.' Goodman, N., *Ways of Worldmaking*, p. 6. Similarly, Harris sees culture as a narrative: Harris, M., *Theories of Culture in Postmodern Times*.

214 Rejecting this view and summarizing communities as 'phantom' communities thus claiming the impossibility of such a project, Durham just ignores the vivid argument that all the Internet communities provide. Durham, S., *Phantom Communities: The Simulacrum and the Limits of Postmodernism.* As 'markets consist of conversations' an open and multiple exchange between persons of some common ground provide the stability of a network This is the secret of success of the Internet. Siegel, D., *Futurize your Enterprise*, p. 5 and p. 43.

215 Synonymous terms are: Self-supporting, autopoietisch, endogenous, network-like, rhizomatic, fractal, self-organizing, self-referential.

216 Rorty R., *Habermas and Lyotard on Postmodernity*, p. 161; cf. Feyerabend, P., *Erkenntnis für freie Menschen*, p. 73ff.

217 Among others: Popcorn, F., *The Popcorn Report.*

218 Lash, S., *Sociology of Postmodernism*, p. 116 and Kaplan, C., *Questions of Travel: Postmodern Discourses of Displacement.*

219 Refer also to Chapter 2, section III on Habermas.

220 A concise summary of the opposing positions can be found in: Rorty, R., *Habermas and Lyotard on Postmodernity*, p. 161f. Cf. also Lima, L. C., *Tropischer Kontrapunkt der Postmoderne?*, p. 574ff. A detailed overview of similarities between Habermas and Lyotard is offered by Lash, S., *Sociology of Postmodernism*, p. 112ff.

221 Kunneman, H., *Der Wahrheitstrichter*, p. 9.

222 Lyotard, J. F., *La condition postmoderne.*

223 Lyotard, J. F., *La culpabilité allemande*; Lyotard, J. F., *Le contenu social de la lutte algérienne*; Lyotard, J. F., *L'Algérie sept ans aprés*; Lyotard, J. F., *Dérive à partir de Marx et Freud*; Lyotard, J. F., *Petite économie libidinale d'un dispositif narratif*; Lyotard, J. F., *Esquisse d'une économie de'l hyperréalisme.* Apex of this development is seen in Lyotard, J. F., *Economie libidinale.*

224 Lyotard, J. F., *Economie libidinale*, preface.

225 For an exhaustive critique of Lyotard's general position: Perger, J., *Jean-François Lyotard, eine Position mit oder ohne Zukunft?*; Taureck, B., *Wo steht Lyotard?* p. 185f.

226 Lyotard, J. F., *Economie libidinale*, p. 164ff.

227 Nietzsche, F., *Götzendämmerung*, p. 958.

228 Cf. Lyotard, J. F., *Economie libidinale*, p. 311.

229 'The big, unifying theory has lost its credibility.' Lyotard, J. F., *La condition postmoderne*, p. 63. See also: Gibson, A., *Towards a Postmodern Theory of Narrative.*

230 Lyotard, J. F., *La condition postmoderne*, p. 51 and p. 89.

231 P. Feyerabend talks about an 'Ocean of incommensurable alternatives'. Feyerabend, P., *Wider den Methodenzwang*, p. 34.

232 See Whitehouse, I., *A Reading of the Postmodern*, p. 209 or Marsh, J. L., *Strategies of Evasion: The Paradox of Self-referentiality and the Postmodern Critique of Rationality.*

233 Cf. Lyotard, J. F., *La condition postmoderne*, p. 7. Lyotard attacks persistently the incredibility of all grand narrations (grand narratives). By this he describes all 'big stories' like the liberation of man by technology, the emancipation of the proletariate, etc.

234 Derrida, J., *Die Schrift und die Differenz*, p. 446. Derrida conceives this not as negative destruction but as a (subversive) dissection, a new reading of the elements and their novel assembly.

235 Lyotard, J. F., *La condition postmoderne*, p. 66f.

236 Lyotard, J. F., *Le différend*, p. 197. See also Carroll, D., *Paraesthetics: Foucault, Lyotard, Derrida.*

237 Schumpeter, J., *Theorie der wirtschaftlichen Entwicklung*, p. 100f.

238 Lyotard, J. F., *La condition postmoderne*, p. 22f. He describes the basic rules a language game must possess. These can serve as the smallest common denominator for all general contracts in the game of games (games between language games).

239 gr., pará lógou – talking aside; a separate meaning; pará lógon – a reply.

240 Lyotard, J. F., *La condition postmoderne*, p. 96.

241 Lyotard, J. F., *La condition postmoderne*, p. 97.

242 'The postmodern knowledge ... heightens our sensitivity to the nuances and increases our capability to stand the incommensurable.' Lyotard, J. F., *La condition postmoderne*, p. 8f. Hassan points out that the sum of all small narratives is much more innovative and variable that any monotonous unity of no matter what. Hassan, I., *Ideas of Cultural Change*, p. 23.

243 Lyotard, J. F., *La condition postmoderne*, p. 102f.

244 In the context of multinational enterprises M. Casson's remarks on trust and contracts are in accordance with this view. Cf. Chapter 5, section II (systems perspective).

245 Lyotard, J. F., *La condition postmoderne*, p. 107.

246 The enigmatic character of this book may have brought about its fame, potentially just because everybody could use the brilliant analysis as a disguise to manipulate the postmodern debate through interpreting the book according to ones liking.

247 Baudrillard, J., *Oublier Foucault*, p. 9.

248 Reese-Schäfer, W., *Vom Erhabenen zum Sublimen ist es nur ein Schritt*, p. 186.

249 Lyotard, J. F., *Le différend*, p. 10f.

250 Lyotard, J. F., *Le différend*, p. 89. Consequently, Lyotard sees the world as a mesh of signs. 'By world I understand a pool of nouns.' Lyotard, J. F., *Le différend*, p. 121. The term 'the world' is a problem in itself as there is no one, single and unique world: 'There is never just one world but worlds (each with different languages and histories).' Lyotard, J. F., *Le différend*, p. 231.

251 Lyotard, J. F., *Le différend*, p. 31; see also p. 64 and p. 67 as well as Lyotard, J. F., *Economie libidinale*, p. 75ff.

252 'By necessity, deconstruction has work from inside out, using all subversive strategies and economic remnants of the old structures. To uses them in a structural manner, that is using the building blocks without being able to splinter off unwanted parts.' Derrida, J., *Gammatologie*, p. 45.

253 Lash, S., *Sociology of Postmodernism*, p. 194 and p. 279f.; Sassower, R. and Ogaz, C. P., *Philosophical Hierarchies and Lyotard's Dichotomies*.

254 Lyotard, J. F., *Le différend*, p. 227; see also Rojek, C., Turner, B. S. and Lyotard, J. F., *The Politics of Jean Francois: Justice and Political Theory*; Wildermuth, A., *Multikulturelle Gesellschaft*, p. 9.

255 'Differing from a court case, the conflict [différend] is a battle between two (or more) parties where a equitable ruling is impossible due to the lack of rules to judge by the two different arguments. That one of it may be legitimate, does not mean the other is not. ... Any attempt at creating a general rule to judge the different worlds is bound to falter.' Lyotard, J. F., *Le différend*, p. 9.

256 Lyotard, J. F., *Le différend*, p. 189ff.

257 Lyotard, J. F., *Le différend*, p. 223. '[... to search for] a policy for equally treating the quest for justice and for the unknown.' Lyotard, J. F., *La condition postmoderne*, p. 108.

258 This oppression of other paradigms is total and abolutistic, for reality is only the officially allowed, the established one, where the scientific system reigns monopolistically. Lyotard, J. F., *Le différend*, p. 18; see also Wilson, R. A., *Die neue Inquisition*.

259 Lyotard, J. F., *La condition postmoderne*, p. 106.

260 'Let's be pagans!' Lyotard, J. F. and Thebaud, J. L., *Au juste – conversations*, p. 33; Lyotard, J. F., *Instructions paiennes*. This motto is an ideal that Nietzsche would have

approved. Nietzsche, F., *Der Antichrist*, p. 1223 and Nietzsche, F., *Aus dem Nachlass der Achtziger Jahre*, p. 835.

261 Lyotard, J. F., *La condition postmoderne*, p. 14, p. 36ff. p. 52f. p. 84; Lyotard, J. F., *Le différend*, p. 18 and p. 189ff.

262 Lyotard writes about a general 'hegemony of the economic'. Lyotard, J. F., *Le différend*, p. 255. See also Lyotard, J. F., *Le différend*, p. 28 and p. 251ff. and Lyotard, J. F., *La condition postmoderne*, p. 16, p. 73f. p. 79 and p. 84.

263 '... post modern culture is ESSENTIALLY ECONOMIC.' [bold in the original] Newman, C., *The Post-Modern Aura*, p. 197; Harvey, D., *The Condition of Postmodernity*, p. 147ff.; Wagner, B., *PostModerne oder PostFordismus*, p. 119; Koslowski, P., *Die postmoderne Kultur*, p. 104ff.

264 Sarup, M., *An Introductory Guide to Poststructuralism and Postmodernism*, p. 131.

265 Sarup, M., *An Introductory Guide to Poststructuralism and Postmodernism*, p. 119f. F. Jameson is a clear proponent of the thesis that postmodern concepts mirror current economic structures (and vice versa). 'The postmodern is the cultural epidermis of the computer-based multinational capitalism'. Jameson, F., *Postmodernism and Consumer Society*, p. 57. Jameson, F., *Postmoderne – Zur Logik der Kultur im Spätkapitalismus*.

266 Jameson, F., *Postmoderne – Zur Logik der Kultur im Spätkapitalismus*, p. 57.

267 Lyotard, J. F., *L'inhumain: causeries sur le temps*, p. 22.

268 Lyotard, J. F., *Grabmal des Intellektuellen*, p. 37. This commercialization of knowledge, this adaptation of science generated – with the aid of technology – our information society. See also Sarup, M., *An Introductory Guide to Poststructuralism and Postmodernism*, p. 118 and p. 123ff.

269 'The know-how is the main ingredient of production.' Lyotard, J. F., *La condition postmoderne*, p. 14; see also in support p. 16 and p. 82ff.

270 Lyotard, J. F., *La condition postmoderne*, p. 73f.

271 Neef, D., Siesfield, T. and Cefola, J., *The Economic Impact of Knowledge*; Siegel, D., *Futurize your Enterprise*, p. 66.

272 Lyotard, J. F., *La condition postmoderne*, p. 16 and p. 107.

273 Harvey, D., *The Condition of Postmodernity*, p. 20 and p. 159; Wagner, B., *PostModerne oder PostFordismus*, p. 110f.

274 Weizenbaum, J., *Die Macht der Computer und der Ohnmacht der Vernunft*. The state as economic actor will be more and more a by-stander. This is why Lyotard can speak of an end of the history of states. More than anything else, capital is transnational, or more concise: non-national. It thrives on differences (interest rates, currencies, investment climates ...) and uses nations in a truly postmodern manner only as short term resting places. Elaborated in Lyotard, J. F., *Die Mauer des Pazifik*, p. 62 and Lyotard, J. F., *Immaterialität und Postmoderne*, p. 47. This radical utilitarian flexibility weakens constantly the state and will be a contributing cause to the end of nations as such. See also Bell, D., *Die dritte technologische Revolution und ihre möglichen sozioökonomischen Konsequenzen*; Lash, S. and Urry, J., *The End of Organized Capitalism*, p. 208f.; and especially Ohmae, K., *The Borderless World*.

275 Years ago, D. Bell forecasted this: '[T]he big corporations are shifting from an economizing mode of activity in which all aspects of organization are single-mindly reduced to becoming means to the goal of production and profit to a socializing mode.' Bell, D., *The Coming of Postindustrial Society*, p. 284; see also Dwight, T. H., *Quotation: Tracing Postmodernism in Washington*. Sauer and Wayne interpret this development as a tendency towards nihilism, antinationalism and technocracy, which is in a way correct; however the negative connotations are misguiding and should be replaced by more positive ones as paralogy and plurality of standpoints (or nihilism), globality (or antinationalism), and technological breakthroughs (or technocracy) are exactly the features of a postmodern

New Economy. Sauer-Thompson, G. and Wayne Smith, J., *Beyond Economics: Post-modernity, Globalization and National Sustainability*. See also Jameson, F. and Miyoshi, M., *The Cultures of Globalization*.
276 Lyotard, J. F., *Le différend*, p. 296; Bertens, H., *The postmodern Weltanschauung and its Relation with Modernism*, p. 33 and Lash, S., *Sociology of Postmodernism*, p. 96ff. For a more general treatment: Neef, D., Siesfield, T. and Cefola, J., *The Economic Impact of Knowledge*.
277 Welsch, W., *Vernunft im Übergang*, p. 30.
278 Weimann, R., *Das Ende der Moderne?*, p. 10.
279 Whole industries live from packaging with symbols: directly the advertising industry; indirectly the fragrances, beer, fashion, and car industries. Everywhere, where extreme markets are targeted (high-end, luxury or markets with fierce competition), the symbolic is the competitive advantage.
280 Jameson, F., *Postmoderne: zur Logik der Kultur im Spätkapitalismus*, p. 48f.
281 Pêcheux, M., *Les vérités de la palice*, p. 144. M. Foucault talks about 'a pre-coded inter-pretation'. See also Foucault, M., *Les mots et les choses*, p. 12.
282 Three real life examples: CNN has completed its strategy of creating a global network of information to create total simultaneity of all things happening on this planet. In New York some pilot-project shower test-households with over 150 TV-channels on top of a variety of Tele-shopping and Tele-Videostore opportunities. Also in New York an 'Ecology-CNN' ('Alternative Cable Network' – ACN) has started. Soon every possible target group has its own TV-world. And we do not even talk about the devastating effects the Internet brings about ... For more, see Anonymous, *Acht für eine bessere Welt*; also Wildermuth, A., *Postmoderne Aufklärung*, p. 30.
283 Baudrillard, J., *L'échange symbolique et la mort*, p. 28f. and Lash, S., *Sociology of Postmodernism*, p. 195.
284 Baudrillard, J., *L'échange symbolique et la mort*, p. 40f. In Derrida's view there is no privileged reference, no single origin anymore. Derrida, J., *L'écriture et la différence*, p. 419; see also Wagner, B., *PostModerne oder PostFordismus*, p. 117f.
285 Baudrillard, J., *Le systéme des objets*, p. 262ff. and Baudrillard, J., *La société de con-sommation*, p. 21. Supporting: Jameson, F., *Postmodernism, or the Cultural Logic of Late Capitalism*, p. 85f.
286 This is also the reason why brands (and trade marks, logos, generally images often used by a company) are seen as immaterial goods, ready to be developed, traded, copied. A well rounded portfolio of brands (a system of symbols) can alone secure the success of a company. (Coca Cola, Philip Morris, Disney)
287 Lash, S., *Sociology of Postmodernism*, p. 43. and Jameson, F. and Miyoshi, M., *The Cultures of Globalization*. For a discussion on Japan see: Harris, M., *Theories of Culture in Postmodern Times*.
288 Baudrillard, J., *L'échange symbolique et la mort*, p. 369 and Baudrillard, J., *De la séduction*, p. 78. A practical example is the boom on falsified luxury goods like watches, designer clothing or sports cars. Things get more tricky in the art business: fakes of famous counterfeiters are regarded as valuable originals (of this counterfeiter), Copies, that are made with the approval of the artist, are cherished as originals. In what category pictures sold under the name 'Mark Kostabi' fall, requires almost medieval sophism, as the artist uses his brush only to put his signature on the pictures, which were executed by hired manual workers. Perhaps this is the beginning of the application of brand management in art ? E. C. Gattinara demands therefore a 'Phenomenology of the impure'. Gattinara, E. C., *Die Offenheit des Erhabenen in Kunst Philosophie und Wissen-schaft*, p. 136f.; refer also to McLuhan, M., *Understanding Media*, p. 57ff.; Anonymous, *Metamorphosen*.

289 Watson questions the need for countries and nations in times of globality. Yet using Canada as an example, he stresses the need for a common ground (maybe Rorty's campfire is appropriate in the Canadian context). This is how virtual citizens come to existence, while the state dies. Watson, W., *Globalization and the Meaning of Canadian Life*, p. 45 and p. 232.

290 Baudrillard, J., *Oublier Foucault*, p. 41 and Baudrillard, J., *Kool Killer – der Aufstand der Zeichen*, p. 70.

291 It would make an interesting study to analyse the existence of the Japanese idea of a godly king (Tenno) with this tool: a powerful symbol (following the equation: '{Universe = God = Ruler of the world = Emperor = us Japanese}'), that is regarded by the Japanese as unreal and outdated, nevertheless creates the most intense emotions in discussions. For further literature use Schwalbe, H., *Japan*, p. 75ff. and also Bock, F., *Das grosse Fest der Thronbesteigung*; Lokowandt, E., *Das japanische Kaisertum – Religiöse Fundierung und politische Realität*; Anonymous, *Ancient Food Offering Rituals are performed by Emperor*. For the embedded symbolism and its political implications: Kong, K. D., *Tenno Faschismus*, passim and p. 15ff. and 139ff.

292 Fekete, J., *Vampire Value, Infinitive Art, and Literary Theory*, p. 71; Baudrillard, J., *Oublier Foucault*, p. 49.

293 For a deeper insight on the subject see Downs, A., *Beyond the Looking Glass: Overcoming the Seductive Culture of Corporate Narcissism*.

294 Baudrillard, J., *Les stratégies fatales* S 62f.; Baudrillard, J., *L'échange symbolique et la mort*, p. 368; Harvey, D., *The Condition of Postmodernity*, p. 285; Raulet, G., *Die neue Utopie*, p. 300f. In a side argument Baudrillard expands this thought in interpreting this compulsion to liquefy, to float and to circulate to be sexually inspired. Total uninhibitedness is required, no fixations or constraints are allowed. By doing so, Baudrillard promotes the homo sexualis as being equal to the homo oeconomicus. Baudrillard, J., *Oublier Foucault*, p. 41. In support of this: Lyotard, J. F., *Economie libidinale*, p. 54, p. 132 and p. 165. In *Symbolic exchange and death* J. Baudrillard expostulates the existence of an economic subject, of a homo oeconomicus; this fiction existed only in the coding of the economic myths. Baudrillard, J., *L'échange symbolique et la mort*, p. 338.

295 Lyotard, J. F., *Réponse à la question: Qu'est-ce que le Postmoderne?*, p. 357.

296 This passage draws on Baudrillard, J., *Pour une critique de l'économie politique du signe*, p. 130ff.

297 Lyotard criticizes this theory in his economics of desires: Lyotard, J. F., *Economie libidinale*, p. 158f. For a more positive analysis: Jameson, F., *Postmodernism, or the Cultural Logic of Late Capitalism*, p. 395f.

298 Just compare the social status of a Hermes shopping bag to one given out by Wal-Mart.

299 As a business consequence, money is seen in the financial world just as a resource, which can be exploited, refined, processed, and recycled. It is therewith totally incompatible to the everyday money, with which labour is translated into goods. Compare Deleuze, G. and Guattari, F., *L'Anti-Oedipe*, p. 273. Lyotard is somewhat more naïve when talking about trade in non-tradeables, or fluttering prices ('flottant'; floating around). He clearly misjudges the aggressiveness and fierceness of these dynamics. Lyotard, J. F., *Economie libidinale*, p. 124, p. 258 and p. 315ff.

300 Lash, S., *Sociology of Postmodernism*, p. 40ff.

301 Deleuze, G. and Guattari, F., *L'Anti-Oedipe*, p. 9 and p. 36. Quote: p. 64.

302 A candid but more journalistic overview gives Lewis, M., *Liar's Poker*. An excellent deeper analysis of this character is Ellis, B. E., *American Psycho*, p. 90, p. 216 and p. 279. In the dissolution of the subject ('... my mask of sanity was a victim of impending slippage...'. 'I am utterly insane.') coupled with the unfruitful trial of identifying the

self via luxury consumption ('... gently stroking my Rolex ...') this novel resembles
in message and form its Japanese (and female) counterpart 'Nanotaku kuistaru'.
Cf. Chapter 2, section IV.

303   'Justice is dead. ... Reflection is useless, the world is senseless. Evil is its only permanence.
God is not alive. Love cannot be trusted. Surface surface surface was all anyone found
meaning in. ... I want no one to escape ... this is no time for the innocent.' That is the
whole credo of these human beings. The novel's last sentence reads accordingly: 'This is
not an exit.' Ellis, B. E., *American Psycho*, p. 375ff. and p. 399.

304   Nietzsche, F., *Die fröhliche Wissenschaft*, p. 15.

305   Habermas, J., *Modernity versus Postmodernity*, p. 13.

306   Nietzsche, F., *Die fröhliche Wissenschaft*, p. 15; Habermas, J., *Modernity versus
Postmodernity*, p. 13.

307   Lash, S., *Sociology of Postmodernism*, p. 26 and Harvey, D., *The Condition of Postmodernity*, p. 83; Sassower, R. and Ogaz, C. P., *Philosophical Hierarchies and Lyotard's
Dichotomies*.

308   Kunneman, H., *Der Wahrheitstrichter*, p. 3.

309   Compare especially Chapter 4, section III (Japanese decision-making).

310   Young Urban Professional; Dual Income No Kids; European and Raving and
EuroRail; Young, European and Proud of it; and all the other fast changing acronyms.

311   Lash, S., *Sociology of Postmodernism*, p. 112.

312   Bourdieu, P., *Champs intellectuels et projet créateur*, p. 865f. and Bourdieu, P., *Outline of
a Theory of Practice*, p. 14f.

313   Bourdieu, P., *La distinction*, p. 271ff. This can be pushed farther: no truth without
groups. A stringent consequence of the denial of the 'written', the existence of meaning
in texts, is necessarily the impossiblility of meaningful statements about reality if there
were not the reference groups. Cf. Angermüller, J., *Derrida vs. Bourdieu: Sociologizing
Deconstruction, Deconstructing the Social*.

314   Lyotard, J. F. *La condition postmoderne*, p. 34; Lash, S., *Sociology of Postmodernism*,
p. 112. On the settlement of the debate on the subject by dissolving the self: Foucault,
M., *Les mots et les choses*, p. 462.

315   This is equivalent to Lyotard's 'intellectual tourism'. Lyotard, J. F., *Postmodern Fables*.
Cf. Jameson, F., *Postmoderne – Zur Logik der Kultur im Spätkapitalismus*, p. 45f.; Lash,
S., *Sociology of Postmodernism*, p. 22 and p. 153. Kaplan, C., *Question of Travel:
Postmodern Discourses on Displacement*.

316   Welsch, W., *Wege aus der Moderne*, p. 40f. Here, Nietzsche's conviction that the 'I', the
ego is a vain, evasive and ambiguous fiction regains validity. Nietzsche, F., *Jenseits von
Gut und Böse*, p. 565 and Nietzsche, F., *Aus dem Nachlass der Achtziger Jahre*, p. 473
and p. 534.

317   'Everyone is sent back to himself. And everyone knows how little that is.' Each subject,
seen as a information processing unit, is able to make moves in the language game; each
with equal rights (though dependent on their level of information). Lyotard, J. F.,
La condition postmoderne, p. 31f., quote p. 30.

318   Baudrillard, J., *La société de consommation*, p. 25.

319   Toffler, A., *Future Shock*, p. 40 and p. 33; Gappert, G., *Post-Affluent America*; Sennett, R., *The Corrrosion of Character: The Personal Consequence of Work in the New
Capitalism*, p. 116.

320   'This new, postmodern capitalism maintains to have no choice, forced by the convincing
power of the facts (i.e. the world market) but to comply without hesitation and without
legitimation. Therefore, the exhaustion of the social cohesive energy, the destabilization
of the citizen's community is pushed further.' Lyotard, J. F., *Das Erhabene und die
Avantgarde*, p. 273.

321 Bell, D., *The Cultural Contradictions of Capitalism*, p. 197ff.; Harvey, D., *The Condition of Postmodernity*, p. 201; Docherty, T., *After Theory*, p. 200.
322 Compare Lyotard's much cited version of this: Lyotard, J. F., *Réponse à la question: Qu'est-ce que le Post-moderne?*, p. 361; Lyotard, J. F., *Postmoderne für Kinder*, p. 19f. See also Lash, S., *Sociology of Postmodernism*, p. 47f. and p. 106f.
323 Anonymous, *Global Banking*.
324 Schmidt, B., *Postmoderne wird sich nicht vollziehen*, p. 100; Bourdieu, P., *Outline of a Theory of Practice*, p. 163; Raulet, G., *Die neue Utopie*, p. 285; see also Wildermuth, A., *Postmoderne Aufklärung*.
325 Neef, D., Siesfield, T. and Cefola, J., *The Economic Impact of Knowledge*; Siegel, D., *Futurize your Enterprise*, p. 66.
326 'prudence, judiciousness', Lyotard, J. F., *Le différend*, p. 29 and Lyotard, J. F., *Immaterialität und Postmoderne*, p. 43f.
327 Gernalzick stresses the economic nucleus of postmodern concepts of man, and asks for a new catalogue of skills necessary to excel. Gernalzick, N., *Gegen eine Metaphysik der Arbeit: Der Ökonomiebegriff der Dekonstruktion und im Poststrukturalismus [Against a Metaphysics of Work: The Definition of Economic in Deconstructionism and Poststructuralism]*. The counterexamples: Theory X, Theory Y, Theory Z, Leadership theories are catchphrases for this. Details are to be found in the standard pertinent literature: e.g. Wunderer, R. and Grunwald, W., *Führungslehre*, vol. 1, p. 80ff.; Staehle, W. H., *Organisation und Führung soziotechnischer Systeme*, p. 102; Colin, J. M., *After X and Y comes Z*, p. 56f.; Holdt, D. H., *Management*, p. 434ff. and Koontz, H., *The Management Theory*, p. 174f.
328 gr., aisthanomai: to perceive, to sense. Compare Welsch, W., *Postmoderne – Pluralität als ethischer und politischer Wert*, p. 62; Welsch, W., *Postmoderne. Zwischen Indifferenz und Pluralität*, p. 35; Vattimo, G., *La fin de la modernité*, p. 51; generally: Enderle, G., *Ethik und Wirtschaftswissenschaften*, or Ulrich, P., *Transformationen der ökonomischen Vernunft: Fortschrittsperspektiven der modernen Industriegesellschaft*.
329 Baudrillard, J., *Oublier Foucault*, p. 50ff.
330 Baudrillard, J., *Oublier Foucault*, p. 64. See also Pefanis, J., *Heterology and the Postmodern: Bataille, Baudrillard, and Lyotard* and Foster, H., *The Anti-Aesthetic: Essays on Postmodern Culture*, p. 141.
331 For example Lévi-Strauss, C., *Pensée sauvage*, p. 109ff. and p. 296
332 According to Lévi-Strauss this evolution started with reciprocity, followed by 'business-like barter', and ended with 'tailor made contracts'. Lévi-Strauss, C., *Les structures élémentaires de la parenté*, p. 270ff. and p. 294ff. *Quotation* p. 547.
333 See Chapter 2, section III or Rorty. Wildermuth and Sakaya independently stress the linkage of these formative forces with the Enlightenment's concepts on the progress of society. Wildermuth, A., Multikulturelle Gesellschaft; Sakaiya, T., *The Knowledge-Value Revolution*.
334 Especially when 'living online' this need for communities is striking. There, groups form and disintegrate, enriching the individual that can open itself to this dynamics. Yet, some communities are 'sticky', thus creating tribes. This will increase as '[t]ribal behavior ... will become more common.' Siegel, D., *Futurize your Enterprise*, p. 83.; quote: p. 127.
335 This danger of over-interpretation and abusing cliches is mentioned by Pfeiffer, K. L., *Schwebende Referenzen und Verhaltenskultur: Japan und die Praxis der permanenten Postmoderne*, p. 351 and passim. The imaginable concordance between Zen and postmodernism proves to be a misapprehension: In all things vague, open, indifferent, multifaceted, trained in the domains of philosophy, Zen, religion and social interaction, Japan has a superior advantage on an abstract learning curve. This curve unfolds in a

postmodern space with the x-axis being 'chances for survival' or 'potential for dominance'. Further comments are to be found in Chapter 3, section II.

336 For further clarification refer to Manschot, H., *Nietzsche und die Postmoderne in der Philosophie*, p. 478f. Likewise: Schirmacher, W., *Schopenhauer und die Postmoderne*.

337 Fine examples of traditional interpretations of art that are adapted to our contemporary intellectual environment are Izutsu, T. and Izutsu, T., *Die Theorie des Schönen in Japan*; Paul, G., *Die Aktualität der klassischen chinesischen Philosophie*; Kato, S., *A History of Japanese Literature*; Suzuki, T., *Words in Context: A Japanese Perspective on Language and Culture*; Okazaki, T. and Stricevic, M., *The Textbook of Modern Karate*; Nitrobe, I., *Bushido: The Soul of Japan*; Kakuzo, O., *The Book of Tea*.

338 Saito, K., *Meien wo aruku: Muromachi Jidai* [*Japanese Gardens: the Muromachi Period*]; Yoshikawa, I., *Chozubashi: Teien-bi no zokei* [*Stone-rimmed ponds: How to achieve beauty in the garden*]; Ebersole. G., *Ritual Poetry and the Politics of Death in Early Japan*.

339 Ito, T. and Iwamiya, T., *The Japanese Garden: An Approach to Nature*, p. 27ff.

340 Refer to Charrier, I., *La peinture japonaise contemporaine*; Wie-Hsun-Fu, C. and Heine, S., *Japan in Traditional and Postmodern Perspectives*; Degli-Esposti, C., *Postmodernism and the Cinema*, p. 234; Harris, M., *Theories of Culture in Postmodern Times*.

341 This problem is exposed transparently in Paul, G., *Zur Geschichte der Philosophie in Japan und zu ihrer Darstellung*. See also Chapter 3, section III on the No-theatre.

342 Hisamatzu, S. I., *Einführung zu: Eine Erläuterung des Lin-chi-Zen*, p. 228.

343 Ohashi, R., *Zen und Philosophie*, p. 95f.

344 Ohashi, R., *Zen und Philosophie*, p. 98.

345 For an overview of French literature on the subject see Birkett, J. and Kearns, J., *A Guide to French Literature: Early Modern to Postmodern*.

346 Isutzu, T. and Isutzu, T., *Die Theorie des Schönen in Japan*; Heartney, E., *Mixed Messages*.

347 Nakamura, H., *Ways of Thinking of Eastern People*, p. 531ff.

348 Cf. Singer, K., *Mirror, Sword and Jewel: The Geometry of Japanese Life*, p. 90ff. or: Nakane, C., *Japanese Society*, p. 42ff. and McKinney, R. H., *An Entropic Analysis of Postmodernism*.

349 Anonymous, *Wissenschaft in Kyoto*.

350 Even Japanese, such as K. Oe talk about fashion trends among the young intellectuals, whose 'enthusiasm for new cultural theories was short-lived, coming and going after only a short craze.' Oe, K., *Japan's Dual Identity*, p. 199 and p. 203ff.

351 Miyoshi, M. and Harootunian, H. D., *Introduction*, p. viii and p. xi. For a contrary opinion see Tadashi, O. and Latarin, M. and Rappe, G. (Eds.): *Interkulturelle Philosophie und Phänomenologie in Japan* who see parallels between the Japanese constructive ambiguity and postmodern traits.

352 Asada, A., Nakazawa, S. and Itoi, S., *Posutomodan no chisei ga kataru: Kakutitsu zero no koto o kano ni suru, kore ga ha tsu no kyokuchi nan ja nai?* [*This is postmodern intelligentia: To have the impossible possible. Is that not the culmination of know-how?*], p. 54.

353 Arata, I., *Of City, Nation and Style*, p. 47f.; quote: p. 60ff.; Yamamoto, C. and Blume, G., *Keine andere Stadt ist wie Tama*.

354 Mönninger, M., *Vogelfrei im Atrium: Die Emanzipation der Büroarbeit in Tokyo*.

355 Thakara, J., *Japanische Designer-Hotelarchitektur*, p. 28f.

356 Cf. Miyoshi, M., *Against the Native Grain: The Japanese Novel and the 'Postmodern' West*, p. 147.

357 Gebhard, L., *Gegenwelten: Das Inventar des Phantastischen in der modernen japanischen Literatur*.

358 Tanaka, Y., *Nantonaku, kurisutaru* [*Somehow, crystal – Somehow, it is a crystal*]. As a more negative counter-example in Western literature could be cited Aylett, S., *Slaughtermatic*.

359 Miyoshi, M., *Against the Native Grain: The Japanese Novel and the 'Postmodern' West*, p. 157.
360 For more on the identity crisis of the younger generation see Sacks, P., *Generation X Goes to College: An Eye-Opening Account of Teaching in Postmodern America*; Long, J., *Generation Hope: A Strategy for Reaching the Postmodern Generation*; Amato, J., *Bookend: Anatomies of a Virtual Self*. For an in-depth analysis turn to: Hickman, L., *Reading Dewey: Interpretations for a Postmodern Generation*.
361 Field, N., *The Postmodern as Atmosphere*, p. 176. See also Epstein, J., *Youth Culture: Identity in a Postmodern World*.
362 Vattimo, G., *The End of Modernity: Nihilism and Hermeneutics in Post-Modern Culture*, p. xxi ff.; Puhr, K. M., *Postmodernism for High School Students*, p. 64f. Contrary opinion: Featherstone, M., *Perspectives on Consumer Culture*.
363 Jameson, F., *Postmoderne – Zur Logik der Kultur im Spätkapitalismus*, p. 95.
364 Burgin, V., *The End of Theory*, p. 204; Oppermann, M., *The Writer in the Closet, or: Three Scetches of a Postmodern Concept of Identity*.
365 Another example for a clearly postmodern Japanese novel: Murakami, R., *Kagirinaku tomei nichikai buru* [*Blue lines on naked skin*].
366 For example in literature: Oe, K., *Jinsei no shinseki* [*Leaning towards life*]; Shiga, N., *A Dark Nights Passing*; Yoshiyuki, J., *The Dark Room*. Consider also: Pfeiffer, K. L., *Schwebende Referenzen und Verhaltenskultur: Japan und die Praxis der permanenten Postmoderne*, p. 345. Or, more pronounced: Shimomura, T., *Mentalität und Logik der Japaner*, p. 375.
367 Vladislav, L. and Inozemtsev, V. L., *The Constitution of the Post-Economic State: Post Industrial Theories and Post-Economic Trends in the Contemporary World*; Sassen, S., *Losing Control?: Sovereignty in an Age of Globalization*; Ormerod, P., *The Death of Economics*.
368 Ashley, D., *History without a Subject: The Postmodern Condition*; Bell, D., *The Coming of the Postindustrial Society*.
369 See for example, Kiuchi, T., *New Economy*, 4; Lövlie, L., *Postmodern Subjectivity on the Internet*.
370 Siegel, D., *Futurize your Enterprise*, p. 5, p. 43.
371 Siegel, D., *Futurize your Enterprise*, p. 156
372 Siegel, D., *Futurize your Enterprise*, p. 303ff.
373 For an overview of this active notion of postmodern see Ferre, F., *Knowing and Value: Toward a Constructive Postmodern*; or Martens, G., *Broch, Musil und die Grenzen der Moderne*, who sees the postmodern as the ontological correlation, as the abstract construction plan for the New Economy. Jameson likewise sees a transformation of the image of postmodernism. Jameson, F., *Cultural Turn: Selected Writings on the Postmodern*. Supportive of that are also Sakaiya, T., *The Knowledge-Value Revolution*; Lash, S., *Sociology of Postmodernism*, p. 116; Newman, C., *The Post-Modern Aura*, p. 197; Harvey, D., *The Condition of Postmodernity*, p. 147ff.; Wagner, B., *PostModerne oder PostFordismus*, p. 119; Koslowski, P., *Die postmoderne Kultur*, p. 104ff.
374 Geras, N., *Solidarity in the Conversation of Humankind: The Ungroundable Liberalism of Richard Rorty*, p. 65.
375 For more on the subject of flexibility see Sennett, R., *Der Flexible Mensch. Die Kultur des neuen Kapitalismus*.

3 Postmodern Indicators in Japanese Culture

1 A good overview about Japan's modernization is provided by Martin, B., *Japans Weg in die Moderne und das deutsche Vorbild*; a more detailed synopsis is however, Beasley,

W. G., *The Modern History of Japan*, p. 134ff. and Reischauer, E. O. and Craig, A. M., *Japan: Tradition and Transition*.

2   Nakane, C., *The Japanese Society*, Preface.

3   Schwalbe, H., *Japan*, p. 30; and Sansom, G. B., *Japan – A Short Cultural History*.

4   Suzuki, T., *Eine verschlossene Sprache*, p. 17.

5   On the evolution of this term: Paul, G., *Zur Geschichte der Philosophie in Japan und zu ihrer Darstellung*, p. 5ff.

6   Nakamura, H., *Ways of Thinking of Eastern People*, p. 532.

7   Quite often these imports become fully japanned: the strike (of workers) is pronounced in Japanese 'su to ra i ki'. Usage shortened it to 'su to', and it is now regarded as a genuine Japanese word, despite its clear origin as a loanword. More details can be found in: Corff, O., *Zur Frage der Herkunft der japanischen Sprache*, p. 13f.

8   Nakamura, H., *Ways of Thinking of Eastern People*, p. 400.

9   See also Chapter 3, IV.

10 Hijia-Kirschnereit, I., *Vom Nutzen der Exotik*, p. 184.

11 Compare with Suzuki, T., *Eine verschlossene Sprache*, p. 155f.

12 Kumon, S., *Some Principles Governing the Thought and Behavior of Japanists* (Kontextualists), p. 8.

13 Cf. Suzuki, T., *Eine verschlossene Sprache*, p. 97. Another finding, consistent to the argument presented, was that convergence of interpretations increased the longer the texts (i.e. the context) were.

14 Mouer, R. and Sugimoto, Y., *Images of Japanese Society*, p. 153ff.; Steward, J., *A Postmodern Look at Traditional Communication Postulates*.

15 Neustupny, I. v., *A Post-Structural Approach to Language*, p. 41ff.

16 Counter-reactions like the proposal to adopt English as the official language of Japan (proposed around 1885) or French (suggested in 1946), or the recent demands to abolish kanji or at least its Chinese way to read them, or to change Japanese completely into roman letters (romaji) do never deny the in-built advantage of ambiguity, the main reason to change is invariably seen in a greater opening to the Western world. In this debate, writers like S. Naoya bemoan that 'nothing is so imperfect and unpractical as the Japanese language' or more heretically: 'Things clear are not Japanese.' reflecting ironically on the French dictum 'Ce qui n'est pas clair, n'est pas français' [What is imprecise, cannot be French]. Quoted after Suzuki, T., *Eine verschlossene Sprache*, p. 38 and p. 50.

17 Schwalbe, H., *Japan*, p. 275. Against this 'imprecision myth' of the Japanese language argues Reischauer, E. O., *The Japanese*, p. 381ff.

18 See also Nakamura, H., *Ways of Thinking of Eastern People*, p. 552 and p. 573; Schinzinger, R., *Japanisches Denken*, p. 16; Singer, K., *Mirror, Sword and Jewel*, p. 46; Pefanis, J., *Heterology and the Postmodern: Bataille, Baudrillard, and Lyotard*.

19 K. v. Wolferen talks about the necessity to develop 'supra-conversational feelers'. Wolferen, K. v., *The Enigma of Japanese Power*, p. 428. This capability to understand without recourse to language is seen to be of high tactical value. Refer here to the concept of haragei, explained in Chapter 3, IV.

20 The ascending hierarchy of these suffixes is: *-chan*, *-kun*, *-san*, *-sama*: a name is ranked by application of these suffixes. Depending of the context a person e.g. Motoko Ezaki (first name, family name) is called Mokoto-chan (by her mother) or Ezaki-san (by her colleagues). See also Nakane, C., *The Japanese Society*, p. 28.

21 For a minute analysis in the general context refer to: Neustupny, I. v., *A Post-Structural Approach to Language*, p. 186ff. and 214ff. The extreme possibilities to express subtleties by means of honorifics or to advance infinitesimal changes just by addressing a person this or another way is graciously used in the famous classical tales of Prince Genji (around

AD 1000). Murasaki, S., *The Tale of Genji [Genji Monogatari]*. Doi, T., *The Anatomy of Dependence*, p. 61; Nakamura, H., *Ways of Thinking of Eastern People*, p. 552.

22 This is also reflected in poetic arts: The formal poems called *Waka* and *Haiku* have an impressionistic, suggestive and vague ambivalence as their ideal. Cf. Higginson, W. J., *The Haiku Handbook*, p. 6 and p. 181ff.

23 A good introduction into this field is Mitsubishi Corporation: *Tatemae and Honne: Distinguishing Between Good Form and Real Intention in Japanese Business Culture*.

24 Suzuki, T., *Eine verschlossene Sprache*, p. 170. Critically opposing: Seitz, B., *The Identity of the Subject, after Sartre: An Identity Marked by the Denial of Identity*.

25 Doi, T., *The Anatomy of Dependence*, p. 94; Hawthorn, G., *The Impossible Sociology of Postmodern Persons*.

26 Suzuki, T., *Eine verschlossene Sprache*, p. 172.

27 There exists an amazing multitude of variants to denote 'I': *watashi, washi, watakushi, boku, ore, jibuchi, shosei, atai, ware*, just to name a few.

28 Although this may sound confusing to the Westerner it sounds natural to the Japanese. Compare with Emig, R., *Towards a Postmodern Poetics*; Lövlie, L., *Postmodern Subjectivity on the Internet*; Carr, D., *Education, Knowledge, and Truth: Beyond the Postmodern Impasse*.

29 Cf. Nakamura, H., *Ways of Thinking of Eastern People*, p. 574.

30 Nakamura, H., *Ways of Thinking of Eastern People*, p. 576; supporting this view is Morris, R., *Words and Image in Modernism and Postmodernism*.

31 Refer particularly to Suzuki, T., *Eine verschlossene Sprache*, p. 112f.

32 Nakamura, H., *Ways of Thinking of Eastern People*, p. 536.

33 Nakamura, H., *Ways of Thinking of Eastern People*, p. 361.

34 See also the remarks by Mitford, A. B., *Tales of Old Japan*, p. 5f.

35 For more on the relation between religion, spirituality and postmodern position refer to Astell, A. W., *Divine Representations: Postmodernism and Spirituality*; Allen, R. J., Johnston, S. B. and Blaisdell, B. S., *Theology for Preaching: Authority, Truth and Knowledge of God in a Postmodern Ethos*; Murphy, N., *Anglo-American Postmodernity*. The point here is to show that one of the roots of Japanese capabilities to deal with postmodern paradoxies lies in its spiritual tradition and practice.

36 This thesis is also put forth by R. Ohashi. With the demise of the modern and the ascent of the postmodern, Zen will regain in importance (as the rising Western interest in Zen evidences). Ohashi, R., *Zen und Philosophie: Kontinuität der Diskontinuität*, p. 97; Ohashi, R., *Die Philosophie der Kyoto-Schule*, p. 228.

37 Doi, T., *Amae: Freiheit in Geborgenheit*, p. 171.

38 Cf. Rahula, W., *Zen and the Taming of the Bull*, p. 65.

39 This comes close to what W. Anderson calls 'ready-to-wear religion'; see, especially, May, T., *The Moral Theory of Poststructuralism*.

40 See also Schinzinger, R., *Japanisches Denken*, p. 14 and p. 18. D. Suzuki defines Zen as non-mystic, non-religious, non-philosophical. Zen searches not sophisticated systems but is pure praxis of utility. Suzuki, D. T., *An Interpretation of Zen Experience*, p. 122 and p. 131ff. and especially Nakamura, H., *Ways of Thinking of Eastern People*, p. 387f.

41 Suzuki, D. T., *Zen and Japanese Culture*, p. 7 and p. 140; Suzuki, S., *Zen Mind Beginner's Mind*, p. 134f.; Hoover, T., *Die Kultur des Zen*, p. 13.

42 Paul, G., *Zur buddhistischen Logik und ihrer Geschichte in Japan*, p. 2 and p. 37. Use also Paul, G., *Zur Geschichte der Philosophie in Japan und zu ihrer Darstellung*, p. 25 and Paul, G., *Die Aktualität der klassischen chinesischen Philosophie*.

43 Cf. Nakamura, H., *Ways of Thinking of Eastern People*, p. 546ff.

44 Shimomura, T., *Mentalität und Logik der Japaner*, p. 373.
45 Koan originally meant 'relevant official decree' or 'public bulletin'. Suzuki, D., *The Koan*, p. 48f. Probably the most famous collection for Western readers remains Reps, P., *Zen Flesh, Zen Bones*.
46 Kapleau, P., *Die drei Pfeiler des Zen*, p. 104. For another explanation through truth and the dubious see Wie-Hsun-Fu, C. and Heine, S., *Japan in Traditional and Postmodern Perspectives*.
47 See also Petersen W., *Stone Garden*; Izutsu, T. and Izutsu, T., *Die Theorie des Schönen in Japan*, p. 90ff.
48 P. Kapleau names three goals of Zen: (a) practising the virtuous way in everyday life, (b) increasing concentration, (c) illumination. Kapleau, P., *Die drei Pfeiler des Zen*, p. 81.
49 K. Nishida based his thoughts on this kind of worldly pragmatism. His ways of Zen is not a teaching but training, not a theory but a concept of 'real-world transcendence' [gyaku choetsu]. Refer to Ohashi, R., *Die Philosophie der Kyoto Schule*, p. 351.
50 Schinzinger, R., *Japanisches Denken*, p. 21. More centred on the axioms of worldliness and predominance of pragmatic performance: Nakamura, H., *A History of the Development of Japanese Thought*, p. 22. Cf. also: Kapleau, P., *Die drei Pfeiler des Zen*, p. 89 and p. 99. In a more common perspective, the famous '10 pictures of a bull' come to mind. Reps, P., *Zen Flesh, Zen Bones*, p. 186 and the more general explanations in Rahula, W., *Zen and the Taming of the Bull*. S. Hisamatsu refines it to a 'purified Zen' as an aesthetic religion of service (used here in a very abstract sense) to the fellow human. Hisamatsu, S., *Philosophie des Erwachens*.
51 On the subject see also Odin, S., *The Social Self in Zen and American Pragmatism*.
52 Suzuki D. T., *Zen and Japanese Culture*, p. 360.
53 Suzuki, D. T., *Living By Zen*, p. 30ff.
54 See also Suzuki, D. T., *Zen and Japanese Culture*, p. 380f; Takuan, S., *The Unfettered Mind*, p. 59; Pirsig, R. M., *Zen and the Art of Motorcycle Maintenance*, p. 53 and Deshimaru, T., *Zen in den Kampfkünsten Japans*, p. 72ff. and p. 132.
55 Only a few detect here a notion of narrow anti-intellectualism. In their view opportunistic compromises between borrowed cultural goods produce the hushed up result of confused irrelevance in the disguise of mystic wisdom. Nakamura, H., *Ways of Thinking of Eastern People*, p. 400ff.
56 Nakamura, H., *Ways of Thinking of Eastern People*, p. 352. For the Haiku, the poet Bashô developed a theory of the transient beauty as the ideal. Refer to the explication in: Izutsu, T. and Izutsu, T., *Die Theorie des Schönen in Japan*, p. 102.
57 Okakura, K., *Ideale des Ostens*, p. 53 and Suzuki, S., *Zen Mind Beginner's Mind*, p. 113. '*Yurari yurari*' (fluctuating, vibrating and oscillating unsteadiness) is a description often used in Haiku. The pertinent images are flash, dream, echo, voices out from nowhere.
58 See also Pirsig, R. M., *Zen and the Art of Motorcycle Maintenance*, p. 231; Kapleau, P., *Die drei Pfeiler des Zen*, p. 242; Musashi, M., *Das Buch der fünf Ringe*, p. 108. On the subject–object relation see especially Izutsu, T. and Izutsu, T., *Die Theorie des Schönen in Japan*, p. 96ff.
59 Wilson-Ross, N., *The World of Zen*, p. 41.
60 For more reading refer to Reid, T. R., *Confucius Lives Next Door* or: Alford, F. C., *Think No Evil: Korean Values in the Age of Globalization*. Very interesting reading is also Fukami, T., *Successful Business Management Through Shinto*.
61 Reps, P., *Zen Flesh, Zen Bones*, p. 195; Suzuki, D. T., *Zen and Japanese Culture*, p. 158; Suzuki, S., *Zen Mind Beginner's Mind*, p. 9; Wilson-Ross, N., *The World of Zen*; Blofeld, J., *The Zen Teachings of Huan Po on the Transmission of Mind*, p. 68.
62 For an elaboration of this turn to Amato, J., *Bookend: Anatomies of a Virtual Self*; Epstein, J., *Youth Culture: Identity in a Postmodern World*.

63 This keen desire to be the fittest, is not only seen from the emptiness alone but also implies cleverness. Takuan, S., *The Unfettered Mind*, p. 26. Amusing is the account of a warlord that wanted to have him prophesy the outcome of his future battles. He insisted however that loaded dice were used. Reps, P., *Zen Flesh, Zen Bones*, p. 76.

64 Suzuki, D. T., *Zen and Japanese Culture*, p. 14 and p. 107ff.; Siu, R. G. H., *Zen and Science*. R. Barthes found the best characterization: ' "Human spirit", said a Tao-master, "is like a mirror. It does not keep things but it rejects nothing. It accepts everything but nothing sticks to it." ' Barthes, R., *Das Reich der Zeichen*, quote: p. 109.

65 In Chinese: '*wu wei*' or '*mu i*' (passive action; accomplishment by abstention). The Japanese explain it as a 'soft but powerful process', comparable to Judo or Aikido.

66 Suzuki, D. T., *Zen and Japanese Culture*, p. 419. Compare also Reps, P., *Zen Flesh, Zen Bones*, p. 18. This close constellation of No and Zen may be explained by the common interest in the idea of nothingness, Anonymous, *Wissenschaft in Kyoto*.

67 For a historic overview of the ideas underlying No-theater: Ortolani, B., *The Japanese Theatre*, p. 85ff.

68 Contrary to the Greek drama, the No-choir proposes additional interpretations, divergent perspectives to the spectator, the intention being a broadening of the possibility (and burden) of interpretation.

69 Miyoshi, M., *Against the Native Grain*, p. 161; see also Maruoka, D. and Yoshisohi T., *Noh*, p. 102 and p. 108.

70 Good explicative insights provide Zeami (Seami), M., *Die geheime Überlieferung des No*, p. 18ff.; Hoover, T., *Die Kultur des Zen*, p. 160f.; Wilson-Ross, N., *The No-Drama*; or in particular Izutsu, T. and Izutsu, T., *Die Theorie des Schönen in Japan*, p. 41ff. and p. 82f.; Ortolani, B., *Das japanische Theater*, p. 408ff. For a recent critique of the No-theatre refer to: Malkin, J. R., *Memory Theater and Postmodern Drama*.

71 Wilson-Ross, N., *Poetry*, p. 118ff.; and Suzuki, S., *Zen Mind Beginner's Mind*, p. 22 and p. 75.

72 Suzuki, D. T., *Zen and Japanese Culture*, p. 22.

73 Suzuki, D. T., *An Interpretation of Zen Experience*, p. 139.

74 Hoover, T., *Die Kultur des Zen*, p. 18; Yoshida, K., *Betrachtungen aus der Stille*.

75 For more see Izutsu, T. and Izutsu, T., *Die Theorie des Schönen in Japan*, p. 70.

76 Suzuki, D. T., *Living by Zen*, p. 96.

77 Suzuki, D. T., *Living By Zen*, p. 49 and p. 113. Unfortunately, Suzuki does not utilize postmodern abstractions, but merely describes the practical value of this paradox.

78 This view is shared by Immoos, T., *Japan – Archaische Moderne*, p. 43; Popham, P., *Japan*, p. 17; Takuan, S., *The Unfettered Mind*, p. 55; Nitobe, I., *Bushido*, p. 11ff.; Mitford, A. B., *Tales of Old Japan*, p. 80f. and p. 273.

79 For general reference: Kobayashi, H., *Wirtschaftsmacht Japan*, p. 11ff. For the special problem of the process of socialization during childhood and on the acquisition of value systems: Herold, R., *Zur Sozialisation des Kindes im Japan der Tokugawa- und Meiji-Zeit*, p. 43ff.

80 Foreign countries serve in this sense as a pressure valve. Those who want to amuse themselves have to go 'outside' i.e. travel. This is a reason why loud, disrespectful and sometimes shameless and irresponsibly childish behaviour of Japanese groups abroad is often to be predicated. Hundreds of photos and shopping in bulk for souvenirs are just the most harmless form of bringing home the evidence needed to create a story (for themselves and for their audience) in order to create an identity. An observant analysis of this behaviour is given by Schmitt, U., *Die Einsamkeit des Japaners in der Fremde*.

81 Singer, K., *Mirror, Sword and Jewel*, p. 90.

82 Anonymous, *Japan 1987*, p. 94.

83 Harotoonian, H. D., *Visible Discourses – Invisible Ideologies*, p. 63f. and p. 80f.

84 Nakamura, H., *Ways of Thinking of Eastern People*, p. 531. v. Wolferen describes this
    basis as 'warm, wet and illogical'. Wolferen, K. v., *The Enigma of Japanese Power*,
    p. 346.
85 Or, to use a more pathetic quotation: 'Not only were they attached to nature, but they
    kept warm spots in their hearts for companions and never ceased to long for humanity,
    in the midst of their hermitage.' Somehow this resembles the camp fire of R. Rorty.
    Nakamura, H., *Ways of Thinking of Eastern People*, p. 371.
86 Nester, W., *Japan's growing Power over East Asia and the World Economy*, p. 126.
87 Mouer, R. and Sugimoto, Y., *Images of Japanese Society*, p. 231.
88 Mouer, R. and Sugimoto, Y., *Images of Japanese Society*, p. 227. Endorsing this:
    Woronoff, J., *Japan: The Coming Economic Crisis*, p. 34.
89 Many authors cite historic and ethnographic reasons: prehistoric, static farming
    societies had to coordinate for their irrigation projects. The basis necessarily was trust,
    control and close cooperation. This created genealogies of relations, which can be seen
    as the geological sediments of society. For example, Nakamura, H., *Ways of Thinking of
    Eastern People*, p. 341f. and Nakane, C., *Japanese Society*, p. 63. It is in a way inter-
    esting that in Los Angeles today one of the most pressing issues is the question of water
    rights and how to create workable, fair solutions. A problem the Japanese had to tackle
    centuries ago.
90 Pye, L. W., *Das japanische Rätsel: Die Verbindung von Wettbewerb und Konsens*.
91 On the importance of families and their networks in postmodern times: Weidenbaum,
    M. and Hughes, S., *The Bamboo Network*; Stacey, J., *In the Name of the Family:
    Rethinking Family Values in the Postmodern Age*; and: Burggraf, S., *The Feminine
    Economy and Economic Man*. Confucian values in modern and postmodern society as
    the coherence factor are stressed by T. R. Reid: Reid, T. R., *Confucius Lives Next Door*.
92 Pfeiffer, K. L., *Schwebende Referenzen und Verhaltenskultur: Japan und die Praxis per-
    manenter Postmoderne*, p. 348.
93 Pye, L. W., *Das japanische Rätsel: Die Verbindung von Wettbewerb und Konsens*, p. 56;
    Herold, R., *Zur Sozialisation des Kindes im Japan der Tokugawa- und Meiji-Zeit*, p. 44.
94 The concept of '*Ie*' is also very valuable for the analysis of the interior functioning of
    today's multinational enterprises in Japan. Please refer to Chapter 5, section III on
    phenotypes and structural histories of Keiretsu. The economic analogy to the '*Ie*' is the
    task force grouping called '*Ka*' as explained in Chapter 4, section III on decision-making.
95 Kumon, S., *Japan as a Network Society*, p. 123.
96 Nakane, C., *Japanese Society*, p. 4 and p. 9.
97 Exemplary for this stance is H. Kawakami, an economist of the Meiji-period:
    'Individuals are not believed to exist for and of themselves as autonomous entities,
    only the state does.' Kawakami, H., *Kawakami Hajime chosakushu*, p. 190. See also
    Nakane, C., *Japanese Society*, p. 73 and Schwalbe, H., *Japan*, p. 337 and Wolferen,
    K. v., *The Enigma of Japanese Power*, p. 218.
98 DeVos, G. A., *Socialization for Achievement*, p. 361ff. Parallel to this is the postmodern
    rejection of theory of classes (chapter 2, III).
99 Neustupny, I. v., *A Post-Structural Approach to Language*, p. 162, p. 169f. and p. 178.
100 Singer, K., *Mirror, Sword and Jewel*, p. 77 and Nakamura, H., *Ways of Thinking of
    Eastern People*, p. 482; see also Chapter 4, section III (structural units).
101 This matches Chapter 3, section IV (*nihonron*) and Chapter 1, section II ('the focus of
    attention') and Wolferen, K. v., *The Enigma of Japanese Power*, p. 337.
102 Reischauer, E. O., *The Japanese*, p. 136.
103 Hall, E. T. and Reed-Hall, M., *Hidden Differences*, p. 158.
104 Matsumoto, M., *Haragei: The Unspoken Way*, p. 20 and p. 36.

105 Matsumoto, M., *Haragei: The Unspoken Way*, p. 54.
106 Nakane, C., *Japanese Society*, p. 52. K. v. Wolferen is defining '*Wa*' more critical as: '... uninterrupted display of a readiness to sacrifice one's personal interests for the sake of a communal tranquility'. Wolferen, K. v., *The Enigma of Japanese Power*, p. 412.
107 Doi, T., *The Anatomy of Dependence*, p. 28, p. 65 and p. 169f.
108 Doi, T., *The Anatomy of Dependence*, p. 7f. and Lutterjohann, M., *Kulturschock Japan*, p. 27.
109 Hall, E. T. and Reed-Hall, M., *Hidden Differences*, p. 54ff. and p. 157.
110 Hall, E. T. and Reed-Hall, M., *Hidden Differences*, p. 56.
111 Hall, E. T. and Reed-Hall, M., *Hidden Differences*, p. 55 and Doi, T., *The Anatomy of Dependence*, p. 32.
112 Doi, T., *The Anatomy of Dependence*, p. 141 and p. 160. See also Harris as he sees (Japanese) culture as a narrative. Harris, M., *Theories of Culture in Postmodern Times*. For the New Economy perspective: e.g. Siegel, D., *Futurize your Enterprise*, p. 5f. and 65ff.
113 Exhaustive explanations are given for example by Doi, T., *The Anatomy of Dependence*, p. 33ff.; or Reischauer, E., *The Japanese*, p. 144 and Lutterjohann, M., *Kulturschock Japan*, p. 27. Critical views offers: Woronoff, J., *Japan: The Coming Economic Crisis*, p. 33.
114 E. Hall and M. Reed-Hall define this basic common understanding '*ninjo*' as the 'ability to read and experience the feelings of others.' Hall, E. T. and Reed-Hall M., *Hidden Differences*, p. 61.
115 'Many Japanese believe that if they have to use words to communicate their feelings, then they are not truly communicating.' Japan Travel Bureau: *Living Japanese Style*, vol. 2, p. 172.
116 Nakane, C., *Japanese Society*, p. 55f. and p. 126.
117 Through cursory surveys on 'average' employees of a big trading firm or a bank this can be easily corroborated: invariably they proudly list memberships of 20 and more formal and informal groups.
118 Though this might be comparable to the Western 'old boys network' and 'rope teams', the Japanese's network is unequally more important to him in terms of position, power and intensity. K. v. Wolferen maintains even that these informal groupings behind the scenes are the sole decision-making body in Japanese politics and 'big business'. Wolferen, K. v., *The Enigma of Japanese Power*, p. 144, p. 183, p. 493 and Hall, E. T. and Reed-Hall, M., *Hidden Differences*, p. 58.
119 See for more details Mitsubishi Corporation, *Tatemae and Honne: Distinguishing Between Good Form and Real Intention in Japanese Business Culture*.
120 Nakamura, H., *Ways of Thinking of Eastern People*, p. 564.
121 Befu, H., *Japan: An Anthropological Introduction*, p. 96ff. and Earhart, H. B., *Religion in the Japanese Experience*, p. 82f.
122 Nakamura, H., *Ways of Thinking of Eastern People*, p. 412.
123 Doi, T., *The Anatomy of Dependence*, p. 135. E. Reischauer adds: '... greater Japanese tendency to emphasize the group at the expense of the individual ...' and '... satisfying sense of being part of something big and significant'. Reischauer, E. O., *The Japanese*, p. 128 and p. 133. A philosophical basis gives K. Nishida, who sees the Western ego as a simple psychological 'I' which then needs to develop an understanding of its relation to others to be the 'real' self. This can only be defined in relational terms, defining its position in its specific world. For more refer to Schinzinger, R., *Japanisches Denken*, p. 62f. In the postmodern context this loss, or weakening, of the ego is put in the broader context of the 'self' which is seen as a fad of the modern movement. Koshmann, J. V., *Maruyama Masao and the Incomplete Project of Modernity*, p. 124.

124 Nakane, C., *Japanese Society*, p. 10. A spicy description is used by G. Mikes: 'Japanese life has extinguished not only privacy but also the desire for privacy'. Mikes, G., *The Land of the Rising Yen*, p. 53.
125 Nester, W., *Japan's growing Power over East Asia and the World Economy*, p. 127. K. Singer records it likewise: '... the gladness with which the Japanese surrender their wills, granting to circumstances ...'. Singer, K., *Mirror, Sword and Jewel*, p. 38. 'Japanese are brought up to accept that much of their lives will be managed for them.' Wolferen, K. v., *The Enigma of Japanese Power*, p. 66. It seems revealing that the Western word 'privacy' is not translated but rather used as a borrowed term [puraibashi] and bears for the Japanese more of a negative 'egoistical' connotation. See also: Wolferen, K. v., *The Enigma of Japanese Power*, p. 427; Watanabe, T., *Der Wille zur Unfreiheit in der japanischen Gesellschaft*, p. 10.
126 Nakane, C., *Japanese Society*, p. 2. This 'environmentally dependent role-definition' is noted earlier: Kahn, H., *The Emerging Japanese Superstate*, p. 48ff. and also K. Maasaki: *The Status and the Role of the Individual in Japanese Society* or Wolfe, A., *Suicide and the Japanese Postmodern: A Postnarrative Paradigm?*, p. 224f.
127 Pye, L. W., *Das japanische Rätsel: Die Verbindung von Wettbewerb und Konsens*, p. 57.
128 Pfeiffer, K. L., *Schwebende Referenzen und Verhaltenskultur*, p. 349.
129 Miyoshi, M., *Against the Native Grain*, p. 148. He explains this disaggregation by the lack of rational and logical thinking ('logocentricity appears to be one crime Japan is scarcely guilty of'). Consequently for M. Miyoshi, there is no deconstruction as there never has been a 'construct' in Japan. An historic account along with the ties to Zen is provided by Asada, A., Derrida, J. and Karatani, K., *Choshoi shakai to chishikijin no yakuwari* [*The hyper-consumption society and the role of the intellectuals*].
130 Nakamura, H., *Ways of Thinking of Eastern People*, p. 374ff. and p. 563.
131 Nakamura, H., *Ways of Thinking of Eastern People*, p. 384 and p. 402. And also Neustupny, I. v., *A Post-Structural Approach to Language*, p. 174. For a more recent analyis refer to Tachibanaki, T. and Kenkyujo R. S., *Who Runs Japanese Business? Management and Motivation*; or Uekusa, K., *Japan in the New Millennium*, who sees an evolution towards a more entepreneurial risk-taking currently happening as a result of the need to adapt to the New Economy and the preceeding crises. See also Chapter 4.5.
132 Moore, C. A., *The Enigmatic Japanese Mind*, p. 303. Already in the last century this view was adopted: '[The Japanese display] lots of vividness, intelligence and talent, though few principles or character.' Quoted in: Hijia-Kirschnereit, I., *Vom Nutzen der Exotik*, p. 176.
133 Moore, C. A., *The Enigmatic Japanese Mind*, p. 289. Likewise, Nakamura, H., *Ways of Thinking of Eastern People*, p. 372.
134 K. Singer talks about a 'logic of the moment'. Singer, K., *Mirror, Sword and Jewel*, p. 118. S. Kumon uses the term 'soft situational logic'. Kumon, S., *Japan as a Network Society*, p. 123. E. Reischauer describes it as a 'multiplicity and complexity of rules,' that condemn nothing but rather present via consensus what has to be the case. Reischauer, E. O., *The Japanese*, p. 146. W. Nester refers to it as an 'absence of legalistic thoughts'. Nester, W., *Japan's Growing Power over East Asia and the World Economy*, p. 128.
135 Nakamura, H., *Ways of Thinking of Eastern People*, p. 490; see also Coulmas, F., *Land der rituellen Harmonie*.
136 See also Nakane, C., *Japanese Society*, p. 37 and p. 155 as well as Nester, W., *Japan's Growing Power over East Asia and the World Economy*, p. 128.
137 Singer, K., *Mirror, Sword and Jewel*, p. 62.
138 Singer, K., *Mirror, Sword and Jewel*, p. 72.
139 Immoos, T., *Japan Archaische Moderne*, p. 38.
140 Wolferen, K. v., *The Enigma of Japanese Power*, p. 63, p. 357, p. 380 and p. 543 and especially Chapter 2, section III on Lyotard's theoretical framework.

141   Wolferen, K. v., *The Enigma of Japanese Power*, p. 388 and p. 489.
142   Wolferen, K. v., *The Enigma of Japanese Power*, p. 26 and p. 170.
143   Cf. Miyoshi, M. and Harootunian, H. D., *Introduction*, p. viiff.
144   Asada, A., *Infantile Capitalism and Japan's Postmodernism*, p. 276. M. Fujioka remarks
      in his esthetically oriented interpretation of architecture that no single element alone
      is allowed to create beauty, instead the collective beauty of the elements, their rela-
      tions and the space in between them is the work of art. Fujioka, M., *Japanese Castles*,
      p. 51.
145   See in Barthes, R., *Das Reich der Zeichen*, p. 51. For a description of everyday life:
      Mikes, G., *The Land of the Rising Yen*, p. 169ff.; Ellin, N., *Postmodern Urbanism*;
      Colquhoun, A., *Modernity and the Classical Tradition: Architectual Essays 1980–1987*.
      On the impossibility of any rational planning and the 'spatial stress' created by such
      vague systems: Benko, G. and Strohmayer, U., *Space and Social Theory: Interpreting
      Modernity and Postmodernity*.
146   Barthes, R., *Das Reich der Zeichen*, p. 148. Barthes has perceived this 'traditional decon-
      structedness' of Japan very sensitively. Using the example of Japanese dishes he
      elaborates the principles of local harmonies and the mixtures thereof; with the example of
      the Japanese puppet theatre (*Bunraku*) he explains the value of the asymmetrical and the
      principles of simulation in general. Barthes, R., *Das Reich der Zeichen*, p. 33 and p. 74.
147   Thomsen points at a 'overkill by media and by optical effects used in Japanese cities'.
      Thomsen, C. W., *Die Utopie der Städte*, p. 56.
148   Ivy, M., *Critical Texts, Mass Artifacts; The Consumption of Knowledge in Postmodern
      Japan*, p. 38.
149   Karatani, K., *Ri no hihan: shiso ni okeru puremodan to postomodan* [*A confucian critique
      of premodern and postmodern concepts*], p. 40. See also Mouer, R. and Sugimoto, Y.,
      Images of Japanese Society, p. 341.
150   '... le mythe est une parole ...' [myths are just words usable as tools]. Barthes, R.,
      Mythologies, p. 193. See also: p. 254f.
151   Oe, K., *Japan's Dual Identity*, p. 189f.
152   The curious reader might read Kumon, S., *Nationalism of Long Intestine* and Tsunoda, T.,
      Nihonjin no No [*The brain of Japanese human beings*]; Harris, M., *Theories of Culture in
      Postmodern Times*.
153   Wolferen, K. v., *The Enigma of Japanese Power*, p. 359. For further literature on the
      subject see Lodge G. C. and Vogel, E. F., *Ideology and National Competitiveness; An
      Analysis of Nine Countries*.
154   Najita, T., *On Culture and Technology in Postmodern Japan*, p. 6.
155   Hijia-Kirschnereit, I., *Vom Nutzen der Exotik*, p. 180.
156   Sakai, N., *Modernity and its Critique*, p. 105.
157   Watanabe, T., *Der Wille zur Unfreiheit in der japanischen Gesellschaft*, p. 8ff.
158   Mouer, R. and Sugimoto, Y., *Images of Japanese Society*, p. 169. W. Nester adds:
      'Japanese elite have found it advantageous to push the image of Japan's uniqueness
      abroad to ward off Western criticism.' Nester, W., *Japan's Growing Power over East
      Asia and the World Economy*, p. 135. Again, G. Mikes describes this strategy more
      crisply: 'The shoguns ... were clever chaps and knew that people busy with meaningless
      ceremonies had little time for political intrigue and conspiracy'. Mikes, G., *The Land of
      the Rising Yen*, p. 18f.
159   Ichiban – striving to be first – is the grammalogue, the sign for this. That this quest is
      not foreign to the Western soul is graciously put by Homer: 'Always be best and strive
      to be first among others'.
160   On the concept of the 'ruling elite' cf. Chapter 4, section III ('the centre').
161   Kumon, S., *Japan as a Network Society*, p. 126.

162   To take an example: The symbolic view of Japan as one single family is not taken in its abstract but in its very concrete meaning: up to the Second World War, the father of a family was an absolutist chief, the Duke (Daimyo) had a comparable position for his fiefdom, the Grand Duke (Shogun) and the Emperor were totalitarian rulers respectively: '[t]he whole Japanese nation has been regarded as an extended family.' Nakamura, H., *Ways of Thinking of Eastern People*, p. 489 and p. 528. Quote: p. 421. This chain of command is often interpreted as a 'great chain of being'. Using this Buddhist terminology should enhance legitimacy and irreversibility of these structures. Wolferen, K. v., *The Enigma of Japanese Power*, p. 434.

163   This tribal view of the world is gaining momentum. Krotkin sees in an empirical overview the Japanese as the model of a global tribe. Postulating a nexus between ethicity and business success he concedes that the networking ability of the Japanese are unparalleled. Krotkin, J., *Tribes: How Race, Religion, and Identity Determine Success in the New Global Economy*. As tribal structures and behaviour will become more common, this character train will serve the Japanese people well. See also Siegel, D., *Futurize your Enterprise*, p. 127.

164   Murakami, Y. and Rohlen, T. B., *Social Exchange Aspects of the Japanese Political Economy: Culture, Efficiency, and Change*, p. 71f.

165   Refer to the paragraphs on symbolic capital in Chapter 2, section III.

166   See Nakane, C., *Japanese Society*, p. 109 and p. 145; or Kendrick, D. M., *Where Communism Works*, p. 35f.; Deresky, H., *International Management: Managing Across Borders and Cultures*. Hazama points out that the family and group serve as the dominant Japanese management ideology. Hazama, H., *The History of Labour Management in Japan*.

167   Imai, K., *Japan's Corporate Networks*, p. 229.

168   Hall, E. T. and Reed-Hall, M., *Hidden Differences*, p. 75 and p. 114; Nakane, C., *Japanese Society*, p. 50; Mouer, R. and Sugimoto, Y., *Images of Japanese Society*, p. 301. See also Murakami, Y. and Rohlen, T. B., *Social Exchange Aspects of the Japanese Political Economy: Culture, Efficiency, and Change*, p. 78.

169   Smith, R., *The Cultural Context of Japanese Political Economy*, p. 19.

170   Ivy, M., *Critical Texts, Mass Artifacts; The Consumption of Knowledge in Postmodern Japan*, p. 24 and p. 25.

171   Wolferen, K. v., *Das Japan Problem*, p. 10 and p. 17; Hall, E. T. and Reed-Hall, M., *Hidden Differences*, p. 58; Nester, W., *Japan's Growing Power over East Asia and the World Economy*, p. 127; Singer, K., *Mirror, Sword and Jewel*, p. 45; Woronoff, J., *Japan: The Coming Economic Crisis*, p. 53.

172   Nakane, C., *Japanese Society*, p. 136.

173   Wolferen, K. v., *The Enigma of Japanese Power*, p. 301, also p. 571.

174   Quoted from Pye, L. W., *Das japanische Rätsel: Die Verbindung von Wettbewerb und Konsens*, p. 56.

175   Quoted from Kumon, S., *Japan as a Network Society*, p. 125. Chapter 5, section II ('the network approach') provides a deeper analysis.

176   Conglomerates being relatively recent in Japanese economic history, are relatively Western, as they are not yet fully immersed into the Japanese system. As only partially digested, they are still edgy, recognizably Western, and thus a bit apart from the truly Japanese business system. This stigma (Western-ness) is vanishing rapidly. 'This evolution is seen as a gradual loosening of the intercorporate linkage and blurring of corporate boundaries.' Imai, K., *Japan's Corporate Networks*, p. 201ff. Quote: p. 228; Wolferen, K. v., *The Enigma of Japanese Power*, p. 221. See also Chapter 5.3 and 5.4.

177   Imai, K., *Japan's Corporate Networks*, p. 228.

178   Read also Chapter 3, section IV ('the basic social concept').

179 Kumon, S., *Japan as a Network Society*, p. 122f. This philosophy of multiple worlds is also consistent with Japan's cultural history: There were always totally separate worlds (Leipnitz' 'Monaden') (the individual Ie and the fiefdoms) which had their own individual set of values, customs and traditions, often complemented by its own legal system. Wolferen, K. v., *The Enigma of Japanese Power*, p. 20 and Yamazaki, M., *The Impact of Japanese Culture on Management*, p. 33.

180 Kumon, S., *Japan as a Network Society*, p. 131f. and Imai, K., *Japan's Corporate Networks*, p. 227. For the New Economy perspective: e.g. Siegel, D., *Futurize your Enterprise*, p. 5f. and 65ff.

181 Ivy, M., *Critical Texts, Mass Artifacts; The Consumption of Knowledge in Postmodern Japan*, p. 35. Please refer also to Chapter 2, section III on the symbolism of postmodern change.

182 Further literature on the subject of loyalty: Lucas, J. R., *Balance of Power*.

183 Rehfeld, J. E., *Alchemy of a Leader: Combining Western and Japanese Management Skills to Transform Your Company*, p. 270.

4 The Structural Environment Surrounding Japan's Multinational Enterprises – a Driving Force for Change

1 Best, M., *The New Competition*, p. 138. For details on cultural aspects see Chapter 3; Organization of production understood as the coordination of productive processes by means of work-flow organization, management, enterprise structure and cooperation between firms, will be the main topic of the fifth chapter.

2 For further literature on the subject see Morgan, J. C. and Morgan J. M., *Cracking the Japanese Market: Strategies for Success in the New Global Economy*.

3 For example Smith, R., *The Cultural Context of the Japanese Political Economy*. The ways of doing (domestic) business in Japan can generally be seen as extensions of the basic ways of simple arrangements in small communities and neighbourhoods or for private events (like the organization of a party or the orchestration of voluntary community service).

4 This is a specification and application of the findings presented in Chapter 3 insofar as Japan's cultural substructure is providing support for a postmodern reading of Japanese business decision-making principles and processes. This will be further elaborated in the context of structural changes on the microeconomic level (Chapter 4, section IVff).

5 For a good book on the mastering of change see Bergquist, W. H., *The Postmodern Organization: Mastering the Art of Irreversible Change*.

6 'The Japanese also have long shown a keen interest in scanning the external environment for useful knowledge.' Quotes from Rohlen, T., *Learning: The Mobilization of Knowledge in the Japanese Political Economy*, p. 324. See additionally Aoyagi, Y., *Unternehmen und Innovation*, p. 145.

7 This is a parallel thought to the simile used in Chapter 2 between foreign cultures and a rental library (or more contemporary, a video store). Best example is the expeditions by Japanese 'scouts' (usually high nobility with entrepreneurial spirit or members of the intellectual elite); R. Schinzinger refers to these scouts and pathfinders at the end of the nineteenth century as: 'brilliant dilettantes, autodidacts, and encyclopedists'. A predetermined set of reconnaissance tasks was given. (questions on national defence, on the legal system, on technology, the educational systems and so on). When coming back specific practical proposals were expected along with comprehensive descriptions of the exotic things seen. Quotation from Schinzinger, R., *Japanisches Denken*, p. 41.

8   Compare with Nakamura, H., *Ways of Thinking of Eastern People*, p. 400. 'Since the beginning of her history Japan is well trained to adopt and assimilate foreign, "strange" things.' Schwalbe, H., *Japan*, p. 19.
9   Harryson, S., *Japanese Technology and Innovation Management: From Know-How to Know-Who*, p. 78.
10 Telling examples for this cultural multiplicity are the religious sphere, fashion and culinary culture. On religious feast days families do the pilgrimage to their Buddhist monastery, then directly to their Shinto shrine followed by a visit to their Christian church. Changing clothes from kimono to Western dress goes hand in hand with a switch in mentality. When appropriate(!), French cuisine is as equally appreciated as traditional Japanese cooking. See also Chapter 3, section IV ('sketches from everyday life') and, more generally, Charrier, I., *La peinture japonaise contemporaine: de 1750 à notre jours*, Introduction; Werhahn-Mees, K., *Kultur und Wirtschaft, Kategorien für eine adäquatere Länderanalyse*, p. 19.
11 Reischauer, E. O., *The Japanese Today*, p. 79 and Doi, T., *The Anatomy of Dependence*, p. 46. See also D. Siegel's call for permenent, institutionalized learning. Siegel, D., *Futurize your Enterprise*, p. 66ff. Cf. also Beechler, S. L. and Bird, A., *Japanese Multinationals Abroad: Individual and Organizational Learning* and Preskill, H. and Torres, R. T., *Evaluative Inquiry of Learning in Organizations*.
12 Quoted from Prestovitz, C. V., *Trading Places*, p. 113.
13 Mikes, G., *The Land of the Rising Yen*, p. 14. This strategy is still valid today. Colloquially it is called 'gaiatsu' (external pressure benefits internal change; or simply no pains – no gains).
14 For more information about the future of democracy see Martin, H.-P. and Schumann, H., *Der Angriff auf Demokratie und Wohlstand* and Messner, D., *Die Zukunft des Staates und der Politik*.
15 Mikes, G., *The Land of the Rising Yen*, p. 13ff.
16 Here, the explanations of C. A. Moore are insightful; Moore, C. A., *The Enigmatic Japanese Mind*, p. 304.
17 'Japan's capacity to evolve economically and to adapt successfully to an exterior world of superior technology and economic power has rested on an extraordinary capacity for learning.' Rohlen, T. P., *Learning: The Mobilization of Knowledge in the Japanese Economy*, p. 322ff. Quote from p. 363. In this sense, Japan is the prime example of a 'learning society' a serious competitive advantage in postmodern times.
18 Asada, A., *Infantile Capitalism and Japan's Postmodernism*, p. 275.
19 It is easy to find examples for the short sightedness of critical Western comments about Japanese copies in the fifties and sixties of this century: 'For a hundred years and more, Japan has been the most prolific copier of things foreign.' McMillan, C., *The Japanese Industrial System*, p. 325. 'Japanese industrial triumphs have been based largely on efficient borrowing or ingenious adaptations of foreign technology rather than on independent scientific discoveries.' Reischauer, E. O., *The Japanese Today*, p. 200.
20 Westney, D. E., *Imitation and Innovation: The Transfer of Western Organizational Patterns to Meiji-Japan*, p. 24. More general: Goel, R. K., *Economic Models of Technological Change*; Buranen, L. and Roy, A. M., *Perspectives on Plagiarism and Intellectual Property in a Postmodern World* and Beamish, P. W., Delios, A. and Lecraw, D. J., *Japanese Multinationals in the Global Economy*.
21 During and after the catch-up phase (that is after 1868), Japan has always focused its research and development activities on adaptation, modification and improvements and done little in the area of fundamental research. N. Sazaki found that 96 per cent of technologies used for synthetic fibre production is improved (i.e. indirectly imported) technology. The remaining four per cent are either (directly imported) licenses or Japanese patents.

Similar results can be found in other industries (electronics, rubber products, car manufacturing). Bringing research to the market, qualitative and pragmatic improvement of existing products is the desired strength of Japanese R&D activities. Sazaki, N., *Management and Industrial Structure in Japan*, p. 27. Comparable results show the analyses of Grossman, G. M., *Explaining Japan's Innovation and Trade: A Model of Quality Competition and Dynamic Comparative Advantage*, p. 80f.; Okimoto, D. I. and Saxonhouse, G. R., *Technology and the Future of the Economy*, p. 385f. Anonymous, *Cutting your Competitor to the Quick*; Aoyagi, Y. F., *Unternehmen und Innovation*, p. 146.

22   Rohlen, T. P., *Learning: The Mobilization of Knowledge in the Japanese Political Economy*, p. 345. See also Klenner, W., *Grundzüge der wirtschaftspolitischen Entwicklung und Wirtschaftspolitik*.

23   The fact that the free-rider problem is not only applicable to transfer of technology but also to other areas (higher education, defence, humanitarian aid, and so forth) assert several researchers: Ernst, A., *Nach den Handelsfriktionen demnächst Technologiefriktionen?*; Reischauer, E. O., *The United States and Japan in 1991*, p. 75ff. There exists a very instructive study on the monodirectional transfer of knowledge: 'On the surface, the arrangements seem fair and well balanced, indicative of an evolving international economic equilibrium. A closer examination however, shows the deals for what they really are –part of a continuing implicit Japanese strategy to keep the higher paying, higher value-added jobs in Japan and to gain the ... process skills that underlie competitive success.' Reich, R. B. and Mankin, E. D., *Joint Ventures with Japan give Away our Future*, p. 78.

24   The authors use the flashy description of a frontal assault that is comparable to Pearl Harbor in its consequent use of camouflage, surprise and unexpected aggressive moves. Although carried a bit too far the basic thrust of this argument might be considered. Wright, R. W. and Pauli, G. A., *The Second Wave – Japan's Global Assault on Financial Services*, p. 1. Cf. also Naisbitt, J., *Megatrends Asien*. Opposing this view are Krugman, P., *Der Mythos vom globalen Wirtschaftskrieg*; and Minc, A., *Globalisierung*.

25   This interpretation of the Japanese economic strategies in the light of Schumpeter's model of competitive advantage will be further examined in Chapter 4, section IV ('the 1980s and 1990s').

26   Klenner, W., *Grundzüge der wirtschaftspolitischen Entwicklung und Wirtschaftspolitik seit d. Zweiten Weltkrieg*, p. 63. and Michie, J. and Smith, J. G., *Globalization, Growth, and Governance: Creating an Innovative Economy*, p. 52.

27   Yamamura, K., *Success that Soured: Administrative Guidance and Cartel in Japan*, p. 94. See likewise Prestovitz, C. V., *Trading Places*, p. 314; Naumann, N., *Identitätsfindung – das geistige Problem des modernen Japans*, p. 173 and Sullivan, W., *Japan, Shredding Role of Imitator, is Emerging as a Scientific Pioneer*.

28   The possibility of this being a dominant strategy not only for the Japanese but for all global players is stated by Leuenberger, T., *Herrschaftsstruktur und Machtverteilung im politischen System der USA*, p. 187. See also Chapter 5, section II on '"unorthodox" MNE persepctives'.

29   This leadership role is unmistakably demonstrated by the strong growth in patents. In the decade of the eighties more patents were of Japanese origin than the combined sum of England and Germany. To this is added the Japanese patents held in other countries. About a third of all American patents are held by firms like Canon USA, Hitachi USA and Toshiba USA. Broad, W. J., *Novel Technique Shows Japanese Outpace Americans in Innovation*. Tasker, P.; *Inside Japan*, p. 55; Gregory, G., *Die Innovationsbereitschaft der Japaner*, p. 119f.

30   Masataka, K., *Japan's Choices*, p. 78ff. On the disputes about patents read for example, Tasker, P., *Inside Japan*, p. 53.

31 Sansom, G. B., *Japan – A Short Cultural History*, p. 54. The following book also focuses on the evolution of Japan's economy, Kim, K. S. *et al.*, *Acquiring, Adapting and Developing Technologies: Lessons from the Japanese Experience*.

32 For more information refer to Kraus, W., *Die japanische Herausforderung*, p. 111; Hall, E. T. and Reed-Hall, M., *Hidden Differences*, p. 42; Imai, K., *Japan's Corporate Networks*, p. 228; Heitger, B., *Import Protection and Export Performance and their Impact on Economic Growth*, p. 7f. and Cohen, D., *Managing Knowledge in the New Economy*.

33 For a more complete description refer to Wagatsuma, H., *Heritage of Endurance*, p. 28ff.

34 In analysing the fate and career of classmates of the first schooling years (*donen*, the path the class took), R. Benedict reasserts just how strong these bonds can be. 'Donen are closer than a wife.' Benedict, R., *The Chrysanthemum and the Sword*, p. 269.

35 More on Keiretsu in Chapters 4, section IV, 5, section III, and 5, section IV.

36 Stemming from the American antitrust-ideology, Nester maintains the thesis that Keidanren was founded by General MacArthur to get a democratic alternative to the top boards of the Zaibatsu. Nester, W. R., *The Foundation of Japanese Power*, p. 180. See also Chapter 5, section III ('structural history').

37 Kevenhörster, P., *Wirtschaft und Politik in Japan*, p. 30f. and Kobayashi, H., *Wirtschaftsmacht Japan*, p. 96.

38 Refer also to Boyd, R., *Government–Industry Relations in Japan: Access, Communication and Competitive Collaboration*, p. 74f. or to Seifert, W., *Wirtschaftsorganisation und politische Macht*, p. 145.

39 More on Zaibatsu in Chapters 4, section IV, 5, section III, and 5, section IV.

40 Kevenhörster, P., *Wirtschaft und Politik in Japan*, p. 96.

41 The 1999 merger between Mitsubishi Bank and the Bank of Tokyo was not only a cost-saving, synergy-creating defensive move, it has expanded Mitsubishi's reach deep into the insurance sector (Meiji Life & Tokyo Marine).

42 See also the paragraphs on groups, cliques and batzu in Chapter 3, section IV and Chapter 1, section I.

43 Eli, M., *Sogo Shosha*, p. 37.

44 Wolferen, K. v., *The Enigma of Japanese Power*, p. 96; see also Sethi, S. P., *The False Promise of the Japanese Miracle*, p. 22: '... the Diet is generally lacking in initiative and influence and acts largely at the behest of the bureaucracy.'

45 The distinction of mainstream, anti-mainstream, and other fractions, as proposed by P. Kevenhörster shows the conceptual difficulty Westerners have with this type of political action. Kevenhörster, P., *Wirtschaft und Politik in Japan*, p. 80.

46 See Chapters 1, section I ('New Economy') and 3, section IV ('group relationship structures'). For a general treatment, Krotkin, J., *Tribes*.

47 Nester, W. R., *The Foundation of Japanese Power*, p. 179; Kobayashi, H., *Wirtschaftsmacht Japan*, p. 107.

48 Yoshino, M., *Japan's Multinational Enterprises*, p. 13.

49 The monetary flows between business and politics is very intense, complex and meshed. Contributions from the business world (mostly via Zaikai) are coordinated by the Keidanren and then channeled into the LDP either directly through the Society for National Politics (kokuminkyokai), or indirectly through grass roots level organizations. Hence, no trace is visible, no machiavellian action discernible and everything looks like an ideal democracy. A detailed analysis is offered for example by Kevenhörster, P., *Wirtschaft und Politik in Japan*, p. 97.

50 Johnson, C., *MITI and the Japanese Miracle*, p. 50 and p. 238ff.; Katz, R., *Japan, the System that Soured*, p. 321ff.

51 There exists a broad body of literature on the theory of elite in Japan. Some hints are given by Cook, T. F., *Cataclysm and Career Rebirth: The Imperial Military Elite*, p. 135f.;

or Pempel, T. J. and Tsunekawa, K., *Corporatism without Labour: The Japanese Anomaly*, p. 231f.

52 Johnson, C., *MITI and the Japanese Miracle*, p. 58ff.; Boyd, R., *Government–Industry Relations in Japan: Access, Communication and Competitive Collaboration*, p. 67f.; Wolferen, K. v., *Enigma of Japanese Power*, p. 143.

53 Sasaki-Smith, M., *Japanese Industrial Policy in the 1980s*.

54 Wolferen, K. v., *The Enigma of Japanese Power*, p. 144 and p. 493f. It is also clear that this attempt at identifying structures will become harder and harder as the virtual media and communication takes over the role of information exchange.

55 Sasaki-Smith, M., *Japanese Industrial Policy in the 1980s*, p. iv. Similar: Wolferen, K. v., *The Enigma of Japanese Power*, p. 57ff.

56 Mouer, R. and Sugimoto, Y., *Images of Japanese Society*, p. 252 and 265.

57 Woronoff, J., *Japan: The Coming Economic Crisis*, p. 99.

58 Echigo, K., *Japanese Studies of Industrial Organization*, p. 450f.

59 Mouer, R. and Sugimoto, Y., *Images of Japanese Society*, p. 388.

60 Clearly, religious and moral aspects play an important part as underlying forces in these processes. See for example, Fukami, T., *Successful Business through Shinto*; Tachibanaki, T. and Kenyujo, R. S., *Who Runs Japanese Business?* Compare also with Alford, F. C., *Think no Evil*. (Cf. Chapter 3, sections III and IV).

61 Eguchi, Y., *Japanische Gruppenmentalität und ökonomische Konflikte*, p. 183f.

62 Maybe the best example for this is the birth of the microsoft competing software 'Linux': designed as an open software, everyone in the world can contribute to its development. No one owns it, no hierarchies, just sheer performance.

63 Hall, E. T. and Reed-Hall, M., *Hidden Differences*, p. 74. Refer also to Chapter 3, section IV ('the role of the primary group').

64 Comparing social structures between villages and families show clear parallels.

65 Vogel, E. F., *Japan as Number One: Lessons for America*, p. 90; Tachibanaki, T. and Kenyujo, R. S., *Who Runs Japanese Business?*; for an empirical report, Robertson, P. L., *Authority and Control in Modern Industry*. For a general treatment, Warnecker, H. J., *Revolution in der Unternehemenskultur: Das Fraktale Unternehmen*.

66 Wolferen, K. v., *The Enigma of Japanese Power*, p. 27. The basic idea of an empty centre is found throughout this study, p. 26, p. 63, p. 170, p. 527 and p. 543.

67 Wolferen, K. v., *The Enigma of Japanese Power*, p. 68, p. 326 and p. 395ff.

68 Symptomatic are the genuflections of high politicians before the houses of victims of a plane crash, asking for forgiveness, or the frequent symbolic resignations of politicians or high managing directors. As v. Wolferen puts it sardonically: 'nobody is boss but everybody, in some way or the other, has leverage over somebody else'. Wolferen, K. v., *The Enigma of Japanese Power*, p. 54.

69 This curious lack of a strong leadership ideal is regularly mentioned in the literature. Wolferen, K. v., *The Enigma of Japanese Power*, p. 193f.; Drucker, P. F., *Toward the Next Economics*, p. 217; Wright, R. W. and Pauli, G. A., *The Second Wave – Japan's Global Assault on Financial Services*, p. 85. Wright and Pauli define this lack of leader and strategic map in combination with the persistent push towards the tacit common good as a 'termite strategy'.

70 Yamamoto, S., *Ursprünge der japanischen Arbeitsethik*, p. 105f.

71 Aoki, M., *Aspects of the Japanese Firm*, p. 36.

72 Johnson, C., *MITI and the Japanese Miracle*, p. 51; See also Sethi, S. P., *The False Promise of the Japanese Miracle*. For the application of this concept on the Internet cf. Siegel, D., *Futurize your Enterprise*, p. 127 and p. 156ff. and Krotkin, J., *Tribes*.

73 It is a conscious choice that the more formal concepts *oyabun–kobun* are used, rather than utilizing the better known and more informal relational pair *senpai* (the older) and *kohai*

(the younger). Both pairs are more or less similar in representing the ubiquitous dyadic structure of relations.

74   For more material, Gibney, F., *Japan: The Fragile Superpower*, p. 179; Japan Travel Bureau, *Salaryman in Japan*, p. 2ff.; Schwalbe, H., *Japan*, p. 363; Tasker, P., *Inside Japan*, p. 161; Bennett, J. W. and Ishino, I., *Paternalism in the Japanese Economy*, p. 47; Robertson, P. L., *Authority and Control in Modern Industry*; Tachibanaki, T. and Kenyujo, R. S., *Who Runs Japanese Business?*

75   Nakane, C., *Japanese Society*, p. 45 and p. 113 and Kobayashi, H., *Wirtschaftsmacht Japan*, p. 16 and p. 27f.

76   Bobke, M., *Arbeitsstaat Japan*, p. 30.

77   As already noted in Chapter 3, section II ('ambiguity of meaning'), subtle nuances in status, hierarchy or power are expressed through a myriad of expressions. An example: if clearly situated more highly in the company hierarchy our test-person would be called Tanaka-sama, as a direct superior Tanaka-san, among his colleagues it would be Tanaka, as a subordinate he would be addressed Tanaka-kun. See Nakane, C., *Japanese Society*, p. 28; Bennett, J. W. and Ishino, I., *Paternalism in the Japanese Economy*, p. 56 and, especially, Go, M., *Linguistic Analysis of Oyabun–Kobun Relationships*.

78   Bennett, J. W. and Ishino, I., *Paternalism in the Japanese Economy*, p. 48ff. and Nakane, C., *Japanese Society*, p. 49.

79   Nakane, C., *Japanese Society*, p. 35 and p. 126f.

80   On the linking pin theory, Likert, R., *New Patterns of Management*, p. 105ff.

81   The main leadership function of an *oyabun* is the maintenance of some sort of esprit de corps and the encouragement of information-intensive communicative culture. Typically, he will be evaluated on (a) the symbolic leadership he provides for his team, (b) how homogeneous and effective his group is, (c) the performance, and (d) how well the informational (power) network of the *oyabun* is. Sethi, S. P., *The False Promise of the Japanese Miracle*, p. 12 and Nakane, C., *Japanese Society*, p. 66.

82   Bierdümpel, E., *Japanisches Informationsverhalten*, p. 66f.

83   Nakane, C., *Japanese Society*, p. 100 and p. 127; Bennett, J. W. and Ishino, I., *Paternalism in the Japanese Economy*, p. 78. Remark how Wolferen regards this '*jinmyaku*' (network of useful connections) as the constituent factor of the Japanese system. Wolferen, K. v., *The Enigma of Japanese Power, p. 432*.

84   Bennett J. W. and Ishino I., *Paternalism in the Japanese Economy*, p. 244ff. As this is already reality in the physical world, one can only wonder how complex, how performing this system is when applied to the virtual worlds on the Internet.

85   Roberts, J. G., *Mitsui: Three Centuries of Japanese Business*, p. 413. See also Yamamoto, S., *Ursprünge der japanischen Arbeitsethik*, p. 99.

86   Shimizu, R., *Top Management in Japanese Firms*, p. 18 and Abegglen, J. C. and Stalk, G., *Kaisha*, p. 208f.

87   Reischauer, E. O., *The Japanese Today: Change and Continuity*, p. 322; Lu, D. L., *Inside Corporate Japan*, p. 43; Wolferen, K. v., *The Enigma of Japanese Power*, p. 300 and Johnson, C., *MITI and the Japanese Miracle*, p. 71.

88   Wheeler, J. W., Janow, M. E. and Pepper, T., *Japanese Industrial Development Policies in the 1980s*, p. 10.

89   Shimizu classifies the different strategies of *nemawashi* as to whether they are open (several people involved discuss informally) or closed (the initiators negotiate with each person involved separately). For further details refer to Shimizu, R., *Top Management in Japanese Firms*, p. 19.

90   See Hayashi, S., *Culture and Management in Japan*, p. 120ff. Critically to this, Woronoff, J., *Japan: The Coming Economic Crisis*, p. 47.

91   Refer to Chapter 4, section III ('*ringi-seido*').

92 Sethi, S. P., *The False Promise of the Japanese Miracle*, p. 36 and Shimizu, R., *Top Management in Japanese Firms*, p. 207.

93 Contrary to Western negotiations in which you often are able to declare winners and losers, in Japan, the yielding party (the loser) receives special attention. It is not unusual to throw a party for them under the disguise of a debriefing (*nijikai*), the objective being to avoid hurt feelings and to smooth out potential antagonistic forces. More graphically, the effect of a *nemawashi* resembles a joint set whereas the Western result resembles an intersecting curve. Hayashi, S., *Culture and Management in Japan*, p. 132ff.

94 See Yakushiji, T., *The Government Policy in a Spiral Dilemma*, p. 265; Hatch, M. J.: *Organization Theory: Modern, Symbolic, and Postmodern Perspectives*. See also Chapter 2, section V.

95 Wolferen, K. v., *The Enigma of Japanese Power*, p. 441.

96 The following passages draw on Bierdümpel, E., *Japanisches Informationsverhalten*, p. 78. For a more general view, Kevenhörster, P., *Wirtschaft und Politik in Japan*, p. 56f. and Eli, M., *Sogo Shosha*, p. 537ff.

97 A *hanko* is a 5 cm tall pencil-like seal or the imprint of it. It is a personal seal of an official and serves as a confirmation that this official has – if not approved – at least seen the document. In everyday business affairs it is considered more 'valid' than a (Western) signature.

98 Reischauer, E. O., *The Japanese Today*, p. 321.

99 The true breadth of a Japanese seal can only be fully appreciated when mentioning that only the inclusion of a *hanko* renders a legal text or contract valid. Signatures alone are not that important. Practically every person involved in affairs has a *hanko*, a copy of which is deposited at the mayor's office. It has a much higher importance than any Western written form of declaration and can be compared, perhaps, to a signature with one's own blood. This tradition of personal and official seals and the ensuing management style (Management by *Hanko*) has its origin in the Chinese public administration.

100 Wolferen, K. v., *The Enigma of Japanese Power*, p. 443.

101 This method of problem-solving is basically used in all areas. A comprehensive classification is given by Eli, M., *Sogo Shosha*, p. 540 and p. 544ff.

102 As already mentioned (Chapter 3, section IV: 'the basic social context'), the intuitive, non-analytic faculties (*ninjo*, *haragei*, multi channel perception of multi-dimensional spaces) gain paramount importance.

103 Woronoff, J., *Japan: The Coming Economic Crisis*, p. 49.

104 Sethi, S. P., *The False Promise of the Japanese Miracle*, p. 34.

105 See also for further explications, Tsuji, K., *Entscheidungsfindung in der japanischen Regierung*, p. 265 and Woronoff, J., *Japan: The Coming Economic Crisis*, p. 56.

106 Abegglen J. C. and Stalk, G., *Kaisha: The Japanese Corporation*, p. 209.

107 Even in relatively simple democratic procedures (for example elections of a town council), intermediaries, 'go-betweens' (*senkyoya san*) play tremendously important roles. At annual general meetings the *sokaya* (small paid groupings of minority shareholders) gain notoriety because of their aggressive manipulative techniques (not hesitating to intimidate). This further weakens the picture of a homogeneous, rational-consensus-based group: 'Japan is one team toward the outside world and a multitude of factions within; institutions could grow to monstrous sizes and still remain highly fragmented and fragile.' Woronoff, J., *Japan: The Coming Economic Crisis*, p. 51ff.

108 A nice example is Nomura's President, who had to step down in 1990 after the scandals over price fixing on the stock exchange. This much publicized act was only a formal and symbolic routine, as evidenced in the lapidary and aloof fashion he did it. A more hard fact evidence is his promotion to Chairman of the board just a few days after the media hype. Other examples cite Clark, R., *The Japanese Company*, p. 126ff. and also Kevenhörster, P., *Wirtschaft und Politik in Japan*, p. 56.

306 Notes

109 Clark, R., *The Japanese Company*, p. 127; Eli, M., *Sogo Shosha*, p. 538.
110 Complementary reading: Sethi, S. P., *The False Promise of the Japanese Miracle*, p. 50.
111 Generally the real reasons for the need of a secondary source of income in the early years of pension (usually from the age of 55 to 60 or 65) are the inadequate state social security and the socio-economic motives (e.g. the second son reaches college age, the accustomed standard of living shall be maintained, and, not to forget, the indepletable expense accounts are not at his disposition anymore).
112 Johnson, C., *MITI and the Japanese Miracle*, p. 72.
113 Sethi, S. P., *The False Promise of the Japanese Miracle*, p. 18.
114 Johnson, C., *MITI and the Japanese Miracle*, p. 74 and Hikino, T., Kikkawa, T. and Miyajima, H., *Policies for Competitiveness: Comparing Business–Government Relationships in the Golden Age of Capitalism*, p. 85.
115 Wolferen, K. v., *The Enigma of Japanese Power*, p. 157 and p. 357.
116 Wakayama, T., *The Implementation and Effectiveness of MITI's Administrative Guidance*, p. 211.
117 Foljanty-Jost, G., *Informelles Verwaltungshandeln*, p. 172.
118 A working definition is given by Wheeler, J. W., Janow, M. E. and Pepper T., *Japanese Industrial Development Policies in the 1980s*, p. 78ff. On the effects, comments are given by Clark, R., *The Japanese Company*, p. 7.
119 Foljanty-Jost, G., *Informelles Verwaltungshandeln*, p. 175.
120 This picks up the ideas of Chapter 3, section IV ('the basic social context').
121 Compare Chapters 3, section IV (subsections on group relationships and the referenceless society), and Chapter 4, section III (subsections 'individual and organizational elements' and 'selected interpersonal mechanisms'). Real world examples can be found in Upham, F. K., *Die gesetzliche und institutionelle Dynamik der japanischen Kartellpolitik*, p. 298ff.
122 Lack of transparency exists only for the external world. All people involved in decision-making as well as all others deemed necessary have – subject to their role – full information.
123 The legal implications are detailed in Davis, P. A., *Administrative Guidance in Japan*.
124 See also Chapter 4, section III, and especially Mitsubishi Corporation, *Tatemae and Honne*.
125 Foljanty-Jost, G., *Informelles Verwaltungshandeln*, p. 186; Wakayama, T., *The Implementation and Effectiveness of MITI's Administrative Guidance*, p. 226f. Refer also to the recent (1999 and 2000) bank mergers. See also Kim, E. M., *Big Business, Strong State: Collusion and Conflict in South Korean Developments, 1960–1990*.
126 Ueno, H., *Wagakumi Sangyo Seisaku no Hasso to Hyoka* [*Japanese Economic Policy. Structure and Evaluation*], p. 39ff.
127 This comparison is done by Gibney, F., *Japan the Fragile Superpower*, p. 324ff. See for the general case, Agrawal, M., *Global Competitiveness in the Pharmaceutical Industry: The Effect of National Regulatory, Economic, and Market Factors* and Cunningham, J. and Thurow, L. C., *Building Wealth: The New Rules for Individuals, Companies, and Nations in a Knowledge-Based Economy*.
128 Cf. Woronoff, J., *Japan: The Coming Economic Crisis*, p. 116f.; Wolferen, K. v., *Das Japan Problem*, p. 13ff.; Seifert, W., *Wirtschaftsorganisation und politische Macht*, p. 144ff. and Knoke, D. and Tsujinaka, Y., *Comparing Policy Network: Labor Politics in the U.S., Germany, and Japan*.
129 Cf. Murakami, Y. and Rohlen T. P., *Social-Exchange Aspects of the Japanese Political Economy*, p. 64. See also Kevenhörster, P., *Wirtschaft und Politik in Japan*, p. 46.
130 Murakami, Y., *Sengo Nihon no keizai shisutemu* [*Japan's Post-War Economic Structure*], p. 53; Muramatsu, M. and Krause, E., *The Ruling Coalition and its Transformation*,

p. 70f. and Inoguchi, T., *Gendai Nihon seiji keizai no kiko* [*The Current Structure of Japanese Political Economy*].

131 Komiya, R., *Industrial Policy of Japan*; Kosai, Y., *The Reconstruction Period*, p. 36.

132 Prestovitz, C. V., *Trading Places*, p. 214. 'The Zaibatzu's top executives floated back and forth between positions in business and in various government ministries ...' Yoshino, M., *Japan's Multinational Enterprises*, p. 9. Thayer used a more benign description, regarding the business world as an integrative part of the conservative political system. Thayer, D., *How the Conservative Rule Japan*, p. 58. The scope of influence is measurable by the fact that this system is increasingly reaching out globally: Keidanren regularly sends out lobbyists to Washington and Europe and has its feelers in all relevant institutions. Wheeler, J. W., Janow, M. E. and Pepper T., *Japanese Industrial Development Policies in the 1980s*, p. 75ff. For a more general account refer to Choate, P., *Agents of Influence*.

133 For example, Ohmae, K., *Japanische Strategien*, p. 177ff. Quote from Wolferen, K. v., *Das Japan-Problem*, p. 24.

134 OECD, *Economies en Transition – L'ajustement structurel dans le pays de l'OCDE*, p. 141.

135 Muto, H., *Innovative Policies and Administrative Strategies for Intergovernmental Change in Japan*, p. 67. For a Marxist view on this see Vladislav, L. and Inozemtsev, V. L., *The Constitution of the Post-Economic State*.

136 Pape, W., *Die politisch-gesellschaftliche Verflechtung des Unternehmens*, p. 27.

137 'Underneath the dynamic, seemingly, changing life of this highly industrialized and drastically urbanized nation, one can see the continuation of a basic value system and common psychological characteristics which motivate people to stay together and keep their society "intact".' Wagatsuma, H., *Heritage of Endurance*, p. 23.

138 'Japan Inc.', 'Clan plc', 'Japan: the Zaibatzu of Zaibatzu' oder 'Project Nation'. Abegglen, J. C., *The Economic Growth of Japan*, p. 31f.; Dohnanyi, K. v., *Japanische Strategien*, p. 11.

139 Murakami, Y. and Rohlen, T. P., *Social Exchange Aspects of the Japanese Political Economy*, p. 64.

140 Bellah, R. N., *Tokugawa Religion*, p. 98; Kahn, H., *The Emerging Japanese Superstate*, Abegglen, J. C., *An Anatomy of Japan's Miracle Economy* and Abegglen, J. C., *The Economic Growth of Japan*, p. 32f.

141 Wheeler, J. W., Janow, M. E. and Pepper T., *Japanese Industrial Development Policies in the 1980s*, p. 10ff.

142 Komiya, R., *The Japanese Economy: Trade, Industry, and Government*, p. 377ff.

143 For a longer account, Seifert, W., *Wirtschaftsorganisation und politische Macht*, p. 135ff.

144 Note also Chapter 5, section IV ('the keiretsu as a fractal structure').

145 Anonymous, *The Endangered European Market*; McMillan, C., *The Japanese Industrial System*, p. 49.

146 Gardner, A. and Ishii, H., *Fiscal, Monetary, and Related Policies*, p. 246.

147 Johnson, C., *MITI and the Japanese Miracle*, p. 10.

148 Compare Chapter 4, section III and Johnson, C., *MITI and the Japanese Miracle*, p. 74. Quote from p. 265. Upham talks about inter-ministry horse trade. Upham, F. K., *Die gesetzliche und institutionelle Dynamik der japanischen Kartellpolitik*, p. 296. K. v. Wolferen describes this situation as 'bureaucratic wars between natural enemies' in which no '*wa*' (harmony) is noticeable. Wolferen, K. v., *The Enigma of Japanese Power*, p. 414 and Chapter 4, section III on *amakundari*. See also Callon, S., *Divided Sun*. Parallel to this, W. MacDonald sees an evolution from mechanistic bureaucratic models to organic models where formerly opposing parties are now partner and competitor at once. MacDonald, W., *Postmodern Management*.

149 For descriptions of the administrative practices see Kevenhörster, P., *Wirtschaft und Politik in Japan*, p. 50f.

150   For a better comprehension use the analogies to social and cultural fundamentals as developed in Chapter 3, section IV, and the patterns of interaction as presented in Chapter 4, section III on selected interpersonal mechanisms..

151   Wheeler, J. W., Janow, M. E. and Pepper, T., *Japanese Industrial Development Policies in the 1980s*, p. 7.

152   On the practical impact of the more recent visions refer to Chapter 4, sections IV ('the 1980s and 1990s') and VI ('the turn of the millennium').

153   Upham, F. K., *Die gesetzliche und institutionelle Dynamik der japanischen Kartellpolitik*, p. 398; Shinohara, M., *Industrial Growth, Trade, and Dynamic Patterns in the Japanese Economy*, p. 52: 'The general tendency of Japanese government policy makers is to look only to the future ...'.

154   Such a portfolio analysis of the Japanese economy is undertaken by McMillan, C., *The Japanese Industrial System*, p. 82ff.

155   Compare with the analyses by Eccleston, B., *State and Society in Postwar Japan*, p. 42 and by Shinohara, M., *Industrial Growth, Trade and Dynamic Patterns in the Japanese Economy*, p. 25f. Critically, Callon, S., *Divided Sun: MITI and the Breakdown of Japanese High-Tech Industrial Policy*.

156   Imai, K., *Japan's Industrial Structure*, p. 81 and p. 90; Johnson, C., *MITI and the Japanese Miracle*, p. 240; Dohnanyi, K. v., *Japanische Strategien*, p. 86; Eccleston, B., *State and Society in Postwar Japan*, p. 109 and Anonymous, *Die Wirtschaft Japans. Strukturen zwischen Kontinuität und Wandel*, p. 55.

157   Shinohara categorizes the rules of the game for influencing expanding and contracting industries by 3S and 3F strategies: software, systematization, specialization; and fashionization, feedback systems and flexibility. Shinohara, M., *Industrial Growth, Trade, and Dynamic Patterns in the Japanese Economy*, p. 34; see also McMillan, C., *The Japanese Industrial System*, p. 87.

158   This compilation is based on Johnson, C., *MITI and the Japanese Miracle*, p. 311ff.; Eccleston, B., *State and Society in Postwar Japan*, p. 47ff.; Kraus, W., *Die japanische Herausforderung*, p. 25ff. and p. 112ff.; Sekiguchi, S., *Die japanische Industriepolitik: Das Zusammenspiel zwischen Politik und dualistischer Struktur*, p. 243f. and p. 264.; Boyd, R., *Government–Industry Relations in Japan: Access, Communication and Competitive Collaboration*, p. 64; Shinohara, M., *Industrial Growth, Trade, and Dynamic Patterns in the Japanese Economy*, p. 27f.

159   These actions are supported by a myriad of social mechanisms: physical control (coercion; e.g. doors intendedly too narrow), utilitarian control (economic incentives), cognitive control (censorship over informational content and channels), symbolic control (incessant repetition of 'Japanese' esthetic ideals, moral lessons in school [shushin], billboards on the street with phrases almost of Chinese flavour: 'Let's all do X' 'Y is not necessary' or just well picked sayings. For more, see Mouer, R. and Sugimoto, Y., *Images of Japanese Society*, p. 234ff.

160   McMillan, C., *The Japanese Industrial System*, p. 63. Although sometimes called 'Superministry', some grave misjudgments happened, the worst ironically in the car industry and in electronics. In the 1940s, the MITI denied categorically that a Japanese car industry was necessary as farm land was too scarce to waste for streets and the volcanic geomorphology rendered it too difficult to construct roads for individual traffic. In the electronic industry the Sony's struggle to test market its Walkman is already an historical anecdote of its success story. Yves, L. D., *Die Rolle des Staates im globalen Wettbewerb*, p. 291. Keizo Obuchi, then Japanese prime minister said in his eulogy to the late leader of Sony that 'Morita was the engine that pulled the Japanese economy'.

161   Governmental activity is not excessive if compared with other industrial nations: Governmental spending is 33% of GNP in Japan, 34 % on the US, and about 45% in

Germany, France and in the UK The number of bureaucrats per thousand inhabitants is significantly lower than in Germany, Switzerland or in the U.S.A and much lower than in France or England. Dahlby, T., *The Bureaucrats: Sons of the Samurai*, p. 34f. and Pechman, J. and Kaizuka, K., *Taxation*, p. 367f. On the effectiveness of MITI refer to Wakiyama, T., *The Implementation and Effectiveness of MITI's Administrative Guidance.* Critical of that, Feketekuty, G. and Stokes, B., *Trade Strategies for a New Era: Ensuring U.S. Leadership in a Global Economy*; Krugman, P. *The Accidental Theorist.*

162 Further literature on this epoch, Sansom, G. B., *Japan, A Short Cultural History* or Maruyama, M., *Studies in the Intellectual History of Tokugawa Japan.*

163 Webb, M., *Japan 1850–1890*, p. 617ff.

164 Core to the Japanese Elite were the samurai, who were the only ones allowed to carry swords. In a way they were above the law and could act as they pleased, only bound and confined by their code of honour (*Bushido*). Bushido generally means a set of rules for noble behaviour. But it is more than just etiquette, it is more importantly a part of the 'national spirit', an all-encompassing style of life. As European correlates, the German 'Junkertum' or the medieval knight could be cited. Classical books on bushido are Nitobe, I., *Bushido* and Daidoji, Y., *The Code of the Samurai.*

165 Yui, T., *Beziehungen zwischen Regierung und Unternehmen und ihr Einfluss auf die Industrialisierung Japans*, p. 32.

166 Botskor, I., *Technologiepolitik in Japan*, p. 8f.

167 For example, Pye, L. W., *Das japanische Rätsel: Die Verbindung von Wettbewerb und Konsens*, p. 41.

168 With restoration, the re-installation of the Emperor as the highest institutional body and symbol was meant. De facto it meant the abolition of the shogunate, since the shogun was in reality the most powerful person in Tokugawa politics. In that sense the restoration was never a revolution by the people, but a change initiated by the elite, for the driving force was the external military threat (to this very elite) by the Americans. For details refer to Beasley, W. G., *The Modern History of Japan*, p. 76ff.; Reischauer, E. O., *The United States and Japan*, p. 51ff.; Lockwood, W. W., *Economic Development of Japan*, p. 5ff.

169 Nojiri, T., *Wirtschaftsethik und Wirtschaftsentwicklung in Japan*, p. 18.

170 Webb, H., *Japan 1840–1890*, p. 618ff.

171 Pye, L. W., *Das japanische Rätsel: Die Verbindung von Wettbewerb und Konsens*, p. 41.

172 Benedict, R., *The Chrysanthemum and the Sword: Patterns of Japanese Culture*, p. 37.

173 See also Yui, T., *Beziehungen zwischen Regierung und Unternehmen und ihr Einfluss auf die Industrialisierung Japans*, p. 38; Webb, H., *Japan 1840–1890*, p. 638; Yoshino, M. J., *Japan's Multinational Enterprises*, p. 4 and Nakagawa, K., *Business Strategy and Industrial Structure in Pre-World War II Japan*, p. 4ff.

174 Cf. Nakagawa, K., *Strategy and Structure of Big Business*; Nakagawa, K., *Business Strategy and Industrial Structure in Pre-World War II Japan*, p. 3, p. 38 and p. 43ff.

175 Maybe this is where Mitsubishi's slogan comes from: 'We trade in everything: from soba (noodles) to cruise missiles.'

176 Botskor, I., *Technologiepolitik in Japan*; Nakagawa, K., *Business Strategy and Industrial Structure in Pre-World War II Japan*, p. 11 and Yoshino, M., *Japan's Multinational Enterprises.*

177 Johnson, C., *MITI and the Japanese Miracle*, p. 109.

178 The laborious preparation for war was certainly not *ex nihilo*, but was burdened onto the Japanese people: 'the Japanese consumer was hit harder by war than civilians in any other major belligerent country for which data is available.' Jerome, B., *Japan's Economy in War and Reconstruction*, p. 65.

179 Refer also to Chapter 5, section III.
180 Johnson, C., *MITI and the Japanese Miracle*, p. 135ff. and p. 150 ff.; Nakagawa, K., *Strategy and Structure of Big Business*.
181 Already shortly after the war these kind of thoughts were expressed. Refer to the narration of Benedict, R., *The Chrysanthemum and the Sword: Patterns of Japanese Culture*, p. 172ff.
182 For example, Bornschier, V., *Westliche Gesellschaft im Wandel*, p. 349 and p. 363.
183 Johnson, C., *MITI and the Japanese Miracle*, p. 172f. C. Maier maintains that the continuity of actors and the ensuing blurring of delineation between government and the economy are the defining characteristic of the corporatist 1950s and 1960s. Maier, C., *Recasting Burgeois Europe*, p. 196 and p. 582. See also Botskor, I., *Technologiepolitik in Japan*, p. 10 and Yoshino, M., *Japan's Multinational Enterprises*, p. 10.
184 Yoshino, M., *Japan's Multinational Enterprises*, p. 14 and especially Johnson, C., *MITI and the Japanese Miracle*, p. 175ff.; quote from p. 149, and Shinohara, M., *Industrial Growth, Trade, and Dynamic Patterns in the Japanese Economy*, p. 12ff.
185 More in Johnson, C., *MITI and the Japanese Miracle*, p. 200; Kunio, Y., *Sogo Shosha*, p. 100; Tasker, P., *Inside Japan*, p. 41; Woronoff, J., *Japan: The Coming Economic Crisis*, p. 22; Kosai, Y., *The Reconstruction Period*, p. 25.
186 Murakami, Y. and Kosai, Y., *Japan and the Global Community*, p. 9.
187 Cf. Pyle, K. B., *Die Zukunft des japanischen Nationalcharakters*, p. 153.
188 Johnson, C., *MITI and the Japanese Miracle*, p. 211 and p. 229; Miyazaki, Y., *Excessive Competition and the Formation of Keiretzu*, p. 56.
189 The following is mainly based on Johnson, C., *MITI and the Japanese Miracle*, p. 125 and Shinohara, M., *Industrial Growth, Trade, and Dynamic Patterns in the Japanese Economy*, p. 22 and p. 51. See also Baranson, J., *The Japanese Challenge to U.S. Industry*, p. 56.
190 Wheeler, J. W., Janow, M. E. and Pepper T., *Japanese Industrial Development Policies in the 1980s*, p. 4ff. Critical, Prestovitz, C. V., *Trading Places*, p. 311: 'The fact is that while Japan is rich, the Japanese are not.'
191 Cf. OECD, *Economies en transition*, p. 118ff.
192 Literally 'knowledge intensive industrial structure' (*chishiki shuyakuka*) or 'knowledge intensive society' (*joho shakai*).
193 OECD, *Economies en transition*, p. 118 and Johnson, C., *MITI and the Japanese Miracle*, p. 290. Refer also to *Economic Planning Agency: The Basic Directions of Trade and Industrial Policy in the 1970s*.
194 Waragai, T., *Neue Entwicklungen der Analyse industrieller Verflechtungen in Japan und in der Bundesrepublik Deutschland*, p. 36ff.
195 See also Chapter 4, section II.
196 Okita, S., *The Developing Economies and Japan: Lessons in Growth*, p. 95f.
197 For an overview on Japanese business performance since 1945 see Abe, E., Gourvish, T. R. and Gourvish, T., *Japanese Success? British Failure?: Comparisons in Business Performance since 1945* or Kawanishi, H. and Corbett, J., *The Human Face of Industrial Conflict in Post War Japan*.
198 Kaizuka, K., *Shin kontenha sogo no tachiba kara mita seisaku teikei [Policy planning from a neoclassical position]*. This mono-dimensional perspectiveson the Japanese structural polices as being strictly MITI related without letting further arguments come into play are clearly ineffective and do not mirror reality. Wolferen, K. v., *The Enigma of Japanese Power*, p. 163.
199 Patrick, H., *Industrial Policy, Economic Growth and the Competitiveness of US Industry*; Haitani, K., *The Japanese Economic System*, p. 135.
200 Cf. Nations, R., *Pax Pacifica: The Regasone Prosperity Plan*, p. 55f. and Tharp, M., *A Few Steps Further*, p. 56.

201 Vogel, E. F., *Japan as Number One: Lessons for America*, p. 232 and Itoh, M., Kiyono, K. and Okuno, M., *Sangyo Seisaku no Keizai Bunzeki* [*An economic analysis of industrial policy*], p. 134ff.
202 Behrman, J. N., *Industrial Policies: International Restructuring and Transnationals*, p. 11ff. and Shinohara, M., *Industrial Growth, Trade and Dynamic Patterns in the Japanese Economy*, p. 21.
203 Zysman, J., Tyson, L. and Borrus, M., *US and Japanese Trade and Industrial Policies*, p. 7ff.; Vogel, E. F., *Japan as Number One: Lessons for America*, p. 233ff. and Nijno, K., *Gendai Sogyo Seisaku no Kadai* [*Current plans for industrial policies*], p. 11ff.
204 Reich, R., *Beyond Free Trade*, p. 775. Refer also to Reich, R., *The Next American Frontier*.
205 These Sector reviews draw on Grossman, G. M., *Explaining Japan's Innovation and Trade: A Model of Quality Competition and Dynamic Comparative Advantage*, p. 76; Freeman, C., *Technology Policy and Economic Performance: Lessons from Japan*, p. 28 and Economic Planning Agency, *Economic Survey of Japan 1986–1987*, p. 167ff. and p. 208.
206 This aspect is mentioned in Dore, R., Bounine-Cabalé, J. and Tapiola, K., *Japan At Work*, p. 23ff. Contrast this to Economic Planning Agency, *Economic Survey of Japan 1987–1988*, p. 122.
207 Johnson, C., *MITI and the Japanese Miracle*, p. 278. If one looks at the current (2000) 'trade' war' between Europe and the US about bananas, it seems clear that these principles seem to be eternally constant.
208 Johnson, C., *MITI and the Japanese Miracle*, p. 81. See also Itoh, M., *The Globalization of Japan: Japanese Sakoku Mentality and U.S. Efforts to Open Japan*.
209 Helliwell, J. F. and Chung, A., *Globalization, Convergence and the Prospects for Economic Growth*, p. 65.
210 Anonymous, *Just possibly, something to sing about at last*.
211 Some accounts of this drift are: on the change in consumer behaviour, Meeham, M. (Ed.), *The Future ain't what it used to be*; on the Japanese customer overcoming the crisis sentiment: Kiuchi, T., *New Economy* 4. See also Dear, M. J., *The Postmodern Urban Condition*; Inamori, K. and Reid, T. R., *For People – And for Profit: A Business Philosophy for the 21st Century*.
212 Cf. OECD, *Economies en transition*, p. 132; Schmiegelow, M., *Zielerreichung*, p. 369ff.
213 Maury, R., *Die japanischen Manager: Wie sie denken, wie sie handeln, wie sie Weltmärkte erobern*, p. 136.
214 This paragraph is based on Ozawa, T., *Europe 1992 and Japanese Multinationals: Transplanting a Subcontracting System in the Expanded Market*, p. 5ff.
215 Here, the Ricardo–Hicks Theory is applicable as scarce fixed input (land and partially labour) is predominant in the Japanese case. Hicks J. R., *The Mainspring of Economic Growth*, p. 336f.
216 Compare especially, Ozawa, T., *Recycling Japan's Surpluses for Developing Countries*.
217 Anonymous, *Smart Factories: America's Turn?*, p. 142 and p. 148. The advance of the Internet can be seen in this context just as the start of the information or knowledge society Japan has envisioned for more than a decade.
218 Japan's foreign direct investments are an integral part of industrial restructuring: 'For once you achieve this kind of manufacturing plant network in Japan, there is no reason why these factories could not be duplicated at will around the world.' Gunn, T. G., *Manufacturing for Competitive Advantage*, p. 205. A striking example for this 'new phase of virtual imperialism' is the fact that exactly those products (produced by Japanese firms abroad) are imported to Japan with which the Japanese 'export miracle' began: motorbikes, TV-sets, simple electronic parts, Hi-Fi-sets, and cars. Robb, S., *Japan's New Imperialism*, p. 244f. Refer also to Ozawa, T., *Japan*.

219 Recent comparative studies confirm this general notion that Japan is on the brink of a new era. Factors to this are: (i) the notion of a change in general sentiment of the Japanese towards change (instilled by a new vision of Japan); (ii) favourable conditions created by the government (easy money, a low tax burden (29% vs 42% of GDP in the EU); (iii) corporate restructuring is well under way; and (iv) the Internet boom has just started and will change all (vertically organized) industries. The expectation is thus that Japan may clock the fastest growth rate since the 1970's. Anonymous, *Just possibly, something to sing about at last*, p. 77; Reyes, A., *Asia's 1000 Top Blue Chip Companies*.

220 For more information on the knowledge economy see Neef, D., Siesfeld, T. and Cefola, J., *The Economic Impact of Knowledge*.

221 Moltke, H. v., *Militärische Werke*, vol. 1, p. 292. See also Röpke, J., *Vom Nachzügler zum Pionier*, p. 54.

222 Cf. Johnson, C., *MITI and the Japanese Miracle*, p. 257, p. 296 and p. 305.

223 Besters, H., *Internationale Wettbewerbsfähigkeit bei unterschiedlichen Sozialordnungen – USA, Japan, Bundesrepublik Deutschland*, p. 64; Schmiegelow, M., *Schluss*, p. 318 and Ohmae, K., *The Evolving Global Economy: Making Sense of the New World Order*. Supportive on the theoretical level are Bryan, L. and Farrell, D., *Der entfesselte Markt. Die Befreiung des globalen Kapitalismus*; and Metcalfe, S. J., *Evolutionary Economics and Creative Destruction*.

224 These tactics draw on a rich traditional heritage of warfare: soft, flexible strategies coupled with tough actions are preferred over fixed positions and long winded positional strategies. The interested reader can resort to Musashi, M., *Das Buch der fünf Ringe*, p. 77ff. or Nitrobe, I., *Bushido*. On the business application, Ohmae, K., *Japanische Strategien*, p. 181f.

225 Sangyo Kozo Shingikai, *Chukan toshin: nanajuendai no tsusho sangyo seisaku [Interim report: Trade and industrial policies in the Seventies]*, p. 101.

226 Sangyo Kozo Shingikai, *Chukan toshin: nanajuendai no tsusho sangyo seisaku [Interim report: Trade and industrial policies in the Seventies]*, p. 101 and MITI, *White Paper on International Trade 1990*, p. 5. Critical thereof, Ohmae, K., *Die Macht der Triade*, p. 69ff.. Here Ohmae sees Japan's leading role endangered by (a) the impossibility of export of the Japanese management philosophy, (b) the slowing growth of export, and (c) the rising problems with increasing the Japanese production abroad.

227 They actually are quite similar to the postmodern analysis of the Western culture. Matsushita, K., *Policies of Citizens' Participation*, p. 451f. and Johnson, C., *MITI and the Japanese Miracle*, p. 283. An exhaustive analysis of environmental organizations can be found in Mouer, R. and Sugimoto, Y., *Images of Japanese Society*, p. 337ff.

228 Or just short 'karo' in Japanese. The first deaths caused by *karoshi* were reported in the 1960s when over 3000 hrs p.a. were the rule rather than the exception, Estimates range from 100 to 10 000 cases p.a. It is a widespread problem yet it is hidden behind a wall of silence: in the mid-1990s the first court cases were won by the families of employees killed by the enormous workload. Some accounts are for example, Wickert, E., *Der Riese hinter den sieben Bergen*; Fujimoto, K., *Working their Way to a Sudden Death*.

229 Cf. Bennett, J. W. and Levine, S. B., *Industrialization in Social Deprivation: Welfare Environment and the Postindustrial Society in Japan*, p. 457f.; Tasker, P., *Inside Japan*, p. 63; Sennett, R., *The Corrosion of Character: The Personal Consequences of Work in the New Capitalism*, p. 116ff. and Hackner, G., *Die anderen Japaner*.

230 Smith, R. J., *The Cultural Context of the Japanese Political Economy*, p. 30. See also Pegels, C. C., *Japan vs. the West*, p. 181ff.; Simon, D. R. and Henderson, J. H., *Private Troubles and Public Issues: Social Problems in the Postmodern Era*; Coulmas, F., *Japan ausser Kontrolle. Vom Musterknaben zum Problemkind*; Furlough, E. and Strikwerda, C.,

Notes 313

Consumers against Capitalism ? Consumer Cooperation in Europe, North America and Japan, p. 224 and Okumura, H., Japan und seine Unternehmen. Eine Einführung in gegenwärtige Strukturprobleme.

231 Japanese call this kind of traffic stoically *tsukin jigoku* (commuter hell) or *kotsu sensu* (traffic war). Signs and systems that indicate the lengths of traffic jams were first introduced in Japan, and display the common daily horror. Every visitor to Tokyo is invited to witness every evening 80 km long traffic jams on all major highways leaving Tokyo. K. Miyamoto calculated that the energy waste due to commuting equals the use within 4 business hours. Miyamoto, K., *Chiiki kaihatsu wa korede yoika? [Is the current trend in regional development acceptable?]*, p. 17. General studies are Dear, M. J., *The Postmodern Urban Condition*; Sauer-Thompson, G. and Wayne Smith, J., *Beyond Economics: Postmodernity, Globalization and National Sustainability*; Benko, G. and Strohmayer, U., *Space and Social Theory: Interpreting Modernity and Postmodernity* or Sennett, R., *The Corrosion of Character*, p. 116ff.

232 Johnson, C., *MITI and the Japanese Miracle*, p. 293 and MITI, *International Trade and Industrial Policy in the 1990s*, p. 30ff.

233 Cf. Besters, H., *Internationale Wettbewerbsfähigkeit bei unterschiedlichen Sozialordnungen – USA, Japan, Bundesrepublik Deutschland*, p. 99.

234 MITI addressed this problem first in 1990 as 'paradox of prosperity'. MITI, *International Trade and Industrial Policy in the 1990s*, p. 4 and Piore, M. J. and Sabel, C. F., *The Second Industrial Divide: Possibilities for Prosperity*, p. 165ff.

235 Kojima, K., *Japan and a New World Economic Order*, p. 121. See especially, Katz, R., *Japan, the System that Soured*.

236 M. Itoh pleads for a new openness of Japan condemning its '*Sakoku*' [secluded nation] mentality keeping it in a state of parochialism and exclusiveness: Itoh, M., *The Globalization of Japan: Japanese Sakoku Mentality and U.S. Efforts to Open Japan*. See also Carlile, L. E. and Tilton, M., *Is Japan Really Changing its Ways? Regulatory Reform and the Japanese Economy*. For a perspective on the future developments in this regard cf. especially Canton, J., *Technofutures: How Leading-Edge Technology will Transform Business in the 21st Century*; Khan, H., *Technology, Development and Democracy: Limits of National Innovation Systems in the Age of Postmodernism* and Mitchie, J. and Smith, J. G., *Globalization, Growth, and Governance: Creating an Innovative Economy*.

237 Yamamura, K., *Success that Soured: Administrative Guidance and Cartel in Japan*, p. 84f. See also Streib, F., *Wirtschaftsstrategien Japans und der USA im asiatisch-pazifischen Raum*.

238 Thailand and Malaysia were leaders of the boycott against Japanese products and the 'Japanese imperialism' proposing import substitution and export-drive industrialization. Shimano, T., *Cultural Conflict: Japan and South East Asian Countries*; Weinstein, F. B., *Multinational Corporations and the Third World: The Case of Japan and Southeast Asia*.

239 At the beginning of the 1970s, the then president K. Tanaka proposed his concept to restructure the Japanese archipelago that required for the following 15 years an average growth rate of 10%. Tanaka, K., *Nihon retto kaizo ron [Concept to restructure the Japanese archipelago]*, p. 5f.

240 Prime Minister's Office, *Survey on National Lifestyle 1991*.

241 Economic Planning Agency, *Economic Survey of Japan 1991–1992*, p. 316; Tominaga, K., *Rolle des Wertsystems für die Industrialisierung Japans*, p. 22.

242 Cf. Sangyo Kozo Shingikai, *Kyujuendai no tsusho seisaku bijon' [A vision of industrial structures in the Nineties]*, p. 10f. and p. 125f.; Sogo Kenkyu Kaihatsu Kiko, *Jiten: Nihon no kadai [Encyclopedia: Japan's preparations for the 21st Century]*, p. 249ff.

243 Ohkawa, K. and Rosovsky, H., *Japanese Economic Growth: Trend Acceleration in the Twentieth Century*, p. 217f.

244 Nomura Institute, *Kokusai kankyo no henka to Nihon no taio: niju-isseiki eno taigen* [*Dynamics in the international environment and Japan's answers: preparation for the 21st century*]; Piore, M. and Sabel, C. F., *The Second Industrial Divide: Possibilities for Prosperity*, p. 15ff.; Nihon Keizai Kenkyu Senta [Japan Center for Economic Research], *The Study of Socioeconomic Framework for the Analysis of Energy Demand and Supply in the Year 2000*, p. 13f.

245 Naumann, N., *Identitätsfindung – das geistige Problem des modernen Japans*, p. 174.

246 The Japanese value systems are now so instable that a change is inevitable. Applying the Freeze–Unfreeze–Refreeze theory of French and Bell, Japan is at the end of a massive unfreeze phase where dynamic forces are at work. French, W. L. and Bell, C. H., *Organizational Development*, p. 107f.; Bleicher, K., *Integriertes Management*, p. 445. Critical comment, Anonymous, *Japan Glimpses the ... Monitor*. This article cites the lack of self assurance and the fear of poverty as powerful forces to overcome the current limbo and become economically more successful and thus come (economically and personally) closer to invincibility.

247 Murakami, Y. and Kosai, Y., *Japan and the Global Community*, p. 9; Dore, R., *Flexible Rigidities*, p. 11 and p. 29; Ohmae, K., *Japanische Strategien*, p. 149ff.

248 Anonymous, *Just possibly, something to sing about at last*. Even the famous 'zaiteku' financing (in its most utilized form called 'tobashi': camouflaging of losses via derivatives) could not halt the slide, it rather accelerated the crisis, pushing serious players like Credits Suisse, First Boston (Japan) or Yamaichi out of business. A more general account of the reinvigorating international implications of financial crises is given by Allen, R. E., *Financial Crises and Recession in the Global Economy*.

249 Hamlin, M., *The New Asian Corporation*; Minc, A., *La Mondialisation Heureuse* [*Happy Globalization*]; Eichgreen, B., *Towards a New International Financial Architecture*.

250 Uekusa, K., *Japan in the New Millennium*; Allen, R. E., *Financial Crises and Recession in the Global Economy*.

251 The fact that 1999 first quarter profit figures of Yahoo! Japan jumped fivefold to new highs, supports this notion of a changed direction of trends.

252 Economic Planning Agency, *Economic Survey of Japan 1991–1992*, p. 317.

253 Economic Planning Agency, *Economic Survey of Japan 1991–1992*, p. 317f.

254 The final sentence of this study can hardly conceal the pride and the hegemonic interests: 'Japan should be able to occupy a position which commands respect and pres- . tige from the international community as a "truly affluent global state"' Economic Planning Agency, *Economic Survey of Japan 1991–1992*, p. 318f. See also MITI, *International Trade and Industrial Policy 1990*, p. 2: 'Japan has achieved the status as one of the world's strongest economic powers. ... Japan must demonstrate its willingness and ability to take a leading role ...' and EPA, *Economic Survey 1991–1992*, p. 1: '[Japan should play] ... a proper role in the in the international society according to its given power.'

255 Compare this to the concept of transitions between phases developed by Dopfer, K., *Elemente einer Evolutionsökonomik*, p. 40. Cf. also Scott, B., *Can Industry Survive the Welfare State?*, p. 70f. and Abernathy, W., *The New Industrial Competition*, p. 68f.

256 Sasaki-Smith, M., *Japanese Industrial Policy in the 1980s*, p. 37.

257 Sangyo Kozo Shingikai [Committee for Industrial Structure], *Juendai no tsusho seisaku bijon* [*A vision of industrial structures in the Nineties*], p. 4ff.

258 Economic Planning Agency, *Economic Survey of Japan 1989–1990*, p. 2 and p. 44ff.; see also Besters, H., *Internationale Wettbewerbsfähigkeit bei unterschiedlichen Sozialordnungen*, p. 14f.

259 Cf. Kosaka, M., *Japan's Choices*.

260 Economic Planning Agency, *Economic Survey of Japan 1992–1993* and EPA, *Economic Survey of Japan White Paper on the Economy 1991–1992*; EPA, *Economic Survey of Japan 1988–1989*; Sangyo Kozo Shingikai, *Kyujuendai no tsusho seisaku bijon [A vision of industrial structures in the Nineties]*; Kosaka, M., *Japan's Choices*; Kojima, K., *Japan and a New World Economic Order*; MITI, *White Paper on International Trade 1992*.

261 For further insights on new cultural styles see Breidenbach, J. and Zukrigl, I., *Tanz der Kulturen. Kulturelle Identität in einer globalisierten Welt.*

262 Sogo Kenkyu Kaihatsu Kiko, *Jiten: Nihon no kadai [Encyclopedia: Japan's preparations for the 21st century]*, p. 3ff. and p. 249ff.; see also MITI's theses, MITI, *International Trade and Industrial Policy in the 1990s*, p. 8ff. For a general account refer to Sackman, R. B., *Achieving the Promise of Information Technology: Introducing the Transformational Project Paradigm*; Braudo, R. J. and MacIntosh, J. G., *Competitive Industrial Development in the Age of Information: The Role of Co-operation in the Technology Sector.*

263 Sangyo Kozo Shingikai, *Hachijuendai no tsusho seisaku bijon [A vision of industrial structures in the Eighties]*, p. 48f.; Sangyo Kozo Shingikai, *Kyujuendai no tsusho seisaku bijon [A vision of industrial structures in the Nineties]*, p. 4 and p. 182ff.; Economic Planning Agency, *Economic Survey of Japan 1991–1992*, p. 15; Mowery, D. C., *U.S. Industry in 2000: Studies in Competitive Performance*, p. 45.

264 Many authors regard this new strategic orientation as another example of a giant master plan, that used the Modernity and its industry as theatrical tools to deceive the West. Goal remains to install the Emperor and Japan as the main power in the world. T. Immoos cites examples from the most symbolic area, the sphere of the imperial house: the founding of modern state shall be 'harmonized' with ancient Japanese mythology, the funeral rites of the last emperor Hirohito were orchestrated as high ceremonies by the state, the reintroduction of (nationalistically tainted) courses on ethics in schools, the holy rites at the enthronement of the Heisei-emperor in 1990 as mega-media events. All these symbolic acts by the imperial house are designed to reinstall the symbol of the Tenno as the god-like 'Uebervater' of the Japanese nation. Immoos, T., *Japan – Archaische Moderne*, p. 100ff.

265 This is the base-line of Japanese economic theory, but is now explicitly styled as the way for the future. Shinohara, M., *Issetsu: Nihon kabushiki kaisha-ron [Against the discussion on Japan Inc.]*, p. 114.

266 Sasaki-Smith, M., *Japan's Leasing Industry*, p. 80f.

267 Cf. Economic Planning Agency, *Economic Survey of Japan 1991–1992*, p. 2.

268 Economic Planning Agency, *Economic Survey of Japan 1991–1992*, p. 315 and MITI, *White Paper on International Trade 1991* and MITI, *International Trade and Industrial Policy in the 1990s*, p. 11ff.

269 Economic Planning Agency, *Economic Survey of Japan 1998–1999*

270 The Economic Planning Agency takes simple statistics to measure such a sophistication: 'consumption-based diversification of lifestyles, higher living standards, increased data sensitiveness in industries and the centralization of technology [i.e. Japan as the technological center].' Economic Planning Agency, *Economic Survey of Japan 1991–1992*, p. 315.

271 Friedman, G. and LeBard, M., *The Coming War with Japan*; Manegold, C. S., *A Military Power, too?* and Chapter 1, section II ('Japan as the focus of attention').

272 Economic Planning Agency, *Economic Survey of Japan 1991–1992*, p. 315.

273 This leads all arguments of Japan being isolated *ad absurdum*. For more refer to Miyoshi, M., *Against the Native Grain*, p. 158.

274   The U.S. National Association of Securities Dealers expresses even hopes to see the new
      role model, blockbuster companies (like Amazon and Yahoo of the 1990s) to come from
      Japan.
275   Matsui, K., Suzuki, H. and Ushio, Y., *Millennium Metamorphosis: From Old to New
      Japan*, p.6
276   This confirms the Economic Planning Agency's approach to construct a 'New Japan'
      (IT, Communication, knowledge-based services) distinguishing it from the 'Old Japan'
      of Machinery and good production and from the 'antique Japan' (Construction and
      Heavy Metal). Uekusa, K., *Japan in the New Millennium*.
277   Uekusa, K., *Japan in the New Millennium*. Still, Japan has the highest total access cost
      when it comes to the Internet (25% more expensive than Germany, more than double
      the USA and almost three times as high as Italy), but this is bound to change.
      Anonymous, *Just possibly, something to sing about at last*, p.75
278   Compare with Chapter 2, section IV and hypothesis 1 in Chapter 1, section V. See also
      Wolfe, A., *Suicide and the Japanese Postmodern*, p.228.
279   Harootunian, H. D., *Visible Discourses Invisible Ideologies*, p.68.
280   This is now a combination of Japanese spirit and Western technology, which was
      searched since the opening of the country in the last century. Nakane, C., *Japanese
      Society*, p.119.
281   Asada, A., *Infantile Capitalism and Japan's Postmodernism*, p.276.
282   Miyoshi, M., *Against the Native Grain*, p.158.
283   Miyoshi, M., *Against the Native Grain*, p.148. Supportingly on a more general level,
      Boyd, G. and Dunning, J. H., *Structural Change and Cooperation in the Global
      Economy*; Cohen, B. J. and Lipson, C., *Issues and Agents in the International Political
      Economy: An International Organization Reader*.
284   On the intertemporal dominance of the trickle down hypothesis, Ozawa, T., *Japan's
      Technological Challenge to the West*; Gardner, A. and Ishii, H., *Fiscal, Monetary and
      Related Policies*, p.158ff.; Pempel, T. J., *Japanese Foreign Policy: The Domestic Bases
      for International Behavior*, p.143.
285   Imai, K., *Japan's Corporate Networks*, p.204ff.; see also Yoshino, M. Y., *Japan's
      Multinational Enterprises*, p.4.
286   Tasker, P., *Inside Japan*, p.261. For international aspects refer to Brewer, T. L. and
      Young, S., *The Multilateral Investment System and Multinational Enterprises* and Weid-
      enbaum, M. L., *Business and Government in the Global Marketplace*. Opposing view has
      K. Cox who writes against the 'myths of postnational enterprises' as driving forces.
      Cox, K. R., *Spaces of Globalization: Reasserting the Power of the Local*, p.89.
287   On the intra-company shift of labour between sectors, Dore, R., Bounine-Cabalé, J.
      and Tapiola, K., *Japan at Work*, p.12f.; Tasker, P., *Inside Japan*, p.220 and p.259 and
      Alic, J. A., Herzenberg, S. and Wial, H., *New Rules for a New Economy: Employment
      and Opportunity in Postindustrial America*. Quote from Eccleston, B., *State and Society
      in Postwar Japa*n, p.41f.
288   In this '*benchaa buumu*' (venture boom) the shortage of entrepreneurs is overcome by a
      guided educational effort: in schools for the middle aged, top managers learn to accept the
      Internet as their main tool for work, while 'sun kids', four to seven-year-old pupils (!), learn
      at the Tokyo Center for Enterpreneurial Students how to be successful entrepreneurs.
289   '... banks rid themselves of cross shareholdings but the conclusion that Keiretsu are
      dead is erroneous.' Anonymous, *Just possibly, something to sing about at last*, p.75
290   Matsui, K., Suzuki, H. and Ushio, Y., *Millennium Metamorphosis: From Old to New
      Japan*, p.8
291   Tasker, P., *Inside Japan*, p.273. N. Chomsky puts it even sharper when stating that the
      architects of the global society are not the countries but the companies. Chomsky, N.,

and Dietrich, H., *Globalisierung im Cybespace. Globale Gesellschaft: Märkte, Demo-kratie und Erziehung*; supportive of that are Münch, R., *Globale Dynamik, lokale Lebenswelten. Der schwierige Weg in die Weltgesellschaft* and Elazar, D. J., *Constitutionalizing Globalization: The Postmodern Revival of Confederal Arrangements.*

292   Shimizu, R., *Top Management in Japanese Firms*, p. 7.
293   Tasker, P., *Inside Japan*, p. 269.
294   Cf. Yoshino, M. Y., *Japan's Multinational Enterprises*, p. 69 and Shinohara, M., *Industrial Growth, Trade, and Dynamic Patterns in the Japanese Economy*, p. 45.
295   Hymer, S., *The United States' Multinational Corporations and Japanese Competition*, p. 4.
296   Sugarman, D., *Governance, Industrial Organization, and Efficiency in a Post-Modern World*, p. 13.
297   Compare with the theories on internalization in Chapter 5, section II ('the theory of internationalization').
298   Sugarman, D., *Governance, Industrial Organization, and Efficiency in a Post-Modern World*, p. 13. An empirical analysis is offered by Pettaway, R., Sicherman, N. W. and Yamada, T., *Japanese Mergers*, p. 181f.
299   Cf. Emmott, B., *Japan's Global Reach*, p. 130; Anonymous, *Global Localization*, p. 7f. See also Rowntree, L., *Diversity Amid Globalization: World Regions, Environment, Development.*

5   Keiretsu: Japanese Multinational Enterprises and the Postmodern

1   Best, M., *The New Competition*, p. 138 and Tsutsui, W. M., *Manufacturing Ideologies: Scientific Management in Twentieth-Century Japan*, p. 170.
2   For more on Honda see Mayo, R., Moody, P. E. and Nelson, D., *Powered by Honda: Developing Excellence in the Global Enterprise.*
3   Eli, M., *Sogo Shosha*, p. 581. M. Emori opposes maintaining that the Japanese MNE are just a copy of the U.S. style MNE. Emori, M., *The Japanese Trading Company*, p. 1. Here, Japanese sources are systematically downplaying the importance, even the existence of groupings, Keiretsu, of a more serious kind: the Japan Company Handbook as a standard reference on listed companies, categorically uses only the deflecting word 'association' when talking about any kind of linkage. Likewise the web-presence of Mitsubishi (www.mitsubishi.co.jp).
4   Wright, R. W. and Pauli, G. W., *The Second Wave*, p. 32; Toagi, Y., *Comments*, p. 104; Miyasaki, Y., *Excessive Competition and the Formation of Keiretzu*, p. 53.
5   Nagata, K., *The World of Mitsubishi – Mighty Mitsubishi.*
6   There are still linguistic confusions, as some authors use 'Zaibatsu' to refer to the contemporary companies' structures or try to describe the trading companies isolated from their surrounding network. See for example Clark, R., *The Japanese Company*, p. 73f.
7   Refer to Chapters 3 and 4.
8   Ballon, R. J. and Tomita, I., *The Financial Behavior of Japanese Corporations*, p. 58; Yui, T., *Die Beziehungen zwischen Regierung und Unternehmen und ihr Einfluss auf die Industrialisierung Japans*, p. 45; Reischauer, E. O., *The Japanese*, p. 306.
9   Very often one finds an ahistorical view on the new forms of Japanese organization, propagating them as the Japanese 'secret', that should be (superficially) adapted, tried as it is the new recipe for success. This view obviously forgets the impact of the developments after World War II and neglects to incorporate the fact that rapid growth had also taken place during the Meiji era. The numerous booklets and training courses on Kanban, Kaizen and other 'Japanese management systems' are examples of this shallow view.

10 Cf. Ozawa, T., *Multinationalism Japanese Style* and Beamish, P. *et al.*, *Japanese Multinationals in the Global Economy*.

11 Further literature about multinational enterprises in other Asian countries: Van Hoesel, R., *New Multinational Enterprises from Korea and Taiwan: Beyond Export-Led Growth*.

12 Miyasaki, Y. *Excessive Competition and the Formation of Keiretzu*, p. 55f.; Reischauer, E. O., *The Japanese*, p. 308; Quote from Yasumuro, K., *The Contribution of Sogo Shosha to the Multinationalization of Japanese Industrial Enterprises in Historical Perspective*, p. 297; Eli, M., *Sogo Shosha*, p. 582.

13 Abegglen, J. C. and Stalk, G., *Kaisha*, p. 181 and p. 286ff.; quote from p. 286. An update is given by Yoshimura, N., Anderson, P. and Yoshimura, N., *Inside the Kaisha*.

14 See also Chapter 1, section I ('the business revolution').

15 Compare with Davidow, W. H. and Mulone, M. S., *The Virtual Corporation: Structuring and Revitalizing the Corporation for the 21st Century*; Howard, W. G. and Guile, B. R., *Profiting from Innovation*; Brown, D., *An Institutionalist Look at Postmodernism*.

16 R. Kusiel describes this French strategy, known there as 'Système Motte': Kusiel, R. F., *Capitalism and the State in Modern France: Revolution and Economic Management in the Twentieth Century*, p. 5ff. and p. 152; see also Burstein, D., *Euroquake*, p. 288 and Michalet, C. A. and Chevallier, T., *France*. The German quasi-Keiretsu (coalition of enterprises) are examined in Zimbalist, A., Sherman, H. J. and Brown, S., *Comparing Economic Systems*, p. 34f.; Grou, P., *The Financial Structure of Multinational Capitalism*, p.128ff. and in Johnson, C., *MITI and the Japanese Miracle*, p. 199f. Anonymous, *Italien will sich am Modell der Hausbank orientieren*.

17 The Swedish Wallenberg conglomerate has a clearly defined holding strategy to maintain the Wallenberg family in control. The Deutsche Bank- and Dresdner Bank-'Keiretsu' are structured likewise and thus contrast to the hierarchy-free, open flexible structures of the Keiretsu. Anonymous, *Mighty Mitsubishi is on the Move*, p. 40; *Structural Impediment Initiative Talks 1991: Opinions on the Keiretzu Issue*, p. 286ff.; Pfeiffer, H., *Das Imperium der Deutschen Bank*.

18 Yoshino, M. Y. and Lifson, T. B., *The Invisible Link*, p. 45; Young, A. K., *The Sogo Shosha – Japans Multinational Trading Companies*, p. 17ff.; Nakatanki, I., *The Economic Role of Financial Corporate Grouping*, p. 80.

19 Womack, J. P., Johnes, D. T. and Roos, D., *Die zweite Revolution in der Autoindustrie*, p. 274; Gilroy, B. M., *Networking in Multinational Enterprises*, p. 159ff.; Engardio, P., *Building a Hong Kong Empire from a Japanese Blueprint*, p. 23; Chu, C. N., *The Asian Mind Game*, p. 225.

20 Grou, P., *The Financial Structure of Multinational Capitalism*, p. 29ff.; Clegg, L. J., *The Determinants of Multinational Enterprise: A Comparative Study of the US, Japan, UK, Sweden, and West Germany*, p. 605f.; OECD, *International Investment and MNE*, p. 23ff.; UNCTAD, *World Investment Report 1993*; Anonymous, *Der Umsatz der 'Multis' ist höher als das Welthandelsvolumen*.

21 Hedlund, G., *Autonomy of Subsidiaries and Formalism of Headquarter–Subsidiary Relationships in Swedish Multinational Enterprises*; see also Negandhi A. R. and Welge, M. K., *Beyond Theory Z: Global Rationalization – Strategies of American, German and Japanese Multinational Companies*.

22 Takamiya, M., *Conclusions and Policy Implications*, p. 188ff.; Kobayashi, N., *The Patterns of Management Style Developing in Japanese Multinationals in the 1980's*.

23 For more about todays globalization see Waters, M., *Globalization*.

24 See also Teece, D. J., *Technology Transfer by Multinational Firms: The Resource Cost of Transferring Technological Know How*, p. 249f. D. Teece, contrasting the Japanese approach with the American, observes significant differences in the area of top-management strategy, product strategies, and production methods, sourcing, industrial

relations R&D and controlling. See also Ftatsugi, Y., *Kigyo kan kankei no sokutei* [*The relations of a company with other companies*], p. 38; and Chapter 5, section III.

25 Relevant general culture-based explanations are De Mente, B., *The Kata Factor*, or De Mente, B., *Japanese Etiquette in Ethics and Business*; see also Chapter 3.

26 Negandhi, A. R., *External and Internal Functioning of American, German, and Japanese Multinational Corporations: Decision-making and Policy Issues*, p. 561ff.

27 Wolferen, K. v., *The Enigma of Japanese Power*, p. 303. This view is supported by M. Moran, regarding the Japanese MNE as pathbreaking models of company culture, as they are useful everywhere, but are always strongly related with value systems that are expertly elaborated and lived in Japan. Moran, M., *The Politics of International Business*.

28 The reader is reminded of the late A. Morita's quote: 'Japanese and American management is 95% the same and differs in all important aspects' quoted after Kiechl, R., *Ethnokultur und Unternehmenskultur*, p. 107.

29 C. Johnson quoted in Neff, R. and Holstein, W. J., *Mighty Mitsubishi is on the Move*, p. 40.

30 Yoshino, M. Y., *Japan's Multinational Enterprises*, p. 69ff.

31 Ozawa, T., *Multinationalism Japanese Style*, p. 186f.; see also Kojima, K., *Nihon gata takokuseiki kigyo no arikata* [*The special type of the Japanese MNE*]; Mataji, M., Togai, Y. and Mishima, Y., *Sogo shosha keieishi* [*History of the Sogo Shosha*]; Nakano, H., *Sogo shosha no honshitsu to nihon gata takokuseki kigyo* [*The nature of the Sogo Shosha and the Japanese MNE*].

32 Shimizu, R., *Top Management in Japanese Firms*, p. 7; see also Chu, N. C., *The Asian Mind Game*.

33 The importance of loyalty and family is stressed in Schneidewind, D., *Das japanische Unternehmen – Uchi no kaisha*, p. 178f.; Hayashi, S., *Culture and Management in Japan*, p. 68ff.; Glazer, N., *Social and Cultural Factors in Japanese Economic Growth*, p. 874ff.; Roberts, J. G., *Mitsui*, p. 128 and p. 496; Yasuoka, S., *The Tradition of Family Business in the Strategic Decision Process and Management Structure of Zaibatzu Business*.

34 Trust as a strong component is examined in Casson, M., *Enterprise and Competitiveness*, p. 114 and Wagatsuma, H., *Heritage of Endurance*, p. 23.

35 The relevance of long-term strategies stress: Aoki, M., *Aspects of the Japanese Firm*, p. 24; Nakatani, I., *The Japanese Firm in Transition*, p. 32; and Kester, W. K., *Japanese Takeovers – The Global Contest for Corporate Control*, p. 54.

36 Special attention to competition as a cornerstone is drawn by Sazaki, N., *Management and Industrial Structure in Japan*, p. 103ff.; Drucker, P. F., *Towards the Next Economics*, p. 144; Johnson, C., *MITI and the Japanese Miracle*, p. 221ff.; Rapaport, C., *Why Japan keeps on Winning*; Ito, M., Siyono, K., Okuno, M. and Suzumura, K., *Industrial Policy as a Corrective to Market Failures*, p. 233ff.

37 See also Krackhard, D. and Hanson, J. R., *Informelle Netze – Die heimlichen Kraftquellen*; Liker, J. K., Fruin, W. M. and Adler, P. S., *Remade in America: Transplanting and Transforming Japanese Management Systems*; Tachibanaki, T. and Kenkyujo, R. S., *Who Runs Japanese Business? Management and Motivation*; Sumi, A., *Japanese Industrial Transplants in the United States: Organizational Practices and Relations of Power*; Beamish, P. W., Delios, A. and Lecraw, D. J., *Japanese Multinationals in the Global Economy*.

38 For more information on strategies for multinationals see Cullen, J. B., *Multinational Management: A Strategic Approach*.

39 It could be argued that only with the new (though sometimes latent) tool of postmodern thoughts an integrative understanding of the Japanese MNE was rendered possible, as all the diverging details were impossible to mould into one framework. Research of the Seventies had to concede: '... the deeper they [the researchers] go in the probe into those sogo shosha, the greater the enigma proves to be. So gigantic is the scale of the sogo shosha that their identity remains difficult to grasp.' Mainichi Daily News, *The Mitsui Group*, p. 44.

40   Casson, M., *The Firm and the Market*, p. 1; Ott, A. E., *Industrieökonomik*, p. 319; Casson, M., *Enterprise and Competitiveness*, p. 2. A concise overview is given by Dunning, J., *Multinational Enterprises and the Global Economy*, p. 68ff.
41   Bain, J. S., *Barriers to New Competition*.
42   Sawyer, M. C., *The Economics of Industries and Firms*, p. 18; Scherer, F. M., *On the Current State of Knowledge in Industrial Organization*.
43   W. G. Shepherd opposes strongly. Shepherd, W. G., *On the Core Concepts of Industrial Economics*, p. 24.
44   A shorter overview of these developments is to be found in Ozawa, T., *Multinationalism, Japanese Style*, p. 42ff.; see also Gilroy, B. M., *Economic Issues of Multinational Enterprises*.
45   One basic neoclassical thesis is: '... big business emerged purely for reasons of production efficiency.' Best, M., *The New Competition*, p. 59.
46   Galbraith, J. K., *Economics and the Public Purpose*, p. 209ff. and Galbraith, J. K., *American Capitalism*, p. 168ff.
47   McCraw, T. K., *Mercantilism and the Market*, p. 41.
48   Hymer, S., *The International Operations of National Firms*.
49   Kindleberger and Hymer talk about a 'compensating advantage'. Buckley P. J., *The Economic Theory of the Multinational Enterprise*; and Buckley P. J., *A Critical View of Theories of the Multinational Enterprise*, p. 2.
50   This theory (in combination with Hymer's ideas) was also propagated by C. Kindleberger: Kindleberger, C. P., *American Business Abroad*.
51   Hennart, J. F., *The Transaction Cost Theory of the Multinational Enterprise*.
52   Casson, M., *The Firm and the Market*, p. 6ff. and Gilroy, B. M., *Multinational Enterprise and Trade Structure*, p. 5.
53   On a formal level S. Hirsch deals with this interdependency of environment and MNE. Hirsch, S., *An International Trade and Investment Theory of the Firm*. See also Helpman, E., *A Theory of Multinational Corporations and the Structure of Foreign Trade*. For Hymer's approach, its relevance today is stressed in Yamin, M., *A Reassessment of Hymer's Contribution to the Transnational Cooperation*.
54   Vernon, R., *International Investment and International Trade in the Product Cycle*; Hirsch, S., *The Location of Industry and International Competitiveness*.
55   Buckley, P. J., *The Economic Theory of the Multinational Enterprise*; Buckley, P. J., *A Critical View of Theories of the Multinational Enterprise*, p. 13ff.
56   Ozawa, T., *Multinationalism, Japanese Style*, p. 48ff.; see also Vernon, R., *Storm over the Multinationals*, p. 244.
57   Praised as the discoverer of globalization (he called it rather 'globalism' a term comparable to the current fad of 'globality') and for his ideas on collaboration between the political and economic spheres he was awarded by Japan the Order of the Rising Sun. Vernon, R., *In the Hurricane's Eye: The Troubled Prospects of Multinational Enterprises*.
58   Casson, M., *The Firm and the Market*, p. 7; Pitelis, C. and Sudgen, R., *On the Theory of the Transnational Firm*.
59   Williamson, O. E., *The Modern Corporation: Origins, Evolution, Attributes*; Williamson, O. E., *The Economic Institutions of Capitalism: Firms – Markets – Relational Contracting*; Masten, S. E., *The Organization of Production*; Masten, S. E., *Institutional Choice and the Organization of Production*.
60   Williamson, O. E., *The Logic of Economic Organization*, p. 91.
61   On the origins of transaction cost economics: Schmalensee, R. and Willig, R. D., *Handbook of Industrial Organization*; Williamson, O. E., *Transaction Cost Economics*, p. 137ff. There one can find a simple algebraic model as well as case studies. See also Williamson, O. E., *The Economic Institutions of Capitalism*, p. 15ff.

62 Rugman, A., *New Theories of the MNE*. For an overview on recent findings: Carroll, G. and Teece, D., *Firms, Markets, and Hierarchies*.
63 Williamson, O. E., *The Economic Institutions of Capitalism*, p. 22.
64 Arrow, K., *The Organization of Economic Activity*.
65 Buchanan, J. M., *A Contractarian Paradigm for Applying Economic Theory*, p. 229.
66 Williamson, O. E., *The Economic Institutions of Capitalism*, p. 32.
67 Williamson, O. E., *The Economic Institutions of Capitalism*, p. 43ff.
68 On the economic concept of 'bounded rationality' see especially H. A. Simon, who describes it as 'intendedly rational but only limitedly so'. Simon, H. A., *Administrative Behavior*, p. xxiv. For further extensions of the economic concept of human behaviour see e.g., Ormerod, P., *The Death of Economics*; Hollstein, B., *Der Arbeitsbegriff inder ökonomischen Theorie und das Ehrenamt*.
69 Williamson, O. E., *The Economic Institutions of Capitalism*, p. 68ff.
70 This changes the variables from quantifiable rational parameters to more fuzzy things like credible responsibility, threats, hostages and reciprocity. For details revert to Williamson, O. E., *The Economic Institutions of Capitalism*, p. 164ff.; Casson, M., *Enterprise and Competitiveness*, p. 43; Williamson, O. E., *Credible Commitments Using Hostages to Support Exchange*; Williamson, O. E., *Transaction Cost Economics: The Governance of Contractual Relations*, p. 233ff.
71 Williamson, O. E., *The Economic Institutions of Capitalism*, p. 68ff. and more elaborately, Fox, A., *Beyond Contractwork Power and Trust Relations*, p. 74ff.
72 Kitagawa, Z., *Contract Law in General*, p. 3; see also Chapter 3, section IV.
73 C.f. Imai, K., *The Legitimacy of Japan's Corporate Groups* and Kojima, K. and Ozawa, T., *Japan's General Trading Companies*, p. 11ff.
74 Chandler, A. D., *The Visible Hand*, p. 257; Williamson, O. E., *The Economic Institutions of Capitalism*, p. 56; Cantwell, J., *A Survey of Theories of International Production*.
75 It has to be noted that the subjective nature of all cost definitions (or rather their meta-economic character) has been stressed much earlier (1946): 'It should hardly be necessary to mention that all the relevant magnitudes involved – cost, revenue, profits – are subjective . . . rather than objective. . . . Marginal analysis of the firm should not be understood to imply anything but subjective estimates, guesses and hunches.' Machlup, F., *Marginal Analysis and Empirical Research*, p. 521f. M. Friedman stressed the non-monetary and non-contractual cost as driving forces: Friedman, M., *Price Theory*, p. 99.
76 Casson, M., *Enterprise and Competitiveness*, p. 9ff.
77 Rugman, A., *Internalization as a General Theory of Foreign Direct Investment*, p. 376. An in-depth overview is provided by Brewer, T. L. and Young, S., *The Multilateral Investment System and Multinational Enterprises*. See also Rugman, A., *Inside the Multinationals: The Economics of Internal Markets*; Fukao, M., *Financial Integration, Corporate Governance, and the Performance of Multinational Companies* and especially, Casson, M., *Internalization Theory and Beyond*.
78 More exhaustive studies of the internationalization are Buckley, P. J., *New Horizons in International Business*; Gilroy, B. M., *Multinational Enterprise and Trade Structure: The Role of Intrafirm Trade*; Grubel, M. G. and Loyd, P. G., *Intra-Industry Trade: The Theory and Measurement of International Trade in Differentiated Products*. Formal models are developed in Ethier, W., *Internationally Decreasing Costs of World Trade*; Ethier, W., *National and International Returns to Scale in the Modern Theory of International Trade*; Helpman, E., *International Trade in the Present Product Differentiation, Economies of Scale and Monopolistic Competition*; and Helpman, E., *Increasing Returns, Imperfect Markets, and Trade Theory*.
79 Quote from Casson, M., *The Firm and the Market*, p. 6; see also Pitelis, C. and Sudgen, R., *On the Theory of the Transnational Firm*.

80	Lichtenberg, F. R. and Pushner, G. M., *Ownership and Corporate Performance in Japan*; Takamiya, M., *The Degree of Organizational Centralization in Multinational Corporations*; Tasker, P., *Inside Japan*, p. 263; Imai, K., *The Legitimacy of Japan's Corporate Groups*; Imai, K., *Japan's Industrial Structure*, p. 108. For the general case, Williamson, O. E., *The Economic Institutions of Capitalism*, p. 287.
81	Broll, U. and Gilroy, B. M., *Aussenwirtschaftstheorie*, p. 149 and p. 159; quote from p. 235.
82	This approach grounds itself on the works of R. Coase. As early as 1937 he asked explicitly where the firm stops and the market begins. Also he wondered which form of relations should be maintained between economic actors: cooperative or market mechanisms. Thirdly, he questioned the need for companies as such favouring a network of cooperative individuals. According to Coase, the main reason for the existence of firms are the cost of price discovery (search, negotiation, taxes) and the short duration of market transaction which opposes longer-term coordination: '... the operation of a market costs something and by forming an organization and allowing some authority ('entrepreneur') to direct the resources, certain marketing cost are saved.' Coase, R. H., *The Nature of the Firm*, p. 19ff.
83	Coase, R. H., *The Nature of the Firm*, p. 18f.
84	Casson, M., *Enterprise and Competitiveness*, p. 43 and p. 54; Williamson, O. E., *The Economic Institutions of Capitalism*, p. 96f.
85	Quote from Siegel, D., *Futurize your Enterprise*, p. 5. For recent adaptations of the inernalization theory: Putterman, L. and Kroszner, R., *The Economic Nature of the Firm*; Spulber, D., *Market Microstructure: Intermediaries and the Theory of the Firm*; Poirier, C. C., *Advanced Supply Chain Management: How to Build a Sustained Competition*; Kay, N. M., *The Boundaries of the Firm: Critiques, Strategies and Policies*; Dubois, A., *Organizing Industrial Activities across Firm Boundaries*.
86	Kojima, K., *Direct Foreign Investment: A Japanese Model of Multinational Business Operations*; Kojima, K., *Macroeconomic versus International Business Approach to Direct Foreign Investment* and Ozawa, T., *A Newer Type of Foreign Investment in Third World Resource Development*. For an empirical study refer to Beamish, P. W., Delios, A. and Lecraw, D. J., *Japanese Multinationals in the Global Economy*.
87	Ruffin, R. J. and Rassekh, F., *The Role of Foreign Direct Investment in US Capital Outflows*; Martin, S., *Industrial Economics: Economic Analysis and Public Policy*.
88	Ozawa, T., *Multinationalism, Japanese Style*, p. 69; quote, p. 63. Read especially, Kojima, K. and Ozawa, T., *Towards a Theory of Industrial Restructuring and Dynamic Comparative Advantage*; Delener, N., *Strategic Planning and Multinational Trading Blocs*. See also Berry, B. J., Conkling, E. C., Ray, M. D. and Berry, B., *Global Economy in Transition*.
89	This is disputed as local strengths have more weight than globally acting forces. Though no concept of a nation is rekindled, territories (or local spaces, remining of Porter's cluster of excellence, e.g. Silicon Valley) play a more dominant role than MNEs: Cox, K. R., *Spaces of Globalization: Reasserting the Power of the Local*, p. 89ff.; Agrawal, M., *Global Competitiveness in the Pharmaceutical Industry: The Effect of National Regulatory, Economic, and Market Factors*.
90	This is the reason why proponents of a macroeconomic approach see themselves in the Hymer–Kindleberger–Caves tradition, and consequently dismiss Vernon's theory (and its critique of the macroeconomic approach). See also Ozawa, T., *Multinationalism Japanese Style*, p. 50.
91	'One cannot have an economic theory of the MNE that includes both the neoclassical theory of location and a realistic theory of management.' Casson, M., *The Firm and the Market*, p. 40.
92	A good overview of the arguments against a normative theory of capital arbitrage is provided by Borner, S., *New Forms of Internationalization*, p. 104ff.

93   A general critique of the macroeconomic approach is given by Buckley, P. J., *Macroeconomic versus International Business Approach: A Reply*.

94   For an overview on intra-industry trade see Stone, L. L., *The Growth of Intra-Industry Trade: New Trade Patterns in a Changing Global Economy*.

95   Ballon, R. J. and Tomita, I., *The Financial Behavior of Japanese Corporations*, p. 23; and Gilroy, B. M., *Multinational Enterprise and Trade Structure: The Role of Intrafirm Trade*, p. 20ff. According to Ozawa, Japan is best able to use the macroeconomic trends in combination with the general trend to multinational combination of firms. Ozawa, T., *Multinationalism Japanese Style*, p. 235.

96   A case study on Japan is Price, J., *Japan Works*.

97   Dunning, J., *Introduction*, p. 3; Ganovetter, M., *Economic Action and Social Structure*, p. 36ff.

98   R. Brenner even maintains that all the usual terms like 'firm', 'profit maximization', 'short-term', 'long-term', 'organizational structure' etc. are not clearly defined if one would be honest. Brenner, R., *Rivalry: In Business, Science, among Nations*, p. 11.

99   Cantwell, J., *A Survey of the Theories of International Production*, p. 17 and p. 29.

100 This flexible modular way of generating theories is favoured by Shepherd, W. G., *On the Core Concepts of Industrial Economics*, p. 26.

101 Dunning, J., *The Eclectic Paradigm of International Production: A Personal Perspective*, p. 133.

102 The advantages were discovered early, for example, Cherkes, M., *The Theory of Multinational Enterprise in Manufacturing Enterprises*, p. 7.

103 For the derivation see Dunning, J., *The Eclectic Paradigm of International Production: A Personal Perspective*, p. 120ff. or Buckley, P. J., *The Economic Theory of the Multinational Enterprise;* Buckley, P. J., *A Critical View of the Theory of the Multinational Enterprise*, p. 13.

104 Dunning, J., *Introduction*, p. 6f.; Casson, M., *The Firm and the Market*, p. 32 and Dunning, J., *Multinational Enterprises and the Global Economy*, p. 54ff. and p. 261ff. Ownership advantages (also called competitive or monopolistic advantages) are all specific and (if only temporary) secured competitive advantages of a firm. Examples are management, better organization of production, rights and patents, or technologies. But also more intangible competencies like experience, local knowledge and a well oiled network are ownership advantages. Locations effects as second category are all advantages resulting from a better choice of location for a given economic activity. Here the connection to the old theory of location is obvious. Advantages of internalization result from an optimized integration (and externalization) of international activities by MNEs (cf. Chapter 5, section II above on 'the theory of internationalization' and 'the macroeconomic explanation'). See also Dunning, J., *Trade, Location of Economic Activity, and the MNE: A Search for an Eclectic Approach*; Dunning, J., *The Eclectic Paradigm of International Production: A Restatement*, p. 2; Cantwell, J., *A Survey of the Theories of International Production*, p. 27; and Schütte, C., *Drohung erlaubt*.

105 Dunning, J., *Multinationals, Technology and Competitiveness*, p. 3.

106 Dunning, J., *Some Conclusions and Policy Implications*, p. 408 and p. 417. Given this point of view, Japan and its MNEs are regarded in empirical analyses as very successful, especially in the efficiency to adapt. Compare with Chapter 4, section III ('the links between . . .') and section IV ('overview of Japan's . . .').

107 Dunning, J., *Multinationals, Technology and Competitiveness*, p. 251; Dunning, J., *Multinational Enterprises and the Global Economy*, p. 578ff. and Shepherd, W. G., *On the Core Concepts of Industrial Economics*, p. 41.

108   'Dunning's eclectic theory implicitly denies the original powerful insight of Coase, which
       is that internalization is the raison d'être of the firm.' Casson, M., *The Firm and the
       Market*, p. 35; see also Buckley, P. J., *The Economic Theory of the Multinational Enter-
       prise*, p. 18 and Itaki, M., *Critical Assessment of the Eclectic Theory of the Multinational
       Enterprise*.
109   A macroeconomic critique is given by Kojima, K., *Macroeconomic versus International
       Business Approach*; the reply is served by Dunning, J., *The Eclectic Paradigm of Inter-
       national Production: A Personal Perspective*; and by Buckley, P. J., *Macroeconomic
       versus International Business Approach: A Comment*.
110   J. Dunning meets the criticism of a 'shopping list of variables', and their inter-
       dependency and static nature with the general argument that every focused theory can
       only answer focused questions. Moreover, reality has interdependencies and antinomies
       that can only be combined into one picture if the eclectic approach is used. This enables
       the research to be consistent from the level of a single company up to the international
       complex network. Undisputed is the call for a further development of the eclectic para-
       digm and its theories, especially for the dynamic aspects of it. This is attempted in
       combining transaction cost economics, theories of entrepreneurship and innovation
       in a dynamic framework of international production. For example, Dunning, J., *The
       Eclectic Paradigm of International Production: A Personal Perspective*, p. 123ff.; Buckley,
       P. J. and Casson, M., *The Optimal Timing of a Foreign Direct Investment*; and Nicholas,
       S. J., *Multinationals, Transaction Costs and Choice of Institutional Form*. Dunning
       updated his views recently in Boyd, G. and Dunning, J. H., *Structural Change and
       Cooperation in the Global Economy*.
111   Cf. Brown, D., *An Institutionalist Look at Postmodernism*, p. 92f.
112   Casson, M., *Enterprise and Competitiveness*, p. vii.
113   Casson, M., *The Economics of Business Culture*, p. 257.
114   M. Casson distinguishes between the complexities of goals, choices, structures, the net-
       works themselves, external influences, time-preferences, general dynamics and strategies.
       Casson, M., *Enterprise and Competitiveness*, p. 54.
115   Buckley, P. J. and Casson, M., *The Future of the Multinational Enterprise*, p. 56.
116   Casson, M., *Enterprise and Competitiveness*, p. 107; see also Casson, M., *Internalization
       Theory and Beyond*, p. 9ff.
117   Hall, E. T. and Reed-Hall, M., *Hidden Differences*.
118   Casson, M., *Enterprise and Competitiveness*, p. 114. See also for the Asian case, Alford,
       F. C., *Think No Evil: Korean Values in the Age of Globalization*; Fukami, T., *Successful
       Business Management Through Shinto*.
119   Casson, M., *The Economics of Business Culture*, p. 11.
120   Here, game theory is fruitful with its theories of repeated games and non-cooperative
       games. Further reading is Axelrod, R., *The Evolution of Cooperation*, p. 27ff.; Rasmussen,
       E., *Games and Information: An Introduction to Game Theory*; Philips, L., *Applied
       Industrial Economics* and Martin, S., *Advanced Industrial Economics*.
121   Casson, M., *The Economics of Business Culture*, p. 120ff., p. 199 and p. 255; see also
       Brenner, R., *Betting on Ideas*, p. 53f.
122   Parallels to the symbol-economy of Baudrillard (cf. Chapter 2, section III on 'the
       symbolism of postmodern change') are near at hand, making the application in a case
       study on Japan easier and smoother.
123   Casson, M., *The Economics of Business Culture*, p. 23. Supportive of that are Preskill, H.
       and Torres, R. T., *Evaluative Inquiry of Learning in Organizations* or Aamodt, M. G.,
       Applied Industrial and Organizational Psychology.
124   Brenner, R., *Rivalry: In Business, Science, among Nations*, p. 15f. See also Hatch, M. J.,
       Organization Theory: Modern, Symbolic, and Postmodern Perspectives; Gee, J. P., *The*

New Work Order: Behind the Language of the New Capitalism; Marcus, G., *Corporate Futures: The Diffusion of the Culturally Sensitive Corporate Form.*

125 This competition between nations and the differentiating cultures is seen as potentially dangerous: 'With cultures so diffuse and fragmented, and with distrust a persistent theme, there is a danger that the 1990s could become a decade of despair, with no moral foundation by which even a basic code of business behavior can be legitimated.' Casson, M., *The Economics of Business Culture*, p. 262 and Casson, M., *Entrepreneurial Culture as a Competitive Advantage.*

126 Casson, M., *Enterprise and Competitiveness*, p. 84 and p. 94ff.; Casson, M., *The Economics of Business Culture*, p. 86ff. and p. 91. A theoretical foundation is attempted by Brenner, R., *Betting on Ideas*; Simon, H. A., *Theories in Decision Making in Economics and Behavioral Sciences*; Friedman, M., *Price Theory*, p. 99.

127 Further literature on the importance of values is Curtler, H. M., *Rediscovering Values: Coming to Terms with Postmodernism.*

128 Casson, M., *Enterprise and Competitiveness*, p. 98 and p. 105. See also Chapter 4, section III on 'selected interpersonal mechanisms'. Kester, C. W., *Japanese Takeovers – The Global Contest for Corporate Control*, p. 53 and p. 64. H. Baum talks in this context about a general 'giri-norm of interpreting contracts'. Baum, H., *Aspekte japanischen Rechts*, p. 117.

129 Cf. Chapter 3, section IV.

130 Roberts, J. G., *Mitsui*, S. 149, p. 439f.; Yoshiaki, S., *Consensus Management in Japanese Industry*, p. 203; Kitagawa, Z., *Contract Law in General*; Williamson, O. E., *The Economic Institutions of Capitalism*, p. 3. See also Chapter 3, section IV.

131 'Trust cannot be overemphasized in any explanation of how Japanese big business works.' Reischauer, E. O., *The Japanese*, p. 338. Refer also to Holstein, W. B., *Hands across America: The Rise of Mitsubishi*, p. 43; Sender, H., *The Humbling of Nomura*, p. 52; Yoshino, M. Y., *Japan's Multinational Enterprises*, p. 71.

132 Casson, M., *Enterprise and Competitiveness*, p. 105; Aoki, M., *Information, Incentives, and Bargaining in the Japanese Economy*; Kono, T., *Strategy and Structure of Japanese Enterprises*; Morishima, M., *Why has Japan Succeeded? Western Technology and Japanese Ethos*; Williamson O. E., *The Economic Institutions of Capitalism.*

133 Similar conclusions are reached by T. Ozawa combining a standard industrial economic approach with Galbraithian spices (technological structure, knowledge clusters etc.). Ozawa, T., *Multinationalism Japanese Style*, p. 48.

134 Recent conceptual developments of business administration with regards to corporate identity and the research of M. Casson could be read as precursors of a wider post-modern approach to corporate culture.

135 Jameson, F. and Miyoshi, M., *The Cultures of Globalization*, p. 245.

136 C.f. Brown, D., *An Institutionalist Look at Postmodernism.*

137 Ezeala-Harrison, F., *Theory and Policy of International Competitiveness.*

138 Orlowski, D., *Die internationale Wettbewerbsfähigkeit einer Volkswirtschaft*, p. 11.

139 Porter, M. E., *The Competitive Advantage of Nations.*

140 Blattner, N., Maurer, M. and Weber, M., *Voraussetzungen der schweizerischen Wettbewerbsfähigkeit.*

141 Borner, S. and Porter, M. E., *Internationale Wettbewerbsvorteile: Ein strategisches Konzept für die Schweiz*, p. 22; cf. Borner, S., *Internationalization of Industry: An Assessment in the Light of a Small Open Economy*; Bärlocher, E., Gartmann, P., Hess, T., Höhn, T. and Wügler, H., *Internationale Wettbewerbsfähigkeit: eine Literaturübersicht mit besonderer Berücksichtigung der Schweiz*; Suntum, U. v., *Internationale Wettbewerbsfähigkeit einer Volkswirtschaft. Ein sinnvolles wirtschaftpolitisches Ziel?*; Preusse, H. G., *Ist die Frage nach der Wettbewerbsfähigkeit einer Volkswirtschaft überholt?*

142 Porter's theory is embedded into the pertinent theoretical context by Weder, R. and Borner, S., *International Competitiveness of Nations and Firms.*
143 Porter, M. E., *Competitive Strategy*, p. 3ff.; cf. Böbel, I., *Wettbewerb und Industriestruktur*, p. 113f.; McDonald, W., *Postmodern Management*, p. 123.
144 An industry is defined by Porter not as a general category for similar companies but rather a narrowly defined group of firms that create a cluster and segment which is internationally competitive. A similar, but not comparable set of firms would not be competitive internationally. (Example: German successful high-end camera production vs the optical high-tech industry).
145 For further reading see Brenner, R., *Betting on Ideas*, p. 66.
146 On the definition of competitiveness see Porter, M. E. and Fuller, B., *Coalitions and Global Strategy.*
147 Nishiguchi, T., *Strategic Dualism*, p. 55.
148 Fendra, R. C., *Trade Policies for International Competitiveness*, p. 170.
149 Compare with Porter's thesis: 'Strategies are not just reactions to the environment but are also attempts to manipulate this environment.' Porter, M. E., *Wettbewerbsvorteile*, p. 20.
150 Enough rivalry among firms is one of the main factors, as this is not only limited to local interaction but is also felt on the international stage: only a fierce competition with the (local) arch-rival mobilized all forces; stagnating monopolies are thus impossible. It is interesting to refer here to the vast Japanese literature on 'excessive competition'. T. Ozawa regards this rivalry as one of the motors of the multinationalization of Japan. Ozawa, T., *Multinationalism Japanese Style*, p. 73
151 Cf. Porter, M. E., *The Competitive Advantage of Nations*, p. 71ff.; Porter, M. E., *Globaler Wettbewerb: Strategien der neuen Internationalisierung*, p. 442; Borner, S. and Porter, M. E., *Internationale Wettbewerbsvorteile: Ein strategisches Konzept für die Schweiz*, p. 61ff. Only the existence of a wide net of successful firms, suppliers and supporting service-companies render a cluster internationally successful too.
152 On the concept of an economic region see Best, M., *The New Competition*, p. 203ff. and p. 227ff.
153 Porter, M. E., *The Competitive Advantage of Nations*. Compare this with the cascade model by Ohmae, K., *Beyond National Borders*, p. 85
154 Rostow, W. W., *The Stages of Economic Growth.*
155 Critical arguments against Porter's theses can be summarized as follows: anecdotal case studies, no falsification possible, no empirically testable models, superficiality of underlying concepts and 'comprehensive laundry lists'. Further reading is Hill, W., *How can Swiss Companies apply Michael Porter's Strategy Concept?*; Borner, S., *Swiss competitiveness: Where do we stand and where are we heading?*; Porter, M. E., *Globaler Wettbewerb*, p. 442. Quote: Anonymous, *Oh Mr. Porter, what shall we do?*, p. 111.
156 Neither Porter nor Ohmae comment on this point. T. Sakaiya develops Ohmae's ideas with regard to the transgression of a wealth-oriented society. Sakaiya, T., *The Knowledge-Value Revolution*. See also Ohmae, K., *Beyond National Borders*, p. 123f.; Baudrillard, J., *L' Echange symbolique et la mort* and Chapter 4, section V.
157 Siegel, D., *Futurize your Enterprise*, p. 303.
158 There is a vast body of literature on this. More or less 'opposing' globalization are Ramonet, I., *Die neuen Herren der Welt. Globale Politik an der Jahrtausendwende*; Barnes, J., *Capitalism's World Disorder*; Greider, W., *One World, Ready or Not: The Manic Logic of Global Capitalism*; Cohen, B. J. and Lipson, C., *Issues and Agents in the International Political Economy: An International Organization Reader*. Interesting reading 'in favour of' globalization might be Sassen, S., *Losing Control?: Sovereignty in an Age of Globalization*; Rowntree, L., *Diversity Amid Globalization: World Regions, Environment, Development*; Krugman, P., *Der Mythos vom globalen Wirtschaftskrieg.*

Notes 327

Eine Abrechnung mit den Pop-Ökonomen; Hood, N. and Young, S., *The Globalization of Multinational Enterprise Activity and Economic Development.*
159 Some of the more popular voices of this are Minc, A., *Globalisierung. Chance der Zukunft* [*Globalization*]; Minc, A., *La Mondialisation Heureuse* [*Happy Globalization*]; Krugman, P., *The Accidental Theorist.* For a theoretical basis see Dominique, C. R., *Unfettered Globalization.*
160 On this, see especially Chomsky, N. and Dietrich, H., *Globalisierung im Cybespace. Globale Gesellschaft: Märkte, Demokratie und Erziehung*; Bryan, L. and Farrell, D., *Der entfesselte Markt. Die Befreiung des globalen Kapitalismus*; Münch, R., *Globale Dynamik, lokale Lebenswelten. Der schwierige Weg in die Weltgesellschaft.*
161 Braudo, R. J. and MacIntosh, J. G., *Competitive Industrial Development in the Age of Information: The Role of Co-operation in the Technology Sector*; Spulber, D., *Market Microstructure: Intermediaries and the Theory of the Firm;* Fransman, M., *Japan's Computer and Communications Industry: The Evolution of Industrial Giants and Global Competitiveness.*
162 On the seemingly divergent positions of K. Ohmae and M. Porter in relation to the functions of nations see Anonymous, *Porter v Ohmae*, p. 55. M. Porter's home-based arguments (nation and national character reinforce the international competitiveness) can be contrasted with K. Ohmae's globalization arguments (states as obstacles in the development of the 'global citizenship' of consumers and companies). In a synthesis, the 'Porter-world' can be seen as the initial stage of an 'Ohmae-world.' In which the diminishing advantages of local (home-based) knowledge are dynamically equilibrated by the growing knowledge of 'foreign' markets. Experience then transforms the 'Porter-world' into an 'Ohmae-world'. Approving of this is Porter, M. E., *Competitive Strategy*, p. 295.
163 Porter, M. E., *The Competitive Advantage of Nations*, p. 596f.; Porter, M. E., *Globaler Wettbewerb: Strategien der neuen Internationalisierung*; Porter, M. E., *Der Wettbewerb auf globalen Märkten: Ein Rahmenkonzept*, p. 7; Kverneland, A., *Japan's Industry Structure – Barriers to Global Competition.*
164 This general view is documented by several studies. Refer to Sazaki, N., *Management and Industrial Structure in Japan*, p. 92; Hayashi, S., *Culture and Management in Japan*, p. 99 and p. 101; or Kenrick, D. M., *Where Communism Works*, p. 30 and Chapter 3, section IV.
165 Unfortunately, Porter comments only marginally on Japan. Contrast with Bartlett, C. A., *Aufbau und Management der transnationalen Organisationsstruktur*, p. 433.
166 Borner, S. and Porter, M. E., *Internationale Wettbewerbsvorteile*, p. 253.
167 On the definition and description of the symptoms see Morozumi, Y., *Sangyo seisaku no riron* [*The logic of industrial policy*]; Morozumi, Y., *Sangyo taisei no sai* [*Reorganization of the industrial structure*], p. 167; on the theoretical analysis in the Cournot–Nash framework, Itoh, M., Okuno, M., Kiyono, K. and Suzumura, K., *Industrial Policy as a Corrective to Market Failures*, p. 248ff. Antitrust and the current level of cut-throat competition in the Japanese market is not in accordance with Confucian ideals of an industry: few companies exist with rather stable market share and with a clearly defined place in the (sales-, profit-, prestige-) hierarchies, only competing for the better quality. Komiya, R., *The Japanese Economy: Trade, Industry, and Government*, p. 298.
168 The more advanced definitions of these forms are Casson, M., *Enterprise and Competitiveness*, p. 15; and Brenner, R., *Rivalry: In Business, Science, among Nations*, p. 46ff.
169 Pyle, K. B., *Die Zukunft des japanischen Nationalcharakters*, p. 161. In Western industrial nations this symbolic competition is likewise well known: Coca Cola vs Pepsi, BMW vs Mercedes Benz, Apple vs IBM are just some examples.

170 Porter, M. E., *Globaler Wettbewerb: Strategien der neuen Internationalisierung*; Porter, M. E., *Der Wettbewerb auf globalen Märkten: Ein Rahmenkonzept*, p. 5ff. and p. 21.
171 Doz, Y., *Die Rolle des Staates im globalen Wettbewerb*, p. 292.
172 Bartlett, C. A., *Aufbau und Management der transnationalen Organisationsstruktur*, p. 438. See also Dunning, J., *Multinational Enterprises and the Global Economy*, p. 578ff.; Dunning, J., *Governments, Globalization, and International Business* and McDonald, W., *Postmodern Management*, p. 155ff.
173 Cf. Chapter 5, sections III and IV.
174 See also Chapter 2., section III on 'the symbolism of postmodern change' and 'postmodern man as an economic agent'.
175 M. Porter's opinion of the Japanese success being a result of clever market entry tactics and good timing is certainly too simple. Porter, M. E., *Der Wettbewerb auf globalen Märkten: Ein Rahmenkonzept*, p. 42f.
176 Ohmae, K., *Triad Power*.
177 In 1992, K. Ohmae founded Heisei-Ishin-No-Kai-Partei [Party with the goal to establish the Heisei-reforms]. See also Chapter 1, section II ('Japan as the focus of attention') and Chapter 4, section IV ('the 1980s and 1990s' and 'Overview of ...'). and section VI. Ohmae, K., *Japan vs Japan: Only the Strong Survive*, p. 20.
178 Ohmae, K., *Die Macht der Triade*, p. 35ff. and p. 39ff.
179 Ohmae, K., *Die Macht der Triade*, p. 85f. and p. 171. It fits that a slogan of a global IT firm claimed to have mastered 'the art of being local everywhere'. The reader is also reminded of A. Morita's term 'global localization'.
180 Ohmae, K., *Beyond National Borders*, p. 4f.
181 Ohmae, K., *Beyond National Borders*, p. 24 and p. 80. Updated in Ohmae, K., *The Evolving Global Economy: Making Sense of the New World Order*. See also Siegel, D., *Futurize your Enterprize*.
182 Ohmae, K., *Beyond National Borders*, p. 128; see also the theoretical considerations by P. N. Giraud on the regional differentiation of economic activities. Giraud, P. N., *Resaux, territoires et modes de croissance des entreprises*. On the role of the MNE in devaluing the concepts of a nation see Kegley, C. and Wittkopf, E. R., *The Multinational Corporation in World Politics*, p. 270. For a critical view on the 'openness' of developing countries economy see Rodrik, D., *The New Global Economy and Developing Countries: Making Openness Work*. Critical observers mention the nihilistic and technocratic aspects of this tendency: e.g., Sauer-Thompson, G. and Wayne Smith, J., *Beyond Economics: Postmodernity, Globalization and National Sustainability*.
183 Ohmae, K., *The Borderless World*, p. xi supported by Dunning, J., *Multinational Enterprises and the Global Economy*, p. 586ff. and Dunning, J., *Governments, Globalization, and International Business*. Critical to the idea of a complex interdependency of all political-economic systems: Gilpin, R., *Can Interdependent World Political Economy Survive?* or O'Keohane, R. and Nye, J. S., *Complex Interdependence, Transnational Relations, and Realism*.
184 Itoh, M., *The Globalization of Japan: Japanese Sakoku Mentality and U.S. Efforts to Open Japan*.
185 Ohmae, K., *The Borderless World*, p. viii. See also Meeham, M. (Ed.), *The Future ain't what it used to be*.
186 Ohmae, K., *The Borderless World*, p. 99, p. 87; Moore, J. F., *Wie Unternehmen in Lebensgemeinschaften prosperieren*; see also Brown, D., *An Institutionalist Look at Postmodernism*, p. 97f. Compare also Chapter 2, section V and Chapter 4, section VII.
187 M. Foucault quoted in Lash, S., *Sociology of Postmodernism*, p. 100.
188 On the problems defining economic networks see Gilroy, B. M., *Networking in Multinational Enterprises*, p. 19ff.

189   Doll, D. R., *Data Communications: Facilities, Networks, and Systems Design*; Diebold, J., *Information Technology as a Competitive Weapon*.

190   Lipnack, J. and Stamps, J., *Networking: The First Report*, p. 1.

191   R. Mueller describes the general character of networks as: '... the fuzzy, ambiguous, equivocal, evanescent, sub-rosa, qualitative, dynamic, personal, empowering, buzz-wordy, confusing nature of networking.' Mueller distinguishes seven types of networks: families, scientific-institutional, informal shadows, overlays, markets, emotional, special interest groups. Relevant to this study are the informal and overlay types of networks. Mueller, R. K., *Corporate Networking*, p. 59; quote from p. 115. Other definitions can be found for example in Hagström, P., *The 'Wired' MNC*, p. 31f.

192   Blois, K. J., *Transaction Costs and Networks*.

193   Ciborra, C. U., *Markets, Bureaucracies and Groups in the Information Society*; Antonelli, C., *A New Industrial Organization Approach*.

194   Veseth, M., *Selling Globalization: The Myth of the Global Economy*, p. 72.

195   Kanter, R. M., *Bis zum Horizont und weiter. Management in neuen Dimensionen*, p. 88.

196   Mueller, R. K., *Corporate Networking*, p. 35, p. 116 and *passim*; see also Thomson, G., *Markets, Hierarchies, and Networks*; Gilroy, B. M., *Networking in Multinational Enterprises*, p. 140ff.

197   For example, Földi, T., *Networks and Information in Social Science Information*; Doz, Y. and Shuen, A., *A Process Framework for Analyzing Cooperation between Firms*; Chichilnisky, G., *Networks and Coalition Formation*; Kolduff, M., *A Dispositional Approach to Social Networks*. Connections between the theory of networks and management literature is manifold: for example Gomez, P. and Probst, G. J. B., *Vernetztes Denken im Management*.

198   The link between network theory and the image of the rhizome is provided by Cooke, P. and Morgan, K., *The Associational Economy: Firms, Religions, and Innovation*; and Korten, D. C., *The Post Corporate World: Life After Capitalism*.

199   An exhaustive economic analysis of the reasons for and use of networks in the context of firms can be found in Gilroy, B. M., *Networking in Multinational Enterprises*, p. 101ff. See also Metcalfe, S. J., *Evolutionary Economics and Creative Destruction*.

200   Williamson, O. E., *The Modern Corporation: Origins, Evolution, Attributes*; Chandler, A., *The M-Form: Industrial Groups, American Style*; Auerbach, P., *Competition*.

201   Auerbach, P., *Competition*, p. 131f.; see also Streek, W., *Basic Categories of a Socio-logical Theory of Industrial Relations*.

202   Gilroy, B. M., *Economic Issues of Multinational Enterprises*, p. 36; Jarillo, J. C., *On Strategic Networks*; Bartlett, C. A., *Building and Managing the Transnational: The New Organizational Challenge*, p. 374ff.; Sproull, L. and Kiesler, S., *Connections: New Ways of Working in the Networked Organization*; Savage, C., *Fifth Generation Management: Integrating Enterprises through Human Networking*.

203   Ghoshal, S. and Nohria, N., *Multinational Corporations as Differentiated Networks*; Ghoshal, S. and Nohria, N., *Distributed Innovation in the 'Differentiated Network' Multinational*. For an empirical overview of existing network structures see Gilroy, B. M., *Networking in Multinational Enterprises*, p. 28ff. and p. 43ff. The update is Nohria, N. and Ghoshal, S., *The Differentiated Network: Organizing Multinational Corporations for Value Creation*.

204   The individual characteristics are (1) clan: medium centralization, weak formalization, high socialization, high complexity and feeble resources; (2) federation: low centralization, high formalization, weak socialization, low complexity and medium resources; (3) hierarchy: high centralization, medium formalization, weak socialization, low complexity and high resources; (4) integrated form: low centralization, medium formalization, high socialization, high complexity and high resources.

205 Hatch, M. J., *Organization Theory: Modern, Symbolic, and Postmodern Perspectives*, p. 67.
206 Viner, J., *Cost Curves and Supply Curves*, p. 24ff.
207 Penrose, E., *Theory of the Growth of the Firm*, p. 17f.
208 Comprehensive overviews are in Jensen, M. and Meckling, W., *Theories of the Firm: Managerial Behavior, Agency Cost, and Ownership Structure* and Fama, E., *Agency Problems and the Theory of the Firm*.
209 Williamson, O. E., *The Firm as a Nexus of Treaties: An Introduction*.
210 This disintegration is a precursor to the fractal economy (as described in Chapter 5, section III): 'Since corporate groups are hybrid arrangements between contract and organization, the autopoiesis paradigm might find here another field of application.' Teubner, G., *Unitas Multiplex: Corporate Governance in Group Enterprises*, p. 67. See also Dunning, J., *Multinational Enterprises and the Global Economy*, p. 462; Hawryszkiewycz, I., *Designing the Networked Enterprise*; Poirier, C. C., *Advanced Supply Chain Management: How to Build a Sustained Competition*; Hope, J. and Hope, T., *Competing in the Third Wave: The Ten Key Management Issues of the Information Age*; Gunn, T. G., *21st Century Manufacturing: Creating Winning Business Performance*.
211 Boorman, S. A., *A Combinatorial Optimization Model for Transmission of Job Information through Contact Networks*; Best, M., *The New Competition*, p. 15f., p. 232ff. and p. 262.
212 Hakansson, H. and Johanson, J., *Formal and Informal Cooperation Strategies in International Industrial Networks*, p. 369.
213 Gilroy, B. M., *Economic Issues of Multinational Enterprises*, p. 35 and p. 43; cf. Porter, M. E., *Wettbewerbsvorteile*; Boorman, S. A., *A Combinatorial Optimization Model for Transmission of Job Information through Contact Networks*.
214 In this sense, D. Bell, although critical of this development (eclipse of distance, communication overload), welcomes this 'capitalism without capitalists'. Bell, D., *The Coming of the Post-Industrial Society*.
215 Johanson, J. and Mattsson, L. G., *Internationalization in Industrial Systems – A Network Approach*, p. 291ff. and p. 308. For models of a fractal organization of production see Howard, W. G. and Guile, B. R., *Profiting from Innovation*; Harmon, R. J., *Reinventing the Factory*.
216 The basic theory of non-cooperative games is explained in Axelrod, R., *Effective Choice in the Prisoner's Dilemma*; Axelrod, R., *The Evolution of Cooperation among Egoists* and Axelrod, R. and Hamilton, W. D., *The Evolution of Cooperation*.
217 For example, Davidow, W. H. and Mulone, M. S., *The Virtual Corporation; On the influence of the Internet*; Hawryszkiewycz, I., *Designing the Networked Enterprise*.
218 Radner, R., *A Behavioral Model of Cost Reduction*; Radner, R., *Monitoring Cooperative Agreements in a Repeated Principal-Agent Relationship*; see also Gilroy, B. M., *Economic Issues of Multinational Enterprises*, p. 35. Critical remarks on the effectiveness of networks are in Kadushin, C. and Brimm, M., *Why Networking Fails*.
219 Quote from Gilroy, B. M., *Economic Issues of Multinational Enterprises*, p. 47; see also Johnston, R. and Lawrence, P. R., *Beyond Vertical Integration – The Rise of the Value-Adding Principle*. P. N. Giraud, sees a gradual transition between firm and surrounding regional environment: Giraud, P. N., *Reseaux, territoires et modes de croissance des entreprises*; this is acknowledged by Best, M., *The New Competition*, p. 203ff. and p. 227ff.
220 Henrici, P., Lazlo, E. and Lomeiko, V., *Netzwerke: Globales Denken oder Isolation*, p. 53f. and Sugarman, D., *Corporate Groups in Europe: Governance, Industrial Organization, and Efficiency in a Post-Modern World*.
221 Industrial development and economic growth in their relation to the micro-fundamentals of business activity are not yet thoroughly researched; only a few studies exist. These

see networks in the tradition of Wicksell, Marshall, and Schumpeter as the only driving force of developmental growth. Carlsson, B., *Industrial Dynamics: An Overview*; Wilks, S. and Wright, M., *Conclusion: Comparing Government–Industry Relations: States, Sectors, Networks*, p. 275. For a good survey see Steel, D., *Review Article: Government and Industry in Britain*; Boyd, R., *Government–Industry Relations in Japan: A Review of Literature* and Giraud, P. N., *Reseaux, territoires, modes de croissance des entreprises.*

222 Reve, T., *The Firm as a Nexus of Internal and External Contracts.*

223 This foundation is maintained by internal contracts, internal organizational motivation, core skills and by dedicated assets.

224 General literature: (1) On horizontal integration: Haitani, K., *Comparative Economic Systems*, p. 10f.; Broll, U. and Gilroy, B. M., *Aussenwirtschaftstheorie*, p. 128ff.; empirical example: Best, M., *The New Competition*, p. 203ff. (2) On vertical integration: Williamson, O. E., *The Vertical Integration of Production*; Williamson, O. E., *Transaction Cost Economics: The Governance of Contractual Relations*; Klein, B., Crawford, R. and Alchian, A., *Vertical Integration, Appropriate Rents, and the Competitive Contracting Process*; Williamson, O. E., *The Economics of Organization: The Transaction Cost Approach*; Riordan, M. and Williamson, O. E., *Asset Specificity and Economic Organization.*

225 Priority of vertical integration is discussed in Williamson, O. E., *The Economic Institutions of Capitalism*, p. 121; Kojima, K. and Ozawa, T., *Japan's General Trading Companies*; Ozawa, T., *Japan*, p. 171. Horizontal relations are stressed by Krug, B., *Die Entzauberung der Samurai*; Best, M., *The New Competition*, p. 137ff.; Sazaki, N., *Management and Industrial Structure in Japan*, p. 92.

226 Cf., Kenrick, D. M., *Where Communism Works*, p. 30; Ballon, R. J. and Tomita, I., *The Financial Behavior of Japanese Corporations*, p. 2; Kverneland, A., *Japan's Industry Structure*, p. 233ff.

227 Williamson, O. E., *The Firm as a Nexus of Treaties*, p. 7. On the connection between strategic alliances and networking see Gilroy, B. M., *Networking in Multinational Enterprises*, p. 16, p. 112f. and p. 151ff.

228 Critical of the theory of strategic alliances is Womack, J. P., Johnes, D. T. and Roos, D., *Die zweite Revolution in der Autoindustrie*, p. 231. On the historical context of alliances in Japan see Tasker, P. *Inside Japan*, p. 106ff.; Bennett, J. W. and Ishino, I., *Paternalism in the Japanese Economy*, p. 90ff.

229 On the objectives of strategic alliances see Backhaus, K. and Plinke, W., *Strategische Allianzen als Antwort auf veränderte Wettbewerbsstrukturen*; Müller, K. and Goldberger, E., *Unternehmenskooperation bringt Wettbewerbsvorteile*; Hanan, M., *Growth Partnering: How to Manage Strategic Alliances for Mutual Profit*, p. 17f. and p. 26; Müller-Stevens, G. and Hillig, A., *Motive zur Bildung strategischer Allianzen*. On the network character of alliances see Gerlach, M., *Business Alliances and the Strategy of the Japanese Firm*, p. 134; Gilroy, B. M., *Networking in Multinational Enterprises*, p. 160; also Broll, U. and Gilroy, B. M., *Aussenwirtschaftstheorie*, p. 158 or Ethier, W., *The Multinational Firm.*

230 Empirical studies in knowledge intensive industries show that alliances need not be only on the company level, they can also exist on the interpersonal level of individuals. Hippel, E. v., *Cooperation between Rivals: Informal Know-How-Trading.*

231 Romme, G., *The Formation of Firm Strategy as Self-Organization.*

232 Refer to Porter's concept of systemic competition between MNEs. The better organization of production, the better system wins. Porter, M. E., *Competitive Strategy*, p. 293; Kojima, K. and Ozawa, T., *Japan's General Trading Companies*, p. 80

233 Parallels to autopoiesis (self-organization as co-evolution with the surrounding environment) as well as to chaos-theory (Changes in the structure of alliances as bifurcations within the respective development of business relations) are near at hand, though they

are not well represented in mainstream research. Maturana, H. and Varela, F., *Der Baum der Erkenntnis*; Stevenson, H. H. and Harmeling, S., *Entrepreneurial Management's Need For a More Chaotic Theory*; Sterman, J. D., *Deterministic Chaos*.

234   'Both the business organization and the entire economy have to be presented as economic systems with a memory, or as path-dependent economies.' Elisasson, G., *The Dynamics of Supply and Economic Growth*, p. 38.

235   Klimecki, R., Probst, G. J. B. and Eberl, P., *Perspektiven eines entwicklungsorientierten Managements*; Orton, J. D. and Weick, K. E., *Loosely Coupled Systems: A Reconceptualization*. Cf., Schonberger, R. J., *Japanese Manufacturing Techniques*, p. 132ff.

236   H. Hakansson and J. Johanson emphasize an overlooked topic, relating the dynamics of MNE of today with the psychology of the Japanese individual (compare this with Chapter 3, section II ('blurring of the subject') and Chapter 3, section IV ('the individual and the group')): in the process of self-organization and relational definition the (Japanese) enterprise is constantly in search for itself, not unlike the Japanese individual. Hakansson, H. and Johanson, J., *Formal and Informal Cooperation Strategies in International Industrial Networks*, p. 375. Compare this with T. Ozawa's 'geocentric enterprise', that is nowhere at home except in itself. Ozawa, T., *Multinationalism, Japanese Style*, p. 231.

237   Piore, M. J. and Sabel, C. F., *Das Ende der Massenproduktion*, p. 5, p. 37f. and p. 194ff.

238   Imai, K., *The Legitimacy of Japan's Corporate Groups*. Quote from Kojima, K. and Ozawa, T., *Japan's General Trading Companies*, p. 75; Saunders, C. T., *Industrial Policies and Structural Change*; Cook, L., *R&D Networks and Markets in a Complex Industry* and Casson, M., *Enterprise and Competitiveness*, p. 41.

239   Quote from Auerbach, P., *Competition*, p. 122; see also Hakansson, H., *Industrial Technological Development*; Karlsson, C., *Knowledge and Material Flow in Future Industrial Networks*.

240   Gilroy, B. M., *Economic Issues of Multinational Enterprises*, p. 45.

241   Johanson, J. and Mattsson, L. G., *Internationalization in Industrial Systems – A Network Approach*, p. 287 and p. 307; Reve, T., *The Firm as a Nexus of Internal and External Contracts*, p. 136ff. and p. 152; see also Miles, R. E. and Snow, C. C., *Network Organizations: New Concepts for New Forms*.

242   Kumon, S., *Japan as a Network Society* p. 110; MITI, *White Paper on International Trade 1992*, p. 97 and p. 105ff.

243   Wilks, S. and Wright, M., *Conclusion: Comparing Government–Industry Relations: States, Sectors, Networks*, p. 278 and p. 295; Katzenstein, P., *Conclusion: Domestic Structures and Strategies of Foreign Economic Policy*; Dunning, J., *Multinational Enterprises and the Global Economy*, p. 462ff. and p. 528ff. and Dunning, J., *Governments, Globalization, and International Business*.

244   Wilks, S. and Wright, M., *Conclusion: Comparing Government–Industry Relations: States, Sectors, Networks*, p. 308 and Streek, W., *Industrial Relations in West Germany*, p. 149; Marin, B. and Mayntz, R., *Policy Networks: Empirical Evidence and Theoretical Considerations*.

245   For further explanation the reader can turn to the concepts of a fractal economy and rhizome economy (Chapter 5, section III).

246   Comparable attempts for other industrialized nations are e.g., Wolf, G., *Wirtschafts- und finanzpolitische Machtstrukturen in der Bundesrepublik Deutschland: Issuespezifische Netzwerkanalysen*; Stockman, F. N., *Networks of Corporate Power: A Comparison of Ten Countries*.

247   Murakami, Y. and Rohlen, T. P., *Social Exchange Aspects of the Japanese Political Economy*, p. 65ff.; quote, p. 71. Compare with Chapter 3, section IV, and Wolferen, K. v., *Das Japan Problem*, p. 16.

248   Kumon, S., *Japan as a Network Society*, p. 110ff.

249 '... Japanese corporate networks [are primarily to be understood] as a system of learning and information exchange.' Imai, K., *Japan's Corporate Networks*, p. 230.

250 Imai, K., *Evolution of Japan's Corporate and Industrial Networks*, p. 125; Nakatami, I., *The Japanese Firm in Transition*.

251 Imai, K., *Japan's Corporate Networks*, p. 212 and p. 229; Gilroy, B. M., *Networking in Multinational Enterprises*, p. 193ff.

252 Imai, K., *The Evolution of Japan's Corporate and Industrial Networks*, p. 123; Nakatami, I., *The Japanese Firm in Transition*, p. 91.

253 Womack, J. P., Johnes, D. T. and Roos, D., *Die zweite Revolution in der Autoindustrie*, p. 99; see also earlier studies on Toyota: Abegglen, J. C. and Stalk, G., *Kaisha: The Japanese Company* and recently, Friedman, T., *The Lexus and the Olive Tree*.

254 Cf., Ftatsugi, Y., *Kigyo kan kankei no sokutei [The relations of firms to other firms]*; Yoshino, M. Y., *Japan's Multinational Enterprises*, p. 115 and Yoshino, M. Y. and Rangan, U. S., *Strategic Alliances: An Entrepreneurial Approach to Globalization*.

255 Womack, J. P., Johnes, D. T. and Roos, D., *Die zweite Revolution in der Autoindustrie*, p. 99.

256 Casson, M., *Enterprise and Competitiveness*, p. 25.

257 Womack, J. P., Johnes, D. T. and Roos, D., *Die zweite Revolution in der Autoindustrie*, p. 258.

258 Borner, S. and Porter, M. E., *Internationale Wettbewerbsvorteile: Ein strategisches Konzept für die Schweiz*, p. 253.

259 Vernon, R., *Storm over the Multinationals: Problems and Prospects*, p. 245; Emmott, B., *Japan's Global Reach*, p. 130; Powell, B., *Sayonara, America*; or Leuenberger, T., *A World Scenario: The Emergence of Three Main Trading Zones*. Beechler, S. L. and Bird, A., *Japanese Multinationals Abroad: Individual and Organizational Learning*. See also Chapter 1, section II.

260 The recourse to contrasting the 'Japanese firm' with 'American ideal firms' by means of 'alphabet-theories' (theory X, Y, Z; J-firm vs. A-firm etc. ...) is omitted here, as these lists are overly nation-oriented. These theories will die out the more global the positions become. Classics of these 'alphabet-theories' are Aoki, M., *Decentralization–Centralization in Japanese Organization*; Aoki, M., *Information, Incentives, and Bargaining in the Japanese Economy*, p. 11ff.; Ouchi, W. G., *Theory Z: How American Business can Meet the Japanese Challenge*; Athos, A. G. and Pascale, R. T., *The Art of Japanese Management*, p. 33ff.; Alston, J. P., *The American Samurai*.

261 For the general case cf. Davies, S. and Meyer, C., *Das Prinzip Unschärfe*; Pickover, C. A., *Fractal Horizons: The Future Use of Fractals*; Warnecker, H.-J., *Revolution der Unternehmenskultur. Das Fraktale Unternehmen*.

262 Ashley, D., *History without a Subject: The Postmodern Condition*.

263 As an analogy the case of the adaptation of Italy to mobile telephony might be cited: being probably the most intense communicators in Europe, the absolute amount and the growth of mobile phone utilization is dwarfing any other nation. The Internet penetration of Japan can be assumed to be equal to this. With the Internet being a more complex instrument than the mobile phone, the positive impact on society in terms of performativity and flexibility can only be underestimated.

264 Metcalfe, S. J., *Evolutionary Economics and Creative Destruction*; Tachibanaki, T. and Kenkyujo, R. S., *Who Runs Japanese Business?: Management and Motivation in the Firm*; Japan Commission on Industrial Performance, *Made in Japan: Revitalizing Japanese Manufacturing for Economic Growth*; Ekstedt, E., Lundin, R. A. and Soderholm, A., *Neo Industrial Organizing: Renewal by Action and Knowledge Formation in a Project-Intensive Economy*. On the evolutionary aspects of Japanese industrial sectors see Fransman, M., *Japan's Computer and Communications Industry: The Evolution of*

Industrial Giants and Global Competitiveness; Den Hertog, F. J. and Huizenga, E., *The Knowledge of Enterprise; Implementation of Intelligent Business Strategies.*

265 On the theoretical aspects read Kumon, S., *Japan as a Network Society*, p. 124; a detailed empirical analysis of Keiretsu-networks remains Dodwell, *Industrial Groupings in Japan*, p. 312ff.; see also Chapter 5, section II.

266 Casson, M., *Enterprise and Competitiveness*, p. 98; Yoshino, M. Y. and Lifson, T. B., *Sogo Shosha*, p. 203ff. and Yoshino, M. Y. and Rangan, U. S., *Strategic Alliances: An Entrepreneurial Approach to Globalization.*

267 Supportive are Tsurumi, Y. and Tsurumi, R., *Sogo Shosha*; Aoyama, N., *The Role of Japanese Sogo Shosha*, p. 212; Aoki, M., *Aspects of the Japanese Firm*, p. 24.

268 Schneidewind, D., *Das Unternehmen im Markt*, p. 163.

269 Nakane, C., *Japanese Society*, p. 144; Kumon, S., *Japan as a Network Society*, p. 125; Higachi, C. and Lauter, P. G., *The Internationalization of the Japanese Economy*, p. 113; Yoshino, M. Y., *Japan's Multinational Enterprises*, p. 71 and Yoshino, M. Y. and Rangan, U. S., *Strategic Alliances: An Entrepreneurial Approach to Globalization.*

270 Nakane, C., *Japanese Society*, p. 98 and p. 138; Hall, E. T. and Reed-Hall, M., *Hidden Differences*, p. 58; Nester, W., *Japan's Growing Power over East Asia and the World Economy*, p. 127; Singer, K., *Mirror, Sword and Jewel*, p. 45; Woronoff, J., *Japan: The Coming Economic Crisis*, p. 53.

271 Yoshino, M. Y., *Japans Multinational Enterprises*, p. 161ff.

272 Ballon, R. J. and Tomita I., *The Financial Behavior of Japanese Corporations*, p. 2ff.

273 Kawamoto, I., *Neue Entwicklungen im Bereich des Gesellschaftsrechts in Japan*, p. 220ff.

274 The most thorough analysis and complete description of all different terms and types of Keiretsu, based on the Japanese publications remains Eli, M., *Sogo Shosha*, p. 171ff.

275 Seen with a strict logic, the use of the basic proposition of companies being the elementary module of analysis, is misleading, as explained in Chapter 5, section IV (see also Chapter 4, section III). There, a fractal understanding of business organization is proposed, which takes into account the absence of clear boundaries of the firm and is able to incorporate the multidimensional linkages of organizational entities (economy, Keiretsu, company, departments, groups, interpersonal relations etc.). Further literature sustaining this view is Ashkenas, R. *et al.*, *The Boundaryless Organization Field Guide: Practical Tools for Building the New Organization.* Contrary to this opinion is Clark, R., *The Japanese Company*, p. 49.

276 An interesting comparative analysis would be to contrast the Japanese developoment with other Asian dynamics (e.g. the Korean Chaebol): for example, Kim, E. M., *Big Business, Strong State* or Clark, G. L. and Kim, W. B., *Asian NIEs and the Global Economy.*

277 Hadley, E. O. M., *Antitrust in Japan*, p. 301ff.

278 Komiya, R., *The Japanese Economy*, p. 185.

279 An interesting lecture about the charismatic director of the Mitsui conglomerate is Guth, C. M. E., *Art, Tea, and Industry: Masuda Takashi and the Mitsui Circle.*

280 Clark, R., *The Japanese Company*, p. 42 and p. 44.

281 Imai, K., *The Legitimacy of Japan's Corporate Groups.*

282 More about Mitsubishi in Mishima, Y. *et al.*, *Mitsubishi: Its Challenge and Strategy.*

283 Dodwell Marketing Consultants, *Industrial Groupings in Japan.*

284 More on the taxonomy can be found in Dolles, H. and Jung, H. F., *Subcontracting in Japan*; Okumura, H., *Interfirm Relations in an Enterprise Group*, p. 55ff.

285 Kowalewsky, R. and Satori, A., *Mitsubishi*, p. 222.

286 The web-sites of Mitsubishi are rigid in their wording: virtually everywhere, size, power, and complexity are radically downplayed presumably by a joint committee on PR and

corporate strategy: 'Mitsubishi is more than 40 independent companies [sic!] who share a common ancestry. The companies conduct business separately but cooperate in areas like philantropy and public affairs.' Quotes from www.mitsubishi.or.jp.

287   Shinohara, M., *Industrial Growth, Trade, and Dynamic Patterns in the Japanese Economy*, p. 41; Echigo, K., *Japanese Studies of Industrial Organization*; Imai, K., *Japan's Industrial Structure*, p. 107; Kionari, T. and Nakamura, H., *The Establishment of the Big Business System*, p. 264.

288   This is especially true if one takes the current changes in entrepreneurial culture und attitudes towards busines organization into consideration: From a family-centered structure to a tight group ideal to a loose group paradigm to a network idea the development went and is now enhanced by technology fully using the network advantages. Uekusa, K., *Japan in the New Millennium*; Hart, R., Kawasaki, S. and Hart, R. A., *Work and Pay in Japan*. Both sources reject the Western view that Keiretsu are a tight 'club', but now rather the material from which the new organizational forms are created.

289   For a recent overview of the Japanese Keiretsu landscape see Osono, T., *Charting Japanese Industry: A Graphical Guide to Corporate and Market Structures*.

290   Eli, M., *Sogo Shosha*, p. 5. It is important to notice that in any Japanese publication the connection or the reference to the Sogo Shosha's cluster of surrounding companies is intentionally omitted.

291   Young, A. K., *The Sogo Shosha – Japan's Multinational Trading Companies*, p. 90.

292   Here again the many names are vexing the amateur bystander: Sogo Shosha (general trading company) is contrasted to Senmon Shosha (special trading company), foreign trade companies and producing trading firms. For more detail refer to Takamiya, S., *Organisation des japanischen Aussenhandels und die Bedeutung der Grosshandelsgesellschaften*, p. 183ff.

293   Yoshino, M. Y. and Lifson, T. B., *The Invisible Link*, p. 101f.; Kobayashi, M., *Wirtschaftsmacht Japan*, p. 31ff.

294   Kunio, Y., *Sogo Shosha*, p. 12ff.; Yoshino, M. Y. and Lifson, T. B.,*The Invisible Link*, p. 102; quote from Tsurumi, Y. and Tsurumi, R., *Sogo Shosha*, p. 91; see Chapter 5, section III ('the functions of the Keiretsu') and section IV ('the composition of the core structure').

295   Johnson, C., *MITI and the Japanese Miracle*, p. 23.

296   Hall, E. T. and Reed-Hall, M., *Hidden Differences*, p. 160.

297   Roberts, J. G., *Mitsui*, p. 130 and p. 224.

298   Piore, M. J. and Sabel, C. F., *Das Ende der Massenproduktion*, p. 177.

299   Piore, M. J. and Sabel, C. F., *Das Ende der Massenproduktion*, p. 177ff.

300   Naturally, these moral obligations were flanked by draconian physical and social penalties, which were deployed for the smaller misdemeanours.

301   See especially Chapter 4.

302   Schwalbe, H., *Japan*, p. 391.

303   Gibney, F., *Japan: The Fragile Superpower*, p. 169.

304   Piore, M. J. and Sabel, C. F., *Das Ende der Massenproduktion*, p. 179; Shale, T., *Reawakening the Sleeping Giant*, p. 14; Tasker, P., *Inside Japan*, p. 265.

305   'Now the wheel is turning full circle and the Zaibatzu are being recreated out of the Keiretzu system.' Shale, T., *Reawakening the Sleeping Giant*, p. 17.

306   Johnson, C., *MITI and the Japanese Miracle*, p. 204; Wolferen, K. v., *The Enigma of Japanese Power*, p. 61; Miyazaki, Y., *Excessive Competition and the Formation of the Keiretzu*.

307   Ballon, R. J. and Tomita, I., *The Financial Behavior of Japanese Corporations*, p. 58. 'It would not be correct if one would interpret the Kigyo Keiretsu as a recycling of the former Zaibatzu. There is a strong movement against the notion that Kigyo Keiretzu are the reincorporation of the traditional Zaibatzu. This is for several reasons: (a) traditional

Zaibatsu had a holding company structure which is against the current antitrust law; (b) The total control by a family has been abolished by the Holding Company Liquidation Commission, that monitored all share holdings; (c) that holding company subsequently sold all shares on the stock exchanges to diversified bidders; (d) the family and their *bantos* were requested to step down from all offices.' Quote from Eli, M., *Sogo Shosha*, p. 173.

308 Clark, R., *The Japanese Company*, p. 73.
309 Sethi, S. P., *The False Promise of the Japanese Miracle*, p. 21.
310 Shimizu, T., *Strukturanalyse der japanischen Verbundunternehmung*, p. 17f.
311 Aoki, M., *Information, Incentives, and Bargaining in the Japanese Economy*, p. 204.
312 Toyota has 122 'first tier subcontractors', 5437 'second tier subcontractors' and about 45 000 'third tier suppliers' (!). Aoki, M., *Information, Incentives, and Bargaining in the Japanese Economy*, p. 204. This fractal business approach is examined in Chapter 5, section IV.
313 Especially this last aspect reminds us of the traditional concepts as explained in Chapter 4, section III.
314 Parent companies (*oyako kaisha*) have clearly defined tasks and responsibilities: '... the authority of the parent is not formulated in writing and, in some sense, independent operations by the child are expected. Yet one should not mistake this for freedom in which there is no commitment to the parent.' Ballon, R. J. and Tomita, I., *The Financial Behavior of Japanese Corporations*, p. 3; see also the exhaustive discussion in Smith, C., *Corporate Identity Crisis*.
315 S. Saba, (past) Chairman of Toshiba quoted in Rapaport, R., *Why Japan keeps on Winning*, p. 45.
316 Focusing the argument on this dimension R. Komiya is able to state: 'These industrial groups are, therefore, more imaginary than real.' Komiya, R., *The Japanese Economy*, p. 186. Such statements seem to be guided by political strategy as (a) Komiya is close to MITI; (b) the text in which this statement appears has been written only for the Western readership; (c) at the time of his writing Keiretsu were a sore point in the bilateral trade debates between Japan and the U.S.; (d) the general intent to play down the role of the Keiretsu etc.
317 Piore, M. J. and Sabel, C. F., *Das Ende der Massenproduktion*, p. 42f. Quotes from Anchordoguy, M., *A Brief History of Japan's Keiretzu*, p. 58; Prestovitz, C. V., *Trading Places*, p. 308.
318 Roberts, J. G., *Mitsui*, p. 492; supporting this notion is Imai, K., *The Legitimacy of Japan's Corporate Groups*, p. 17.
319 Cf. Chapter 3, section IV, Chapter 4, sections III and IV, and Chapter 5, section III.
320 On the relationship between a global and fractal economy see Menzel, U., *Globalisierung versus Fragmentierung*.
321 McHugh *et al.* propose also the term 'holonic enterprise', understanding the MNE as an integrative force consisting of myriads of fractal business units. Therefore, the term has the same explanatory power as the term 'fractal enterprise' and is thus not used further. McHugh, P., Wheeler W. and Merli, G., *Beyond Business Process Reengineering*.
322 Interesting first attempts are: Pickover, C. A., *Fractal Horizons: The Future Use of Fractals*; Davies, S. and Meyer, C., *Das Prinzip Unschärfe*; Warnecker, H.-J., *Revolution der Unternehmenskultur. Das Fraktale Unternehmen* [*Revolution in the Corporate Culture*].
323 This chapter focuses on the historical development of the Zaibatsu and Keiretsu. A general account of the macro-economic developments surrounding the Zaibatsu and Keiretsu can be found in Chapter 4, section IV; a case study is presented in Chapter 4, section VI.

324 Caves, R. and Uesuka, M., *Industrial Organization in Japan*, p. 2: 'The Zaibatzu represent yet another persistent legacy of the Meiji era ...' Contrary opinion is voiced by T. Ozawa, 'Japanese corporations have emerged as multinationals, both suddenly and recently ...'. Here, Ozawa takes a simple definition of MNE (production in more than one country) as a starting point without taking into account the longer-term strategies used by the groupings. Ozawa, T., *Multinationalism – Japanese Style*, p. 3.

325 For earlier history refer to Hurst, C. C., *The Structure of the Heian Court: Some Thoughts on the Nature of Familial Authority*, p. 39ff. or Hall, J. W. and Mass, J. P., *Medieval Japan: Essays in Institutional History*; and Vogel, E. F., *Japan as Number One – Lessons for America*, p. 132f.

326 'It may sound strange to alienate the emergence of free capitalism with the beginning of the Zaibatzu in the 17th century, but at the core of both were the financing families, which by reinvesting profits let the companies grow not only in size but also in dependency of the core family.' Pape, W., *Die politisch-gesellschaftliche Verflechtung des Unternehmens, p. 24.*

327 'The 'Zaibatzu' was not founded by the traditional ruling elite but is a product of the political reforms in the Meiji restoration. At the start were entrepreneurs who had helped by introducing the politics of industrialization and were now supported by the government.' Yui, T., *Zaibatzu*, p. 45.

328 The conditions, the general atmosphere and the pressure to change at the end of the Tokugawa era, that led to revolution and a new era are sketched out well in Maruyama, M., *Studies in the Intellectual History of Tokugawa Japan*, p. 274ff. and p. 341ff.; see also Beasely, W. G., *The Modern History of Japan*.

329 Caves, R. and Uesuka, M., *Industrial Organization in Japan*, p. 7; Yasuo, H., *The Role of the Ie in the Economic Modernization of Japan*, p. 9f.; McMillan, C., *The Japanese Industrial System*, p. 37; Roberts, J. G., *Mitsui*, p. 28 and p. 35; Wolferen, K. v., *The Enigma of Japanese Power*, p. 68. Fascinating are the company histories of Fruin, M., *Kikkoman* or Roberts, J. G., *Mitsui*. For a survey see Glazer, N., *Social and Cultural Factors in Japanese Economic Growth* or Reischauer, E. O., *The Japanese*, p. 306. For a discussion of familism as a management ideology refer to Hazama, H., *The History of Labour Management in Japan*. See also Chapter 3, section IV ('the role of the primary groups').

330 Cf.. Eli, M., *Sogo Shosha*, p. 10; Eccleston, B., *State and Society in Postwar Japan*, p. 109; Tsurumi, Y. and Tsurumi, R., *Sogo Shosha*, p. 20.

331 This knowledge-elite stemmed from families which had close links to government. Even in Tokugawa times houses like Mitsui were almost a governmental executive body (e.g. tax collecting). Mitsui also financed the Tokugawa government, which did not hinder the family from assisting in its fall, though. Roberts, J. G., *Mitsui*, p. viii and p. 79f. The current situation is examined in Chapter 4, section II.

332 Clark, R., *The Japanese Company*, p. 20.

333 Although tempting, no one has so far developed the hypothesis that the 'hegemonic national elite', which controlled government and the important family groupings, used at first the government as a change agent, to come only in the second step with the economic interests of the private sector to counterbalancê the public demands. This strategy would have defended them from any accusation of being greedy. The enormous tactical competence of these families (e.g. the naming of the revolution as a restoration of the Emperor) and their business acumen could advocate such a hypothesis, which can only be studied in later research.

334 Yoshino, M. Y., *Japan's Multinational Enterprises*, p. 4; Eccleston, B., *State and Society in Postwar Japan*, p. 42.

335 Firms like the German Krupp and governments like the German Empire were the models for the Zaibatsu feudalism. Tsurumi, Y. and Tsurumi, R., *Sogo Shosha*, p. 127 and p. 185; Nakagawa, K., *Business Strategy and Industrial Structure in Pre-World-War-II Japan*, p. 19; see also Chapter 4, section II.
336 Yoshino, M. Y. and Lifson, T. B., *The Invisible Link*, p. 14.
337 Tsurumi, Y. and Tsurumi, R., *Sogo Shosha*, p. 15ff.; Nester, W., *The Foundation of Japanese Power*, p. 182.
338 A. Young estimates that around 1860 96% of all foreign trade was dominated by foreign companies. Young, A. K., *The Sogo Shosha*, p. 24. This is supported by Shibagaki, K., *Zaibatzu*, p. 5.
339 Yoshino, M. Y., *Japan's Multinational Enterprises*, p. 3: 'The merchant class, thrust into the rather chaotic political and economic environment of the era and totally lacking prior experience in manufacturing, was reluctant to take new industrial ventures.' See also Tominaga, K., *Die Rolle des Wertsystems für die Industrialisierung Japans.* Shibagaki cites the high sums and the big risk involved in such investments as the main reasons for the reluctance of the families. Shibagaki, K., *Zaibatzu*, p. 7.
340 Roberts, J. G., *Mitsui*, p. 3.
341 Only reference can be made to the complex and interesting history of organizational development in Japan. On the development of management systems in Japan see Tsurumi, Y. and Tsurumi, R., *Sogo Shosha*, p. 22; Morikawa, H., *Management Structures and Control Devices for Diversified Zaibatzu Business* and Yasuoka, S., *The Tradition of Family Business in the Strategic Decision Process and Management Structure of Zaibatzu Business*. For a more general description of organizational development from a MNE perspective see Kobayashi, T., *Nihon no takokuseki kigyo [Japanese MNE]*.
342 Caves, R. and Uesuka, M., *Industrial Organization in Japan*, p. 61f.
343 Eli, M., *Sogo Shosha*, p. 10f.; Noda, K., *Zaibatzu, keieisha ni miru shotai [Current plans for industrial policy]*, p. 5; Roberts, J. G., *Mitsui*, p. 306, p. 348, p. 372.
344 Roberts, J. G., *Mitsui*, p. 115, p. 134, p. 196, p. 244, p. 251; Beasley, W. G., *The Modern History of Japan*, p. 227; Hall, J. W., *Japan*, p. 316.
345 See also Woronoff, J., *Japan: The Coming Economic Crisis*, p. 20.
346 Wright, R. W. and Pauli, G. A., *The Second Wave – Japan's Global Assault on Financial Services*, p. 32; Beasley, W. G., *The Modern History of Japan*, p. 304.
347 Shibagaki, K., *Zaibatzu*, p. 9.
348 The American 'trustbuster' could be interpreted as an unconscious catalyst of change, thus enabling Japan to regain its leading position again. Reischauer, E. O., *The Japanese*, p. 395; Tasker, P., *Inside Japan*, p. 205.
349 Roberts, J. G., *Mitsui*, p. 372ff.
350 J. Robinson, member of the SCAP as quoted in Roberts, J. G., *Mitsui*, p. 394.
351 The Japanese Fair Trade Commission calculated that already in 1955 the top ten trading companies had over 40 % share of foreign trade. Eli, M., *Sogo Shosha*, p. 12f. 'It is a fact that an economic constellation of power existed which was very similar to the pre-war settings, then dominated by the Zaibatzu.' Roberts maintains that the Zaibatsu were never de facto abolished: 'Despite the breakup of the Zaibatzu holding companies, the corporate pattern of Japan remained very much as it has been in the past.' Roberts, J. G., *Mitsui*, p. 412f.; supported by Yoshino, M. Y., *Japan's Multinational Enterprises*, p. 14ff.
352 Clark, R., *The Japanese Company*, p. 73f.
353 MITI is generally held responsible for organizing the re-consolidation of the 2800 firms created by General MacArthur. This institution guided this concentration with informal guidance, tax incentives and direct transfer payments. Refer to Chapter 4, section IV.
354 Yoshino, M. Y., *Japan's Multinational Enterprises*, p. 16.

355 Around 1953 Mitsubishi was reinstated as Mitsui in 1959. Tasker, P., *Inside Japan*, p. 205 and Takamiya, S., *Organisation des japanischen Aussenhandels und die Bedeutung der Grosshandelsgesellschaften*, p. 188.

356 This refers to the six to ten companies stemming from century-old families: Mitsui, Mitsubishi, Sumitomo, Yasuda, Asano, Okura, Suzuki, Itoh, Nissan. Within this 'classic' group, two sets are separated: the old Zaibatsu centred around the primary sector (coal, paper) and the new Zaibatsu, concentrated on heavy industry and chemicals. Sakudo, Y., *Comment*, p. 43; opposing, Seifert, W., *Wirtschaftsorganisation and polit. Macht*, p. 143.

357 Young, A. K., *The Sogo Shosha*, p. 36.

358 Ozawa, T., *Multinationalism, Japanese Style*, p. 236.

359 Eccleston, B., *State and Society in Postwar Japan*, p. 40; Endo, K., *The Sogo Shosha Shuffle*, p. 4.

360 Takamiya, S., *Organisation des japanischen Aussenhandels und die Bedeutung der Grosshandelsgesellschaften*, p. 184f.; Yoshino, M. Y., *Japan's Multinational Enterprises*, p. 115f.

361 Kojima, R., *The Japanese Economy*; Komiya, K., *Direct Foreign Investment*.

362 Saucier, P., *New Conditions for Competition between Japanese and European Firms in the Post-1992 Unified Market*, p. 3.

363 Seitz, K., *Die japanisch-amerikanische Herausforderung*, p. 262.

364 Saucier, P., *New Conditions for Competition between Japanese and European Firms in the Post-1992 Unified Market*, p. 3; see also Anonymous, *Japan's FDI in Europe*. Also refer to Chapter 1, section II ('Japan as the focus of attention').

365 Seitz, K., *Die japanisch-amerikanische Herausforderung*, p. 262.

366 This argument is strengthened by the fact that Japan uses an effective strategy of focused portfolio investments and the West rather uses a shotgun approach, undifferentiated and unorchestrated, across all industries.

367 Yoshino, M. Y., *Japan's Multinational Enterprises*, p. 19.

368 The importance of accelerated research efforts for future success stress: Cunningham, J. and Thurow, L. C., *Building Wealth: The New Rules for Individuals, Companies, and Nations in a Knowledge-Based Economy*; Sackman, R. B., *Achieving the Promise of Information Technology: Introducing the Transformational Project Paradigm* and Goel, R. K., *Economic Models of Technological Change*. Critical aspects of the total availability of all information mentions Buranen, L. and Roy, A. M., *Perspectives on Plagiarism and Intellectual Property in a Postmodern World*.

369 Tasker, P., *Inside Japan*, p. 253ff. Cf. Chapter 4, section VI on 'the role of the Zaibatsu amd Keiretsu'.

370 The term 'globalization' means in Japan an internationalization of Japanese firms and the increased recycling of profits generated abroad in foreign direct (and indirect) investments. Economic Planning Agency, *Economic Survey of Japan 1989*, p. 123f.

371 For more refer to Wolferen, K. v., *The Enigma of Japanese Power*, p. 520; Porter, M. E., *Einführung: Der Wettbewerb auf globalen Märkten: Ein Rahmenkonzept*, p. 50.

372 The recurrent theses about Japanese firms being relatively little internationalized and being far from the global model of a multinational firm are in fact misleading about the advanced status of organizational development. This is rooted in the fact that these studies often idolize the American business model, or partially look at only one firm without the network around it. Refer to Kobayashi, N., *The Patterns of Management Style Developing in Japanese Multinational Companies*, p. 249; Kuroda, M., *Japan in a Changing World*.

373 Imai, K., *The Legitimacy of Japan's Corporate Groups*, p. 20f.; Ferguson, C., *Computers and the Coming of the US Keiretzu*; Johnson, C., *MITI and the Japanese Miracle*, p. 110.

374   Ozawa, T., *Europe 1992 and Japanese Multinationals: Transplanting a Subcontracting
      System in the Expanded Market*; and Saucier, P., *New Conditions for Competition between
      Japanese and European Firms in the Post-1992 Unified Market*; see also Ozawa, T., *Japan*.

375   This fits seamlessly into the symbolism of the Heisei era, which is described as the 'last
      major effort to enter the peaceful ages'. See Chapter 4, section IV ('the 1980s and 1990s')
      and section VI ('the turn of the millennium concept').

376   Sazaki, N., *Management and Industrial Structure in Japan*, p. 143.

377   Economic Planning Agency, *Economic Survey of Japan 1986–1987*, p. 172.

378   Also on the Board level, internationalization is moving forward having had its first non-
      Japanese in a leading firm (the Swiss H. Schmuckli at Sony). David, F., *In erlauchtem
      Kreise*.

379   Yoshino, M. Y. and Lifson, T. B., *The Invisible Link*, p. 35; Emmott, B., *Japan's Global
      Reach*; Roberts, J. G., *Mitsui*, p. 35 and p. 66; Tasker, P., *Inside Japan*, p. 265.

380   For explanations of the offices of 'Shogun' (Grand Duke) and 'Daiymo' (Duke) see
      Chapter 3, section IV on 'Japanese social network' and Roberts, J. G., *Mitsui*, p. 244ff.

381   By the externally induced development of Japanese corporate finance, a huge demand
      for financial products was created, fueling the growth of the financial sector. Core
      Keiretsu firms define themselves rather as 'sophisticated investment holding companies'
      and achieve a big part of their profits in complex financial transactions (called 'Zaitecku'
      playing on the combination of Zaibatsu and high-tech). During the Nineties, Mitsubishi
      Corp. had 30% of its profits coming from this area, other firms have even higher
      percentages. (Toyota, Toshiba, Hitachi).

382   Anonymous, *The Giants that Refused to Die*. See also Chapter 4, section II and section
      VI on 'the role of the Zaibatsu and Keiretsu'.

383   Endo, K., *The Sogo Shosha Shuffle*, p. 1.

384   Burstein, D., *Yen*, p. 257; for casual reading take the entertaining yet accurate novel
      Crichton, M., *Rising Sun*.

385   Anonymous, *Inside the Charmed Circle* and Rapaport, C., *Why Japan keeps on Winning*.
      On the parallel defence strategy of market entry barriers see Kverneland, A., *Japan's
      Industrial Structure – Barriers to Global Competition*.

386   Ferguson, C., *Computers and the Coming of the US Keiretzu*.

387   Kelly, K., *Learning from Japan*; Ferguson, C., *Computers and the Coming of the US
      Keiretzu*.

388   Anonymous, *A New Study Fuels the Clash over Keiretzu*. 'Keiretzu is ... a good to be
      imitated.' Quote from Rapaport, C., *Why Japan keeps on Winning*, p. 49.

389   More information on these ventures can be found in Van Hoesel, R., *New Multinational
      Enterprises from Korea and Taiwan: Beyond Export-Led Growth*.

390   Tsurumi, Y. and Tsurumi, R., *Sogo Shosha*, p. 59ff. and Gilroy, B. M., *Networking in
      Multinational Enterprises*, p. 159f.

391   Hailed in 1995 as the alliance of the decade covering about 750 000 employees, with the
      aim of integrating two industrial giants into the closest coalition save a merger. 'The alli-
      ance covers nothing less than the future of the auto-, aerospace-, and electronics industries;
      a German–Japanese alliance made up of two of the world's biggest and most outstanding
      industrial companies is on the (economic) warpath – and is headed for their markets.'
      Burstein, D., *Euroquake*, p. 27. Anonymous, *Daimler Benz flirtet mit Mitsubishi*. The first
      years' analyses were critical as the alliance was enacted only in marginal and unimportant
      areas. Cf. Heisman, G., *Die Flops*; or Pries, L., *Auf dem Weg zu Global operierenden
      Konzernen?*. This prenuptial period has lasted now for over five years and was slowed down
      after the first months of enthusiasm. Then an alliance with Chrysler gave Mitsubishi access
      to U.S. know-how. After the Daimler Benz Chrysler merger, Mitsubishi is reappearing as
      the potential partner in what could be the global power house of 'traditional' industry.

414   Mitsubishi Research Institute, *Some Theses on Interactions Pertinent to Innovation*, p. 55.
415   Kojima, K. and Ozawa, T., *Japan's General Trading Companies*, p. 14 and p. 25; Yoshino, M. Y. and Lifson, T. B., *The Invisible Link*, p. 81; Reischauer, E. O., *The Japanese*, p. 306 and especially, Imai, K., *The Legitimacy of Japan's Corporate Groups*, p. 21.
416   In that sense the Internet functions like an unorganized, open and rather anarchic Keiretsu.
417   Nakatani, I., *The Japanese Firm in Transition*, p. 87 and Eli, M., *Sogo Shosha*, p. 96.
418   Tasker, P., *Inside Japan*, p. 269. The reader is reminded that Tasker's study was undertaken before the advent of networked PCs and the Internet.
419   Mitsubishi Corporation, *The Mitsubishi Group*, p. 27. This ambition to remain the leader in Japan for cutting edge information technology is unbroken.
420   Bierdümpel, E., *Japanisches Informationsverhalten*, p. 83ff.
421   Tsurumi, Y. and Tsurumi, R., *Sogo Shosha*, p. 3.
422   Real-life examples can be found in Young, A. K., *The Sogo Shosha*, p. 63.
423   For the mathematical derivation refer to Aoki, M., *Risk Sharing in the Corporate Group*.
424   Aoki, M., *Aspects of the Japanese Firm*, p. 24.
425   Nakatani, I., *The Japanese Firm in Transition*, p. 47ff. and Nakatani, I., *The Economic Role of Financial Corporate Grouping*, p. 228ff. Concluding just the opposite is Adams, T. F. M. and Kobayashi, N., *The World of Japanese Business*, p. 48f.
426   High dividends are regarded as undesirable given taxation and strategic considerations (cross holdings).
427   Nakatani, I., *The Economic Role of Financial Corporate Groupings*, p. 245f.
428   Empirical Analysis of intra-group preferential trade: Zichinski, R., *Unequal Equities*, p. 37 or Ballon, R. J. and Tomita, I., *The Financial Behavior of Japanese Corporations*, p. 18.
429   Further critical studies are Caves, R. and Uekusa, M., *Industrial Organization*, p. 496f. Seen from the American perspective, this risk-minimizing strategy represents a trade barrier, so that a permanent conflict is not to be avoided. Bergsten, C. F. and Cline, W. R., *The United States–Japan Economic Problem*, p. 3; Kverneland, A., *Japan's Industrial Structure – Barriers to Global Competition*.
430   See Chapter 5, section III ('phenotypes . . .') and Chapter 5, section IV ('the composition of the core structure').
431   Cf. Wolferen, K. v., *The Enigma of Japanese Power*, p. 503; Nakamura, T., *The Postwar Japanese Economy*, p. 16ff.
432   Nakatani, I., *The Japanese Firm in Transition*, p. 45; Tasker, P., *Inside Japan*, p. 270 and Young, A. K., *The Sogo Shosha*, p. 67. This is also a reason why the Euro-Yen bond market and the CHF market for Japanese borrowers were growing exponentially in the 1980s and beginning 1990s.
433   The institutional structure of a Keiretsu is dissected in Chapter 5, IV. Generally speaking a financing institution is at the core, fueling growth, often in collaboration with a trade facilitator, organizing the flow. 'Each "Zaibatzu" [and Keiretzu] contained a bank, a trust company and an insurance company to provide funds and financial services, and a trading company to buy and sell goods on behalf of the member firms.' Clark, R., *The Japanese Company*, p. 73. See also Kester, W. C., *Japanese Takeovers*, p. 68.
434   Gibney, F., *Japan: The Fragile Superpower*, p. 164; Piore, M. J. and Sabel, C. F., *Das Ende der Massenproduktion*, p. 177.
435   Yoshino, M. Y. and Lifson, T. B., *The Invisible Link*, p. 52.
436   Young, A. K., *The Sogo Shosha*, p. 58; Johnson, C., *MITI and the Japanese Miracle*, p. 205; Eli, M., *Sogo Shosha*, p. 5ff.

437 Kojima, K. and Ozawa, T., *Japan's General Trading Companies*, p. 14.

438 Lichtenberg, F. R. and Pushner, G. M., *Ownership and Corporate Performance in Japan*.

439 Originally this refers to the disassociation of the nations of the Balkan at the beginning (and end) of this century, which resulted in upheaval and anarchy. Here it means a dissolution of financial markets into intransparent inhomogeneous micromarkets with restrictive access. This process of Balkanization would counteract the trends to globality and more efficient financial markets. In this context refer to the vast literature on efficiency of financial markets and their globalization.

440 Nakatani, I., *The Japanese Firm in Transition*, p. 48f.; Nakatani I., *The Economic Role of Financial Corporate Groupings*, p. 231.

441 Kojima, K. and Ozawa, T., *Japan's General Trading Companies*, p. 75.

442 Yoshino, M. Y. and Lifson, T. B., *The Invisible Link*, p. 79; Chapter 5, section IV ('the composition . . .', and 'the relationship network'); on the general case see Teubner, G., *Unitas Multiplex: Corporate Governance in Group Enterprises*.

443 These relations do not stop at transactions between firms but include industries, governmental spheres, academia and entities abroad. Mitsubishi Research Institute, *Some Theses on Interactions Pertinent to Innovation*, p. 55 and p. 280; see also Batelle Institut, *Innovationsprozesse und Innovationspolitik in Japan*.

444 Ozawa, T., *Europe 1992 and Japanese Multinationals: Transplanting a Subcontracting System in the Expanded Market* and Imai, K., *The Legitimacy of Japan's Corporate Groups*, p. 16.

445 Eccleston, B., *State and Society in Postwar Japan*, p. 109; Nakatani, I., *The Japanese Firm in Transition*, p. 87.

446 K. Imai concludes that the Keiretsu system intensifies rather than suffocates the general competitive situation. Imai, K., *The Legitimacy of Japan's Corporate Groups*, p. 16ff. Yui regards cartels and industrial groupings as reactions to extreme competition within an industry. Yui, T., *Beziehungen zwischen Regierung und Unternehmen und ihr Einfluss auf die Industrialisierung Japans*, p. 38; Yamamaru, K., *Economic Policy in Postwar Japan*, p. 107; Anchordoguy, M., *A Brief History of Japan's Keiretzu*, p. 59 and Wolferen, K. v., *The Enigma of Japanese Power*, p. 520.

447 Usually this takes place in the form of share exchanges, that are only some per cent in each case but aggregated, fix a large part of the share capital (about 30% on average). Taking the large networks into account Anchordoguy estimates that 60 to 80% of all Keiretsu shares never touched the official stock exchange. Anchordoguy, M., *A Brief History of Japan's Keiretzu*, p. 59; Shale, T., *Reawakening the Sleeping Giant*, p. 16; Ballon, R. J. and Tomita, I., *The Financial Behavior of Japanese Corporations*, p. 16f.

448 M. Yoshikazu's empirical studies on the top 500 companies (or 0.07% of all Japanese firms) demonstrate that these firms rule over more than half of the total sum of Japan's market capitalization via strategic shareholdings, directorships or indirectly via business relations or loan agreements. Yoshikazu, M., *Kasen [Japanese Oligopoly]*, p. 19. Lichtenberg, F. R. and Pushner, G. M., *Ownership and Corporate Performance in Japan*.

449 Neff, R. and Holstein, W. J., *Mighty Mitsubishi is on the Move*, p. 41.

450 See also Hazama, H., *The History of Labour Management in Japan*; Ashley, D., *History without a Subject: The Postmodern Condition*.

451 Roberts, J. G., *Mitsui*, p. 492 and Yoshino, M. Y. and Lifson, T. B., *The Invisible Link*, p. 94.

452 Cf. Chapter 3, section IV, and Chapter 4, section III.

453 Clark, R., *The Japanese Company*, p. 83. A more general perspective of the company as an (additional) family is Schneidewind, D., *Das japanische Unternehmen – Uchi no kaisha*, p. 63ff and p. 91.

454 Refer also to Casson's concept of structurally induced trust ('engineering of trust'). Casson, M., *Internalization Theory and Beyond*, p. 11.
455 James, B. G., *Wirtschaftsmacht Japan*, p. 208; and Porter: 'Strategies are not just reactions on the environment but attempts to actively shape the surroundings.' Porter, M. E., *Wettbewerbsvorteile*, p. 20.
456 Takamiya is referring to the fact that the dynamic growth of Japan's economy rendered rigid structures, over-specialization and orthodoxy impossible, instead calling for flexibility, openness and performance orientedness. Takamiya, S., *Organisation des japanischen Aussenhandels und die Bedeutung der Grosshandelsgesellschaften*, p. 191.
457 For example Piore, M. J. and Sabel, C. F., *Das Ende der Massenproduktion*, p. 177 or Hirschmeier, J. and Yui, T., *The Development of Japanese Business: 1600–1973*, pp. 70–144.
458 Eli, M., *Sogo Shosha*, p. 111.
459 See Chapter 4, sections II, IV and VI.
460 Tasker, P., *Inside Japan*, p. 269.
461 Young, A. K., *The Sogo Shosha*, p. 230ff.
462 Good historical summaries of the Mitsubishi family and its firms can be found in Yoshino, M. Y. and Lifson, T. B., *The Invisible Link*, p. 15ff. and Kunio, Y., *Sogo Shosha*, p. 32ff. Standard reference for the earlier history remains Mitsubishi Shoji, *Ritsugyo boeki-roku* [*History of the development of foreign trade*]. Western literature is scarce: Mitsubishi Sha, *Mitsubishi Kaisha*; Mitsubishi Sha, *An Outline of the Mitsubishi Enterprise*. Recent history covers Chihara Shobo, *Zusetzu Mitsubishi Shoji* [*Diagrammatic overview Mitsubishi trading company*]; Mainichi Shinbun, *Nippon no shosha Mitsubishi Shoji* [*Japan's trading company: Mitsubishi*].
463 Johnson, C., *MITI and the Japanese Miracle*, p. 287.
464 Just to compare sizes: one central company (in this case Mitsubishi Corporation) regularly has a higher turnover than the Exxon group as a whole. Taking the core Mitsubishi Keiretsu, it compares well with GDPs of medium-sized countries like Brazil. Smaller countries like Austria, Denmark or Indonesia are left far behind. Sazaki, N., *Management and Industrial Structure in Japan*, p. 116f.; Anonymous, *Japan Company Handbook 1988*; Anonymous, *Japan Company Handbook 1999*; Roberts, J. G., *Mitsui*, p. 491.
465 Zichinski, R., *Unequal Equities*, p. 34. Mitsubishi is proud to trade in everything, 'from Noodles to Atomic Power'. Sazaki, N., *Management and Industrial Structure in Japan*, p. 103.
466 Roberts, J. G., *Mitsui*, p. 415; Schwalbe, H., *Japan*, p. 411.
467 This Iwasaki Yotaro was the son of a farmer, who bought a noble title, and built within a very short period an aggressive clan and an even more aggressive and successful enterprise. Schwalbe, H., *Japan*, p. 413; Kojima, K. and Ozawa, T., *Japan's General Trading Companies*, p. 18; Clark, R., *The Japanese Company*, p. 22.
468 This nucleus company still exists as Nippon Yusen Kaisha and remains Japan's most prestigious shipping company. Anonymous, *Japan Company Handbook 1990*, p. 1216; see also Takamiya, S., *Organisation des japanischen Aussenhandels und die Bedeutung der Grosshandelsgesellschaften*, p. 185.
469 Y. Iwasaki is sometimes directly addressed as a 'government protégé': Yoshino, M. Y. and Lifson, T. B., *The Invisible Link*, p. 15; Clark, R., *The Japanese Company*, p. 22f.
470 Kunio, Y., *Sogo Shosha*, p. 34. This battle between Mitsubishi and Mitsui is still virulent: 'the epic battle between the two giants has provided the most exciting episodes in modern Japanese business history, and is still raging.' Roberts, J. G., *Mitsui*, p. 119.
471 Morikawa, H., *Management Structure and Control Devices for Diversified Zaibatsu Business*, p. 56.
472 Morikawa, H., *Management Structure and Control Devices for Diversified Zaibatsu Business*, p. 58. Relevant for the MNE research is the fact that, based on this study,

Chandler's Thesis of the first multidivisional system which was invented in 1921 in the U.S. seems refuted. Chandler, A. and Yasuo, M., *Comments*, p. 63.

473 Mitsubishi Group, *A Century of Progress – A Bigger Century to Come*, p. 17.

474 This is a historically consistent business philosophy. Already in 1876 Iwasaki wrote: 'If we succeed it will not only be an accomplishment for our company alone, but also a glorious event for our Japanese Empire, which shall let its light shine to all four corners of the earth. We can succeed or fail, and it depends on your effort or lack of it. Do your utmost in this endeavor.' Cf. Lu, D., *Sources of Japanese History*, p. 81f. Today this would be understood as a kind of 'philosophy of corporate citizenship' as was done by M. Makihara, Mitsubishi Corp. Chairman in the mid-nineties. Mitsubishi Corporation, *Annual Report 1992*, p. 5.

475 Consequently, M. Eli characterized Mitsubishi as the 'most dangerous war agent among all Zaibatzu.' Eli, M., *Sogo Shosha*, p. 182.

476 This percentage remained relatively constant over time despite all changes. Gibney, F., *Japan: The Fragile Superpower*, p. 166.

477 A thorough description of the dissolution of Mitsubishi and its reconstruction is included in Caves, R. and Uekusa, M., *Industrial Organization in Japan*, p. 62ff. and in Mitsubishi Group, *The Mitsubishi Group*, p. 15; see also Kojima K. and Ozawa, T., *Japan's General Trading Companies*, p. 20.

478 Persistence, speed and indirectness of strategy implementation is exemplified with the gradual assembly of the main trading house: Mitsubishi Shoji, *Mitsubishi Shoji: sono ayumi: 20-shunen kinen-go [Mitsubishi Trading Company: its development In commemoration of the 20th anniversary]*, p. 22ff.

479 Dodwell Marketing Consultants, *Industrial Groupings in Japan*, p. 24ff. and Eli, M., *Sogo Shosha*, p. 184.

480 Mitsubishi Corporation, *Annual Report 1992*, p. 2. Interestingly, this company report is sub-titled 'How does Mitsubishi Corporation Ride the Wave of Change'.

481 Eli, M., *Sogo Shosha*, p. 180 and Kunio, Y., *Sogo Shosha*, p. 42ff. A shorter overview of the evolutionary diversification of Mitsubishi is Tsurumi, Y. and Tsurumi, R., *Sogo Shosha*, p. 30ff.

482 Neff, R. and Holstein, W. J., *Mighty Mitsubishi is on the Move*, p. 38.

483 In that sense Mitsubishi is exactly applying the most advanced ideas in corporate strategy leveraging its change on the basis of IT that drives strategies rather than vice versa. Magretta, J., *Managing in the New Economy*

484 For explanations of the offices of 'Shogun' (Grand Duke) and 'Daimyo' (Duke) see Chapter 3, section IV on 'Japan as a social network' and Roberts, J. G., *Mitsui*, p. 244ff.

485 The finding that the key success drivers in the New Economy are knowledge based can serve as a further argument that Japan's enterprises are practically the only ones that have experienced this kind of postmodern environment many times over, leaving them in a pole position for the New Economy. Burton-Jones, A., *Knowledge Capitalism*.

486 For the sake of brevity and clarity we will still refer to the 'Mitsubishi Bank–Bank of Tokyo' as the 'Mitsubishi Bank'.

487 More on the history of this company see Rudlin, P., *The History of Mitsubishi Corporation in London*.

488 Anonymous, *Japan Company Handbook 1990*, p. 900.

489 Eli, M., *Sogo Shosha*, p. 195 and Mitsubishi Corporation, *Mitsubishi Corporation 1993*, p. 8f.

490 Mishima, Y. and Yamaguchi E., *Mitsubishi: Its Challenge and Strategy*, p. 60.

491 Mitsubishi Corporation, *Annual Report 1992*, p. 68.

492 Anonymous, *Japan Company Handbook 1975*, p. 395; Anonymous, *Japan Company Handbook 1990*, p. 900 and Anonymous, *Japan Company Handbook 1995*, p. 891.

493   Young, A. K., *The Sogo Shosha*, p. 51.

494   Mitsubishi Corporation, *Mitsubishi Corporation 1993*, p. 10.

495   As a consequence of the (deliberate) blurring of the nucleus, Mitsubishi speaks now of four 'principal financial institutions among the Mitsubishi companies': Bank of Tokyo– Mitsubishi Bank, Mitsubishi Trust and Banking, Tokyo Marine and Meiji Life. www.mitsubishi.or.jp.

496   Anonymous, *Japan Company Handbook 1990*, p. 1918; Anonymous, *Japan Company Handbook 1995*, p. 891; Mitsubishi Group, *A Century of Progress – A Bigger Century to Come* (Tokyo: Mitsubishi Corporation 1970).

497   Tasker, P., *Inside Japan*, p. 205. See also Chapter 5, III.

498   Ballon, R. J. and Tomita, I., *The Financial Behavior of Japanese Corporations*, p. 61 and Neff, R. and Holstein, W. J., *Mighty Mitsubishi is on the Move*, p. 41.

499   Arnold, R., *The World of Mitsubishi*, p. 35; see also Neff, R. and Holstein, W. J., *Mighty Mitsubishi is on the Move*, p. 41.

500   Eli, M., *Sogo Shosha*, p. 175; Okamura, H., *Interfirm Relations in an Enterprise Group: The Case of Mitsubishi*; Morikawa, H., *Management Structure and Control Devices for Diversified Zaibatzu Business*.

501   This could happen since the Sogo Shosha were disassembled, but the banks remained intact. Cf. Chapter 4, section 4; Roberts, J. G., *Mitsui*, p. 435 and Zichinski, R., *Unequal Equities*, p. 42.

502   Quickly after that, the strength was back: 'Mitsubishi corporation is the virtual leader of the mighty Mitsubishi group.' Anonymous, *Japan Company Handbook 1991*, p. 726.

503   Anonymous, *Japan Company Handbook 1990*, p. 750, p. 900, p. 1018.

504   www.mitsubishi.or.jp.

505   Anonymous, *Japan Company Handbook 1991*, p. 758.

506   Johnson, C., *MITI and the Japanese Miracle*, p. 157 and Clark, R., *The Japanese Company*, p. 56.

507   Roberts, J. G., *Mitsui*, p. 326 and p. 354.

508   Roberts, R., *Mitsui*; see also Takashi, K., *Dokumento Tsusan-sho I: shinkanryo no jidai* [*Documentary on MITI part I: the era of the new bureaucrats*], p. 73ff.

509   Anonymous, *Japan Company Handbook 1990*, p. 758.

510   A more detailed description of the company relations can be found in the section, 'the Keiretsu enterprise', this chapter.

511   Dodwell Marketing Consultants, *Industrial Groupings in Japan*, p. 199. Quote from Okamura, H., *Interfirm Relations in an Enterprise Group: the Case of Mitsubishi*, p. 55.

512   Neff, R. and Holstein, W. J., *Mighty Mitsubishi is on the Move*, p. 40.

513   Cf. Chapter 4, section IV, and Chapter 5, section III.

514   W. Tajitsu, former President of Mitsubishi Bank as quoted in Eli, M., *Sogo Shosha*, p. 193.

515   Cf. Shimizu, T., *Strukturanalyse der japanischen Verbundunternehmung*, p. 5f.

516   Eli, M., *Sogo Shosha*, p. 184. For a practical application by Mitubishi of this strategy of having strong ties behind the façade while downplaying it and still explaining it to foreigners in a plausible way: Mitsubishi Corporation, *Tatemae and Honne: Distinguishing Between Good Form and Real Intention in Japanese Business Culture*.

517   Krisher, B., *Mitsubishi, a Giant Reborn*, p. 32.

518   Top-Management is not meant hierarchically but is understood simply as membership in different commissions, clubs, etc. See also Chapter 4, section III ('basic structural units').

519   Anonymous, *Japan Company Handbook 1990*; Anonymous, *Japan Company Handbook 1999*. The constancy of these relations reveal the figures of 1980. FTC, *Annual Report 1982*, p. 5ff.

520 Sazaki, N., *Management and Industrial Structure in Japan*, p. 116f.; Anonymous, *Japan Company Handbook 1988* and Anonymous, *Japan Company Handbook 1999*. These calculations are based on long term average exchange rates of about 120 yen to the US dollar.

521 The same argument holds on the personal level, where a collective form of diffuse responsibility is always preferred. See Chapter 3, section IV, and Chapter 4, sections on nemawashi and ringi seido.

522 These clubs and associations transcend all grouping and reach far into the privacy of the employee, e.g. the Diamond Family Club, which is a kind of marriage facilitator within the Mitsubishi Keiretsu. Sazaki, N., *Management and Industrial Structure in Japan*, p. 105.

523 Cf. Chapter 4, section III ('basic structural units').

524 Sazaki, N., *Management and Industrial Structures in Japan*, p. 17; Nakatami, I., *The Economic Role of Financial Corporate Grouping*, p. 250; Dodwell Marketing Consultants, *Industrial Groupings in Japan*, p. 50f.

525 Political strategies are also coordinated here. Dodwell explicitly mentions the 'allocation of political contributions' as one of the main tasks of these meetings. Dodwell Marketing Consultants, *Industrial Groupings in Japan*, p. 48.

526 Okamura, H., *Interfirm Relations in an Enterprise Group: The Case of Mitsubishi*, p. 21.

527 Yoshino, M. Y. and Lifson, T. B., *The Invisible Link*, p. 121 and Roberts, J. G., *Mitsui*, p. 354.

528 Cf. Neff, R. and Holstein, W. J., *Mighty Mitsubishi is on the Move*, p. 41.

529 Yoshino, M. Y. and Lifson, T. B., *The Invisible Link*, p. 123.

530 In the analysis of cross shareholdings within the Mitsubishi-Keiretsu by A. Young the exponential growth in numbers of companies affiliated is clearly visible: 3 core companies, 27 Kinyokai-firms, 399 subsidiaries, 1460 third level affiliates, etc. Young, A. K., *The Sogo Shosha*, p. 38; compare with the section following on 'the Keiretsu enterprise as a fractal structure'.

531 Y. Mimura, former president, Mitsubishi Corporation, as quoted in Yoshino, M. Y. and Lifson, T. B., *The Invisible Link*, p. 7.

532 Neff, R. and Holstein, W. J., *Mighty Mitsubishi is on the Move*, p. 40.

533 K. Nagata reports of a kind of 80 : 20 rule: despite the inherent conflict between family and best buy, at least 20% of business should be done within the Mitsubishi family of firms. Nagata, K., *The World of Mitsubishi – Mighty Mitsubishi*.

534 Tasker, P., *Inside Japan*, p. 260.

535 Mitsubishi Corporation, *Annual Report 1993*, p. 1.

536 Tasker, P., *Inside Japan*, p. 261f.

537 Nagata, K., *The World of Mitsubishi – Mighty Mitsubishi*.

538 Holstein, W. J. *et al.*, *Hands across America: The Rise of Mitsubishi*, p. 45: 'The conspiracies form naturally within a Keiretzu, and they are conducted informally. Word of mouth is sacred. Nobody breaks the deal. They don't need lawyers.'

539 Tasker, P., *Inside Japan*, p. 262.

540 Clark, R., *The Japanese Company*, p. 74.

541 M. Makihara, former president, Mitsubishi Corporation, as quoted in Holstein, W. J. *et al.*, *Hands across America: The Rise of Mitsubishi*, p. 43.

542 Kojima, K. and Ozawa, T., *Japan's General Trading Companies*, p. 21.

543 Evans and Wurster see the deconstruction of industries (vertically and horizontally) as the main challenge of leading companies: 'the glue that holds today's value chains and supply chains together is melting'. Those companies that can embrace this openness and are able to effectively create a 'habitat', a network of relations will stay abreast of the dynamics. Parallels to postmodern positions (cf. Chapter 2) are obvious. Here,

these are then supported by practical examples, as Mitsubishi is excellent at exactly this creation of fractal economies. Evans, P. and Wurster, T. S., *Blown to Bits*, p.124f.

544 Arnold, R., *The World of Mitsubishi*.

545 Gibney, F., *Japan: The Fragile Superpower*, p.176; and also Mitsubishi Corporation, *Annual Report 1993*, p.32 or Roberts, J. G., *Mitsui*, p.425. On the general topic of per-ceived worlds created by the surrounding environment see Munéva, G., *Radical Knowledge*.

546 In former times in a business setting a Japanese addressed an unacquainted person with the name of the respective company he worked for: Mitsubishi-san or Toyota-san; Glazer, N., *Social and Cultural Factors in Japanese Economic Growth*, p.879. On the identification of employees with their firm see Young, A. K., *The Sogo Shosha*, p.46. Both sources stress the fact that this system creates isolated worlds of Keiretsu: the world of 'we' and the world of 'they'; see also Chapter 3, section IV on 'the web of individual relationships'.

547 C. Johnson as quoted in Neff, R. and Holstein, W. J., *Mighty Mitsubishi is on the Move*, p.41. Please refer also to Kegley, C. and Wittkopf, E. R., *The Multinational Corporation in World Politics*.

548 Dodwell Marketing Consultants, *Industrial Groupings in Japan*, p.53ff.

549 There is no consensus on the number of Keiretsu firms. Even Mitsubishi employees are unable to give defined figures as they all face the problem of where to set the boundaries. But this is not only a contemporary phenomenon: in the dissolution of Zaibatsu after World War II, the Americans maintained that 336 companies were in the Mitsui clan, whereas Mitsui claimed only 272; after lengthy negotiations the compromise was 294. Roberts, J. G., *Mitsui*, p.371f.

550 A detailed quantitative analysis of the intricate network of Mitsubishi in comparison with other Keiretsu is Dodwell Marketing Consultants, *Industrial Groupings in Japan*, p.312ff. For a more general analysis see Okumura, H., *Interfirm Relations in an Enter-prise Group: The Case of Mitsubishi*.

551 For an interesting theoretical overview of linkages between sectors refer to Richards, D. J. and Pearson, G., *The Ecology of Industry: Sectors and Linkages*, p.131ff. These ideas of an ecology between sectors in an economy can also be integrated into a consistent view of one group of firms where different sectors are represented in a orchestrated manner. Further literature on evolutionary aspects of industries include Fujimoto, T., *The Evolu-tion of a Manufacturing System at Toyota*; Fransman, M., *Japan's Computer and Com-munications Industry: The Evolution of Industrial Giants and Global Competitiveness*, but they invariably fail to address the topic of an intra-group ecology.

552 Anonymous, *Japanese Company Handbook 1991*, p.759.

553 Dodwell Marketing Consultants, *Industrial Groupings in Japan*, p.200f.

554 Anonymous, *Japan Company Handbook 1991*, p.775.

555 In contrast to Nissan, that lost most of its identity, Mitsubishi Motors remains a Mitsubishi Company that now adjusts to tactical structural failures committed in the 1990s. When Fuji and IBJ sold their shares in Nissan (about 40%) to the French Renault the Fuyo Keiretsu practically abandoned the car maker. Renault manager Carlos Ghon announced in one of his first speeches job cuts of 21 000 by 2002 with classical Japanese determination: 'there is no alternative. Failure is not an option') thus making it clear that Renault is in the driver's seat. Mitsubishi Motors could avoid such deconstruction. Besides, having major Non-Japanese shareholders is seen in Japan not as a negative: Ford was first in the Japanese car market with its 12% stake in Mazda acquired in 1988. Usually the Japanese view these deals as measures to get better access to technology and distribution.

556 Mitsubishi Electric, *Annual Report 1991*, p. 6.
557 Kiuchi, T., *New Economy*, **4**; see also Siegel, D., *Futurize your Enterprise*.
558 See for example Kelly, K., *New Rules for the New Economy*; MacDonald, W., *Postmodern Management*; Evans, P. and Wurster, T. S., *Blown to Bits*.
559 Kuttner, R., *Everything for Sale: The Virtues and Limits of Markets*; Burton-Jones, A., *Knowledge Capitalism*; Inamori, K. and Reid, T. R., *For People – And for Profit: A Business Philosophy for the 21st Century*; Japan Commission on Industrial Performance, *Made in Japan: Revitalizing Japanese Manufacturing for Economic Growth*.
560 For an account on the American part of this structuring of a new kind of industrial cooperation see Chapman, M. L., Elhance, A. P. and Wenum, J. D., *Mitsubishi Motors in Illinois*.
561 Refer to Chapter 2, section III and Vattimo, G., *La fin de la modernité*.
562 For example Ross, D. N., *Keiretzu: Global Manager's Unseen Rivals*.
563 Kagono, T., Nonaka, I., Okumura, A. *et al.*, *Mechanistic vs. Organic Management Systems*.
564 Some of the concepts of successful firms in competitive markets ('fractal production', 'virtual company', 'efficient information processing in the total value chain', 'net business' etc.) are already amply covered by Western research. Howard, W. G. and Guile, B. R., *Profiting from Innovation*; Harmon, R. L., *Reinventing the Factory II*; Davidoff, W. H. and Mulone, M. S., *The Virtual Corporation: Structuring and Re-vitalizing the Corporation for the 21st Century*; Teubner, G., *Unitas Multiplex: Corporate Governance in Group Enterprises*; Schmidtheini, S., *Kurswechsel*, p. 118ff.
565 Beechler, S. C. and Bird, A., *Japanese Multinationals Abroad: Individual and Organizational Learning*, p. 167.
566 Gernalzick, N., *Gegen eine Metaphysik der Arbeit: Der Ökonomiebegriff der Dekonstruktion und im Poststrukturalismus*; Martens, G., *Broch, Musil und die Grenzen der Moderne*; Oppermann, M., *The Writer in the Closet*; Ashley, D., *History without a Subject: The Postmodern Condition*.

6 Postscript: Bringing it all Together – Postmodern–New Economy Japan–MNE

1 Maybe in some areas of the social sciences, bankruptcy should be declared, but as an economic idea the postmodern proves quite useful to fill the void in the concepts of the emerging New Economy paradigm. See also Oppermann, M., *The Writer in the Closet*; Martens, G., *Broch, Musil und die Grenzen der Moderne* and Christensen, P., *Minding the Underworld*.
2 J. Naisbitt calls this 'technology intoxication'. Naisbitt, J., *High Tech High Touch*.
3 Kelly, K., *New Rules for the New Economy*.
4 Thurow, L., *Creating Wealth*.
5 On the aspect of values and 'dreams' and their impact on Japanese business see Yoshimura, N. and Anderson, P., *Inside the Kaisha*; Matsui, K., Suzuki, H. and Ushio, Y., *Millennium Metamorphosis: From Old to New Japan*, p.4; Friedman, T., *The Lexus and the Olive Tree*. An interesting attempt at bridging Confucian Traditions and postmodern society is provided in Reid, T. R., *Confucius Lives Next Door*.
6 An extensive net-search on Mitsubishi exemplifies all the arguments of this book. One can find almost 30 times as many references to Mitsubishi if compared with other global companies such as GM, Coca Cola, or DaimlerChrysler. Likewise there is no structure at all in the overall structure of appearance. Contrary to the American and European sites, the sites of Mitsubishi all tone down the size and power of the group and stress the

importance of the local and the small things. Truly a rhizome, it is impossible for a novice to this jungle of sites to grasp the whole of Mitsubishi. This is especially true in the Japanese language sites where an almost 'visceral' feeling of fractal community is fostered by the individual sites.

7   See for example, Kiuchi, T., *New Economy*, **4**; or Siegel, D., *Futurize your Enterprise*.

Bibliography

Note: Titles of non-English language sources have been translated for better understanding. If an English language edition is currently available, it is mentioned.

Aamodt, M. G. (1999) *Applied Industrial/Organizational Psychology* (New York: Wadsworth).
Abe, E., Gourvish, T. and Gourvish, T. R. (1997) *Japanese Success? British Failure?: Comparisons in Business Performance since 1945* (Oxford: Oxford University Press).
Abegglen, J. C. (1970) 'The Economic Growth of Japan', *Scientific American*, March, pp. 31–7.
— (1970) 'An Anatomy of Japan's Miracle Economy', *Washington Post*, 15 March.
Abegglen, J. C. and Stalk, G. (1990) *Kaisha: The Japanese Corporation* (Tokyo: Tuttle).
Abernathy, W. (1982) 'The New Industrial Competition', *Harvard Business Review*, September, pp. 68–81.
Ackoff, R. L. (1973) 'Science in the Systems Age', *Operations Research*, April, pp. 661–71.
Adams, T. F. M. and Kobayashi, N. (1969) *The World of Japanese Business* (Tokyo: Kodansha).
Adorno, T. and Horkheimer, M. (1973) *Dialektik der Aufklärung* (Frankfurt: Fischer), *Dialectic of Enlightenment* (Continuum, 1976).
Agger, B. (1992) *The Discourse of Domination: From the Frankfurt School to Postmodernism* (Evanston, Ill: Northwestern University Press).
Agrawal, M. (1999) *Global Competitiveness in the Pharmaceutical Industry: The Effect of National Regulatory, Economic, and Market Factors* (New York: Haworth).
Alford, F. C. (1999) *Think No Evil: Korean Values in the Age of Globalization* (Cornell, NY: Cornell University Press).
Alic, J. A., Herzenberger, S. and Wial, H. (1997) *New Rules for a New Economy: Employment and Opportunity in Postindustrial America* (Ithaca, NY: Cornell University Press).
Allan, S. (1999) *Modernity and Postmodern Culture. News Culture* (London: Open University Press).
Allen, R. E. (1999) *Financial Crises and Recession in the Global Economy* (Aldershot: Elgar).
Allen, R. J., Johnston, S. B. and Blaisdell, B. S. (1997) *Theology for Preaching: Authority, Truth and Knowledge of God in a Postmodern Ethos* (London: Abingdon).
Alston, J. P. (1986) *The American Samurai: Blending American and Japanese Managerial Practices* (Berlin: De Gruyter).
Amato, J. (1997) *Bookend: Anatomies of a Virtual Self* (Albany, NY: SUNY Press).
Anchordoguy, M. (1990) 'A Brief History of Japan's Keiretzu', *Harvard Business Review*, July, pp. 58–9.
Anders, G. (1956) *Die Antiquiertheit des Menschen* [*The outdatedness of the human being*] (Munich: Beck).
Anderson, W. (1992) *Reality isn't what it used to be* (San Francisco: Harper).
— (1998) *The Future of the Self: Inventing the Postmodern Person* (New York: Putnam).
Angermüller, J. (1999) 'Derrida vs. Bourdieu: Sociologizing Deconstruction, Deconstructing the Social', Paper presented at: Postmodern Perspectives: Second International Graduate and Postgraduate Conference, Erlangen, November 19–21, 1999.
Anonymous (1975) *Japan Company Handbook*, First Section (Tokyo: Toyo Keizai, April).
— (1987) 'Global Banking', *Financial Times*, May.
— (1988) *Japan Company Handbook*, First Section (Tokyo: Toyo Keizai, April).

351

352 Bibliography

— (1988) 'Japan glimpses the ... Monitor', *New York Times*, April.
— (1988) 'Cutting your Competitor to the Quick', *Wall Street Journal*, November.
— (1988) '1992: Europe's Counterattack: Japanese Industry will be shut out', *Nikkei Business*, December, pp. 6–8.
— (1989) *Témoigner du différend – Quand phraser ne se peut. Autour de Jean-François Lyotard* [*Testify the difference: around Jean-François Lyotard*] (Paris).
— (1989) 'Japan's FDI in Europe', *Japan Economic Journal*, April, p. 8.
— (1989) 'Smart Factories: America's Turn?', *Business Week*, May, pp. 142–8.
— (1989) 'Global Localization', *Schweizerische Handelszeitung*, August.
— (1989) 'Pornographie für US-Handelspolitiker' [Pornography for US-trade negotiators], *Neue Züricher Zeitung*, December.
— (1990) 'Daimler Benz flirtet mit Mitsubishi' [Daimler Benz flirts with Mitsubishi], *Baseler Zeitung*, March.
— (1990) *Japan Company Handbook*, First Section (Tokyo: Toyo Keizai, April).
— (1990) 'Porter v Ohmae', *The Economist*, April, p. 55.
— (1990) 'Oh Mr Porter, what shall we do?', *The Economist*, May, p. 111.
— (1990) 'Ancient Food Offering Rituals are Performed by Emperor', *Japan Times*, October.
— (1990) 'Emperor's Enthronement, Part 1', *Japan Times Special Issue*, October.
— (1990) 'Emperor's Enthronement, Part 2', *Japan Times Special Issue*, October.
— (1991) 'Inside the Charmed Circle', *The Economist*, January, p. 56.
— (1991) 'Japan's Working Woman the most Dissatisfied', *Japan Economic Journal*, February, pp. 28.
— (1991) 'A New Study Fuels the Clash over Keiretzu', *Washington Post*, April.
— (1991) *Japan Company Handbook*, First Section (Tokyo: Toyo Keizai, April).
— (1991) 'Japan may be the last Economic Power', *Japan Times*, July.
— (1992) *Metamorphosen* (Hannover: Sprengel Museum, Ausstellungskatalog).
— (1992) *Japan Company Handbook*, First Section (Tokyo: Toyo Keizai, April).
— (1992) 'Wissenschaft in Kyoto' [Science in Kyoto], *Neue Züricher Zeitung*, April.
— (1992) 'Acht für eine bessere Welt [Eight for a better world]', *Ambiente*, September, pp. 34–41.
— (1993) *Japan Company Handbook*, First Section (Tokyo: Toyo Keizai, February).
— (1993) 'Italien will sich am Modell der Hausbank orientieren' [Italy will take on the 'Housebank' model], *Frankfurter Allgemeine Zeitung*, June.
— (1993) 'Der Umsatz der "Multis" ist höher als das Welthandelsvolumen' [Sales of MNE is higher than world trade trade], *Frankfurter Allgemeine Zeitung*, July.
— (1993) 'Japans Banken behaupten Spitzenpositionen' [Japan's banks are top], *Bank Magazin*, September, p. 6.
— (1995) *Japan Company Handbook*, First Section (Tokyo: Toyo Keizai, April).
— (1998) *Die Wirtschaft Japans. Strukturen zwischen Kontinuität und Wandel Wandel* [*Japan's Economy: Structures between Continuity and Change*] (Hamburg: Springer).
— (1999) *Japan Company Handbook*, First Section (Tokyo: Toyo Keizai, February).
— (1999) 'Obituary: Akio Morita', *The Economist*, October, p. 135.
— (2000) *Japan Company Handbook*, First Section (Tokyo: Toyo Keizai, January).
— (2000) 'Hard Truths for Softbank', *The Economist*, March, pp. 65–7.
— (2000) 'Just possibly, something to sing about at last', *The Economist*, March, pp. 75–9.
— (2000) 'Japans Handelshäuser im Krebsgang, Höhere Widerstandskraft der Keiretzu Unternehmen' [Japan's Trading Companies in Slow Motion: Stronger Endurance of the Keiretzu], *Neue Züricher Zeitung*, May.
Antonelli, C. (1988) 'A New Industrial Organization Approach', in: Antonelli, C. (Ed.) *New Information Technology and Industrial Change* (Boston, MA: Kluwer), pp. 1–12.
Aoki, M. (1980) 'Decentralization–Centralization in Japanese Organization', in: Sato, K. (Ed.) *Industry and Business in Japan* (White Plains, NY: Sharpe), pp. 143–54.

— (1984) 'Aspects of the Japanese Firm', in: Aoki, M. (Ed.) *The Economic Analysis of the Japanese Firm* (Amsterdam: Elsevier), pp. 3–46.

— (1984) 'Risk Sharing in the Corporate Group', in: Aoki, M. (Ed.) *The Economic Analysis of the Japanese Firm* (Amsterdam: North Holland), pp. 259–64.

— (1988) *Information, Incentives, and Bargaining in the Japanese Economy* (Cambridge: Cambridge University Press).

Aoyagi, Y. F. (1986) 'Unternehmen und Innovation', in: Herold, R. (Ed.) *Das Industrieunternehmen in Japan* (Berlin: Schmidt), pp. 145–63.

Aoyama, N. (1982) 'The Role of Japanese Sogo Shosha', in: Lee, S. M. and Schwendiman, G. (Eds.) *Management by Japanese Systems* (New York: Praeger), pp. 210–14.

Arata, I. (1989) 'Of City, Nation and Style', in: Miyoshi, M. and Harootunian, H. D. (Eds.) *Postmodernism and Japan* (Durham, NC: Duke University Press), pp. 47–63.

Arato, A. and Rosenfeld, M. (1998) *Habermas on Law and Democracy: Critical Exchanges* (Berkeley, CA: University of California Press).

Arbeitsgruppe Soziologie (1986) *Denkweisen und Grundbegriffe der Soziologie* [*Methodology and basic terminology of sociology*] (Frankfurt: Campus Press).

Armin, H. H. v. (1980) *Volkswirtschaftspolitik* [*Economic Policy*] (Frankfurt: Metzner).

Arnold, R. (1989) 'The World of Mitsubishi', *Bilanz*, August, pp. 34–8.

Arrow, K. J. (1992) 'The Organization of Economic Activity', in: US Joint Economic Committee (1991 Congress) (Ed.) *The Analysis and Evaluation of Public Expenditure*, vol. 1 (Washington, DC: US Government Printing Office), pp. 59–73.

Asada, A. (1989) 'Infantile Capitalism and Japan's Postmodernism', in: Miyoshi, M. and Harootunian, H. D. (Eds.) *Postmodernism and Japan* (Durham, NC: Duke University Press), pp. 273–8.

— Derrida, J. and Karatani, K. (1984) 'Choshoi shakai to chishikijin no yakuwari' [The hyperconsumption society and the role of the intellectuals], *Asahi Jaanaru* [*Asahi Journal*], May, pp. 6–14.

— Nakazawa, S. and Itoi, S. (1986) 'Posutomodan no chisei ga kataru: Kakutitsu zero no koto o kano ni suru, kore ga ha tsu no kyokuchi nan ja nai?' [This is the postmodern intelligentsia: to render the impossible possible. Is this not the culmination of know-how?], *Samu appu* [*Thumbs up*], April, pp. 52–4.

Ashley, D. (1997) *History without a Subject: The Postmodern Condition* (Boulder, CO: Westview).

Astell, A. W. (1994) *Divine Representations: Postmodernism and Spirituality* (San Francisco: Paulist Press).

Ashkenas, R., Jick, T., Paul-Chowdhury, C. and Ulrich, D. (1999) *The Boundaryless Organization Field Guide: Practical Tools for Building the New Organization* (Hong Kong: Jossey-Bass).

Athos, A. G. and Pascale, R. T. (1981) *The Art of Japanese Mangement* (New York: Simon & Schuster).

Auerbach, P. (1988) *Competition* (Oxford: Blackwell).

Awanohara, S. (1991) 'Paradigm Paranoia', *Far Eastern Economic Review*, June, p. 78.

Axelrod, R. (1980) 'Effective Choice in the Prisoner's Dilemma', *Journal of Conflict Resolution*, **1**, 3–25.

— (1981) 'The Evolution of Cooperation among Egoists', *American Political Science Review*, **75**, pp. 306–18.

— (1984) *The Evolution of Cooperation* (New York: Basic Books).

— and Hamilton, W. D. (1981) 'The Evolution of Cooperation', *Science*, **27**, pp. 1390–6.

Aylett, S. (1998) *Slaughtermatic* (Four Walls Eight Windows).

Backhaus, K. and Plinke, W. (1990) 'Strategische Allianzen als Antwort auf veränderte Wettbewerbsstrukturen' [Strategic alliances as answer to changing competitive structures], in: Backhaus, K. (Ed.) *Strategische Allianzen* [*Strategic alliances*] (Sonderheft, Zeitschrift für betriebswirtschaftliche Forschung 27) pp. 21–34.

Baghai, M., Coley, S. and White D. (1999) *The Alchemy of Growth* (New York: Perseus Books).

Bain, J. S. (1956) *Barriers to New Competition* (Cambridge, MA: Harvard University Press).

Ballon, R. J. and Tomita, I. (1988) *The Financial Behavior of Japanese Corporations* (Tokyo: Kodansha).

Baranson, J. (1981) *The Japanese Challenge to the U.S. Industry* (Lexington, MA: Heath).

Barker, S. (1995) *Signs of Change: Premodern–Modern–Postmodern* (Albany, NY: SUNY Press).

Bärlocher, E., Gartmann, P., Hess, T., Höhn, T. and Wügler, H. (1990) 'Internationale Wettbewerbsfähigkeit: eine Literaturübersicht mit besonderer Berücksichtigung der Schweiz' [International competitiveness: a literature survey with special reference to Switzerland], in: Schelbert, H. and Inderbitzin, W. (Eds.) *Internationale Wettbewerbsfähigkeit* [*International competitiveness*] (Diessenhofen: Rüegger).

Barnes, J. (1999) *Capitalism's World Disorder* (New York: Pathfinder Press).

Barsky, N. (1992) 'What will become of Skylines without Edifice Complexes', *Wall Street Journal*, January.

Barthes, R. (1981) *Das Reich der Zeichen* (Frankfurt: Suhrkamp) [*The Empire of the Sign* (Noonaday 1983)].

— (1990) *Mythologies* (Paris: Seuil).

Bartlett, C. A. (1990) 'Building and Managing the Transnational: The New Organizational Challenge', in: Porter, M. E. (Ed.) *Competition in Global Industries* (Boston, MA: Harvard Business School Press), pp. 367–405.

Batelle Institut (1983) *Innovationsprozesse und Innovationspolitik in Japan* [*Processes and policies for innovation*] (Bonn: Bundesministerium für Wirtschaft).

Bateson, G. (1980) *Mind and Nature* (London: Fontana).

Baudrillard, J. (1968) *Le systéme des objets* (Paris: Gallimard) [*The System of Objects* (London: Verso)].

— (1972) *Pour une critique de l'économie politique du signe* (Paris: Gallimard) [*A Critique of the Political Economy of the Sign* (Tevlos)].

— (1976) *L'échange symbolique et la mort* (Paris: Gallimard) [*The Symbolic Exchange and Death* (Sage)].

— (1978) *Kool Killer – der Aufstand der Zeichen* (Berlin: Merve) [*Kool Killer* (London: Verso)].

— (1978) *La société de consommation* (Paris: Gallimard) [*Society of Consumption* (Sage)].

— (1978) *Oublier Foucault* (Paris: Galilée) [*Forget Foucault* (Autonomedia)].

— (1979) *De la seduction* (Paris: Galilée) [*On Seduction* (New York: St. Martin's Press)].

— (1982) *Der symbolische Tausch und der Tod* (München: Mathes & Seitz) [*The Symbolic Exchange and Death* (Sage)].

— (1983) *Les stratégies fatales* [*Fatal strategies*] (Paris: Grasset).

— (1987) *Simulacra and Simulations* (New York: Semiotexte).

Baum, H. (1990) 'Aspekte japanischen Rechts' [Some aspects of Japanese law], in: Redaktion Japan Brief (Ed.) *Japan Perspektiven* [*Perspectives on Japan*] (Frankfurt: Frankfurter Allgemeine Zeitung), pp. 112–57.

Beamish, P. W., Delios, A. and Lecraw, D. J. (1997) *Japanese Multinationals in the Global Economy* (Aldershot: Elgar).

Beasley, W. G. (1986) *The Modern History of Japan* (Tokyo: Tuttle).

Beechler, S. C. and Bird, A. (1999) *Japanese Multinationals Abroad: Individual and Organizational Learning* (Oxford: Oxford University Press).

Befu, H. (1971) *Japan: An Anthropological Introduction* (San Francisco: Chandler).

Behrman, J. N. (1984) *Industrial Policies: International Restructuring and Transnationals* (Lexington, MA: Lexington Books).

Bell, D. (1974) *The Coming of the Postindustrial Society* (London: Heinemann).
— (1976) *The Cultural Contradictions of Capitalism* (New York: Basic Books).
— (1990) 'Die dritte technologische Revolution und ihre möglichen sozioökonomischen Konsequenzen' [The third technological revolution and its possible social and economic consequences], *Merkur*, **1**, 28–47.
— (1999) *The Coming of the Post-Industrial Society 2* (New York: Basic Books).
Bellah, R. N. (1957) *Tokugawa Religion: The Values of Pre-Industrial Japan* (Glencoe, Ill: Free Press).
Benedict, R. (1946) *The Chrysanthemum and the Sword: Patterns of Japanese Culture* (New York: Houghton & Miflin).
Benko, G. and Strohmayer, U. (1997) *Space and Social Theory: Interpreting Modernity and Postmodernity* (London: Blackwell).
Bennett, J. W. and Ishino, I. (1963) *Paternalism in the Japanese Economy* (Westport, CN: Greenwood).
— and Levine, S. B. (1976) 'Industrialization in Social Deprivation: Welfare Environment and the Postindustrial Society in Japan', in: Patrick, H. (Ed.) *Japanese Industrialization and its Social Consequences* (Berkley, CA: University of California Press), pp. 457–90.
Bergquist, W. H. (1993) *The Postmodern Organization: Mastering the Art of Irreversible Change* (Hong Kong: Jossey-Bass).
Bergsten, F. C. and Cline, W. R. (1987) *The United States–Japan Economic Problem* (Washington, DC: Institute for International Economics).
Berman, M. (1982) *All that is Solid Melts into Air* (New York: Free Press).
Berndt, J. (1992) 'Bilderwelten – Popularität des Manga und Visualitätskultur' [A pictorial universe – popularity of manga and visual culture], Paper presented at 3rd OAG Japanologist Conference, Tokyo, October.
Bernstein, R. J. (1983) *Beyond Objectivism and Relativism: Science Hermeneutics and Praxis* (Philadelphia, PA: University of Pennsylvania Press).
— (1985) *Habermas and Modernity* (Cambridge, MA: MIT).
Berry, B. J., Conkling, E. C., Ray, M. D. and Berry, B. (1996) *Global Economy in Transition* (Englewood Cliffs, NJ: Prentice Hall).
Bertens, H. (1986) 'The postmodern Weltanschauung and its Relations with Modernism', in: Fokkema, D. and Bertens, H. (Eds.) *Approaching Postmodernism* (Amsterdam: Benjamins), pp. 9–51.
Best, M. (1990) *The New Competition: Institutions of Industrial Restructuring* (Cambridge, MA: Polity Press).
Besters, H. (1982) *Internationale Wettbewerbsfähigkeit bei unterschiedlichen Sozialordnungen – USA, Japan, Bundesrepublik Deutschland* [*International competitiveness with different social systems – USA, Japan, Germany*] (Baden-Baden: Nomos).
Bierdümpel, E. (1987) *Japanisches Informationsverhalten* [*Japanese strategies for acqusition of information*] (Bergisch Gladbach: Eul).
Birkenkamp, F. (1936) *Deutsche Industrieanlagen im Ausland* [*German foreign direct investment*] (Würzburg: Universität Würzburg, Diss.).
Birkett, J. and Kearns, J. (1997) *A Guide to French Literature: Early Modern to Postmodern* (New York: St. Martin's Press).
Blattner, N., Maurer, M. and Weber, M. (1987) *Voraussetzungen der schweizerischen Wettbewerbsfähigkeit* [*Conditions for the competitiveness of Switzerland*] (Bern: Haupt).
Bleicher, K. (1991) *Integriertes Management* [*Integrated management*] (Frankfurt: Campus).
Blofeld, J. (1960) 'The Zen Teachings of Huan Po on the Transmission of Mind', in: Wilson-Ross, N. (Ed.) *The World of Zen* (New York: Vintage Press), pp. 65–74.
Blois, K. J. (1989) *Transaction Costs and Networks* (Oxford: Templeton College Press).
Bloom, A. (1987) *The Closing of the American Mind* (New York: Simon & Schuster).

Böbel, I. (1984) *Wettbewerb und Industriestruktur* [*Competition and industrial organization*] (Berlin: Springer).

Bobke, M. (1990) *Arbeitsstaat Japan: Arbeitsbeziehungen Arbeitszeit und Arbeitsrecht* [*Workplace Japan: labor relations, time and law*] (Munich: Bund).

Bock, F. (1990) *Das grosse Fest der Thronbesteigung* [*The big spectacle of the coronation*] (Tokyo: OAG).

Bogue, R. (1990) 'Gilles Deleuze: Postmodern Philosopher?', *Criticism*, **4**, pp. 401–19.

Boland, L. A. (1981) 'On the Futility of Criticizing the Neoclassical Maximization Hypothesis', *American Economic Review*, **71**, pp. 1031–6.

Boorman, S. A. (1975) 'A Combinatorial Optimization Model for Transmission of Job Information through Contact Networks', *Bell Journal of Economics*, **81**, pp. 216–50.

Borner S. (1985) *New Forms of Internationalization* (Zürich: Forschungsbericht NFP 11).

— (1986) *Internationalization of Industry: An Assessment in the Light of a Small Open Economy* (Berlin: Springer).

— (1989) *Swiss Competitiveness: Where do we stand and where are we heading?* (Tagungsbeitrag: International Competitiveness of Switzerland, Basle).

— and Porter, M. E. (1991) *Internationale Wettbewerbsvorteile: Ein strategisches Konzept für die Schweiz* [*International competitive advantage: a strategic concept for Switzerland*] (Frankfurt: Campus).

Bornschier, V. (1988) *Westliche Gesellschaft im Wandel* [*Changing Western society*] (Frankfurt: Campus).

Botskor, I. (1990) *Technologiepolitik in Japan* [*Politics of technology in Japan*] (Bonn: Europa Union).

Bourdieu, P. (1966) 'Champs intellectuels et projet créateur' [Intellectual fields and the project of creation], *Les temps modernes*, **10**, pp. 865–906.

— (1977) *Outline of a Theory of Practice* (Cambridge: Cambridge University Press).

— (1979) *La Distinction* (Paris: Minuit) [*The Distinction* (Harvard University Press)].

Boyd, G. and Dunning, J. H. (1999) *Structural Change and Cooperation in the Global Economy* (Aldershot: Elgar).

Boyd, R. (1986) *Government–Industry Relations in Japan: A Review of Literature* (London: ESRC).

— (1989) 'Government–Industry Relations in Japan: Access, Communication and Competitive Collaboration', in: Wilks, S. R. M. and Wright, M. (Eds.) *Comparative Government–Industry Relations* (Oxford: Oxford University Press), pp. 61–90.

Brandes, W. (1985) *Über die Grenzen der Schreibtischökonomie* [*transgressing the limits of theoretical economy*] (Tübingen: J. C. B. Mohr).

Braudo, R. J. and MacIntosh, J. G. (1999) *Competitive Industrial Development in the Age of Information: The Role of Co-operation in the Technology Sector* (London: Routledge).

Breidenbach, J. and Zukrigl, I. (1998) *Tanz der Kulturen. Kulturelle Identität in einer globalisierten Welt* [*Dance of Cultures: Cultural Identity in a Globalized World*] (Berlin: Kunstmann).

Brenner, R. (1985) *Betting on Ideas* (Chicago: University of Chicago Press).

— (1987) *Rivalry: In Business, Science, among Nations* (Cambridge: Cambridge University Press).

Brewer, T. L. and Young, S. (1998) *The Multilateral Investment System and Multinational Enterprises* (Oxford: Oxford University Press).

Bricmont, J. and Sokal, A. (1998) *Fashionable Nonsense: Postmodern Intellectuals' Abuse of Science* (London: Picador).

Broad, W. J. (1988) 'Novel Technique Shows Japanese Outpace Americans in Innovation', *New York Times*, March.

Broadbridge, S. (1968) *Industrial Dualism in Japan* (Oxford: Oxford University, Diss.).

Brock, B. (1988) 'Selbstanmache' [Masturbation], in: Anonymous, *Programmheft zur Essener Neuinszenierung von Giuseppe Verdis 'Don Carlos'* (Essen). p. 70.

Broll, U. and Gilroy, B. M. (1989) *Aussenwirtschaftstheorie [International economics]* (Munich: Oldenbourg).

Brown, D. (1991) 'An Institutionalist Look at Postmodernism', *Journal of Economic Issues*, **12**, pp. 243–57.

Bryan, L. and Farrell, D. (1997) *Der entfesselte Markt. Die Befreiung des globalen Kapitalismus [The Unchained Market]* (Ueberreuter).

Buchanan, J. M. (1975) 'A Contractarian Paradigm for Applying Economic Theory', *American Economic Review*, **65**, pp. 225–30.

Buckley, P. J. (1981) 'A Critical Review of Theories of Multinational Enterprises', *Aussenwirtschaft*, January, pp. 70–87.

— (1983) 'Macroeconomic vs. International Business Approach to Direct Foreign Investment: A Comment', *Hitotsubashi Journal*, **1**, pp. 95–100.

— (1983) 'New Horizons in International Business', in: Buckley, P. J. (Ed.) *Internalization Theory and Beyond* (London: Macmillan Press) pp. 4–28.

— (1985) 'A Critical View of Multinational Enterprises', in: Buckley P. J. and Casson, M. (Eds.) *The Economic Theory of the Multinational Enterprise* (London: Macmillan Press), pp. 1–20.

— and Casson, M. (1976) *The Future of Multinational Enterprise* (London: Macmillan Press).

— and — (1985) 'The Optimal Timing of a Foreign Direct Investment', in: Buckley P. J. and Casson, M. (Eds.) *The Economic Theory of the Multinational Enterprise* (London: Macmillan Press), pp. 98–113.

Buranen, L. and Roy, A. M. (1999) *Perspectives on Plagiarism and Intellectual Property in a Postmodern World* (Albany, NJ: SUNY Press).

Bureau of Statistics (1992) *The Labor Force Survey 1991* (Tokyo: Government Printing Office).

Burggraf, S. (1999) *The Feminine Economy and Economic Man* (Boston, MA: Perseus).

Burgin, V. (1986) *The End of Theory* (Atlantic Highlands, NJ: Prentice-Hall).

Burstein, D. (1988) *Yen!* (New York: Simon & Schuster).

— (1991) *Euroquake* (New York: Simon & Schuster).

Burton-Jones, A. (1999) *Knowledge Capitalism* (Oxford: Oxford University Press).

Cadrière, P. (1987) 'Die rationale Funktion der relativen Ethik in Webers Theorie der Moderne' [The rational function of relative ethics in Weber's theory of the modern], in: Le Rider, J. and Raulet, G. (Eds.) *Verabschiedung der Postmoderne [Good-byes to the postmodern]* (Tübingen: Narr), pp. 39–63.

Callinicos, A. (1989) *Against Postmodernism* (Cambridge, MA: Polity Press).

Callon, S. (1997) *Divided Sun: MITI and the Breakdown of Japanese High-Tech Industrial Policy* (Stanford: Stanford University Press).

Canton, J. (1999) *Technofutures: How Leading-Edge Technology will Transform Business in the 21st Century* (Hay House).

Cantwell, J. (1987) *A Dynamic Model of the Postwar Growth of International Economic Activity in Europe and the US* (Reading: University of Reading Discussion Papers 104).

— (1991) 'A Survey of the Theories of International Production', in: Pitelis, C. and Sudgen, R. (Eds.) *The Nature of the Transnational Firm* (London: Routledge), pp. 16–64.

— and Randaccio, F. S. (1990) *Growth and Multinationality amongst the World's Largest Firms* (Reading: University of Reading Discussion Paper 134).

Capra, F. (1975) *The Tao of Physics* (Berkeley, CA: University of California Press).

— (1987) *Das neue Denken [The new way of thinking]* (München: Scherz).

— (1988) *Wendezeit* (München: Scherz 1984) [*The Turning Point* (Bantam)].

Carlile, L. E. and Tilton, M. (1998) *Is Japan Really Changing its Ways? Regulatory Reform and the Japanese Economy* (Washington DC: Brookings Institution).

Carlsson, B. (1989) 'Industrial Dynamics: An Overview', in: Carlsson, B. (Ed.) *Industrial Dynamics* (Boston, MA: Kluwer), pp. 1–20.

Carr, D. (1999) *Education, Knowledge, and Truth: Beyond the Postmodern Impasse* (London: Routledge).

Carroll, D. (1997) *Paraesthetics: Foucault, Lyotard, Derrida* (London: Routledge).

Carroll, G. R. and Teece, D. J. (1998) *Firms, Markets, and Hierarchies* (Oxford: Oxford University Press).

Carver, T. (1999) *The Postmodern Marx* (Philadelphia, PA: Pennsylvania State University Press).

Casson, M. (1985) 'Transaction Cost and the Theory of the Multinational Enterprise', in: Buckley, P. J. and Casson, M. (Eds.) *The Economic Theory of the Multinational Enterprise* (London: Macmillan), pp. 20–38.

— (1986) 'General Theory of the Multinational Enterprise', in: Hertner, P. and Jones, G. (Eds.) *Multinationals: Theory and History* (Aldershot: Gower), pp. 42–63.

— (1987) *The Firm and the Market* (Cambridge, MA: MIT Press).

— (1989) *Entrepreneurial Culture as a Competitive Advantage* (Reading: University of Reading Discussion Paper 124).

— (1990) *Enterprise and Competitiveness: A Systems View of International Business* (Oxford: Clarendon).

— (1990) *Internalization Theory and Beyond* (Reading: University of Reading Discussion Paper 148).

— (1991) *The Economics of Business Culture* (Oxford: Oxford University Press).

Caves, R. and Uekusa, M. (1976) *Industrial Organization in Japan* (Washington, DC: Brookings Institution).

— and — (1976) 'Industrial Organization', in: Patrick, H. and Rosovsky, H. (Eds.) *Asia's New Giant: How the Japanese Economy Works* (Washington, DC: Brookings Institution), pp. 459–524.

Cefola, J., Neef, D. and Siesfeld, T. (1998) *The Economic Impact of Knowledge* (London: Butterworth Heinemann).

Chandler, A. D. (1977) *The Visible Hand: The Managerial Revolution in American Business* (Cambridge, MA: Bellknap Press).

— (1980) 'The Growth of the Transnational Firm in the United States and the United Kingdom: A Comparative Analysis', *Economic History Review*, **33**, pp. 396–410.

— (1982) 'The M-Form: Industrial Groups, American Style', *European Review*, **9**, pp. 3–23.

— and Mishima, Y. (1980) 'Comments', in: Nakagawa, K. (Ed.) *Strategy and Structure of Big Business* (Tokyo: University of Tokyo Press), pp. 61–64.

Chapman, M. L., Elhance, A. P. and Wenum, J. D. (1995) *Mitsubishi Motors in Illinois* (Westport, CN: Greenwood).

Charrier, I. (1991) *La peinture japonaise contemporaine* [*Japanese contemporary painting*] (Besançon: La Manufracture).

Cherkes, M. (1984) *The Theory of the Multinational Enterprise in Manufacturing Industries* (Philadelphia, PA: University of Pennsylvania Press).

Chichilnisky, G. (1990) *Networks and Coalition Formation* (New York: Columbia University Working Paper 496).

Chihara Shobo (1979) *Zusetzu Mitsubishi Shoji* [*Diagrammatic overview Mitsubishi trading company*] (Tokyo: Chihara Shobo).

Cho, H. T. (1990) *Postmodern Philosophy, Relativism, and a Renewed Vision of Education* (Urbana, Ill: University of Illinois, Diss.).

Choate, P. (1990) *Agents of Influence* (New York: Knopf).

Chomsky, N. and Dietrich, H. (1996) *Globalisierung im Cyberspace. Globale Gesellschaft: Märkte, Demokratie und Erziehung [Globalization in Cyberspace]* (Horlemann).

Christensen, P. (1990) *Minding the Underworld: Clayton Eshleman and Late Postmodernism* (Black Sparrow Press).

Chu, C. N. (1991) *The Asian Mind Game* (New York: Rawson).

Ciborra, C. U. (1983) 'Markets, Bureaucracies and Groups in the Information Society', *Information Economics and Policy*, 2, pp. 145–60.

Clancy, T. (1998) *Rainbow Six* (London: Penguin).

Clark, G. L. and Kim, W. B. (1995) *Asian NIEs and the Global Economy: Industrial Restructuring and Corporate Strategy in the 1990s* (Washington DC: Johns Hopkins University Press).

Clark, R. (1988) *The Japanese Company* (Tokyo: Tuttle).

Clegg, L. J. (1990) 'The Determinants of Multinational Enterprise: A Comparative Study of the US, Japan, UK, Sweden and West Germany', in: Casson, M. (Ed.) *Multinational Corporations* (Aldershot: Elgar), pp. 578–609.

Cloyd, J. T. (1992) 'Introduction: Postmodern Praxis in Politics', in: Cloyd, J. T. (Ed.) *Politics' Postmodern Paralysis* (Nashville: Vanderbilt University Press), pp. 1–21.

Coase, R. H. (1991) 'The Nature of the Firm', in: Williamson, O. E. and Winter, S. G. (Eds.) *The Nature of the Firm* (Oxford: Oxford University 1991), pp. 18–33 [Reprint, first edition 1937].

Cohen, B. J. and Lipson, C. (1999) *Issues and Agents in the International Political Economy: An International Organization Reader* (Cambridge, MA: MIT Press).

Cohen, D. (1998) *Managing Knowledge in the New Economy* (Washington DC: Conference Board).

Colin, J. M. (1971) 'After X and Y comes Z', *Personnel Journal*, 50, pp. 56–61.

Collins, J. (1989) *Uncommon Cultures* (New York: Routledge).

Colquhoun, A. (1989) *Modernity and the Classical Tradition: Architectual Essays 1980–1987* (Cambridge, MA: MIT Press).

Connoly, W. (1984) *The Terms of Political Discourse* (Princeton, NJ: Princeton University Press).

Cook, T. F. (1983) 'Cataclysm and Career Rebirth: The Imperial Military Elite', in: Plath, D. W. (Ed.) *Work and Lifecourse in Japan* (Albany, NY: New York State University) pp. 135–52.

Cooke, M. and Habermas, J. (1998) *On the Pragmatics of Communication* (Boston, MA: MIT Press).

Cooke, P. and Morgan, K. (1998) *The Associational Economy: Firms, Religions, and Innovation* (Oxford: Oxford University Press).

Corff, O. (1991) *Zur Frage der Herkunft der japanischen Sprache [On the origins of the Japanese Language]* (Tokyo: OAG).

Coulmas, F. (1993) *Das Land der rituellen Harmonie [Land of ritual harmony]* (Munich: Campus).

— (1998) *Japan ausser Kontrolle. Vom Musterknaben zum Problemkind [Japan out of Control]* (Darmstadt: Primus).

Cox, K. R. (1997) *Spaces of Globalization: Reasserting the Power of the Local* (New York: Guilford).

Crichton, M. (1992) *Rising Sun* (New York: Knopf).

Critchley, S., Derrida, J., Laclau, E. and Rorty, R. (1996) *Deconstruction and Pragmatism* (London: Routledge).

Cronin, C., De Greiff, P. and Habermas, J. (1998) *The Inclusion of the Other: Studies in Political Theory* (Boston, MA: MIT Press).

Cullen, J. B. (1998) *Multinational Management: A Strategic Approach* (Phoenix, AZ: South-Western).

Cunningham, J. and Thurow, L. C. (1999) *Building Wealth: The New Rules for Individuals, Companies, and Nations in a Knowledge-Based Economy* (Cambridge, MA: MIT Press).

Curtler, H. M. (1997) *Rediscovering Values: Coming to Terms with Postmodernism* (M. E. Sharpe).

Dacey, R. (1981) 'Some Implications of Theory Absorption for Economic Theory and the Economics of Information', in: Pitt, J. C. (Ed.) *Philosophy in Economics* (Dordrecht: Reidel), pp. 111–36.

Dahlby, T. (1991) 'The Bureaucrats: Sons of the Samurai', *Far Eastern Economic Review*, March, pp. 34–40.

Daidoji, Y. (1990) *The Code of the Samurai* (Tokyo: Tuttle).

Danger, M. (1985) *Adventures of a Gaijin* (Tokyo: Tuttle).

David, F. (1990) 'In erlauchtem Kreise' [In high circles], *Wirtschaftswoche*, September, pp. 57–60.

Davidow, W. H. and Malone, M. S. (1992) *The Virtual Corporation: Structuring and Revitalizing the Corporation for the 21st Century* (San Francisco: Harper).

Davies, S. and Meyer, C. (1998) *Das Prinzip Unschärfe* [*The Fractal Principle*] (Wiesbaden: Gabler).

Davis, P. A. (1972) *Administrative Guidance in Japan* (Tokio: Sophia University Press).

Dear, M. J. (1999) *The Postmodern Urban Condition* (London: Blackwell).

Decisions in Organizations Group (1979) 'A Comparative Study in Britain, the Netherlands, and Yugoslavia', *Industrial Relations*, **18**, pp. 49–68.

— (1983) 'A Contingency Model of Participative Decision Making', *Journal of Occupational Psychology*, **56**, pp. 1–18.

Degli-Esposti, C. (1998) *Postmodernism and the Cinema* (San Francisco: Berghan).

Delener, N. (1990) *Strategic Planning and Multinational Trading Blocs* (New York: Quorum Books).

Deleuze, G. (1968) *Différence et répétition* (Paris: PUF) [*Difference and Repetition* (Columbia University Press)].

— and Guattari, F. (1976) *Rhizom* (Paris: Galilée).

— and — (1985) *L'Anti-Oedipe* (Paris: Minuit) [*Anti Oedipus* (University of Minnesota Press)].

De Mente, B. (1987) *Bachelor's Japan* (Tokyo: Tuttle).

— (1987) *Japanese Etiquette in Ethics and Business* (Phoenix, AZ: Phoenix).

— (1990) *The Kata Factor* (Phoenix, AZ: Phoenix).

Den Hertog, F. J. and Huizenga, E. (1999) *The Knowledge of Enterprise; Implementation of Intelligent Business Strategies* (London: Imperial College Press).

Deresky, H. (1999) *International Management: Managing Across Borders and Cultures* (Wokingham: Addison-Wesley).

Derrida, J. (1967) *L'écriture et la différence* (Paris: Minuit) [*The Writing and the Difference* (University of Chicago Press)].

— (1976) *Die Schrift und die Differenz* (Frankfurt: Suhrkamp) [*The Writing and the Difference* (University of Chicago)].

— (1981) *Disseminations* (Chicago: University of Chicago Press).

— (1998) *Grammatologie* (Frankfurt: Suhrkamp) [*Grammatology* (Johns Hopkins University Press)].

Deshimaru, T. (1978) *Zen in den Kampfkünsten Japans* (Munich: Knaur) [*Zen and Martial Arts in Japan* (New York: E. P. Dutton)].

DeVos, G. A. (1973) *Socialization for Achievement* (Berkeley, CA: University of California Press).

Dewey, J. (1929) *The Quest for Certainty: A Study of the Relation of Knowledge and Action* (New York: Putnam).

— (1938) *Logic: The Theory of Inquiry* (New York: Holt).

Dews, P. (1999) *Habermas: A Critical Reader* (Oxford: Blackwell).

Diebold, J. (1986) 'Information Technology as a Competitive Weapon', *Advance Technology Alert System Bulletin*, **6**, pp. 104–6.

Docherty, T. (1997) *After Theory* (Edinburgh: Edinburgh University Press).

Dodwell Marketing Consultants (1992) *Industrial Groupings in Japan* (Tokyo: Dodwell).

— (1995) *Industrial Groupings in Japan* (Tokyo: Dodwell).

Dohnanyi, K. v. (1990) *Japanische Strategien* (Munich: Piper).

Doi, T. (1989) 'Amae: Freiheit in Geborgenheit' [Amae: freedom in comfort], in: Hijia-Kirschnereit, I. and Schmölers, C. (Eds.) *Japan* (Frankfurt: Insel), pp. 169–74.

— (1990) The Anatomy of Dependence (Tokyo: Kodansha)

Doll, D. R. (1978) *Data Communications: Facilities, Networks, and Systems Design* (New York: Wiley).

Dolles, H. and Jung, H. F. (1990) *Subcontracting in Japan* (Nürnberg: Universität Nürnberg Working Paper).

Dominique, C. R. (1999) *Unfettered Globalization* (New York: Praeger).

Donne, J. (1912) 'Anatomy of the World', in: Grierson, H. J. (Ed.) *Poems of John Donne*, vol. 1 (Oxford: Oxford University Press).

Dopfer, K. (1970) *Ost–West Konvergenz* [*East–West convergence*] (Zürich: Polygraphischer Verlag).

— (1989) 'Mechanistisches Denken und seine Überwindung in der Ökonomie' [Mechanistical thinking and its transgression in economics], in: Dubs, R., Hangartner, Y. and Nydegger, A. (Eds.) *Der Kanton St. Gallen und seine Hochschule* [*The canton St. Gallen and its university*] (St. Gallen: Hochschule St. Gallen), pp. 400–7.

— (1990) 'Elemente einer Evolutionsökonomik' [Elements of evolutionary economics], in: Witt, U. (Ed.) *Studien zur evolutorischen Entwicklung*, vol. 1 [Studies in evolutionary devlopments] (Berlin: Dunker & Humblot), pp. 19–48.

Dore, R. (1986) *Flexible Rigidities* (Stanford, CA: Stanford University Press).

Dore, R., Bounine-Cabalé, J. and Tapiola, K. (1989) *Japan at Work* (Paris: OECD).

Downs, A. (1997) *Beyond the Looking Glass: Overcoming the Seductive Culture of Corporate Narcissism* (New York: Amacom).

Doz, Y. (1989) 'Die Rolle des Staates im globalen Wettbewerb' [The role of the state in the global competition], in: Porter, M. E. (Ed.) *Globaler Wettbewerb: Strategien der neuen Internationalisierung* [*Global competition: strategies of a new internationalization*] (Wiesbaden: Gabler), pp. 257–306.

— and Pralahad, C. K. (1988) 'Quality of Management: An Emerging Source of Global Advantage?', in: Hood, N. and Vahlne, J. E. (Eds.) *Strategies in Global Competition* (London: Croom Helm), pp. 345–69.

— and Shuen, A. (1987) *A Process Framework for Analyzing Cooperation between Firms* (Fontainbleau: INSEAD Working Paper 33).

Droughty, A. (1991) *Japan 2000* (Rochester, NY: Rochester Institute of Technology Press).

Drucker, P. F. (1991) *Toward the Next Economics* (New York: Harper & Row).

Dubois, A. (1998) *Organizing Industrial Activities across Firm Boundaries* (London: Routledge).

Dunning, J. H. (1974) *Economic Analysis and the Multinational Enterprise* (London: Macmillan Press).

— (1977) 'Trade, Location of Economic Activity and the MNE: A Search for an Eclectic Approach', in: Ohlin, B., Hesselborn, P. O. and Wijkman, P. M. (Eds.) *The International Allocation of Economic Activity: Proceedings of a Nobel Symposium Held at Stockholm* (London: Macmillan Press), pp. 395–418.

— (1985) 'Introduction', in: Dunning, J. H. (Ed.) *Multinational Enterprises, Economic Structure and International Competitiveness* (New York: Wiley), pp. 1–13.

— (1985) 'Some Conclusions and Policy Implications', in: Dunning, J. H. (Ed.) *Multinational Enterprises, Economic Structure and International Competitiveness* (New York: Wiley), pp. 407–31.

— (1988) 'The Eclectic Paradigm of International Production: A Restatement and some possible Extensions', *Journal of International Business Studies*, 1, pp. 1–31.

— (1988) *Multinationals, Technology and Competitiveness* (London: Unwin).

— (1991) 'The Eclectic Paradigm of International Production: A Personal Perspective', in: Pitelis, C. and Sudgen, R. (Eds.) *The Nature of the Transnational Firm* (London: Routledge), pp. 117–36.

— (1993) *Multinational Enterprises and the Global Economy* (Wokingham: Addison Wesley).

— (1997) *Governments, Globalization, and International Business* (Oxford: Oxford University Press).

— and Cantwell, J. A. (1990) *Japanese Manufacturing Direct Investment in the EEC, post-1992: Some Alternative Scenarios* (Reading: University of Reading Discussion Paper 132).

Durham, S. (1998) *Phantom Communities: The Simulacrum and the Limits of Postmodernism* (Stanford, CA: Stanford University Press).

Dwight, T. H. (1992) 'Quotation: Tracing Postmodernism in Washington', in: Cloyd, J. T. (Ed.) *Politics' Postmodern Paralysis* (Nashville: Vanderbilt University Press), pp. 56–121.

Earhart, H. B. (1974) *Religion in the Japanese Experience* (Belmont, CA: Dickinson).

Ebersole, G. (1992) *Ritual Poetry and the Politics of Death in Early Japan* (Princeton: Princeton University Press).

EC Commission on International Trade (1989) *The Group of Thirty: 1992: The External Dimension* (London).

Eccleston, B. (1989) *State and Society in Postwar Japan* (Cambridge, MA: Polity Press).

Echigo, K. (1980) 'Japanese Studies of Industrial Organization', in: Sato, K. (Ed.) *Industry and Business in Japan* (White Plains, NY: Sharpe), pp. 450–63.

Eco, U. (1988) *Nachschrift zu 'Im Namen der Rose'* [*Postscriptum to 'In the Name of the Rose'*] (Munich: DTV).

Economic Planning Agency (1971) *The Basic Directions of Trade and Industrial Policy in the 1970s* (Tokyo: EPA).

— (1987) *Economic Survey of Japan 1986–1987* (Tokyo: Government Printing Office)

— (1988) *Economic Survey of Japan 1987–1988* (Tokyo: Government Printing Office).

— (1989) *Economic Survey of Japan 1988–1989* (Tokyo: Government Printing Office).

— (1990) *Economic Survey of Japan 1989–1990* (Tokyo: Government Printing Office).

— (1992) *Economic Survey of Japan 1991–1992* (Tokyo: Government Printing Office).

— (1993) *Economic Survey of Japan 1992–1993* (Tokyo: Government Printing Office).

— (1999) *Economic Survey of Japan 1998–1999* (Tokyo: Government Printing Office).

Economist (1987) *Japan* (London: *The Economist*).

Eguchi, Y. (1986) 'Japanische Gruppenmentalität und ökonomische Konflikte' [Japanese group mentality and economic conflicts]', in: Barloewen, C. v. and Werhahn-Mees, K. (Eds.) *Japan und der Westen*, vol. 2 [*Japan and the West*] (Frankfurt: Fischer), pp. 181–90.

Eichgreen, B. (1999) *Towards a New International Financial Architecture: A Practical Post-Asia Agenda* (Washington, DC: Institute for International Economics).

Ekstedt, E., Lundin, R. A. and Soderholm, A. (1999) *Neo Industrial Organizing: Renewal by Action and Knowledge Formation in a Project-Intensive Economy* (London: Routledge).

Elazar, D. J. (1998) *Constitutionalizing Globalization: The Postmodern Revival of Confederal Arrangements* (London: Rowan & Littlefield).

Eli, M. (1977) *Sogo Shosha* (Düsseldorf: Econ).

Ellin, N. (1999) *Postmodern Urbanism* (Princeton, NJ: Princeton Architectural Press).

Elisasson, G. (1989) 'The Dynamics of Supply and Economic Growth', in: Carlsson, B. *Industrial Dynamics* (Boston, MA: Kluwer), pp. 21–54.

Ellis, B. E. (1991) *American Psycho* (New York: Vintage).

Emig, R. (1999) *Towards a Postmodern Poetics* (New York: St. Martin's Press).

Emmott, B. (1992) *Japan's Global Reach* (London: Century).

Emori, M. (1968) *The Japanese Trading Company* (Tokyo: Speech, US Embassy, October).

Enderle, G. (1985) *Ethik und Wirtschaftswissenschaften* (Berlin: Springer).

Endo, K. (1988) *The Sogo Shosha Shuffle* (Tokyo: Nomura).

Engardio, P. (1991) 'Building a Hong Kong Empire from a Japanese Blueprint', *Business Week*, August, p. 23.

Engelmann, P. (1989) 'Zur Ambivalenz von Moderne und Postmoderne' [On the ambivalence of modern and postmodern], in: Schirmacher, W. (Ed.) *Schopenhauer in der Postmoderne* [*Schopenhauer in postmodern times*] (Graz: Passagen), pp. 21–33.

Epstein, J. (1998) *Youth Culture: Identity in a Postmodern World* (Oxford: Blackwell).

Ernst, A. (1989) 'Nach den Handelsfriktionen demnächst Technologiefriktionen?' [After frictions in trade now conflicts about technology?], *Japaninfo*, **4**, p. 11.

Ertel, E. (1930) *Internationale Kartelle und Konzerne der Industrie* [*International cartels and industrial concerns*] (Stuttgart: Poeschel).

Esposito, E. (1991) 'Paradoxien als Unterscheidungen von Unterscheidungen' [Paradoxa as differences within differences], in: Gumbrecht, H. U. and Pfeiffer, K. L. (Eds.) *Paradoxien, Dissonanzen, Zusammenbrüche: Situationen offener Epistemologie* [*Paradoxa, dissonances, implosions: situations of open epistemology*] (Frankfurt: Suhrkamp), pp. 35–57.

Ethier, W. (1979) 'Internationally Decreasing Costs of World Trade', *Journal of International Economics*, **2**, 1–24.

— (1982) 'National and International Returns to Scale in the Modern Theory of International Trade,' *American Economic Review*, **6**, 389–405.

— (1986) 'The Multinational Firm', *Quarterly Journal of Economics*, **101**, 805–33.

Evans, P. and Wurster, T. S. (1999) *Blown to Bits* (Boston: Harvard Business School Press).

Ezeala-Harrison, F. (1999) *Theory and Policy of International Competitiveness* (New York: Praeger).

Fama, E. (1980) 'Agency Problems and the Theory of the Firm', *Journal of Political Economy*, **4**, pp. 288–307.

Featherstone, M. (1990) 'Perspectives on Consumer Culture', *Sociology*, **1**, pp. 5–23.

Federal Trade Commission (1983) *Annual Report 1982* (Tokyo: Government Printing Office).

Fekete, J. (1988) 'Vampire Value, Infinitive Art, and Literary Theory', in: Fekete, J. (Ed.) *Life After Postmodernism* (London: Macmillan Press), pp. 54–85.

Feketekuty, G. and Stokes, B. (1998) *Trade Strategies for a New Era: Ensuring U.S. Leadership in a Global Economy* (London: Council on Foreign Relations).

Felperin, H. (1988) *Beyond Deconstruction: The Uses and Abuses of Literary Theory* (London: Unwin).

Fendra, R. C. (1989) *Trade Policies for International Competitiveness* (Chicago: University of Chicago Press).

Ferguson, C. (1990) 'Computers and the Coming of the US Keiretzu', *Harvard Business Review*, **7**, pp. 55–70.

Ferguson, M. (1980) *The Aquarian Conspiracy* (Los Angeles: Tarcher).

Fernandez, S. (1999) *Gustavo Sainz: Postmodernism and the Mexican Novel* (Frankfurt: Lang).

Ferre, F. (1998) *Knowing and Value: Toward a Constructive Postmodern* (Albany, NY: SUNY Press).

Festenstein, M. (1990) *Pragmatism and Political Theory: From Dewey to Rorty* (Chicago, Ill: University of Chicago Press).

Feyerabend, P. (1980) *Erkenntnis für freie Menschen* [*Knowledge for free men*] (Frankfurt: Suhrkamp).
— (1986) *Wider den Methodenzwang* (Frankfurt: Suhrkamp) [*Against Method* (London: Verso)].
Fiedler, L. (1965) 'The New Mutants', *Partisan Review*, **32**, pp. 505–25.
Field, N. (1989) 'The Postmodern as Atmosphere', in: Miyoshi, M. and Harootunian, H. D. (Eds.) *Postmodernism and Japan* (Durham, NC: Duke University Press), pp. 169–88.
Figlestahler, P. (1979) 'Zwischen Ghetto und Metropolis' [Between ghetto and metropolis], *Neue Züricher Zeitung*, October.
Flierl, B. (1991) 'Postmoderne Architektur [Postmodern architecture]', in: Weimann, R., Gumbrecht, H. U. and Wagner, B. (Eds.) *Postmoderne – Globale Differenz* [*The postmodern – global difference*] (Frankfurt: Suhrkamp), pp. 211–45.
Flossdorf, B. (1978) 'Wie kommt die Wissenschaft zu ihrem Wissen [How science gets its knowledge], *Psychologie Heute*, **5**, pp. 65–78.
Fokkema, D. (1986) 'Semantic and Syntactic Organization of Postmodern Texts', in: Fokkema, D. (Ed.) *Approaching Postmodernism* (Amsterdam: Benjamins), pp. 81–98.
Földt, T. (1984) *Networks and Networking in Social Science Information* (Budapest: Hungarian Academy of Science Press).
Foljanty-Jost, G. (1989) 'Informelles Verwaltungshandeln [Informal administrative action]', in: Menzel, U. (Ed.) *Im Schatten des Siegers*, vol. 2 [*In the shadow of the winner*] (Frankfurt: Suhrkamp), pp. 171–90.
Foster, H. (1998) *The Anti-Aesthetic: Essays on Postmodern Culture* (The New Press).
Foucault, M. (1966) Les mots et les choses (Paris: Gallimard) [The Words and the Things (Schoenenhof, 1990)].
— (1970) *The Order of Things* (London: Travistock).
— (1977) *Languages, Counter-Memory, Practice* (Oxford: Blackwell).
— (1986) 'Of other Spaces', *Diacritics*, **16**, pp. 22–7.
— and Raulet, G. (1983) 'Um welchen Preis sagt die Vernunft die Wahrheit?' [At what price reason speaks truth?], *Spuren*, **1**, pp. 2–19.
Fox, A. (1974) *Beyond Contractwork Power and Trust Relations* (London: Faber and Faber).
Fraenkel, B. (1990) 'The Cultural Contradictions of Postmodernity', in: Milner, A. (Ed.) *Postmodern Conditions* (Oxford: Berg), pp. 95–112.
Frank, M. (1984) *Was ist Neostrukturalismus?* [*What is neostructuralism?*] (Frankfurt: Suhrkamp).
— (1988) *Die Grenzen der Verständigung* [*Limits of communication*] (Frankfurt: Suhrkamp).
Fransman, M. (1995) *Japan's Computer and Communications Industry: The Evolution of Industrial Giants and Global Competitiveness* (Oxford: Oxford University Press).
Freeman, C. (1987) *Technology Policy and Economic Performance: Lessons from Japan* (London: Pinter).
French, W. L. and Bell, C. H. (1978) *Organizational Development* (Englewood Cliffs, NJ: Prentice Hall).
Friedman, G. and LeBard, M. (1991) *The Coming War with Japan* (New York: St. Meredith).
Friedman, M. (1951) *Essays in Postitive Economics* (Chicago: University of Chicago Press).
— (1975) *Price Theory* (Chicago: Aldine).
Friedman, T. L. (1999) *The Lexus and the Olive Tree: Understanding Globalization* (New York: Simon and Schuster).
Frischkorn, T. (1990) *Zazen für Arbeitnehmer. Zur Symptomatologie zen-buddhistischer Rituale in Japans Wirtschaft* [*Zazen for employees: symptomatology of zen-buddhist rituals in Japanese business*] (Berlin: Freie Universität, Diss.).
Fruin, M. (1991) *Kikkoman, Clan, Company* (Tokyo: Kodansha).

Ftatsugi, Y. (1969) 'Kigyo kan kankei no sokutei' [The relations of firms to other firms], *Kikan Riron Keizagaku* [*Economic studies*], **2**, pp. 37–49.

Fujimoto, K. (1990) 'Working their Way to a Sudden Death', *Japan Times*, December.

Fujimoto, T. (1999) *The Evolution of a Manufacturing System at Toyota* (Oxford: Oxford University Press).

Fujioka, M. (1990) *Japanese Castles* (Osaka: Hoikusha).

Fukami, T. (1998) *Successful Business Management Through Shinto* (Tokyo: toExcel).

Fukao, M. (1994) *Financial Integration, Corporate Governance, and the Performance of Multinational Companies* (Washington DC: Brookings Institution).

Furlough, E. and Strikwerda, C. (1999) *Consumers against Capitalism? Consumer Cooperation in Europe, North America and Japan* (London: Rowman & Littlefield).

Gadamer, H.-G. (1996) *Wahrheit und Methode* (Tübingen: J. C. B. Mohr 1960) [Truth and Method (Continuum, 1993)].

— (1971) *Begriffsgeschichte und die Sprache der Philosophie* [*History of concepts and the language of philosophy*] (Opladen: Westdeutscher Vlg.).

Galbraith, J. K. (1952) *American Capitalism* (Boston: Houghton Miflin).

— (1973) *Economics and the Public Purpose* (Boston: Houghton Miflin).

— (1988) *Die Entmythologisierung der Wirtschaft* [*De-mystifying business*] (Wien: Zsolany).

Gander, E. (1998) *The Last Conceptual Revolution: A Critique of Richard Rorty's Political Philosophy* (Albany, NY; State University of New York Press).

Gantenbein, D. (1990) 'Architecture: Arthur Erickson', *Architectural Digest*, **3**, pp. 220–7.

Gappert, G. (1979) *Post-Affluent America* (New York: Watts).

Gardbaum, S. A. (1989) *Liberalism, Postmodernism, Antimodernism* (New York: Columbia University Press).

Gardner, A. and Ishii, H. (1976) 'Fiscal, Monetary and Related Policies', in: Patrick, H. and Rosovsky, H. (Eds.) *Asia's New Giant* (Washington DC: Brookings Institution), pp. 153–249.

Gasché, R. (1987) 'Infrastructures and Systematicity', in: Sallis, J. (Ed.) *Deconstruction and Philosophy* (Chicago: University of Chicago Press), pp. 3–21.

Gattinara, E. C. (1990) 'Die Offenheit des Erhabenen in Kunst, Philosophie und Wissenschaft' [The openness of the noble in the arts], in: Reese-Schäfer, W. and Taureck B. H. F. (Eds.) *Jean-François Lyotard* (Cuxhaven: Junghans), pp. 136–56.

Gebhardt, E. (1991) *Abschied von der Autorität: Die Manager der Postmoderne* [*Good-bye to authority: managers in postmodern times*] (Wiesbaden: Gabler).

Gebhardt, L. (1993) *Gegenwelten: Das Inventar des Phantastischen in der modernen japanischen Literatur* [*Counter-worlds: the treasure of the phantastic in modern Japanese literature*] (Tokyo: Vortrag, OAG).

Gee, J. P. (1996) *The New Work Order: Behind the Language of the New Capitalism* (Boulder, CO: Westview).

Georgescou-Roegen, N. (1971) *The Entropy Law and the Economic Process* (Cambridge, MA: Harvard University).

Geras, N. (1995) *Solidarity in the Conversation of Humankind: The Ungroundable Liberalism of Richard Rorty* (London: Verso).

Gergen, K. J. (1985) 'The Social Constructionist Movement in Modern Psychology', *American Psychologist*, **3**, pp. 266–75.

Gerken, G. (1987) *Die Zukunft des Handels* [*The future of trade*] (Freiburg: Haufe).

Gerlach, M. (1987) 'Business Alliances and the Strategy of the Japanese Firm', *California Management Review*, **4**, pp. 126–42.

Gernalzick, N. (1999) 'Gegen eine Metaphysik der Arbeit: Der Ökonomiebegriff der Dekonstruktion und im Poststrukturalismus' [Against a Metaphysics of Work: The Definition of Economic in Deconstructionalism and Poststructuralism], Paper presented at:

366 *Bibliography*

Postmodern Perspectives: Second International Graduate And Postgraduate Conference, Erlangen, November 19–21.

Ghoshal, S. and Nohria, N. (1987) *Multinational Corporations as Differentiated Networks* (Fontainbleau: Insead Working Paper 13).

— and — (1991) *Distributed Innovation in the 'Differentiated Network' Multinational* (Fontainbleau: Insead Working Paper 44).

Gibney, F. (1988) *Japan: The Fragile Superpower* (Tokyo: Tuttle).

Gibbons, M. T. (1991) 'The Ethic of Postmodernism', *Political Theory*, **1**, pp. 96–103.

Gibson, A. (1990) *Towards a Postmodern Theory of Narrative* (Edinburgh: Edinburgh University Press).

Giddens, A. (1985) 'Reason without Revolution', in: Bernstein, R. J. (Ed.) *Habermas and Modernity* (Cambridge, MA: MIT Press), pp. 95–160.

Giddy, I. H. (1978) 'The Demise of the Product Cycle Model in International Business Theory', *Columbia Journal of World Business*, **1/13**, s. 90–7.

Gilpin, R. (1984) 'Can Interdependent World Political Economy Survive?', in: Kegley, C. W. and Wittkopf, E. R. (Eds.) *The Global Agenda* (New York: Random House), pp. 224–44.

Gilroy, B. M. (1987) *Multinational Enterprise and Trade Structure – The Role of Intra Firm Trade* (HSG Discussion Paper 51/87).

— (1990) *Economic Issues of Multinational Enterprises* (Konstanz: Hartung-Gorre).

— (1992) *Networking in Multinational Enterprises* (Columbia, SC: University of South Carolina).

Girardo, D. (1996) *Architecture After Modernism* (London: Thames and Hudson).

Giraud, P. N. (1992) *Reseaux, territoires et modes de croissance des entreprises [Resources, territories and forms of growth of the enterprise]* (Paris: Ecole Supérieure des Mines Working Paper 9).

Glazer, N. (1976) 'Social and Cultural Factors in Japanese Economic Growth', in: Patrick, H. and Rosovsky, H. (Eds.) *Asia's New Giant* (Washington DC: Brookings Institution), pp. 813–97.

Go, M. (1963) 'Linguistic Analysis of Oyabun–Kobun Relationships', in: Bennett, J. W. and Ishino, I. (Eds.) *Paternalism in the Japanese Economy* (Westport, CN: Greenwood), pp. 273–94.

Goel, R. K. (1999) *Economic Models of Technological Change* (New York: Quorum Books).

Gomez, P. and Probst, G. J. B. (1987) *Vernetztes Denken im Management [Network thinking in management]* (Bern: Die Orientierung 29).

Goodman, N. (1972) 'The Way the World is', in: Goodman, N. (Ed.) *Problems and Projects* (Indianapolis, IN: Hackett), pp. 14–32.

— (1977) *The Structure of Appearance* (Dordrecht: Reidel).

— (1978) *Ways of Worldmaking* (Indianapolis, IN: Hackett).

— (1984) *Of Mind and Other Matters* (Cambridge, MA: Harvard University).

Grabow, S. (1983) *The Search for a New Paradigm in Architecture* (Boston: Oriel).

Graff, G. (1979) *Literature Against Itself: Literary Ideas in Modern Society* (Chicago: Chicago University Press).

Granovetter, M. (1983) 'Economic Action and Social Structure', *American Journal of Sociology*, 36–51.

Gregory, G. (1989) 'Die Innovationsbereitschaft der Japaner – Elektronik als Beispiel' [Japans willingness to innovate – a case study in electronics], in: Menzel, U. (Ed.) *Japan und der Westen*, vol. 2 *[Japan and the West]* (Frankfurt: Fischer), pp. 110–40.

Greider, W. (1998) *One World, Ready or Not: The Manic Logic of Global Capitalism* (Touchstone).

Greiner, B. (1989) 'Die Hamletmaschine' [The automatic Hamlet], in: Deutsch-Amerikanisches Institut Freiburg (Ed.) *Die Postmoderne – Ende der Avangarde oder Neubeginn [The postmodern – end of the Avant-garde or a new beginning]* (Eggingen: Isele), pp. 75–96.

Grilliches, Z. (1990) 'Data and Econometricians – The Uneasy Alliance', *American Economic Review*, **5**, pp. 196–200.

Gronlund, L. (1975) *New Economy* (London: Hyperion).

Grossman, G. M. (1990) 'Explaining Japan's Innovation and Trade: A Model of Quality Competition and Dynamic Comparative Advantage', *Monetary and Economic Studies*, **9**, pp. 75–100.

Grou, P. (1985) *The Financial Structure of Multinational Capitalism* (Oxford: Berg).

Grubel, M. G. and Loyd, P. G. (1975) *Intra-Industry Trade: The Theory and Measurement of International Trade in Differentiated Products* (London: Macmillan Press).

Guillaume, M. (1989) 'Post-Moderne Effekte der Moderne' [Post-modern effects of the modern], in: Reese-Schäfer, W. and Taurek, B. H. F. (Eds.) *Jean-François Lyotard* (Cuxhaven: Junghans), pp. 75–88.

Gumbrecht, H. U. (1991) 'nachMODERNE ZEITENräume' [post-modern time-spaces], in: Weimann, R., Gumbrecht, H. U. and Wagner, B. (Eds.) *Postmoderne – Globale Differenz* [*Postmodern – global difference*] (Frankfurt: Suhrkamp), pp. 54–72.

Guth, C. M. E. (1993) *Art, Tea, and Industry: Masuda Takashi and the Mitsui Circle* (Princeton; NJ: Princeton University Press).

Gunn, T. G. (1995) *21st Century Manufacturing: Creating Winning Business Performance* (London: Wiley).

— (1987) *Manufacturing for Competitive Advantage* (Cambridge, MA: Ballinger).

Gutting, G. (1999) *Pragmatic Liberalism and the Critique of Modernity* (Cambridge: Cambridge University Press).

Habermas, J. (1962) *Strukturwandel der Öffentlichkeit* (Neuwied: Luchterhand) [*Structural Change of the Public* (MIT Press)].

— (1971) *Theorie und Praxis* [*Theory and praxis*] (Frankfurt: Suhrkamp).

— (1977) *Legitimationsprobleme im Spätkapitalismus* [*Problems of legitimacy in late capitalism*] (Frankfurt: Suhrkamp).

— (1981) 'Modernity versus Postmodernity', *New German Critique*, **22**, pp. 11–28.

— (1983) 'Modernity – an Incomplete Project', in: Forster, H. (Ed.) *The Anti-Esthetic: Essays on Postmodern Culture* (Port Townsend, WA: Bay Press), pp. 58–83.

— (1985) *Der philosophische Diskurs der Moderne* (Frankfurt: Suhrkamp), [*The Philosophical Discourse of the Modern* (MIT Press)].

— (1985) *Theorie des kommunikativen Handelns*, 2 vols (Frankfurt: Suhrkamp 1981) [*Theory of Communicative Action* (New York: Beacon)].

— (1988) 'Die Moderne – ein unvollendetes Projekt' [Modernity – an incomplete project], in: Welsch, W. (Ed.) *Wege aus der Moderne* [*Escape from the modern*] (Weinheim: VCH), pp. 177–192.

— (1992) *Faktizität und Geltung* [*Facts and validity*] (Frankfurt: Suhrkamp).

— (1992) 'Die Zweite Lebenslüge der Bundesrepublik: wir sind wieder normal geworden' [The second big lie of Germany: we are normal again], *Die Zeit*, December.

Hadley, E. O. M. (1970) *Antitrust in Japan* (Princeton, NJ: Princeton University Press).

Haft, A. J., White J. G., White, R. J. and Haft, A. T. (1999) *The Key to the Name of the Rose: Including Translations of all Non-English Passages* (Ann Arbor, MI: University of Michigan Press).

Hagiwara, S. (1990) *Doing Business in Japan* (Tokyo: Japan Legal Publishers).

Hagström, P. (1991) *The 'Wired' MNC* (Stockholm: Stockholm School of Economics, Diss.).

Haire, M. and Ghiselli, E. (1968) *Managerial Thinking* (New York: Morrow).

Haitani, K. (1976) *The Japanese Economic System* (Lexington, MA: Lexington Books).

— (1986) *Comparative Economic Systems* (Englewood Cliffs, NJ: Prentice Hall).

Hakansson, H. (1989) *Industrial Technological Development: A Network Approach* (London: Routledge).

— and Johanson, J. (1989) 'Formal and Informal Cooperation Strategies in International Industrial Networks', in: Neghandi, A. R. and Savara, A. (Eds.) *International Strategic Management* (Lexington, MA: Lexington Books), pp. 369–79.

Hall, E. T. and Reed-Hall, M. (1987) *Hidden Differences* (New York, NY: Anchor).

Hall, J. W. (1986) *Japan: From Prehistory to Modern Times* (Tokyo: Tuttle).

Hall, J. W. and Mass, J. P. (Eds.) (1974) *Medieval Japan: Essays in Institutional History* (Stanford, CA: Stanford University Press).

Hamel, G. and Prahalad, C. K. (1983) 'Managing Strategic Responsibility in the Multinational Corporation', *Strategic Management Journal*, **4**, pp. 341–52.

Hamlin, M. (1999) *The New Asian Corporation* (Hong Kong: Jossey Bass).

Hanan, M. (1986) *Growth Partnering: How to Manage Strategic Alliances for Mutual Profit* (New York: American Management Association).

Hannigan, J. (1998) *Fantasy City: Pleasure and Profit in the Postmodern Metropolis* (London: Routledge).

Harmon, R. L. (1992) *Reinventing the Factory II* (New York: Free Press).

Harootunian, H. D. (1989) 'Visible Discourses – Invisible Ideologies', in: Miyoshi, M. and Harootunian, H. D. (Eds.) *Postmodernism and Japan* (Durham, NC: Duke University Press), pp. 63–92.

Harper, B. B. (1993) *Framing the Margins: The Social Logic of Postmodern Culture* (Oxford: Oxford University Press).

Harris, M. (1998) *Theories of Culture in Postmodern Times* (Altamira Press).

Hart, R., Kawasaki, S. and Hart, R. A. (1990) *Work and Pay in Japan* (Tokyo: Japan Legal Publishers).

Harryson, S. (1998) *Japanese Technology and Innovation Management: From Know-How to Know-Who* (Aldershot: Elgar).

Harvey, D. (1989) *The Condition of Postmodernity* (Oxford: Blackwell).

Hassan, I. (1971) 'POSTmodernISM', *New Literary History*, **1**, pp. 5–30.

— (1975) *Paracriticisms: Seven Speculations of the Times* (Urbana, Ill: University of Illinois Press).

— (1983) 'Ideas of Cultural Change', in: Hassan, I. and Hassan, S. (Eds.) *Innovation Renovation* (Madison, WI: University of Wisconsin Press), pp. 15–39.

— (1987) 'Pluralism in Postmodern Perspective', in: Calinescu, M. and Fokkema, D. (Eds.) *Exploring Postmodernism* (Amsterdam: Benjamin), pp. 17–39.

— (1987) *The Postmodern Turn* (Columbus, OH: Ohio State University Press).

Hatch, M. J. (1997) *Organization Theory: Modern, Symbolic, and Postmodern Perspectives* (Oxford: Oxford University Press).

Haury, S. (1989) *Grundzüge einer ökonomischen Theorie der lateralen Kooperation* [*Fundamentals of a theory on lateral cooperation*] (St. Gallen: Hochschule St. Gallen, Diss.).

Hawthorn, G. (1990) 'The Impossible Sociology of Postmodern Persons', *Australian Journal of Anthropology*, **1**, pp. 168–80.

Hawryszkiewycz, I. (1997) *Designing the Networked Enterprise* (New York: Artech House).

Hayashi, S. (1988) *Culture and Management in Japan* (Tokyo: University of Tokyo Press).

Hazama, H. (1997) *The History of Labour Management in Japan* (New York: St. Martin's Press).

Heartney, E. (1990) 'Mixed Messages: Western Influence in Postmodern Japanese Art', *Art in America*, **4**, pp. 212–20.

Hedlund, G. (1981) 'Autonomy of Subsidiaries and Formalism of Headquarter – Subsidiary Relationships in Swedish Multinational Enterprises', in: Otterbeck, L. (Ed.) *The Management of Headquarter-Subsidiary Relationships in Multinational Corporations* (Stockholm: Grover), pp. 25–78.

Heisman, G. (1992) 'Die Flops' [The loser], *Wirtschaftswoche*, October, p. 222.

Heitger, B. (1987) 'Import Protection and Export Performance and their Impact on Economic Growth', *Weltwirtschaftliches Archiv*, **123**, pp. 249–61.

Heller, F. A. (1985) 'Some Problems in Multinational Research on Organizations', in: Takamiya, S. and Thurley, K. (Eds.) *Japan's Emerging Multinationals* (Tokyo: University of Tokyo Press), pp. 21–34.

Helliwell, J. F. and Chung, A. (1991) 'Globalization, Convergence and the Prospects for Economic Growth, in: Cornwall, J. (Ed.) *The Capitalist Economies: Prospects for the 1990s* (Aldershot: Elgar), pp. 63–91.

Helpman, E. (1981) 'Increasing Returns, Imperfect Markets, and Trade Theory', in: Jones, R. W. and Kennan, P. B. (Eds.) *Handbook of International Economics* (Amsterdam: North Holland), pp. 1012–20.

— (1981) 'International Trade in the Present Product Differentiation, Economies Scale and Monopolistic Competition', *Journal of International Economics*, **8**, pp. 305–400.

— (1983) *A Theory of Multinational Corporations and the Structure of Foreign Trade* (HIER Discussion Papers 961).

Henderson, H. (1988) 'Global Denken, lokal Handeln' [Global thought, local action], in: Lutz, R. (Ed.) *Pläne für eine menschliche Zukunft* [*Sketches of a human future*] (Weinheim: Belz), pp. 268–87.

Hennart, J. F. (1985) 'The Transaction Cost Theory of the Multinational Enterprise', in: Dunning, J. H. (Ed.) *Multinational Enterprises, Economic Structure, and International Competiveness* (New York: Wiley), pp. 81–116.

Henrici, P., Lazlo, E. and Lomeiko, V. (1989) *Netzwerke: Globales Denken oder Isolation* [*Networks: global thinking or isolation*] (Münsingen: Fischer).

Herold, R. (1993) *Zur Sozialisation des Kinder im Japan der Tokugawa- und Meiji-Zeit* [*On the socialization of children during the Tokugawa and Meiji periods*] (Tokyo: OAG).

Hickman, L. (1998) *Reading Dewey: Interpretations for a Postmodern Generation* (Bloomington, IN: Indiana University Press).

Hicks J. R. (1973) 'The Mainspring of Economic Growth', *Swedish Journal of Economics*, **75**, pp. 336–48.

Higashi, C. and Lauter, G. P. (1987) *The Internationalization of the Japanese Economy* (Boston, MA: Kluwer).

Higginson, W. J. (1990) *The Haiku Handbook* (Tokyo: Kodansha).

Hijia-Kirschnereit, I. (1989) 'Vom Nutzen der Exotik' [The utility of exotics], in: Hijia-Kirschnereit, I. and Schmölers, C. (Eds.) *Japan* (Frankfurt: Insel), pp. 174–90.

Hikino, T., Kikkawa, T. and Miyajima, H. (1999) *Policies for Competitiveness: Comparing Business–Government Relationships in the Golden Age of Capitalism* (Oxford: Oxford University Press).

Hilb, M. (1985) *Personalpolitik für multinationale Unternehmen* [*Human resources policies for MNE*] (Zürich: Verlag Industrielle Organisation).

Hill, W. (1989) *How can Swiss Companies apply Michael Porter's Strategy Concept?* (Tagungsbeitrag: International Competitiveness of Switzerland, Basle).

Hippel, E. v. (1989) 'Cooperation between Rivals: Informal Know-How-Trading', in: Carlsson, B. (Ed.) *Industrial Dynamics* (Boston: Kluwer), pp. 157–75.

Hiraiwa, G. (1991) 'Rethinking Japanese Culture', *Keidanren Review on Japanese Economy*, **6**, p. 2.

Hirsch, S. (1967) *The Location of Industry and International Competitiveness* (Oxford: Oxford University Press).

— (1976) 'An International Trade and Investment Theory of the Firm', *Oxford Economic Papers*, **28**, pp. 258–69.

Hirschmeier, J. and Yui, T. (1975) *The Development of Japanese Business: 1600–1973* (Cambridge, MA: Harvard University Press).

Hirshleifer, J. (1985) 'The Expanding Domain of Economics', *American Economic Review*, **12**, pp. 53–68.

Hisamatsu, S. (1990) *Philosophie des Erwachens* [*Philosophy of awakening*] (Munich: Theseus).

— (1990) 'Einführung zu: Eine Erläuterung des Lin-chi-Zen' [Introduction to: an explanation of Lin-chi-zen], in: Ohashi, R. (Ed.) *Die Philosophie der Kyoto Schule* [*The philosophy of the Kyoto school*] (Freiburg: Alber), pp. 227–32.

Hofmann, W. (1987) 'Emanzipation der Dissonanzen' [Emanicpation of the dissonances], in: Le Rider, J. and Raulet, G. (Eds.) *Verabschiedung der Postmoderne* [*Good-bye to the postmodern*] (Tübingen: Narr), pp. 117–31.

Hofstädter, D. (1999) *Gödel, Escher, Bach* (Stuttgart: Klett Cotta) [*Goedel, Escher, Bach* (Basic Books)].

Hofstede, G. (1980) *Culture's Consequences: International Differences in Work Related Values* (London: Sage).

— and Kassem, S. (1976) *European Contributions to Organizational Theory* (Amsterdam: Assen).

Hohmann, W. L. (1990) 'Einige Überlegungen zur Einführung' [Some thoughts for starters], in: Bering, K. (Ed.) *Wie postmodern ist die Postmoderne?* [*Just how postmodern is post-modernity*] (Essen: Die blaue Eule), pp. 1–24.

Holdt, D. H. (1987) *Management* (Englewood Cliffs, NJ: Prentice Hall).

Holesovsky, V. (1977) *Economic Systems: Analysis and Comparison* (New York: McGraw-Hill).

Hollstein, B. (1999) 'Der Arbeitsbegriff inder ökonomischen Theorie und das Ehrenamt' [The Concept of Work in Economic Theory and Non-Profit Work] Paper presented at: Postmodern Perspectives: Second International Graduate and Postgraduate Conference, Erlangen, November 19–21.

Holstein, W. J. *et al.* (1990) 'Hands across America – The Rise of Mitsubishi', *Business Week*, October, pp. 42–5.

Hood, N. and Young, S. (1999) *The Globalization of Multinational Enterprise Activity and Economic Development* (New York: St. Martin's).

Hoover, T. (1986) *Die Kultur des Zen* [*The culture of Zen*] (Munich: Diederichs).

Hope, J. and Hope, T. (1997) *Competing in the Third Wave: The Ten Key Management Issues of the Information Age* (Cambridge, MA: Harvard Business School Press).

Horvitch, M. (1992) *Postmodern Strategic Management* (New York: Free Press).

Howard, W. G. and Guile, B. R. (1992) *Profiting from Innovation* (New York: Free Press).

Howe, I. (1959) 'Mass Society and Post-Modern Fiction', *Partisan Review*, **26**, pp. 420–36.

Howe, S. (1991) 'Dead Ends', *New Statesman & Society*, April.

Hübner, K. (1978) *Kritik der wissenschaftlichen Vernunft* [*A critique of scientific reason*] (Freiburg: Alber).

Hudson, W. (1987) 'Zur Frage postmoderner Philosophie' [On the question of a postmodern philosophy], in: Kamper, D. and Reijen, W. v. (Eds.) *Die unvollendete Vernunft* [*Incomplete reason*] (Frankfurt: Suhrkamp), pp. 122–56.

Hurst, C. C. (1984) 'The Structure of the Heian Court: Some Thoughts on the Nature of Familial Authority', in: Hurst, C. C. (Ed.) *Sociology of Early Japan* (New Haven, CN: Yale University Press), pp. 39–60.

Hutcheon, L. (1988) *A Poetics of Postmodernism* (London: Routledge).

Huyssen, A. (1984) 'Mapping the Postmodern', *New German Critique*, Fall, pp. 5–52.

— (1986) *After the Great Divide* (New York: Columbia University Press).

Hymer, S. (1960) *The International Operations of National Firms* (Cambridge, MA: Massachusetts Institute of Technology, Diss.).

— (1970) 'The United States' Multinational Corporations and Japanese Competition in the Pacific', Paper presented at the Conferencia del Pacifica, Vina del Mar, Chile, October.

Ichihara, K. and Takamiya, S. (Eds.) (1977) *Die japanische Unternehmung – Strukturwandlungen in einer wachsenden Wirtschaft* [*The Japanese enterprise – structural changes in a growing economy*] (Opladen: Westdeutscher Verlag).

Imai, K. (1980) 'Japan's Industrial Structure', in: Sato, K. (Ed.) *Industry and Business in Japan* (White Plains, NY: Sharpe), pp. 74–135.

— (1989) 'Evolution of Japan's Corporate and Industrial Networks', in: Carlsson, B. (Ed.) *Industrial Dynamics* (Boston, MA: Kluver), pp. 123–56.

— (1990) 'The Legitimacy of Japan's Corporate Groups', *Economic Eye*, 3, 16–22.

— (1992) 'Japan's Corporate Networks', in: Kumon, S. and Rosovsky, H. (Eds.) *The Political Economy of Japan*, vol. 3 (Stanford, CA: Stanford University Press), pp. 198–230.

Immoos, T. (1990) *Japan – Archaische Moderne* [*Japan – archaic modernity*] (Munich: Kindt).

Inamori, K. and Reid, T. R. (1997) *For People – And for Profit: A Business Philosophy for the 21st Century* (Tokyo: Kodansha).

Inglehart, R. (1997) *Modernization and Postmodernization: Cultural Economic and Political Change* (Princeton, NJ: Princeton University Press).

Inoguchi, T. (1983) *Gendai Nihon seiji keizai no kiko* [*The Current Structure of Japanese Political Economy*] (Tokyo: Nihon Keizai Shinbun).

Ishihara, S. (1989) *The Japan that can say 'No'* (New York: Simon & Schuster).

Itaki, M. (1990) *A Critical Assessment of the Eclectic Theory of the Multinational Enterprise* (Reading: University of Reading Discussion Paper 129).

Ito, M., Kiyono, K., Okuno, M. and Suzumura, K. (1988) 'Industrial Policy as a Corrective to Market Failures', in: Komiya, R. (Ed.) *Industrial Policy of Japan* (Tokyo: Academic Press Japan), pp. 233–56.

—, — and — (1988) *Sangyo Seisaku no Keizai Bunzeki* [*An economic analysis of industrial policy*] (Tokyo: University of Tokyo Press).

Ito, T. and Iwamiya, T. (1972) *The Japanese Garden: An Approach to Nature* (New Haven, CN: Yale University Press).

Itoh, M. (1998) *The Globalization of Japan: Japanese Sakoku Mentality and U.S. Efforts to Open Japan* (New York: St. Martin's).

Ivy, M. (1989) 'Critical Texts, Mass Artifacts: The Consumption of Knowledge in Postmodern Japan', in: Miyoshi, M. and Harootunian, H. D. (Eds.) *Postmodernism and Japan* (Durham, NC: Duke University Press), pp. 21–47.

Izutsu, T. and Izutsu, T. (1988) *Die Theorie des Schönen in Japan* [*Theory of beauty in Japan*] (Köln: Dumont).

Jäger, M. (1989) 'Das Problem der Namen bei Lyotard' [The problem of names in Lyotard], in: Reese-Schäfer, W. and Taurek, B. H. F. (Eds.) *Jean-François Lyotard* (Cuxhaven: Junghans), pp. 87–104.

James, B. G. (1991) *Wirtschaftsmacht Japan: Das trojanische Pferd* (Freiburg: Haufe) [*Trojan Horse* (Mercury)].

Jameson, F. (1984) 'Postmodernism and Consumer Society', *Amerikastudien*, 2, 55–77.

— (1989) 'Postmoderne – zur Logik der Kultur im Spätkapitalismus', in: Huyssen, A. and Schrep, K. (Eds.) *Postmoderne – Zeichen eines kulturellen Wandels* [*Postmodernity – signs of a cultural change*] (Hamburg: Rowohlt), pp. 45–103.

— (1991) 'Postmoderne und Utopie [Postmodern and utopia]', in: Weimann, R., Gumbrecht, H. U. and Wagner, B. (Eds.) *Postmoderne – Globale Differenz* [*Postmodernity – global difference*] (Frankfurt: Suhrkamp), pp. 73–109.

— (1991) *Postmodernism, or the Cultural Logic of Late Capitalism* (Durham, NC: Duke University).

— (1998) *Cultural Turn: Selected Writings on the Postmodern 1998* (London: Verso).

— and Miyoshi, M. (1998) *The Cultures of Globalization* (Durham, NC: Duke University Press).

Jantsch, E. (1988) 'Die Grenzen westlicher Rationalität' [Limits of Western rationality], in: Lutz, R. (Ed.) *Pläne für eine menschliche Zukunft* [*Sketches for a human future*] (Weinheim: Belz), pp. 47–59.

Japan Commission on Industrial Performance (1998) *Made in Japan: Revitalizing Japanese Manufacturing for Economic Growth* (Cambridge, MA: MIT Press).

Japan Travel Bureau (1990) *Salaryman in Japan* (Tokyo: JTB).

— (1991) *Living Japanese Style*, vol. 2 (Tokyo: JTB).

Jarillo, J. C. (1988) 'On Strategic Networks', *California Management Journal*, **9**, pp. 31–41.

Jay, M. (1984) 'Habermas and Modernism', *Praxis International*, **4**, pp. 1–14.

Jencks, C. (1984) *The Language of Postmodern Architecture* (London: Academy Editions).

— (1996) *Was ist Postmoderne?* (Zürich: Artemis) [*What is Postmodern?* (New York: Wiley)].

— and Anderson, K. (1990) 'Architectual Dialogue', *Architectural Digest*, **12**, pp. 31–40.

Jensen, M. and Meckling, W. (1976) 'Theories of the Firm: Managerial Behavior, Agency Cost, and Ownership Structure', *Journal of Financial Economics*, **10**, pp. 305–60.

Jerome, B. (1949) *Japan's Economy in War and Reconstruction* (Mineapolis, MN: University of Minnesota Press).

Johanssen, A. M. (1992) *Applied Anthropology and Postmodernist Ethnography* (Human Organization 1) pp. 71–82.

Johanson, J. and Mattsson, L. G. (1988) 'Internationalization in Industrial Systems – A Network Approach', in: Hood, N. and Vahlne, J. E. (Eds.) *Strategies in Global Competition* (Beckenham: Croom Helm), pp. 287–314.

— and Nonaka, I. (1997) *Relentless: The Japanese Way of Marketing* (San Francisco: Harper Collins).

Johnson, C. (1991) *MITI and the Japanese Miracle* (Tokyo: Tuttle).

Johnson, G. L. (1978) 'Philosophic Foundations of Agricultural Economics Thought', *American Association of Agricultural Economists Literature Review*, **5**, pp. 86–128.

Johnson-Lenz, P. and Johnson-Lenz, T. (1988) 'Soziale Vernetzung' [Social networks], in: Lutz, R. (Ed.) *Pläne für eine menschliche Zukunft* [*Sketches for a human future*] (Weinheim: Belz), pp. 342–61.

Johnston, R. and Lawrence, P. R. (1988) 'Beyond Vertical Integration – The Rise of the Value-Adding Principle', *Harvard Business Review*, **7**, pp. 94–105.

Joswig-Kühl, G., Hölzel, K. *et al.* (Eds.) (1984) Gablers Wirtschaftslexikon, vol. 6 [*Gabler's encyclopedia of business*] (Wiesbaden: Gabler).

Kadushin, C. and Brimm, M. (1992) *Why Networking Fails: Double Binds and the Limitations of Shadow Networks* (Fontainbleau: INSEAD Working Paper).

Kagono, T., Nonaka, I., Okumura, A. *et al.* (1984) 'Mechanistic vs. Organic Management Systems', in: Sato, K. and Yasuo, H. (Eds.) *The Anatomy of Japanese Business* (Armonk, NY: Sharpe), pp. 27–69.

Kahn, H. (1970) *Bald werden sie die Ersten sein: Japan 2000 – Zukunftsmodell der Herren der Welt* [*Soon they will be first: Japan 2000 – modelling the future masters of the world*] (Wien: Molden).

— (1970) *The Emerging Japanese Superstate* (Englewood Cliffs, NJ: Prentice Hall).

— (1977) *Vor uns die guten Jahre* [*Good years ahead*] (Wien: Molden).

Kaizuka, K. (1990) 'Shin kontenha sogo no tachiba kara mita seisaku teikei' [Policy planning from a neoclassical position], *Shukan Toyo Keizai Rinji Zokan*, December.

Kakuzo, O. (1990) *The Book of Tea* (Tokyo: Kodansha).

Kamper, D. (1987) 'Aufklärung – Was sonst?' [Enlightenment – what else?], in: Kamper, D. and Reijen, W. v. (Eds.) *Die unvollendete Vernunft* [*Incomplete reason*] (Frankfurt: Suhrkamp), pp. 37–44.

Kanter, R. M. (1998) *Bis zum Horizont und weiter. Management in neuen Dimensionen* [*To Horizon and Further. Management in a New Dimension*] (Munich: Hanser).

Kaplan, A. (1964) *The Conduct of Inquiry* (San Francisco: Chandler).

Kaplan, C. (1996) *Questions of Travel: Postmodern Discourses on Displacement* (Durham, NC: Duke University Press).

Kaplan, E. J. (1972) *Japan: The Government–Business Relationship* (Washington, DC: Department of Commerce).

Kapleau, P. (1989) *Die drei Pfeiler des Zen* (Munich: Barth) [*The Three Pillars of Zen* (New York: Anchor Books 1989)].

Karatani, K. (1985) 'Ri no hihan: Shiso ni okeru puremodan to postomodan' [A confucian critique of premodern and postmodern concepts], *Gendaishi Techo*, **5**, 40.

— (1990) 'One Spirit, Two Nineteenth Centuries', in: Miyoshi, M. and Harootunian, H. D. (Eds.) *Postmodernism and Japan* (Durham, NC: Duke University Press), pp. 259–72.

Karlsson, C. (1991) *Knowledge and Material Flow in Future Industrial Networks* (Brussels: European Institute for Advanced Studies in Management Working Paper 20).

Kato, S. (1991) *A History of Japanese Literature*, 3 vols (Tokyo: Kodansha).

Katz, R. (1998) *Japan, the System that Soured* (New York: M. E. Sharpe).

Katzenstein, P. (1978) 'Conclusion: Domestic Structures and Strategies of Foreign Economic Policy', in: Katzenstein, P. (Ed.) *Between Power and Plenty* (Cambridge, MA: Harvard University), pp. 323–35.

Kawakami, H. (1964) *Kawakami Hajime chosakushu* [*Collected Works*], vol. 8 (Tokyo: Chikuma Shobo).

Kawamoto, I. (1990) 'Neue Entwicklungen im Bereich des Gesellschaftsrechts in Japan' [Recent developments in company law in Japan], in: Coing, H. (Ed.) *Die Japanisierung des westlichen Rechts* [*The Japanization of Western Law*] (Tübingen: J. C. B. Mohr), pp. 213–26.

Kawanishi, H. and Corbett, J. (1998) *The Human Face of Industrial Conflict in Post War Japan* (London: Kegan Paul).

Kay, N. M. (1999) *The Boundaries of the Firm: Critiques, Strategies and Policies* (New York: St. Martin's Press).

Keidanren (1989) 'Brief an die Staatsoberhäupter der EG-Mitgliedsstaaten vom 05.03.1987' [Letter to the heads of state of the EC nations, dated 05.03.1987], in: *Keidanren: Official Statements* (Tokyo: Keidanren, MS).

Kellerer, C. (1982) *Der Sprung ins Leere: Objét trouvé, Surrealismus, Zen* [*The jump into the void: Objét trouvé, Surrealism, Zen*] (Köln: Dumont).

Kelly, K. (1992) 'Learning from Japan', *Business Week*, October, pp. 52–60.

— (1999) *New Rules for the New Economy* (New York: Penguin).

Kendrick, D. M. (1990) *Where Communism Works* (Tokyo: Tuttle).

Kennedy, P. (1987) *The Rise and Fall of the Great Nations* (New York: Random House).

Kermode, F. (1986) *Continuities* (London: Routledge).

— (1988) *History and Value* (Oxford: Blackwell).

Kester, W. C. (1991) *Japanese Takeovers – The Global Contest for Corporate Control* (Cambridge, MA: Harvard Business School Press).

Kevenhörster, P. (1973) *Wirtschaft und Politik in Japan* [*Economic and politics in Japan*] (Wiesbaden: Harrassowitz).

Khan, H. (1998) *Technology, Development and Democracy: Limits of National Innovation Systems in the Age of Postmodernism* (Aldershot: Elgar).

Kiechl, R. (1990) 'Ethnokultur und Unternehmenskultur' [Ethnoculture and corporate culture], in: Lattmann, C. (Ed.) *Die Unternehmenskultur* [*Corporate culture*] (Heidelberg: Physica), pp. 107–130.

Kilduff, M. (1989) *A Dispositional Approach to Social Networks* (Fontainbleau: INSEAD Working Paper 36).

Kim, E. M. (1997) *Big Business, Strong State: Collusion and Conflict in South Korean Developments, 1960–1990* (Albany, NY: SUNY Press).

Kim, K. S., Minami, R. and Seo, J.-H. (1994) *Acquiring, Adapting and Developing Technologies: Lessons from the Japanese Experience* (New York: St. Martin's Press).

Kindleberger, C. P. (1969) *American Business Abroad: Six Lessons on Direct Investment* (New Haven, CN: Yale University Press).

King, U. (1998) *Faith and Praxis in a Postmodern Age* (London: Cassell).

Kionari, T. and Nakamura, H. (1980) 'The Establishment of the Big Business System', in: Sato, K. (Ed.) *Industry and Business in Japan* (White Plains, NY: Sharpe), pp. 247–84.

Kitagawa, Z. (1980) 'Contract Law in General', in: Hagiwara, S. (Ed.) *Doing Business in Japan* (Tokyo: Japan Legal Publishers), pp. 1–24.

Kiuchi, T. (1990) *New Economy*, 4 (Tokyo: toExcel).

Kiyonari, T. and Nakamura, H. (1976) 'Daikigyo taisei no kakuritzu' [The emergence of the industrial organization in company groupings], in: Iida, T. (Ed.) *Gendai Nihon keizai shi – sengo sanjunen no ayumi* [*Japan's contemporary economic history: developments in the 30 post-war years*], vol. 2 (Tokyo: Chikuma Shobo), pp. 5–37.

Klein, B., Crawford, R. and Alchian, A. (1978) 'Vertical Integration, Appropriate Rents, and the Competitive Contracting Process', *Journal of Law and Economics*, **22**, pp. 297–326.

Klenner, W. (1989) 'Grundzüge der wirtschaftspolitischen Entwicklung und Wirtschaftspolitik seit dem Zweiten Weltkrieg', in: Menzel, U. (Ed.) *Im Schatten des Siegers*, vol. 3 [*In the shadow of the winner*] (Frankfurt: Suhrkamp), pp. 63–88.

— (1990) 'Administrative Guidance: Barrieren und Chancen für ausländische Unternehmen' [Administrative Guidance: obstacles and chances for foreign companies], in: Frankfurter Allgemeine Zeitung (Ed.) *Japan Perspektiven* [*Perspectives on Japan*] (Frankfurt: Frankfurter Allgemeine Zeitung), pp. 57–62.

Klimecki, R. G. (1985) *Laterale Kooperation* (Bern: Haupt).

—, Probst, G. J. B. and Eberl, P. (1991) *Perspektiven eines entwicklungsorientierten Managements* [*Perspectives on evolutionary management*] (Genève: Université de Genève Working Paper).

Klotz, H. (1988) 'Moderne und Postmoderne' [Modernity and postmodernity], in: Welsch, W. (Ed.) *Wege aus der Moderne* [*Escape from the Modern*] (Weinheim: VCH), pp. 99–109.

Knipes, B. J. (1988) *Corporate Reputation and Strategic Performance* (Amherst, MA: University of Massachusetts, Diss.).

Knoke, D. and Tsujinaka, Y. (1996) *Comparing Policy Network: Labor Politics in the U.S., Germany, and Japan* (Cambridge: Cambridge University Press).

Kobayashi, H. (1980) *Wirtschaftsmacht Japan* [*Economic power Japan*] (Köln: Deutscher Instituts Verlag).

Kobayashi, N. (1985) 'The Patterns of Management Style Developing in Japanese Multinational Companies', in: Takamiya, S. and Thurley, K. (Eds.) *Japan's Emerging Multinationals* (Tokyo: University of Tokyo), pp. 229–64.

Kobayashi, T. (1980) *Nihon no takokuseki kigyo* [*Japanese MNE*] (Tokyo: Chuo Keizaisha).

Köhler, M. (1977) 'Postmodernismus: ein begriffsgeschichtlicher Überblick' [Postmodernism: history of its terminology], *Amerikastudien*, **22**, 8–18.

Kojima, K. (1975) 'Nihon gata takokuseiki kigyo no arikata' [The special type of the Japanese MNE], *Sekai Keizai Hyoron*, August, pp. 43–52.

— (1977) *Japan and a New World Economic Order* (Boulder, CO: Westview).

— (1978) *Direct Foreign Investment: A Japanese Model of Multinational Business Operations* (London: Croom Helm).

— (1982) 'Macroeconomic versus International Business Approach to Direct Foreign Investment', *Hitotsubashi Journal of Economics*, **23/1**, pp. 1–19.

— and Ozawa, T. (1984) *Japan's General Trading Companies* (Paris: OECD).

— and — (1985) 'Towards a Theory of Industrial Restructuring and Dynamic Comparative Advantage', *Hitotsubashi Journal of Economics*, **26/2**, 179–202.

Komiya, R. (1988) *Industrial Policy of Japan* (Tokyo: Academic Press Japan).

— (1988) 'Japan's Foreign Direct Investment: Facts and Theoretical Considerations', in: Borner, S. (Ed.) *International Finance and Trade in a Polycentric World* (London: Macmillan), pp. 247–89.

— (1990) *The Japanese Economy: Trade, Industry, and Government* (Tokyo: University of Tokyo).

Kong, K. D. (1982) *Tenno Faschismus – Zur Entstehung, Struktur, Ideologie und Funktion des Herrschaftssystems in Japan* [*Tenno fashism: on the origins, structure, ideology and function of this system of dominance in Japan*] (Marburg: Universität Marburg, Diss.).

Kono, T. (1984) *Strategy and Structure of Japanese Enterprises* (London: Macmillan).

Koontz, H. (1961) 'The Management Theory', *Academy of Management Journal*, **12**, pp. 174–8.

Korten, D. C. (1999) *The Post Corporate World: Life After Capitalism* (Berrett-Koehler).

Kosai, Y. (1988) 'The Reconstruction Period', in: Komiya R. (Ed.) *Industrial Policy of Japan* (Tokyo: Academic Press), pp. 25–48.

Kosaka, M. (1987) 'The Status and the Role of the Individual in Japanese Society', in: Moore, C. A. and Morris, A. (Eds.) *The Japanese Mind* (Honolulu, HI: University of Hawaii), pp. 245–61.

— (1989) *Japan's Choices* (London: Pinter).

Koshmann, J. V. (1989) 'Maruyama Masao and the Incomplete Project of Modernity', in: Miyoshi, M. and Harootunian, H. D. (Eds.) *Postmodernism and Japan* (Durham, NC: Duke University Press), pp. 123–41.

Koslowski, P. (1987) *Die postmoderne Kultur* [*Postmodern culture*] (München: Beck).

— (1989) *Wirtschaft als Kultur* [*Business as culture*] (Graz: Passagen).

— (1989) *Prüfungen der Neuzeit* [*Examination of the modern times*] (Graz: Passagen).

Kowalewsky, R. and Satori, A. (1992) 'Mitsubishi', *Wirtschaftswoche*, October, pp. 220–2.

Kraus, W. (1982) *Die japanische Herausforderung* [*The Japanese challenge*] (Berlin: Dunker & Humblot).

Kray, R. and Pfeiffer, K. L. (1991) 'Vom Ende und Fortgang der Provokationen', in: Gumbrecht, H. U. and Pfeiffer, K. L. (Eds.) *Paradoxien, Dissonanzen, Zusammenbrüche: Situationen offener Epistemologie* [*Paradoxa, dissonances, implosions: situations of open epistemology*] (Frankfurt: Suhrkamp), pp. 13–31.

Krisher, B. (1973) 'Mitsubishi a Giant Reborn', *Newsweek*, April, p. 32.

Krohn, W. and Küppers, G. (1989) 'Rekursives Durcheinander' [*Recursive chaos*], *Kursbuch*, **98**, 69–83.

Krotkin, J. (1994) *Tribes: How Race, Religion, and Identity Determine Success in the New Global Economy* (New York: Random House).

Krug, B. (1993) 'Die Entzauberung der Samurai' [*De-mystification of the samurai*], *Frankfurter Allgemeine Zeitung*, April.

Krugman, P. (1990) *The Accidental Theorist* (New York: Penguin).

— (1999) *Der Mythos vom globalen Wirtschaftskrieg. Eine Abrechnung mit den Pop-Ökonomen* [*The Myth of a Global Economic War*] (Hamburg: Campus).

Kuhn, T. S. (1970) *The Structure of Scientific Revolutions* (Chicago: University of Chicago Press).

Kumon, S. (1982) 'Some Principles Governing the Thought and Behavior of Japanists (Kontextualists)', *Journal of Japanese Studies*, **8**, pp. 5–28.

— (1988) 'Nationalism of Long Intestine', *Japan Times*, February.

— (1992) 'Japan as a Network Society', in: Kumon, S. and Rosovsky, H. (Eds.) *The Political Economy of Japan*, vol. 3 (Stanford, CA: Stanford University Press), pp. 109–41.

Kunio, Y. (1982) *Sogo Shosha – The Vanguard of the Japanese Economy* (Oxford: Oxford University Press).

Kunneman, H. (1991) *Der Wahrheitstrichter* [*The tunnel towards truth*] (Frankfurt: Campus).

Kuntz-Brenner, R. (1992) 'Ästhetik verkommt zum Lebensstil' [Esthetic degrades to a lifestyle], *Deutsche Universitätszeitung*, November.

Kuroda, M. (1990) *Japan in a Changing World* (Tokyo: Speech, Mitsubishi Bank Forum, October).

Kusiel, R. F. (1981) *Capitalism and the State in Modern France: Revolution and Economic Management in the Twentieth Century* (Cambridge: Cambridge University Press).

Küster, R. (1990) 'Richard Wagner – oder die Geschwätzigkeit der Postmoderne' [Richard Wagner – or the talkative postmodernity], in: Bering, K. (Ed.) *Wie postmodern ist die Postmoderne? [Just how postmodern is postmodernity]* (Essen: Die blaue Eule), pp. 89–102.

Kuttner, R. (1999) *Everything for Sale: The Virtues and Limits of Markets* (Chicago, Ill: University of Chicago Press).

Kverneland, A. (1988) 'Japan's Industrial Structure – Barriers to Global Competition', in: Hood, N. and Vahlne, J. E. (Eds.) *Strategies in Global Competition* (Beckenham: Croom Helm), pp. 225–55.

Lakatos, I. (1970) 'Falsification and the Methodology of Scientific Research Programs', in: Lakatos, I. and Musgrave, A. *Criticism and the Growth of Knowledge* (Cambridge, MA: Harvard University Press), pp. 91–196.

— (1970) 'History of Science and its Rational Reconstructions', *Boston Studies in the Philosophy of Science*, **8**, pp. 1–53.

Lall, S. (1978) 'The Pattern of Intra-Firm Exports by US Multinationals', *Oxford Bulletin of Economics and Statistics*, **3**, pp. 209–22.

Lall, S. and Streeten, P. (1967) *Foreign Investment, Transnationals, and Developing Countries* (London: Macmillan Press).

Lash, S. (1991) *Sociology of Postmodernism* (London: Routledge).

— and Urry, J. (1987) *The End of Organized Capitalism* (Cambridge, MA: Polity Press).

Lee, J. and Powell J. N. (1998) *Postmodernism for Beginners* (New York: Writers and Readers).

Leontiades, M. (1986) *Managing the Unmanageable: Strategies for Success within the Conglomerate* (Reading, MA: Wesley).

Leuenberger, T. (1981) *Herrschaftsstruktur und Machtverteilung im politischen System der USA [Power: structures and distribution in the political system of the USA]* (Berlin: Duncker & Humblot).

— (1990) 'A World Scenario: The Emergence of Three Main Trading Zones: The European Community, Japan – East Asia – Pacific, USA – Canada', in: Kulessa, M. (Ed.) *The Newly Industrializing Economies of Asia* (Berlin: Springer) pp. 197–210.

Levi-Strauss, C. (1966) *La pensée sauvage* (Paris: Plou) [*The Savage Mind* (University of Chicago Press)].

— (1971) *Les structures élémentaires de la parenté* (Paris: Mouton) [*The Structures of Kinship* (New York: Beacon)].

Levin, C. (1988) 'Art and the Sociological Ego', in: Fekete, J. (Ed.) *Life After Postmodernism* (Basingstoke: Macmillan), pp. 22–64.

Levin, H. (1966) 'What was Modernism?', *Massachusetts Review*, **1**, pp. 609–30) [also as: Levin, H. 'What was Modernism?', in: Levin, H. *Refractions: Essays in Comparative Literature* (New York: Oxford University Press), pp. 271–295].

Lewis, M. (1989) *Liar's Poker* (Sevenoaks: Hodder & Stoughton).

— (1991) *The Money Culture* (New York: Norton).

Li, V. (1991) 'Naming the System: Fredric Jameson's Postmodernism', *Ariel*, **10**, pp. 131–42.

Lichtenberg, F. R. and Pushner, G. M. (1992) *Ownership and Corporate Performance in Japan* (NBER Working Paper 4092).

Liker, J. K., Fruin, W. M. and Adler, P. S. (1999) *Remade in America: Transplanting and Transforming Japanese Management Systems* (Oxford: Oxford University Press).

Likert, R. (1961) *New Patterns of Management* (New York: McGraw-Hill).

Lilla, M. (1984) 'On Goodman, Putnam and Rorty: The Return to the 'Given'', *Partisan*, **51/2**, pp. 220–35.

Lima, L. C. (1991) 'Tropischer Kontrapunkt der Postmoderne?' [Tropical counterpoint of postmodernity], in: Gumbrecht, H. U. and Pfeiffer, K. L. (Eds.) *Paradoxien, Dissonanzen, Zusammenbrüche: Situationen offener Epistemologie* [*Paradoxa, dissonances, implosions: situations of open epistemology*] (Frankfurt: Suhrkamp), pp. 571–88.

Lipnack, J. and Stamps, J. (1982) *Networking: The First Report* (New York: Doubleday).

Lockwood, W. W. (1953) *Economic Development for Japan* (Princeton, NJ: Princeton University Press).

Lodge, G. C. and Vogel, E. F. (1998) *Ideology and National Competitiveness; An Analysis of Nine Countries* (Boston, MA: Harvard Business School Press).

Lokowandt, E. (1989) *Das japanische Kaisertum – Religiöse Fundierung und politische Realität* [*The Japanese emperor – religious base and political reality*] (Tokyo: OAG).

Long, J. (1997) *Generating Hope: A Strategy for Reaching the Postmodern Generation* (Chicago, IL: Intervarsity Press).

Lorenzen, P. (1987) *Lehrbuch der konstruktiven Wissenschaftstheorie* [*Textbook on a constructivistic theory of science*] (Mannheim: Bibliographisches Institut).

Lövlie, L. (1999) 'Postmodern Subjectivity on the Internet' (Speech 18.3.1998 Universität Hamburg).

Lu, D. (1974) *Sources of Japanese History* (New York: McGraw-Hill).

—— (1989) *Inside Corporate Japan* (Tokyo: Tuttle).

Lucas, J. R. (1998) *Balance of Power* (Washington DC: American Management Association).

Lutterjohann, M. (1987) *Kulturschock Japan* [*Culture shock Japan*] (Bielefeld: Rump).

Lutz, R. (1988) 'Das Paradigma als Weltanschauung der Wissenschaften' [The paradigm as a view of the world for sciences], in: Lutz, R. (Ed.) *Pläne für eine menschliche Zukunft* [*Sketches for a human future*] (Weinheim: Belz), pp. 207–17.

—— (1988) 'Die unbewusste Revolution' [Revolution unconscious], in: Lutz, R. (Ed.) *Pläne für eine menschliche Zukunft* [*Sketches for a human future*] (Weinheim: Belz), pp. 60–76.

Lyotard, J. F. (1948) 'La culpabilité allemande' [The German guiltiness], *L'Age Nouveau*, **28**, pp. 90–4.

—— (1959) 'Le contenu social de la lutte Algérienne' [The social context of the Algerian war], *Socialisme ou Barbarie*, **29**, pp. 1–38.

—— (1962) 'L'Algérie sept ans après' [Algeria seven years later], *Socialisme ou Barbarie*, **33**, pp. 10–16).

—— (1973) *Dérive á partir de Marx et Freud* [*Deriving from Marx and Freud*] (Paris: Union Générale d'Editions).

—— (1973) 'Esquisse d'une économie de'l hyperréalisme' [Expression of a hyperrealistic economy], *L'Art Vivant*, **36**, pp. 9–12.

—— (1973) 'Petite économie libidinale d'un dispositif narratif' [Little libidinal economy in an explanatory fashion], in: Lyotard, J. F. *Des dispositifs pulsionnels* [*The pulsing way*] (Paris: Union Générale d'Editions), pp. 179–224.

—— (1974) *Economie libidinale* (Paris: Minuit) [*Libidinal Economy* (Bloomington, IN: Indiana University Press)].

—— (1977) *Instructions paiennes* [*Pagan lessons*] (Paris: Galilée).

—— (1979) *La condition postmoderne* (Paris: Minuit) [*The Postmodern Condition* (Minneapolis, MN: University of Minnesota Press)].

—— (1982) 'Réponse á la question: "Qu'est-ce que le Postmoderne?"' [Response to the question: what is postmodernity], *Critique*, **419**, pp. 357–67.

—— (1983) *Le différend* (Paris: Minuit) [*The conflict* (Minneapolis, MN: University of Minnesota Press)].

— (1985) 'Histoire universelle et différences culturelles' [Universal history and cultural differences], *Critique*, **456**, pp. 559–68.

— (1985) *Grabmal des Intellektuellen* [*Tombstone of the intellectual*] (Graz: Passagen).

— (1985) *Die Mauer des Pazifik* [*The wall of the pacific*] (Graz: Passagen).

— (1985) *Immaterialität und Postmoderne* [*Immateriality and postmodernity*] (Berlin: Merve).

— (1987) 'Das Erhabene und die Avantgarde' [The noble and the Avant-garde], in: Le Rider, J. and Raulet, G. (Eds.) *Verabschiedung der (Post-)Moderne?* [*Good-byes to the postmodern*] (Tübingen: Narr), pp. 251–92.

— (1987) *Postmoderne für Kinder* [*Postmodernity for children*] (Graz: Passagen).

— (1988) *L'inhumain: causeries sur le temps* (Paris: Galilée) [*The Inhuman: reflection of Time* (Stanford University Press)].

— (1991) 'Eine post-moderne Fabel über die Postmoderne' [A postmodern fable on postmodernity], in: Weimann, R., Gumbrecht, H. U. and Wagner, B. (Eds.) *Postmoderne – Globale Differenz* [*Postmodernity – global difference*] (Frankfurt: Suhrkamp), pp. 291–304.

— (1997) *Postmodern Fables* (Minneapolis, MN: University of Minnesota Press).

— and Thebaud, J. L. (1979) *Au juste – conversations* [*Exactly – conversations*] (Paris: Bourgois).

Maasaki, K. (1987) 'The Status and the Role of the Individual in Japanese Society', in: Moore, C. A. and Morris, A. *The Japanese Mind* (Honolulu: University of Hawaii Press), pp. 245–61.

MacDonald, W. (1998) *Postmodern Management* (New York: Quorum Books).

Macharzina, K. (Ed.) (1984) *Diskontinuitätenmanagement* [*Management of discontinuities*] (Berlin: Schmidt).

Machlup, F. (1946) 'Marginal Analysis and Empirical Research', *American Economic Review*, **36**, pp. 519–54.

Magretta, J. (1999) *Managing in the New Economy* (Boston, MA: Harvard Business School Press).

Maier, C. (1975) *Recasting Bourgeois Europe* (Princeton, NJ: Princeton University Press).

Mainichi Daily News (Ed.) (1971) *The Mitsui Group* (Tokyo: Mainichi Daily News).

Mainichi Shinbun (1973) *Nippon no shosha: Mitsubishi shoji* [*Japan's trading company: Mitsubishi*] (Tokyo: Mainichi Shinbunsha).

Malkin, J. R. (1999) *Memory Theater and Postmodern Drama* (Ann Arbor: University of Michigan Press).

Malraux, A. (1991) *Liberation*; quoted after: Scholl Latour, P. (1990) *Leben mit Frankreich* [*To live with France*] (Munich: DTV), pp. 208.

Manegold, C. S. (1991) 'A Military Power, too?', *Newsweek*, August, pp. 57–65.

Mann, C. L. (1989) 'Determinants of Japanese Direct Investment in US Manufacturing Industries' (Washington, DC: Board of Governors of the Federal Reserve Systems International Finance Discussion Papers 362).

Manschot, H. (1987) 'Nietzsche und die Postmoderne in der Philosophie' [Nietzsche and the postmodern in philosophy], in: Kamper, D. and Reijen, W. v. (Eds.) *Die unvollendete Vernunft* [*The incomplete reason*] (Frankfurt: Suhrkamp), pp. 478–96.

Marcus, G. (1998) *Corporate Futures: The Diffusion of the Culturally Sensitive Corporate Form* (Chicago, IL: University of Chicago Press).

Marcuse, H. (1972) *Der eindimensionale Mensch* (Neuwied: Luchterhand) [*The One-Dimensional Man* (New York: Beacon)].

Marin, B. and Mayntz, R. (1991) *Policy Networks: Empirical Evidence and Theoretical Considerations* (Frankfurt: Campus).

Marsh, J. L. (1989) 'Strategies of Evasion: The Paradox of Self-Referentiality and the Postmodern Critique of Rationality', *International Philosophical Quarterly*, **3**, pp. 339–50.

Martens, G. (1999) 'Broch, Musil und die Grenzen der Moderne' [Broch, Musil, and the Boundaries of the Modern], Paper presented at: Postmodern Perspectives: Second International Graduate and Postgraduate Conference, Erlangen, November 19–21.

Martin, B. (1987) 'Japans Weg in die Moderne und das deutsche Vorbild' [Japan's way into modernity and the German example], in: Martin, B. (Ed.) *Japans Weg in die Moderne* [*Japan's way into modernity*] (Frankfurt: Campus), pp. 17–45.

Martin, H.-P. and Schumann, H. (1998) *Der Angriff auf Demokratie und Wohlstand* [*Assault on Democracy and Wealth*] (Reinbeck: Rowohlt).

Martin, S. (1993) *Advanced Industrial Economics* (Oxford: Blackwell).

— (1993) *Industrial Economics: Economic Analysis and Public Policy* (Englewood Cliffs, NJ: Prentice Hall).

Martland, T. R. (1991) 'Post-Modernism – or what's become of us, Tarzan?', *Antioch Review*, 3, pp. 587–99.

Maruoka, D. and Yoshiksohi T. (1990) *Noh* (Osaka: Hoikusha).

Maruyama, M. (1974) *Studies in the Intellectual History of Tokugawa Japan* (Tokyo: University of Tokyo Press).

Masataka, K. (1989) *Japan's Choices, New Globalism and Cultural Orientations in an Industrial State* (London: Pinter).

Masten, S. E. (1984) 'The Organization of Production', *Journal of Law and Economics*, 27, pp. 403–17.

— (1986) 'Institutional Choice and the Organization of Production', *Zeitschrift für die Gesamte Staatswissenschaft*, 3, pp. 493–510.

Mataji, M., Togai, Y. and Mishima, Y. (Eds.) (1976) *Sogo shosha keieishi* [*History of the Sogo Shosha*] (Tokyo: Toyo Keizai Shimposha).

Matsuda, T. (1982) 'Die Entwicklung der Wirtschaft nach 1868', in: Hammitzsch, H. (Ed.) *Japan Handbuch* (Stuttgart: DVA), pp. 200–27.

Matsui, K., Suzuki, H. and Ushio, Y. (1999) *Millennium Metamorphosis: From Old to New Japan* (Goldman Sachs Market Strategy).

Matsumoto, M. (1989) *Haragei: The Unspoken Way – Silence in Japanese Business and Society* (Tokyo: Kodansha).

Matsushita, K. (1975) 'Policies of Citizens' Participation', *The Japan Interpreter*, 1, 451–519.

— (1988) 'The Secret is Shared', *Manufacturing Engineering*, 2, 100.

Maturana, H. and Varela, F. (1987) *Der Baum der Erkenntnis: Die biologischen Wurzeln des menschlichen Erkennens* (Bern: Scherz) [*The Tree of Knowledge* (Shambhala)].

Maury, R. (1991) *Die japanischen Manager: Wie sie denken, wie sie handeln, wie sie Weltmärkte erobern* [*Japanese Managers: how they think and how they conquer global markets*] (Wiesbaden: Gabler).

May, T. (1995) *The Moral Theory of Poststructuralism* (Philadelphia, PA: Pennsylvania State University Press).

Mayo, R., Moody, P. E. and Nelson, D. (1998) *Powered by Honda: Developing Excellence in the Global Enterprise* (New York: Wiley).

McCallum, D. (1996) *The Death of Truth: What's Wrong with Multiculturalism, the Rejection of Reason and the New Postmodern Diversity* (London: Bethany House).

McCraw, T. K. (1986) 'Mercantilism and the Market', in: Barfield, C. E. and Schambra, W. A. (Eds.) *The Politics of Industrial Policy* (Washington, DC: American Enterprise Institute), pp. 258–88.

McDonald Wallace, W. (1998) *Postmodern Management* (New York: Quorum Books).

McGuigan, J. (1999) *Modernity and Postmodern Culture* (London: Open University).

McHale, B. (1982) 'Writing about Postmodern Writing', *Poetics Today*, 3, pp. 211–27.

— (1987) *Postmodern Fiction* (New York: Methuen).

McHugh, P., Wheeler W. and Merli, G. (1995) *Beyond Business Process Reengineering* (New York: Wiley).

McKinney, R. H. (1989) 'The Origins of Postmodernism', *Philosophy Today*, **3**, pp. 232–45.

— (1990) 'An Entropic Analysis of Postmodernism', *Philosophy Today*,**2**, pp. 163–75.

McLuhan, M. (1965) *Understanding Media: The Extensions of Man* (New York: McGraw-Hill).

McMillan, C. (1989) *The Japanese Industrial System* (Berlin: De Gruyter).

Meeham, M. (Ed.) (1999) *The Future ain't what it used to be* (New York: Penguin).

Melkonian, M. (1999) *Richard Rorty's Politics: Liberalism at the End of the American Century* (New York: Humanity Books).

Mellard, J. M. (1980) *The Exploded Form: The Modernist Novel in America* (Urbana, IL: University of Illinois).

Melville, H. (1981) Letter to Duyckinck, quoted after: Walcut, C. C. 'Introduction to Moby Dick', in: Melville, H. *Moby Dick* (Toronto: Bantam), pp. viii–xii.

Menzel, U. (1998) *Globalisierung versus Fragmentierung* [*Globalization vs. Fragmatation*] (Frankfurt: Suhrkamp).

— (1989) 'Einleitung [Introduction]', in: Menzel, U. (Ed.) *Im Schatten des Siegers*, vol. 1 [*In the shadow of the winner*] (Frankfurt: Suhrkamp), pp. 9–40.

Messner, D. (1998) *Die Zukunft des Staates und der Politik* [*The Future of State and Politics*] (Bonn: Dietz).

Metcalfe, S. J. (1998) *Evolutionary Economics and Creative Destruction* (London: Routledge).

Michalet, C. A. and Chevallier, T. (1985) 'France', in: Dunning, J. H. (Ed.) *Multinational Enterprises, Economic Structures and International Competitiveness* (New York: Wiley), pp. 91–127.

Michie, J. and Smith, J. G. (1998) *Globalization, Growth, and Governance: Creating an Innovative Economy* (Oxford: Oxford University Press).

Mikes, G. (1973) *The Land of the Rising Yen* (London: Penguin).

Miles, R. E. and Snow, C. C. (1986) 'Network Organizations: New Concepts for New Forms', *California Management Review*, **28**, pp. 62–73.

Miller, R. (1990) 'Putting on the Glitz: Architecture after Postmodernism', *Dissent*, **1**, pp. 27–36.

Mills, C. A. (1990) 'Creating a Disney World', *Geographical Magazine*, **12**, pp. 40–4.

Minc, A. (1998) *Globalisierung. Chance der Zukunft* [*Globalization*] (Wien: Zsolnay).

— (1998) *La Mondialisation Heureuse* [*Happy Globalization*] (Paris: Plon).

Mishima, Y. and Yamaguchi, E. (1990) *Mitsubishi: Its Challenge and Strategy* (Tokyo: JAI).

Mitchie, J. and Smith, J. G. (1999) *Globalization, Growth, and Governance: Creating an Innovative Economy* (Oxford: Oxford University Press).

Mitford, A. B. (1989) *Tales of Old Japan* (Tokyo: Tuttle).

MITI (1990) *International Trade and Industrial Policy in the 1990s* (Tokyo: MITI).

— (1990) *White Paper on International Trade 1990* (Tokyo: Jetro).

— (1992) *White Paper on International Trade 1992* (Tokyo: Jetro).

Mitsubishi Corporation (1970) *The Mitsubishi Group* (Tokyo: Mitsubishi Corporation).

— (1992) *Annual Report 1992* (Tokyo: Mitsubishi Corporation).

— (1993) *Annual Report 1993* (Tokyo: Mitsubishi Corporation).

— (1998) *Annual Report 1998* (Tokyo: Mitsubishi Corporation).

— (1998) *Tatemae and Honne: Distinguishing Between Good Form and Real Intention in Japanese Business Culture* (Tokyo: Mitsubishi).

Mitsubishi Electric (1991) *Annual Report 1991* (Tokyo: Mitsubishi Electric).

Mitsubishi Group (1970) *A Century of Progress – A Bigger Century to Come* (Tokyo: Mitsubishi Corporation).

— (2000) *Mitsubishi Monitor* (Internet presence: www.mitsubishi.or.jp).

Mitsubishi Research Institute (1982) *Some Theses on Interactions Pertinent to Innovation* (Tokyo: Mitsubishi Research Institute).

Mitsubishi Sha (1910) *Mitsubishi Kaisha* (Tokyo: Mitsubishi).

— (1935) *An Outline of the Mitsubishi Enterprise* (Tokyo: Mitsubishi Sha).

Mitsubishi Shoji (1958) *Ritsugyo boeki-roku* [*History of the development of foreign trade*] (Tokyo: Mitsubishi Shoji).

— (1974) *Mitsubishi Shoji: sono ayumi: 20-shunen kinen-go* [*Mitsubishi Trading Company: its development – In commemoration of the 20th anniversary*] (Tokyo: Mitsubishi Shoji).

Miyamoto, K. (1973) *Chiiki kaihatsu wa korede yoika?* [*Is the current trend in regional development acceptable?*] (Tokyo: Iwanami Shoten).

Miyasaki, Y. (1972) *Kasen* [*The Japanese Oligopoly*] (Tokyo: Iwanami Shoten).

— (1980) 'Excessive Competition and the Formation of Keiretzu', in: Sato, K. (Ed.) *Industry and Business in Japan* (White Plains, NY: Sharpe), pp. 53–73.

Miyoshi, M. (1989) 'Against The Native Grain: The Japanese Novel and the "Postmodern" West', in: Miyoshi, M. and Harootunian, H. D. (Eds.) *Postmodernism and Japan* (Durham, NC: Duke University Press), pp. 143–69.

— and Harootunian, H. D. (1989) 'Introduction', in: Miyoshi M. and Harootunian, H. D. (Eds.) *Postmodernism and Japan* (Durham, NC: Duke University Press), pp. vii–xxi.

Moltke, H. v. (1892) *Militärische Werke*, vol. 1 [*Military writings*] (Berlin: Grosser Generalstab).

Monden, Y. (1999) *Japanese Cost Management* (World Scientific).

Mönninger, M. (1992) *Vogelfrei im Atrium: Die Emanzipation der Büroarbeit in Tokyo* [*Cut loose in the hall: emancipation of the office work in Tokyo*] (Frankfurter Allgemeine Zeitung).

Moore, C. A. (1987) 'The Enigmatic Japanese Mind', in: Moore, C. A. and Morris, A. (Eds.) *The Japanese Mind* (Honolulu, HI: University of Hawaii Press), pp. 288–313.

Moran, M. (1978) 'The Politics of International Business', *British Journal of Political Science*, **8**, 217–36.

Morgan, J. C. and Morgan, J. J. (1991) *Cracking the Japanese Market: Strategies for Success in the New Global Economy* (New York: Free Press).

Morgenstern, O. (1950) *On the Accuracy of Economic Observations* (Princeton, NJ: Princeton University Press).

— (1972) 'Descriptive, Predictive, and Normative Theory', *Kyklos*, **25**, pp. 699–714.

Mori, S. (1990) 'Yet Again, there is Reverse Culture Shock', *Nippon View*, **11**, p. 9.

Morikawa, H. (1980) 'Management Structure and Control Devices for Diversified Zaibatzu Business', in: Nakagawa, K. (Ed.) *Strategy and Structure of Big Business* (Tokyo: University of Tokyo Press), pp. 45–60.

Morishima, M. (1982) *Why has Japan Succeeded? Western Technology and Japanese Ethos* (Cambridge: Cambridge University Press).

Morozumi, Y. (1966) *Sangyo seisaku no riron* [*The logic of industrial policy*] (Tokyo: Nohin Keizai Shinbun Sha).

— (1973) *Sangyo taisei no sai* [*Reorganizing industrial structures*] (Tokyo: Shunjusha).

Morris, R. (1989) 'Words and Images in Modernism and Postmodernism', *Critical Inquiry*, **2**, pp. 337–48.

Mouer, R. and Sugimoto, Y. (1986) *Images of Japanese Society* (London: KPI).

Mounce, H. O. (1997) *The Two Pragmatisms: From Peirce to Rorty* (London: Routledge).

MOW (1981) 'The Meaning of Working', in: Dlugor, G. and Weirmair, K. (Eds.) *Management under Different Value Systems* (Berlin: De Gruyter), pp. 289–305.

Mowery, D. C. (1999) *U.S. Industry in 2000: Studies in Competitive Performance* (Washington, DC: National Academy).

Mueller, R. K. (1986) *Corporate Networking* (New York: Free Press).

Müller, K. and Goldberger, E. (1986) *Unternehmenskooperation bringt Wettbewerbsvorteile* [*Cooperation for competitiveness*] (Zürich: Orell Füssli).

Müller-Stewens, G. and Hillig, A. (1992) 'Motive zur Bildung strategischer Allianzen' [Motives for strategic alliances], in: Bronder, C. and Pritzl, R. (Eds.) *Wegweiser für strategische Allianzen* [*Guidelines for strategic alliances*] (Wiesbaden: Gabler), pp. 63–102.

Münch, R. (1998) *Globale Dynamik, lokale Lebenswelten. Der schwierige Weg in die Welt-gesellschaft* [*Global Dynamics – Local Life*] (Frankfurt: Suhrkamp).

Munéva, G. (1975) 'Radical Knowledge' (Berkeley, CA: University of California, Diss.).

Murakami, R. (1976) *Kagirinaku tomei nichikai buru* [*Blue lines on naked skin*] (Tokyo: Kodansha).

Murakami, Y. (1982) 'Sengo Nihon no keizai shisutemu' [Japan's post war economic system], *The Economist (Japan)*, June, pp. 38–54.

— and Kosai, Y. (Eds.) (1986) *Japan in the Global Community* (Tokyo: Tokyo University Press).

— and Rohlen T. B. (1992) 'Social Exchange Aspects of the Japanese Political Economy: Culture, Efficiency, and Change', in: Kumon, S. and Rosovsky, H. (Eds.) *The Political Economy of Japan*, vol. 3 (Stanford, CA: Stanford University Press), pp. 63–105.

Muramatsu, M. and Krause, E. (1984) 'The Ruling Coalition and its Transformation', *Chuo Koron*, **11**, pp. 70–3.

Murasaki, S. (1976) *The Tale of Genji* [*Genji Monogatari*] (New York: Knopf).

Murphy, N. (1997) *Anglo-American Postmodernity* (Boulder: Westview).

Musashi, M. (1983) *Das Buch der fünf Ringe* (Munich: Knaur) [*The Book of Five Rings* (Bantam)].

Musgrave, A. (1981) ' "Unreal Assumptions" in Economic Theory', *Kyklos*, **34**, pp. 777–87.

Muto, H. (1996) 'Innovative Policies and Administrative Strategies for Intergovernmental Change in Japan', in: Jun, J. S. and Wright, D. S. *Globalization and Decentralization: Institutional Context Policy Issues, and Intergovernmental Relations in Japan and the United States* (Washington, DC: Georgetown University).

Nagata, K. (1991) 'The World of Mitsubishi – Mighty Mitsubishi', Paper presented at the Special Roundtable Discussion on Cross Cultural Management, Keidanren Guest House, Gotemba, January.

Naisbitt, J. (1995) *Megatrends Asien. Acht Megatrends, die unsere Welt verändern* [*Megatrends Asia*] (Wien: Signum).

— (1999) *High Tech High Touch* (London: Brealey).

— and Aburdene, P. (1990) *Megatrends 2000* (Düsseldorf: Econ).

— and — (1993) *Megatrends Frauen* [*Megatrends Women*] (Düsseldorf: Econ).

Najita, T. (1990) 'On Culture and Technology in Postmodern Japan', in: Miyoshi, M. and Harootunian, H. D. (Eds.) *Postmodernism and Japan* (Durham, NC: Duke University Press), pp. 3–21.

Nakagawa, K. (1980) 'Business Strategy and Industrial Structure in Pre-World-War-II Japan', in: Nakagawa, K. (Ed.) *Strategy and Structure of Big Business* (Tokyo: University of Tokyo Press), pp. 3–38.

Nakamura, H. (1969) *A History of the Development of Japanese Thought* (Tokyo: Iwanami Shoten).

— (1971) *Ways of Thinking of Eastern People* (Honolulu, HI: University of Hawaii Press).

— (1986) 'Der religionsgeschichtliche Hintergrund der Entwicklung Japans in der neuen Zeit' [Religion as a background for Japan's development in the recent times], in: Barloewen, C. v. and Werhahn-Mees, K. (Eds.) *Japan und der Westen*, vol. 1 [*Japan and the West*] (Frankfurt: Fischer), pp. 56–94.

Nakamura, T. (1981) *The Postwar Japanese Economy* (Tokyo: Tokyo University Press).

Nakane, C. (1989) 'Die Struktur der japanischen Gesellschaft' [Structure of the Japanese society], in: Hijia-Kirschnereit, I. and Schmölers, C. (Eds.) *Japan* (Frankfurt: Insel), pp. 164–8.

— (1990) *The Japanese Society* (Tokyo: Tuttle).

Nakano, H. (1976) 'Sogo shosha no honshitsu to nihon gata taokokuseki kigyo' [The nature of the Sogo Shosha and the Japanese MNE], *Seikai Keizai Hyoron*, February, pp. 71–9.

Nakatani, I. (1984) 'The Economic Role of Financial Corporate Grouping', in: Aoki, M. (Ed.) *The Economic Analysis of the Japanese Firm* (Amsterdam: Elsevier), pp. 227–58.

— (1988) *The Japanese Firm in Transition* (Tokyo: Asian Productivity Organization).

Naohiro, A. (1970) *MITI* (Toyko: Sophia University Press).

Nash, C. (1987) *World Games* (London: Methuen).

Nations, R. (1983) 'Pax Pacifica: The Regasone Prosperity Plan', *Far Eastern Economic Review*, July, pp. 55–6.

Naumann, N. (1987) 'Identitätsfindung – das geistige Problem des modernen Japans' [Finding one's identity – the spiritual problem of Japan], in: Martin, B. (Ed.) *Japans Weg in die Moderne [Japan's path into modernity]* (Frankfurt: Campus), pp. 173–91.

Neef, D., Siesfield, T. and Cefola, J. (1998) *The Economic Impact of Knowledge* (London: Heinemann).

Neff, R. and Holstein, W. J. (1990) 'Mighty Mitsubishi is on the Move', *Business Week*, December, pp. 38–41.

Negandhi, A. R. (1990) 'External and Internal Functioning of American, German, and Japanese Multinational Corporations: Decision making and Policy Issues', in: Casson, M. (Ed.) *Multinational Corporations* (Aldershot: Elgar), pp. 557–77.

— and Welge, M. K. (1984) *Beyond Theory Z: Global Rationalization Strategies of American, German and Japanese Multinational Companies* (Greenwich, CN: JAI).

Nester, W. R. (1990) *The Foundation of Japanese Power: Continuities, Changes, Challenges* (London: Macmillan).

— (1990) *Japan's Growing Power over East Asia and the World Economy* (London: Macmillan).

Neumann, J. v. and Morgenstern, O. (1953) *Theory of Games and Economic Behavior* (Princeton, NJ: Princeton University Press).

Neustupny, I. v. (1978) *A Post-Structural Approach to Language* (Tokyo: University of Tokyo Press).

Newman, C. (1985) *The Post-Modern Aura* (Evanston, IL: Northwestern University Press).

Nicholas, S. J. (1986) 'Multinationals, Transaction Costs and Choice of Institutional Form' (University of Reading Discussion Papers 97).

Nietzsche, F. (1979) 'Aus dem Nachlass der Achtziger Jahre' [Posthumous works of the eighties], *Gesammelte Werke [Collected works]*, vol. 3 (Frankfurt: Ullstein).

— (1979) 'Der Antichrist', *Gesammelte Werke*, vol. 2 (Frankfurt: Ullstein) [*The Antichrist* (LPC)].

— (1979) 'Die fröhliche Wissenschaft' [Serene science], *Gesammelte Werke*, vol. 2 [*Collected works*] (Frankfurt: Ullstein).

— (1979) 'Götzendämmerung' [Dawning of the idols], *Gesammelte Werke*, vol. 2 [Collected works], (Frankfurt: Ullstein)

— (1997) 'Jenseits von Gut und Böse', *Gesammelte Werke*, vol. 3, (Frankfurt: Ullstein) [*Beyond Good and Evil* (Vintage 1989)].

Nihon Keizai Kenkyu Senta [Japan Center for Economic Research] (1976) *The Study of Socioeconomic Framework for the Analysis of Energy Demand and Supply in the Year 2000* (Tokyo: Nihon Keizai Kenkyu Senta).

Nijno, K. (1988) *Gendai Sangyo Seisaku no Kadai [Current plans for industrial policy]* (Tokyo: Keiso Shob).

Nishiguchi, T. (1989) 'Strategic Dualism' (Oxford: Oxford University, Diss.).

Nitrobe, I. (1969) *Bushido: The Soul of Japan* (Tokyo: Tuttle).

Noda, K. (1967) *Zaibatzu, keieisha ni miru shotai* (Tokyo: Toyo Keizai Shimposha).

Nohria, N. and Ghoshal, S. (1997) *The Differentiated Network: Organizing Multinational Corporations for Value Creation* (San Diego, CA: Jossey-Bass).

Nojiri, T. (1989) 'Wirtschaftsentwicklung und Wirtschaftsethik in Japan' [Economic development and business ethic], in: Menzel, U. (Ed.) *Japan und der Westen*, vol. 2 [*Japan and the West*] (Frankfurt: Fischer), pp. 17–40.

Nomura Institute (Ed.) (1978) *Kokusai kankyo no henka to Nihon no taio: Niju-isseiki eno taigen* [*Dynamics in the international environment and Japan's answers: preparation for the 21st century*] (Kamakura: Nomura Institute).

Norris, C. (1990) *What's wrong with Postmodernism?* (New York: Harvester Wheatsheaf).

North, R. and Holsti, O. (1963) *Content Analysis: A Handbook with Applications for the Study of International Crisis* (Evanston, IL: Northwestern University Press).

Nuyen, A. T. (1991) 'Postmodern Theology and Postmodern Philosophy', *International Journal for Philosophy of Religion*, 10, pp. 65–77.

Odin, S. (1995) *The Social Self in Zen and American Pragmatism* (Albany, NY: State University of New York Press).

Oe, K. (1989) 'Japan's Dual Identity', in: Miyoshi, M. and Harootunian, H. D. (Eds.) *Postmodernism and Japan* (Durham, NC: Duke University Press), pp. 189–214.

— (1989) *Jinsei no shinseki* [*Leaning towards life*] (Tokyo: Hototogisu).

OECD (1987) *International Investment and MNE* (Paris: OECD).

— (1989) *Economies en transition* [*Economies in transition*] (Paris: OECD).

Ohashi, R. (1988) 'Zen und Philosophie: Kontinuität der Diskontinuität' [Zen and Philosophy: continuity of discontinuity], in: Wimmer, F. M. (Ed.) *Vier Fragen zur Philosophie in Afrika, Asien und Lateinamerika* [*Four question on philosophy in Africa, Asia and Latin America*] (Graz: Passagen), pp. 95–116.

— (Ed.) (1990) *Die Philosophie der Kyoto-Schule* [*The philosophy of the Kyoto school*] (Freiburg: Alber).

Ohkawa, K. and Rosovsky, H. (1973) *Japanese Economic Growth: Trend Acceleration in the Twentieth Century* (Stanford, CA: Stanford University Press).

Ohmae, K. (1981) Japan vs. Japan: Only the Strong Survive, *WSJ*, 26 January, p. 20.

— (1985) *Die Macht der Triade* (Wiesbaden: Gabler).

— (1985) *Triad Power: The Coming Shape of Global Competition* (New York: Free Press).

— (1986) *Japanische Strategien* [*Japanese strategies*] (Hamburg: McGraw-Hill).

— (1987) *Beyond National Borders* (Tokyo: Kodansha).

— (1990) *The Borderless World: Power and Strategy in the Interlinked Economy* (London: Collins).

— (1995) *The Evolving Global Economy: Making Sense of the New World Order* (Cambridge, MA: Harvard Business School Press).

Okakura, K. (1922) Ideale des Ostens [Ideals of the East] (Leipzig: Insel).

Okamura, H. (1982) 'Interfirm Relations in an Enterprise Group: The Case of Mitsubishi', *Japanese Economic Studies*, 2, pp. 53–82.

Okawa, K., Shinohara, M. and Meissner, L. (1979) *Patterns of Japanese Economic Development* (New Haven, CN: Yale University Press).

Okazaki, T. and Stricevic, M. (1990) *The Textbook of Modern Karate* (Tokyo: Kodansha).

O'Keohane, R. and Nye, J. S. (1984) 'Complex Interdependence, Transnational Relations and Realism', in: Kegley, C. W. and Wittkopf, E. R. (Eds.) *The Global Agenda* (New York: Random House), pp. 245–61.

Okimoto, D. I. and Saxonhouse, G. R. (1987) 'Technology and the Future of the Economy', in: Yamamura, K. and Yasuba, Y. (Eds.) *The Political Economy of Japan*, vol. 1. (Stanford, CA: Stanford University Press), pp. 385–421.

Okita, S. (1980) *The Developing Economies and Japan: Lessons in Growth* (Tokyo: Tokyo University Press).

Okumura, H. (1998) *Japan und seine Unternehmen. Eine Einführung in gegenwärtige Strukturprobleme* [*Japan and its Companies: Introduction into the Current Structural Problems*] (Frankfurt: Oldenbourg).

Oppermann, M. (1999) 'The Writer in the Closet, or: Three Sketches of a Postmodern Concept of Identity', Paper presented at: Postmodern Perspectives: Second International Graduate and Postgraduate Conference, Erlangen, November 19–21.

Orlowski, D. (1982) *Die Internationale Wettbewerbsfähigkeit einer Volkswirtschaft* [*International competitiveness of a nation*] (Göttingen: Schwartz).

Ormerod, P. (1997) *The Death of Economics* (New York: Wiley).

— (2000) *Butterfly Economics* (London: Pantheon).

Ortolani, B. (1966) 'Das japanische Theater' [The Japanese Theater], in: Kindermann, H. (Ed.) *Fernöstliches Theater* [*East-Asia theater*] (Stuttgart: Kröner), pp. 391–521.

— (1990) *The Japanese Theatre* (Leiden: Brill).

Orton, J. D. and Weick, K. E. (1990) 'Loosely Coupled Systems: A Reconceptualization', *Academy of Management Review*, 115, pp. 203–23.

Osono, T. (1996) *Charting Japanese Industry: A Graphical Guide to Corporate and Market Structures* (London: Cassell).

Ott, A. E. (1985) 'Industrieökonomik' [Industrial organization], in: Bombach, G. (Ed.) *Industrieökonomik* [*Industrial organization*] (Tübingen: J. C. B. Mohr), pp. 319–33.

Ouchi, W. G. (1981) *Theory Z: How American Business can Meet the Japanese Challenge* (Reading, MA: Wesley).

Ozawa, T. (1974) *Japan's Technological Challenge to the West* (Cambridge, MA: MIT Press).

— (1979) *Multinationalism, Japanese Style* (Princeton, NJ: Princeton University Press).

— (1982) 'A Newer Type of Foreign Investment in Third World Resource Development', *Rivista Internationale di Szience Economiche e Commerciali*, 29, pp. 1133–51.

— (1985) 'Japan', in: Dunning, J. H. (Ed.) *Multinational Enterprises, Economic Structures, and International Competitiveness* (New York: Wiley), pp. 255–187.

— (1989) 'Europe 1992 and Japanese Multinationals: Transplanting a Subcontracting System in the Expanded Market', Gèneve: Université de Gènève Working Paper 5.

— (1989) *Recycling Japan's Surpluses for Developing Countries* (Paris: OECD).

— (1992) 'Japanese Multinationals and 1992', in: Bürgenmeister, B. and Muccielli, J. L. (Eds.) *Multinationals and Europe 1992: Strategies for the Future* (London: Routledge), pp. 135–51.

Pape, W. (1986) 'Die politischgesellschaftliche Verflechtung des Unternehmens' [The political and social connections of a company], in: Herold, R. (Ed.) *Das Industrieunternehmen in Japan* [*The industrial enterprise in Japan*] (Berlin: Schmidt) pp. 23–37.

Pascale, R. T. and Athos, A. G. (1981) *The Art of Japanese Management* (New York: Simon & Schuster).

Patrick, H. (1983) *Industrial Policy, Economic Growth and the Competitiveness of US Industry* (Washington, DC: US-Government Printing Office).

Paul, G. (1986) *Zur Geschichte der Philosophie in Japan und zu ihrer Darstellung* [*On the history of philosophy and its presentation*] (Tokyo: OAG).

— (1987) *Die Aktualität der klassischen chinesischen Philosophie* [*Chinese philosophy is up-to date*] (Munich: Iudicium).

— (1992) *Zur buddhistischen Logik und ihrer Geschichte in Japan* [*On buddhist logic and its history in Japan*] (Tokyo: OAG).

Pêcheux, M. (1975) *Les vérités de la palice* [*The truth of paleness*] (Paris: Galilée).

Pechman, J. and Kaizuka, K. (1976) 'Taxation', in: Patrick, H. and Rosovsky, H. (Eds.) *Asia's New Giant* (Washington, DC: Brookings Institution), pp. 317–82.

Pefanis, J. (1991) *Heterology and the Postmodern: Bataille, Baudrillard, and Lyotard* (Durham, NC: Duke University Press).

Pegels, C. C. (1984) *Japan vs. the West* (Hingham, MA: Kluwer).

Pempel, T. J. (1977) 'Japanese Foreign Policy: The Domestic Bases for International Behavior', in: Katzenstein, P. J. (Ed.) *Between Power and Plenty* (Madison, WI: University of Wisconsin Press). pp. 130–90.

— and Tsunekawa, K. (1979) 'Corporatism without Labour: The Japanese Anomaly', in: Schmitter, P. C. and Lembruch, G. (Eds.) *Trends toward Corporatist Intermediation* (London: Sage), pp. 231–70.

Penrose, E. (1959) *Theory of the Growth of the Firm* (Oxford: Blackwell).

Perger, J. (1990) 'Jean-François Lyotard, eine Position mit oder ohne Zukunft?' [Jean-François Lyotard, a position with or without a future?], in: Reese-Schäfer, W. and Taureck, B. H. F. (Eds.) *Jean-François Lyotard* (Cuxhaven: Junghans), pp. 157–69.

Petersen, W. (1960) 'Stone Garden', in: Wilson-Ross, N. (Ed.) *The World of Zen* (New York: Vintage), pp. 104–11.

Pettaway, R., Sicherman, N. W. and Yamada, T. (1990) 'Japanese Mergers', in: *1st Annual Pacific Basin Finance Conference: Pacific Basin Capital Markets Research* (Amsterdam: Elsevier), pp. 181–202.

Pfeiffer, H. (1987) *Das Imperium der Deutschen Bank* [*The Deutsche Bank empire*] (Frankfurt: Campus).

Pfeiffer, K. L. (1991) 'Schwebende Referenzen und Verhaltenskultur: Japan und die Praxis permanenter Postmoderne' [Floating references and behavioral culture: Japan and the praxis of permanent postmodernity] in: Weimann, R., Gumbrecht, H. U. and Wagner, B. (Eds.) *Postmoderne – Globale Differenz* [*Postmodernity – global difference*] (Frankfurt: Suhrkamp), pp. 344–53.

Philips, L. (1998) *Applied Industrial Economics* (Cambridge: Cambridge University Press).

Pickover, C. A. (1996) *Fractal Horizons: The Future Use of Fractals* (New York: St. Martin's Press).

Piore, M. J. and Sabel, C. F. (1984) *The Second Industrial Divide: Possibilites for Prosperity* (New York: Basic Books).

— and — (1989) *Das Ende der Massenproduktion* [*The end of mass production* (Frankfurt: Fischer).

Pirsig, R. M. (1974) *Zen And the Art of Motorcycle Maintenance* (London: Corgi).

Pitelis, C. and Sudgen, R. (1991) 'On the Theory of the Transnational Firm', in: Pitelis, C. and Sudgen, R. (Eds.) *The Nature of the Transnational Firm* (London: Routledge), pp. 9–16.

Pohl, M. (Ed.) (1990) *Japan 1989/90: Politik und Wirtschaft* [*Japan 1989/1990: politics and economics*] (Hamburg: Institut für Asienkunde).

Poirier, C. C. (1999) *Advanced Supply Chain Management: How to Build a Sustained Competition* (Berrett-Koehler).

Popcorn, F. (1993) *The Popcorn Report* (Munich: Heyne).

Popham, P. (1986) *Japan* (Hong Kong: CFW).

Popper, K. R. (1966) *Logik der Forschung* (Tübingen: J. C. B. Mohr) [*Logic of Scientifc Discovery* (Routledge, 1992)].

— (1974) 'Die Normalwissenschaften und ihren Gefahren' [Normal science and its dangers], in: Lakatos, I. (Ed.) *Kritik und Erkenntnisfortschritt* [*Critique and epistemological progress*] (Braunschweig: Viehweg), pp. 51–84.

Porter, M. E. (1980) *Competitive Strategy* (New York: Free Press).

— (1986) *Wettbewerbsvorteile* [*Competitive Strategy*] (Frankfurt: Campus).

— (1989) *The Competitive Advantage of Nations* (Tagungsbeitrag: International Competitiveness of Switzerland, Basle, December).

— (1989) 'Einführung: Der Wettbewerb auf globalen Märkten: Ein Rahmenkonzept' [Introduction: global competition: a basic framework], in: Porter, M. E. (Ed.) *Globaler Wettbewerb: Strategien der neuen Internationalisierung* [*Global competition: strategies of a new internationalization*] (Wiesbaden: Gabler), pp. 1–69.

— (1990) *The Competitive Advantage of Nations* (New York: Free Press).

— and Fuller, B. (1986) 'Coalitions and Global Strategy', in: Porter, M. E. (Ed.) *Competition in Global Industries* (Cambridge, MA: Harvard Business School Press), pp. 315–43.

Portoghesi, P. (1982) *After Modern Architecture* (New York: Rizzoli).
— (1983) *The Postmodern* (New York: Rizzoli).
Postman, N. (1999) *Building a Bridge to the 18th Century: How the Past can Improve our Future* (New York: Knopf).
Powell, B. (1991) 'Sayonara, America', *Newsweek*, August, pp. 16–17.
Preskill, H. and Torres, R. T. (1998) *Evaluative Inquiry of Learning in Organizations* (New York: Sage).
Prestovitz, C. V. (1989) *Trading Places* (New York: Basic Books).
Preusse, H. G. (1990) 'Ist die Frage nach der Wettbewerbsfähigkeit einer Volkswirtschaft überholt?' [Is the question: What is the competitiveness if a nation outdated?], *Aussenwirtschaft*, **1**, pp. 81–103.
Price, J. (1996) *Japan Works: Power and Paradox in Postwar Industrial Relations* (Cornell, NY: University Press).
Pries, L. (1999) *Auf dem Weg zu Global operierenden Konzernen? [On the Way to Globally Operating Conglomerates?]* (Hampp).
Prime Minister's Office (1991) *Survey on National Life Style* (Tokyo: Government Printing Office).
Puhr, K. M. (1992) 'Postmodernism for High School Students', *English Journal*, **1**, pp. 64–7.
Putterman, L. and Kroszner, R. (1996) *The Economic Nature of the Firm* (Cambridge: Cambridge University Press).
Pye, L. W. (1989) 'Das japanische Rätsel: Die Verbindung von Wettbewerb und Konsens' [The Japanese enigma: the connex of competition and consensus], in: Menzel, U. (Ed.) *Im Schatten des Siegers*, vol. 1 *[In the shadow of the winner]* (Frankfurt: Suhrkamp), pp. 41–75.
Pyle, K. B. (1987) 'The Pursuit of a Grand Design: Nakasone Between the Past and the Future', in: Society of Japanese Studies (Ed.) *The Trade Crisis – How will Japan respond* (Seattle, WA: Society of Japanese Studies), pp. 9–83.
— (1989) 'Die Zukunft des japanischen Nationalcharakters' [The future of the Japanese national character] in: Menzel, U. (Ed.) *Im Schatten des Siegers*, vol. 3 *[In the shadow of the winner]* (Frankfurt: Suhrkamp), pp. 146–96.
Radner, R. (1975) 'A Behavioral Model of Cost Reduction', *Bell Journal of Economics*, **6**, pp. 196–216.
— (1981) 'Monitoring Cooperative Agreements in a Repeated Principal-Agent Relationship', *Econometrica*, **9**, pp. 1127–48.
Rahula, W. (1978) *Zen and the Taming of the Bull* (London: Fraser).
Raja, T. and Sarup, M. (1996) *Identity, Culture and the Postmodern World* (Atlanta, GA: University of Georgia Press).
Ramonet, I. (1998) *Die neuen Herren der Welt. Globale Politik an der Jahrtausendwende [The New Masters of the World]* (Zürich: Rotpunktverlag).
Rapaport, C. (1991) 'Why Japan keeps on Winning', *Fortune*, July, pp. 44–9.
Rasmussen, E. (1989) *Games and Information: An Introduction to Game Theory* (Oxford: Blackwell).
Ratti, O. and Westbrook, A. (1973) *Secrets of the Samurai* (Tokyo: Tuttle),
Raulet, G. (1983) 'La fin de la raison dans l'histoire' [The end of reason in history], *Revue Canadienne de Philosophie*, **12**, pp. 631–46.
— (1984) 'Modernes et postmodernes' [The moderns and the postmoderns], in: Raulet, G. (Ed.) *Weimar ou l'explosion de la modernité [Weimar or the explosion of modernity]* (Paris: Minuit), pp. 303–23.
— (1984) 'From Modernity as a One-Way Street to Postmodernity as a Dead End', *New German Critique*, **33**, pp. 27–63.

— (1987) 'Singuläre Geschichten und pluralistische Ratio' [Singular stories and pluralistic reason], in: Le Rider, J. and Raulet, G. (Eds.) *Verabschiedung der Postmoderne* [*Good-byes to the postmodern*] (Tübingen: Narr), pp. 275–92.

— (1988) 'Die neue Utopie' [The new utopia], in: Frank, M., Raulet, G. and Reijen, W. v. (Eds.) *Die Frage nach dem Subjekt* [*The question for the subject*] (Frankfurt: Suhrkam), pp. 283–316.

Reddies, B. (1989) *Der Recruit Skandal in Japan: Modernisierungskrise einer Wirtschaftsmacht* [*The Recruit scandal in Japan: crisis of modernization*] (Tokyo: OAG).

Reese-Schäfer, W. (1989) 'Vom Erhabenen zum Sublimen ist es nur ein Schritt' [From the noble to the sublime is sometimes just a step], in: Reese-Schäfer, W. and Taurek, B. H. F. (Eds.) *Jean-François Lyotard* (Cuxhaven: Junghans), pp. 169–83.

Rehfeld, J. E. (1994) *Alchemy of a Leader: Combining Western and Japanese Management Skills to Transform Your Company* (New York: Wiley).

Reich, R. (1983) *The Next American Frontier* (New York: New York Times Book).

— (1983) 'Beyond Free Trade', *Foreign Affairs*, 1, pp. 773–804.

— and Mankin, E. D. (1986) 'Joint Ventures with Japan give Away our Future', *Harvard Business Review*, 3, 78–86.

Reid, T. R. (1992) 'Tokyo Officials call U.S. "Subcontractor" to Japanese Economy', *International Herald Tribune*, January.

— (1999) *Confucius Lives Next Door* (New York: Random House).

Reijen, W. v. (1987) 'Einleitung [Introduction]', in: Kamper, D. and Reijen, W. v. (Eds.) *Die unvollendete Vernunft* [*The incomplete reason*] (Frankfurt: Suhrkamp), pp. 1–36.

— (1987) 'Miss Marx, Terminals und Grands Récits oder: Kratzt Habermas, wo es nicht juckt?' [Miss Marx terminals and grand narrations: is Habermas scratching where it does not itch?] in: Kamper, D. and Reijen, W. v. (Eds.) *Die unvollendete Vernunft* [*The incomplete reason*] (Frankfurt: Suhrkamp), pp. 536–69.

Reischauer, E. O. (1965) *The United States and Japan* (Cambridge, MA: Harvard University Press).

— (1991) *The Japanese Today: Change and Continuity* (Tokyo: Tuttle).

— (1992) *The United States and Japan in 1991* (Washington, DC: Center for East Asian Studies.

— and Craig, A. M. (1978) *Japan: Tradition and Transition* (Boston, MA: Houghton Mifflin).

Reps, P. (1989) *Zen Flesh, Zen Bones* (Tokyo: Tuttle).

Reve, T. (1990) 'The Firm as a Nexus of Internal and External Contracts', in: Aoki, M. and Gustafson, B. (Eds.) *The Firm as a Nexus of Treaties* (London: Sage), pp. 133–61.

Reyes, A. (1998) *Asia's 1000 Top Blue Chip Companies* (New York: Wiley).

Richards, D. J. and Pearson, G. (1998) *The Ecology of Industry: Sectors and Linkages* (Washington, DC: National Academy Press).

Richardson, B. M. and Flanagan, S. C. (1984) *Politics in Japan* (Boston, MA: Little & Brown).

Riordan, M. and Williamson, O. E. (1985) 'Asset Specificity and Economic Organization', *International Journal of Industrial Organization*, 3, pp. 365–78.

Robb, S. (1990) *Japan's New Imperialism* (London: Macmillan Press).

Roberts, J. G. (1989) *Mitsui: Three Centuries of Japanese Business* (New York: Weatherhill).

Robertson, P. L. (1999) *Authority and Control in Modern Industry* (London: Routledge).

Rodrik, D. (1999) *The New Global Economy and Developing Countries: Making Openness Work* (London: Overseas Development Council).

Rohlen, T. (1992) 'Learning: The Mobilization of Knowledge in the Japanese Political Economy' in: Kumon, S. and Rosovsky, H. (Eds.) *The Political Economy of Japan*, vol. 3 (Stanford, CA: Stanford University Press), pp. 321–63.

Rojek, C., Turner, B. S. and Lyotard, J. F. (1998) *The Politics of Jean Francois: Justice and Political Theory* (London: Routledge).

Rokkan, S. (1968) *Comparative Research across Cultures and Nations* (Den Haag: Mouton).
Romme, G. (1990) 'The Formation of Firm Strategy as Self-Organization', in: Freeman, C. and Soete, L. (Eds.) *New Explorations in the Economics of Technical Change* (London: Pinter), pp. 38–53.
Röpke, J. (1989) 'Vom Nachzügler zum Pionier' [From latecomer to pioneer], in: Menzel, U. (Ed.) *Im Schatten des Siegers*, vol. 3 [*In the shadow of the winner*] (Frankfurt: Suhrkamp), pp. 29–55.
Rorty, R. (1972) 'The World well lost', *Journal of Philosophy*, **69**, 649–65.
— (1979) *Philosophy and the Mirror of Nature* (Princeton, NJ: Princeton University Press).
— (1980) 'Philosophy as a Kind of Writing', in: Rorty, R. *Consequences of Pragmatism* (Princeton, NJ: Princeton University Press), pp. 89–109.
— (1982) *Consequences of Pragmatism* (Minneapolis, MN: University of Minnesota Press).
— (1982) 'Hermeneutics, General Studies, and Teaching', *Synergos Seminars: Selected Papers*, **2**, 1–15.
— (1985) 'Habermas and Lyotard on Postmodernity', in: Bernstein, R. J. (Ed.) *Habermas and Modernity* (Cambridge, MA: Massachusetts Institute of Technology Press), pp. 161–75.
— (1989) *Contingency, Irony, and Solidarity* (Cambridge: Cambridge University Press).
— (1998) *Truth and Progress* (Cambridge: Cambridge University Press).
— (1999) *Achieving Our Country: Leftist Thought in Twentieth Century America* (Cambridge, MA: Harvard University Press).
— (1999) *Philosophy and Social Hope* (London: Penguin).
Ross, D. N. (1991) 'Keiretzu: Global Managers' Unseen Rivals' in: Prasad, S. B. and Peterson, R. B. (Eds.) *Advances in International Comparative Management: A Research Annual* (London: JAI), pp. 20–23.
Rostow, W. W. (1971) *The Stages of Economic Growth* (Cambridge, MA: Harvard University Press).
Roszak, T. (1969) *The Making of a Counter Culture: Reflections on the Technocratic Society and its Youthful Opposition* (New York: Anchor).
Rothleder, D. (1999) *The Work of Friendship: Rorty, His Critics, and the Project of Solidarity* (Albany, NY: SUNY Press).
Rowley, A. (1991) 'Odd Man Out', *Far Eastern Economic Review*, October, p. 57.
Rowntree, L. (1999) *Diversity Amid Globalization: World Regions, Environment, Development* (Englewood Cliffs, NJ: Prentice Hall).
Rudlin, P. (2000) *The History of Mitsubishi Corporation in London* (London: Routledge).
Ruffin, R. J. and Rassekh, F. (1986) 'The Role of Foreign Direct Investment in US Capital Outflows', *American Economic Review*, **76**, pp. 1126–30.
Rugman, A. (1980) 'Internalization as a General Theory of Foreign Direct Investment', *Weltwirtschaftliches Archiv*, **2**, 365–79.
— (1981) *Inside the Multinationals – The Economics of Internal Markets* (New York: Columbia University Press.
— (1982) *New Theories of the MNE* (London: Croom Helm).
Ruhloff, J. (1990) 'Widerstreitende statt harmonische Bildung – Grundzüge eines postmodernen pädagogischen Konzepts' [Education rather combatant than harmonic: principles of a postmodern educational concept] in: Bering, K. (Ed.) *Wie postmodern ist die Postmoderne?* [*Just how postmodern is postmodernity?*] (Essen: Die blaue Eule), pp. 25–39.
Sackman, R. B. (1998) *Achieving the Promise of Information Technology: Introducing the Transformational Project Paradigm* (Project Management Institute).
Sacks, P. (1996) *Generation X Goes to College: An Eye-Opening Account of Teaching in Postmodern America* (Open Court).
Safdie, M. (1988) 'Architectural Trends', *New York Times*, May.

Saito, K. (1988) *Meien wo aruku: Muromachi jidai* [*Japanese Gardens: the Muromachi Period*] (Tokyo: Mainichi Shimbunsha).

Sakai, N. (1989) 'Modernity and its Critique', in: Miyoshi, M. and Harootunian, H. D. (Eds.) *Postmodernism and Japan* (Durham, NC: Duke University Press), pp. 93–122.

Sakaiya, T. (1991) *The Knowledge-Value Revolution: A History of the Future* (Tokyo: Kodansha).

Sakudo, Y. (1980) 'Comment', in: Nakagawa, K. (Ed.) *Strategy and Structure of Big Business* (Tokyo: University of Tokyo Press), pp. 42–4.

Salanti, A. (1987) 'Falsificationism and Fallibilism as Epistemic Foundations of Economics: A Critical View', *Kyklos*, **40**, pp. 368–92.

Sangyo Kozo Shingikai [Committee for Industrial Structure] (1971) *Chukan toshin: Nanajuendai no tsusho sangyo seisaku* [*Interim report: trade and industrial policies in the Seventies*] (Tokyo: MITI).

— (1980) *Hachijuendai no tsusho seisaku bijon* [*A vision of industrial structures in the Eighties*] (Tokyo: MITI).

— (1990) *Kyujuendai no tsusho seisaku bijon* [*A vision of industrial structures in the Nineties*] (Tokyo: MITI).

Sansom, G. B. (1952) *Japan – A Short Cultural History* (London: Cresset).

Sapelli, G. (1990) 'A Historical Typology of Group Enterprises', in: Sugarman, D. and Teubner, G. (Eds.) *Regulating Corporate Groups in Europe* (Baden-Baden: Nomos), pp. 193–216.

Sardar, Z. (1991) 'Total Recall: Aliens, "Others" and Amnesia in Postmodernist Thought', *Futures*, **3**, pp. 189–204.

Sartorius v. Waltershausen, A. (1907) *Das volkswirtschaftliche System der Kapitalanlage im Auslande* [*The economics of foreign direct investments*] (Berlin: Reimer).

Sarup, M. (1988) *An Introductory Guide to Poststructuralism and Postmodernism* (Hemel Hempstead: Wheatsheaf)

Sasaki-Smith, M. (1990) *Japan's Leasing Industry* (Tokyo: Credit Suisse Japan).

— (1990) *Japanese Industrial Policy in the 1980s* (Tokyo: MS).

Sassen, S. (1996) *Losing Control?: Sovereignty in an Age of Globalization* (New York: Columbia University Press).

Sassower, R. (1995) *Cultural Collisions: Postmodern Technoscience* (London: Routledge).

— and Ogaz, C. P. (1992) 'Philosophical Hierarchies and Lyotard's Dichotomies', *Philosophy Today*, **2**, pp. 153–61.

Saucier, P. (1989) 'New Conditions for Competition between Japanese and European Firms in the Post-1992 Unified Market' (Genève: Université de Genève Working Paper).

Sauer-Thompson, G. and Wayne Smith, J. (1996) *Beyond Economics: Postmodernity, Globalization and National Sustainability* (London: Avebury).

Saunders, C. T. (1987) *Industrial Policies and Structural Change* (New York: St. Martin's Press).

Savage, C. M. (1990) *Fifth Generation Management: Integrating Enterprises through Human Networking* (Bedford, MA: Digital).

Sawyer, M. C. (1981) *The Economics of Industries and Firms* (London: Croom Helm).

Sazaki, N. (1990) *Management and Industrial Structure in Japan* (Oxford: Pergamon).

Schaede, U. (1990) *Der neue japanische Kapitalmarkt* [*The new Japanese capital market*] (Wiesbaden: Gabler).

Schaumann, W. (1992) ' "The Book of Tea" oder: Das schöne Japan', Paper presented at 3rd OAG Japanologist Conference, Tokyo, March.

Schepe, D. (1988) *Oskar Schlemmer: Das Triadische Ballett und die Bauhausbühne* [*Oskar Schlemmer: the triad ballet: and the Bauhaus*] (Berlin: Schriftenreihe der Akademie der Künste).

Scherer, F. M. (1986) 'On the Current State of Knowledge in Industrial Organization', in: De Jong, H. W. and Shepherd, W. G. (Eds.) *Mainstreams in Industrial Organization* (Dordrecht: Nijhoff), pp. 5–22.

Schinzinger, R. (1983) *Japanisches Denken* [*Japanese thinking*] (Tokyo: OAG).
Schirmacher, W. (1989) *Schopenhauer und die Postmoderne* [*Schopenhauer and the postmodern*] (Graz: Passagen).
Schmid, G. (1989) 'Geschichtsbilder und die unendliche Schreibbarkeit' [Views on history and the neverending writing], in: Pries, C. (Ed.) *Das Erhabene* [*The noble*] (Weinheim: VCH), pp. 293–310.
Schmidheini, S. (1992) *Kurswechsel* [*Changing directions*] (Munich: Artemis und Winkler).
Schmidt, B. (1989) 'Die Postmoderne wird sich nicht vollziehen' [The postmodern will not happen for long], in: Burtscher, P. and Donner. W. (Eds.) *Postmoderne – Philosophem und Arabeske* [*Postmodernity: philosophical topic and arabesque*] (Frankfurt: Lang), pp. 100–19.
Schmiegelow, M. (1989) 'Schluss' [Postscript], in: Schmiegelow, M. (Ed.) *Japans Antwort auf Krise und Wandel in der Weltwirtschaft* [*Japan's answer to crisis and change in the global economy*] (Hamburg: McGraw-Hill), pp. 317–19.
— (1989) 'Zielerreichung' [Did we reach the objective?], in: Schmiegelow, M. (Ed.) *Japans Antwort auf Krise und Wandel in der Weltwirtschaft* [*Japan's answer to crisis and change in the global economy*] (Hamburg: McGraw-Hill), pp. 360–75.
Schmitt, U. (1992) 'Die Einsamkeit des Japaners in der Fremde' [The loneliness of a Japanese in foreign countries], *Frankfurter Allgemeine Zeitung*, November.
Schneidewind, D. (1986) 'Das Unternehmen im Markt' [The enterprise in its market], in: Herold, R. (Ed.) *Das Industrieunternehmen in Japan* [*The Japanese enterprise*] (Berlin: Schmidt), pp. 163–82.
— (1991) *Das japanische Unternehmen – Uchi no kaisha* [*The Japanese enterprise*] (Berlin: Springer).
Schonberger, R. J. (1982) *Japanese Manufacturing Techniques* (New York: Free Press).
Schönherr, H. M. (1989) *Die Technik und die Schwäche* [*Technology and weakness*] (Graz: Passagen).
Schopenhauer, A. (1975) *Gesammelte Werke*, vol. 4 [*Collected works*] (Frankfurt: Kremer).
Schrag, C. O. (1986) *Communicative Praxis and the Space of Activity* (Bloomington, IN: Indiana University Press).
Schumpeter, J. (1964) *Theorie der wirtschaftlichen Entwicklung* (Berlin: Duncker & Humblot) [*Theory of Economic Development* (Transaction Pub.)].
Schuster, H. G. (1989) *Deterministic Chaos* (Weinheim: VCH).
Schütte, C. (1993) 'Drohung erlaubt' [Threat is allowed], *Wirtschaftswoche*, April, pp. 46–9.
Schütz, A. (1981) *Theorie der Lebensformen* [*Theory of lifestyles*] (Frankfurt: Suhrkamp).
Schwalbe, H. (1985) *Japan* (Munich: Prestel).
Schwarz, S. (1990) 'Wettbewerbspotentiale politischer Kulturen am Beispiel der Vereinigten Staaten und Japan' [The competitive potential of political cultures: case study Japan – USA] (St. Gallen: Hochschule St. Gallen, Diss.).
Schwengel, H. (1988) 'Nach dem Subjekt oder nach der Politik fragen' [To ask for the subject or for the object], in: Frank, M. (Ed.) *Die Frage nach dem Subjekt* [*Searching for the subject*] (Frankfurt: Suhrkamp), pp. 317–46.
Scobel, G. (1989) 'Chaos, Selbstorganisation und das Erhabene' [Chaos, Self-organization and the noble], in: Preis, C. (Ed.) *Das Erhabene* [*The noble*] (Weinheim: VCH), pp. 277–94.
Scott, B. (1982) 'Can Industry Survive the Welfare State', *Harvard Business Review*, September, pp. 70–84.
Seidman, S. (1998) *Contested Knowledge: Social Theory in the Postmodern Era* (London: Blackwell).
Seifert, W. (1989) 'Wirtschaftsorganisation und politische Macht' [Industrial organization and political power] in: Menzel, U. (Ed.) *Im Schatten des Siegers*, vol. 3 [*In the shadow of the winner*] (Frankfurt: Suhrkamp), pp. 134–69.

392 Bibliography

Seifritz, W. (1987) *Wachstum, Rückkoppelung und Chaos* [*Growth, feedback and chaos*] (Munich: Hanser).
Seitz, B. (1990) 'The Identity of the Subject, after Sartre: An Identity Marked by the Denial of Identity', *Philosophy Today*, **4**, pp. 362–73.
Seitz, K. (1991) *Die japanisch–amerikanische Herausforderung: Deutschlands Hoch-Technologie-Industrien kämpfen ums Überleben* [*The Japanese–American challenge: Germany's high-tech industries fight for survival*] (Munich: Bonn Aktuell).
Sekiguchi, S. (1989) 'Die japanische Industriepolitik: Das Zusammenspiel zwischen Politik und dualistischer Struktur', in: Schmiegelow, M. (Ed.) *Japans Antwort auf Krise und Wandel in der Weltwirtschaft* [*Japan's answer to crisis and change in the global economy*] (Hamburg: McGraw-Hill), pp. 242–68.
Semsch, K. (1999) 'Prolegomena zu einer texttheoretischen Diskurslogik zwischen Moderne und Postmoderne' [Prolegomena for a text-based Logic of the Discourse: Between Modern and Postmodern], Paper presented at: Postmodern Perspectives: Second International Graduate and Postgraduate Conference, Erlangen, November 19–21.
Sender, H. (1992) 'The Humbling of Nomura', *Institutional Investor*, **1**, pp. 45–52.
Sennett, R. (1998) *The Corrrosion of Character: The Personal Consequence of Work in the New Capitalism* (New York: Norton).
— (1998) *Der flexible Mensch. Die Kultur des neuen Kapitalismus* [*The Flexible Human. The Culture of the New Capitalism*] (Berlin: Berlin).
Servan-Schreiber, J. J. (1968) *Die amerikanische Herausforderung* [*The American challenge*] (Hamburg: Hoffmann & Campe).
Sethi, S. P. (1984) *The False Promise of the Japanese Miracle* (London: Pitman).
Shale, T. (1990) 'Reawakening the Sleeping Giant', *Euromoney*, **11**, pp. 14–23.
Shapiro, S. G. (1992) 'Teaching Modernism and Postmodernism in a Values Elective', *English Journal*, **1**, pp. 60–4.
Shepherd, W. G. (1986) 'On the Core Concepts of Industrial Economics', in: De Jong, H. W. and Shepherd, W. G. (Eds.) *Mainstreams in Industrial Organization* (Dordrecht: Nijhoff), pp. 23–67.
Shibagaki, K. (1985) *Zaibatzu* (Berlin: Schiller).
Shiga, N. (1990) *A Dark Nights Passing* (Tokyo: Kodansha).
Shimabukuro, Y. (1987) *Consensus Management in Japanese Industry* (Tokyo: ISS).
Shimano, T. (1980) 'Cultural Conflict: Japan and South East Asian Countries' (Tokyo: Gakushuin University Occasional Papers 11).
Shimizu, R. (1986) *Top Management in Japanese Firms* (Tokyo: Chikura Shobo).
— (1989) *The Japanese Business Success Factors* (Tokyo: Chikura Shobo).
Shimizu, T. (1970) 'Strukturanalyse der japanischen Verbundunternehmung [Structural analysis of the Japanese connected company] (Köln: Universität Köln, Diss.).
Shimomura, T. (1990) 'Mentalität und Logik der Japaner' [Mentality and logic of the Japanese] in: Ohashi, R. (Ed.) *Die Philosophie der Kyoto-Schule* [*The philosophy of the Kyoto school*] (Freiburg, Br.: Alber), pp. 369–85.
Shinohara, M. (1976) 'Issetsu: Nihon kabushiki kaisha-ron' [Against the discussion on Japan Inc.], *The Economist* [Japan. edition], November, pp. 114.
— (1982) *Industrial Growth, Trade, and Dynamic Patterns in the Japanese Economy* (Tokyo: University of Tokyo Press).
Siegel, D. (1999) *Futurize your Enterprise* (New York: Wiley).
Sim, S. (1996) *Jean-Francois Lyotard* (Hempstead: Wheatsheaf).
— (1999) *Derrida and the End of History* (Totem Books).
— (1999) *The Routledge Critical Dictionary of Postmodern Thought* (London: Routledge).
Simon, D. R. and Henderson, J. H. (1997) *Private Troubles and Public Issues: Social Problems in the Postmodern Era* (San Diego, CA: Harcourt Brace).

Simon, H. A. (1959) 'Theories in Decision Making in Economics and Behavioral Sciences', in: Mansfield, E. (Ed.) *Microeconomics* (New York: Macmillan), pp. 85–98.

— (1961) *Administrative Behavior* (New York: Macmillan Press).

— (1986) 'The Failure of Armchair Economics', *Challenge*, **6**, pp. 18–25.

Singer, K. (1990) *Mirror, Sword and Jewel: The Geometry of Japanese Life* (Tokyo: Kodansha).

Siu, R. G. H. (1960) 'Zen and Science', in: Wilson-Ross: N. (Ed.) *The World of Zen* (New York: Vintage), pp. 308–17.

Slemon, S. (1989) 'Modernism's last Post', *Ariel*, **10**, pp. 3–18.

Smith, B. (1988) 'Value without Truth-Value', in: Fekete, J. (Ed.) *Life After Postmodernism* (Basingstoke: Macmillan Press), pp. 1–22.

Smith, C. (1987) 'Corporate Identity Crisis', *Far Eastern Economic Review*, December, p. 118.

Smith, L. (1991) 'Why Japan's Surplus is Rising', *Fortune*, December, pp. 79–81.

Smith, R. J. (1992) 'The Cultural Context of Japanese Political Economy', in: Kumon, S. and Rosovsky, H. (Eds.) *The Political Economy of Japan*, vol. 3 (Stanford, CA: Stanford University Press), pp. 13–31.

Snyder, J. R. (1990) 'A Study in Canadian Postmodernism' (Thunder Bay: University of Western Ontario, Diss).

Sobchack, V. (1991) 'All-Theorien: Reflexion über Chaos, Fraktale und die Differenz, die zu Indifferenz führt' in: Gumbrecht, H. U. and Pfeiffer, K. L. (Eds.) *Paradoxien, Dissonanzen, Zusammenbrüche: Situationen offener Epistemologie* [*Paradoxa, dissonances, implosions: situations of open epistemology*] (Frankfurt: Suhrkamp), pp. 809–22.

Sogo Kenkyu Kaihatsu Kiko (1978) *Jiten: Nihon no kadai* [*Encyclopedia: Japan's preparations for the 21st Century*] (Tokyo: Gakuyo Shobo).

Sokal, A. and Bricmont, J. (1998) *Intellectual Impostures* (London: Profile Books).

Sombart, W. (1927) *Die Ordnung des Wirtschaftslebens* [*The order of business life*] (Berlin: Springer).

Sonntag, S. (1967) *Against Interpretation* (London: Eyre & Spottiswoode).

Soper, K. (1991) 'Postmodern and its Discontents', *Feminist Review*, Autumn, pp. 97–109.

Spaemann, R. (1983)' Unter welchen Umständen kann man noch von Fortschritt sprechen?' [Under which circumstances can it be called progress?], in: Spaemann, R. *Philosophische Essays* [*Philosophical essays*] (Stuttgart: Reclam), pp. 130–50.

Spiethoff, A. (1932) 'Die allgemeine Volkswirtschaftslehre als geschichtliche Theorie' [General economics as historical theory], *Schmollers Jahrbuch*, **2**, pp. 910–23.

Sproull, L. and Kiesler, S. (1991) *Connections: New Ways of Working in the Networked Organization* (Cambridge, MA: MIT Press).

Spulber, D. (1998) *Market Microstructure: Intermediaries and the Theory of the Firm* (Cambridge: Cambridge University Press).

Staehle, W. H. (1973) *Organisation und Führung soziotechnischer Systeme* [*Organization and management of socio-technical systems*] (Stuttgart: Haupt).

Stacey, J. (1996) *In the Name of the Family: Rethinking Family Values in the Postmodern Age* (New York: Beacon).

Stam, R. (1988) 'Mikhail Bakthin and the Left Cultural Critique', in: Kaplan, A. E. (Ed.) *Postmodernism and its Discontents* (London: Verso), pp. 116–45.

Steel, D. (1983) 'Review Article: Government and Industry in Britain', *British Journal of Political Science*, **12**, pp. 449–503.

Stegmüller, W. (1973) *Probleme und Resultate der Wissenschaftstheorie und analytischen Philosophie*, vol. 4 [*Problems and results of methodology and analytical philosophy*] (Berlin: Springer).

Sterman, J. D. (1988) 'Deterministic Chaos in an Experimental System' (Cambridge, MA: MIT Working Paper 2040).

Stevenson, H. H. and Harmeling, S. (1989) 'Enterpreneurial Management's Need For a More Chaotic Theory' (Cambridge, MA: Harvard Business School Working Paper 61).

Stewart, C. (1989) 'Die japanische Friedensbewegung: Zersplitterung statt Solidarität' [The Japanese peace movement: disintegration not solidarity], in: Hackner, G. (Ed.) *Die anderen Japaner* [*The other Japanese*] (Munich: Iudicium), pp. 94–118.

Steward, J. (1991) 'A Postmodern Look at Traditional Communication Postulates', *Western Journal of Speech Communication*, **4**, pp. 354–80.

Stockman, F. N. (1985) *Networks of Corporate Power: A Comparison of Ten Countries* (Oxford: Blackwell).

Stone, L. L. (1997) *The Growth of Intra-Industry Trade: New Trade Patterns in a Changing Global Economy* (New York: Garland).

Stopford, J. M. and Dunning, J. H. (1982) *The World Directory of Multinational Enterprises* (London: Macmillan).

Streek, W. (1984) *Industrial Relations in West Germany* (London: Heinemann).

Streib, F. (1993) *Wirtschaftsstrategien Japans und der USA im asiatisch-pazifischen Raum* [*Economic strategies of the US and Japan in the Asian-pacific sphere*] (Tokyo: OAG Vortrag).

Structural Impediments Initiative Talks 1991 (Ed.) *1992: Opinions on the Keiretzu Issue* (Washington, DC: US Government Printing Office).

Sugarman, D. (1990) 'Corporate Groups in Europe: Governance, Industrial Organization, and Efficiency in a Post-Modern World' in: Sugarman, D. and Teubner, G. (Eds.) *Regulating Corporate Groups in Europe* (Baden Baden: Nomos), pp. 13–66.

Sullivan, W. (1987) 'Japan, Shredding Role of Imitator, is Emerging as a Scientific Pioneer', *New York Times*, September.

Sumi, A. (1998) *Japanese Industrial Transplants in the United States: Organizational Practices and Relations of Power* (New York: Garland).

Suntum, U. v. (1986) 'Internationale Wettbewerbsfähigkeit einer Volkswirtschaft – Ein sinnvolles wirtschafts-politisches Ziel?' [International competitiveness – a sensible goal for economic policy?], *Zeitschrift für Wirtschafts- und Sozialwissenschaften*, **106**, pp. 495–507.

Suzuki, D. T. (1960) 'The Koan', in: Wilson-Ross N. (Ed.) *The World of Zen* (New York: Vintage), pp. 48–56.

— (1972) *Living By Zen* (London: Rider).

— (1987) 'An Interpretation of Zen Experience', in: Moore, C. A. and Morris, A. (Eds.) *The Japanese Mind* (Honolulu, HI: University of Hawaii Press), pp. 122–42.

— (1988) *Zen and Japanese Culture* (Tokyo: Tuttle).

Suzuki, S. (1990) 'Ausblick über die europäische Geschichte' [Survey of the European history], in: Ohashi, R. (Ed.) *Die Philosophie der Kyoto- Schule* [*The philosophy of the Kyoto school*] (Freiburg: Alber), pp. 391–417.

— (1990) *Zen Mind Beginner's Mind* (Tokyo: Weatherhill).

Suzuki, T. (1990) *Eine verschlossene Sprache* [*A tight language*] (Munich: Iudicium).

— (1991) *Words in Context: A Japanese Perspective on Language and Culture* (Tokyo: Kodansha).

Swindal, J. C. (1999) *Reflection Revisited: Jurgen Habermas's Discursive Theory of the Truth* (New York: Fordham University Press).

Swirski, P. (1992) 'Playing a Game of Ontology: a Postmodern Reading of the Futurological Congress', *Extrapolation*, **1**, pp. 32–41.

Tachibanaki, T. and Kenkyujo R. S. (1998) *Who Runs Japanese Business? Management and Motivation in the Firm* (Aldershot: Elgar).

Tadashi, O., Latarin, M. and Rappe, G. (Eds.) (1998) Interkulturelle Philosophie und Phänomenologie in Japan [Intercultural Philosophy and Phenomenology in Japan] (Munich: Iudicium).

Takamiya, M. (1985) 'The Degree of Organizational Centralization in Multinational Corporations' in: Takamiya, S. and Thurley, K. *Japanese Emerging Multinationals* (Tokyo: Tokyo University Press), pp. 35–49.

— (1985) 'Conclusions and Policy Implications', in: Takamiya, S. and Thurley, K. *Japanese Emerging Multinationals* (Tokyo: Tokyo University Press), pp. 183–201.

Takamiya, S. (1977) 'Organisation des japanischen Aussenhandels und die Bedeutung der Grosshandels-gesellschaften' [Organization of foreign trade and the importance of the trading houses] in: Ichihara, K. and Takamiya, S. (Eds.) *Die japanische Unternehmung – Strukturwandlungen in einer wachsenden Wirtschaft* [*The Japanese enterprise – structural changes in a growing economy*] (Opladen: Westdeutscher Verlag), pp. 183–94.

— (1977) 'Entwicklung des Management-Systems der japanischen Unternehmungen' [Development of management systems of Japanese enterprise] in: Ichihara, K. and Takamiya, S. (Eds.) *Die japanische Unternehmung – Strukturwandlungen in einer wachsenden Wirtschaft* [*The Japanese enterprise – structural changes in a growing economy*] (Opladen: Westdeutscher Verlag), pp. 299–319.

Takashi, K. (1979) *Dokumento Tsusan-sho I: Shinkanryo no jidai* [*Documentary on MITI part I: the era of the new bureaucrats*] (Kyoto: Kenkyu Jo).

Takuan, S. (1990) *The Unfettered Mind* (Tokyo: Kodansha).

Tanaka, K. (1972) *Nihon retto kaizo ron* [*Concept to restructure the Japanese archipelago*] (Tokyo: Nikkan Kogyo Shinbunsha).

Tanaka, S. (1992) 'Konichi no Nihon no seji/keizai ni mirareru Nihon no bigaku no kozai' [Influences of 'Japanese Esthetic' on business and politics in contemporary Japan], Paper presented at 3rd OAG Japanologist Conference, Tokyo, March.

Tanaka, Y. (1980) *Nantonaku, Kurisutaru* [*Somehow crystal*] (Tokyo: Bungei).

Tasker, P. (1987) *Inside Japan* (London: Sigwick & Jackson).

Taureck, B. H. F. (1990) 'Wo steht Lyotard?' [What position has Lyotard?] in: Reese-Schäfer, W. and Taureck, B. H. F. (Eds.) *Jean-François Lyotard* (Cuxhaven: Junghans), pp. 185–204.

Taylor, C. (1985) *Human Agency and Language* (Cambridge: Cambridge University Press.)

Teece, D. J. (1977) 'Technology Transfer by Multinational Firms: The Resource Cost of Transferring Technological Know How', *Economic Journal*, **87**, pp. 242–61.

Tetsuya Chikushi (1999) *News 23* (Tokyo: TV Tetsuya Chikushi).

Teubner, G. (1990) 'Unitas Multiplex: Corporate Governance in Group Enterprises', in: Sugarman, D. and Teubner, G. (Eds.) *Regulating Corporate Groups in Europe* (Baden Baden: Nomos), pp. 66–104.

Thakara, J. (1992) 'Japanische Designer-Hotelarchitektur' [Japanese designer hotel architecture], *Ambiente*, **6**, pp. 28–40.

Tharp, M. (1983) 'A Few Steps Further', *Far Eastern Economic Review*, March, p. 56.

Thayer, D. (1969) *How the Conservative Rule Japan* (Princeton, NJ: Princeton University Press).

Thomsen, C. W. (1992) 'Die Utopie der Städte' [Urban utopia], *Ambiente*, **9**, pp. 48–56.

Thomson, G. (1991) *Markets, Hierarchies, and Networks: The Coordination of Social Life* (London: Sage).

Thurow, L. (1999) *Creating Wealth* (Boston, MA: Brealey).

Tirole, J. (1986) 'Hierarchies and Bureaucracies', *Journal of Law, Economics, and Organization*, **2**, 181–214.

Toffler, A. (1970) *Future Shock* (New York: Bantam).

Togai, Y. (1980) 'Comments', in: Nakagawa, N. (Ed.) *Strategy and Structure of Big Business* (Tokyo: University of Tokyo Press), pp. 102–105.

Tominaga, K. (1977) 'Rolle des Wertsystems für die Industrialisierung Japans' [The role of value systems in the industrialization of Japan] in: Ichihara, K. and Takamiya, S. (Eds.) *Die japanische Unternehmung – Strukturwandlungen in einer wachsenden Wirtschaft* [*The Japanese enterprise – structural changes in a growing economy*] (Opladen: Westdeutscher Verlag), pp. 21–9.

Toulmin, S. (1972) *Human Understanding* (Princeton, NJ: Princeton University Press).

Tran, D. (1992) 'Securities Markets in Asia and Oceania' in: The Asean Securities' Analysts Council (Ed.) *Proceedings 1992* (Hong Kong: The Asean Securities' Analysts Council), pp. 239–310.

Tsuji, K. (1989) 'Entscheidungsfindung in der japanischen Regierung' [Decision making in the Japanese Government] in: Menzel, U. (Ed.) *Im Schatten des Siegers*, vol. 2 [*In the shadow of the winner*] (Frankfurt: Suhrkamp), pp. 256–75.

Tsutsui, W. M. (1998) *Manufacturing Ideology: Scientific Management in Twentieth-Century Japan* (Princeton, NJ: Princeton University Press).

Tsunoda, T. (1978) *Nihonjin no No* [*The Japanese's brain*] (Tokyo: Taishukan Shoten).

Tsurumi, Y. and Tsurumi, R. (1980) *Sogo Shosha: Engines of Export-Based Growth* (Montreal: Institute for Research on Public Policy).

Uekusa, K. (1999) 'Japan in the New Millennium', Paper presented at the Global Hedge Fund Conference, Tokyo, 29–30 November.

Ueno, H. (1976) 'Wagakumi sangyo seisaku no hasso to hyoka' [Japanese Economic Policy. Structure and Evaluation], *Kikan Riron Keizagaku* [*Economic studies quarterly*], 4, pp. 3–63.

Ulrich, P. (1986) *Transformation der ökonomischen Vernunft – Fortschrittsperspektiven der modernen Industriegesellschaft* [*Transformation of economic reasoning – perspectives for progress in modern industrial society*] (Bern: Haupt).

— and Hill, W. (1976) 'Wissenschaftstheoretische Grundlagen der Betriebswirtschaftslehre' [Methodological foundations of business administration], *Wirtschaftswissenschaftliches Studium*, 7, pp. 304–9 (Teil 1) and *Wirtschaftswissenschaftliches Studium*, 8, pp. 345–50 (Teil 2)).

UNCTAD (1993) *World Investment Report 1993* (Genève: UNCTAD).

Upham, F. K. (1989) 'Die gesetzliche und institutionelle Dynamik der japanischen Kartellpolitik', [Legal and institutional dynamics of Japanese cartel policy] in: Schmiegelow, M. (Ed.) *Japans Antwort auf Krise und Wandel in der Weltwirtschaft* [*Japan's answer to crisis and change in the global economy*] (Hamburg: McGraw-Hill), pp. 289–316.

Van Hoesel, R. (1999) *New Multinational Enterprises from Korea and Taiwan: Beyond Export-Led Growth* (London: Routledge).

Vattimo, G. (1987) *La fin de la modernité* (Paris: Editions du Seuil) [*The End of Modernity* (Johns Hopkins University, 1991)].

Venturi, R. (1988) 'Komplexität und Widerspruch in der Architektur' [Complexity and opposition in Architecture] in: Welsch, W. (Ed.) *Wege aus der Moderne* [*Escape from the modern*] (Weinheim: VCH), pp. 79–84.

Vernon, R. (1966) 'International Investment and International Trade in the Product Cycle', *Quarterly Journal of Economics*, 2, 190–207.

— (1977) 'Storm over the Multinationals: Problems and Prospects', *Foreign Affairs*, 1, 243–62.

— (1979) 'The Product Cycle Hypothesis in a New International Environment', *Oxford Bulletin of Economics and Statistics*, 4/41, 255–67.

— (1998) *In the Hurricane's Eye: The Troubled Prospects of Multinational Enterprises* (Boston: Harvard University Press).

Veseth, M. (1998) *Selling Globalization: The Myth of the Global Economy* (Oslo: Lynne Rienner).

Vester, H. G. (1989) 'Moderne – Postmoderne und Retour' [From modernity to postmodernity and back] in: Deutsch-Amerikanisches Institut Freiburg (Ed.) *Die Postmoderne: Ende der Avangarde oder Neubeginn* [*The postmodern – end of the Avant-garde or a new beginning*] (Eggingen: Isele), pp. 13–31.

Viner, J. (1931) 'Cost Curves and Supply Curves', *Zeitschrift für Nationalökonomie*, 3, pp. 23–46.

Vladislav, L. and Inozemtsev, V. L. (1998) *The Constitution of the Post-Economic State: Post Industrial Theories and Post-Economic Trends in the Contemporary World* (London: Ashgate).

Vogel, E. F. (1979) *Japan as Number One: Lessons for America* (Cambridge, MA: Harvard University Press).

Vondereau, R. (1992) 'Cultural Gap Experienced by a Gajin Engineer', *Mechanical Engineering-CIME*, 1, pp. 70–3.

Wagatsuma, H. (1984) *Heritage of Endurance* (Berkeley, CA: University of California).

Wagner, B. (1991) 'PostModerne oder PostFordismus' [Postmodernity or postfordism], in: Weimann, R., Gumbrecht, H. U. and Wagner, B. (Eds.) *Postmoderne – Globale Differenz* [*Postmodernity – global difference*] (Frankfurt: Suhrkamp), pp. 110–20.

Wagstyl, S. (1992) 'Sensitivity over Surplus', *Financial Times*, July.

Wakayama, T. (1989) 'The Implementation and Effectiveness of MITI's Administrative Guidance' in: Wilks, S. and Wright, M. (Eds.) *Comparing Government-Industry Relations* (Oxford: Oxford University Press), pp. 211–32.

Waragai, T. (1989) 'Neue Entwicklungen der Analyse industrieller Verflechtungen in Japan und in der Bundesrepublik Deutschland' [Recent developments in the analysis of business networks in Japan and Germany] in: Schmidt, K. H. (Ed.) *Organisation und Finanzierung des Strukturwandels der Wirtschaft in Japan und in der Bundesrepublik Deutschland* [*Organization and financing of structural change in Japan and Germany*] (Paderborn: Gesamthochschule Paderborn), pp. 35–45.

Warnecker, H. J. (1993) *Revolution in der Unternehmenskultur: Das fraktale Unternehmen* [*Revolution in Corporate Culture: The Fractal Enterprise*] (Hamburg: Springer).

Watanabe, T. (1992) 'Der Wille zur Unfreiheit in der japanischen Gesellschaft' [Japanese society and the desire to be restricted], *OAG Mitteilungen*, 11, pp. 8–11.

Waterman, R. H. (1988) *Leistung durch Innovation: Strategien zur unternehmerischen Zukunftssicherung* [*Innovation induced performance: strategies for enterprises to maintain competitiveness*] (Hamburg: Hoffmann & Campe).

Waters, M. (1995) *Globalization* (London: Routledge).

Watson, W. (1998) *Globalization and the Meaning of Canadian Life* (Toronto: University of Toronto Press).

Webb, H. (1964) 'Japan 1850–1890' in: Mann, G. (Ed.) *Propyläen Weltgeschichte*, vol. 8 [*Propyläen history of the world*] (Frankfurt: Propyläen), pp. 614–47.

Webb, M. (1949) *Gesammelte Aufsätze zur Wissenschaftslehre* (Tübingen: J. C. B. Mohr) [*Methodology of Social Sciences* (Free Press)].

— (1990) 'Architecture: Cesar Pelli', *Architectural Digest*, 7, 124–9.

Weber, M. (1983) *Gesammelte Aufsatze zur Wissenschaftslehre* (Tübingen: J. C. B. Mohr 1988).

Weder, R. and Borner, S. (1990) 'International Competitiveness of Nations and Firms' (Universität Basel Working Paper WWZ 19).

Weidenbaum, M. L. (1990) *Business and Government in the Global Marketplace* (Englewood Cliffs NJ: Prentice Hall).

— and Hughes, S. (1996) *The Bamboo Network* (New York: Free Press).

Weimann, R. (1991) 'Das Ende der Moderne?' [The end of modernity?] in: Weimann, R., Gumbrecht, H. U. and Wagner, B. (Eds.) *Postmoderne – Globale Differenz* [*Postmodernity – global difference*] (Frankfurt: Suhrkamp), pp. 9–53.

Weinstein, F. B. (1990) 'Multinational Corporations and the Third World: The Case of Japan and Southeast Asia', *International Organization*, 2, pp. 373–404.

Weizenbaum, J. (1976) *Die Macht der Computer und die Ohnmacht der Vernunft* (Frankfurt: Suhrkamp) [*Computer Power and Human Reason* (San Francisco: W. H. Freeman)].

Welge, M. K. (1990) 'Multinational Corporations' in: Grochla, E. and Gaugler, E. (Eds.) *Handbook of German Business Management* (Stuttgart: Poeschel), pp. 1499–1510.

Wellmer, A. (1985) 'Zur Dialektik von Moderne und Postmoderne: Vernunftkritik nach Adorno' [On the dialectics of modernity and postmodernity: critique of reason after Adorno] in: Wellmer, A. *Zur Dialektik von Moderne und Postmoderne Adorno* [*On the dialectics of modernity and postmodernity*] (Frankfurt: Suhrkamp), pp. 48–114.

Welsch, W. (1986) 'Nach welcher Moderne' [After which modernity], in: Koslowski, P., Spaemann, R. and Löw, R. (Eds.) *Moderne oder Postmoderne?* [*Modern or Postmodern?*] (Weinheim, VCH), pp. 237–57.

— (1987) *Unsere postmoderne Moderne* [*Our postmodern modernity*] (Weinheim: VCH).

— (1987) 'Vielheit ohne Einheit? Zum gegenwärtigen Spektrum der philosophischen Diskussion um die "Postmoderne"' [*Multiplicity without unity? On the current spectrum of philosophical discussions around the postmodern*], *Philosophisches Jahrbuch*, **94**, 111–41.

— (1988) 'Postmoderne – Pluralität als ethischer und politischer Wert' [*Postmodernity – plurality as ethical and political value*] (Köln: Walter Raymond Stiftung, Kleine Reihe 45, Wirtschaftsverlag Bachem).

— (1989) 'Postmoderne – Zwischen Indifferenz und Pluralität' [Postmodernity – between indifference and plurality], in: Burtscher, P. and Donner, W. (Eds.) *Postmoderne – Philosophem und Arabeske* [*Postmodernity: philosophical topic and arabesque*] (Frankfurt: Lang), pp. 21–35.

— (1989) 'Vernunft im Übergang' [Changing reason], in: Reese-Schäfer, W. and Taurek, B. H. F. (Eds.) *Jean-François Lyotard* (Cuxhaven: Junghans), pp. 1–39.

— (1990) 'Rückblickend auf einen Streit, der ein Widerstreit bleibt' [Review of a debate that remained a discord], in: Wildermuth, A. and Klein, U. (Eds.) *Postmoderne – Ende in Sicht* [*Postmodernity – the end is near*] (Heiden: Rosenberg). pp. 1–26.

— (1990) 'Die Geburt der postmodernen Philosophie aus dem Geist der modernen Kunst' [The birth of postmodern philosophy from the spirit of modern art], *Philosophisches Jahrbuch*, **1**, 15–38.

Werhahn-Mees, K. (1986) 'Kultur und Wirtschaft: Kategorien für eine adäquatere Länderanalyse' [Culture and business: categories for a better country analysis] in: Barloewen, C. v. and Werhahn-Mees, K. (Eds.) *Japan und der Westen*, vol. 2 [*Japan and the West*] (Frankfurt: Fischer), pp. 11–57.

Westney, D. E. (1987) *Imitation and Innovation: The Transfer of Western Organizational Patterns to Meiji-Japan* (Cambridge, MA: Harvard University Press).

Wheeler, J. W., Janow, M. E. and Pepper, T. (Eds.) (1982) *Japanese Industrial Development Policies in the 1980s* (Croton-on-Hudson, NY: Hudson Institute Press).

Whitehouse, I. (1989) *A Reading of the Postmodern* (Cardiff: University of Wales Press).

Whorf, B. L. (1984) *Sprache – Denken – Wirklichkeit* [*Language – Thought – Reality*] (Hamburg: Rowohlt).

Wickert, E. (1992) 'Der Riese hinter den sieben Bergen' [The giant behind the seven hills], *Frankfurter Allgemeine Zeitung*, June.

Wie-Hsun-Fu, C. and Heine, S. (1995) *Japan in Traditional and Postmodern Perspectives* (Albany, NY: SUNY Press).

Wilber, C. K. and Harrison, R. S. (1978) 'The Methodological Basis of Institutional Economics: Pattern Model, Storytelling, and Holism', *Journal of Economic Issues*, **12**, pp. 61–90.

Wildermuth, A. (1990) 'Postmoderne Aufklärung [Postmodern Enlightenment]', in: Wildermuth, A. and Klein, U. (Eds.) *Postmoderne – Ende in Sicht* [*Postmodernity – the end is near*] (Heiden: Niggli), pp. 26–50.

— (1991) 'Multikulturelle Gesellschaft' [Multicultural society], *Prisma*, **5**, 5–12.

Wilke, S. (1990) 'Adorno and Derrida as Readers of Husserl: Some Reflections on the Historical Context of Modernism and Postmodernism', *Boundary*, **2**, pp. 77–91.

Wilkins, M. (1986) 'Japanese Multinational Enterprises before 1914', *Business History Review*, **60**, pp. 199–231.

— (1988) 'European and North American Multinationals, 1870–1914: Comparisons and Contrasts', *Business History*, **30**, pp. 8–45.

Wilkinson, M. (1991) *The Growth of Multinationals* (Aldershot: Elgar).

Wilks, S. and Wright, M. (1989) 'Conclusion: Comparing Government–Industry Relations: States, Sectors, Networks' in: Wilks, S. and Wright, M. (Eds.) *Comparing Government–Industry Relations* (Oxford: Oxford University Press), pp. 274–313.

Williams, J. (1998) *Lyotard: Towards a Modern Philosophy* (Cambridge, MA: Polity Press).

Williamson, O. E. (1971) 'The Vertical Integration of Production', *American Economic Review*, **63**, pp. 112–23.

— (1979) 'Transaction Cost Economics: The Governance of Contractual Relations', *Journal of Law and Economics*, **2**, 233–61.

— (1981) 'The Economics of Organisation: The Transaction Cost Approach', *American Journal of Sociology*, **87**, 548–77.

— (1981) 'The Modern Corporation: Origins, Evolution, Attributes', *Journal of Economic Literature*, **19**, 1537–68.

— (1983) 'Credible Commitments Using Hostages to Support Exchange', *American Economic Review*, **73**, 519–40.

— (1985) *The Economic Institutions of Capitalism* (New York: Free Press).

— (1986) 'The Logic of Economic Organization', in: Williamson, O. E. (Ed.) *Economic Organization: Firms, Markets, and Policy Control* (Brighton: Wheatsheaf), pp. 90–116.

— (1989) 'Transaction Cost Economics', in: Schmalensee, R. and Willig, R. D. (Eds.) *Handbook of Industrial Organization*, vol. 1 (Amsterdam: North Holland), pp. 135–82.

— (1990) 'The Firm as a Nexus of Treaties: An Introduction', in: Aoki, M. and Gustafson, B. (Eds.) *The Firm as a Nexus of Treaties* (London: Sage), pp. 1–25.

— (1990) Industrial Organization (Aldershot: Elgar).

Willms, B. (1989) 'Postmoderne und Politik' [Postmodernity and politics], *Der Staat*, **3**, pp. 321–51.

Wilson, R. A. (1992) *Die neue Inquisition* (Frankfurt: Zweitausendeins) [*The New Inquisition* (Falcon)].

Wilson-Ross, N. (1960) 'Poetry' in: Wilson-Ross: N. (Ed.) *The World of Zen* (New York: Vintage), pp. 112–20.

— (1960) 'The No-Drama' in: Wilson-Ross, N. (Ed.) *The World of Zen* (New York: Vintage), pp. 167–70.

Wolf, G. (1987) 'Wirtschafts- und finanzpolitische Machtstrukturen in der Bundesrepublik Deutschland: Issuespezifische Netzwerkanalyse' [Power structures in business and politics in Germany: a focused network analysis (Mannheim: Universität Mannheim, Diss.)].

Wolf, M. J. (1984) *The Japanese Conspiracy: Their Plot to Dominate Industry Worldwide* (Sevenoaks: New English Library).

Wolfe, A. (1989) 'Suicide and the Japanese Postmodern: A Postnarrative Paradigm?' in: Miyoshi, M. and Harootunian, H. D. (Eds.) *Postmodernism and Japan* (Durham, NC: Duke University Press), pp. 215–34.

Wolfe, T. (1987) *The Bonfire of the Vanities* (New York: Bantam).

Wolferen, K. v. (1989) 'Das Japan Problem' [The Problem of Japan] in: Menzel, U. (Ed.) *Im Schatten des Siegers*, vol. 3 [*In the shadow of the winner*] (Frankfurt: Suhrkamp), pp. 9–27.

— (1990) *The Enigma of Japanese Power* (London: Macmillan Press).

Womack, J. P., Jones, D. T. and Roos, D. (1990) *Die zweite Revolution in der Autoindustrie* (Frankfurt: Campus) [*The Machine that Changed the World* (Rawson)].

Woronoff, J. (1982) *Japan: The Coming Economic Crisis* (Tokyo: Lotus).

Wright, R. W. and Pauli, G. A. (1987) *The Second Wave – Japan's Global Assault on Financial Services* (New York: St. Martin's Press).

Wunderer, R. and Grunwald, W. (1980) *Führungslehre*, vol. 1 [*Management Theory*] (Berlin: De Gruyter).

Yakushiji, T. (1984) 'The Government Policy in a Spiral Dilemma', in: Aoki, M. (Ed.) *The Economic Analysis of the Japanese Firm* (Amsterdam: Elsevier), pp. 265–311.

Yamamaru, K. (1967) *Economic Policy in Postwar Japan* (Berkeley, CA: University of California Press).

Yamamoto, C. and Blume, G. (1991) *Keine andere Stadt ist wie Tama: Tokyos postmoderne Vorstadt [No other town like this: Tokyo's postmodern suburb]* (Die Rheinpfalz)

Yamamoto, S. (1986) 'Ursprünge der japanischen Arbeitsethik' [Origins of Japanese attitudes towards work] in: Barloewen, C. v. and Werhahn-Mees, K. (Eds.) *Japan und der Westen*, vol. 1 *[Japan and the West]* (Frankfurt: Fischer), pp. 95–129.

Yamamura, K. (1982) 'Success that Soured: Administrative Guidance and Cartel in Japan' in: Yamamura, K. (Ed.) *Policy and Trade Issues of the Japanese Economy* (Seattle, WA: University of Washington Press), pp. 83–123.

Yamazaki, M. (1985) 'The Impact of Japanese Culture on Management' in: Thurow, L. C. (Ed.) *Management: Japan* (Cambridge, MA: MIT Press), pp. 31–41.

Yamin, M. (1991) 'A Reassessment of Hymer's Contribution to the Transnational Cooperation' in: Pitelis, C. and Sudgen, R. (Eds.) *The Nature of the Transnational Firm* (London: Routledge), pp. 64–81.

Yasumuro, K. (1984) 'The Contribution of Sogo Shosha to the Multinationalization of Japanese Industrial Enterprise in Historical Perspective' in: Okochi, A. and Inoue, T. *Overseas Business Activities* (Tokyo: University of Tokyo Press), pp. 65–92.

Yasuo, H. (1966) 'The Role of the Ie in the Economic Modernization of Japan', *Kyoto University Economic Review*, **4**, pp. 1–16.

Yasuoka, S. (1980) 'The Tradition of Family Business in the Strategic Decision Process and Management Structure of Zaibatsu Business' in: Nakagawa, N. (Ed.) *Strategy and Structure of Big Business* (Tokyo: University of Tokyo Press), pp. 81–101.

Yoshida, K. (1989) 'Betrachtungen aus der Stille' [Quiet reflections] in: Hijia-Kirschnereit, I. and Schmölers, C. (Eds.) *Japan* (Frankfurt: Insel), pp. 13–15.

Yoshihara, K. (1979) *Japanese Economic Development: A Shorter Introduction* (Oxford: Oxford University Press).

Yoshikawa, I. (1989) *Chozubashi: Teien-bi no zokei [Stone-rimmed ponds: How to achieve beauty in the garden]* (Tokyo: Graphic-sha).

Yoshimura, N., Anderson, P. and Yoshimura, N. (1997) *Inside the Kaisha: Demystifying Japanese Business* (Boston, MA: Harvard Business School Press).

Yoshino, M. Y. (1976) *Japan's Multinational Enterprises* (Cambridge, MA: Harvard University Press).

— (1981) 'Emerging Japanese Multinational Enterprises' in: Vogel, E. (Ed.) *Modern Japanese Organization and Decision Making* (Tokyo: Tuttle), pp. 146–73.

— and Lifson, T. B. (1986) *The Invisible Link* (Cambridge, MA: MIT Press).

— and Rangan, U. S. (1995) Strategic Alliances: An Entrepreneurial Approach to Globalization (Cambridge, MA: Harvard Business School Press).

Yoshiyuki, J. (1990) *The Dark Room* (Tokyo: Kodansha).

Young A. K. (1990) *The Sogo Shosha – Japans Multinational Trading Companies* (Toyko: Tuttle).

Yui, T. (1974) 'Beziehungen zwischen Regierung und Unternehmen und Ihr Einfluss auf die Industrialisierung Japans' [The relations between government and companies and its influence on the industrialization of Japan] in: Ichihara, K. and Takamiya, S. (Eds.) *Die japanische Unternehmung – Strukturwandlungen in einer wachsenden Wirtschaft [The Japanese enterprise – structural changes in a growing economy]* (Opladen: Westdeutscher Verlag), pp. 31–42.

— (1977) 'Zaibatzu', in: Ichihara, K. and Takamiya, S. (Eds.): *Die japanische Unternehmung – Strukturwandlungen in einer wachsenden Wirtschaft [The Japanese enterprise – structural changes in a growing economy]* (Opladen: Westdeutscher Verlag), pp. 45–55.

Yves, L. D. (1989) 'Die Rolle des Staates im globalen Wettbewerb' [The role of the state in global competition] in: Porter, M. E. (Ed.) *Globaler Wettbewerb: Strategien der neuen Internationalisierung* [*Global competition: strategies of a new internationaliization*] (Wiesbaden: Gabler) pp. 257–306.

Zeami (Seami), M. (1989) 'Die geheime Ueberlieferung des No' [The secret tradition of Noh] in: Hijia-Kirschnereit, I. and Schmölers, C. (Eds.) *Japan* (Frankfurt: Insel), pp. 18–25.

Zengage, T. R. and Ratcliffe, C. T. (1988) *The Japanese Century* (Hong Kong: Longman).

Zichinski, R. (1991) *Unequal Equities – Power and Risk in the Japanese Stock Market* (Tokyo: Kodansha).

Zimbalist, A. H., Sherman, J. and Brown, S. (1989) *Comparing Economic Systems* (San Diego, CA: Harcourt Brace Jovanovitch).

Zweigle, F. (1993) 'Topoi der Rotationslyrik: Ein kritischer Beitrag zur Analyse überstrukturierter Texte' [Topics of rotational lyrics: critical notes on the analysis of structured texts] (Radolfszell: MS).

Zysman, J., Tyson, L. and Borrus, M. (1994) *US and Japanese Trade and Industrial Policies* (Berkeley, CA: Berkeley Roundtable on the International Economy).

Index

previous research, 15
theory, 173f., 178ff.
Modern *v.* Postmodern, 9, 33ff., 42ff.,
47ff., 69, 257
Modernism, 33ff., 37, 39ff., 72, 165
excess, 40, 49f., 156f.
Modernity, end of, 42, 44ff., 64, 72
and Japan, 67
Modernization, 148, 153, 156, 232
MoF (Ministry of Finance), 115f., 130,
138, 171
Mondo, 84
Money, 58f., 61f., 63, 163, 190
Mouer, R., 80, 89
Multiculturalism, 37, 106
Multidimensionalism, 9, 37, 50, 65, 83,
100, 122, 128, 142, 191, 202, 256
Murakami, R., 133

Nagasaki, 109, 231
Nakamura, H., 68, 80, 82, 94
Nakane, C., 93, 98
Nakatani, I., 224, 226
Narrative, 16, 41, 55, 57, 91, 126, 131, 134
National culture, 11, 78f., 96f., 161,
176, 187, 189, 192, 258f.
Naumann, N., 158
NEC, 6, 203f.
Negandhi, A. R., 177
Nemawashi, 99, 112, 122ff., 128, 131f.,
136, 170
Network, 4, 48f., 71, 73, 89, 97ff., 171,
173f., 178, 181, 185ff., 200f., 253,
256, 262
state, 64, 99f., 103, 198f.
theory, 193ff., 200f., 258f.
see also Social network
Networking, 34, 51, 91ff., 102, 113, 121,
163, 168
Neustupny, I., 80
New economy and postmodern, 3, 7ff.,
10, 17, 21f., 46, 50f., 58, 71, 103,
171f., 174, 233, 253, 261
New Economy and Zen, 85
New Japan, 156, 158, 165, 220
Nietzsche, F., 44, 48, 52, 54, 63
Nihonjinron, 13, 96ff.
Nihonron, 96ff., 100, 102
Nijno, K., 149
Nikkeiren, 112
Nishida, K., 165

Nissan, 14, 203, 206, 216
Nissho–Iwai, 209, 219
Nohriah, N., 196
No-theatre, 76, 86, 101
Nucleus, 21, 50, 65, 90ff., 101, 115ff.,
138, 167ff., 183, 192ff., 203, 212,
218, 225, 233, 235, 239ff., 249f.,
253, 257, 259, 262

Ohashi, R., 67
Ohmae, K., 12, 192ff., 256
Okimoto, D. I., 99
Okumura, H., 232
OLI paradigm (ownership advantages,
location, internalization), 186f.
On, 91f., 131
One-set principle, 207
Organization, 6, 14, 18, 22, 47, 73f.,
98ff., 104, 111f., 117ff., 121, 133,
168, 173ff., 181, 188, 191ff., 199ff.,
215, 222ff., 245, 253, 256ff.
Orlowski, D., 189
Oyabun–kobun relationship, 91, 112,
120ff., 130, 132, 170, 181, 207, 246
Ozawa, T., 177, 180

Paradigm change, 7, 14, 19, 37, 139,
158, 161, 168, 220, 257, 260
Paradigm leader, 105, 172, 255, 262
Paradox, 36, 68, 84, 94, 259
Paul, G., 84
Pauli, G., 107
Penrose, E., 196
'Perpetual now', 107
Piore, M. J., 205
Pluralism, 4, 35f. 106, 133, 142, 165, 171
Popper, K. R., 4
Porter, M., 189ff., 191, 194, 200, 256
Portoghesi, P., 34
Post-industrial society, 31, 34, 54f., 230,
257
Postmodern and new economy, 3, 7ff.,
10, 17, 21f., 46, 50f., 58, 71, 103,
171f., 174, 233, 253, 261
Postmodern and science, 35ff, 55f., 65
Postmodern building, 34f.
Postmodern company, 174ff., 178, 208,
258f.
Postmodern economic model, 21f., 27,
31, 53ff., 66, 71, 171

·